REGIONAL INTEGRATION AND TRADE LIBERALIZATION IN SUBSAHARAN AFRICA

Volume 2: Country Case-Studies

REGIONAL INTEGRATION AND TRADE LIBERALIZATION IN SUBSAHARAN AFRICA

VOLUME 1: FRAMEWORK, ISSUES AND METHODOLOGICAL PERSPECTIVES
Edited by Ademola Oyejide, Ibrahim Elbadawi and Paul Collier

VOLUME 2: COUNTRY CASE-STUDIES
Edited by Ademola Oyejide, Benno Ndulu and Jan Willem Gunning

VOLUME 3: REGIONAL CASE-STUDIES
Edited by Ademola Oyejide, Ibrahim Elbadawi and Stephen Yeo

VOLUME 4: SYNTHESIS AND REVIEW
Edited by Ademola Oyejide, Benno Ndulu and David Greenaway

Regional Integration and Trade Liberalization in SubSaharan Africa

Volume 2: Country Case-Studies

Edited by

Ademola Oyejide
Professor of Economics and Director of
the Trade Policy Research and Training Programme
University of Ibadan
Nigeria

Benno Ndulu
The World Bank Group
Tanzania

and

Jan Willem Gunning
Professor of Development Economics
Free University
Amsterdam
The Netherlands

First published in Great Britain 1999 by
MACMILLAN PRESS LTD
Houndmills, Basingstoke, Hampshire RG21 6XS and London
Companies and representatives throughout the world

A catalogue record for this book is available from the British Library.

ISBN 0–333–66105–2

First published in the United States of America 1999 by
ST. MARTIN'S PRESS, INC.,
Scholarly and Reference Division,
175 Fifth Avenue, New York, N.Y. 10010

ISBN 0–312–21769–2

Library of Congress Cataloging-in-Publication Data
Regional integration and trade liberalization in subsaharan Africa.
v.<2>;cm.
Includes bibliographical references and index.
Contents: — Vol. 1. Framework, issues and methodological Perspectives / edited by Ademola Oyejide, Ibrahim Elbadawi and Paul Collier — Vol. 2. Country case-studies / edited by Ademola Oyejide, Benno Ndulu and Jan Willem Gunning — Vol. 3. Regional case-studies / edited by Ademola Oyejide, Ibrahahim Elbadawi and Stephen Yeo — Vol. 4. Synthesis and review / edited by Ademola Oyejide, Benno Ndulu and David Greenaway
ISBN 0–312–17321–0 (v. 1).—ISBN 0–312–21769–2 (v. 2).—ISBN 0–312–21771–4 (v. 3).—ISBN 0–312–21772–2 (v. 4)
1. Africa, Sub-Saharan—Economic integration. 2. Africa, Sub-Saharan—Economic policy. 3. Africa, Sub-Saharan—Foreign economic relations. I. Oyejide, T. Ademola. II. Elbadawi, Ibrahim. III. Collier, Paul.
HC800.R448 1997
337.67—dc21 96–49387
CIP

This book is printed on paper suitable for recycling and made from fully managed and sustained forest sources.

10 9 8 7 6 5 4 3 2 1
08 07 06 05 04 03 02 01 00 99

Printed and bound in Great Britain by Antony Rowe Ltd, Chippenham, Wiltshire

Contents

List of Figures

List of Tables

List of Contributors

Christopher Adam University of Oxford
Olu Ajakaiye University of Ibadan
Bouabré Bohoun University of Abidjan
Michael Bleaney University of Nottingham
Paul Collier University of Oxford; The World Bank, Washington
Beealasingh Dabee University of Mauritius
David Fielding University of Nottingham
Jan Willem Gunning Centre for the Study of African Economies, Free University of Amsterdam
Alan Hirsch University of Cape Town
Merle Holden University of Natal
Carolyn Jenkins University of Oxford
Oussou Kouassy University of Abidjan
A.V.Y. Mbelle University of Dar es Salaam
Andrew McKay University of Nottingham
Chris Milner University of Nottingham
Kupukile Mlambo University of Zimbabwe
Flora Musonda COMESA Secretariat, Zambia
Francis Mwega University of Nairobi
Mthuli Ncube London School of Economics
Benno Ndulu Former Executive Director (African Economic Research Consortium); The World Bank Group, Tanzania
Abena Oduro University of Ghana
Ademola Oyejide University of Ibadan
Joseph Semboja University of Dar es Salaam
Adedoyin Soyibo University of Ibadan
Germina Ssemogerere Makerere University
Kwadwo Tutu University of Ghana

1 Introduction and Overview

Ademola Oyejide, Benno Ndulu and Jan Willem Gunning

1.1 INTRODUCTION

This volume analyses the trade liberalization experiences of 10 subSaharan African countries: Côte d'Ivoire, Ghana, Kenya, Mauritius, Nigeria, South Africa, Tanzania, Uganda, Zambia and Zimbabwe. The volume is part of a series of four that contain papers generated by the collaborative project on Regional Integration and Trade Liberalization in subSaharan Africa sponsored by the African Economic Research Consortium (AERC) and other collaborating institutions. Volume I of the series focuses on conceptual issues and methodological perspectives; Volume III presents an analysis of regional integration experiences; while Volume IV contains the synthesis. The country studies presented in this volume have a close family resemblance, since a common methodology was applied. This is described in detail in Volume I, but a few aspects of the methodology should be reviewed here.

First, in the country studies trade liberalization was defined in terms of objective measures: changes in policy and observed changes in prices and quantities. This differs, for example, from the massive World Bank study of trade liberalization (Papageorgiou *et al.*, 1991). That study used an index of trade liberalization that was partly based on the authors' subjective judgements (Greenaway, 1993).

For this collaborative project, authors were asked to measure trade policy by a number of continuous variables. Three of these are price measures: the implicit tariff rate (derived from a comparison of domestic and world prices of importables), the ratio of the implicit tariff rate and the implicit export tax rate, and the premium in the parallel market for foreign exchange. In addition to these price measures, the country studies report on changes in three types of quantity measures. The simplest quantity measure is trade intensity – the ratio of total external trade (imports plus exports) to GDP. The second type of quantity measure is the change in resource allocation; this is measured by shifts of investment and employment between sectors. Finally, quantity changes were measured by comparing observed import volumes with counterfactuals constructed on the basis of unchanged policies.

The country studies not only measure changes in prices and quantities, they also describe trade policy changes in 'policy accounts'. Country authors concentrated on trade liberalization 'episodes' – periods marked by substantial policy changes and changes in the various price and quantity measures. Any study of trade liberalization faces the fundamental problem that the policy account may not be corroborated by changes in the chosen quantitative indicators. For example, if trade policy involves quotas, a fall in real income, say as a result of a terms-of-trade loss, will lead to lower quota rents as demand for imports falls. If the government does not adjust the quotas, the policy account will record no change in trade policy, while one of the price measures, the implicit tariff rate, will indicate trade liberalization. Obviously, the price measure correctly suggests that there is an incentive for less production and more consumption of importables. However, a trade liberalization episode thus defined is problematic, since policy-makers may be totally unaware of a change in policy. In the country studies a period is treated as a trade liberalization episode only if both policy changes and the price and quantity measures indicate liberalization.

Secondly, the country studies all attempted to assess the credibility of trade liberalization attempts. African trade liberalizations have often been considered as incredible and the country studies report on a series of diagnostics of incredibility (Table 1.1). One way in which incredibility can arise is if the policy stance is seen as incompatible, leading either to an unsustainable balance of payments deficit (payments incompatibility) or to an unsustainable budget deficit (fiscal incompatibility). An obvious diagnostic of payments incompatibility is a fall in the level of reserves. Since subSaharan Africa foreign exchange reserves are typically very low, a fall is usually a good indicator that the policy stance is unsustainable. The usefulness of reserves as an indicator of sustainability depends on what policies the government chooses to ensure compatibility.

If the effect of trade liberalization on money demand is offset by a devaluation, then incompatibility (which might arise if the devaluation is too small relative to the trade reform) will show up immediately as a loss of reserves. Conversely, if compatibility is achieved through extra aid (Collier and Gunning, 1992), then reserves are a poor indicator; incompatibility will show up as a loss of reserves only when the aid runs out. This leads to a second diagnostic: the current account balance. When aid (or commercial borrowing) is the instrument used, the current account should initially deteriorate (reflecting the extra capital inflow). A third diagnostic is the volume of imports. An increase in imports is likely to reflect incompatibility (except when extra capital flows have been obtained, as in the case of aid-supported trade liberalization). Finally, since payments incompatibility arises from the effect of trade liberalization on

Table 1.1 Indicators of incredibility

	Indicators
Payments incompatibility	
(a) Results	level of reserves current account volume of imports price level
(b) Policies	exchange rate indirect taxes liquidity ratio budget deficit
(c) Exogenous changes	for example, terms of trade, drought
Fiscal incompatibility	budget deficit
Forecastability	endogenous trade policy
Time inconsistency	for example, donor support

the price level, the most direct diagnostic is the price level itself (or possibly a price index restricted to imported consumer goods). A fall in the price level (relative to a counterfactual) would indicate incompatibility.

These indicators of payments incompatibility have in common that results are measured. Alternatively, one can directly observe policies that might be changed to ensure compatibility. This calls for monitoring the exchange rate (in a fixed exchange rate regime), the average rate of indirect taxes, the minimum liquidity ratio imposed on commercial banks and the budget deficit. Finally, exogenous events other than policy changes (for example, a terms-of-trade improvement or a drought) may make a policy stance payments compatible or incompatible. The budget deficit is an indicator not just of balance of payments compatibility (since budget deficit is an indicator not just of balance of payments compatibility – a government savings effort will reduce money supply, thereby offsetting the effect on money demand of the trade reform) but also of fiscal compatibility; a reform may well lead to an unsustainable budget deficit: for example, by lowering government tariff revenue.

Private agents may expect trade liberalization to be reversed even if they consider the policy stance as compatible. First, a policy reversal is predictable if the liberalization is seen as resulting from the application of an endogenous trade policy rule. For example, if the government maintains a fixed exchange rate and adjusts to terms-of-trade shocks by liberalizing or tightening trade policy, then private agents, recognizing the policy rule, are able to forecast changes in trade policy. When the government liberalizes trade restrictions in response to a temporary commodity boom, private agents will – if they realize the boom is not permanent – expect a subsequent tightening. Secondly, agents may see the liberalization as time inconsistent. Authors were therefore asked to investigate whether the government had an incentive to reverse the liberalization.

A possible reason for time inconsistency is donor involvement. If private agents suspect that the government has decided to liberalize trade only because it thereby gains access to extra aid, then they will expect the liberalization to be reversed when the aid runs out.

When private agents perceive liberalization as incredible (because they perceive incompatibility, because there is systematic forecastability or because of time inconsistency), they will try to profit from the expected policy reversal. This may be observed in various forms, such as the stockpiling of import licenses or increases in stocks of imports in warehouses.

Thirdly, the country authors were asked to present a common set of performance indicators, by which the impact of trade liberalization could be judged. This includes time series of GDP and employment (and their sectoral composition), investment, and the growth and composition of external trade.

Finally, surveys were carried out among industrial firms in the 10 countries. The surveys focused on whether or not firms were exporting, the effects of regional integration on their export performance, and the financing of investment. The surveys also included questions on expectations, which may be used to assess credibility directly.

The country studies are therefore characterized by four complementary methodological approaches: the definition of liberalization episodes in terms of quantitative measures, the assessment (in terms of the Table 1.1 diagnostics) of credibility, the use of a common set of performance indicators and the use of survey data.

In the next section, we summarize the studies' description of the liberalization episodes. Section 1.3 considers the evidence on compatibility, credibility and policy reversals. The impact of the liberalization together with the evidence on regional issues and the results of the surveys are discussed in section 1.4. Section 1.5 concludes.

1.2 A REVIEW OF EXPERIENCES WITH TRADE LIBERALIZATION: WHAT HAPPENED?

The basic questions we attempt to answer in this section relate to whether trade liberalization took place in the 10 countries covered by this study.

How did it happen? What was the impetus for it? What is the evidence?

We draw insights from the policy accounts presented in each chapter. These focus on policy measures adopted towards liberalization, describe the key features of each of the multiple episodes of liberalization experiences and provide the motivation behind each of the episodes. In assessing whether trade liberalization took place or not, we refer to the objective measures of liberalization adopted commonly by the studies pertaining to changes in relative prices and quantities as described above.

Table 1.2 summarizes the key features of the liberalization experience, highlighting the measures taken, the motivation for these measures, and their effectiveness. We will refer to it throughout this section. We begin by characterizing briefly the dominant features of the trade regimes that were subjected to change in the liberalization episodes. This allows us to draw out clearly the main pressures behind the frequent reversals observed. We then identify the stimuli for change. Next we characterize the cumulative effects of the policy changes before drawing conclusions from the experience.

The Main Factors behind Trade Restrictions

The key features of the restrictive trade regimes obtaining in all the 10 countries prior to liberalization were determined by four main considerations. First were the protective needs of the widely adopted import-substitution industrialization strategy (ISI). Among the 10 countries, the trade regimes in South Africa and Mauritius were particularly influenced by this concern. High tariff walls, import controls, subsidies to ISI industries via controlled interest rates and over-valued currencies, and complex tariff rate structures to target protection to specific commodities were among the main trade instruments explicitly applied for this purpose. Trade confinement to public entities covering a wide range of import substitutes, and 'no objection' certificates (for example, in Tanzania and Kenya) were also applied to control importation of competing goods. The strongest resistance to import liberalization, not surprisingly, would thus come from the beneficiaries of the ISI strategy. Protection rates are important indicators for tracking a shift away from this regime via liberalization.

Second, with revenues from external trade taxes being a significant source of financing public expenditures, high tariffs were also levied for revenue generation purposes. As the policy accounts in the case-studies show, a large number of partial reversals of liberalization episodes resulted from fiscal pressures. This is notwithstanding the fact that there was little if any correlation between high scheduled tariff rates and actual collection success, as Pritchett and Sethi (1994) showed.

Third, invariably import controls and foreign exchange allocation systems/exchange controls – including the CFA franc zone countries – were

Table 1.2 Trade liberalization in sub-Saharan Africa: summary of findings of Regional Integration and Trade Liberalization Project

	Kenya	*Uganda*	*Mauritius*	*Nigeria*	*Ghana*	*South Africa*	*Tanzania*	*Zambia*	*Côte d'Ivoire*	*Zimbabwe*
1 *Trade liberalization – Did trade liberalization take place?* (Yes/No)	Yes	Yes	Yes	Yes, very limited	Yes	Yes	Yes	Yes	Yes	Yes (limited)
1.1 Tarification of QRs										
Exchange rate premium decline (%)	100	100	n.a.	n.a.	90	n.a.	99	97	n.a.	n.a.
1.2 Imports covered by licensing										
Reduction (%)	100	64	100	n.a.	100	100	100	n.a.	22	n.a.
1.3 Payment liberalization (reduction of exchange controls)	Yes	Yes	Yes	Yes	Yes	Yes	Yes	Yes	n.a.	n.a.
1.4 Tariff liberalization				Yes	Yes					Yes
Reduction in tariffs (%)	76	n.a.	85	n.a.	5–10	38	70	67	36	n.a.
Tariff structure compression (%)	76	n.a.	85	n.a.	n.a.	41	70	50	44	n.a.
1.5 Effective rates of protection										
Reduction	Yes	No	Yes	No	Yes	Yes	Yes	Yes	Yes	Yes
(%)	n.a.	n.a.	n.a.	n.a.	60	n.a.	50	58	n.a.	n.a.
1.6 Export taxes										
Reduction	Yes	Yes	Yes	n.a.	No	Yes	Yes	Yes	Yes	n.a.
(%)	n.a.	n.a.	n.a.	n.a.	n.a.	n.a.	100	100	100	n.a.
2 *Macroeconomic adjustment – Did macroeconomic adjustment accompany liberalization?* (Yes/No)										
2.1 Exchange rate depreciation? (Yes/No)	Yes	Yes	Yes	Yes	Yes	Yes	Yes	Yes	Yes	Yes
Depreciation (nominal local: foreign (%)	364	436	45	80	1700	45	530	4800	100	165
2.2 Fiscal reform? (Yes/No)	Yes	Yes	Yes	No	No	n.a.	Yes	Yes	No	No
Reduction of deficit/GDP (%)	n.a.	n.a.	n.a.	–28	n.a.	n.a.	44	n.a.	1	n.a.

3 *Impetus for liberalization – What was the impetus for liberalization?*										
3.1 Positive commodity price shocks? (Yes/No)	Yes	No	Yes	No	No	No	Yes	No	No	No
3.2 When?	1976/77							1976/77		
Commodity linked to reform? (Yes/No)	Yes	Yes	Yes	Yes	Yes	No	Yes	Yes	Yes	Yes
3.3 Beginning when?	1980	1987	1979	1986	1983		1986	1983	1984	1990
3.4 Membership in a regional scheme? (Yes/No)	Yes	Yes	No	No	No	No	Yes	Yes	No	Yes
3.5 Own initiative to better performance? (Yes/No)	No	No	Yes	Yes	Yes	Yes	Yes	No	No	Yes
4 *Impact of liberalization – What impact did liberalization have (+ or –) on:*							*Real	*Real		
4.1 imports (imports/GDP)?*	38	123	35	–67	1088	min	–4	–36	–29	mix
4.2 exports (exports/GDP)?	62	9	46	min	723	min	26	–31	–14	+
4.3 output (real GDP growth)?	5	6.4	6	min	4	min	4.2	–1.1	n.a.	3.4
4.4 employment?	+	min	33	min	.	min	n.a.	.	.	18
4.5 industrial efficiency?	n.s.c.	n.a.	n.a.	n.a.	n.a.	n.a.	+	n.a.	n.a.	n.a.
5 *Sustainability of liberalization – Was liberalization sustained?*										
5.1 Number of episodes	7	3	2	4	2	3	4	2	3	4
5.2 Any reversals? (Yes/No)	Yes	Yes	No	Yes	Yes	No	Yes	Yes	Yes	No
5.3 Were reversal partial (P) or total (T)?	P	n/a	n/a	T	P	P	P	P	P	n.a.
5.4 Did survey results indicate confidence/support? (Yes/No)	Yes	n.a.	Yes	No	No	Yes	Yes	Yes	No	Yes

Notes:
min: negligible
mix: mixed
pts: percentage points on all imports except luxury goods
n.a.: not available
n.a.: not applicable
n.s.c.: no significant correlation
*: nominal unless otherwise stated

Where information is not quantified, qualitative indicators are used if available.

also used as instruments for managing balance of payments crises when they arose. This was particularly the case during the late 1970s and the first half of the 1980s when crises were triggered by the collapse of commodity prices, reduction of aid flows and world recession. Tightening of import restrictions and exchange controls during crises is documented in virtually all cases covered in this volume. With exchange rates more or less fixed, protection of foreign exchange reserves was pursued mainly through this route. It would thus be reasonable to expect that pressures against liberalization would subside with the adoption of flexible exchange rate regimes for managing the balance of payments.

A fourth feature of the pre-liberalization trade regime is the ambivalent coexistence of an anti-export bias prompted by the above features, and a pursuit of explicit export promotion measures particularly for manufacturers. This ambivalence can be traced to attempts to deal with the inherent inconsistency of ISI strategy, in that on the one hand, it vastly expanded the demand for production and capital goods imports, while on the other it stifled import capacity through the disincentive to export it spawned. Over-valued exchange rates buttressed this unsustainable situation of expanding import requirements in the face of deteriorating export performance. Among the arguably early measures of 'liberalization' as referred to by all case-studies were compensatory arrangements for exporters of manufacturers to ameliorate the disincentive effects of the ISI strategy. These arrangements variably appeared as export subsidy schemes, foreign exchange retention schemes and tax rebates. A few examples will illuminate these arrangement. In South Africa the instruments included cash grants to exporters, tax concessions and rebates, and rail rates concessions; later, economy-wide export incentives were provided under the General Export Incentive Scheme based on value added and local content of inputs. In Kenya and Tanzania, they included a 10 per cent cash subsidy on value of exports and 10–25 per cent export rebate, respectively. In Mauritius, the most significant of these measures was to create a free-trade enclave (export-processing zone) for manufacturing for export.

It is curious to note that in spite of the awareness of the distortive impacts of ISIs on exports, the compensatory arrangements were confined only to exporters of manufactures; other exporters, who were easily in the majority, continued to be severely taxed. We can only speculate on the overriding strength of the manufacturing lobby and the devotion of various governments to ISI. Needless to note that for most part these contemporary arrangements were judged by the authors to be inadequate, particularly in the face of grossly over-valued domestic currencies. In any case, as exchange controls and import restrictions were dismantled, local currencies depreciated and duty levels lowered, these compensatory arrangements became superfluous and the treatment of different categories of exporters more even. To be sure, export promotion should to be redesigned in the context of changes in the trading environment.

Impetus for Liberalization

We identify four main types of stimuli for liberalization of trade regimes in the countries covered by this volume (see Table 1.2). The most prevalent among these is related to conditions imposed for gaining access to external finance under the structural adjustment programmes. The only exception to date among the countries is South Africa, which has not relied on external official assistance for pursuing its reform programmes.

Typically, the policy framework papers (PFP), which are the main instruments for setting and monitoring changes in economic policy agreed to under the programmes, have included various aspects of trade liberalization as part of the conditions to be fulfilled in order to qualify for adjustment finance. These have invariably included import and export liberalization, the related liberalization of the domestic trade environment (particularly dismantling of public trade monopolies), and payments liberalization. Import liberalization has entailed compression of the tariff structure to achieve sectoral uniformity of protection and simplification, reduction of duty rates, and removal of non-tariff barriers to imports particularly import licensing. The thrust of the sequence in this respect is tarrification of quantitative restrictions and then reduction of the tariff rates. Export liberalization has entailed reduction in export taxes and simplification of administrative procedures for exporting. Payments liberalization was mainly demanded in terms of dismantling exchange controls. Liberalization of the domestic trading environment mainly included deconfinement of local trade away from public monopolies and the decontrol of the pricing system. Often these were translated into benchmarks to be achieved over an agreed schedule. Industrial sector credit facilities of the World Bank more directly addressed trade liberalization policies by targeting protection levels and structure.

Complementary macroeconomic adjustment measures have also been part of the negotiated programmes. These included establishing appropriate values of local currencies via depreciation, reducing fiscal deficits to sustainable levels and holding a lid on/reducing monetary expansion. These measures are deemed not only to be consistent with the above liberalization measures but also necessary for sustaining the process of liberalization.

To a very large extent, the close similarities in the design of the liberalization episodes since the mid-1980s across the nine case countries (excluding South Africa) is due to the fact that they were all pursuing structural adjustment programmes that included the above mentioned elements. Mauritius and Kenya were the earliest of the nine to adopt these programmes, in 1979 and 1980, respectively; they were followed by Côte d'Ivoire, Ghana, Zambia, Tanzania, Nigeria, Uganda and Zimbabwe in that sequence from 1981. Along the way, five of these experienced partial reversals entailing temporary suspension of programmes (Zambia, Uganda, Tanzania, Côte d'Ivoire, Kenya, Zimbabwe); Nigeria experienced total reversal in 1988, while Mauritius and Ghana have pursued the programmes persistently.

The second stimulus for temporary and partial liberalization of the trade regimes is positive external shock. Kenya's and Tanzania's cases are well documented not only by the studies included in this volume but also a series of studies to assess the impacts of commodity booms of 1976–7 by Bevan *et al.* (1987, 1989, 1989). Liberalization pursued in response to this type of stimulus was mainly in the form of temporary relaxation of import restrictions and exchange controls. The legal provisions for controls were maintained in the books and all policy fundamentals left untouched. These episodes were typically short-lived as fortunes reversed quickly with the commodity price collapse of 1979–80 ushering in more severe restrictions compared to the pre-liberalization status.

A third stimulus operative in different countries and at different points in time can be categorized under the broad term of 'own initiative'. Most significant among the cases reviewed here is that of South Africa. Liberalization in South Africa began with the Reynders Commission of Inquiry in 1972 that focused on initiatives to reduce anti-export bias particularly for manufacturing resulting from the avid pursuit of ISI strategy. Various policy reviews between 1983 and 1993 led to a new industrial strategy under a more neutral trade regime with tarrification of QRs and a simpler, more transparent tariff structure. South Africa's trade liberalization process prior to 1995 was largely pursued in the context of the country's own sectoral adjustment programmes. It is instructive to note that in 1995, South Africa consolidated these changes through accession to GATT terms for binding its tariff system and is seeking further binding under a negotiated free-trade agreement with the European Union.

To a lesser extent Mauritius seriously pursued reduction in anti-export bias effects of ISI between 1970 and 1979 prior to SAL-induced trade liberalization episodes of the 1980s. Although many of the countries in this study undertook measures aimed at the same objective, the sheer scale and effectiveness of this pursuit in Mauritius distinguishes her from the rest.

At a different level of intensity of own initiative were the partial import liberalization schemes pursued in Tanzania (1984–6) and Zambia under the Own Funded Import schemes (to bring in goods with own finance, no questions being asked as to its source), which were mainly aimed at ameliorating shortages of essential goods. The significance of these episodes lies more in preparing the ground for the more intense liberalization process under SAPs. Lastly under this category of stimulus is included the Nigerian liberalization episode of 1970–6, which was partly helped along by the discovery of oil. The study identifies attempts to control imported inflation and facilitate ISI strategy as the main impetus behind import liberalization during this period, particularly for intermediate and capital goods. Ghana likewise had its first episode during 1967–72 that was characterized by import liberalization; preceded by a *coup d'état*, the episode made little use of exchange rate policy as a supporting policy measure.

The last and least significant stimulus for trade liberalization among the case-studies is membership in a sub-regional economic integration scheme. The stimulus was in the form of preferential trade arrangements among members belonging to such schemes. At best the SACU members enjoyed a virtual free-trade area status partly extended to Zimbabwe and Botswana under bilateral agreements with South Africa. Its insignificance lies in the fact that the individual countries, including South Africa, traded predominantly with countries outside the area. Membership within PTA also accorded preferential tariff treatment. In the case of Mauritius, such preference is currently accorded at 70 per cent below its international schedule for regional imports without a similar level of reciprocation from other members. The problem, as in the previous case, is that of the minuscule share of intra-regional trade for such preferences to have significant effect on overall liberalization. Moreover, pursuit of more intense unilateral liberalization recently seems to have overshadowed this preferential treatment as tariff rates were brought down more steeply via this route.

It is clear that the dominant stimuli for trade liberalization in the region are linked to conditions imposed by structural adjustment programmes. More than 80 per cent of the liberalization episodes identified by the policy accounts were prompted by this stimulus. To date this category of episodes represents the longest sustained and most comprehensive among liberalization initiatives.

Did Trade Liberalization Take Place?

The first section of Table 1.2 presents the cumulative effects of trade liberalization measures undertaken in each of the 10 countries included in the study. Section 2 of the table presents the cumulative effects of the trade-related macroeconomic adjustment measures. The table clearly abstracts away from the numerous partial and total reversals intervening in the liberalization process and hence assesses the effectiveness of the process between the first and the last episodes. Fortunately, in most cases some of the aspects of liberalization achieved earlier remained – even after reversals.

The individual chapters in this volume present more in-depth analysis of the price and quantity changes that signal whether liberalization actually took place or not. The link with the policy accounts helps to map out attribution of the changes in the indicators to the policy action taken. From Table 1.2 and the more detailed analysis in the individual case-studies we can make the following broad observations.

In the 10 countries, quantitative restrictions have been either completely or partly converted to tariffs. Mauritius abolished import permits in 1991, Ghana did the same in 1989, Tanzania by 1993, Zambia by 1992, and Kenya by 1993. South Africa reduced 85 per cent of restrictions by 1990. In these countries, there has been a switch from a positive list of permitted imports to a small negative list of mostly prohibited items or those considered too luxurious for the countries. The remaining countries achieved significant reduction in the proportion of imports covered by licensing. The typical sequence followed in the changes was first to levy import surcharges, and then to adjust the minimum and maximum tariffs prior to abolishing restrictions. This change was strengthened by abolition or reduction in exchange controls in virtually all countries of this study with the exception of South Africa and Nigeria after reversal. A good indicator of amelioration of the stringency of the exchange regimes where applicable, is the sharp decline in the premium on the official exchange rate (see Table 1.2). This partly reflects the extent to which imports (and hence demand for foreign exchange) are now less restricted by controls. Virtual elimination of exchange rate premiums has been achieved in Kenya, Uganda, Ghana, Tanzania and Zambia, where buying and selling of foreign exchange is now market-based and previous restrictions on current account transactions have been abolished. These numbers may not do full justice to the quantum leap in trade facilitation the changes have made possible, as well as the very significant reduction in the transactions costs for importation.

Tariff structures in all countries have been compressed. Mauritius compressed its structure from 60 to 10 tariff categories. Tanzania brought its large number of categories to essentially 3, Kenya from 25 down to 6, Côte d'Ivoire from 10 to 6, and Zambia down to 3. South Africa just began a similar rationalization of its tariff structure in 1995 and Nigeria pursued this effort during 1986/7. The process of compressing the tariff structure has been gradual and intensifying across episodes. The significance of the compression is that the protective structure for industries has become much less varied and it has also significantly reduced the scope for discretionary granting of protection to specific activities. As part of tariff liberalization, duty rates were significantly lowered, again across virtually all 10 countries. Maximum rates have been reduced from 250 per cent to 100 per cent in Mauritius; in Ghana duty rates now range between 10 per cent and 40 per cent. Maximum rates in Tanzania fell from 200 per cent to 60 per cent; in Zambia from 150 per cent to 50 per cent; and in Kenya from 170 per cent to 40 per cent. In Zimbabwe the rates now range from 5 per cent to 30 per cent. Overall, the reduction in tariff rates did not negatively affect revenue collection from this source, partly because of the simultaneous expansion of the tax base made possible by larger programme-funded imports and a steep rise of the local currency value of imports due to large currency depreciations. Moreover, revenue increases may have been induced by the tarrification of quantitative restrictions and increased compliance from tax payers because of the lowering of the scheduled rates.

The effectiveness of the tariff and non-tariff reforms described above is also measured in the case studies in terms of the effective rates of protection (ERP). Liberalization will be construed to have taken place if ERP has fallen. This measure is particularly pertinent to those countries where the overwhelming concern addressed by trade liberalization was the negative incentive effects of protective measures under the ISI strategy. The broad trends of the rates of protection and their structures have been reviewed in each of the studies. In seven out of the ten countries, significant reduction in effective rates of protection (see Table 1.2) as well as rationalization were achieved. Nigeria appears to be the only case of total reversal in this regard, with the average ERP first falling from its 33 per cent pre-SAP levels to 23 per cent in 1986/87, and then climbing back to 41 per cent in 1991 as SAP was abandoned.

Another measure widely used by the case-studies to confirm whether trade liberalization took place is the anti-export bias related to the application of both tariff and non-tariff barriers mainly for protective purposes. These were measured broadly as the ratio of domestic to world terms of trade, with neutrality implying non-existence of wedges related to trade policies. Both trends and structural breaks coinciding with liberalization episodes were investigated. The results for cumulative effects of the various liberalization episodes appear to confirm that anti-export bias has generally declined, particularly if one takes into account steep declines in exchange rate premiums as quantitative restrictions were dismantled and import tariff rates fell. More neutrality of the trade regime has been gained particularly in the 1990s. In the case of Kenya and South Africa, the analysis included testing for structural breaks in the observed trends. These confirm weak effectiveness of particular liberalization episodes.

Overall it would be reasonable to conclude that a significant relaxation of trade restrictions has been achieved across the majority of the countries included in this study. In 1995, there were far fewer import restrictions than in the periods of most stringent application of these in each country. The switch to the use of exchange rate policy for clearing disequilibrium in the market for foreign exchange has considerably reduced the need to use trade policy instruments for managing balance of payments pressures. The critical question is whether this momentum can be sustained in view of the fact that the process of liberalization has been largely prompted by external pressure and sustained to a significant extent by large inflows of external resources to ameliorate adjustment costs. In the next section we assess the sustainability of the liberalization initiatives based on their design, assessment of their credibility and learning from past policy reversals.

1.3 POTENTIAL FOR SUSTAINABILITY OF LIBERALIZATION

That trade reform is often not sustained in Africa is illustrated dramatically by our sample. In only three countries, Uganda, Mauritius and Zimbabwe, have there been no policy reversals. Even in those cases there have been substantial doubts about sustainability. For example, Zimbabwe sharply raised statutory tariffs in January 1995. While this was not in effect a policy reversal, it was widely interpreted as such. In the seven countries where reform was reversed the reversal was total in two cases: Nigeria totally reversed its 1986–94 liberalization in 1994 and Zambia completely changed course after the 1986 collapse of its foreign exchange auction. Many of the partial liberalizations are almost as dramatic. For example, Chapter 5, the case-study on Kenya, identifies no fewer than seven liberalization episodes, most of them separated by large partial reversals. Less dramatically, in Ghana the 1967–70 liberalization was followed by a long period (1972–82) of trade controls and then a new liberalization. Within the control period there was a short, half-hearted liberalization attempt in 1977/78. Therefore within a period of about 15 years Ghana experienced five shifts in trade policy: in 1967 (liberalization), 1970 (reversal), 1977 (liberalization), 1978 (reversal) and 1983 (liberalization). Obviously, frequent policy changes undermine the credibility of subsequent liberalization attempts.

Within our sample Mauritius appears to have been most successful in achieving credibility. This case is in many ways unique. First, of the two liberalization episodes identified in Chapter 6 (in 1979–85 and in 1991–4), the first was characterized by stabilization and exchange rate adjustment, with initially very little change in trade policy measures. The phasing out of QRs did not take place until 1983–5. A possible interpretation of Mauritius' successful trade liberalization is that the government had established credibility by first showing its determination in a traditional stabilization programme. This included showing its willingness to adjust the exchange rate; there were large devaluations in 1979 (23 per cent) and 1981 (17 per cent). By contrast, in many other African countries trade reform was attempted early on, by governments that it was difficult to see as credible because the trade controls were often their own creation and, unlike Mauritius, they had not built up a reputation with policy reform in areas other than trade policy.

This interpretation is necessarily speculative, but other ingredients of Mauritius' success are easy to document. As the authors of Chapter 6 point out, 'sustainability was accorded the highest priority by government'. The government's efforts to ensure compatibility included substantial further exchange rate adjustment (a depreciation of 45 per cent in 1981–5) and the use of import surcharges. One way of viewing the Mauritius reform is to note that initially it only emphasized tariffication; QRs were abolished, but the government took great pains (through a combination of devaluations and surcharges) to ensure that domestic prices of importables did not fall. The issue of payments compatibility therefore simply did not arise. Indeed, the government deliberately overshot. Import volumes substantially decreased (from $529 m in 1980 to only $390 m six years later) and there was a large improvement in the current account. Signalling its determination to the private sector, the government advertised the (rising) level of foreign exchange reserves and repaid an IMF loan ahead of schedule. Given these signals, the fact that the whole machinery of import licensing was left intact until 1991 was interpreted (as the government intended it to be) as an indication that any incipient payments crisis could be dealt with quickly rather than an indication that the government might be willing and able to reverse the reform. Tax changes were announced years ahead, making it easier to interpret them as elements of a long-term strategy. The company tax rate had just been lowered from 35 per cent to only 15 per cent prior to our survey. The survey data confirm the view that the reform programme is seen as fully credible. In particular, respondents indicate that they did not expect a reversal of the tax reduction. The government's awareness of the possibility of incompatibility was shown clearly in 1988, when it refused to accept a World Bank recommendation for early tariff reductions, arguing that this would lead to fiscal incompatibility.

The Uganda case is similar in one respect: the early emphasis on eliminating distortions in the foreign exchange market. Uganda first devalued, then moved to an auction system and then introduced foreign exchange bureaus. By the end of 1994 the foreign exchange rate premium in the parallel market had completely disappeared, a remarkable achievement. In other ways Uganda is quite different from most of the countries in our sample, in particular in having a president who is committed to reform, not identified with the previous control regime and willing to rely on the advice of 'technopols'. Williamson's (1994) study of the political economy of policy reform does not cover Africa, but Uganda seems to satisfy many of the conditions for successful reform he identified for Latin America and Eastern Europe.

Zimbabwe is very unusual in having postponed liberalization longer than any other country in the sample. Structural adjustment did not start until 1991. In the early part of the reform programme compatibility was not achieved. Imports were artificially cheap and private agents responded with speculation. Ncube *et al.* estimate in Chapter 11 that in 1992 the balance of payments deficit may have amounted to an astonishing 20 per cent of GDP. This coincided with very high real interest rates making speculative responses such as hoarding of imports (Calvo, 1988) extremely costly. Compatibility was subsequently achieved with a large devaluation. By 1993 the foreign exchange rate premium had virtually disappeared.

Zimbabwe's case is somewhat unusual in two respects. First, while the reform has been aid-supported and indeed ESAP, as the structural adjustment programme is known in Zimbabwe, is strongly identified with the World Bank, the government was not desperate for aid money. Donor involvement has not led to a perception of time inconsistency, as for example, happened in Kenya in the 1980s. Secondly, there was a domestic constituency for reform outside the government. The CZI (Confederation of Zimbabwe Industries) became convinced of the need for reform as early as 1987 on the basis of evidence from its members that import controls held back industrial output. Similarly, the influential Commercial Farmers Union adopted a pro-reform stance at an early stage. In the ESAP period there have been some policy reversals. Notably, items were moved on and off OGIL (the Open General Import Licence) and in January 1995 a large number of statutory tariff rates were raised, in many cases to 100 per cent. While the tariff changes did not constitute a policy reversal, (but at most the possibility of a reversal), they were so interpreted.

The fiscal effects of Zimbabwe's reform are difficult to assess. As usual, the effect on tariff revenue was strong and positive as QRs were replaced by tariffs and the tariff base expanded through exchange rate adjustment. However, this was offset by the government being a net buyer of foreign exchange. Since 1994 the fiscal deficit has grown alarmingly, for reasons largely unrelated to the trade liberalization. This has been reflected in high interest rates. The survey evidence suggests that this is now holding back investment. While the survey data suggest substantial resource reallocation since 1991, as measured by changes in the sectoral distribution of employment and investment, this has slowed in 1995. The fiscal development could well lead to a policy reversal, but the survey data suggest that this is not what private agents expect. Respondents apparently anticipate fiscal adjustment after the elections.

In the case of Nigeria, the 1986 liberalization involved a simultaneous move from QRs to tariffs and a substantial devaluation. Some reversal occurred early on as domestic firms lobbied successfully for protection in 1988. However, this reversal was modest and in spite of the government's rigging of the foreign exchange 'auction' the post-1986 reforms were largely considered credible. The evidence in Chapter 4 indicates that none of the incredibility measures would be a good predictor of reversals of trade liberalizations, with one exception, the budget deficit. However, though the fiscal deficit was serious in 1993, it is not a sufficient explanation for the 1994 policy reversal. That reversal, which took most observers by surprise, remains a poignant reminder that even credible liberalizations can be reversed.

Ghana's first liberalization (1967–70) initially achieved both payments and fiscal compatibility. Indeed, the government probably overshot, the combination of a sharp devaluation and a dramatic cut in public expenditures leading to a substantial improvement in the current account. However, this was short-lived. The exchange rate was subsequently maintained in the face of fiscal expansion and a terms-of-trade deterioration and by 1970 payments incompatibility was obvious. The second liberalization episode, starting in 1983, achieved compatibility with a combination of frequent exchange rate adjustments and extra aid in support of the structural adjustment programme. However, Ghana has run large fiscal deficits since 1992 and the survey results suggest that the programme is presently not seen as fully credible.

Kenya, as noted above, frequently reversed trade liberalizations. In most cases the government was forced to reverse policies by incompatibility. The most important reason appears to have been the government's reluctance to use exchange rate adjustment. Large trade liberalizations were combined with modest devaluations, sometimes complemented with aid or indirect tax changes. Chapter 5 stresses the lack of incompatibility in 1988/89 when aid fell but the exchange rate adjustment that had become necessary was delayed. Kenya offers the most striking example of the effect of donor involvement on credibility. The first two liberalization attempts in the 1980s were widely seen as time inconsistent, a reluctant government having agreed to trade liberalization and then defaulting on the aid conditions. While Kenya's initial reform (1982/83) was incredible, the donors' stance became credible when Kenya was offered aid again, largely for agreeing to execute measures it had agreed to before. Kenya's subsequent relations with the donor community were stormy. All aid was suspended in 1991–3. In this period the government, desperate for a resumption of aid, moved far in the direction desired by the donors. The incident has therefore become famous as an example of the failure of aid conditions as traditionally practiced.

Kenya offers considerable evidence on private agents' responses to perceived incredibility. Both stockpiling of import licenses and large increases in imports held in bonded warehouses were observed. In addition, as Reinikka (1993) showed, the Kenyan liberalizations of 1976/77, 1982/83 and 1988/89 were typically marked by declining foreign exchange reserves, rising foreign exchange rate premiums and deferral of fixed investment. Unlike the previous ones, the liberalization of 1993/94 was compatible, partly as a result of a very strict monetary policy, but also because from 1994 it was supported by a terms-of-trade improvement, a coffee boom. The current account moved into surplus in 1993. While lack of credibility has plagued Kenya for a long time, at present private agents do not expect a policy reversal. For example, the vast majority of the firms in our survey do not expect increases in tariffs (Table 5 below). At present it is unclear to what extent the resumption of aid can offset the inevitable fall of coffee prices as the boom recedes. There is therefore still doubt on the sustainability of the present reform.

In Tanzania the first liberalization occurred in 1978/79. This was a response to the coffee boom, as in Kenya. It was therefore not credible as a permanent liberalization; private agents could easily recognize that the endogenous trade policy rule that led to trade liberalization when the terms of trade improved would dictate a tightening of controls when the boom was over. Chapter 7 describes how, in the 1980s, Tanzania adopted a series of liberalization measures: export retention schemes, exchange rate adjustment, an own-funded imports scheme, dismantling of QRs and introduction of foreign exchange bureaus. The premium came down from an astonishing 477 per cent in 1985 to 5 per cent in 1993 (Table 7.4 below). The Tanzania reform may be considered successful; the reform was sustained and Ndulu *et al.* show that the regime is now virtually neutral. Though tariffs were raised in 1993, this was for fiscal reasons and was perceived as such rather than as a policy reversal. Compatibility was largely achieved by a very large adjustment of the exchange rate: 85 per cent in real terms over an eight-year period. In addition, there was substantial fiscal tightening so that monetary growth was reduced. The most recent tariff reductions (in 1993) may have gone too far; there is a danger of fiscal incompatibility and a need to reduce tax exemptions and to fight tax evasion. Also, as in Zimbabwe, interest rates now are high, threatening to slow the process of resource reallocation.

Côte d'Ivoire offers an example of serious policy reversal. In the first liberalization episode (1984–7) QRs were dismantled and some tariffs were reduced. This was followed by a two-year period of reversal (1987–9). It appears that the liberalization became incompatible through two exogenous events: a terms of trade deterioration and a growing fiscal deficit. In addition, domestic firms lobbied for a return to protection.

Bohoun *et al.* show in Chapter 2 that in both the first and the second liberalization episode (1990–3) government revenue fell sharply, suggesting fiscal incompatibility.

There were two liberalization episodes in Zambia, the first from 1983 to 1987 and the second from 1989 onwards. The two periods are separated by the dramatic 1987–9 interlude when liberalization was completely reversed. As noted in Chapter 10, the first liberalization started out as credible. Compatibility was achieved through exchange rate adjustment, with the foreign exchange auction the centrepiece of the reform and a striking departure from the period of exchange controls. The failure of this first liberalization attempt was due to a growing fiscal deficit. However, this was not a case of fiscal incompatibility; the growth of the deficit cannot be attributed to the reform. Indeed, since tariff rates were not changed, exchange rate adjustment had a very strong positive effect on government revenue, with devaluations increasing the tariff base.

There is fairly clear evidence that Zambia's first liberalization period quickly became incredible. Musonda *et al.* show (Figure 10.11) that changes in inventories quickly rose, reaching a massive 10 per cent of GDP in 1986. In that year inventory accumulation substantially exceeded total gross fixed capital formation. In the auction period lack of fiscal discipline showed up as exchange rate depreciation. The results were considered politically unacceptable, with the president instructing the central bank to ensure that the *kwacha* did not depreciate further. At that stage the policy stance became completely incredible.

The post-1989 reform has been characterized by Draconian fiscal tightening and has thereby become credible. Expenditure was reduced by the equivalent of 8 per cent of GDP in two years. There appears to have been a period of inventory accumulation in response to the reform but this was short-lived. The reform is currently probably credible but plagued by high interest rates. The resource reallocation that the liberalization is meant to encourage will be slowed, as in Zimbabwe and Tanzania, by high capital costs.

The judgement on liberalization in South Africa is necessarily preliminary, since it is very recent. Measures to reduce anti-export bias have been taken since 1982 and in 1983 QRs were replaced by tariffs. But effective protection was still high in 1994 and substantial tariff reductions started only in 1995. Bleaney *et al.* argue in Chapter 9 that the effect on import quantities is as yet very modest. Credibility does not appear to be an issue. There now has been a period of seven years in which lobbying by domestic industries has been successfully resisted. Also, QRs have not been used for macroeconomic management for a long time. For example, in 1985, a payments crisis led to the introduction of surcharges rather than to tightening of quantitative restrictions. However, the present government may find it difficult to resist labour union pressure. The bilateral treaty between South Africa and Zimbabwe has not been renewed and this creates some doubt about the sustainability of trade liberalization. Lock-in of reform could conceivably be achieved through the free trade area that the European Union has offered South Africa, but at the time of writing the FTA negotiations had not yet started.

The country studies suggest a few generalizations. First, exchange rate adjustment appears critical. The successful liberalizations involved large devaluations and some of the policy reversal in other countries, for example Kenya, can be traced to a reluctance to make sufficient use of exchange rate adjustment. It should be noted that the importance of exchange rate adjustment does not follow from the theoretical literature; compatibility can after all be achieved in other ways. However, the alternatives (for example, the use of programme aid) may well undermine credibility. Conversely, precisely in African economies that had long refused to change the exchange rate, as in Tanzania, Zimbabwe or Zambia, a large devaluation is a very powerful signal of the government's determination.

Second, many liberalizations have been derailed by fiscal problems but usually these were not cases of fiscal incompatibility. The evidence on the fiscal effects of trade reform is not very clear but appears to be positive in many cases, as a result of the replacement of quantitative restrictions by tariffs.

Third, in several countries (for example, Zambia, Tanzania and Zimbabwe) trade reform has been accompanied by high real interest rates, sometimes the result of peculiarities of financial liberalization programmes. The result may be a fall in investment, as suggested by our survey data for Zimbabwe, and hence a slow reallocation of resources. As yet there is no evidence that this has undermined credibility in the countries concerned, but it is clear that support may wane if the benefits of liberation fail to materialize quickly.

Finally, most (but not all) policy reversals in our sample were triggered by incompatibility and governments clearly differed in the importance they attached to achieving compatibility. In both Ghana and Mauritius there was overshooting. In addition, Mauritius simply refused to accept World Bank advice when the government thought this would endanger compatibility. The importance of compatibility is a key conclusion.

1.4 THE CONSEQUENCES OF TRADE LIBERALIZATION

The impacts of trade liberalization are assessed here against the expectations drawn from received wisdom. These are fourfold.

(1) The most widely cited is that liberalization provides expanded market opportunities that when coupled with reduced discrimination against exports allow exploitation of comparative advantage, which permits greater capacity utilization and exploitation of scale economies.
(2) Liberalization, through reducing anti-export bias, stimulates export performance, particularly of non-traditional exports. Openness to international trade and complementary macroeconomic policies are regarded as key to successful export-led industrialization and rapid growth. Southeast Asian success is often cited as a clear example (Krueger, 1995).
(3) Studies that relate trade regimes to export growth in turn also link export growth to income and employment growth in an indirect causation (see Edwards, 1993, for a comprehensive review). This conclusion is tempered by a strong critique that points to the weakness of empirical evidence to verify such a link. The proposed alternative link offered instead is through the alleviation of the foreign exchange constraints to growth (Helleiner, 1986, 1990, 1995; Esfahami, 1991).
(4) Increased competition from abroad and enhanced access to better technology made possible by liberalization induce technological innovation and higher productivity (Feder, 1983; Edwards, 1993; Baldwin, 1995).

A fundamental problem in assessing the impacts of trade liberalization lies in the attribution of observed post-liberalization changes in economic performance to changes in trade policies. The before-and-after comparisons of selected macroeconomic aggregates as used widely in the case-studies, are prone to the now well-established criticism of lacking appropriate counterfactuals. Nevertheless they do shed some light on the consequences of the liberalization initiatives and remain important in gauging perceptions of the various interest groups as to the success of liberalization. Two other related problems in assessing consequences should be noted. The effects of trade policies and trade-liberalizing macroeconomic adjustment are difficult to separate. Furthermore, it is also important to distinguish circumstances under which quantitative restrictions are being applied predominantly for the purpose of managing balance of payments problems and when they are used for protective purposes (Rodrik, 1992), as the consequences may differ. Although the liberalization experiences reviewed in this volume may be too recent and too broken by reversals to allow an accurate assessment of their impacts, we do nevertheless present below the preliminary assessments of their consequences and highlight the attributions to liberalization where the studies have attempted to make them. We focus on resource allocation effects and supply responsiveness.

The case of Mauritius is perhaps the best documented in view of the longevity and effectiveness of its liberalization process. The case study concludes that liberalization has had positive consequences on trade, output and employment. Between 1979 and 1990, the ratio of imports to GDP increased by 35 per cent, while the proportion of GDP exported increased by 46 per cent. The success in raising export orientation of the economy is most notable in this regard. Employment also registered significant gains over the same period with the rate of unemployment falling from 28 per cent in 1982 to 4 per cent in 1991. Employment in the manufacturing sector particularly mirrored periods of intense liberalization. Real GDP growth has been maintained at an average rate of 5.6 per cent through the 1990s. Dabee and Milner, however, caution attribution of this impressive performance solely to the sustained liberalization. They single out very favourable prices (three to five times the world price) for the export item, sugar, under the Lome Agreement; expansion of the tourist industry; and a large increase in foreign direct investment. Macroeconomic stability and the growth enhancing supply-side policies (including trade liberalization) were nevertheless the principal stimulus for taking advantage of these opportunities. The Mauritian experience with liberalization has been credible as confirmed by the upbeat expectations of firms surveyed in the study; respondents indicate that the liberalized environment would stay on course and anticipate higher activity and employment. Gradual implementation, announcement of planned changes well in advance and consensus building around anticipated changes are considered important factors behind the largely supported and sustained liberalization process.

Ghana's case is much less impressive in spite of the fairly long period of uninterrupted liberalization. The retrenchment of the manufacturing sector and the poor response of the private sector to liberalization programmes, partly blamed on overshooting of the liberalization speed, has had adverse effects on real wages and employment. The response of non-traditional exports (excluding gold) has been modest (rising from 4 per cent of total exports to 14.8 per cent) resulting in significantly less diversification of the export basket than anticipated. The most significant stimulus for improved export supply response was identified as the exchange rate depreciation. Overall real growth, however, averaged in excess of 4 per cent, led by revival of agriculture, mining and service sectors, which significantly gained from reduced anti-export bias and considerable infusion of external resources.

Sectoral composition of output shifted away from import substituting and non-tradeable sectors to tradeable sectors as anticipated. Export levels more generally have responded to the adopted measures. The modest revival of investment followed a similar pattern to overall resource reallocation and reflects closely the composition of growth mentioned earlier. Perhaps the most worrisome pressure on sustained liberalization remains the high unemployment linked to the deindustrialization consequences of trade liberalization and public sector retrenchment programmes.

Regional integration has not been an impetus for liberalization, nor has Ghana's liberalization had significant effects on trade with ECOWAS member states. Liberalization has led to increased government revenues and collection. Excessive spending, however, resulted in a huge budget deficit in 1992, which has only been contained in recent years by divestiture earnings from gold and other public investments. Excessive government financing is a threat to the liberalization programme, and a lack of support for the programme has been expressed in certain quarters where the concern is that liberalization has gone too far.

In Kenya, liberalization is assessed to have had positive effects on growth in imports, exports, output and employment. Nominal imports as a percentage of GDP increased by approximately 38 per cent from 26 per cent of GDP in 1972 to 36 per cent in 1993. The ratio of exports to GDP increased by 62 per cent, from 26 per cent to 42 per cent over the same period. Real GDP growth, which averaged 5 per cent in 1988 and 1989, declined thereafter, to revive back to 5 per cent in 1995. There is, however, no significant correlation between liberalization and industrial efficiency, nor have any conclusive observations been made on the effect of liberalization on the government budget deficit. It is predicted that liberalization is likely to improve revenue collection from tariffs, a broader tax base and reduced incentives to avoid duties.

The study reveals support and confidence in Kenya's current liberalization episode. Given the government's past history of reversals, however, and that the current episode is based on temporary balance of payments support, there is a risk that this episode may not be credible. It is nevertheless possible that this episode could be sustained over a period of time before there is substantial pressure on foreign exchange reserves, if commodity prices remain buoyant, growth in import demand is checked by moderate economic growth, and increased official capital inflows are sustained.

In Tanzania's case, liberalization of the exchange regime has been identified as the single most important factor in increased import, export and output growth. Nominal imports to GDP and export to GDP ratios increased by 90 per cent and 78 per cent, respectively, between 1986 and 1993. Real exports to GDP increased over the same period by 26 per cent, from 11.7 per cent to 14.7 per cent. It is observed, however, that tariff liberalization and relaxation of import restrictions have not had a significant effect on real import growth, which has declined marginally, by 4.25 per cent. This is attributed partly to import saving response as costs of imported inputs rose with depreciated currency, a reduction in stockpiling of imports and some deindustrialization. The impact of scrapping explicit taxes on export growth has been insignificant relative to that of the real exchange rate. A simulation exercise to distinguish the effects of macroeconomic adjustment and trade policies confirms this. Real GDP growth averaged 4.25 per annum between 1987 and 1992.

Increased availability of foreign exchange has led to improved industrial efficiency by increasing capacity utilization (albeit from very low levels) and reducing the need to hold excessive stocks. Depreciation of the shilling has also entailed allocative efficiency in response to changes in input prices. In addition, the study indicates that the exporting firms registered higher increases in labour productivity with liberalization.

The government budget deficit as a proportion of GDP declined by 44 per cent, from an average of 10 per cent from 1980–5 to 5.6 per cent after 1985. This reduction has largely been the result of an increase in revenue collection, particularly from imports, and a deceleration of growth in government expenditure. Increased aid flows and borrowing from the public have facilitated reduced recourse to monetization of the deficit.

The main threats to Tanzania's liberalization, which has been credible, relate to the high real interest rate resulting from large sales of treasury bills to diversify sources of government finance and mop up excess liquidity. This may entail a significant real appreciation of the shilling and may breed fiscal indiscipline. As well, the build-up of domestic public debt represents a future burden that may necessitate higher taxes to service.

Liberalization measures in Zambia are assessed to have had only a marginal effect on the performance of the economy. The ratios of imports and exports to GDP declined over this period, output growth was marginal, and unemployment increased. Real GDP growth averaged –1.1 per cent between 1989 and 1991. The decade from 1983 saw a decline in real imports as a percentage of GDP of 36 per cent, from 52 per cent to 33 per cent. Real exports to GDP declined by 31 per cent, from 29 per cent to 20 per cent, over the same period.

Failure to stimulate exports is largely attributed to the predominance of copper as the major export. Copper production is entirely owned by government, and is subject to externally determined prices. Nor would this sector generate a significant increase in the demand for imported inputs. Failure to stimulate output growth is attributed to macroeconomic instability. The suspension of aid flows in 1993 prompted the government to resort to domestic debt financing, which led to a sharp rise in nominal and real domestic interest rates. This high cost of credit has prohibited output growth, as investment has been more speculative than real.

Despite an established positive correlation between liberalization and government revenues and a reduction in the government deficit, limited response of target sectors to liberalization measures poses a credibility threat to the liberalization process.

The effects of trade liberalization measures in Zimbabwe are difficult to isolate from those of financial liberalization and the internal negative shock of drought that occurred during the short period under consideration. The study pays particular attention to the impact on the manufacturing sector, positing that it is likely to be the most affected by liberalization.

The first phase of liberalization (1990/91) led to an increase in the value and quantity of imports, as this sector benefited from liberalization of imported inputs, in the context of an over-valued exchange rate and continued protection. In the second phase (1991–3), imports declined as a result of increased trade, financial liberalization and the drought, which caused a collapse in demand. The devaluation reduced the inputs subsidy, and financial liberalization caused interest rates to more than triple, from 10 per cent to over 30.5 per cent. The value of the Zimbabwean dollar fell by 165 per cent between 1990 and 1993, from Z$2.45:US$ to Z$6.50:US$. The third phase (1993–4) coincided with the end of the drought and was one of recovery; both imports and output increased. Nominal interest rates declined, and the depreciation of the official exchange rate was countered by a real appreciation of the commercial bank rate. Recovery was not uniform, however, as substantial parts of the manufacturing sector are intrinsically uncompetitive. The current phase has been one of renewed contraction as a result of the reversal in the decline of the interest rate. Real GDP growth in the early 1990s averaged 3.4 per cent per annum, but drought caused a drop of 7.7 per cent in 1992.

The survey shows that the manufacturing export sector grew by 19 per cent in real terms in the four years from 1990/91 to 1994/95. This growth has been modest in terms of value, however, with large inter-sectoral differences. The food and wood sectors have shown rapid growth, the metal sector shows no real trend, and textiles and garments, the dominant sector, has grown by approximately 16 per cent over this period.

The administered wage policy, prior to liberalization, maintained artificially high wages, and consequently high unemployment. Financial liberalization, which has been accompanied by inflation, and trade liberalization has led to a reduction in real wages and increased employment. It is estimated that employment increased by 18.4 per cent between 1991 and 1995.

The study concludes that the effect of trade and financial liberalization on the manufacturing sector has been mixed with regard to imports and output growth, that exports have grown, although modestly, and that liberalization has had a positive effect on employment.

The South African liberalization experience prior to 1995 largely focused on export promotion measures to counter the negative consequences of the ISI strategy. Tarrification of QRs was pursued vigorously during the 1980s, liberalization was pursued only recently. The effect of export subsidies, the principal instrument of export promotion, has been a contribution to the decline in the relative price of non-gold exports. The analysis suggests that these measures in combination with depreciation of the rand stimulated a significant growth of the volume of non-gold exports traded, averaging 7.7 per cent annually between 1984 and 1990. Following the rapid expansion of the 1970s, economic growth has been stagnant, productivity declined in the final years of apartheid, and unemployment remains high.

In Uganda's case, the evidence on the impact of the recent liberalization experience is rather speculative. The lack of accurate historical data precludes conclusive time series analysis. The study does predict that in view of still high tariff levels, liberalization is not expected to encourage import or export growth. The ratio of nominal imports of GDP increased by 123 per cent, from 9 per cent to 20 per cent, between 1989 and 1993, facilitated by revival of the collapsed industrial sector and massive inflows of official and private external resources. Nominal exports to GDP did not increase over this period and remained at 5 per cent. Real GDP grew by an annual average of 6.4 per cent between 1991 and 1995 (with a wide annual dispersion of 3.1 per cent to 10 per cent) partly reflective of the very low base the growth process began from and partly due to macroeconomic adjustment measures being pursued in earnest.

Despite an increase in tax revenues as a percentage of GDP from 7 per cent to 12 per cent over the study period, the study emphasizes that fiscal expenditure has not been effectively rationalized and suggests that trade reform is likely to coincide with an increase in the budget deficit, putting the long-term sustainability of reform into question.

In Nigeria liberalization has not had a significant effect on output, employment, income generation or imports. This is consistent with the very short-lived liberalization attempt that was subsequently reversed. The ratio of imports to GDP has, in fact, declined by 67 per cent, from 15 per cent to 5 per cent, but this is largely influenced by the performance of the oil sector, which has been the dominant economic sector since the 1970s with limited import requirements. Real imports have increased eightfold over this period. This is attributed to the high demand for imports induced by persistent over-valuation of the naira. A deterioration in the government budget deficit (as a percentage of GDP) has preceded reversals in liberalization episodes. These have entailed the return to restrictive import policies, putting the sustainability of liberalization into question. We note that the government budget deficit deteriorated by 28 per cent, from 12.5 per cent to 16 per cent of GDP, between 1970 and 1993. Nigeria's trade policy has not been influenced by its membership in ECOWAS. The strong lobby of local producers is unlikely to support policies that reduce protection. As witnessed in 1988, the lobby was able to secure reversals of such policies.

Evidence for resource reallocation is the very significant deindustrialization, which has taken place in some of these countries as inefficient firms fail to withstand the competitive pressure. As some of the case-studies show, however, large inter-sectoral dispersion of growth performance in manufacturing suggests that the experience is not uniform. Indeed, those firms that could quickly adapt to the more stringent competitive requirements of the liberalized regime have registered impressive growth. The Zimbabwe and Mauritius case-studies provide strong evidence of surviving and thriving firms.

As observed in the case of Ghana and Zimbabwe, sectoral composition of investment has also followed a similar pattern to that of overall resource reallocation. Tradeables and particularly sectors engaged in exporting have attracted a growing share of the modest revival in investment. The significance of this lies in its likely future influence in tilting the structure of production further towards tradeables.

The survey data include interesting evidence on the determinants of investment. As discussed in Chapter 11, two expectational variables are highly significant in a regression analysis of differences between firms in investment rates. Entrepreneurs who expect reductions in regional trade barriers are more likely to invest and invest more than others. Also, those who expect exchange rate depreciation invest more. Hence the surveys suggest a link (via expectations) from trade and exchange rate policies to investment. The effect of the lowering of regional trade barriers on investment is an important effect which so far has received no attention.

Surprisingly – and contrary to the popular view – more than half of the case-studies reviewed here indicate either a positive or unchanged situation as far as employment is concerned. Where the unemployment problem has been attributed to liberalization gone too far, such as is the case of Ghana, public sector retrenchment schemes as well as the stoppage of budget subsidies to public enterprises have contributed significantly to this deterioration.

1.5 CONCLUSIONS

The restrictive trade regimes of the case study countries prior to liberalization were influenced by several key factors. These include the protective needs of the widely adopted import-substitution strategy, the heavy reliance on external trade taxes, and the management of balance-of-payments crises through the use of import controls and foreign exchange rationing mechanisms. The most dominant stimulus for trade liberalization emanated from conditions imposed for gaining access to external resources in the context of structural adjustment programs. While other stimuli such as positive external shocks and 'own initiative' played a role in this respect, the trade liberalization episodes they induced were often short-lived. The least significant of the stimuli for trade liberalization was membership in a regional integration scheme. Clearly, there was hardly any overlap between national-level trade liberalization initiatives driven primarily by SAPs and trade liberalization protocols agreed to in the context of regional integration arrangements.

A significant relaxation of trade restrictions has been achieved in most of the countries covered in this project. But African trade liberalization remains fragile and subject to problems of credibility and sustainability that are associated with payments and fiscal incompatibility. Thus, trade reform has been reversed, partially or fully, at one time or the other, by many of the case-study countries, while in the others there have been substantial doubts about sustainability. Exchange rate adjustment appears critical in this respect. Many of the more successful liberalization attempts involved large devaluations, while some of the policy reversals can be traced to a reluctance to make sufficient use of exchange rate adjustment.

Over the relatively short periods of trade liberalization in the case-study countries, there has generally been a shift in the allocation of resources towards tradeables and away from non-tradeables and import substitution in response to the liberalization measures. This is reflected in the positive though modest response of exports. In particular, export orientation has increased and trade shares are higher. But significant deindustrialization has also taken place in some of these countries as inefficient firms have failed to withstand new competitive pressures. On the whole, however, employment levels have not been significantly affected by trade liberalization measures.

References

Baldwin, R. E. (1995) 'Review of Theoretical Development on Regional Integration', mimeo, AERC, Nairobi.

Bevan, D., P. Collier and J. W. Gunning (1987) 'Consequences of a Commodity Boom in a Controlled Economy: Accumulation and Redistribution in Kenya 1975–83', *World Bank Economic Review*, **1**(3):489–513.

Bevan, D. L., P. Collier and J. W. Gunning (1989) 'Fiscal Response to a Temporary Trade Shock: The Aftermath of the Kenyan Coffee Boom', *World Bank Economic Review*, **3**(3):359–78.

Bevan, D., P. Collier and J. W. Gunning (1989) *Peasants and Governments: An Economic Analysis* (Oxford: Clarendon).

Calvo, G. A. (1988) 'Costly Trade Liberalizations: Durable Goods and Capital Mobility', *IMF Staff Papers*, **35**:461–73.

Collier, P. and J. W. Gunning (1992) 'Aid and Exchange Rate Adjustment in African Trade Liberalisations', *Economic Journal*, **102**:925–39.

Edwards, S. (1993) 'Openness, Trade Liberalization and Growth in Developing Countries', *Journal of Economic Literature*, **21**:1358–93.

Esfahami, H. S. (1991) 'Exports, Imports and Economic Growth in Semi-industrialized Countries', *Journal of Development Economics*, **35**(1):93–116.

Feder, H. (1983) 'On Exports and Economic Growth', *Journal of Development Economics*, **12**(1/2):59–73.

Greenaway, D. (1993) 'Liberalising Foreign Trade through Rose Tinted Glasses', *Economic Journal*, **103**:208–222.

Helleiner, G. K. (1986) 'Outward Orientation, Import Instability and African Economic Growth: An Empirical Investigation', in S. Lall and F. Stewart (eds), *Theory and Reality in Development: Essays in Honour of Paul Streeten* (New York: St. Martin's Press).

Helleiner, G. K. (1990) 'Trade Strategy in the Medium-Term Adjustment', *World Development*, **18**(6).

Helleiner, G. K. (1995) 'Manufacturing for Export in the Developing World: Problems and Possibilities'. mimeo, Toronto.

Krueger, A. (1995) *Trade Policies and Developing Nations* (INE Series, Brookings Institution).

Papageorgiou, D., M. Michaely and A. Choksi (1991) *Liberalising Foreign Trade*, 7 vol. (Oxford: Blackwell).

Pritchett, L. and G. Sethi (1994) 'Tariff Rates, Tariff Revenue and Tariff Reform: Some New Facts', *World Bank Economic Review*, **8**(1).

Reinikka, R. S. (1993) 'Credibility, Speculation and the Speed of Trade Liberalisation with an Application to Kenya', unpublished D Phil thesis, University of Oxford.

Rodrik, D. (1992) 'Closing the Productivity Gap: Does Trade Liberalization Really Help?', in G. K. Helleiner (ed.), *Trade Policy, Industrialization, and Development: New Perspectives* (Oxford: Clarendon).

Williamson, J. (ed.) (1994) *The Political Economy of Policy Reform* (Washington: Institute of International Economics).

2 Evaluating Trade Liberalization Episodes in Côte d'Ivoire*

Andrew McKay, Oussou Kouassy and Bouabré Bohoun

2.1 INTRODUCTION

Since the beginning of the 1980s, economic liberalization has become an increasingly important item on the agenda of economic policies undertaken in developed as well as developing countries. Liberalization of foreign trade has been an important component of such policies in most cases, where in general this has meant a movement from inward-orientated policies based on import substitution towards outward-orientated policies. In the developing world, the first countries to embark on such trade liberalizing policies were generally in Latin America and Asia. According to Papageorgieu, Michaely and Choksi (1991), the records achieved by many of these countries in liberalizing their foreign trade were generally positive.

African countries tended to move towards liberalization of their economies in general, and of foreign trade in particular, later than other developing regions. The World Bank report, *Accelerated Development in Sub-Saharan Africa Countries*, published in 1981, can be regarded as the starting point of these policies. Indeed, one of its major conclusions was the necessity to liberalize African economies in order to enhance development strategies, representing a reversal of the policy stance of the previous two decades. Economic liberalization in general, and the liberalization

* Final research report prepared for the African Economic Research Consortium (AERC). We are grateful to the AERC for the financial support to enable us to undertake this research, which was conducted as part of their collaborative research project on Trade Liberalization and Regional Integration in subSaharan Africa. An earlier version of this paper was presented at the AERC workshop on this theme held in Harare in March 1995. We gratefully acknowledge the helpful comments received from resource persons and other participants at this workshop, especially those of the paper's official discussant, Jack London.

of foreign trade in particular, became one of the most important components of the IMF and World Bank-supported adjustment programmes implemented in Africa.

Two subsequent World Bank reports on African economies (*Sub-Saharan Africa: From Crisis to Sustainable Growth* [1985]; and *Adjustment in Africa: Reforms, Results, and the Road Ahead* [1993]) have come to the same conclusions: those African economies that have adopted liberalization measures consistently are the ones that have achieved better results in their reforms.

Côte d'Ivoire was one of the first African countries to embark on structural adjustment programmes (SAPs), in response to the economic crisis the country experienced at the beginning of the 1980s. (The ongoing structural adjustment programme – 1994–6 – is the fifth since 1981.) Some of these programmes have involved trade policy reforms, which in principle were intended to liberalize foreign trade. So far, however, there has been relatively limited systematic assessment of the reality, extent and impacts of these trade liberalization reforms. On the one hand, it is necessary to assess the extent to which the trade policy reforms conceived in the SAPs were in fact liberalizing measures, and the extent to which the measures were implemented and sustained. On the other hand, it is important to examine the impacts of the trade reforms that were actually implemented. According to conventional theory, trade liberalization can be expected to affect factor utilization (transitional effects), factor allocation (short-term to medium-term effects) and factor accumulation (long-term effects). To what extent are these effects observed in the Ivorian case?

Concurrently with the structural adjustment process in Africa, there is a growing concern about regional integration. Referring to the 1980 OAU Lagos Economic Summit, the interest in regional integration in West Africa is now shown in the reactivation of ECOWAS (Economic Community of West African States) and the transition from UMOA (West African Monetary Union) to UEMOA (Economic and Monetary Union of West Africa) in the francophone countries. This raises the question of the compatibility of the regional integration and trade liberalization processes. This chapter also tries to deal with the issue of the interactions between regional integration and trade liberalization in the specific case of Côte d'Ivoire, considering to what extent they are consistent or contradictory.

The structure of this chapter is as follows. In section 2.2, we briefly summarize the macroeconomic background and set out the specific issues that arise in examining trade policy in the case of Côte d'Ivoire. Sections 2.3 and 2.4 represent the main body of the chapter, the assessment of the extent to which trade liberalization measures were in fact implemented and pursued; this is discussed in Section 2.3 by means of a descriptive policy account and in Section 2.4 by quantitative measures that can be considered as indicators of trade policy stance (following the arguments set out by Collier, Greenaway and Gunning, 1994). It is argued here that though a number of trade policy measures were undertaken, some of which were apparently liberalizing, often these were not sustained. Section 2.5 examines the impact of those trade policy measures that were undertaken and discusses the factors that led to some policy reversals. Section 2.6 then considers trade policy issues from a firm-level perspective on trade liberalization, based on the preliminary results of a survey of manufacturing firms. Section 2.7 addresses the issue of the consistency of the regional integration arrangements to which Côte d'Ivoire is a party, discussing whether or not these adversely affected measures to liberalize trade policy. Section 2.8 concludes.

2.2 OVERVIEW OF TRADE POLICY ISSUES IN CÔTE D'IVOIRE

Macroeconomic Background

From independence in 1960 until 1977, macroeconomic performance in Côte d'Ivoire was impressive. Based on outward-orientated policies, and centred around the export of primary commodities (coffee, cocoa), the economy grew rapidly, while inflation was kept under control by membership in UMOA. However, macroeconomic performance deteriorated sharply following the end of the commodity price boom of 1976/77. The government response to the significant increases in cocoa and coffee prices in the boom years was to launch a large public investment programme, a programme that was not curtailed following the collapse of commodity prices after 1977.

The consequence was a significant increase in the fiscal deficit, some of which was financed by monetary expansion, leading to increased inflation; much of the deficit was financed externally, however, leading to an increased debt burden. As a result (and given the fixed nominal exchange rate), the real exchange rate became increasingly over-valued, a phenomenon that can be explained in terms of a 'Dutch disease' effect (Devarajan and de Melo, 1987; Chamley, 1991). There was also a large current account deficit.

The situation was clearly becoming unsustainable; in response, the government undertook a series of structural adjustment programmes in the 1980s and early 1990s, the objectives of which were initially to restore fiscal and external balance. Achieving these objectives required a depreciation of the over-valued real exchange rate, but membership in UMOA meant that the government did not have the policy option of unilaterally devaluing the nominal exchange rate. In these circumstances other mechanisms are required to achieve a real devaluation, such as fiscal and monetary contraction and the use of trade policy instruments. Heavy reliance was therefore placed on controlling public expenditure and on monetary contraction. Trade policy measures were also used to try to adjust the real exchange rate towards its equilibrium level (Bohoun and Kouassy, 1993).

In practice, it proved very difficult to attain a sustained depreciation of the real exchange rate. Initially, the policy measures taken, along with a fortuitous depreciation of the French franc, enabled a significant real exchange rate depreciation over the period 1980–4, but by 1986 the real exchange rate again began to appreciate. This was due in part to external factors such as adverse terms of trade movements and the appreciation of the French franc. The economy moved into a sharp decline from 1987 until the early 1990s and remained relatively stagnant until 1994.

January 1994 saw the devaluation of the CFA franc (from CFAF 50 = FF1 to CFAF 100 = FF 1), largely or completely eliminating the overvaluation of the real exchange rate. The issue now, of course is the extent to which it will be possible to maintain the real exchange rate close to its equilibrium level, avoiding the problems of severe over-valuation that plagued the 1980s and early 1990s. While it is still early to know the definitive answer to this question, there is plenty of evidence to suggest that immediately following the devaluation, economic activity and trade picked up sharply.

Specific Trade Policy Issues in the Case of Côte d'Ivoire

In the conduct of trade policy in Côte d'Ivoire, a number of specific issues arise that must be taken into account in considering the trade policy reforms actually undertaken. Such issues are important because they may reduce the degree of freedom to the government has to pursue trade liberalization. Potentially, also, they have an important impact on the credibility of any steps actually taken.

The Fixed Nominal Exchange Rate

One of the most important issues is the consequence of Côte d'Ivoire's membership in UMOA, in which the CFA franc is pegged at a fixed rate to the French franc. Consequently, the nominal exchange rate relative to the French franc and to all currencies outside the CFA franc zone is not a policy instrument for the government. Thus, the authorities are not able to control one of the most obvious variables affecting the real exchange rate, a key variable for trade policy. However, a number of alternative mechanisms do exist for influencing the real exchange rate, notably fiscal policy and trade policy itself.

Given the importance of maintaining the real exchange rate at something close to its equilibrium level, these other policy options are of heightened importance in the case of members of UMOA. Fiscal policy is capable of influencing the real exchange rate through its impact on the domestic price level, a contractionary fiscal policy serving to drive down the domestic price level relative to the foreign price level (or to reduce the price of non-tradeables relative to tradeables), leading to a more competitive real exchange rate. Expansionary fiscal policy will have the reverse effect, leading to real exchange rate over-valuation. Similar principles apply to monetary policy, though as discussed below UMOA membership imposes certain constraints on monetary policy. Trade policy measures can operate on the real exchange rate through changing the price of tradeable goods relative to non-tradeable goods. Both import tariffs and export subsidies are likely to increase the domestic price of tradeable goods relative to non-tradeable goods, thereby increasing domestic competitiveness (increasing the incentive to produce, and reducing the incentive to consume, tradeables). The policy of simultaneously introducing import tariffs and export subsidies is commonly referred to as a 'mock devaluation', since it attempts to achieve the same effects on incentives to export and import as a devaluation of the nominal exchange rate would.

While measures involving the introduction of import tariffs and export subsidies appear at first sight to be a movement away from neutrality rather than a liberalization, the appropriate definitions of neutrality and liberalization are more complex in this case. If the real exchange rate is indeed over-valued, then the price of tradeable goods will be too low relative to the price of non-tradeable goods; this represents a deviation from neutrality that may be offset by appropriate levels of import tariffs and export subsidies. The basic point is that an evaluation of the structure of protection should take into account any potential real exchange rate over-valuation as well as commercial policy interventions. Only by considering both can we arrive at an appropriate concept of neutrality.

In discussing the mock devaluation, an important question may be raised as to whether commercial policy interventions will have a lasting impact on the price of tradeables relative to non-tradeables, or whether the effect will be merely temporary. This arises because of the impact of export subsidies and import tariffs on the price of non-tradeable goods. Theoretically, under reasonable assumptions, Milner and McKay (1996) demonstrate that the price of a composite non-tradeable good will rise by the weighted average of the increases in the price of the composite exportable and composite importable goods, with the weights summing to one. Hence, overall, the real exchange rate may not change in the long run, although the real exchange rates for the export sector or for the import sector may change. At a practical level, increases in the price of tradeable goods, notably importables, may create upward pressure on wages and ultimately on the price of non-tradeable goods. Either way, the increase in the price of non-tradeable goods will at least partly offset the increase in the relative price of tradeable goods.

If these concerns are legitimate, then the mock devaluation may ultimately not be successful in adjusting the real exchange rate, or may be successful only if accompanied by appropriate fiscal and/or monetary policy (contractionary in the situation of real exchange rate over-valuation). It should also be recognized that the mock devaluation itself will have consequences for the fiscal balance, but the direction of this effect is ambiguous *ex ante*. These fiscal consequences may enhance or reduce the effectiveness of the mock devaluation on the real exchange rate, depending on the relative magnitudes of the resulting increases in tariff revenue and expenditure on export subsidies.

Fiscal Policy

Fiscal policy plays a key role in this discussion not just because it is potentially a means (albeit blunt) of correcting for misalignments of the real exchange rate, but also because trade policy inevitably has fiscal consequences. Côte d'Ivoire is a country that has been bedevilled by fiscal deficits for a long time, and this has probably been an important factor contributing to real exchange rate over-valuation. Moreover, trade taxes are an important source of revenue for the government (and subsidies an element of expenditure). Changes in trade policy measures therefore have significant fiscal consequences. Trade liberalization may result in a loss of fiscal revenue, which may lead to domestic inflation and a tendency towards over-valuation of the real exchange rate.

It should be recognized, however, that trade liberalization does not necessarily have adverse fiscal consequences. Where trade liberalization involves the reduction of tariffs that are already higher than the revenue maximizing tariffs, a lowering of these tariffs may in fact have beneficial fiscal consequences. The replacement of quantitative restrictions by tariffs (often considered a liberalizing move) will have beneficial effects on fiscal revenue. So it is not necessarily and always the case that trade liberalization has adverse fiscal consequences.

The overall point is that changes in commercial policy interventions will have fiscal consequences that have implications for other key variables in the economy. Given the long history of fiscal deficits in Côte d'Ivoire, this issue of fiscal consequences is particularly important in this case. They may act to limit degrees of freedom in pursuing trade strategy.

Monetary Policy

Membership in UMOA places certain restrictions on the monetary policy that can be pursued by member countries. In particular, the arrangement places a ceiling on the amount of credit the central bank (BCEAO: *Banque Centrale des Etats de l'Afrique de l'Ouest*) can give to member countries, which severely limits the countries' ability to engage in seigniorage. If member countries pass this ceiling they pay a punitive interest rate; this has happened in the case of Côte d'Ivoire, but there is a clear incentive for countries to avoid putting themselves in this position. While obviously members countries do have other mechanisms through which they can finance spending, their limited ability to engage in seigniorage has meant that inflation performance among UMOA countries has been significantly better than in a number of neighbouring countries outside UMOA. Other things being equal, this obviously has a beneficial impact on the competitiveness of member countries.

In short, UMOA arrangements constrain a country's ability to engage in expansionary monetary policy, but do not limit countries wishing to pursue a tight monetary policy.

2.3 A DESCRIPTIVE ACCOUNT OF TRADE POLICY IN CÔTE D'IVOIRE

The consideration of trade liberalization as a specific and explicit policy measure is a very recent phenomenon in the history of Côte d'Ivoire. The establishment of a comprehensive and coherent trade liberalization programme was closely related to the adjustment programmes of the 1980s and early 1990s, supported by the international donors (mainly the World Bank, the IMF and the French government).

In reality, the objective of trade liberalization did not proceed on an uninterrupted basis, but experienced many breaks and reversals. In part, as we shall see later, this is related to issues discussed in the previous section and to questions of credibility. First, however, we provide a policy account that describes this process, focusing on the measures relating to tariffs, quantitative restrictions (QRs) and other non-tariff barriers (NTBs) that were actually applied. Of course, an increase in any of these instruments normally indicates a tendency to increase the protection of the economy and a decrease signals liberalization efforts or attempts, though as we have already seen, this all needs to be considered in the context of the evolution of the real exchange rate.

Before coming to the policy account, we discuss briefly the instruments of trade policy used by the government in the past and/or at present.

The tariff structure in Côte d'Ivoire is very complex, as can be seen in Table 2.1. There are various entry duties and taxes, with imported products, for instance, being subject to at least to 3 to 4 types of taxes (custom duties, fiscal duties, VAT, specific entry tax, etc.). Each tax generally has many rates according to the sector and the status of taxpayers (there are 3200 tariff positions and many exemptions). Although less complex, export duties also vary according to the sector and the taxpayer.

By the end of the 1980s the nominal tariff varied between 0 and 151 per cent, with an average of 33 per cent. In addition to tariff protection, Côte d'Ivoire has also set up a wide range of NTBs, including licences and quotas, reference prices and set values (mainly for imported goods). This wide range of trade measures allows for an interesting discussion and analysis of trade policy in the country. We consider now the evolution of these trade policy measures over time, considering the period from 1971 to the present.

1971–80: Tariff Discrimination, QRs and Other NTBs

Prior to the era of the SAPs, the first deliberate trade-related measures were undertaken between 1971 and 1973. Following the recommendations of the World Bank, the Ivorian government introduced escalating import taxes (taxes were higher for more finished products), as well as licences and other NTBs (setting values and quotas). In line with the orthodoxy at the time, this first wave of protection was presented as the best way to strengthen the import substitution industries, while at the same time starting up a complementary export-orientated strategy.

By 1973 these measures had resulted in a growing and discriminatory effective protection across sectors. According to Michel and Noël (1984), while the nominal rate of protection (NRP) remained stable between 1971 and 1978, the effective rate of protection (ERP) rose on average from 39 per cent to 76 per cent. Their study also showed a big dispersion of the ERPs across sectors over this period. Indeed, the ERP of the cereal processing sector increased from 18 per cent to 52 per cent and that of beverages and food processing increased from 71 per cent to 118 per cent, while the sectors of cooking fats (38 per cent to 22.5 per cent), other food industries and tobacco (106 per cent to 82 per cent), building materials (25.6 per cent to 5.5 per cent) and the rubber industry (22.5 per cent to –9 per cent) became less protected or disprotected. The situation of the remaining sectors remained unchanged.

Textiles did not benefit very much from the tariff changes of 1971–3, but this industry was the one most protected by NTBs. Out of the 86 products under import licences in 1973, 41 were in the textiles sector. In 1976, the number of textile products under this restriction increased to

Table 2.1 Trade policy instruments in Côte d'Ivoire

(a) Imports	
(1) Direct taxes	
Customs duties (*Droits de douane*)	Ad valorem tax on c.i.f. value of 5 per cent–10 per cent. A number of exemptions, including food products, capital goods, raw materials and imports from CEAO countries.
Fiscal entry duties (*Droit fiscal d'entrée*)	Major revenue source; charged on c.i.f. value at rates of
Surtaxes and surcharges	Introduced to replace QRs on certain products
Statistic tax (*taxe statistique*)	Applies at a uniform rate of 2 per cent on products under temporary admission.
Preferential tax (TCR – *Taux de Coopération Régionale*)	Reduced entry tax for products from CEAO countries, which do not pay fiscal duties or customs duties
(2) Indirect taxes	
Value added tax (TVA – *taxe valeur ajouté*)	Charged on c.i.f. values of imports including all import duties; three rates: reduced, normal and increased.
Specific taxes	Specific taxes on particular products: alcoholic drinks, motor fuels, and so on.
(3) Non-tariff barriers	
Licences	Quotas determined by Directorate of External Trade and shared out among importers
Prior authorization	Importers need prior approval from Ministry of Commerce; functions like a licence
Declaration of intention to import	Imports need declaration of intention to import by importers, but volumes are not controlled.
Reference prices	Set prices for competitive imports to ensure international price is similar to domestic price
(b) Exports	
Exit duty (*Droit unique de sortie*)	Charged on most products at rates from 0 to 30 per cent; exemptions for priority enterprises in agriculture and mining
Export subsidies	
Special tax for OIC and CICE	0.6 per cent; coffee and cocoa exempted

Source: Compiled by the authors.

147 out of a total of 310, and in 1982 this number passed to 182 of 424. In fact, the textile sector has consistently had the highest number of products subject to QRs since the beginning of this policy in 1971.

Over this period the government also set up many public enterprises. More than 250 of the 400 public enterprises listed in 1981 were set up during this period.

1981–3: the First SAP

Faced with all the macroeconomic problems described in section 2.2, the government in 1981 signed its first structural adjustment loan (SAL 1) with the World Bank and a standby agreement with the IMF. This first SAP was dominated by macroeconomic measures, aiming above all to eliminate the external and internal macro imbalances (balance of payments and fiscal deficits) of the late 1970s and early 1980s. But this first SAP also contained some specific measures relating to agricultural activities, in the areas of prices and incentives, reform of the agricultural development agencies, and sectoral investments. The macro underpinning and pro-agriculture orientation of these first measures did not prevent them from affecting other sectors, and in turn trade performance and incentives. But such effects were indirect, rather than the result of deliberate, targeted policy.

The macro objectives were achieved through a traditional public spending cut package, with most of the effort directed towards spending cuts in public investment. Additionally, some specific measures were taken, such as the suppression of housing benefit for teachers of all levels, a slow down in the recruitment of new civil servants and a limitation on the increase in the budget of 1 per cent from year to year. The government also spelt out its privatization strategy and started to list public enterprises likely to be reformed or privatized later.

The reform of agricultural incentives was achieved through an increase in producer prices, the elimination of subsidies for expanding plantation (cocoa) and for the acquisition of fertilizer for most agricultural products, the elimination of the rebate of 15 FCFA/kg on cotton fibre sold to domestic manufacturers, and so on. Though this package included both positive and negative measures for the agricultural sector, on balance the net effects were positive.

These measures, although not directly related to trade liberalization, generated some effects in terms of costs or relative prices (industry *vis-à-vis* agriculture), affecting the competitiveness of Ivorian industry. The increase in producer prices of agricultural products resulted in increasing costs for the manufacturers using these products as raw materials, while the public spending cutbacks, combined with the elimination of subsidies on fertilizers, led to a sharp fall in domestic demand. This lack of demand pushed firms towards more export activities as shown by Bohoun and Kouassy (1993). On the other hand, the success of fiscal reform (public spending cutbacks and the reduction of the fiscal deficit) was seen as likely to stop or reverse the over-valuation of the real exchange rate. Therefore, the stabilization of the economy was expected to generate, in addition to its positive fiscal effects, appropriate conditions for industrial competitiveness.

But given the strong deterioration of the terms of trade and the relatively small increase in other domestic government revenues, the fiscal improvements did not last very long, whereas the adverse effects of the reforms were more long lasting. This situation required a complete industrial reform, with trade reform measures being a major component. It was in the second SAP that explicit trade policy reforms were introduced.

1984–mid 1987: the First Deliberate Liberalization Episode

The tariff changes undertaken concerned the introduction of temporary tariffs (surcharges and surtaxes) as a means of transforming QRs into tariffs. The government also introduced an export subsidy (*prime à l'exportation*) and a VAT reimbursement on imported inputs used for exported goods. These two last measures formed an important part of the mock devaluation referred to previously. Attempts were made to lower and harmonize tariff levels in order to get average effective rates of protection of 40 per cent in industry and 20 per cent in agriculture.

The surcharges and surtaxes introduced were limited to agro-industries at the beginning. They were extended later to all of the industrial sector (Decree 87–1278, June 1985) and to some agricultural sectors (Decree 87–17278, October 87).

The changes in NTBs concerned the dismantling of QRs, mentioned above. The list of products subject to NTBs fell from 320 in 1984 to 250 by the end of 1987.

Mid 1987–89: Reversal of the First Liberalization Attempt

Over this period, there was again an increase in tariff and non-tariff protection. New taxes were introduced and some taxes were increased. For instance, in August 1987 the entry duties were increased by 30 per cent, and the objective of 40 per cent ERP for the industrial sector was adjusted upwards to 52 per cent. 1988 saw the introduction of new entry duties, DSE, on some goods (40 per cent for capital goods and 20 per cent for agricultural goods), and an increase in the tariffs for some specific products (some fibres, rice, iron, tobacco), followed in 1989 by the introduction of the *taxe statistique* or statistic tax (at a uniform rate of 2 per cent on products on the temporary admission regime). Moreover, the government extended the list of products under QRs in response to pressure from industrial firms in the textile industry. Indeed, in 1988, as a result of the reintroduction of reference prices and the placing of QRs on 300 products including footwear and textiles, along with other factors, the World Bank interrupted its adjustment loans.

Clearly over this period Côte d'Ivoire experienced a break in its liberalization programme. This major reversal can be explained by the financial constraints (the disastrous fiscal situation of the government, facing a sharp decline in international prices of commodities) and the pressure from local firms, which generally benefited from the protection of the domestic market.

1990–3: the Second Liberalization Episode

This second liberalization episode was characterized by an acceleration of tariff changes, as well as of the privatization programme.

Tariff changes included the suppression in 1990 of the DSE, which had been in place since 1988. In 1993 the custom duties were collapsed into one rate (5 per cent) from the three that had applied previously (10 per cent, 5 per cent and 2 per cent). The government also eliminated most of the export duties (DUS – *droit unique de sortie* on coffee and cocoa). It also introduced a single office (*guichet unique*) to deal with all export regulation and export incentives (export subsidies, export procedures, VAT reduction and special regimes for imported inputs used in exporting activities, and so on). This period was also marked by a limitation and a simplification of the set value scheme, where all the past authorizations and price and quality controls were gradually replaced by a single check exerted by SGS (*Société Générale de Surveillance*) once for all. The willingness of the government to move again towards a more liberalized and export-orientated regime can be seen in these measures.

Nevertheless, it is important to note that this period was very disrupted because of political and social movements. Following the failure of the government to implement a general salary cut measure, President Houphouet was forced to reintroduce a multi-party system. The coming of Alassane Ouattara to the economic scene, and the launch of a new adjustment programme with a consistent macroeconomic framework, did improve the adjustment scheme as a whole. But it brought in too many measures at the same time. The few things that were done on the side of trade liberalization were sketching a policy analysis matrix, tackling the issue of the dismantling of NTBs and seeking to make the tariff structure of Côte d'Ivoire more transparent.

Since 1994: Devaluation and the Accompanying Programme

This last liberalization episode takes place in a peculiar context: the devaluation of the CFA franc after more than 45 years of stability. The discussion above mentioned the non-availability of the exchange rate instrument in countries, like Côte d'Ivoire, that belong to a monetary union. Other measures to control the real exchange rate were generally not effective (see above); the ability to control the nominal exchange rate was therefore required in this case in order to correct the misalignment and over-valuation of the currency, which had become serious obstacles to the adjustment process. In January 1994, the CFA franc was devalued by 50 per cent in foreign currency terms, and a set of measures were taken to mitigate the expected negative effects and maximize the positive impacts of the devaluation.

Given the inflation surge of 32.5 per cent in 1994, the huge devaluation of the CFA franc should have improved the competitiveness of Ivorian production by at least 47.5 per cent for exportables (the elimination of export subsidies and the reintroduction of export taxes having eroded the gains of this sector). But adjusting for the previous over-valuation, ranging from 15 per cent to 30 per cent, the economy ended up with a competitiveness gain from 50 per cent to 32 per cent for importables and from 33 per cent to 17.5 per cent for exportables. Without appropriate correcting policies, the devaluation would have been more beneficial to the importables sector than to the exportables sector, conflicting with the stated desire of the government for more export orientation. Besides this, there was a need for a correction of fiscal imbalances and for a control of inflationary pressures, requiring accompanying policy measures in order to maximize the global gains of the devaluation.

The correcting measures relating to trade policy concern tariffs and customs reforms, VAT and other domestic tax reforms, the new investment code, and the privatization programme. After the devaluation, custom duties, which had amounted to 18 per cent on average beforehand, were brought down to 13 per cent (a fall of nearly one-third). Also, the maximum tariff fell from 55 per cent to 70 per cent before the devaluation to 35 per cent afterwards, while the number of duties fell from ten to 6 per cent. The maximum VAT rate of 35 per cent was abolished, and the standard 25 per cent rate was reduced to 20 per cent (a reduction of 20 per cent). Combining these two sets of measures yielded a substantial reduction in import taxes and duties, of 53.3 per cent. Other tax reforms involved the elimination of the employer tax on local staff, the reduction of expatriate staff, and changes in taxation of exports (suppression of the export subsidies and the VAT drawback for export activities, and the reintroduction of the export tax on coffee and cocoa).

At the same time the programme of replacing NTBs by tariffs was accelerated. Indeed, following the devaluation measure, the government planned to eliminate most of the remaining NTBs in a two-year period, except for a short list of products excluded for health and security reasons. The specific plan for the elimination of NTBs was set out according to the following phases: 33 products to be liberalized in 1994, 55 products in January 1995, and 86 products in January 1996. This programme omits 175 products out of the 291 subject to NTBs in January 1994, mostly in the following sectors: health (56 products), the coffee sector (49 products), textiles (20 products) and the security sector (20 products). Nonetheless, the intention remains to accelerate the elimination of NTBs, most of which will be replaced quickly by standard tariffs.

The new investment code, adopted in 1994, extends the advantages to smaller investors and simplifies the application procedure. It distinguishes two regimes for investments depending only on their amount: investments below CFA 500 million are classified in the declaration regime, which allows automatically for tax rebates and holidays and other tax advantages. Above CFA 500 million, investments are classified in the preferential regime (*agrément*), with higher rebates and advantages subject to government authorization and scrutiny. This new code reduces the discrimination in access to the tax advantages relating to investments that had previously been suffered by small business, particularly important for the duties and taxes on trade.

The post-devaluation era is also characterized by an acceleration of the privatization programme of the Ivorian government. During the initial privatization programme launched at the end of the 1980s, 60 public entities were to be sold. Five were sold between 1990 and 1992, four in 1993, five in 1994 and eight in 1995; eleven were planned for 1996. This acceleration of the privatization programme is likely to support the liberalization process by increasing the pace of introducing market forces and competition in the different markets.

The devaluation of the currency and the accompanying programme are typical liberalization measures. The devaluation has improved the relative prices of tradeable goods, particularly for importables. The accompanying programme tries to correct the incentive structure toward more export orientation and financial improvement for production activities. At the same time, there is an acceleration of the liberalization and privatization programmes.

2.4 QUANTITATIVE INDICATORS OF THE STANCE OF TRADE POLICY

The previous section summarized trade policy measures undertaken by the government in the period since 1970. We now turn to an assessment of changes in trade policy for a number of different quantitative measures, based on a subset of those proposed by Collier, Greenaway and Gunning (1994).

Changes in Prices

Besides the descriptive trade policy accounts set out above, changes in trade policy can also be considered by monitoring changes in appropriate prices, in other words prices that will change when trade policy changes. In one respect this is a more objective measure of the extent to which trade liberalization was implemented, because it is possible to follow how prices directly related to trade changed in practice. On the other hand, it is necessary to remember that other factors besides trade policy influence the evolution of prices.

Measurements of the changes in prices associated with trade liberalization are commonly based on three indicators: (1) the implicit tariff; (2) various relative price measures; and (when relevant) (3) the parallel market premium. The methodological arguments underlying the use of these measures are set out by Collier, Greenaway and Gunning (1994). Since the parallel market is not important in the CFA zone countries, the parallel market premium measure does not make much sense in the case of Côte d'Ivoire, so we restrict our attention to the other two.

Implicit Tariff Measures

Implicit tariff measures, which can be defined for both importable and exportable goods, are usually derived from the following domestic price equation:

$$P_j = P_j^* \, e \, (1 + t_j) \qquad (2.1)$$

where P_j^* denotes the world price of importables/exportables (in dollars), P_j their domestic price (in local currency), e the exchange rate (local currency per dollar) and t_j the implicit tariff rate. In the case of Côte d'Ivoire, as a member of the CFA zone, the nominal exchange rate relative to the French franc is fixed; however, its value relative to a basket of currencies of trading partners varies as these currencies fluctuate relative to the French franc. The world price P_j^* can be considered as exogenous.

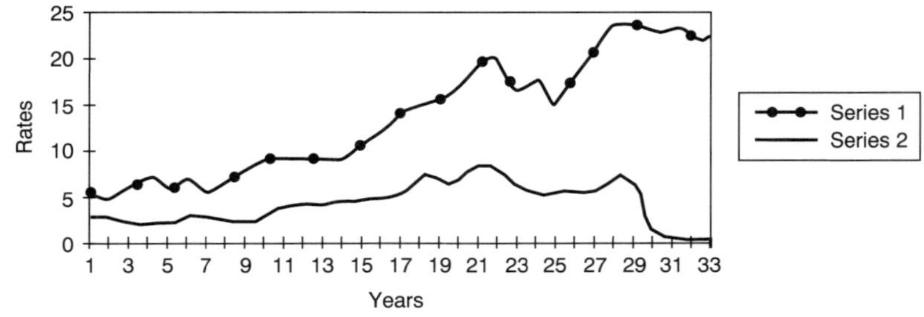

Figure 2.1 Implicit tariff of import (1) and export (2), 1960–92

Given the domestic price level P_j, it is then possible to work out the implicit tariff rate, which can be used to evaluate domestic trade policy. In normal circumstances, trade liberalization can be measured as a reduction in the implicit tariff measure.

The calculation of this index requires the availability of c.i.f. import price data, and the domestic price index at an aggregate level. These data are not particularly easy to obtain on reliable basis for countries like Côte d'Ivoire. To overcome that problem we decided to derive the implicit tariff from the following equation:

$$t_j = \frac{Dt_j}{TR_j} \tag{2.2}$$

where Dt_j denotes the value of tax payments on exports or imports (as appropriate); TR_j is the volume of exports or imports; and *tj* is the implicit tariff.

Figure 2.1, relating to implicit tariffs (exports, labelled as series 2, and imports, labelled series 1), shows their evolution over the period 1960–92, which covers most of the implementation period of the structural adjustment programmes. The following observations can be made.

(1) The implicit import tariff has been higher than the implicit export tariff over the entire period. This is to say that government trade policy has a large focus on taxation of imports. The gap is greater by the end of the period.
(2) The relatively flat form of the implicit export tariff chart indicates largely constant measures on the exports side, in contrast to the import side where the implicit tariff is more volatile, and generally with an increasing trend over time. This volatility is evident, for example,

during the first half of the 1980s, where the negative slope indicates a significant reduction in tariff on imports (refer to the discussion of policy accounts above). This is followed by a significant upward movement from 1985 to 1988, corresponding to the reversal of the trade liberalization.

(3) The last point is about the implicit tariff rate on imports compared to the nominal tariff. While the nominal tariff averaged 60 per cent or more in the 1980s, the implicit tariff on imports was about 21–23 per cent. This is despite the presence of a large number of NTBs in addition to tariff measures. It may reflect a number of factors, including cross-border smuggling and the number of exemptions applying to tariffs.[1]

Despite the fact that a number of trade liberalization measures were taken as part of the SAPs in the 1980s, the implicit tariff on imports in fact increases from a rate approaching 20 per cent at the end of the 1970s to 23 per cent by 1992. This is despite the liberalization of the early 1980s, whose impact appears to have been quite modest while it lasted, and then promptly reversed. This seems to reveal (confirm) the difficulties of implementing trade liberalization in the country, as already indicated in the policy accounts.

Relative Price Measures

While the implicit tariff rate is intuitively attractive in view of its similarity to the nominal tariff rate, it does not measure changes in the incentives facing either producers or consumers. This is because it does not take account of alternatives; it considers policy relating to exports and imports in isolation, not considering relative incentives. It does not consider changes in the price of non-tradeable goods, which may change for reasons related or unrelated to trade policy, but which in either case affect relative incentives. It can therefore be supplemented by relative price measures that take some of these issues into account.

To analyse incentive impacts in the small open economy, theory suggests consideration of three sectors: importables (M); exportables (X); and non-tradeables (N). Then incentives can be summarized by two main relative prices: the external relative price, which is the so-called external terms of trade ($TOT = P_x/P_m$), and the domestic relative price (DRP) or domestic terms of trade (P_m/P_n).

The TOT measure is presented in Figure 2.2 (series 2) for the period 1960–92. This measure remains largely static in the 1960s and the first half of the 1970s, but displays a significant upward movement from 1975–7, largely due to the improvement of the world prices of the main crops (cocoa and coffee) produced by the country. The TOT measure then

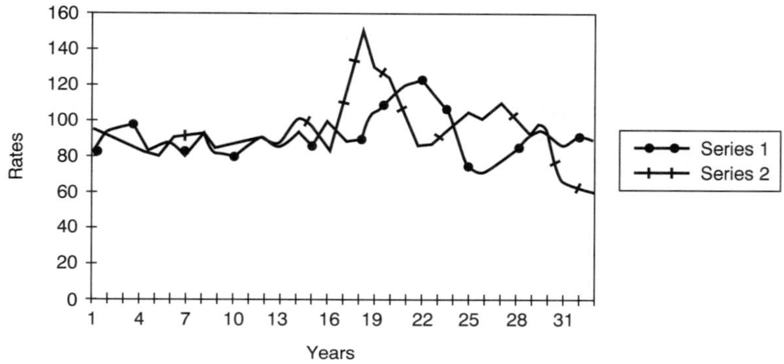

Figure 2.2 Competitiveness indexes: DRP (1) and TOT (2), 1960–92

declines until the early 1980s. It improves slowly up to about 1986 (the period of the cocoa and coffee mini-boom), before declining more sharply from 1986 until the end of the period. Again, this may reflect both the reversal of the trade liberalization from 1987 onwards (which can be expected to drive the price of importables up), as well as adverse commodity price shocks.

As well as considering the relative price of exportable and importable goods, it is also necessary to consider the relative price of tradeable and non-tradeable goods. A convenient way of doing this is by examining the real exchange rate. This is a good indicator of the competitiveness of the economy, particularly for small open economies, at the aggregate level (Edwards, 1989). It also measures an aspect of the relative incentives facing producers and consumers. A straightforward measure of the real exchange rate is obtained from the theoretical model of a two-sector economy, comprising the tradeable sector (*T*), constituting both the importable and the exportable sectors, and the non-tradeable sector (*N*). If we suppose P_t and P_n are the price indexes in the tradeable and non-tradeable sectors, respectively, the real exchange rate index (RER) is calculated as follows:[2]

$$RER = \frac{P_n}{P_t} \tag{2.3}$$

The results of calculating the real exchange rate for Côte d'Ivoire are presented in Figure 2.3, along with the TOT index again (for comparison). Note that the way the RER is calculated, lower magnitudes represent

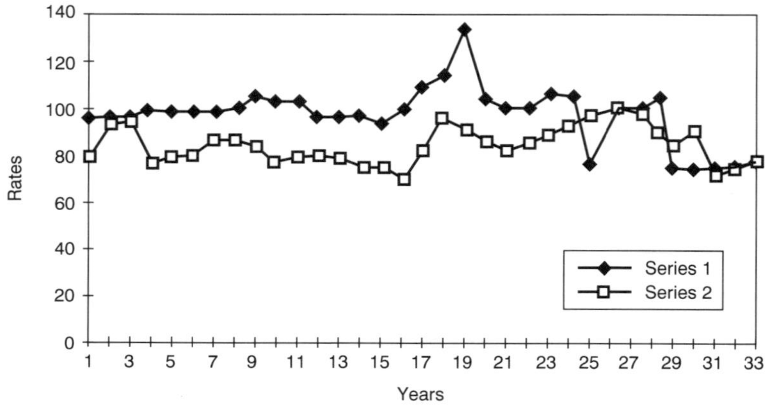

Figure 2.3 Competitiveness indexes: TOT (1) and RER (2), 1960–92

a more appreciated value. On the basis of this figure the following conclusions can be drawn.

First, by comparing the TOT and RER movements it is obvious that the TOT and RER indexes have largely the same pattern over the period 1960–92. That is, the periods of improvement in the TOT correspond broadly to those of real depreciation or competitiveness gains for the Ivorian economy, whereas the periods in which the TOT measure falls are the same ones in which there is a real appreciation of the exchange rate.[3] This result reveals the relative dependence of the Ivorian economy on international trade performance and its exposure to external shocks. Thus government policy, including liberalization measures, is very important given its expected impact on prices in the tradeable sector (*M* and *X*).

Second, referring to the liberalization episodes (particularly during the 1980s) as noted above, it is clear that the different attempts to reduce the effective protection of the economy did not positively affect competitiveness as might be expected. It is true that the RER depreciated in the first half of the 1980s, including through the liberalization episode, but the depreciation was modest and quickly reversed.

Following the same approach to evaluating the competitiveness of the economy at the aggregate level, we may address similarly the issue of the competitiveness at sectoral level. We shall then calculate a domestic relative price index (*drp*) that involves the agricultural (*agr*) sector on one hand and the industrial sector (*ind*) on the other:

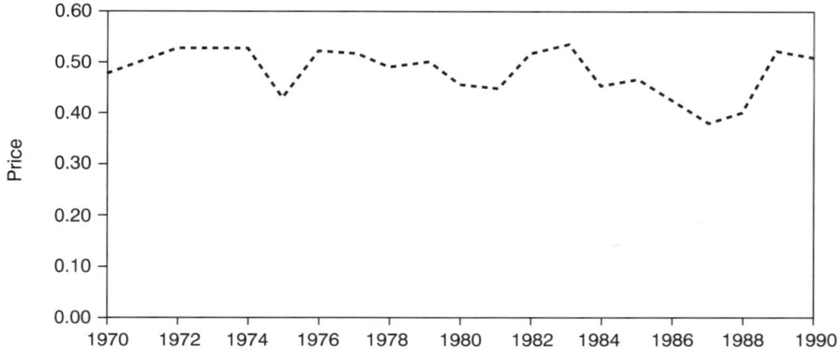

Figure 2.4 Relative prices of industrial goods

$$DRP = \frac{P_{ind}}{P_{agr}} \tag{2.4}$$

where P_{agr} and P_{ind} denote respectively the price indexes in the agricultural and industrial sectors. The purpose of calculating these indexes is to see if liberalization measures affect each sector differently, and hence relative incentives.

The results of this calculation are presented in Figure 2.4. This relative price does not display any significant upward or downward trend over time. The first trade liberalization episode is associated with an increase in the price of agricultural commodities relative to industrial commodities, partly reflecting the nature of the changes in trade policy at that time and partly reflecting a relatively favourable movement in commodity prices. From 1986 onwards this is reversed, with incentives shifting against agriculture. This tends to suggest that trade liberalization benefited the agricultural sector relative to the industrial sector.

Overall, the direction and timing of movements in price-based measures of liberalization appear to tie in quite well with the policy account. However, the trade policy measures undertaken by the government seem to have affected fairly modestly the behaviour of the main relative price indexes. And the changes in relative prices that did occur partly reflect exogenous changes in the country's terms of trade.

Changes in Quantities

Trade Intensity Measures

Trade intensity measures are the first step in measuring changes in quantities. Usually trade intensity is measured as the ratio of trade (imports plus exports) to GDP (op = $(M + X)/GDP$). It is a measure of the openness of the economy to international trade, in other words, a measure of the degree of outward orientation. We could note that, following Collier *et al.* (1994), 'one objection to trade intensity measures is that imports are financed both by export revenue and by capital flows. Therefore, a change in the trade intensity measure may simply pick up an increase in aid flows.' Also, as noted by the same authors, the use of the GDP variable is difficult to defend. Finally, it is not clear whether this measure should be seen as an indicator of a change in trade policy or a measure of its effects. Notwithstanding these limitations, it is of interest to examine the behaviour of this measure, as well as to look separately of exports and imports as a proportion of GDP ($exp = X/GDP$ and $imp = M/GDP$) in order to see which is the primary contributor to changes in the openness measure.

The results of calculating these measures are displayed in Figure 2.5 for the openness measure, and in Figure 2.6 for the export and import ratios. These show that while the *op* and *imp* indexes are relatively stable over the period, the *exp* index fluctuates a lot, particularly over the period of the 1980s. From its lowest level of 20 per cent in 1980, *exp* moved above 45 per cent in 1986. It then declined sharply for the rest of the 1980s, before recovering in the 1990s to achieve levels again in excess of 45 per cent. In the 1990s *imp* was around 23 per cent, having declined slightly from higher levels in the late 1970s and the 1980s.

The index *op* displays a peak in 1985 (a year of a rise in international prices of raw materials), but falls to 65 per cent in 1990 and 1991. The last year, 1992, registered an improvement in the index. Is trade liberalization responsible for such evolution?

Import Counterfactuals (Import Demand Model)

The last variant of trade intensity measures we consider is that of import demand counterfactuals. Using this methodology, the effect of trade policy is measured by comparing actual import volumes with counterfactual volumes given by appropriate import demand function. The import demand M_d is usually derived as a logarithmic function of real income y and some relative price variable, say the external relative price variable like the RER index (defined above):

$$\log(M^d) = \alpha + \beta \log(y) + \mu \log(RER) \qquad (2.5)$$

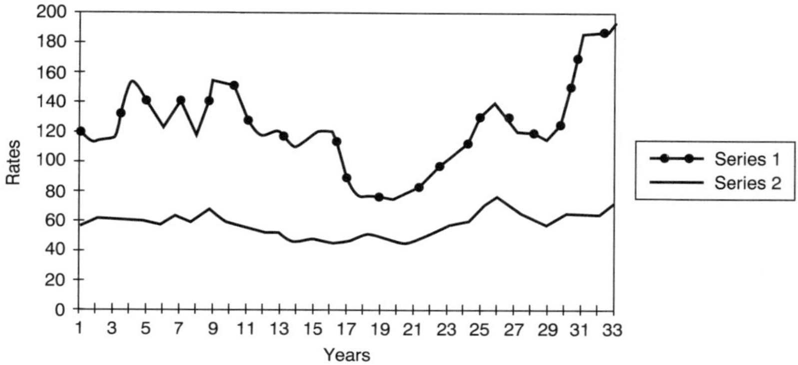

Figure 2.5 Trade balance (1) and openness (2), 1960–92

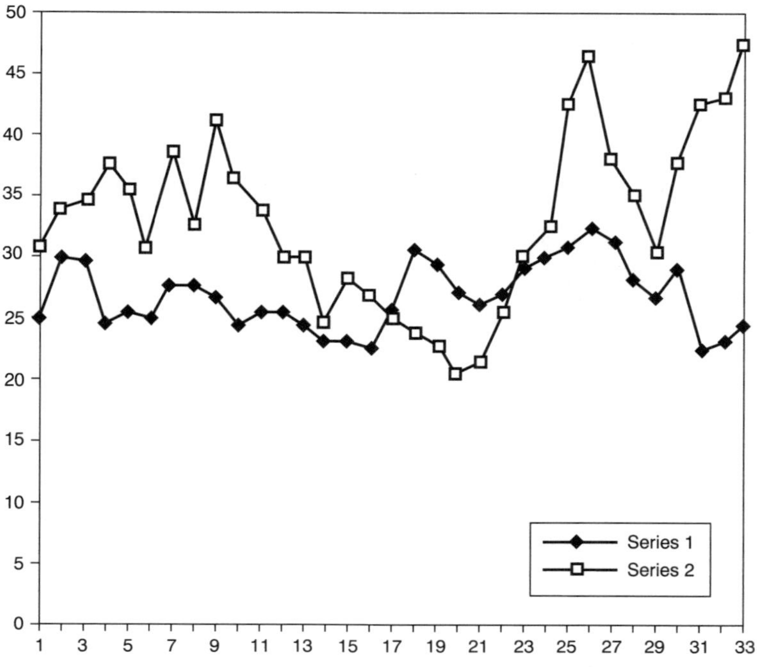

Figure 2.6 Trade intensity: export rate (2) and import rate (1), 1960–92

Table 2.2 Results of estimation of import demand function

Variable	*Value of coefficient*	*T-ratio*
Intercept	–1.95	–1.72
Real income	1.08	7.23
Relative price	–0.05	–0.93
Dummy variable	0.01	0.24

Dependent variable: Annual value of real imports

where

$$u_t = 0.56\, u_{t-i} + v_t$$

R2 adjusted = 0.96; F(4,27) = 214.2; DW = 1.55.

Given the counterfactual defined by that import demand function, which means the parameters a, β and μ are known or estimated using an appropriate method, one can then derive a measure of trade restrictiveness. The deviation of counterfactual volumes predicted by the import demand function from the actual volumes is the indirect measure of import restrictiveness. If actual imports are found to be lower than the demand function predicts, then as suggested by Collier *et al.* (1994), the difference is deemed to be the result of trade policy.[4]

The problem that arises is identifying plausible values for the elasticities. Narasimhan and Pritchett (1993) imposed elasticities derived from other empirical studies for the income elasticity β and price elasticity μ (β = 1.25, and $\mu = -1$). An alternative approach is to estimate the elasticities econometrically. This method is clearly preferable where the data are adequate, and is the approach used here.

An import demand function of the form of Equation 2.5 has previously been estimated for Côte d'Ivoire by M'Bet (1990), but using a PPP-based relative price measure in place of the RER. The estimated elasticities were $a = 1.48$, $\beta = -0.011$ and $\mu = 1.56$.

Various different relative price measures are used in import demand functions in the literature, but their theoretical background is not always obvious. In the case of our own estimation, we calculate the external relative price as P, which is the price of imports to the price of domestic goods:

$$P = \frac{P_m}{P_d} \qquad (2.6)$$

Table 2.3 The implied import restrictiveness index over the period 1961–92

1961 –62	*1963–5*	*1966–7*	*1968–* 69	*1970–1*	*1972–* 75	*1976–8*	*1979–* 80	*1981–6*	*1987–* 88	*1989*	*1990–* 92
(+)	(−)	(+)	(−)	(+)	(−)	(+)	(−)	(+)	(−)	(+)	(−)

where P_m and P_d stand, respectively, for the price index of imports and of domestic production, which is supposed to be an imperfect substitute for imports (Bohoun, 1996).

Then, using the Cochrane–Orcutt estimation procedure in TSP, with an AR(1) error term, the estimation of the import demand function gives the results presented in Table 2.2.

The purpose of the use of the dummy variable (M1) is to allow for the shifts in public policy measures relative to external trade.

The results of the estimation show significant coefficients of the real income variable ($\beta = 1.08$) though not of the relative price variable ($\mu = -0.05$), respectively the income and price elasticities of demand. An index of implied import restrictiveness (IIIR) is then calculated as follows:

$$IIIR = \log (M^d) - \log (M^{d*}) \tag{2.7}$$

where $\log(M^{d*})$ and $\log(M^d)$ are the predicted and the actual import volumes in log terms.

The results of the computed index using Equation 2.7 are given in Table 2.3.

These results are disappointing, in that they do not show any particularly strong feature due to the trade policy during the SAPs implementation period. A positive sign, meaning that imports are above their expected level based on the equation, might be interpreted as denoting the impacts of the liberalization programme; this is observed over the period 1981–6 when many of the trade liberalizing measures were implemented. The negative sign of the index over most of the period from 1987 to 1992 can be interpreted as the effect of the policy reversals consisting of an increase of protection and incentives after the period of reduction of protection.

2.5 THE CONSEQUENCES OF TRADE LIBERALIZATION

At the outset it must be recognized that the distinction between variables that might be considered as measures of the extent of liberalization and variables that can be used to consider the consequences of liberalization is a slightly artificial one, and may also depend on the theoretical

Table 2.4 Selected macroeconomic indicators for Côte d'Ivoire, 1980–95

Year	*1980–4*	*1985–7*	*1988*	*1989*	*1990*	*1991*	*1992*	*1993*	*1994*	*1995**
Overall fiscal deficit (% of GDP)	13.3	3.5	5.7	10.0	11.6	12.0	12.4	11.0	7.8	5.5
Public arrears (% of GDP)	–	–	9.3	17.2	27.5	37.0	45.3	60.0	66.0	62.0
Private investment (% of GDP)	10.9	7.6	6.8	5.7	4.5	5.0	7.5	5.3	7.7	9.0
Real exchange rate	97.7	101.8	72.6	72.9	73.4	73.4	73.7	–	–	–
Per capita GDP growth (%)	–2.7	–1.6	–6.0	–4.7	–3.8	–4.5	–3.8	–4.9	–2.0	2.7

*projection.

Source: Authors' computation based on data from MEFP/CI, the IMF and the World Bank.

perspective. For example, the openness measures considered in the previous section might be considered as indicators of trade liberalization, but the changes in exports and imports implicit in these measures might rather be considered as consequences of the trade policy changes. From this perspective it could be argued that changes in trade policy capture changes in incentives, which may be represented by the real exchange rate, for example. The response of exports and imports to the change in incentives is more properly regarded as a consequence of trade policy.

While recognizing this problem, we look at in this section factors that may more confidently be classified as consequences of trade policy measures, focusing in turn on (1) changes in the level and composition of exports and imports over the period; (2) changes in the use of factors of production (labour and capital); and (3) issues of credibility, which we argue are central to understanding the the trade policy changes that took place in Côte d'Ivoire. Before discussing these more specific issues we first briefly discuss the general evolution of the macroeconomy over the period of the SAPs, focusing on those aspects of direct relevance to the evaluation of trade policy in the period since 1980.

General Macroeconomic Characteristics

Table 2.4 summarizes the evolution of some key macroeconomic variables over the period of the SAPs, allowing an examination of the relationship between these variables and the trade liberalization episodes and reversals previously identified. The first SAP was dominated by stabilization measures, with only a few specific liberalization measures.

Over this period the fiscal deficit was very high (13.3 per cent of GDP) and per capita GDP fell (−2.7 per cent), but the level of private investment is reasonable (10.9 per cent of GDP). The next period, covering the second SAP and the coffee and cocoa mini-boom of 1985–6, was characterized by an improvement in the fiscal position (the fiscal deficit having fallen to only 3.5 per cent of GDP), and a reduction in the rate of decline of per capita GDP growth. Over the same period the share of private investment in GDP fell, while the real exchange rate depreciated modestly. This latter movement in the real exchange rate may be related to the trade liberalization measures put in place over this period, including the mock devaluation, and this depreciation may have been a contributory factor to the decline in investment.

From 1988, one can see the deterioration of the fiscal situation, with particularly large increases in the fiscal deficit from 1988 to 1990. The fiscal deficit increased from only 3.5 per cent of GDP over the period 1985–7 to 11.6 per cent of GDP by 1990; in fact, over the period 1989–93 the average fiscal deficit was in excess of 11.5 per cent of GDP. The same period was characterized by a large accumulation of public arrears, beginning in 1988 when public arrears amounted to 9.3 per cent of GDP. The stock of public arrears increased consistently over the next few years, reaching 60 per cent of GDP in 1993. This serious decline in the fiscal position over 1988–90 was clearly a major factor explaining the reversal of the trade liberalization programme at this time. While the decline in the fiscal position was largely contained after 1990, the level of the deficit remained very high and the accumulation of public arrears continued. The other macroeconomic indicators in Table 2.4 also performed badly over this period: the real exchange rate remained over-valued although stable (26–27 per cent over-valuation on average between 1989 and 1993), private investment was unstable and with a decreasing trend, and per capita GDP declined. Though repeated attempts were also made to curtail public expenditures, it was against this background of macroeconomic crisis that the trade liberalization reversals occurred.

It is clear from the ongoing discussion that the terms of trade, the fiscal developments and the real exchange rate are the most important macroeconomic variables of interest in analysing the impacts of trade liberalization.

To consider the relationship between trade policy and the fiscal deficit, it is important to recognize that taxation of foreign trade represents a very important source of revenue for the Ivorian government. This comes mainly from taxes on imports, taxes on exports and the net profits of the stabilization fund for cocoa and coffee. In general, taxes on imports represent the major source of revenue from taxation of trade, but this tends to fluctuate less widely than the other components. Indeed, revenue from the taxation of imports did not fall during the first trade liberalization episode at all, while revenue from other sources of trade taxes increased. The reversal of this trade liberalization was then associated with a significant decline in revenue from export taxes and a large decline in revenue from the surplus of the stabilization fund; this latter reflected the revolution of world prices for cocoa and coffee.

There is evidence that revenues from all sources of trade taxation improved sharply in 1994 following the devaluation of the CFA franc.

Impact on Trade Flows

Table 2.5 summarizes the evolution of the level and composition of exports and imports in Côte d'Ivoire over the period 1980–91. The aggregate level of exports is observed to decline over the period 1980–3, but then to recover between 1984 and 1986, so that by 1986 the value of exports exceeds that in 1980. This pattern is largely mirrored by real exports, indicating that changes in the unit value of exports did not play a major role in explained aggregate changes over this period. Examination at the sectoral level demonstrates the dominant contribution made by primary products to exports in Côte d'Ivoire, with manufactured exports accounting for only a small portion of total exports in 1980. The decline in export values between 1980 and 1983 was predominantly due to a decline in the export revenue from primary commodities, with manufacturing exports remaining relatively stable. On the other hand, the recovery in exports between 1983 and 1986 was due to increases in exports of both primary commodities and manufactured goods.

1986 represents the peak year for exports of both primary and manufactured commodities, at least in value terms. Over the period 1987–9 the value of exports declined, a decline not entirely matched by export volumes, indicating adverse export price movements over the period. At the sectoral level, this decline was much sharper among primary commodities than in the manufacturing sector; in large measure this reflects adverse movements in primary commodity prices over this period. Exports are then observed to increase again in 1989–91, especially in volume terms, indicating favourable movements in the unit value of exports over this period. This time both the primary commodity and the manufacturing sectors contributed to the improvement in export performance. The improvement over this period canceled out a large proportion of the decline that occurred from 1987–9.

Turning to imports, the pattern at the aggregate level for 1980–6 is very similar to that for exports; in both value and volume terms total imports declined from 1980 to 1984, but then increased again from 1984 to 1987; here, however, the improvement fell a long way short of offset-

Table 2.5 Evolution of the level and composition of merchandise trade, Côte d'Ivoire, 1980–91 (in $US)

	1980	*1981*	*1982*	*1983*	*1984*	*1985*	*1986*	*1987*	*1988*	*1989*	*1990*	*1991*
(1) Value of exports												
Total	3142.0	2535.2	2288.0	2103.7	2710.0	2720.9	3351.0	3092.0	2696.0	2611.0	3082.0	3011.3
Primary	2903.1	2273.0	2041.3	1868.7	2412.8	2447.4	2991.3	2760.1	2406.6	2330.7	2751.2	2688.0
Manufactures	238.9	262.2	246.7	235.0	297.2	273.5	359.7	331.9	289.4	280.3	330.8	323.2
(2) Volume of exports (Total)	2585.2	2418.0	2276.0	2046.9	2455.2	2605.3	3065.9	3092.0	2595.8	2842.3	3852.7	4013.5
(3) Value of imports												
Total	2967.2	2393.1	2183.7	1813.5	1524.0	1733.8	2048.0	2242.0	2081.0	2111.0	2098.0	1671.0
Primary	808.0	1072.6	938.2	749.9	658.4	724.5	862.1	943.8	876.0	888.6	883.2	703.4
Manufactures	2159.3	1320.5	1245.6	1063.6	865.6	1009.3	1185.9	1298.2	1205.0	1222.4	1214.8	967.0
(4) Volume of imports (Total)	2791.3	2197.8	2142.5	1844.1	1566.5	1819.1	2239.4	2242.0	2095.1	2130.9	1823.6	1484.4

Source: Demery and Castillo (1995).

ting the decline. At the sectoral level, manufactured goods accounted for around two-thirds of the total, and these accounted for the large majority of the movements in total imports over the period. The movements in primary commodity imports were smaller, and by 1986 imports of primary commodities moved above their 1980 level.

After 1987, changes in the level of imports were relatively small compared with those for exports. The value and volume of imports did decline slightly from 1987 to 1988, but then changed little for the following two years, before declining significantly in 1991. Again, the evolution of imports of primary commodities and of manufactured goods remained largely similar over this period.

While macroeconomic factors undoubtedly played an important part, at least on the import side, these patterns of change in the evolution of the level and composition of exports and imports in Côte d'Ivoire are largely what might be predicted from the characterization of trade policy set out in Section 2.4. The first SAP (1981–3) did not involve any explicit trade liberalization policies, though undoubtedly some of the policy measures taken did affect foreign trade. The data presented here suggest that these impacts were predominantly negative, with both exports and imports declining over this period in both value and volume terms. However, the second (1984–6) and third (1986–8) SAPs did involve explicit trade policy measures that were intended to be liberalizing. Though the implementation of these measures was piecemeal, they still seem to have resulted in significant increases in both exports and imports up until 1986 or 1987. For the remainder of the 1980s, the increase in imports was not sustained (and declined in volume terms), and export values also decline significantly. In some way this may be related to the about-face in trade policy from 1987 to 1989, but other factors are likely to have played a very important role: adverse terms of trade movements, the increasing over-valuation of the real exchange rate and the increasingly unsustainable fiscal position. These factors probably contributed to the reversal in trade policy, but they are also likely to have had direct impacts on trade incentives and indirect impacts through the adverse macroeconomic circumstances they brought about.

The data presented here are not really sufficient to assess the impact of the more liberalized trade policy measures the government sought to introduce from 1990 onwards, but there is no evidence that these led to an immediate recovery in import values or volumes.

In broad terms, then, the movements in exports and imports in Côte d'Ivoire over the period 1980–91 are broadly consistent with the changing patterns of incentives described in Section 2.4, with the liberalization of 1984–6 leading to increases in export and import values and volumes, and the trade policy reversal of 1987–9 contributing to a cessation of the growth of imports and a decline in the growth of exports. While these effects should not be attributed to explicit trade policy measures alone, there is significant evidence that changes in the stance of trade policy did have an impact, in the expected direction, on levels of trade.

Changes in Factor Use

Here we discuss the changes in capital and labour use and of the capital–labour ratio in aggregate, and then across sectors. Looking first at the capital stock, this is observed to decline over much of the liberalization period. Prior to this there had been a significant increase in investment during the coffee price boom (1976/7), but increases in the capital stock were more modest in the following years. However, following the beginning of the economic crisis from 1981 onwards, the year-on-year changes in the capital stock were consistently and increasingly negative until 1984. 1985 saw a recovery of investment in line with the partial recovery of the economy, but from then until 1990 the level of the capital stock continued to decline gradually. In this period of relative economic stagnation, little new investment took place, to replace depreciated capital.

Variations in formal sector employment were less stark over the liberalization period, but demonstrated some of the same features. The magnitude of the increase in employment from 1979 to 1980 and the subsequent fall from 1980 to 1981 are difficult to accept, though the directions of change they indicate are credible. In particular, it is entirely credible that there was a significant decline in formal sector employment with the onset of the crisis in 1981. Over most of the rest of the liberalization period formal sector employment generally declined marginally, the partial recovery of 1985/6 only temporarily arresting the compression of formal sector employment. This general compression in formal sector employment reflects both the extent of layoffs in the public sector and the lack of confidence among private sector employers over much of this period (note also the declining investment in this sector).

Notwithstanding these falls in employment, the capital–labour ratio in the formal sector is observed to decline consistently from 1981 onwards, with the decline being particularly sharp over the period 1982–4. But in some ways this is largely a reversal of the unsustainable increases in the level of capital intensity during the period of the commodity price boom (1976–8), when investment increased sharply.

Turning to the disaggregated level, for this purpose the economy is decomposed into five sectors: (1) food related agriculture, forestry and fish sectors; (2) export and industrial agriculture; (3) manufacturing sector; (4) other industry; and (5) service sectors. Apart from agricultural sectors, in which changes in employment due to liberalization were small, the other sectors experienced a sharp reduction in employment over the liberalization period. The changes were largest in the other industrial sector and during the post-1990 liberalization episode.

Capital use, measured by changes in investment, shows a different pattern. In agricultural activities liberalization periods are associated with an increase in investment (that is, in capital use), whereas in industrial activities, apart from manufacturing during 1984, liberalization is associated with a decline in investment (that is, in capital use).

The changes in labour and capital use clearly explain the evolution of the capital–labour ratio. The latter increased in agricultural activities during the liberalization periods, increased in industrial activities during the 1984 liberalization episode, and declined during the 1990 liberalization period, particularly in manufacturing (passing from 0.77 in 1988 to an average of 0.65 between 1989 and 1991).

Credibility of Trade Policy Measures

A critical issue in assessing the trade liberalization episodes in Côte d'Ivoire, and their reversal, is whether the reforms implemented were in fact credible. There are two aspects to this (Collier, *et al.*, 1994), which are discussed in turn. Did the reforms display macroeconomic compatibility? And were they time consistent?

Macro Incompatibility

Trade Liberalization and the Balance of Payments Trade liberalization, by lowering or eliminating import taxes, or relaxing or removing QRs, makes imported goods more available and lowers the domestic price of importables. This process can be expected to create an increase in the demand for imports if the loss of income due to tariff cuts and the relaxation of QRs (fall in tax revenue for the government and in rents from import quotas for the private agents) does not offset the decrease in the prices of importables as in a barter model (Collier, *et al.*, 1994). The increase in import demand takes place when economic agents have an optimal hoarding level and the excess of cash balances available to them is directed towards the acquisition of imported goods, which are now cheaper.

At the same time, trade liberalization is intended to create an increased incentive to export instead of engaging in the production of import substitutes. This, however, requires a sufficient supply response on the part of the export sector. If this is not sufficient then the increased demand for imports will exert pressure on foreign official reserves and result in balance of payments problems. In the case of Côte d'Ivoire, this situation is aggravated by the non-availability of a number of the mitigating instruments (monetary and credit measures for private agents' increased demand for cash balances or government cash balance supply).

The indicators used to assess the compatibility of balance of payments situation are changes in the official reserves and the extra use of central bank facilities.

Regarding official reserves, the two liberalization episodes are characterized by a sharp fall in their level in the first year of the liberalization (from FCFA 2.444 bn to FCFA 1.951 bn between 1984 and 1985 and from FCFA 3.727 bn to FCFA 1.021 bn between 1989 and 1990), followed by a quick recovery.

The situation of the use of the central bank facilities was a bit different. The 1984 liberalization episode was preceded and accompanied by a sharp increase in extra-facilities (from less than FCFA 6 bn in 1979, the facilities amounted to more than FCFA 310 bn in 1983, FCFA 335 bn in 1984 and FCFA 347 bn in 1985 against the normal level, which should be around FCFA 80 bn). The 1990 liberalization episode did not affect the level of the extra facilities of the central bank.

Fiscal Constraints The first effect of trade liberalization on fiscal variables relates to tax revenue. Indeed, liberalization by tariff cuts or relaxation of QRs is likely to result in the short term in losses of tax revenue. However, the removal of QRs might generate new tax revenue if they are replaced by tariffs (even if these are usually transitory). Given this latter feature, governments are often keener to remove QRs than to remove tariffs; however, the economic agents who benefit from QRs are strongly opposed to this.

The net effect depends on the nature of the liberalization programme. In the case of Côte d'Ivoire, two kinds of measures have been used. It seems that there has been a net negative effect of trade liberalization on government revenue. Over the two liberalization episodes total government revenue as well as tax revenue, fell sharply. For instance, total revenue passed from FCFA 798 bn in 1984 to 795 bn in 1985 and 693 bn in 1986. Tax revenue passed from FCFA 589 bn in 1983 to 412 bn in 1984 and 400 bn in 1985. Total revenue (–1.2 per cent) and tax revenue (–6.5 per cent) also fell between 1989 and 1990.

This has resulted in high fiscal deficits over the liberalization periods (15 per cent of GDP between 1983 and 1984 and 9 per cent of GDP between 1989 and 1990). High fiscal deficits during liberalization periods raise the issue of the sustainability of such measures. The sustainability problem seems more serious during the 1984 episode. A further problem with high fiscal deficits is their tendency to lead to real exchange rate over-valuation. These fiscal problems potentially played a major role in the reversal in 1988 of the first trade liberalization attempt.

Time Inconsistency

Policy Reversals The history of trade policies in Côte d'Ivoire shows breaks and reversals in the major reforms. For instance, over the years following the shift of 1984 one could have expected a tendency to consolidate liberalization trends. This was not the case. In 1988 and 1989 the government went back to tariff and non-tariff barriers. In large measure this was probably a response to fiscal revenue constraints, but it sent the wrong signals to economic agents. Such behaviour can be expected to undermine the credibility of later trade liberalization measures, and lack of credibility is likely to mean that trade liberalization will be less effective.

Time Lag Effects One expects trade liberalization to affect fiscal variables. When the liberalization is done through removing QRs, it is likely to increase tax revenue if QRs are replaced by tariffs. But when the liberalization is achieved by tariff suppression or lowering, the immediate consequence is a loss of tax revenue for the government. It is often argued that the revenue loss, due mostly to a shrinking average tax rate, might be compensated by the widening of the tax base brought about by a boom in economic activity. But, this effect generally takes time and is rarely fully compensating. Therefore there might be a lag effect between the decline in tax revenue and its recovery following the subsequent boom in economic activity (assuming one comes about).

In the case of Côte d'Ivoire, the two liberalization episodes were followed by a fall in government revenue. The first liberalization episode, dominated by an elimination of QRs, resulted in a moderate fall in government revenue (from FCFA 798.2 bn in 1984 to 795 bn in 1985 and 693.1 bn in 1986). The second liberalization episode, dominated by tariff changes, resulted in a sharper fall in government revenue (from FCFA 679.1 bn in 1989 to 639 bn in 1990 and 589.4 bn in 1991).

It is important that trade liberalization measures take account of the constraints under which government operates. Especially in the case of Côte d'Ivoire, there are implications for the fiscal deficit and the real exchange rate. It is equally important that governments be willing to undertake the necessary supporting policy measures. In Côte d'Ivoire it was clearly necessary to take measures to prevent the development of an unmanageable fiscal deficit or of real exchange rate over-valuation. There is evidence that this was not done. However, in view of the serious problems the government faced in this period, among other things due to its inability to adjust its nominal exchange rate, the type of corrective policy measures required might have been quite severe.

2.6 FIRM LEVEL EVIDENCE ON THE EXTENT AND IMPACT OF TRADE LIBERALIZATION

So far, the quantitative evaluation of trade liberalization in Côte d'Ivoire has been based on macroeconomic data from official sources. We now supplement this discussion with microeconomic data based on recent surveys conducted at the firm level, to see to what extent this provides an additional or different perspective.

The data used as the basis for this section are based on a combination of the results of two surveys of manufacturing enterprises. The first is a sub-sample of the data collected by the World Bank's Regional Programme on Enterprise Development (RPED). This was a detailed survey of formal and informal enterprises in the environs of Abidjan and in the cities of Bouaké and San Pedro, covering the following sectors: metals, food processing, textiles and wood. Although the total sample size was 210, at the time of writing sufficiently complete and reliable data are only available for around 80 enterprises; these results are used here. The second source is the sample survey of manufacturing enterprises conducted as part of the AERC collaborative project, using the standard questionnaire. This was intended to be a supplement to the RPED data base, covering sectors not covered by the RPED, and in particular collecting more detailed information on the impact of trade policy than was available from the RPED questionnaire. This second survey was based on an intended sample size of 50 formal manufacturing enterprises covering the following sectors: chemicals, plastics, natural rubber, paper and refining of grains; however, given that a number of firms refused to respond for various reasons,[5] and that the responses for some other firms were incomplete or otherwise unsatisfactory, we restrict our attention to 21 enterprises for which we have reasonable confidence in the results.

We also restrict our attention to only the parts of the questionnaires of direct interest to this study, which means in particular that we do not use the vast majority of the information available in the RPED questionnaire. We focus on those questions relating to trade policy. As a number of questions in the AERC questionnaire are essentially the same as those in the RPED questionnaire, we merged the two sets of responses in these cases. However, some information of relevance and importance for this study is only available from the AERC questionnaire (the RPED questionnaire being rather sketchy in the information it collects on trade-related issues). In these cases, therefore, we need to recognize the restrictions imposed by the small sample size.

We consider first the information based on those issues for which we could merge the two surveys. Some summary frequency distributions relating to profit rates and orientation to international trade are presented in Table 2.6. This table is calculated on the basis of all firms responding to the relevant questions.

Looking first at profit rates, 40 per cent of firms earn gross profits in excess of 5 per cent of their output in the year in question, with over 20 per cent earning profits in excess of 25 per cent of output. Expressed as a proportion of sales, 37.5 per cent of firms earned gross profits in excess of 10 per cent of their sales, and more than 20 per cent earned gross profits in excess of 25 per cent of sales.

The data in the third to sixth rows of the table relate to the orientation of the surveyed firms to international trade. The measures are again calculated as ratios and expressed in the same frequency classes. Around a quarter of the surveyed firms exported in excess of 10 per cent of their output in the year in question, most of whom exported at least 25 per cent. On the other hand, two-thirds of firms either did not export at all or only exported a negligible quantity of their output.

Of those firms that exported anything in the reference period, the next two rows give the frequency distributions of the proportions that were exported within the UMOA sub-region (row 4) and the proportion that was exported to other African countries (row 5). Only a quarter of those firms reported that 5 per cent or more of their exports were destined for the UMOA market; on the other hand, among these firms, for more than half of them UMOA represents the majority of their export sales. Thus around 90 per cent of the firms in the sample do not export to any significant extent within UMOA; however, but for the remaining 10 per cent of firms UMOA is a very important export market. By contrast, African countries outside of UMOA represent an important export market for very few exporting firms (although, of course, there may be some indirect exporting to these countries through UMOA countries).

The next row (row 6) gives the percentage of raw materials that are imported. More than 30 per cent of responding firms import at least 10 per cent of their raw materials, with nearly 30 per cent importing at least a quarter of their raw materials.

The final three rows relate to the channels used by exporting firms to sell abroad. The most important mechanism is by selling directly to foreign buyers; in particular very few firms export through either government or private marketing agencies to any significant extent.

Tables were also constructed based on the same sample of firms indicating the relationship between profitability and the export orientation of firms. Unfortunately, no strong pattern emerges from such tables; there is no evidence, for example, of significant differences in profitability between those firms that are highly export-orientated and those producing predominantly for the domestic market. Similar remarks apply on the

Table 2.6 Summary characteristics of surveyed firms and their orientation towards trade

% of firms surveyed	*Non-declared*	*0–5*	*5–10*	*10–25*	*25–50*	*>50*	*No. of valid observations*
(1) Profits of firms							
Profits as % of sales	31*	33	11	19	19	7	89
Profit as % of output	26*	46	2	5	5	36	94
(2) Trade orientation							
Exports as % of output	20	65	6	4	25	0	100
% of exports to UMOA		48	4	6	1	12	71
% of exports to Africa outside UMOA		56	1	2	1	3	63
% of raw materials imported		62	7	3	30	0	102
(3) Marketing channels							
% of output sold directly to foreign buyers		49	0	1	27	0	77
% of output sold through government agencies		62	0	0	2	0	64
% of output sold through private marketing agents		59	1	3	3	0	66

Source: Industrial survey.

import side; there is no evidence that the firms which are highly dependent on imported raw materials are necessarily more or less profitable than those with lower levels of import dependence.

This largely exhausts the most useful information of trade-related issues available from the RPED questionnaire for Côte d'Ivoire. We now focus on the firms that responded to the questionnaire specifically designed for the AERC project, bearing in mind always the small sample size on which our results are based. Most of these firms are predominantly orientated to the domestic market; seven of the twenty-one enterprises do not export at all, and only five export a quarter of their output or more. In the domestic market, one-third of the firms said that they do not have any competitors at all, while for most of the remainder their main competitors are domestic firms. Only for one firm is the main competitor an importer.

Firms were also asked whether they had experienced increased competition in the preceding year, either from other domestic firms or from imports within or outside the region. In the majority of cases the response was negative, particularly so with regard to import competition. This confirms the impression that many firms are operating in relatively uncompetitive domestic markets, and that for those in more competitive markets, the main source of competition is other domestic firms and not imports.

An important set of questions collected information on barriers to exporting and importing faced by firms. On the export side, seven of the twenty firms that responded to the question said they do experience barriers to exporting in the region, including tariffs and an unspecified miscellaneous category. On the import side as well, five of the sixteen responding firms report the existence of barriers to importing, again in the form of tariffs and an unspecified miscellaneous category. In both cases, quotas, licensing arrangements and foreign exchange were reported not to be problems for the firms in question. On the other hand, virtually all firms experiencing barriers to importing and/or exporting say that they would import or export more in the absence of these barriers.

A majority of the firms did report having observed policy changes relating to the regional dimensions of their trade but no systematic pattern emerges in the firms' assessment of the importance of these changes. Some consider changes in barriers to trade to be very important, but unfortunately the questionnaire does not collect information as to whether these were positive or negative changes. It does give the information that at least some firms appear to be quite responsive to changes in trade barriers.

The questionnaire also sought information on trade incentives, regulations and taxes. Though most firms reported being familiar with incentive schemes such as import duty drawback, export tax rebates, export retention and various tax privileges, in fact in each case only a small minority of firms currently benefit from such schemes. On the other hand, a majority of the responding firms reported possessing import licences, though fewer firms hold export licences than import licences.

The overall impression that emerges from the survey results analysed to date is of a large number of firms apparently reliant to a significant extent on imported raw materials, which they then use to produce predominantly for the domestic market. In general, there appears to be relatively little evidence of export orientation among the surveyed firms. From the rather general information available from the survey, there is little evidence of either unilateral or regional incentives having a significant influence on the decision of firms to export. Among those firms that do export, however, there are a number whose exporting activities are focused predominantly on the UMOA market; exports to non-UMOA African countries appear to be of very little importance, which may seem surprising given that many of the larger potential markets close to Côte d'Ivoire are in fact in non-UMOA countries (for example, Ghana, Nigeria).

2.7 THE CONSISTENCY OF TRADE LIBERALIZATION WITH REGIONAL INTEGRATION INITIATIVES

The single-country model is the conventional approach to trade liberalization studies but recent developments tending to bring to the agenda of policy design regional integration and policy convergence in EU countries, North America and Africa, have taken us back to the issues of preferential trade areas, optimal zones, and so on. On the trade side, these latter concerns raise the issues of unilateral versus multilateral trade policy (or trade liberalization more narrowly) as contemplated by UDEAC countries (Decaluwé, 1995; World Bank, 1992), or planned in the UEMOA protocol (BCEAO, 1994). The need for region-wide reforms can be justified by the traditional scale advantages and the additional pressures they would generate for the enforcement of reform measures. It has also been argued that highly protectionist national trade policies pursued in Africa were among the most serious obstacles to the success of regional integration within the region (Elbadawi, 1995).

In countries belonging to a monetary union, the need for harmonization of the policies affecting management of the common currency is an additional reason for regional co-operation.

This issue of compatibility also runs from regional integration to trade liberalization. In this study we discuss this last problem. Côte d'Ivoire belongs to a monetary union (UMOA) and two regional trade arrangements (ECOWAS and CEAO–UEMOA). Viewing the commitments taken by member countries within these regional trade arrangements, their compatibility with the liberalization programme of the Ivorian government are also considered. Then, some impacts of regional integration on trade and trade policy are traced through trade flows and reserves saving within the pooled reserves management of the franc zone scheme.

Exchange Rate-related Issues (UMOA)

As indicated above, Côte d'Ivoire belongs to a monetary union, UMOA (*Union Monétaire de l'Afrique de l'Ouest*), composed of six West African francophone countries (Benin, Burkina Faso, Niger, Senegal, Togo and Côte d'Ivoire). This situation creates some constraints in terms of the availability of exchange rate and other monetary instruments (interest rates, credit policy, and so on), as well as having some potentially beneficial aspects.

The objective of UMOA is to set up a monetary union through the use of a common currency (CFA franc), pegged to the French franc; the pooling and common management of international reserves; and the conduct of a common exchange rate, monetary and credit policies. The CFA franc is pegged to the French currency through an explicit arrangement by which the French government provides for a guarantee for the value and the rate of the CFA franc while the African countries agree to deposit a high proportion of their foreign reserves in an account in the French treasury (*Compte d'Opération*, or CO). The modified rate of the CFA franc cannot be changed without the consent of all the member countries as well as France. The credit allocation, the setting of the level of money supply in each country and in the union, the determination of interest rates, and the monetary and financial operations (bank supervision, the intermediation scheme, status and activities of non-bank financial institutions and informal financial institutions, and so on) are the responsibility of the board of UMOA, which includes French representatives. UMOA is also supposed to assist the member countries in organizing their money and financial markets, in better co-ordinating their development plans, in creating complementaries between their production bases and in encouraging intra-regional trade. The UMOA protocol also stipulates a free capital movement within the member countries and between them and France.

Actually, UMOA is a subset of the franc zone, which originated in colonial times in order to organize the monetary relations between France and its colonies. The zone has evolved into two distinctive monetary unions (UMOA for West Africa and UDEAC for Central Africa). The current UMOA treaty was signed in 1973. At that date it was decided to transfer the headquarters of the common central bank (BCEAO – *Banque Centrale des Etats de l'Afrique de l'Ouest*) to Africa (Dakar, Senegal), to increase the proportion of international reserves held and managed by the member countries themselves (now 35 per cent), and to compensate for losses due to a devaluation of the French currency. Another change introduced in 1973 concerned the remuneration of the surplus of the CO, which is now based on the base rate of the *Banque de France*.

These changes brought more flexibility to the UMOA system, allowing for the accumulation of more foreign currency by the countries and reducing the opportunity cost of holding resources in the CO. The 1994 devaluation of the CFA franc also put an end to the lasting fixity of this currency *vis-à-vis* the French franc, adding to the policy instruments available to the countries. Current efforts of financial liberalization underway in most UMOA countries are likely to give more means to governments to use monetary instruments in order to mitigate some of the effects of liberalization measures. But, as it is now UMOA generates serious limitations in the use of monetary instruments.

Trade Preferential Issues

CEAO–UEMOA

According to the terms of the treaty signed in January 1974, the ultimate objective of CEAO (*Communauté Economique de l'Afrique de l'Ouest*) was to set up a full custom union within a 12-year period. In addition, CEAO aimed to set up co-operation and common policies in the areas of agricultural development, fisheries, livestock, industry, transport, communication and tourism. CEAO covers an area of 4330 million kilometres square and has a total population of more than 50 million – up from 30.7 million in 1977.

The instrument of the custom union was intended to be a common custom tariff. The agricultural and other primary products were immediately free to trade, but industrial and processed goods remained subject to a preferential tariff scheme, TCR (*Taxe de Coopération Régionale*), during the transitional period. For the eligible products (those having more than 40 per cent of local value added content), the TCR replaced custom duties and taxes (for products with full eligibility), or the custom duties only (for products meeting the rule of origin but which had not accomplished the eligibility procedure).

The TCR mechanism is also based on the principle of compensation for tax revenue loss. Indeed, the government that loses tax revenue due to the lowering of tax rates applied to products coming from the CEAO is eligible for TCR compensation. But only two-thirds of the tax losses are compensated and the mechanism is fuelled by funds drawn from the gains of the beneficiary countries (exporters). The remaining third is recorded as resources for the financing of the development of the community. Actually, for exporting countries, subject to the payments to the FCD (*Fonds Communautaire de Développement*) of the tax gains due to the TCR, the scheme creates additional pressures on government spending.

Regarding the link with trade liberalization, the CEAO protocol is compatible with the unilateral liberalization programme adopted by the Ivorian government. The ultimate objective of a common union and the preferential tariff of the transitory period can be seen as the lower boundary of custom tariffs. Hence there is not any conflict between the CEAO scheme and the larger trade liberalization (reduction and clarification of tariffs, elimination or relaxation of NTBs, devaluation, and so on). However, the first years of the CEAO agreement (1974–8) were characterized by a wave of protection, through an increase in NTBs starting from 1976. Similarly, the second wave of protection of 1989–90 took place over a period well beyond the projected date for the full accomplishment of CEAO. Despite these conflicts, the CEAO commitments in themselves cannot be seen as being opposed to the general liberalization process. On the contrary, they are more liberalization-induced and time consistent.

The other issue relating the CEAO protocol to trade liberalization concerns the impacts on infrastructure and structural changes of community projects (handled by the FCD and FOSIDEC, *Fonds de Solidarité et d'Intervention pour le Développement Economique de la Communauté*). The FCD projects target technical education and training (four out of the seven projects of the institution between 1976 and 1983 were directed towards this aim[6]), and industrial development, particularly at national level. The aim of FOSIDEC is to help the development of projects at both the national and community levels by providing assistance to fund raising and contributing directly to the financing of some projects. Its activities include project studies, subsidies to specific projects, provision of credit guarantees, lending for buying shares, and so on. By the end of 1980, FOSIDEC, which amounted to CFA 13 bn, was dominated by project subsidies and credit bonuses and guarantees (more than 93 per cent of the total), of which community projects represented 75 per cent. Although Côte d'Ivoire did not benefit very much from FCD and FOSIDEC projects at national level (only 2 per cent of FCD projects), the improvement that they have brought about in some inland countries (Niger, 25 per cent; Burkina Faso, 23 per cent; Mali, 23 per cent) did help to strengthen the community market, while the community projects have improved the physical and social infrastructure of CEAO.

In these various respects (preferential tariffs and project co-operation) we can say that CEAO has strengthened the market bases of member countries and of the community as a whole. But since there was not any macro policy commitment in the protocol (like on fiscal and balance of payments deficits, counter-inflationary objectives, and so on), its impact on trade liberalization was limited, at least in the short term, to those of the TCR and some of the project assistance schemes.

It is such limitations that UEMOA tried to correct. But the UEMOA protocol did not take over the project assistance activities of CEAO. The commitment to policy convergence in addition to the monetary union is the paramount feature of this new treaty. UEMOA takes up the custom union objective through a common tariff (TEC: *Tarif Extérieur Commun*), but goes beyond this by setting an objective of a full common market aiming at free movement of people, goods and services including capital. Although the framework and details of the process have not yet been clearly stated, some immediate decisions have been taken in the area of trade policy: the member countries are urged not to take any new restrictive decisions relating to others and to make sure that within the new GATT any member of the union is not treated worse than countries outside.

The UEMOA treaty is not, however, likely to speed up the customs union and/or the common market. But its objective of attaining full integration (economic, monetary, institutional, and so on) and the gradualism adopted through the process of convergence are very interesting. The introduction of an executive for the community under the form of a supranational commission and the proposals for balancing institutions like a court of justice (*cours de justice*) and an accounts checking court (*cours des comptes*) pave the road to a more realistic and transparent approach than in the past.

ECOWAS

The protocol for ECOWAS (the Economic Community of West African States, CEDEAO in French) was signed in 1976 and put in place in 1979. It is composed of 16 countries, covering an area of 6440 million square kilometres and having a population of nearly 200 million. The stated objectives of ECOWAS are very similar to those of CEAO–UEMOA: the creation of a customs union and a common market, with a quick achievement of the free movement of persons. On the trade side ECOWAS aims to eliminate custom duties and taxes among the member countries and establish a common external tariff. Moreover, ECOWAS objectives include harmonization of economic and sectoral policies of the member countries. The latter was thought to be accelerated by the conduct of common programmes and projects.

These objectives were planned to be achieved within a 15-year period, starting from 1979. During this period transitory measures deemed to help members to move gradually toward these objectives were set up: free movement of persons, free movement for agricultural and other primary products within a period of two years from the agreement. On the existing tariffs the focus is on the exchange of custom information. Regarding industrial products, the protocol stipulated the elimination of custom tariffs and NTBs within a period of 2–10 years. Although the detailed framework and operation of the common market were not explicit in the protocol, its achievement was to be obtained within the 15 years.

The main instruments of the ECOWAS arrangement – tariff reduction, revenue loss compensation, project assistance and financing, credit guarantees and assistance for capital mobilization, and so on – are handled by FCCDC (*Fonds de Coopération, de Compensation et de Développement de la CEDEAO*). Tariff lowering is based on a rule of origin principle similar to that of CEAO (40 per cent domestic share of the value added), extended to the re-exports within the area. The compensation account receives the payments of the exporting countries, which are used to reimburse the losses of importing countries. FCCDC also assists the member countries in identification of foreign financing, project preparation and in investment guarantees, as well as in contributing to projects and programmes through direct financing at both country and community levels.

The trade-related measures of ECOWAS concern tariff lowering, re-exporting facilities, and so on. The other activities that indirectly affect trade are the free movement of people, project financing and investment support. Regarding the performance of ECOWAS, the only data available to us go back to 1986. There is no report of compensation payments, which is strange. Project financing is dominated by loans and grants to countries in infrastructural sectors (telecommunications sector, US$24.50 bn, 37.14 per cent of the total operational expenditure; transport sector, US $8.16 bn, 12.4 per cent of the total). The other important support to productive activities is through the financing of Ecobank, a private community bank (US$5.8 bn, 8.9 per cent of the total). But the strangest thing is the amount of resources allocated to the building of offices and headquarters of ECOWAS (US$15 bn, 39.1 per cent of the total).

On the free movement of persons and goods, it seems that ECOWAS has made some progress, in that in theory natives of any member country are allowed to move freely to another one, and goods circulate freely between the countries (cars, for example). But in practice this is more debatable for goods and even persons, given the recent tight conditions of entry and immigration regulations adopted by most of the countries.

Regarding trade liberalization, the commitments of Côte d'Ivoire to ECOWAS are not in conflict with its unilateral trade liberalization measures. But ECOWAS membership does not appear to aid trade liberalization either, as could have been expected from a naïve reading of the protocol. Furthermore, now that UEMOA has been established, it overlaps with the objectives of ECOWAS much more than CEAO did. It must be debatable whether there are benefits to Côte d'Ivoire of being a member of the two organizations simultaneously.

The Impacts of Regional Integration on Trade and Trade Policy

Trade Flows

Table 2.7 shows the evolution of trade flows of Côte d'Ivoire, expressed as a proportion of GDP, over the period considered in this study, with a

Table 2.7 Trade flows (as % of GDP)

	Before SAP	*SAP I 1981–83*	*SAP II 1984–87*	*SAP III 1988–90*	*SAP IV 1991–93*	*SAP V 1994–95*
Total trade						
Total flows	60.1	58.3	59.4	48.5	45.9	
Imports	28.1	28.1	22.8	20.5	20.0	
Exports	32.0	30.2	36.6	28.1	25.9	
CFA Zone						
Total flows	5.1	4.9	5.1	3.8	4.3	
Imports	1.2	1.1	1.3	0.4	0.3	
Exports	4.0	3.8	3.8	3.4	4.0	
Other Africa (Non-CFA)						
Total flows	2.7	3.6	4.8	7.4	8.8	
Imports	1.4	2.3	2.9	4.0	4.9	
Exports	1.3	1.3	1.9	3.3	3.9	

Source: Computed by the authors.

partial disaggregation by geographic region to enable an assessment of the importance of intra-regional trade. The first rows of the table refer to the total trade of the country; these are the openness measures considered in section 2.4.

The importance of trade as a proportion of GDP remained relatively stable at around 60 per cent of GDP until 1987, but then declined significantly between 1988 and 1993 (the last year for which we have reliable information). This break is associated with the major policy reversal previously referred to; the move towards increased protection adversely affected both export and import levels, but particularly the former, which fell from 36.5 per cent of GDP over 1984–7 to 28.1 per cent from 1988–90. By contrast, the importance of imports as a proportion of GDP had already begun to decline in the era of SAP 2.

Table 2.7 reveals the small proportion of the total volume of trade accounted for by other African countries, whether within or outside the franc zone. Trade with franc zone countries rarely accounts for more than 10 per cent of Côte d'Ivoire's total volume of trade, and most of this takes place on the export side. Indeed, less than 5 per cent of Côte d'Ivoire's imports come from franc zone countries, whereas the region accounts for around 10 per cent of exports. Over time, though, the proportion of Côte d'Ivoire's total exports that are sold to franc zone countries

Table 2.8 Trade flows for Côte d'Ivoire after 1992 (US$m)

	1992	*1993*	*1994*	*1995 (6 months)*
Imports	1629.3	1983.5	1834.5	1417.3
Main primary products	221.2	308.3	319.6	156.8
Main manufactured products	758.6	927.5	827.7	661.7
Exports	2099.8	2640.6	2757.4	1616.4
Main primary products	929.9	1276.4	1240.4	1005.8
Main manufactured products	450.8	544.0	636.9	371.6

Source: MEFP/INS (1995–6).

has increased marginally, while the corresponding proportion for imports has fallen sharply. However, there is anecdotal evidence that, following the devaluation of the CFA franc in January 1994, the importance of Africa in general, and UEMOA countries in particular, as a market for Côte d'Ivoire's exports has increased.

However, the importance of trade with African countries outside of the franc zone has increased more rapidly over the period than trade with countries within it, this increase occurring both on the export and import side. This is largely accounted for by transactions with Nigeria, Ghana and North Africa. Unlike within the franc zone, here exports and imports are more closely balanced.

These features are well depicted by the recent trends in trade flows. Imports are dominated by manufactured goods (See Table 2.8). The main manufactured products account for more than 45 per cent of the total imports over the period despite the slight change during the year of the devaluation. This feature is reinforced in 1995, with the main manufactured products of the first semester accounting for more than 77 per cent of the level of 1994, whereas the corresponding figure for the main primary products is 49 per cent.

Looking more carefully at the structure of the imports of manufactured goods in 1995, it appears that they consisted mainly of equipment and intermediate goods (the import of machineries of the first semester 1995 represents 75.7 per cent of the level of 1994; those of metal goods, 74.2 per cent chemicals, 63.6 per cent; and papers 61.8 per cent) (MEFP/INS, 1996). This is a sign of the reconstitution of industrial capacities and of growth of production activities. By contrast, Côte d'Ivoire's imports from other African countries are dominated by final consumption as shown in Table 2.9.

The exports are dominated by primary goods. The latter account for

Table 2.9 Import flows (as % of GDP)

	1970–80	*1981–83*	*1984–87*	*1988–90*	*1991–93*	*1994–95*
CFA zone						
Food (1)	0.04	0.04	0.05	0.01	0.01	
Final consumption (2)	0.05	0.05	0.06	0.01	0.01	
Intermediate (3)	0.01	0.01	0.01	0.05	0.04	
Other final consumption (4)	0.02	0.02	0.02	0.08	0.07	
Other Africa						
Food (1)	0.01	0.02	0.02	0.03	0.04	
Final consumption (2)	0.01	0.02	0.02	0.03	0.04	
Intermediate (3)	0.01	0.02	0.02	0.03	0.05	
Other final consumption (4)	0.01	0.02	0.04	0.02	0.06	

more than 64 per cent of the total exports over the period except in 1992. This domination of primary goods was accentuated after the devaluation. The main primary products represent a greater share of total exports in 1994 and 1995 (64.4 per cent in 1993, 67.6 per cent in 1994 and 71 per cent in 1995). Over the first semester of 1995, the exports of main primary products represented more than 81 per cent of their level of 1994, the figure for the manufactured goods is 58.3 per cent. Côte d'Ivoire's exports to African countries were also dominated by primary goods as can be seen from Table 2.10.

The CFA franc devaluation has affected the trade flows of Côte d'Ivoire. In 1994, imports experienced their first fall (−7.5 per cent), but quickly recovered in 1995. Exports have done well (+4.1 per cent). But the traditional structure of the trade flows of the country have been accentuated (domination of imports by manufactured foods and domination of exports by primary goods). Clearly this last liberalization episode has not adversely affected the trade flows, but has not reversed their existing structure.

The figures in Table 2.11 show important net reserves gains for Côte d'Ivoire from 1981 to 1988. In particular, the gains jumped from less than 1 per cent of tax revenue in 1983 more than 9 per cent in 1984. Another increase occured between 1985 and 1986, from 9.2 per cent to 13.5 per cent. These jumps in reserves gains (deficit of the CO) coincide with the starting years of the liberalization episodes. This means that fiscal pressures of liberalization measures could have been eased by financing from the French treasury through the CO deficit, extending the overdraft facilities of BCEAO to Côte d'Ivoire. This source of financing accounted for 9 per cent–13.5 per cent of tax revenue between 1984 and 1985. It seems clear the UMOA membership has provided for extended overdraft facilities (BCEAO and French treasury), which have probably

Table 2.10 Export flows (as a % of GDP)

	1970–80	*1981–83*	*1984–87*	*1988–90*	*1991–93*	*1994–95*
CFA zone						
Primary goods	0.08	0.07	0.07	0.06	0.07	
Manufactured	0.03	0.03	0.03	0.02	0.03	
Other Africa						
Primary goods	0.01	0.01	0.02	0.03	0.04	
Manufactured	0.01	0.01	0.01	0.02	0.03	

helped the country to face the adverse fiscal effects of liberalization measures. Côte d'Ivoire's dominant role in UMOA has added to the extent of the use of these facilities, resulting in the country's loose fiscal policy (Fielding, 1994).

2.8 CONCLUSIONS

Trade liberalization in Côte d'Ivoire took place in a particular situation, that of the economic crisis faced by the country in the 1980s – a period serious problems imposed by the over-valuation of the real exchange rate and serious fiscal imbalances that plagued the country into the early 1990s. This meant that the trade liberalization initiatives attempted during periods of relatively favourable terms of trade (such as 1984–6) were abandoned as soon as the terms of trade started to move adversely, in response to growing fiscal imbalances and the pressures of domestic firms.

The problems of exchange rate over-valuation have been at least temporarily relaxed by the devaluation of the CFA franc in January 1994, but, as is well known, the problem will be to sustain the real exchange rate close to its equilibrium level. Although there is not yet sufficient quantitative information to assess the impact of the devaluation on trade flows, anecdotal evidence suggests that they have increased markedly. This is to be expected. But whether or not these benefits are temporary or permanent depends largely on whether or not the real exchange rate devaluation can be maintained. In other words, will the government take the policy measures necessary to ensure that non-tradeables prices are kept under control and fiscal discipline is maintained?

In terms of the regional dimension of trade policy, it is clear that Côte d'Ivoire trades much more with countries outside of Africa than those within Africa, including within the regional integration arrangements to which the country is a party. The most significant such arrangement is

Table 2.11 Reserves gains for Côte d'Ivoire from the pooling scheme of UMO and tax revenue

Year	*RNGAINS*	*TAXR*	*EVRNGAINF (%)*
1981	4 273	358 520	1.19
1982	1 909	407 399	0.47
1983	4 033	410 698	0.98
1984	47 467	511 965	9.27
1985	40 206	501 815	8.01
1986	69 577	514 618	13.52
1987	70 866	541 806	13.08
1988	49 466	527 480	9.38
Mean	35 975	471 788	6.98

Note: Net reserves gains (RNGAINS) is defined as the difference between the average deficit of the *Compte d'Opération* (CO) minus the opportunity cost of its surpluses. TAXREV is total tax revenue; RNGAINE is reserves gains as a percentage of TAXREV.

Sources: M'Bet and Niamkey (1994) and the authors' calculations.

UEMOA, which includes both monetary and trade dimensions. In and of itself membership in UEMOA does not conflict with a policy objective of trade liberalization, as long as the appropriate policy measures are taken to ensure that the fixed nominal exchange rate does not once again lead to real exchange rate misalignment. In trade terms, membership in UEMOA may imply an increasing focus on trade within the region in future. There is some evidence that this has happened since the devaluation.

Notes

1. In 1998 for example, about 57 per cent of imported goods benefited from exemption regime.
2. Note that if $P_t = F(P_x, P_m)$ is an homogenous function of first degree, then $P_t = f(TOT) \cdot P_m$ where *TOT* is defined as above (the external terms of trade). For more details about the issue of the real exchange rate in a small open economy, see Bohoun and Kouassy (1993). In an application to the case of Côte d'Ivoire, the authors showed that public policy impacts on the competitiveness of the economy through demand substitution effects on the real exchange rate.
3. The Ivorian economy is then characterized by substitution effects as noted in the study of Bohoun and Kouassy (1993). It should be added that the substitution effects identified here relate closely to the behaviour of the government

which captures most of the premium accruing from the improvement of the terms of trade through the activities of marketing boards. The substitution effects are linked here to the extent to which the latter allocates the additional means to incentives and cost-reducing policies.

4. If a measure in price space is desired, the import demand function is in fact inverted to derive (given the chosen values of the elasticities) the implicit (relative) price change from the observed changes in real income and in the volume of imports.
5. Significant problems of obtaining an adequate response arose from the need to conduct this survey during August, during which time senior members of many firms were absent on holiday. Other firms refused to co-operate because they felt they had been 'oversurveyed' recently (reflecting the number of enterprise surveys which have been conducted in the country recently).
6. The major educational and training projects are: *Centre Africain d'Etudes supérieures en Gestion* (CESAG), (High School of Management); *Ecole des Mines et Géologie* (EMIG) (High School for Mining and Geological Techniques); *Institut des Sciences et Techniques Halieutiques* (ISSTH), and *Ecole Supérieure des Industries Textiles* (ESITEX) (High School of the Textile Industry).

References

BCEAO (*Banque Centrale des Etats de l'Afrique de l'Ouest*) (1994) 'La transition de l'Union Monétaire Ouest Africaine (UMOA) à l'Union Economique Monétaire Ouest Africaine (UEMOA)', presentation to the Workshop on *Macroeconomic Adjustment in Côte d'Ivoire*, Bingerville, April.

Bohoun, B. (1996) *Essai d'analyse de la demande d'importation: application à l'économie ivoirienne* (Abidjan: Université Nationale de Côte d'Ivoire).

Bohoun, B. and O. Kouassy (1993) 'Budgetary adjustment and the real exchange rate dynamic in the WAMU countries, Research Report, Nairobi, Kenya, AERC.

CAPEC–CIRES (1995) 'Suivi devaluation en Côte d'Ivoire', DT no. 15, CIRES–National University of Côte d'Ivoire.

Chamley, C. (1991) 'Côte d'Ivoire: The failure of structural adjustment', in V. Thomas *et al.* (eds), *Restructuring Economies in Distress: Policy Reform and the World Bank* (Oxford University Press for the World Bank).

Collier, P., D. Greenaway and J. Gunning (1994) 'Evaluating trade liberalization: A methodological framework', paper represented at AERC Conference on *Regional Integration and Trade Liberalization in Sub-Saharan Africa*, Nairobi, December 1993.

Decaluwé B., D. Jinkeu and L. Bela (1994) 'Collaborative project on Regional Integration and Trade Liberalization in sub-Saharan Africa: UDEAC, Case Study', paper presented at an AERC workshop, Harare, March.

Demery, L. and G. Castillo (1995) 'Trade reform under macroeconomic instability: The case of Côte d'Ivoire', TEP Study on Trade Policy Reforms in Sub-Saharan Africa, World Bank.

Devarajan, S. and J. de Melo (1987) 'Adjustment with a fixed exchange rate: Cameroon, Côte d'Ivoire and Senegal', *World Bank Economic Review*, **1**: 447–88.

Edwards, S. (1989) *Real Exchange Rates, Devaluation and Adjustment* (MIT Press).
Elbadawi, I. (1995) 'The impact of regional trade/monetary schemes on intra-sub-saharan Africa trade', paper presented at the AERC research workshop on *Regional Integration And Trade Liberalization in SSA*, Harare, March.
Fielding, D. (1994) 'Assymetries in the behaviour of members of a monetary union: A game-theoretic model with an application to West Africa', CREDIT Research Paper no. 94/11, University of Nottingham, November.
M'Bet, A. (1990) 'L'analyse du comportement des importations de la Côte d'Ivoire en période d'adjustement structurel', Paris, PUF Sorbonne-France.
M'Bet, A. and M. Niamkey (1994) 'Evaluating the net gains of the membership of the franc zone', *World Development*, **7** (22).
MEFP/INS (1995/1996) Bulletin in *Trimestriel*, 7 (June 1995) and 8 (October 1996).
Michel, G. and M. Noël (1984) 'Short-term responses to trade and incentive policies in the Ivory Coast: Comparative static simulations in a computable general equilibrium model, World Bank Staff Working Paper, no. 647, Washington, DC.
Milner, C. R. and A. McKay (1996) 'Neutrality and export promotion: Evidence, issues and policy implications', forthcoming in V. Balasubramaniam and D. Greenaway (eds), *International Trade and Development: Essays in Honour of Jagdish Bhagwati* (London: Macmillan).
Narasimhan, B. and L. Pritchett (1993) 'The evolution of import restrictions in sub-Saharan Africa in the 1980s: An empirical analysis'.
Papageorgiou, D., M. Michaely and A. Choksi (1991) *Liberalizing Foreign Trade*, 7 vols (Oxford: Blackwell).
World Bank (1992) *Intra-Regional Trade in Sub-Saharan Africa*. Washington, DC: The World Bank.

3 Trade Liberalization in Ghana

Kwadwo Tutu and Abena Oduro

3.1 INTRODUCTION

Almost all African countries have been moving towards more open trading systems since the mid-1980s, after years of strict controls on international trade that had been introduced for balance of payments, industrialization and revenue purposes. The switch towards more liberal trading systems occurred when the countries adopted World Bank and IMF adjustment programmes to address the problems of declining growth and severe foreign exchange constraints. The economic deterioration has been attributed among other things to trade and exchange rate controls. Liberalization of the trade and payments regime was therefore a central component of these adjustment programmes.

At the theoretical level, it is argued that the imposition of controls on international trade may result in both micro and macro-level distortions leading to misallocation of resources and poor economic performance. A liberalized trade regime removes these distortions and creates an enabling environment that is conducive to better economic performance.

Trade liberalization has implications for employment, economic growth, balance of payments, investment and government budget. In general, studies on trade and payments liberalization show favourable effects on employment, economic growth and the balance of payments (Papageorgiou *et al.*, 1992; Jebuni, Oduro and Tutu, 1994).

This study examines Ghana's experience with trade liberalization. It begins in section 3.2, by identifying trade liberalization episodes. The credibility of the trade liberalization programme is important in determining its sustainability; this is the subject of section 3.3. Section 3.4 presents a discussion of the characteristics of the sample of firms in the survey. The consequences of the programme are investigated in section 3.5 by looking at developments in output, investment, the external account, employment and the fiscal balance. The link between unilateral trade liberalization and regional integration is the focus of section 3.6 which tries to answer the question of whether or not trade liberalization will strengthen regional integration efforts. The paper concludes with policy recommendations. This is particularly pertinent for Ghana since there is domestic discontent with the current trade liberalization programme because it is perceived by some as having gone too far.

3.2 IDENTIFYING LIBERALIZED TRADE REGIMES

A liberalized trade regime may be described as one in which:

(1) tariffs rather than quantitative restrictions are the major instruments of trade intervention;
(2) there is a reduction in the level and dispersal of average import tariff rates; and
(3) export incentives are improved so that any bias against exporting is reduced or removed altogether.

A devaluation of the currency (without the accompanying tariff reductions) can result in a liberalization of the trade regime if it absorbs the import premium of the import licences. If the devaluation absorbs the import premium, and is accompanied by inflows of external finance that allow an increase in import volumes, the reduction in the domestic price of importables that occurs can contribute to a fall in the anti-export bias (Krueger, 1978, pp. 93 and 100).

In this study a trade regime may be described as being liberalized if conditions (1) and (2) hold and if there are moves towards achieving condition (3).

In order to determine whether a trade regime is liberalized, developments in certain indicators can be monitored. These are the bias in the trade regime, parallel market premium, relative prices, trade intensity measures and import counter-factuals.

Liberalization of the trade regime is likely to result in a decline of the black market premium. It is necessary to avoid a worsening of the balance of payments position when trade liberalization is embarked upon in order to reduce the possibility of a reversal of the programme. One way to ensure this is to reduce real money balances by a devaluation of the nominal exchange rate, or increasing indirect taxes, or contracting the nominal money supply. These measures should contribute to reducing the size of the premium as real money balances fall. In the medium term a devaluation should encourage exports through a positive supply response and a reduction in smuggling. The increase in the official supply of foreign exchange should reduce the gap between the parallel and the official exchange rate.

A reduction of import tariffs accompanied by a devaluation can cause the effective exchange rate of imports relative to exports to fall. It is possible, however, that if the objective of the trade liberalization is to create a neutral trade regime, the effective exchange rate of exports will increase as well. The net effect will be to increase the effective exchange rate for exports relative to imports. Thus the bias in the trade regime against exports should decline with a liberalization of the trade regime.

Movements in the ratio of exports and imports to GDP (that is, the trade intensity measure) will depend upon what happens to relative prices in the domestic economy. The trade intensity coefficient may change even if there is no change in policy because of an increase in the availability of foreign exchange, thus making it possible to increase import volumes.

Trade liberalization may also be identified by examining the differences between actual import volumes and predicted import volumes obtained from an estimated import demand function.

These indicators and policy accounts will be used to identify episodes of trade liberalization in Ghana.

Trade Liberalization Episodes in Ghana

In July 1961, Ghana's rapidly dwindling foreign exchange reserves forced the government to introduce trade controls by passing the exchange Control Act (Act 71) as part of a policy package to control and conserve foreign exchange. The Act made drastic changes in the existing foreign exchange market. Foreign exchange controls were extended, and comprehensive import licensing was introduced by December 1961. The imposition of trade controls in 1961 was in response to balance of payments difficulties. The import-licensing regime and tariffs were also used to achieve the import substitution, industrialization and revenue objectives of government.

By 1965, however, the economy was facing a severe balance of payments constraint, with trade and current account deficits of 5.72 per cent and 10.8 per cent of GDP, respectively. The effect of the trade controls was to increase the anti-export bias and reduce market intensity coefficients, and by 1966 a substantial black market premium had emerged. There was a change in government through a *coup d'état* in 1966. The new government accepted the IMF/World Bank stabilization package and set about trying to stabilize the economy and control inflation by using both deflationary fiscal and monetary policies and decontrolling state production. The system for allocating import licences was altered to ensure efficient mobilization of domestic resources and adequate supplies of essential commodities for consumers.

The First Liberalization Episode

Policy Accounts: Import Liberalization In 1967 the exchange rate was devalued by 43 per cent and import duties were either removed altogether or lowered on selected essential commodities. Between 1967 and 1971 import duties were lowered on a number of items to counteract the price-raising effect of the devaluation. The wholesale price index for imported food remained below its 1965 levels until 1968. The import-licensing system was liberalized further in 1968 as the proportion of items that could enter the country under the Open General Licence (which allowed importation without prior approval) was increased to 17 per cent in 1968 from 3 per cent in 1967 (Killick, 1978). This process was continued in subsequent years so that by 1970, 57 per cent of imports could enter under the Open General Licence.

In 1969 the demand for imports increased as the government pursued expansionary fiscal policies and the nominal exchange rate remained fixed. To stem the demand for imports, a 5 per cent temporary import surcharge on all items except goods imported for or by the government was introduced. The surcharge was raised in 1970 in order to try to control the demand for imports and to raise revenue for the government. The increase in the surcharge was an attempt by the government to transfer the import premium to itself. Five schedules were applicable, ranging from 5 per cent to 40 per cent for the first four schedules and 11 per cent to 150 per cent for the fifth. The rates were adjusted again in 1971 and government agencies were no longer exempt.

Export Promotion An export promotion package was introduced in 1969 to encourage the export of manufactured goods. It had four components:

(1) an income tax rebate scheme for manufacturing firms – the size of the rebate received depending on the share of total output exported;
(2) an export bonus scheme, providing producers with a bonus equivalent to 10 per cent of the value of the increase in export earnings over the previous year. The export bonus scheme was revised in the 1970/71 budget to 25 per cent of the value of exports;
(3) the automatic renewal of import licences for raw materials; and
(4) a waiver of local taxes.

The introduction of the package did not result in any significant improvement in the effective exchange rate for exports. Cocoa tax rates increased after 1967 and the export bonus scheme was not implemented until about 1971. Thus not much headway was achieved in providing a neutral trade regime.

Cocoa prices slumped in 1971, leading to a deterioration of the balance of payments. There was a build-up in arrears on short-term debt, and expected foreign resource inflows did not materialize. The exchange rate was devalued in 1971 and with the devaluation the import surcharges were removed. Another *coup d'état* took place in January 1972. Trade liberalization was brought to a halt with the tightening of trade restrictions, and part of the 1971 devaluation was reversed in February.

Indicators of Trade Liberalization The account of policy changes is suggestive of a liberalization of the trade regime between 1967 and 1971 compared to what prevailed in the period between 1961 and 1967. It is important to determine whether these policy changes brought about the expected changes in relative prices in order to stimulate the required resource flows.

An examination of the indicators of trade liberalization finds that the black market premium declined between 1967 and 1970 (Table 3.1). Relative prices moved in favour of exports between 1967 and 1970. The ratio of the wholesale price of exports to the wholesale price of manufactured articles improved continuously between 1967 and 1970. The bias in the trade regime did not change significantly in favour of total exports, however. This was because of the increase in the cocoa tax rate from 25 per cent in 1967 to 61 per cent in 1971. Estimates of the bias in the trade regime excluding cocoa exports show that it moved in favour of non-cocoa exports during the liberalization period (Table 3.1). The trade intensity coefficients picked up between 1967 and 1970, largely because of a rise in the export–GDP ratio as cocoa prices improved. The largest increase in the export–GDP ratio was in 1970 when cocoa prices rose substantially. An examination of import counterfactuals during the period finds that predicted import volumes were lower than actual volumes from 1968 to 1970, suggestive of the expansionary effect of the liberalizing measures on imports (Table 3.2).

The policy accounts and indicators of trade liberalization indicate that there was an attempt at liberalization of the trade regime between 1967 and 1971. It was not a complete liberalization, however; Leith (1974) describes it as 'cautious'. The liberalization was not complete because the import-licensing system was maintained and utilized to reign in imports when it was thought necessary. The initial decline in import tariffs was later counteracted by the imposition of surcharges. The discussion of credibility will show that this was because of inconsistencies between the macroeconomic framework and the trade liberalization programme.

The Interlude of Controls: 1972–82

The reversal of trade liberalization in 1972 ushered in a 10-year period characterized by a plethora of instruments to achieve government's objectives.[1] There was increasing dependence on the use of import licences and other non-tariff measures to control imports and achieve the balance of payments and import-substitution objectives. The exchange rate

Table 3.1 Indicators of trade liberalization

	Trade bias					
	Ratio of EERX to EERM	*Ratio of non-cocoa EERX to EERM*	*Black market premium (%)**	*Trade intensity coefficient (%)*†	*Ratio of imports to GDP (%)*	*Ratio of exports to GDP (%)*
1960	0.715	0.839	1.006	55.59	28.38	27.21
1966	0.636	0.693	2.996	28.11	15.00	13.11
1967	0.621	0.722	1.915	31.79	15.35	16.44
1968	0.626	0.802	1.720	34.14	15.88	18.26
1969	0.655	0.810	1.720	32.67	15.07	17.60
1970	0.499	0.792	1.607	36.22	16.94	19.28
1971	0.520	0.782	1.703	28.94	15.16	13.78
1972	0.677	0.856	1.232	28.69	10.53	18.16
1982	0.813	0.812	12.120	3.80	1.87	1.93
1983	0.608	0.834	8.686	4.50	2.40	2.11
1984	0.681	0.825	2.687	14.62	7.09	7.53
1985	0.637	0.857	2.415	20.62	10.60	10.02
1986	0.719	0.872	2.074	25.92	12.43	13.49
1987	0.728	0.891	1.380	38.71	20.71	18.00
1988	0.776	0.881	1.367	36.08	19.12	16.96
1989	0.778	0.877	1.280	34.47	19.09	15.38
1990	0.784	0.861	1.056	33.56	19.26	14.30
1991	0.794	0.857		33.09	18.84	14.25
1992	0.805	0.876		35.49	21.16	14.33
1993‡	0.842	0.886		45.85	28.51	17.34

Notes:
* Black market premium is the ratio of black market rate to official exchange rate.
† Trade intensity co-efficient is the ratio of the sum of the value of exports and imports to the GDP.
‡ Provisional

Sources: Calculated using information obtained from: Ghana Statistical Services, *Quarterly Digest of Statistics*, various issues and IMF, *International Financial Statistics Yearbook*, various issues (Accra).

Table 3.2 Import counter-factuals, 1966–71 (in logarithms)

	1966	*1967*	*1968*	*1969*	*1970*	*1971*
Predicted volumes*	5.185	5.249	5.206	5.384	5.417	5.45
Actual volumes	5.301	5.242	5.524	5.452	5.548	5.374

* Predicted values obtained from estimated import demand equation.

Source: Estimated by the authors from Table 3.19, Equation (3).

was not used as a policy instrument and remained fixed for long periods when the rate of inflation was rising. The real exchange rate began to appreciate in 1975 (Appendix, Table 3A.1). Estimates of the purchasing power parity exchange rate and the ratio of the black market rate to the official rate indicate the extent of the distortions created by the exchange rate policy (Appendix, Table 3A.1). Import tariff rates were high during most of the period and the schedules were changed quite frequently as the government tried to achieve its revenue objective. It failed to do this because of the prevalence of tax evasion through the misclassification of commodities, the misuse of tax exemption provisions and the increasing dependence on the import-licensing mechanism.

There was a half-hearted attempt at liberalization in 1977 and 1978. This is described as half-hearted because the import-licensing system was not dismantled. The easing of licensing requirements on the importation of raw materials and spare parts only applied to a limited number of companies that had been identified by the government in its budget. The range of import duty schedules was reduced from 5–150 per cent to two rates of 35 per cent for all items that had rates of less than 60 per cent and 60 per cent for all items that had rates of more than 60 per cent. The import licence levy was abolished. A major determinant of the restructuring of the tariff schedules was the need to increase tax collection rates. The wide schedule of tax rates had created the possibility of tax evasion.

By 1982, import volumes, real government revenue and cocoa export volumes were at their lowest levels since the 1960s. Most economic variables had negative growth rates and the economy faced a severe foreign exchange crisis. Between 1972 and 1982 merchandise exports contributed on average 69 per cent to total gross foreign exchange inflows. In some years in the 1970s the contribution was as high as 85 per cent. The decline in the growth of export values and the dependence on foreign exchange earnings from merchandise exports for a significant proportion of foreign exchange inflows meant that the capacity to import had declined over the period 1972–82.

The domestic manufacturing sector is highly import-dependent, with most sectors depending on imported raw materials for a significant proportion of total requirements. Shortages in required raw materials, spare parts, and capital goods were identified as being important determinants of excess capacity in the manufacturing sector (MDPI, 1974). The problem was not limited to the manufacturing sector. The cocoa sector, for example, was adversely affected by inadequate supplies of insecticides, pesticides and spraying cans (Nyanteng, 1980).

The alleviation of the stranglehold the import shortages had on the Ghanaian economy could only occur if there was an improvement in the performance of the export sector and an increase in external financial inflows. In order for there to be such an improvement, it was necessary that the incentive structure for exports in particular be improved. Theoretical analysis has shown that export sector activities are affected by policy towards imports (Clements and Sjaastad, 1984). Econometric evidence for Ghana has found that 74–85 per cent of the import tax is shifted to exports (Jebuni, Oduro, Asante and Tsikata, 1992). A restrictive import trade regime with an anti-export bias will only serve to discourage export production. There was therefore a need to liberalize the trade regime and remove the anti-export bias.

The trade liberalization process that began in 1983 was part of a broad macroeconomic programme, the objective of which was to reverse the decline in major economic indicators and to deal with the severe foreign exchange crisis facing the economy.

The Second Liberalization Episode

Policy Account: Import Liberalization The move towards trade liberalization began in April 1983 with the introduction of a multiple exchange rate system. The nominal exchange rate remained fixed at its 1978 level, but a system of bonuses and surcharges was introduced that increased the effective exchange rate. Traditional exports, as well as imports of crude oil, essential raw materials, basic foodstuffs and capital goods were subject to an effective exchange rate of 23.75 *cedis* (C) to one US$. Non-traditional exports and other imports faced a rate of 25.975 cedis to the US$. The exchange rate was unified in October 1983 at C30.00 to US$1.00. Three nominal devaluations took place in 1984 and 1985. The currency was devalued again in January 1986 from C60.00 to C90.00 to the US$.[2]

The real exchange rate depreciated as the nominal exchange rate was devalued (Appendix, Table 3A.1). The devaluations were also accompanied by a reduction in the gap between the official rate and parallel market rate. The frequent changes in the rate during the three-year period beginning from October 1983 would have contributed to generating confidence that the liberalization programme would be maintained.

Import programming and the import-licensing system that was in operation prior to 1983 were maintained until 1986 when the new exchange rate system was introduced. There was a re-definition of import licence categories, with three types in operation.

(1) The 'A' licence allowed the holder to bid for foreign exchange at the Bank of Ghana auction. Items that could be imported using this category were pharmaceutical goods, raw materials, spare parts and other producer goods.
(2) The 'S' licence allowed individuals with access to their own sources of foreign exchange to import goods. Holders of this licence could not bid for foreign exchange at the Bank of Ghana auction. These licences were valid for six months.
(3) The 'G' licence was issued to government organizations for the importation of essential goods and services. It was allocated to the ministries, which submitted licences to the Ministry of Trade and Tourism. This licence allowed government organizations to use foreign exchange without making recourse to the auction.

The tax schedules were adjusted downwards in 1983 with the introduction of the bonuses and surcharges. The tax structure remained fairly stable over the period 1983–5 (Table 3.3). The major significant change in the structure of taxes during that time was the increased tax on special licences. In 1986 there was a decline of between 5 and 10 percentage points in the tax rates for all import categories except for luxury goods. A licence tax of 0.1 per cent was levied on the 'A' licence. Holders of the 'S' licence were required to pay a 20 per cent advance income tax. However, importers of agriculture-related items were exempt from paying this tax.

In 1986 import duties were reduced further on all items except luxury goods. Sales taxes were reduced in all categories. An escalating tariff structure was established, with raw materials and capital goods having a lower import tariff rate than did consumer goods and luxury goods. The effect of this was to increase the effective rate of protection of the domestic import-substituting (consumer goods) industries compared to the previous period.

The exchange rates were unified in 1987 with the closure of the first window at the Bank of Ghana. Henceforth all transactions had to take place at the Bank of Ghana auction. Approximately 70 per cent of the goods that had previously not been on the 'A' licence list were transferred to that list from the 'S' licence. Import duties and sales taxes on capital goods, consumer goods and luxury items were adjusted upwards

Table 3.3 Import tax schedules (%)

	1983	*1984*	*1985*	*1986*	*1987*	*1988*	*1989*	*1990*	
Import Duties									
Concessionary	[10–20]	[10–20]	[20–25]	[10–20]	[10–25]	[10–25]	10	10	
Basic raw materials	25	25	25	10	15	10	10	10	
Other raw materials	30	30	30	20	20	15	15	10	
Capital goods	30	30	30	20	25	15	15	10	
Consumer goods	30	30	30	25	35	20	20	20	
Luxury items	30	30	30	30	30	25	25	25	
Import Sales Tax									
Concessionary	[10–15]	10	[10–20]	10	10	10	7.5	15	
Basic consumer goods		20	10	35	25	22.5	22.5	17.5	15
Luxury goods		70	20	45	35	35	35	35	35
Special Development Tax									
Special Licences	10	20	50	50	50	50	0	0	
Import Licence Fee									
Special Licence*	20	20	20	20	20	20	0	0	
‘A’ Licence				0.1	0.5	0.5	0	0	

* Advance income tax

Source: National Revenue Secretariat, Accra, and Budget Statements 1992 and 1994.

in 1987 but reduced in 1988, so that they were below the rates prevailing prior to 1986. The lowering of import duty and sales tax rates continued into the early 1990s. The escalating tariff structure was maintained. The basis on which the sales tax was calculated was adjusted in the 1988 budget. It was formerly calculated as a percentage of the c.i.f. value; the new method calculated the sales tax as a percentage of the c.i.f. value plus the import duty value. Both domestic and imported items were made subject to the same sales tax rate.

Several significant changes took place in 1988.

(1) Forex bureaux were introduced, which could sell foreign exchange freely to importers and other users of foreign exchange and could purchase foreign exchange from non-traditional exporters and recipients of remittances from abroad. The exchange rate was determined by the demand and supply of foreign exchange. With the introduction of the forex bureaus there were two ‘market determined’ official exchange rates.
(2) Exchange control regulations were relaxed; residents could take a maximum of US$3000 out of the country.
(3) The liberalization of access to the Bank of Ghana foreign exchange

> auction was extended when the remaining holders of the 'S' licence, who had previously been excluded, became eligible to bid for foreign exchange at the auction.

In January 1989, the import-licensing system was removed. This was because:

> recent economic measures like the foreign exchange auction and the establishment of the forex bureaux no longer justify the continued operation of the import licensing system. (K. Botchwey, in his 1989 Budget Statement)

With the end of the import-licensing system the exchange rate and the international trade taxes became the major instruments for the implementation of trade policy.

The cost of importing was reduced for most items because of the elimination of the special development tax and import licence fees in 1989. The tax rates on other raw materials and capital goods were reduced in 1990, thus contributing to increasing further the effective rate of protection of the consumer goods industry.

In order to protect selected industries, duty protection rates ranging from 10 per cent to 40 per cent were imposed on selected items. In 1992 a single rate of 10 per cent was applied.

Policy Account: Export Promotion Policy At the time of the introduction of the Economic Recovery Programme there was already an export promotion package in place, although most of its components were hardly utilized. The export bonus scheme was abolished when the currency was devalued in 1983. In 1981 an export retention programme was introduced that allowed all, except for cocoa exporters, to retain 20 per cent of their foreign exchange earnings. Restrictions were initially placed on the use of these monies. The percentage of foreign exchange that could be retained by the exporter was increased to 35 per cent in 1987 and the limitations on the uses to which these monies could be put were relaxed.

The incentives of the export promotion programme have become more attractive over time as the income tax rebates have increased and been extended to the agricultural sector, the customs duty drawback has been raised from 95 per cent to 100 per cent, and the export retention has been raised to 100 per cent for non-traditional exporters. Except for the export retention scheme, the export promotion package has not had much of an impact on encouraging non-traditional exports. This is because most exporters are ignorant of the different components of the package and when they do know about it they do not utilize the benefits because of

Table 3.4 Import counter-factuals, 1983–90 (1980=100)

	*Predicted volumes**	*Actual volumes*
1983	4.235	4.06
1984	4.312	4.302
1985	4.395	4.409
1986	4.463	4.542
1987	4.718	4.663
1988	4.759	4.709
1989	4.732	4.778
1990	4.854	4.804

* Predicted values obtained from estimated import demand equation; see Table 3.19, Equation (3).

the cumbersome bureaucratic procedures involved in obtaining them (Jebuni, Oduro, Asante and Tsikata, 1992). The foreign exchange retentions scheme was widely advertised by the authorities, unlike the income tax rebate scheme or customs duty drawback schemes, for example. The retention scheme also directly addressed a problem faced by almost all producers in Ghana – the need to obtain foreign exchange.

Indicators of Trade Liberalization

Estimates of the bias in the trade regime indicate that there has been some decline in the anti-export bias since 1983 (Table 3.1). The improvement has been much greater for non-cocoa exports, which have hardly been taxed during this period (Table 3.1). The improvement in the incentive structure has also come about because of the decline in import taxes. Because of the difficulty in calculating the import premiums during the period of controls, the extent of the improvement in the bias towards exporting between 1983 and 1988 compared to the period of controls has been underestimated. The black market premium has declined continuously since 1983, so that there is now no effective parallel market in operation. The trade intensity coefficient has increased. However, the increase in the import–GDP ratio cannot be attributed solely to import liberalization because liberalization has been accompanied by significant increases in aid and other external financial inflows. The import counter-factual shows that in most of the years since 1983 the actual import volumes have been lower than those predicted by the import demand equation (Table 3.4). Between 1983 and 1988 this may be explained by the import programming that was still in place.

Conclusion

The policy accounts and some indicators have confirmed that Ghana has gone through two distinct periods of trade liberalization. The first started in 1967 and ended in 1971. Import duties were lowered and import licensing was relaxed but not removed. The exchange rate was not used as a policy tool except in 1967 and 1971. Thus the liberalization was not extensive.

The second liberalization, which is more extensive than the first, began in 1983. The exchange rate has been liberalized, tariffs and taxes have been lowered and narrowed, all quantitative restrictions on imports have been eliminated and import licensing has been removed: The process of trade liberalization is a continuing one, as measures are currently being taken to reduce the bottlenecks in exporting procedures.

3.3 CREDIBILITY OF THE TRADE LIBERALIZATION EPISODES

It is recognized that the credibility of a programme is important in determining whether the programme will be sustained. Three necessary conditions for a trade liberalization to be credible are: (1) macroeconomic compatibility; (2) the absence of systematic forecastability; and (3) time inconsistency.

Macroeconomic Compatibility

Macroeconomic compatibility has two components, balance of payments and fiscal. Liberalization of the trade regime will tend to worsen the balance of payments position. This is because the price level falls as import duties are reduced and this causes increases in real money balances, which can cause the balance of payments to deteriorate. In Ghana, trade liberalization was adopted when the balance of payments was in a weak position. Trade liberalization that further weakened the balance of payments would not be long-lived. The probability of the liberalization exercise being sustained would only increase if it was accompanied by policies that restrained the increase in real money balances. A devaluation, an increase in indirect taxes, or contractionary fiscal and monetary policies are appropriate to support the liberalization to ensure it is payment compatible.

Most developing countries have long depended on trade taxes for a substantial proportion of their government revenues. Fiscal incompatibility will occur if an import liberalization programme reduces trade and total

Table 3.5 Developments in balance of payments

Year	*Total exports ($US m.)*	*Total imports ($US m.)*	*Trade balance ($US m.)*	*CA. def (surp. ($US m.)*	*Total reserves ($US m.)*	*Export volume index**	*Import volume index**
1960	333.8	348.1	–14.3	–108.30	272.2		184.88
1966	280.3	320.7	–40.4	–125.10	105.5	257.96	200.62
1967	284.2	265.4	18.8	–84.90	77.1	235.63	189.20
1968	304.4	264.6	39.8	–56.10	90.3	241.23	250.83
1969	345.0	295.0	49.7	–60.10	66.2	199.38	233.28
1970	427.0	375.1	51.9	–67.70	36.6	220.90	256.90
1971	334.6	368.2	–33.6	–145.80	36.1	155.20	215.8
1972	384.3	222.9	161.4	108.20	93.7	186.60	111.5
1982	607.0	588.7	18.3	–108.60	138.9	116.50	64.4
1983	439.1	499.7	–60.6	–174.10	144.8	74.00	58.2
1984	565.9	533.0	32.9	–38.80	301.6	85.70	73.9
1985	632.4	668.7	–36.3	–134.20	478.5	103.70	82.2
1986	773.4	712.5	60.9	–43.00	513.0	114.90	93.9
1987	826.8	951.5	–124.7	–96.90	195.1	123.80	106.0
1988	881.0	993.4	–112.4	–65.80	221.3	189.00	111.0
1989	807.2	1002.2	–195.0	–98.60	347.0	166.60	118.9
1990	890.6	1198.9	–308.3	–228.50	218.8	176.90	122.1
1991	997.6	1318.7	–321.1	–252.70	550.2		
1992	986.4	1456.7	–470.3	–377.80	319.9		
1993	1050.9	1727.86	–676.96	–571.55	341.2		

Note:
* 1980=100.

Source: International Monetary Fund, *International Financial Statistics Yearbooks*, various issues and IMF files; Ghana Statistical Services, *Quarterly Digest of Statistics*, various issues (Accra).

revenue. The liberalization will be reversed if the government has no immediate alternative sources of revenue. The government could either increase import taxes to their pre-liberalization level or run a budget deficit, which if financed by borrowing from the banking system would increase money supply and worsen the balance of payments position.

Compatibility of the 1967–71 Liberalization

The liberalization of 1967–71 was preceded by a sharp cut in government expenditures of 27 per cent in 1966. Although revenues declined as well, the size of the budget deficit was cut in half and the budget deficit–GDP ratio fell to 2.5 per cent in 1966. Import volumes did not increase in 1967, but fell by 57 per cent (Table 3.5). This suggests that the fiscal

Table 3.6 Growth of output, 1960–93

Year	GDP growth	Agriculture GDP growth	Industry GDP growth	Services GDP growth
1960				
1961	6.17			
1962	4.83			
1963	3.47			
1964	2.15			
1965	1.36			
1966	0.09			
1967	–3.00			
1968	6.43			
1969	5.88			
1970	6.76			
1971	5.56			
1972	–2.49			
1973	15.25	–1.994	19.552	2.066
1974	3.39	8.812	–0.569	8.503
1975	–12.86	–19.933	–0.956	–7.441
1976	–3.52	–4.849	–2.589	–1.008
1977	2.26	–2.233	3.778	7.936
1978	8.48	19.051	–7.237	4.379
1979	–7.82	5.318	–21.037	–8.134
1980	6.24	0.674	9.027	5.235
1981	–3.49	–2.570	–15.978	3.343
1982	–6.92	–5.449	–17.021	–3.618
1983	–4.56	–6.975	–11.859	2.275
1984	8.65	9.696	8.964	6.618
1985	5.09	0.648	17.604	7.522
1986	5.20	3.306	7.562	6.496
1987	4.80	0.031	11.489	9.380
1988	5.62	3.583	7.253	7.834
1989	5.09	4.251	2.592	6.678
1990	3.33	–2.018	6.989	7.929
1991	5.30	4.740	3.719	6.273
1992	3.90	–0.655	5.717	7.670
1993	4.98	2.859	4.308	7.007

Source: Calculated using information obtained from Ghana Statistical Services, *Quarterly Digest of Statistics*, various issues (Accra).

restraint of the preceding year plus the devaluation must have constrained import demand. The current account deficit fell and the trade balance moved into surplus in 1967 for the first time in five years (Table 3.6). However, the failure to devalue the exchange rate as the liberalization process was continued, and the accompanying expansionary fiscal policies, put pressure on the external account. This was not reflected in a worsening current account or trade balance because of the improvement in the terms of trade as cocoa prices increased. In order to maintain payments compatibility an import surcharge of 5 per cent was introduced in 1969 and some items that had been exempt were made subject to the surcharge. The export promotion package was also introduced as a measure to sustain the import liberalization programme.

In 1970 the terms of trade worsened, and there was a sharp increase in import volumes. Macroeconomic incompatibility became quite obvious. The exchange rate had still not been adjusted, and the import surcharges were not adequate to restrain the demand for imports because the government 'when succumbing to political pressures . . . exempted a number of importers from surcharges and granted stretch out payment terms to others' (Ofori-Atta, 1975, p. 18). Killick (1978) estimates that if the surcharges had been collected fully they would have been equivalent to 13 per cent and 15 per cent of the value of imports in 1970 and 1971 respectively. Because of the exemptions and possible tax evasion, the actual collection rates were 2.7 per cent and 6.2 per cent of the value of total imports in those years.

Total reserves began to fall sharply in 1968, indicating the possibility of payments incompatibility. Reserves fell by 26.6 per cent in 1969, 44.7 per cent in 1970 and 1.3 per cent in 1971. Short-term debts increased by US$79.2m between September 1969 and June 1971 (Frimpong-Ansah, 1991). The terms of trade deteriorated a further 26 per cent by 1971. The size of the current account deficit doubled and the trade balance went into deficit for the first time since liberalization had begun. Unfortunately, before the measures undertaken by government could take effect, that is, the devaluation of December 1971, there was a reversal in policy by the new government that had come into power through a *coup d'état*.

Compatibility of the Present Liberalization Episode

Problems of macroeconomic incompatibility have been avoided in the current liberalization exercise because of the real devaluations that were achieved in the early years; the initial fiscal restraint that characterized the structural adjustment programme; the ability to widen the tax base and so reduce dependence on trade taxes; and the inflows of external financing.

Payments compatibility was achieved through frequent nominal devaluations, which contributed to a real depreciation of the currency. The decline in the budget deficit ratio also reduced expansionary pressures on the money supply. By the time the pace of the liberalization had quickened in 1989, the budget was in surplus. Aid flows increased in each year from 1985 to 1989. There was a substantial build-up of international reserves between 1983 and 1986 (Table 3.6); they declined in 1987 and 1988 but picked up again in 1989. Thus the current account deficit, inclusive of official transfers, decreased between 1985 and 1989.

However, from 1989 certain indicators seem to suggest that the programme was becoming payments incompatible. The current account deficit began to rise significantly and continued to do so until 1993. The payments incompatibility was accommodated by the increase in reserves as a result of inflow of loans and grants. Matters got worse in 1992 and the issue of balance of payments compatibility had emerged due to the inability to prevent the appreciation of the real exchange rate because of the emergence of large fiscal deficits. As a result of the expansionary fiscal programme pursued by the government in 1992, a huge budget deficit was recorded. The current account deficit rose to approximately 9.6 per cent of GDP and the money supply increased by 59 per cent. The failure of the export prices of the major export commodities to increase significantly had become important as aid flows sometimes fall below expectations. In response to these developments indirect taxes were increased and special levies introduced to try to refrain from resorting to the use of quantitative restrictions.

The liberalization is on course because of the continuing inflow of foreign resources. However, if government policies do not generate significant improvement in the economy and stem the inflationary pressures, the programme may finally become incompatible.

The liberalization has been fiscally compatible in so far as it has not resulted in any significant decline in government revenue in either real or nominal terms.

Systematic Forecastibility

Some aspects of macroeconomic policy may be systematically forecastable, and this could alter the efficacy of policy. Trade policy can be endogenous when, as a result of improvements in the foreign reserves or balance of payments, trade policy is relaxed. Liberalizations that are responses under an endogenous trade policy rule can be predicted to be reversed and hence are incredible.

In Ghana the government has initiated liberalization programmes as a means to address poor economic performance. During the first liberalization, trade policy was endogenous to the performance of the economy. In the second period, liberalization had continued irrespective of the performance of the economy. When the terms of trade, foreign reserves and current account started to deteriorate from 1988, it did not lead to changes in trade policy or exchange rate policy. The liberalizations continued. As the balance of trade deficits increased from 1990, the liberalization has not been reversed. Thus this liberalization so far has been credible as far as systematic forecastibility is concerned.

Time Consistency

This is a situation where the private sector views liberalization as transitory and liable to change. For instance, the reduction of the tax on cocoa might be seen by farmers as a short-term measure. If this were so, they would not invest by planting new cocoa trees. The questions to be asked are:

(1) What are the reasons for maintaining the trade restrictions?
(2) Why did the government liberalize?
(3) Did private agents act on the assumption that the policy would be permanent: and
(4) Was there at any time in the liberalization episode good reason to expect that future political equilibrium or trade policy would be different from that in the past?

It was mentioned earlier that trade restrictions were imposed to correct balance of payments deficits and to protect import-substituting industries. The liberalization was undertaken because initially the economy had reached its lowest level and only such a policy package could lead to receipt of assistance from multilateral sources.

Consequences of Incredibility

The incredibility of a liberalization programme can be tested by examining how private agents behave towards the programme. The basic theory is due to Calvo (1987) and Dixit (1989). Calvo postulates that if agents anticipate increases in implicit tariffs, they will hoard imports and sell them when the tariffs are raised. Dixit argues that, faced with uncertainty about how relative prices might evolve, agents will defer irreversible investments until the uncertainty is resolved, preferring liquid assets.

Changes in the stockpile of import licences and imports in bonded warehouses are indicators of credibility, but the import-licensing system was removed in 1989. The two indicators will not be good measures.

Some of the disturbing issues of the current liberalization are the deterioration in the current account, depreciation of the local currency and inflation. Private agents' behaviour in the face of these outcomes, which reflect incredibility, will be to stay liquid and invest in foreign exchange. The proportion of money supply outside the banking system can be an indication of staying liquid. The currency outside the banking system averaged 36 per cent during the first liberalization. During the high inflationary periods, the currency outside the banks started increasing in 1977 to a high of 55 per cent in 1984 before falling to a low of 26 per cent in 1991.

The currency was devalued by large amounts between 1984 and 1986. A fixed exchange rate regime was in operation during this period. The exchange rate was more or less determined by market forces with the introduction of the auction in 1986 and the forex bureaus in 1988. After 1986 the rate of depreciation declined to a low of 13 per cent in 1990 before increasing again. These indications show that private agents were behaving in a way that showed credibility in the programme until 1992. The macroeconomic instability that has occurred since 1992 led to large depreciation of the *cedi* in 1992 and 1993 and an increase in the proportion of the currency held outside the banks. As indicated above, developments since 1992 cast doubts on the credibility of the programme.

The response to output growth from the cocoa sector confirms that the private sector does not see the reduction in the export tax as temporary. Since 1986/7 when the real producer price of cocoa began to increase, farmers have responded positively by increasing the output of cocoa to a high level of 300 000 tonnes in 1988/89; output then began to fall as real prices declined (see Appendix, Table 3A.2).

There have been instances since 1991 when the private sector argued against what they perceived to be 'over-liberalization' of trade and the need to control it. Although the accusation of dumping is still made, the government has stuck to its liberalization pace.

Macroeconomic incompatibility was an important reason for the reversal of the 1967–71 liberalization. In an assessment of the liberalization, Leith (1974) attributes its failure to 'the broader failure of general economic policy in Ghana'. The emerging balance of payments incompatibility could derail the present liberalization exercise. A great deal depends on the government's commitment to correcting the fiscal imbalances at the heart of the incompatibility problem as well as its commitment to the ideals of a liberalized economy *per se*. The ability of domestic manufacturers to survive in the new environment is another important determinant. The private sector has in the past asked that the liberalization exercise be reconsidered. What this suggests is that not only is macro-consistency necessary for the sustainability of a trade liberalization programme, but that it is also necessary that micro-level issues be addressed (for example, the level and state of productive capacity of the firms and their ability to create the capacity to exist in a liberalized environment).

3.4 THE SURVEY

The survey began in August 1995. Given the time constraint facing the researchers, the field work had to be completed in November 1995. Some 95 firms were contracted, of which approximately 21 per cent were exporters. It had been intended that at least 40 per cent of the firms in the sample would be exporting firms. The *Ghana Business Directory* published by the Ghana Chamber of Commerce and a list of exporting enterprises drawn up by the Ghana Export Promotion Council (GEPC) were used to produce the sample of firms.

Problems Encountered

A problem with the *Business Directory* was that some firms were listed as exporters when they were not; some that had been exporters had ceased to export. The problem with the list of enterprises obtained from the GEPC was that some of the enterprises listed as exporters were not manufacturers but export agencies. However, this information was not indicated in the list. It was only when the field work began that all these problems became apparent.

Another difficulty encountered was the unwillingness of firm owners, managers and accountants to co-operate with the interviewers. Some owners and/or managers decided which questions they wanted to answer. In one instance, the questionnaire was filled in by a manager who refused to meet the interviewer. Other problems encountered were the closure of firms reported as exporters, and the relocation of some of these firms to new premises that could not be found by the interviewers.

Thus at the end of the first round of interviews it was found that only 14 of the firms interviewed were currently exporting. The development plan of the GEPC reports that a small number of firms are responsible for a large proportion of the non-traditional exports. Two firms dominate the export of furniture and one firm dominates the export of aluminium products. A recent television report based on information provided by GEPC stated that the number of firms involved in non-traditional exports declined in 1994.

Table 3.7 Sector distribution of firms

Sector	*Value*	*Frequency*	*(%)*	*Valid (%)*	*Cum (%)*
Food	1	4	4.2	4.2	4.2
Beverages	2	2	2.1	2.1	6.3
Textiles	3	8	8.4	8.4	14.7
Garments	4	6	6.3	6.3	21.0
Leather	5	6	6.3	6.3	28.4
Wood	6	5	5.3	5.3	33.7
Furniture	7	26	27.4	27.4	60.1
Paper	8	1	1.1	1.1	61.2
Chemical	9	9	9.5	9.5	70.7
Rubber and Plastics	10	9	9.5	9.5	80.2
Pottery and Glass	11	1	1.1	1.1	81.3
Metal	12	15	15.8	15.8	97.1
Miscellaneous	13	3	2.9	2.9	100.0
Total		95	100.0	100.0	

Source: Survey results.

Characteristics of the Sample

The sample covered a wide range of sectors but the largest group of firms (27 per cent) were in the furniture industry (Table 3.7). The other significant industries represented in the sample were metal (15.8 per cent), rubber and plastics, and pottery and glass; the latter two sectors were 9.5 per cent each.

The firms were classified on the basis of size (Table 3.8). Micro firms which employ fewer than five workers made up 28.1 per cent of the sample. Small-scale firms (those employing between 5 and 29 workers) made up 32.6 per cent and medium-sized firms, which employ between 30 and 99 workers, made up 20 per cent of the sample. Firms employing at least 100 workers were designated as large firms; they made up 14.8 per cent of the sample.

Just under half of the firms were limited liabilities and 43 per cent were sole proprietorships. A majority of the firms in the sample – that is, 60 per cent – were established prior to liberalization of the trade regime (1985).

Table 3.8 Size distribution of firms

	Frequency	*(%)*
Less than 5 workers	25	26.3
5–29 workers	31	32.6
30–99 workers	19	20.0
100 or more workers	14	14.8

Note: There were six missing observations

Source: Survey results.

3.5 ECONOMIC PERFORMANCE FOLLOWING LIBERALIZATION

The relative price changes accompanying trade liberalization have implications for resource allocation in the domestic economy. Liberalization can be expected to affect output, trade, investment, productivity of capital and the fiscal balance. The performance of the economy as a result of liberalization will be assessed by examining the behaviour of the data series of the relevant variables and data obtained from the firm-level survey conducted in 1995. We shall look at the results of some of the estimated functions based on the time series data for imports, exports, productivity of capital, per capita GDP and gross fixed capital formation. We used variables indicated by basic theory and then added policy variables relating to the trade and payments regime.

Two measures were used as trade and payments policy variables. The first measure was the bias in the trade regime. This is defined as the ratio of the effective exchange rate of exports to the effective exchange rate of imports. The second measure is the black market premium defined as the ratio of the black market rate to the official exchange rate. A similar procedure has been used in Roubini and Sala-i-Martin (1991) in testing the role of the trade regime in economic growth in a cross-section sample of countries. The trade regime could have both a direct and indirect effect on the macroeconomic variables. We used ordinary least squares estimation techniques.

Growth and Sectoral Composition of Output

There is a growing body of theoretical literature attempting to model the effects of trade policy on the long-run growth of the economy. In a detailed review of this literature, Roubini and Sala-i-Martin (1991, p. 7) conclude that 'the relation between the trade regime and economic growth is theoretically very ambiguous. Depending on the structure of the model, the origin of growth and the initial endowments and conditions of the various economies, trade restrictions may or may not reduce economic growth'.

In most of these models the effects of trade policy depend on the 'allocative' effects. Grossman and Helpman (1990) note the different comparative advantages that countries have in research and development activities versus the production of final manufactured goods.

In Khan and Villanueva (1991), liberalizations of foreign trade and direct investment are said to promote long-run growth by improving factor productivity through the removal of barriers to imported inputs and to the inflow of risk capital.

An additional link between trade policy and growth is provided by the existence of rent-seeking activities associated with the restrictive regime. Rent-seeking adversely affects growth in two ways. First, rent-seeking has a negative effect on output by the wasteful use of resources in the pursuit of rents associated with quota, other trade restrictions and the overvalued exchange rate (Krueger, 1974). Second, economic rents are transfers of income or of wealth and hence represent a tax on the means of production. As such rents lower the incentives to invest or work since they reduce the net returns to all factors. (Gallagher, 1991).

The underlying framework for most of this theoretical analysis is the endogenous growth approach started by Romer (1986) through the enhancement of human capital.

The First Liberalization

The period of controls prior to the trade-liberalizing exercise experienced a continuous slow down in the growth of GDP (Table 3.6). Growth of output plummeted in 1967 because of the contractionary fiscal policies pursued. After 1967 growth rates remained positive, averaging 6 per cent between 1968 and 1971. The liberalized period, therefore, saw a reversal of the decline in growth rates during the earlier period of controls between 1961 and 1965 (Table 3.6).

The Second Liberalization

Growth of GDP during the liberalized period has been positive, averaging about 4 per cent over the period. This is a distinct departure from the controlled periods when some years recorded negative growth rates. Table 3.6 shows that this second liberalization period may be sub-divided into two based on the differences in growth performance. Growth rates between 1984 and 1989 averaged 5.7 per cent while they averaged 4.3 per cent between 1990 and 1993.

Table 3.6 also shows sectoral growth rates. Agriculture had the lowest growth rates, which were even negative in 1990 and 1992. Services and industry had consistent high growth rates. The services sector has been the fastest growing sector since 1988.

Within the industrial sub-sector, two significant growth patterns can be seen. The growth of industry was substantially higher during the earlier phase of liberalization compared to the more recent years. It averaged 11 per cent between 1984 and 1987 and 5.09 per cent between 1988 and 1993. While manufacturing showed the highest growth rates up to 1988 and then slowed significantly, mining and construction showed sluggish growth up to 1986 and stepped up. The growth of water and electricity has been remarkable throughout this period. Manufacturing, which is the most important industrial sub-sector, contributing on average 9 per cent of GDP between 1989 and 1993, has seen an average growth rate of only 2.3 per cent since 1989. The manufacturing sector is mainly import-substituting. The liberalization of the trade regime has adversely affected certain sectors within manufacturing. Other reasons explaining the sector's poor performance since 1989 are the recent high budget deficits, the high cost of capital, the lack of long-term capital for investment and the high inflation rate.

The manufacturing sector was plagued by a low level of capacity utilization in the early 1980s. Capacity utilization increased during the mid-1980s from a low of about 32 per cent to an average of about 48 per cent. The problem of low capacity utilization has resurfaced even in the face of the high level of liberalization and that could account for the slowdown of the growth of the manufacturing sector.

The survey shows that only 12.6 per cent of the firms were operating at full capacity (Table 3.9). The most frequently cited reason for this was the lack of demand which 51 firms gave as a reason for the low capacity utilization.

The lack of demand is not necessarily due to increased competition from imports, as would be expected in a liberalized trade regime. Firms were asked to identify their main competitors: 73 per cent listed other domestic firms, only 11.6 per cent of the firms identified imports as the main source of competition, while 5.3 per cent considered foreign firms to be their main competitors. This suggests that the problem of imports is a sector specific one. This echoes the finding of another study on the manufacturing sector in Ghana, which found that only firms in the textiles sector perceived import competition as a severe constraint to performance (Baah-Nuakoh, 1993). The fact that the furniture industry dominated our sample and the competition is from local firms can also partly explain this outcome. Also this may partly be due to the depressed real incomes and a high level of unemployment.

Table 3.9 Reasons for low capacity utilization

Reason	*Frequency*
Lack of demand	51
Finance:	
Lack of credit	33
High cost of credit	32
Foreign exchange:	
Shortage of it	3
High price of it	21
Lack of raw materials	20
Old machinery	9
Expensive labour	7

The second important set of reasons for the low capacity utilization was finance related. For 33 of the firms, the problem was availability of credit, and for 32 of them the problem was the cost of credit. These results do not differ from earlier surveys on the manufacturing sector of Ghana, which find that problems of finance lie behind the problems of firms moving into exporting (Jebuni *et al.*, 1992) or generally expanding production (Baah-Nuakoh, 1993).

With the exchange reforms that have taken place since 1983, problems of access to foreign exchange due to quantity rationing have eased. However, the high cost of foreign exchange was cited as a problem by 32 firms. The large proportion of furniture firms in the sample can explain why the number of firms that cited this as a problem is not higher than expected. Firms working in the wood industry do not have high ratios of imported inputs to total because the major raw material is produced locally.

The relative prices of importables and exportables to the non-tradeables sector improved between 1984 and 1988. The importables price index was proxied by the wholesale price index of the manufacturing sector and the exportables price index was proxied by the wholesale price index of exports. The non-tradeables price index was proxied by the price of stone obtained from the prime building costs price index. These movements in relative prices follow closely movements in the real exchange rate (Appendix Table 3A.1). The decline in the contribution of non-tradeables between 1984 and 1989 can be explained by the changes in the incentives structure resulting from the trade and exchange rate reforms. However, in 1989 and 1990 relative prices fell and the real exchange rate appreciated compared to its 1988 levels. The manufacturing sector in particular performed quite poorly during this period. The change in relative prices

Table 3.10 Composition of nominal GDP, 1968–93

Year	*Share agriculture GDP (%)*	*Share industry GDP (%)*	*Share services GDP (%)*	*Non-traded GDP (%)**
1968	41.78	17.86	40.37	43.2
1969	45.95	17.19	36.95	41.8
1970	46.92	18.27	34.83	40.4
1971	44.14	18.28	35.14	42.7
1972	46.65	18.05	35.03	40.2
1973	48.96	18.60	31.97	36.9
1974	51.07	18.12	29.73	36.0
1975	47.67	20.98	30.99	36.4
1976	35.25	19.22	30.70	35.0
1977	56.21	15.84	27.98	32.2
1978	60.71	11.98	27.31	30.0
1979	60.31	12.26	27.25	30.1
1980	61.00	11.50	27.50	30.4
1981	53.81	9.17	38.60	42.61
1982	57.34	6.25	37.87	40.18
1983	59.73	6.63	34.10	35.82
1984	49.24	10.58	40.31	43.31
1985	44.89	16.68	38.59	42.62
1986	47.77	17.15	34.55	38.83
1987	50.60	16.32	32.88	37.49
1988	49.61	16.57	33.61	38.64
1989	48.97	16.72	33.39	38.26
1990	47.86	15.86	35.82	40.69
1991	48.63	15.99	35.28	40.76
1992	48.58	16.19	34.87	40.47
1993	47.80	16.00	35.70	40.70

* Non-traded GDP is GDP of the services, utilities and construction sectors.

Source: Calculated using information obtained from Ghana Statistical Services, *Quarterly Digest of Statistics*, various issues (Accra).

can therefore explain the increase in the share of non-tradeables in output (Table 3.10) during this period.

Agriculture, especially the food crop sub-sector, has performed badly as a result of lack of credit, marketing and extension services, and the withdrawal of subsidies on inputs. The cocoa and forestry sub-sectors have benefited from the reduction in the bias against exports in the trade regime and have seen significant public support. The increase in export volumes has not been translated equally into earnings as prices fluctuate downwards.

The important sub-sectors of trade and government activity of the service sector continue to experience growth, with wholesale and retail trade growing at an average annual growth of 10 per cent since 1990. The next largest sub-sector, government services, has grown at a fast rate, averaging 6.5 per cent, since 1991.

The service sector, and especially the two sub-sectors mentioned above, has experienced spectacular growth rates, mainly due to the liberalized trade and significant inflow that goes to the public sector for its activity. Furthermore, as a result of the availability of foreign exchange and the shrinking of the manufacturing sector, the local demand for manufactured items is met by increasing imports. Besides, the high interest and foreign exchange cost make unprofitable most productive activities that depend on imported inputs, leaving import trade and very few other sectors lucrative.

Per Capita Growth Equations

We estimated an endogenous growth equation following the formulations by Romer (1986), Fischer (1991) and Roubini *et al.* (1991). The growth Equation (1) in Table 3.11 performed quite well in terms of explanatory power and overall fit, but with unexpected results for some variables. We tried checking for auto-correlation in Equation (2). The only significant variable is the real exchange rate. We considered lag of per capita income, investment ratio and deficit ratio in addition to the trade variables. All the variables were significant. The lag of per capita output and deficit ratio had the expected sign. Lagged investment ratio had the unexpected negative sign. The deficit ratio is a reflection of macroeconomic instability, which in almost all cases results in increased inflation, crowding out private sector sources of investment and thereby having a negative effect on investment and output. However, in Equation (2), the deficit and investment ratios are not significant.

The exchange rate variables have a significant influence on output in both equations. The real exchange rate has a positive and significant effect on output. The exchange rate depreciation has enabled higher producer prices of cocoa to be achieved, thereby increasing output of agricultural export items. It has also allowed significant inflow of both official and private foreign exchange, which has increased output.

The black market premium was not significant in explaining growth in per capita real income but had the right sign in an unreported equation. The bias and its one-period lag were insignificant in Equation (2), where we corrected for auto-correlation. The bias would be likely to have an

Table 3.11 Per capita GDP growth equations, 1961–91

Explanatory variables	*Dependent variable equations* (1)	(2)*
Constant	3.682	6.104
	(3.850)	(31.759)
Real exchange rate	0.104	0.145
	(4.215)	(3.174)
Lagged per capita income	0.411	–
	(2.714)	
Lagged capital formation	–0.056	–0.064
	–(2.030)	(1.323)
Lagged Deficit ratio	–0.009	–0.006
	–(2.044)	(1.080)
Bias	–0.102	–0.035
	–(2.565)	(0.811)
Lagged bias	0.086	–0.003
	(2.315)	(0.062)
R-squared	0.90	
F-statistic	37.43	
D.W.	1.53	

* Calculated using RALS; corrected for second-order serial correlation.

indirect effect on output through investment. The trade and payments regime would affect growth through investment. However, it is possible that the trade and policy variables are not exogenous, as has been assumed here.

The basic endogenous growth model includes human capital which affects growth. We did not include this variable because Jebuni *et al.* (1992), using the secondary school enrolment rate as a proxy for human capital, did not find it as an important variable. The reasons were that there was very little variation in the school enrolment rate, while by the 1970s Ghana had met her secondary school skills requirement. Also, the out-migration of both skilled and unskilled labour in the late 1970s and 1980s suggests a leakage of the expected benefits of spending on secondary school education.

Capital Formation

Liberalization of the trade regime will affect capital formation through its effect on the profitability of investment, certainty of policies and availability of foreign exchange. A priori the net effect of liberalization on investment cannot be determined. For example, depreciation of the real exchange rate will discourage investment if the cost of capital increases. It will on the other hand improve profitability in the exportables sector and therefore encourage investment. However, whether or not investment will increase will depend upon whether the investment is credible. If investment was constrained by the availability of foreign exchange and the liberalization is accompanied by an increase in these flows, then the liberalization may have a positive investment response.

The sectoral allocation of investment will be determined by what happens to relative prices. The devaluation accompanying the liberalization will increase the interest cost of capital so that there may be a shift towards demand for non-traded capital goods.

The First Liberalization

The investment rate fell sharply in 1966 as the government cut back on its spending (in particular capital expenditures) and deflated the economy. The decline in the investment rate continued until 1968, when it fell to 9.75 per cent (Table 3.12). Investment rates increased in 1970 as government spending began to pick up.

The Second Liberalization

Investment rates fell to 3.5 per cent in 1982, rising slightly to 3.76 per cent in 1983. The economic reform programme of 1983 triggered a surge in investment spending (Table 3.12). Investment rates increased continuously until 1989; they then fell in 1990 and remained fairly constant until 1993, when they increased to 14.71 per cent.

Growth in investment has been spread among all sectors of the economy (Table 3.12). The service sector had the largest share of investment, averaging about 60 per cent until the mid-1980s, when it averaged about 50 per cent. This is followed by share of investment in industry, which increased from a low of 17 per cent in 1981 to an average of 35 per cent in the late 1980s (Table 3.12). The sector that experienced the most rapid growth in investment was the industrial sector, in particular manufacturing and utility. Investment in the non-traded goods sector (that is, services, utilities and construction) declined from 79.4 per cent of total investment in 1975 prices to 63.5 per cent in 1987 and 61.9 per cent in 1990. Thus, as is to be expected given the shift in relative prices, the improvement in profitability of the traded goods sector saw an increase in investment in that sector until 1990. There were substantial flows of investment to the mining and the forestry sectors. This is a result of the favourable exchange rate policy for exports and the large inflow of official resources

Table 3.12 Gross fixed capital formation, 1960–93

Year	Investment rate (%)*	*% of total gross fixed capital formation in constant 1975 prices*			*Annual % change of gross fixed capital formation in 1975 prices*		
		Industry	*Agriculture*	*Services*	*Industry*	*Agriculture*	*Services*
1960	22.27						
1961	22.53						
1962	18.46						
1963	19.80						
1964	18.76						
1965	18.14						
1966	12.98						
1967	11.57						
1968	11.00						
1969	9.75						
1970	12.00	30.53	3.50	65.97			
1971	12.44	30.51	3.52	65.97	4.60	5.22	4.68
1972	8.67	24.89	3.04	72.07	–47.10	–43.89	–29.16
1973	7.62	33.80	3.62	62.58	31.34	14.97	–16.02
1974	11.89	31.13	3.86	65.01	42.34	65.09	60.58
1975	11.62	30.51	3.49	66.00	–16.72	–23.30	–13.75
1976	9.82	30.51	3.49	66.00	–6.14	–6.07	–6.12
1977	9.40	30.50	3.50	66.01	19.80	20.40	19.85
1978	6.46	30.53	5.08	64.48	–15.24	22.73	–17.29
1979	6.73	19.94	3.29	42.17	–38.94	–39.39	–38.86
1980	6.10	20.73	8.82	61.38	–1.83	152.78	37.44
1981	4.73	17.20	7.26	50.93	–26.73	–27.25	–26.74
1982	3.53	22.79	9.70	67.51	2.17	3.02	2.24
1983	3.76	22.80	9.70	67.50	–2.00	–2.05	–2.06
1984	6.85	17.51	8.84	73.65	–12.74	3.59	23.97
1985	9.53	21.89	11.47	66.64	56.35	62.14	13.16
1986	9.29	30.26	9.05	60.69	28.57	–26.56	–15.28
1987	10.36	38.00	9.00	53.00	56.06	23.54	8.51
1988	10.86	39.99	9.01	51.00	11.96	6.48	2.37
1989	13.48	40.00	9.00	51.00	36.08	35.98	36.08
1990	12.19	40.00	9.00	51.00	6.17	6.11	6.13
1991	12.68						
1992	12.83						
1993	14.71						

* Investment rate is the ratio of nominal gross fixed capital formation to nominal GDP. Information to calculate this ratio was obtained from Ghana Statistical Services, *Quarterly Digest of Statistics*, various issues (Accra). Information for sectoral distribution of investment in constant 1975 prices was obtained from the Statistical Services files.

Table 3.13 Gross fixed capital formation, 1961–91

Explanatory Variables	*Dependent variable equations* (1)	(2)	(3)
Constant	3.919	1.300	1.253
	(4.665)	(2.401)	(2.651)
Real exchange rate	–	0.386	–
Growth of output	0.402	0.061	0.470
	(0.680)	(0.096)	(0.744)
Lagged capital formation	0.513	0.559	0.638
	(5.080)	(5.767)	(6.824)
Inflation	–0.340	–0.111	–0.863
	–(1.950)	–(0.533)	–(4.103)
Reserves	–0.470	0.039	–
	–(0.760)	(0.576)	
Foreign exchange ratio	–	–	0.234
			(2.835)
Bias	–0.025	–0.034	–0.043
	–(0.972)	–(1.196)	–(1.409)
Black market premium	–0.369	–	–
	–(3.858)		
R-squared	0.95	0.95	0.94
F-statistic	82.46	77.81	82.04
D.W.	2.08	1.76	2.17
Schwartz criterion		–1.34	–1.331

* Calculated using RALS; corrected for third-order serial correlation.

that has made the extraction and export of these raw materials more profitable than value-added processed items. Unfortunately, at the present, a sectoral distribution of investment is not available after 1990 to allow an analysis of what has happened since the change in incentive structure.

Following the modelling of investment through the partial adjustment approach by Matin *et al.* (1992), we obtained an investment equation using the trade variables, inflation, reserves, inflow of foreign exchange, growth of output and lagged capital formation. The results for total gross investment as presented in Table 3.13 are satisfactory.

In all equations our variables explain over 90 per cent of the variation in investment. We tried the lags of all the independent variables but with the exception of the lag of capital formation, none of the variables either singly or together improved our investment equations. We report only three of the equations that performed better. The F-statistic shows that the overall relation is significant. The real exchange rate and the black market premium had a significant influence on the rate of investment. As the exchange rate depreciates, the rate of investment increases. The black market premium representing the divergence between the official and black market exchange rates has a negative effect on investment. As the black market premium increases, access to foreign exchange at the official rate generates rents much higher than returns that could be obtained from investment. As a result, the rate of investment declines.

The bias has a negative sign and is not statistically significant in any of the equations. It seems that the bias might be more important in determining the allocation and therefore the productivity of investment rather than the rate of investment.

Reserves as a proxy for the foreign exchange constraint did not do well in two of our equations. However, foreign exchange inflow had a positive and statistically significant coefficient. This confirms our explanation above, that as the foreign exchange constraint is relaxed, the rate of investment increases. This is particularly important in less-industrialized countries, where a large component of investment may consist of imported machinery and equipment.

Growth in GDP as an indicator of demand has a positive co-efficient but is not significant. Lagged capital formation is significant.

Equation (3) comes out as the best in terms of its ability to explain investment. The factors that are significant are lagged capital formation, inflation and foreign exchange inflow. As argued above, the liberalization affects investment through the availability of foreign exchange. It also shows that macro-instability, which results in inflation, has a negative influence on investment.

Productivity of Capital

Liberalization of the trade regime removes quantitative restrictions and distortions in the exchange rate regime. It is thus expected to induce increased efficiency in the economy and provide a basis for growth. Import duties to protect domestic import-substituting industry represent a tax on exporting activities. For Ghana it is estimated that between 74 per cent and 85 per cent of the tax on imports is shifted to the export sector (Jebuni *et al*., 1992). This reduces the profitability of exporting and shifts investment into import-substituting industries. The change in the structure of incentives as liberalization occurs should shift the economy towards activities in which it has a comparative advantage. It will be expected, then, that a trade liberalization accompanied by a devaluation should improve the productivity of capital. Moreover, the exposure of the economy to international competition through liberalization increases domestic capital productivity. The easing of the import restrictions should increase the

Table 3.14 Incremental output–capital ratio (3-year moving average)

Year	*IOCR*
1962	0.224
1966	–0.039
1967	0.099
1968	0.285
1969	0.547
1970	0.488
1971	0.268
1972	0.587
1982	–2.719
1983	–0.549
1984	0.862
1985	1.290
1986	0.875
1987	0.830
1988	0.713
1989	0.603
1990	0.558
1991	0.511
1992	0.530

availability of complementary inputs necessary to bring about an increase in productivity. A devaluation that increases the cost of capital, compared to the pre-liberalization period, should introduce more rationality in the use of capital; that is, firms will be forced to purchase equipment that they really need rather than install it because it is cheaper than it should be. In the medium to long run, if there is a shift from uncompetitive import-substitution activities into labour-intensive exporting activities in which the country has a competitive advantage, the productivity of capital should increase.

The First Liberalization

The productivity of capital improved in the first three years of the liberalization but declined in 1970 and 1971 (Table 3.14). The policy of government during the years 1966 to 1968 was to control the growth of government spending, particularly on what was perceived to be wasteful capital projects. This rationalization of government spending may explain the improvement in the productivity of capital during these early years. In the years after 1969, with the newly-elected government taking over, it is possible that the restraint on public spending was not adhered to. In fact, during the period when the government was supposed to be divesting itself of state enterprises, some new enterprises were established. It is possible that investment spending of this type may explain the fall in the productivity of capital.

The Second Liberalization

The productivity of capital increased during the first three years of trade liberalization, but has been falling since then. Despite this fall, the productivity of capital since 1983 is higher than it was in the 1970s (Table 3.14). The trend in the productivity of capital may be explained by sectoral distribution of investment. Between 1983 and 1985 the share of investment in constant 1975 prices in the utilities and construction industries declined. A greater proportion of the increase in investment went to directly productive activities. Between 1986 and 1990 (the years for which the relevant information is available) the trend reversed, with the share going to utilities and construction increasing. Investments in these sectors of the economy are crucial; however, they may be accompanied by a decline in the incremental output–capital ratio because they may have longer gestating periods. Second, although they are important co-operative factors for the growth process, an increase in investment in these sectors alone will not bring about growth if there is no corresponding increase in investment in directly productive activities.

The application of econometric techniques to find out the impact of trade liberalization on the productivity of capital finds that the exchange rate variable is a significant determinant (Table 3.15). The productivity of capital improves with depreciation of the real exchange rate. It also improves as the black market premium falls. An increase in foreign exchange reserves has a positive effect on the productivity of capital. The bias in the trade regime is significant, but has the wrong sign, contrary to what was expected. The discussion on the composition of investment may be relevant here. The public investment variable was not significant in any of the equations.

Composition of Employment

Employment in Ghana can be categorized into formal and informal. The informal sector is characterized by low earnings and productivity. The returns to workers in the formal sector in terms of earnings and productivity are higher than those of the informal and have highly organized labour relations. Jobs are offered by both the private and public sectors, with the latter having the largest share of employment (see Table 3.16). We shall confine our analysis to the formal sector because it is relatively easy to obtain data.

Table 3.15 Productivity of capital equations, 1970–91

Explanatory variable	*Equations*			
	*(1)**	*(2)**	*(3)*	*(4)*
Constant	0.548	0.0372	1.279	1.9808
	(0.813)	(0.0471)	(2.3309)	(2.801)
Real exchange rate	0.159	0.014	–	–
	(7.372)	(5.333)	–	
Bias	–3.53	–3.266	–1.4105	–1.452
	–(3.564)	–(3.144)	–(1.791)	–(1.909)
Public investment	–	0.0016	–	–0.0022
	–	(1.0490)	–	–(1.497)
International Reserves	0.0047	0.005	0.0026	0.001
	(6.370)	(5.8623)	(3.532)	(1.928)
Black market premium	–		–(0.219)	–(0.255)
	–		–(6.625)	–(6.386)
R-squared			.79	.81
F-statistic			21.9	18.19
D.W.			1.97	1.90
Schwartz Criterion			–1.34	–1.331

* Calculated using RALS; corrected for third-order serial correlation.

Note: Dependent variable: 3-year moving average of incremental output–capital ratio.

The First Liberalized Regime

Between 1967 and 1971, when the trade regime was liberalized, there was a consistent yearly increase in total employment accounted for by fluctuations in both the public and private sectors with wider variations in the latter. The deflationary policies of 1966 and 1967, including some retrenchment, led to a fall in employment in both sectors. The distribution of employment between the two sectors remained fairly constant, with fluctuations within a narrow band. There was a non-significant increase in the share of labour employed in the traded goods sector after 1968.

The Second Liberalized Regime

Employment in both the public and private sectors increased between 1983 and 1985 but declined to its lowest level of 186 300 in 1991. The lay-off in the public sector was argued on the basis that, as a result of over-establishment, it was impossible to pay commensurate salaries to skilled persons to promote efficiency and increased production in the system.

Table 3.16 Distribution of employment: public, private, traded, and non-traded

Year	*Nos. employed*			*Share of: private*	*Share of public*	*Traded sector*	*Non-traded*	*Share of: traded*	*Share of non-traded*
	All	*Private*	*Public*						
1960	332 898	148 547	184 351	44.62	55.38	110 859	222 039	33.30	66.70
1966	356 054	94 128	261 926	26.44	73.56	109 576	246 478	30.78	69.22
1967	156 111	99 659	256 416	28.00	72.00	75 050	245 867	30.96	69.04
1968	385 291	103 150	282 141	26.77	73.23	117 675	267 616	30.54	69.46
1969	395 172	115 265	279 907	29.17	70.83	124 583	270 589	31.53	68.47
1970	396 000	106 600	289 400	26.92	73.08	126 300	266 700	31.89	67.35
1971	396 600	109 600	287 000	27.63	72.37	125 700	270 900	31.69	68.31
1982	279 600	43 600	236 000	15.59	84.41	75 100	204 500	26.86	73.14
1983	312 000	57 700	254 300	18.49	81.51	114 300	197 700	36.63	63.37
1984	450 800	64 500	386 300	14.31	85.69	128 700	324 100	28.55	71.89
1985	464 300	67 200	397 100	14.47	85.53	133 300	331 000	28.71	71.29
1986	413 700	66 300	347 400	16.03	83.97	119 400	294 300	28.86	71.14
1987	394 300	79 000	315 300	20.04	79.96	138 600	256 800	35.15	65.13
1988	306 900	55 300	251 600	18.02	81.98	92 700	214 100	30.21	69.76
1989	215 100	38 200	176 900	17.76	82.24	60 700	154 200	28.22	71.69
1990	229 600	40 200	189 400	17.51	82.49	60 600	169 200	26.39	73.69
1991	186 300	30 600	155 700	16.43	83.57	52 300	133 900	28.07	71.87

Source: Ghana, Statistical Services, *Quarterly Digest of Statistics*, various issues (Accra).

The decline in employment during this period was due to several factors. First, there was the implementation of the public sector retrenchment exercises that began effectively in 1987. Second, the losses in public sector jobs were not compensated for by expansion of employment in the private sector (Table 3.16). Third, significant investment went into the mining and logging sectors, whose employment capacities are very limited. The mining sector even shrank in terms of employment due to the high capital intensity of the new investments. Agriculture and manufacturing, which could boost employment, have lagged behind in growth. It could also have been that the easing of labour market regulations allowed employers to shed whatever excess labour they were carrying. The rationalization of employment in the context of a changing incentive system may also partly explain the phenomenon. The low level of private investment during the adjustment also accounts for the low level of employment.

The lack of expansion in the private sector has been blamed on overliberalization, which has led to excessive imports. Also, factors such as constant depreciation of the *cedi*, the relatively high inflation rate in the late 1980s and the high cost of credit led to the high cost of production, making most productive sectors uncompetitive. This is in sharp contrast to the controlled period of 1972–82, which recorded a high level of employment. The increasing involvement of government in production and distribution (through the establishment of state-owned enterprises) also saw the maintenance of employment as a social obligation, even though productivity was low.

A division of the formal sector into traded and non-traded sectors finds that employment in the traded sectors contracted during the second liberalized period compared to the controlled period (see Table 3.16). Employment in the traded sectors averaged 33 per cent between 1972 and 1982. The increase in the non-traded share since 1987 suggests that the retrenchment may have hit the traded goods sector much more than the non-traded goods sector. The faster fall in employment in the traded goods sector may also be explained by the relative price changes, which have caused a slower growth in output in that sector. Employment in the manufacturing sector was badly hit, especially in the public sector, where employment in manufacturing in 1991 was estimated at 18 per cent of its 1987 levels.

Unemployment

The International Labour Organization defines unemployment as a pool of people above a specified age (15 years) who are without work, but are currently available for work and are seeking work during a period of reference. The Ghana Statistical Service Census definition comprised all persons who did not work and had no fixed jobs, but were actively looking for work during the seven days preceding census night. It also included any persons who were not looking for work because they believed that no work was available. The Labour Department in the Ministry of Employment and Social Welfare adds a condition that makes an unemployed person register at an employment centre.

Such categorization results in a very low rate of unemployment in Ghana. In the first place, because there are no jobs for those who would register at the employment centres, no one registers. Secondly, any person who did some casual informal job on a farm or anywhere during the reference period but ceased to work thereafter was deemed to be employed. The census estimates of unemployment rates of 7 per cent, 8 per cent and 3 per cent in 1960, 1970 and 1984 respectively, are clearly too low (Census, 1960, 1970, 1984).

On the other hand, several estimates of unemployment rates are high. Dordunoo (1994) estimates an average rate of 19 per cent between 1970 and 1988. Considering that the formal employment in 1990 was only 69 per cent that of 1960 but population has increased by 116 per cent since then, the unemployment rate should have been very high, especially in the second liberalized period.

Unemployment among university graduates has become a major issue of late. A recent advertisement by a local bank for job opportunities for 10 positions that could be filled by high school leavers received 240 responses from unemployed university graduates (Stanchart Training Centre, 1995).

Wages

In the early controlled period, there was a wide differential between the highest-paid and lowest-paid worker. In 1963 it was 34 times, but by 1979, the differential had fallen to 14 times (Abdin *et al.*, 1983). The wage compression continued and by 1983 the differential was only about two times. The objectives of the compression were to maximize job creation and to minimize earning disparities. However, this served as a disincentive for the skilled to be attracted to the public sector, especially the civil service.

The First Liberalization

Real monthly wages were quite high from 1960 up until 1975. From a high real average of C510 between 1960 and 1963, it declined between 1964 and 1966 before rising in 1967. The real average wage started a slight recovery from 1967. This was a result of the relaxation of the controls

Table 3.17 Average monthly earnings: nominal and real wages for all sectors

Year	*Nominal wages*	*W/CPI**
1960	33.00	553.8
1966	42.25	394.5
1967	45.64	453.2
1968	49.67	448.3
1969	52.87	455.0
1970	54.99	403.5
1971	60.73	407.6
1972	67.01	408.8
1982	645.00	60.7
1983	1 110.00	46.9
1984	2 287.00	69.2
1985	3 633.00	99.6
1986	7 433.00	163.6
1987	10 524.00	165.7
1988	13 805.00	165.5
1989	24 257.00	232.1

* W/CPI is the consumption wage; that is, earnings deflated by the consumer price index (CPI). The base year for the CPI is 1977.

Source: Ghana Statistical Services, *Quarterly Digest of Statistics*, various issues (Accra).

and the stabilization policies which held in check the rate of inflation. The real wage averaged around C420 between 1967 and 1971 before falling continuously to C47 in 1983 (Table 3.17).

The Second Liberalized Period

The second liberalized period has seen some improvements in the real wage but these have been marginal. The real wage has not recovered to the levels of the 1960s and 1970s, and in 1989 was one-third the 1960 level. This depicts a considerably reduced standard of living for Ghanaians. The real wage has not recovered strongly, partly because of the resurgence in inflation in the latter part of the period. The other part can be explained by a slowdown in the growth of earnings and depreciation of the *cedi*.

Growth and Composition of Exports and Imports

The First Liberalization

Total export values rose in 1967 primarily because of the increase in cocoa prices. Cocoa volumes, on the other hand, fell in 1966 and continued falling until 1970. The improvement in dollar values was basically a price effect. Export volumes followed a cyclical pattern, falling in three of the years between 1967 and 1971. Export volumes were below their 1967 levels by the time the liberalization was reversed. The real exchange rate gradually appreciated during the liberalization period because the nominal exchange rate was not devalued as the inflation began to pick up. The export promotion package, though attractive, was limited in its impact because of problems of implementation.

There was no significant change in the composition of exports during this period (Table 3.18). Cocoa continued to dominate export earnings. The increase in the shares of non-traditional exports may be explained less by dramatic changes in their values and more by price developments of the traditional exports.

Import dollar value fell in 1968 but began a steady rise between 1969 and 1971. Import volumes were above their 1967 levels by 1971, although it was not a steady increase. Import volumes had a rather ambiguous response to the liberalization. The substantial increase in 1968 was followed by a decline in 1969. This is because despite the loosening of controls through the transfer of goods from the specific to OGL lists, a 5 per cent surcharge had been imposed in 1969. The developments in import volumes may be explained not by the exchange rate, but by the import-licensing system, which was able to restrain the surge of imports in one year but was not quite successful in doing so the following year.

There was no significant change in the composition of imports during this period. The import licensing seemed able to constrain the growth of consumer goods so that their share of total imports never reached the levels attained in 1967. Basically the policy of restructuring imports to protect domestic industry was maintained through the licensing system.

The Second Liberalization

The depreciation of the nominal and real exchange rates, decline in the average import tariff rates and average export tax rates are expected to have a positive impact on exports. The extent of the supply response of the export sector depends also on the existence of capacity that can be utilized, the availability of adequate working capital, the type of exports and imported inputs as well as confidence that the liberalization will not be reversed. The change in officially recorded exports depends upon the

Table 3.18 Composition of exports (% share)

	Cocoa and cocoa products	*Timber and timber products*	*Minerals*	*Non-traded exports*
1960	58.98	13.91	24.35	2.76
1966	62.32	11.23	22.35	4.11
1967	64.93	9.33	18.54	7.20
1968	63.49	8.47	17.33	10.71
1969	62.93	10.00	13.33	13.74
1970	72.04	8.03	10.57	9.36
1971	67.91	9.39	14.08	8.62
1972	59.72	12.12	15.45	12.71
1982	51.30	2.02	15.79	30.90
1983	41.64	2.74	22.95	32.67
1984	70.47	2.32	21.23	5.98
1985	65.86	4.55	17.87	11.72
1986	58.52	6.19	18.15	17.14
1987	59.23	10.85	21.27	8.65
1988	56.07	n/a	32.43	n/a
1989	40.39	n/a	16.90	n/a
1990	40.21	13.16	n/a	n/a
1991	34.73	12.45	35.33	17.49
1992	30.67	11.55	39.40	18.38
1993	26.60	13.58	45.06*	14.76

Notes:
* Gold exports only
n/a not available
The share of non-traditional exports is a residual. It is the difference between the value of total exports and the value of cocoa, timber and mineral exports.

Source: Ghana Statistical Services, *Quarterly Digest of Statistics*, various issues (Accra).

proportion of actual production that was being smuggled. It has been estimated that smuggling in Ghana in 1979 cost the economy the equivalent of approximately 1.4 per cent of GDP.

Export volumes suffered a decline of 28 per cent in 1983. Cocoa bean exports fell by 36 per cent because of bush fires and the difficulty in transporting cocoa from the hinterland. Moreover, when the programme began the cocoa sector had an old, diseased tree stock. Gold production also fell by 16.3 per cent. Real investment in the mining and manufacturing sectors had been declining since 1974 and 1977, respectively. Although capacity utilization in manufacturing was estimated at 30 per cent in 1983, this was not a very good indicator of usable capacity since most firms had old machinery. It is thus not surprising that given these constraints export volumes increased by only 2 per cent in 1984. An increase in exports would have required some investment for rehabilitation purposes. Producers would have had to be sure that there would be no policy reversals before the necessary investment would be undertaken.

Export volumes increased quite rapidly after 1984. Among the traditional exports of cocoa, timber and minerals, the increase in export volumes was concentrated primarily in bauxite, gold and cocoa. The increase in import volumes, which was encouraged by the trade liberalization process as well as the inflows of aid and other financial flows as a result of the liberalization programme, was a boost to exports, in particular the mining sector.

The composition of exports has changed since 1983 (Table 3.18). There has been a gradual erosion of the dominance of cocoa in merchandise exports from 70 per cent of the total in 1984 to an estimated 26.6 per cent in 1993. However, the dominance of cocoa has been replaced by the dominance of gold, which now accounts for approximately 45 per cent of total merchandise export earnings. The share of exports other than cocoa, timber and minerals has increased from 5 per cent of the total to 14.76 per cent in 1993. The developments in the commodity structure of exports can be explained primarily by the decline in cocoa prices that caused cocoa values to fall despite the increase in volumes since 1983. Also important were the increase in volume and value of timber exports and the increased investment in the gold industry, which has facilitated the rapid expansion in the value of gold exports. The depreciation of the real exchange rate had a significant effect on the expansion of the non-traditional exports since 1984 (Jebuni *et al.*, 1992).

Despite the significant increases in export volumes, total export earnings have only slightly increased so that in 1993, 10 years into the liberalization, total export earnings were less than the peak levels of 1979 and 1980.

The survey also throws some light on the contribution to exports by manufacturing firms. It is expected that a liberalized trade regime will encourage an increase in exports because it reduces the indirect taxes on the export sector (some of the import tariffs are transferred to the export sector) and reduces the cost of exporting as the import controls are relaxed and the exporting procedures are made less cumbersome. The survey found that 47.6 per cent of the exporting firms in the sample began to export after 1985, when the trade liberalization began. If 1983, the year in which the implementation of the economic recovery programme began, is chosen as the cut-off point, the proportion of firms that began exporting rises to 52.4 per cent. This could suggest that firms established prior to 1985 were encouraged to export as a result of the change in the incentive structures and/or that contrary to earlier years the liberalization has encouraged the establishment of firms that have an export bias. However, the evidence is not conclusive that on net basis this is the case, since six of the firms which are not currently exporting had done so in the past, while others had collapsed. Of the current non-exporters, 36 would like to export in the future. The questionnaire did not, however, elicit the extent of their commitment to exporting. An earlier study on non-traditional exports (which comprised both agricultural and manufactured exports) also found that the economic reforms, in particular the exchange rate changes, had encouraged a shift into exporting (Jebuni *et al.*, 1992).

The export promotion package comprises income tax rebates, a 100 per cent customs duty drawback scheme, exemption from sales and excise taxes and on taxes paid on packaging materials. The export retention scheme, which allowed non-traditional exporters to retain 35 per cent of their export earnings, is now redundant since there is now 100 per cent retention. Not all firms are aware of the existence of various components of the promotion package and this could be a reason why the expansion of non-traditional exports is not commensurate with the degree of trade liberalization that has occurred. Some 36.8 per cent of the firms did not know of the existence of either the customs duty drawback scheme or the income tax rebate scheme. It must be admitted that this rate of ignorance is an improvement on the figures obtained from a survey of non-traditional exports conducted in 1990 (Jebuni *et al.*, 1992). That study found that 51 per cent (50 per cent) of the firms in the sample did not know of the existence of the income tax rebate (customs duty drawback scheme). Of the sub-set of exporting firms, 53 per cent were unaware of the customs duty drawback scheme and 40 per cent were unaware of the income tax rebate scheme.

Import volume growth rates have been consistently positive despite the significant depreciations of the nominal and real exchange rate. They grew faster than did export volumes between 1983 and 1986. The increase in import volumes despite the large depreciation of the nominal and real exchange rates occurred because the economy for the most part was operating with a parallel exchange rate. The official exchange rate simply caught up with what had already happened. Prior to 1983, import volumes were constrained more by controls than by tariffs, so that relaxation of the import-licensing system allowed for a large surge in imports. Imports volumes also increased because of the inflow of aid and other external financial resources for balance of payments support. It is only since 1988

Table 3.19 Composition of imports

	Consumer imports (%)	*Fuel imports (%)*	*Producer imports (%)*
1960	50.00	4.50	45.50
1961	49.40	4.20	46.40
1966	30.90	4.22	64.88
1967	32.83	5.89	61.29
1968	28.25	7.75	63.40
1969	30.20	6.34	63.40
1970	30.10	5.74	64.10
1971	23.39	6.02	65.85
1972	24.70	11.50	63.80
1982	20.90	35.60	48.47
1983	29.72	10.11	60.16
1984	19.24	34.73	46.01
1985	25.49	29.20	45.29
1986	16.50	15.62	67.87
1987	16.58	14.14	69.27
1988	13.84	13.56	72.59

Source: Ghana Statistical Services.

that there has been any significant drop in the rate of increase in import volumes. External donors and organizations have played a significant role in the moves towards liberalization. The bulk of the finance of the import programme was expected to come from external sources. In the budgets between 1984 and 1988 at least 63 per cent of the available foreign exchange was expected to come from foreign sources.

The high level of investments into the mineral and timber sectors and a reduction in the importance of the cocoa and manufacturing sectors have strong implications for the balance of payments situation. These investments are quite expensive, unlike those in the cocoa sector while the world prices are at best stagnant, which does not improve the net foreign exchange position and hence the balance of payments situation.

The share of producer goods imports increased between 1983 and 1988 (Table 3.19). This was probably in response to the import programming that was in place for most of the period until 1988, which emphasized the importation of items for the development and rehabilitation of the physical infrastructure.

The economy must move from export of raw products into processed and manufactured items so as to gain in terms of trade and in employment.

Table 3.20 Export volume equations, 1962–90

Dependent variable log of exports	*Explanatory variable* (1)	(2)
Constant	5.877	5.881
	(2.211)	(2.413)
Lagged Export	0.524	0.5602
Volumes	(3.092)	(3.653)
Real exchange rate	0.146	–
	(2.611)	–
Real income	–0.510	–0.441
	–(1.961)	–(1.860)
Bias	0.274	0.231
	(1.762)	(1.565)
Import volumes	0.0802	0.065
	(0.582)	(0.498)
Black market premium	–	–0.161
	–	–(3.2101)
R-squared	0.873	0.88
F-statistic	31.62	35.86
D.W.	2.25	2.32
Schwartz criterion	–3.34	–3.45

Generally, the price trend of manufactured items is upwards in contrast to primary products. Such diversification has the chance of ensuring a sustainable growth that de-emphasizes the dependence on loans and grants.

An export volume equation was estimated for the period 1962 to 1990. Unfortunately the data on export volumes end in 1990, hence the truncated estimation period. We used the standard model (Bond, 1985; Moran, 1988), which assumes that producers base their decisions on domestic capacity and the relative profitability of producing for exports rather than for the home market. The basic model expresses exports as a function of domestic capacity constraint proxied by real GDP and price effects. The explanatory variables were the log of lagged export volumes, an exchange rate variable, real GDP, import volumes and the bias in the trade regime. Indicators of trade liberalization were the bias variable and the black market premium. It is expected that as the trade regime is liberalized, the size of the premium will decline. The exchange rate variable used was the real exchange rate. The real exchange rate and the black market premium were not put together in the same equation because of the possibility of multi-collinearity. Import volumes were introduced as a measure of the impact of the foreign exchange constraint on the export sector.

The equations were estimated using ordinary least squares. None of them were found to suffer from first-order or second-order serial correlation. In both equations that were estimated the only variables which were significant with the expected sign were the exchange rate variable, the black market premium and the lagged dependent variable. The bias in the trade regime had the expected sign but was not significant, while the real income variable was significant but had a negative sign. Contrary to expectations import volumes were not an important explanatory variable. Including the level of international reserves instead of imports did not improve the performance of the equation. The results seem to suggest that the removal of the distortions in the exchange rate that accompanied the trade liberalization programmes have been powerful in generating positive responses in the export sector.

For the import demand equation, we followed the formulation based on Khan and Knight (1988) except that the relative price of imports was replaced by trade and exchange rate variables. The explanatory variables are log of real income, international reserves, the real exchange rate, the black market premium and the bias in the trade regime. The only variable that was significant and had the expected sign was the black market premium. The preferred equation for imports was therefore Equation (3) in Table 3.21, which had the black market premium, real income and reserves as explanatory variables. The bias in the trade regime was insignificant with an unexpected sign in all equations. The poor performance of the real income and the bias variables may be explained by the trade regulations in place during most of the period under study. However the real exchange rate and international reserves variables have unexpected signs with the former being significant. This is probably because as an import dependent nation, Ghana's growth must be necessity be made up of high import growth irrespective of the depreciation of the currency. This goes with the finding that producer goods have comprised an increasing share of imports.

Both the export and import equations suggest that the removal of the distortions indicative in the size of the black market premium are important determinants of the export supply and import demand.

The Fiscal Profile

The effect trade liberalization will have on government finances depends upon the type of liberalization (whether it emphasizes only imports or also has an export promotion package); whether tariff rates are at the maximum revenue levels; the proportion of taxable imports that are exempt

Table 3.21 Import volume equations, 1961–90

Dependent variable log of imports	*Explanatory variable* (1)	(2)	(3)
Constant	4.633	4.249	4.629
	(1.619)	(1.489)	(1.651)
Lagged import volumes	0.539	0.543	0.537
	(3.368)	(3.359)	(3.484)
Real exchange rate	–	0.173	–
	–	(2.957)	–
Real income	–0.191	–0.263	–0.190
	–(0.710)	–(0.953)	–(0.721)
Bias	0.014	0.041	–
	(0.0715)	(0.213)	–
International reserves	–0.1205	–0.091	–0.120
	–(1.458)	–(1.489)	–(1.492)
Black market premium	–0.184	–	–0.185
	–(3.043)	–	–(3.192)
R-squared	0.812	0.809	0.812
F-statistic	20.84	20.44	27.12
D.W.	1.99	2.08	1.99
Schwartz criterion	–2.826	–2.81	–2.939

from taxes before and after the liberalization; the proportion of imports that had been restricted by quantitative measures prior to liberalization; the importance of trade taxes in total revenue; and the growth generating effects of the liberalization programme.

The effect of the trade liberalization on revenues may be examined using a formal decomposition analysis following Greenaway and Milner (1993). Using the decomposition analysis, three types of effects of trade liberalization can be analysed:

(1) *the real import effect*, which measures the revenue effect associated with a change in the real (dollar) value of imports;
(2) *the exchange rate effect*, which measures the indirect effect of exchange rate changes on import tax yields through the effect on the tax base;
(3) *the tariff rate effect*, which measures the tariff revenue effect of a real change in average tariff rate for a given tax base.

The First Liberalization

When the liberalization process began in 1967, the ratio of total revenue to GDP was 16.9 per cent (Table 3.22). Trade duties accounted for approximately 53 per cent of total revenues, with import duties contributing the most to trade tax revenues (Table 3.23). Producer goods dominated the composition of imports and most of these were either exempt from trade taxes or subject to low rates. Import licensing had been pervasive in the six-year period prior to liberalization. Thus a trade liberalization which reduced tariff rates, devalued the currency and reduced the use of import quotas would be expected to raise revenues from trade. The export promotion package would probably be expected to have a depressing effect on revenues because of the exemption of imported inputs used in exports from taxes and the other components of the package already discussed. The export bonus scheme would be a drain on the government budget, increasing expenditures as exports increased. However, the imported input–output coefficient of the exporting sector is much lower compared to the import-substituting sector. Moreover, there would be no loss of revenue if the imported inputs had not previously been taxed.

Import tariff revenues declined until 1969 (Table 3.24). This was primarily because of the negative tariff effect, which was not counteracted by substantial increases in import volumes or positive exchange rate effects. The increase in the share of producer goods that are either tax exempt or have low tax rates reduced further import revenues. It was only in 1970 that the revenue effects were positive. That was when the real import effect was substantial and the real tariff effect became positive because of the introduction of temporary surcharges and the extension of these surcharges to government imports.

The Second Liberalization

In 1983 trade taxes accounted for approximately 48 per cent of total revenues, with export duties comprising the bulk of trade revenues (Table 3.22). The heavy dependence on trade taxes notwithstanding, the share of trade taxes to GDP had fallen since 1979. In fact, real total revenues and revenues as a share of GDP had fallen (Table 3.22). The tax base had shrunk as both export and import volumes fell. The heavy dependence on quantitative restrictions that had occurred in the preceding 10-year period had denied the government a substantial amount of tax revenues. Import tax schedules of 35 per cent, 60 per cent and 100 per cent in 1982 were also quite high. The average import duty collection rates were only 22.95 per cent, indicating that taxes were probably above their maximum revenue levels and also suggestive of the incidence of tax evasion. Irresponsible use of tax exemptions could also explain the low collection

Table 3.22 Developments in total revenue and trade taxes

	Revenues as % of GDP			*Real revenues (1985=100 Cm)*			*Share of total revenue (%)*	
Year	*Total revenue*	*Import and sales duties*	*Export duties*	*Real government revenue*	*Real import and sales revenue*	*Real export duties*	*Export duties*	*Import and sales taxes*
1960	17.82	5.20						
1961	18.66	7.06						
1966	15.21	7.33	1.01	72 184.04	34 765.33	4 793.28	6.64	48.16
1967	16.89	6.70	2.22	84 212.76	33 405.26	11 094.47	13.17	39.66
1968	17.52	4.95	4.36	90 003.61	25 426.64	22 416.88	24.91	28.25
1969	16.61	4.14	3.76	95 431.49	23 807.08	21 610.35	22.64	24.94
1970	19.36	4.78	7.70	121 426.20	29 958.79	48 317.44	39.79	24.67
1971	18.02	4.85	4.82	119 134.30	32 050.13	31 879.28	26.76	26.90
1972	14.92	2.29	4.24	92 245.36	14 166.52	26 240.73	28.44	15.35
1982	5.62	0.68	0.00	17 110.34	2 085.59	8.10	0.04	12.18
1983	5.56	1.04	1.59	15 778.68	2 934.62	4 521.64	28.66	18.59
1984	8.37	1.21	1.80	24 976.29	3 613.08	5 376.38	21.52	14.46
1985	11.75	1.92	2.67	40 311.00	6 591.40	9 171.60	22.75	16.35
1986	14.41	2.52	2.77	59 149.27	10 361.72	11 372.71	19.22	17.51
1987	14.88	2.39	3.62	63 719.86	10 225.72	15 510.28	24.34	16.04
1988	14.63	2.39	2.33	67 220.27	11 003.58	10 692.48	15.91	16.37
1989	15.14	3.43	2.20	74 873.64	16 957.49	10 905.10	14.56	22.64
1990	13.16	3.13	1.29	67 992.62	16 192.98	6 659.36	9.79	23.81
1991	15.17	2.95	1.23	84 182.28	16 359.51	6 800.54	8.07	19.43
1992	13.17	2.82	1.28	77 554.96	16 630.32	7 523.58	9.70	21.44
1993	16.90	3.55	0.97	104 097.80	21 860.48	5 986.09	5.75	21.00

Real revenues are nominal revenues deflated by the consumer price index.

Source: Ghana Statistical Services, *Quarterly Digest of Statistics*, various issues (Accra).

Table 3.23 Average import and export tax rates (%)

	Import tax rates	*Export tax rates*	*Cocoa tax rate*	*Non-cocoa tax rate*
1960	17.03	16.32	27.20	1.79
1961	22.23	13.29	20.97	1.73
1962	27.69	11.34	18.57	1.24
1963	28.64	13.43	20.29	1.52
1964	30.16	13.74	21.99	1.41
1965	38.06	10.01	15.78	0.93
1966	44.27	8.25	14.84	0.04
1967	38.53	13.96	25.59	0.02
1968	24.68	22.00	39.95	0.01
1969	23.37	19.24	47.46	0.02
1970	25.75	37.23	57.70	0.40
1971	27.37	33.73	61.46	0.45
1972	16.40	21.16	40.99	0.35
1973	18.81	12.98	26.44	0.94
1974	12.74	20.96	38.07	2.28
1975	11.50	34.12	56.17	1.86
1976	12.82	11.51	19.79	
1977	12.61	24.11		
1978	18.29	18.10		
1979	17.42	66.50	98.14	8.14
1980	12.90	20.20	32.75	0.08
1981	18.81	16.22	39.80	0.30
1982	22.95	0.10	*	0.20
1983	17.26	28.69	70.18	2.16
1984	14.95	21.73	31.08	5.21
1985	13.96	27.38	44.51	2.29
1986	13.82	18.12	33.17	0.77
1987	12.24	18.34	39.77	0.03
1988	13.55	11.89	28.51	0.00
1989	13.99	11.34	30.08	0.00
1990	16.19	8.95	18.28	0.00
1991	15.64	8.18	23.54	0.87
1992	13.34	8.74	28.49	0.70
1993	12.44	5.30	19.91	0.42

* No cocoa taxes were collected in that year.

Source: Ghana Statistical Services, *Quarterly Digest of Statistics*, various issues (Accra).

Table 3.24 Decomposition analysis of changes in tax revenue, 1966–71

	1966	*1967*	*1968*	*1969*	*1970*	*1971*
Actual effect (Cm)	–10.62	–10.45	–16.59	–1.33	25.07	13.38
Predicted effect	–16.47	–9.67	–32.15	3.08	28.99	6.33
Real import effect	–32.07	–17.38	–0.26	7.72	19.02	–1.81
Exchange rate effect	0.00	22.71	15.33	0.00	0.00	0.96
Tariff rate effect	15.59	–15.01	–47.22	–4.64	9.97	7.17

Source: Calculated by the authors.

Table 3.25 Decomposition analysis of changes in tax revenue, 1984–92

	The effects				
	Actual	*Predicted*	*Real import rate*	*Exchange rate*	*Tariff rate*
1984	1370	1887.60	50.75	2342.50	–505.59
1985	3316	1727.87	730.13	1464.58	–466.83
1986	6319	3454.07	332.44	3252.33	–130.70
1987	4903	7388.95	2946.58	7203.88	–2761.52
1988	7363	8051.53	832.72	465.62	256.259
1989	23407	10868.07	241.28	9100.07	1526.72
1990	15086.8	23978.85	7429.94	7897.90	8651.01
1991	12253.7	11705.42	6329.37	8045.52	–2669.47
1992	9021.5	7590.38	7937.86	14294.81	–14642.30

Source: Calculated by the authors.

rates. Given this initial situation, a trade liberalization programme that reduced import tax schedules as this liberalization did, reduced the use of import quotas, and devalued the exchange rate, would most likely result in an improvement in import revenues.

Between 1983 and 1986, as the liberalization gradually got under way, import revenues increased in real terms. Revenues also increased as a share of total revenues and as a share of GDP (Table 3.22). A decomposition of the impact of the trade liberalization on import revenues shows that between 1984 and 1986 import revenues increased due to an increase in the import base and the devaluation of the currency (Table 3.25). However, as the tax schedules were reduced the average duty collected fell, which could suggest a lack of compliance. This would seem an irrational response, since tax schedules had been adjusted considerably downward, but in fact the *cedi* value of the import duties may have increased considerably as a result of the devaluation of the currency. This in turn may have induced the response to reduce the absolute value of cedi payments through the application of lower rates with the connivance of customs officials. Moreover, even though import duties fell in 1985, an import sales tax and special development tax were introduced so that the average rates may not have fallen significantly compared to the pre-1983 situation. Duty collection rates increased between 1988 and 1990 as import duty rates and sales taxes were reduced. The exchange rate effects were important in ensuring that import revenues did not decline with liberalization.

The export promotion package did not make much of a drain on government expenditures nor bring about a fall in revenues. This is because most exporters who could benefit from the scheme did not, either because they were ignorant of its existence or because the bureaucratic procedures were such that they did not perceive it to be worth while. The direct contribution of the export sector to government revenues has fallen during the liberalization period because of the fall in export tax rates. Export taxes have declined in real terms and as a share of GDP since 1989 (Table 3.22). The decline in world cocoa prices has somewhat reduced the revenue that could have been obtained from the cocoa sector. At the same time taxes on exports other than cocoa were removed altogether.

The net effect of the liberalization on trade revenues is that even though import duties have increased in real terms, there has been a fall in total real trade taxes since 1989 and a decline in their share of total revenues and GDP. Total government revenues, on the other hand, have increased in real terms and as a share of GDP. This is because of the increase in efficiency in tax collection, the widening of the tax base and the positive growth in the economy.

The government revenue position has also been assisted by the inflow of grants which have comprised a significant share of total revenues. Grants increased from less than 1 per cent of total revenues in 1983 to 11.45 per cent of revenues in 1990, falling to 5.33 per cent in 1993. The importance of taxes as a source of government revenue also reduced. The improved budgetary balances have been aided significantly by the inflow of aid. The dependence of aid flows, though, is a weakness – since in the 1995 budget, the Minister of Finance stated that the ability to avoid macroeconomic distress was dependent on these external inflows.

3.6 UNILATERAL TRADE LIBERALIZATION AND REGIONAL INTEGRATION

The Links

Should a change in the direction of trade be expected when there is unilateral trade liberalization? Liberalization of the trade regime has been defined as a reduction in tariff rates and the removal of quantitative restrictions. In the short run, it is not expected that there will be a significant change in the direction of trade of exports and imports because it takes time to obtain information about new markets and develop links with new buyers and sellers. A second constraint is the commodity structure of exports. If the commodity concentration index of exports is high (for example, if about 85 per cent of export earnings are from the sale of two primary commodities) then the rate of market diversification will be a positive function of the rate at which exports are diversified. This is because in order to enter new markets it may be necessary to export a new product. The extent to which export diversification occurs depends on whether the liberalization has brought about a decline in the anti-export bias of the trade regime. In the long run, as new entrants enter the export market and if the economy should undergo structural change as manufacturing output increases and product differentiation develops, changes in the direction of trade will most likely occur.

Whether or not unilateral trade liberalization will accelerate the regional trade integration process depends on several variables. The first is whether improvements in the anti-export bias favour those products that can be exported to other members of the regional integration unit. If the incentive structure encourages non-traditional exports, in particular processed goods, this may favour regional trade if these exports tend to go to regional markets. The second is whether the cuts in tariff rates are on goods that are of export interest to member countries. Unilateral trade liberalization will reduce tariff rates and may reduce tariff dispersion. It is possible that an escalated tariff structure may persist. If regional imports tend to be consumer goods, then they would enter under the upper end of the tariff schedule. In this case it would not be unexpected if regional imports did not increase substantially with UTL especially if there is a bias against regional trade in terms of higher transportation and transaction costs. The third factor of importance, therefore, is whether there are regional variations in the non-tariff barriers to trade. Examples of this are whether the unit cost of *intra*-regional transportation is lower than *inter*-regional transportation; the ease with which information about product markets in member countries may be obtained; and the efficiency of payments procedures in the region compared to non-member countries.

Table 3.26 Ghana's trade with ECOWAS

	1980	*1982*	*1984*	*1986*	*1992*	*1994*
Share of exports (%)	0.39	1.66	3.55	3.66	16.13	2.98
Imports (%)	23.84	29.38	39.86	31.80	15.65	7.04
Imports excluding Nigeria (%)	2.16	8.06	5.83	18.49	1.59	0.69

Sources: Ghana Statistical Services *Quarterly Digest of Statistics* (June 1994); *External Trade Statistics* (1992); *External Trade Bulletin* (1994).

In most African countries the creation of regional units preceded the current episodes of unilateral trade liberalization. Unfortunately the regional integration agreements, which usually visualized the formation of free trade areas or customs unions, were never implemented. In the West African sub-region, ECOWAS was signed in 1975 at a time when trade controls in Ghana were being intensified. The move to a more liberalized trade regime in Ghana was not negotiated within the context of ECOWAS, but was a unilateral decision considering only the national interests of Ghana.

Unilateral Trade Liberalization and Regional Integration in Ghana

Trade liberalization in Ghana may be described as a two-track process. The unilateral trade liberalization which began effectively in 1986, occurred with little regard to how it influenced regional integration. The regional trade liberalization process begun in 1990 is very slow and discriminatory. It discriminates between products and between firms. The result of this is that any change in regional trade integration from Ghana's point of view since 1990 has occurred not because of the ECOWAS trade liberalization scheme but in spite of it.

Trade liberalization has not been accompanied by a significant and sustained increase in trade with ECOWAS (Table 3.26). The share of exports going to ECOWAS, in fact, declined dramatically between 1992 and 1994. A significantly larger proportion of imports compared to exports is from ECOWAS. This can be explained by the dominance of oil imports from Nigeria. If imports from Nigeria are excluded, ECOWAS import shares fall quite dramatically. Interestingly, prior to 1992 the tendency was for ECOWAS import shares to be larger than the share of exports to the sub-region. This changed in 1992.

The trade liberalization process in Ghana can explain some of these developments. The trade liberalization and exchange rate reform programme have reduced the anti-export bias of the trade regime. This has encouraged an increase in the value of non-traditional exports since 1983, even though their shares in total exports have not increased dramatically. Ghana's exports are generally biased towards the developed countries. It has been estimated that in 1987 approximately 84.1 per cent of non-traditional exports went to industrial country destinations. This declined to 62.04 per cent in 1990 (Oduro, 1994).

Table 3.27 provides information on the direction of trade for selected exports in 1992 which account for approximately 95 per cent of the value of exports in that year. Primary products dominate Ghana's exports and of these only a small percentage is sent to ECOWAS. None of the minerals are exported to ECOWAS countries and only a minute proportion of lumber exports. On the other hand, of the sample of products in the table, approximately 31 per cent of the processed products go to ECOWAS member countries. ECOWAS markets dominate exports of crude palm oil, frozen tuna, articles of paper, aluminium alloys, household articles made of aluminium and office furniture made of wood. Estimates of the revealed comparative advantage suggest that, of these items, Ghana has a comparative advantage in crude palm oil, aluminium alloys and frozen tuna and skipjack. Thus as the export base becomes more diversified towards processed products, it is expected that trade with ECOWAS will increase.

The decline in the share of exports going to ECOWAS in 1994 may be explained by the mediocre performance of these economies. The annual growth in GDP per capita between 1988 and 1993 was negative for Côte d'Ivoire, Senegal, Benin, Sierra Leone, Liberia, Niger, Mauritania and Togo. As the major ECOWAS destinations for most products are Côte d'Ivoire, Nigeria and Togo, the slowdown in the growth of two of the major trading partners may explain the decline in the ECOWAS shares.

The fall in the proportion of imports from ECOWAS (excluding Nigeria) may be explained by two factors. The first is that as tariff rates are reduced distant markets become attractive. If these distant markets have a cost advantage over ECOWAS markets but producers are unable to penetrate Ghana's markets because of high tariffs, then as these tariffs fall they can compete effectively against goods produced in the sub-region. Second, the mediocre performance of the ECOWAS economies may again be important in explaining the decline in imports from the region. The political instability in Liberia, Sierra Leone and Nigeria are also relevant explanatory variables. Also important is the degree of industrialization of the trading partners and whether they have the capacity to produce what Ghana requires. The degree of industrialization of ECOWAS member countries is limited, in particular the size of the manufacturing sector (Oduro, 1995). These countries may not be able to respond to the new opportunities for exporting to the Ghanaian market.

Table 3.27 Direction of trade of selected export products, 1992

Primary products	*SITC*	*USA*	*EU*	*Japan*	*Developed*	*ECOWAS*	*Other LDC*	*CPE*
Fresh fish	3418	7.96	89.712	0.00	99.22	0.000	0.78	0.000
Frozen shrimps and prawns	3611	0.00	22.044	0.00	22.05	71.547	0.00	0.003
Bananas	5730	0.00	99.563	0.00	99.76	0.097	0.02	0.000
Pineapples	5795	0.92	76.395	0.00	97.39	1.992	0.59	0.012
Cocoa beans	7210	5.83	44.426	6.06	57.52	29.508	0.38	2.604
Pepper	7511	0.30	98.189	0.00	99.17	0.826	0.00	0.000
Crushed ground pepper	7512	11.36	55.979	4.34	72.15	18.327	0.00	0.000
Natural rubber	23110	0.00	97.150	0.00	100.00	0.000	0.00	0.000
Untreated coniferous wood, rough	24740	0.00	8.488	0.00	8.48	0.000	83.02	0.000
Untreated non-coniferous wood	2475152	0.21	96.86	0.02	97.09	0.132	2.00	0.763
Industrial diamonds	27719	0.00	96.79	0.00	96.79	0.000	3.20	0.000
Alum ores	28510	0.00	86.35	0.00	100.00	0.000	0.00	0.000
Bauxite	28511	0.00	69.96	0.00	100.00	0.000	0.00	0.000
Manganese	28770	0.00	39.42	11.762	73.97	0.000	0.00	26.029
Gold	97101	0.00	3.44	0.00	100.00	0.000	0.00	0.000
Processed products								
Frozen tuna, skipjack	3423	3.09	7.87	0.00	10.96	87.59	0.23	0.000
Fish fillets and meat	3451	0.00	39.75	13.20	52.95	47.04	0.00	0.000
Prepared tuna, skipjack	3713	49.55	17.84	0.00	67.39	22.95	0.00	0.000
Sawn wood	24840	0.12	85.90	0.07	86.30	0.61	8.27	4.808
Palm oil, crude	42221	0.00	48.60	0.00	48.60	51.35	0.00	0.000
Refined palm oil	42229	28.25	31.31	0.00	65.42	25.11	0.00	0.000
Veneer sheets, conifers	63411	0.00	95.98	0.00	95.98	4.01	0.00	0.000
Veneer sheets, non-conifers	63412	0.45	58.60	0.00	60.27	19.51	1.07	0.030
Veneer, plywood	63449	0.00	58.52	0.00	59.62	30.62	0.18	0.000

(*continued on page 136*)

Table 3.27 *continued*

Primary products	*SITC*	*USA*	*EU*	*Japan*	*Developed*	*ECOWAS*	*Other LDC*	*CPE*
Pallets	63512	0.00	59.18	0.00	59.18	25.70	0.00	0.000
Casks, barrels, vats	63520	66.33	29.09	0.00	95.95	1.84	2.20	0.000
Tableware wood	63542	0.00	99.89	0.00	99.90	0.09	0.00	0.000
Builders, joinery	63539	0.00	99.91	0.00	99.91	0.00	0.08	0.000
Wood marquetry	63549	36.90	37.75	1.61	81.70	11.06	4.31	0.000
Wooden tools, brooms	63591	0.00	100.00	0.00	100.00	0.00	0.00	0.000
Other wooden articles	63599	1.70	46.36	0.00	46.39	46.61	0.03	0.000
Articles of paper	641642	0.21	25.18	0.00	25.40	74.59	0.00	0.000
Aluminium alloys	68412	0.00	13.50	0.00	13.50	86.49	0.00	0.000
Alum plates, sheets	68423	17.87	6.69	0.00	31.74	41.70	26.54	0.000
Alum household articles	69743	0.00	9.23	0.00	9.23	75.11	15.64	0.000
Office wood furniture	82151	0.00	40.78	0.00	40.78	59.21	0.00	0.000
Wooden furniture	82159	0.45	13.48	0.00	13.48	72.53	13.98	0.000
Furniture other materials	82179	0.00	60.21	0.00	60.21	32.82	0.02	0.000
Parts of furniture	82180	0.00	76.48	0.00	76.48	7.73	0.00	0.000

Notes: Values do not add up to 100 per cent because of rounding and because table does not include the share of exports sold on the high seas.

Source: Calculated from Ghana Statistical Services, *External Trade Statistics* (1992).

Table 3.28 Direction of export trade of sample

	No. of firms exporting to	*No. of firms exporting only to*
ECOWAS	7	2
Other Africa	5	0
Middle East	1	0
Europe	9	4
Asia	1	0
USA	4	2

Source: Survey results.

The information obtained from the survey confirms the economy-wide data that have already been discussed. The direction of export trade of processed goods is more diversified than the direction of trade or primary products. Table 3.28 also confirms the importance of the ECOWAS region as a market for Ghana's manufactured exports.

The ECOWAS region was not an important source of imports for most of the firms in the sample, as 58 of them did not obtain any of their imports from ECOWAS. Only 19 firms imported from ECOWAS; of these, 10 purchased more than 50 per cent of their raw materials from the ECOWAS region and of these 10, 5 reported that they imported entirely from ECOWAS. This contrasts with 53 firms that obtained imports from outside the ECOWAS region, 30 of which sourced more than 50 per cent of their imports from outside the region.

The survey was used to elicit factors that might influence the direction of trade, in particular, regional trade. Firms were asked if there were barriers to exporting to ECOWAS. Sixteen responded in the affirmative, 22 said there were none and 2 did not know. The firms were then classified on the basis of whether or not they exported to ECOWAS. The majority of firms that export to ECOWAS were of the opinion that there are barriers to exporting to the region (Table 3.29). Firms that exported only a small proportion to ECOWAS did not consider that there were any barriers to trade, whereas the two firms that exported solely to the ECOWAS market perceived that there were barriers to regional trade.

For most of the firms, what may be described as standard or orthodox trade barriers were not perceived as barriers to exporting in the region. Table 3.30 shows that the number of firms that did not perceive member country tariffs as a barrier to trade was larger than the number that did.

It would appear that from the firms' point of view there are more barriers to exporting to the region than to importing from the region. Given

Table 3.29 Firms' perception of barriers to exporting to ECOWAS

Firms that export to:	*Barriers exist*	*No barriers*
ECOWAS	4	3
Other African countries	1	1
Middle East	1	0
Europe	3	3
Asia	1	0
USA	1	2

Source: Survey results.

Table 3.30 Firms' perceptions of types of barriers to regional trade

	Barriers to exports		*Barriers to imports*	
	Yes	*No*	*Yes*	*No*
Tariffs	7	12	4	25
Licensing arrangements	3	15	3	26
Quotas	2	15	2	27
Foreign exchange problems	5	13	1	28
Other barriers	8	4		

Source: Survey results.

the extent to which Ghana's trade regime has been liberalized, this is to be expected. As trade barriers fall, import procedures should become easier, irrespective of the source of imports. For eight of the firms the concern was not with the tariffs, quotas, and so on of member countries, but with payment procedures (for example, the speed with which letters of credit can be opened with regional buyers in Southeast Asia) and the lack of an air cargo link along the west coast of Africa. One firm mentioned that their product was competitive in terms of price and quality with European competitors but the lack of an efficient air transport network in the ECOWAS region made them uncompetitive in terms of ability to deliver on schedule.

Fourteen firms indicated they would export more in the absence of barriers. Only eight said they would import more from the sub-region. The large number of firms that would not import more from ECOWAS if trade barriers were removed suggests that ECOWAS member countries do not produce what local manufacturers require on competitive terms, where 'competitive' is defined to include price, quality, and the ability to supply quantity required and meet delivery schedules.

Table 3.31 Importance of incentives to encourage expansion of regional trade

	Very important	*Important*	*Unimportant*
Reductions in regional tariffs	37.9	28.8	33.3
Reductions in general tariffs	40.9	25.8	33.3
Changes in investment rules	18.5	33.3	47.7
Changes in licensing rules	6.2	35.4	58.8

Source: Survey results.

An important point that emerges from the survey is the extent of the lack of information about the ECOWAS sub-region. Some 55 firms did not know if they were competitive with regional firms in terms of availability of capital and production costs. 49 firms did not know whether there had been policy changes affecting regional trade. This lack of awareness about conditions in neighbouring markets may be because of the small size of the firms, because of the small number of firms that export to ECOWAS or because those firms that use imported raw materials (whether from ECOWAS or outside the region) might not import the materials directly but through agents.

A significant proportion of firms do not perceive that changes in the incentive structure would be relevant to their decision to expand regional trade (Table 3.31). This could be because of the general lack of information about conditions in the ECOWAS market. Another reason could be that, given the current decline in trade barriers in ECOWAS as most countries, assisted by the World Bank and IMF, pursue economic reform programmes that have a trade liberalization component, the importance of these variables as obstacles to trade is not as great as it was during the period of trade controls. A third reason is that as a result of the unilateral trade liberalization in most ECOWAS countries, in order for firms to penetrate ECOWAS markets the relevant variables of increasing importance are the internal costs and efficiency of the firms.

To illustrate these points, one of the firms interviewed was not keen on the concept of ECOWAS because it could not compete against the Ivorian firms that were major competitors in the local market. According to this entrepreneur, what was keeping the Ivorian firms out was the language barrier.

With regard to regional trade integration, trade liberalization can facilitate the process and is important as an initial impetus. For the regional trade integration process to be sustained however, two conditions need to be fulfilled. The first is that non-tariff barriers of the type identified in the survey must be removed. The second is that firm-level efficiency must be increased. This is because at the international level efficiency is always improving because of technological change. If our survey of Ghanaian firms is indicative, it is necessary that ECOWAS firms in general catch up with that, change in order to increase and then maintain their shares of the regional market.

3.7 SUMMARY AND CONCLUSION

Ghana has undertaken economic measures in two distinct periods that could be labelled as trade liberalizations. The periods were 1967–71 and 1983 to the present. The first period was mainly an import liberalization with very little active use of the exchange rate as a supporting policy measure. The second liberalization, however, has a policy package that includes an exchange rate liberalization.

We used policy accounts, parallel market premiums, bias, trade intensity coefficients and import counter-factuals to determine whether a liberalization had actually taken place. The evidence shows that liberalization has taken place during the second period.

We also conducted a survey to investigate some of the issues, particularly that of regional integration. We found that firms had low levels of capacity utilization and that this was due to lack of demand. This may generally be due to the depressed real incomes and a high level of unemployment. Barriers to regional trade exist. This is tended to be perceived as a problem for exporting rather than importing. Economy-wide data shows that recorded export trade with ECOWAS is still limited. However, the importance of ECOWAS as a destination for exports is greater for processed goods. Thus a diversification of Ghana's exports into processed goods should enhance regional integration. While unilateral trade liberalization could enhance integration, creation of greater awareness among citizens of the ECOWAS region, especially the stakeholders, is very crucial.

We also investigated whether the liberalization was credible. The second liberalization was found to be both payments compatible and time consistent for most years. However, some element of incredibility was found from 1992 as a result of huge expansionary policies leading to some macroeconomic instability.

Despite the fact that the first liberalization was short-lived and confined to only import liberalization, we analyzed its effects so as to contrast it with the more liberalized programme of the second period.

Growth of output resulting from the liberalization increased in both periods but was more significant in the second period, averaging 4 per cent throughout. However, the sectoral composition of output shows that growth in the manufacturing sector, which was very high in the early part of the second liberalization, has fallen off since 1989 and has been overtaken by mining, utilities and activities in the service sector. Investment in these sectors has also followed closely the movements in the growth of output of the sectors.

While the volume of imports and exports has responded positively to the programme, the deteriorating terms of trade and the lack of diversification into more value-added products have resulted in a smaller growth in export earning. This has culminated in a continuing current account deterioration. The substantial inflow of foreign resources has contributed to increasing the debt stock.

The high level of investments into the mineral and timber sectors and a reduction in the importance of the cocoa and manufacturing sectors have strong implications for the balance of payments situation. These investments are quite expensive, unlike those in the cocoa sector, while the world prices are at best stagnant. They do not improve the net foreign exchange position and hence the balance of payments situation.

The structural change in the economy must move from export of raw products into processed and manufactured items so as to gain in terms of trade and in employment. Generally, manufactured items have upward price trends compared to primary products. Such diversification has the chance of ensuring a sustainable growth and less reliance on borrowing.

Employment is the phenomenon that has not seen any positive response from the liberalization. As a result of public sector retrenchment and the low response of the private sector to the programme, aggregate formal employment has continued to fall. Against the backdrop of a growing labour force, the unemployment rate has significantly increased. Although real wages have recovered marginally since 1984, the wage of 1989 was only about half the average of the early 1970s. The negative social effects of the programme are therefore large.

The fiscal performance was satisfactory until 1992, when huge budget deficits started emerging. It was only in 1994 that the significant out-turn of divestiture earnings from the sale of public investments converted the deficits that would have occurred into surpluses. Since this is a one-time sale, we are not certain that measures are being put into place to address the issue of excessive government expenditures and hence deficit. Besides, it is clearly unsustainable and bad economic management to use the sale of a nation's assets to support the budget when over 80 per cent of the budget is recurrent expenditures.

The liberalization programme has remained on course, though the recent macroeconomic instability caused by excessive government deficit financing could derail it. The unemployment situation and the slow growth of real incomes are areas of concern. The rapid depreciation of the exchange rate as the budget deficits have risen has caused people to wonder whether the liberalization has not gone too far. It has also raised demands in some quarters for a shift to fixed exchange rates. The consistent deterioration of the current account balance since 1990 as the budget position has worsened has serious implications for the build-up of debt, credibility and sustainability of the programme. Finally, other supporting policies must be put in place to boost investment, production and employment.

APPENDIX 3A

Table 3A.1 Exchange rate measures (cedis per $US)

Year	*Nominal rate**	*Black market*	*Equilibrium rate*†	*Real rate*‡
1960	0.710	0.714	0.71	
1961	0.710	0.714	0.72	
1962	0.710	0.714	0.78	105.29
1963	0.710	0.558	0.76	100.36
1964	0.710	0.581	0.81	89.62
1965	0.710	0.653	0.92	74.06
1966	0.710	2.127	0.89	71.69
1967	0.870	1.666	0.93	93.45
1968	1.020	1.754	1.08	102.31
1969	1.020	1.754	1.12	101.15
1970	1.020	1.639	1.18	101.11
1971	1.030	1.754	1.09	100.44
1972	1.330	1.639	1.24	112.75
1973	1.170	1.492	1.38	110.31
1974	1.150	1.724	1.48	103.64
1975	1.150	1.492	1.69	80.22
1976	1.150	1.923	2.17	55.01
1977	1.150	5.263	3.46	26.38
1978	1.760	7.140	4.74	25.14
1979	2.750	10.000	6.99	28.62
1980	2.750	16.660	8.76	21.77
1981	2.750	16.660	12.02	10.99
1982	2.750	33.330	16.03	9.38
1983	8.830	76.700	36.25	13.34
1984	35.990	96.700	64.23	39.89
1985	54.370	131.300	100.90	54.36
1986	89.210	185.000	169.96	69.52
1987	162.370	224.100	233.98	92.92
1988	202.350	276.600	303.09	91.71
1989	270.000	345.600	362.65	102.53

Table 3A.1 – *continued*

Year	*Nominal rate**	*Black market*	*Equilibrium rate*†	*Real rate*‡
1990	326.330	344.700	459.74	93.53
1991	367.780	0.000	–	89.46
1992	437.090	0.000	–	97.207
1993	648.980	0.000	–	117.22

Notes:
* Average for the period
† Calculation of the equilibrium exchange rate uses 1960 as the base year. In this year the trade regime was liberalized. Trade and exchange rate controls were introduced in 1961. The inflation rates used are the wholesale price indices of Ghana and the United States. The wholesale price index for Ghana is only available until 1990.
‡ Real exchange rate is the average nominal rate (C/$) multiplied by the ratio of the US wholesale price index to the domestic consumer price index.

Sources: Nominal rate obtained from IMF, *International Financial Statistics Yearbook 1990 and 1994*; and black market rates obtained from May (1984) and Kapur *et al.* (1991).

Table 3A.2 Production and price for cocoa

Year	*G. Output** *(000 tonnes)*	*W. Output*† *(000 tonnes)*	*Nominal price* *(¢/tonne)*	*Real price* *(1972 prices)*	*Western* *Output (%)*
1975/76	394	n.a.	602	342	n.a.
1978/79	265	46	2 489	235	17
1981/82	225	44	10 628	187	20
1983/84	158	39	20 000	125	25
1986/87	228	76	85 000	291	33
1987/88	188	53	140 000	351	28
1988/89	300	104	165 000	317	35
1989/90	295	112	174 000	271	38
1990/91	265	n.a.	224 000	258	n.a.
1991/92	243	n.a.	251 000	245	n.a.

Notes:
* G. Output = production of cocoa beans in Ghana
† W. Output = production of cocoa beans by Western Region
n.a. = not available

Sources: ISSER, *The State of the Ghanaian Economy 1992 and 1993* (Legon, 1993) p. 90, p. 60; World Bank, *Ghana: Progress on Adjustment* (Washington, DC, 1993) pp. 114–15.

Table 3A.3 Exports of timber, volume and value

Year	*Volume (000 cu.m.)*	*Unit value ($/cu.m.)*	*Total earnings ($m.)*
1984	148	143	21
1985	247	113	28
1986	291	151	44
1987	497	182	90
1988	550	195	107
1989	378	214	81
1990	373	319	119
1991	394	315	124
1992	401	280	114

Sources: World Bank, *Ghana: Progress on Adjustment* (Washington DC, 1991) p. 75; ISSER, *The State of the Ghanaian Economy, 1992 and 1993* (Legon, 1993) p. 62.

Notes

1. See Jebuni, Oduro and Tutu (1994) for a detailed discussion of the evolution of the trade regime during this period.
2. The evolution of the exchange rate system during this period can be found in Jebuni *et al.* (1994).

References

Abdin, R., P. Bennell, O. Fajana, M. Godfrey, and B. Hamdouch (1983) *A World of Differentials: African Pay Structures in a Trans-national Context* (London: Hodder & Stoughton).

Baah-Nuakoh, A. (1993) 'Constraints on the Growth and Expansion of the Manufacturing Sector in Ghana', in A. Baah-Nuakoh and F. Teal, *Economic Reform and the Manufacturing Sector in Ghana*, Final Report (The African Regional Program on Enterprise Development, The World Bank).

Bond, M. E. (1985) 'Export demand and supply for groups of non-oil developing countries', *IMF Staff Papers*, **32**(1):56–7.

Calvo, G. (1987) 'Costly Trade Liberalisations', *IMF Staff Papers*, **35**:461–73.

Clements, K. W. and L. A. Sjaastad (1984) *How Protection Taxes Exports* (London: Trade Policy Research Centre).

Collier, P., D. Greenaway and J. Gunning (1994) *Evaluating Trade Liberalisation: A Methodological Framework*, draft framework paper for AERC project meet-

ing on Regional Integration and Trade Liberalisation in Sub-saharan Africa.
Dixit, A. (1989) 'Intersectoral Capital Reallocation under Price Uncertainty', *Journal of International Economics*, **26**:309–25.
Dordunoo, C. (1994) 'Macroeconomic Analysis of Output and Employment in Ghana' (Accra: Paper for Ministry of Employment).
Fischer, S. (1991) *Growth, Macroeconomics, and Development*, National Bureau of Economic Research, Inc. working paper no. 3702.
Foroutan, F. and L. Pritchett (1993) 'Intra-sub-Saharan Trade: Is it Too Little?' *Journal of African Economies*, **2**(1):74–105.
Frimpong-Ansah, J. (1991) *The Vampire State in Africa. The Political Economy of Decline in Ghana* (London: James Currey).
Gallagher, M. (1991) *Rent-Seeking and Economic Growth in Africa* (Boulder, Colo.: Westview).
Ghana Statistical Service (1962) *1960 Population Census of Ghana: Total Country* (Accra).
Ghana Statistical Service (1972) *1970 Population Census of Ghana: Total Country* (Accra).
Ghana Statistical Service (1987) *1984 Population Census of Ghana: Total Country* (Accra).
Ghana Statistical Services (1992) *External Trade Statistics* (Accra).
Ghana Statistical Services (various issues) *Quarterly Digest of Statistics* (Accra).
Greenaway, D. and C. R. Milner (1987) 'Industrialization and Macroeconomic Performance in Developing Countries under Alternative Trade Strategies', *Kyklos*, **41**:419–36.
Greenaway, D. and C. R. Milner (1993) 'The Fiscal Implications of Trade Policy Reform: Theory and Evidence', UNDP–World Bank Trade Expansion Programme, occasional paper no. 9.
Grossman, G. M. and E. Helpman (1990) 'Comparative Advantage and Long-run Growth', *American Economic Review*, **80**(4):796–815.
ISSER, *The State of the Ghanaian Economy 1992 and 1993* (Legon).
Jebuni, C. D., A. Oduro, Y. Asante and G. K. Tsikata (1992) *Diversifying Exports. The Supply Response of Non-Traditional Exports to Ghana's Economic Recovery Programme*, ODI Research Report (London): Overseas Development Institute and University of Ghana).
Jebuni, C. D., A. D. Oduro and K. A. Tutu (1994) 'Trade, Payments Regime and Economic Performance in Ghana', AERC research report no. 27 (Nairobi).
Kapur, I., M. J. Hadjimichael, P. Holbers, J. Schiff and P. Szymczak (1991) 'Ghana: Adjustment and Growth 1983–1991', IMF occasional paper no. 86 (Washington DC).
Khan, M. S., and M. D. Knight (1988) 'Import Compression and Export Performance in Developing Countries', *Review of Economics and Statistics* (May): 315–21.
Khan, M. and D. Villanueva (1991) 'Macroeconomic Policies and Long-term Growth', AERC special paper no. 13 (Nairobi).
Killick, T. (1978) *Development Policy in Action. A Study of Economic Policies in Ghana* (London: Heinemann).
Krueger, A. (1978) *Liberalisation Attempts and Consequences* (New York: National Bureau of Economic Research).

Leith, J. C. (1974) *Foreign Trade Regimes and Economic Development: Ghana* (New York and London: Columbia University Press).
Matin, K. M. and B. Wasow (1992) 'Adjustment and Private Investment in Kenya' *Policy Research Working Papers*, 878.
May, E (1984) 'Exchange Controls and Parallel Market Activities', World Bank Staff working paper no. 711 (Washington DC).
Moran, C. (1988) 'A structural model for developing countries' manufactured exports', *World Bank Economic Review* **2**(3):321–40.
MDPI (1974) *Utilisation of Installed Capacity in Ghanaian Manufacturing Industry* (Accra: Management Development and Productivity Institute).
Nyanteng, V. K. (1980) *The Declining Cocoa Industry: An Analysis of Some Fundamental Problems*, Technical Publication Series no. 40 (Legon: Institute of Statistical, Social and Economic Research).
Oduro, A. D. (1994) 'The Direction of Ghana's Export Trade in the Nineteen Eighties', *African Journal of Economic Policy* **1**(1):125–40.
Oduro, A. D. (1995) 'An Overview of Economic Trends in the Economic Community of West African States', in K. Ansah Koi and K. Boafor-Arthur (eds), *Regional Integration in West Africa* (Accra: Freidrich Ebert Stiftung).
Ofori-Atta, J. (1975) 'Devaluation-The Prelude to Self-Reliance in Ghana', *Economic Bulletin of Ghana*, 3rd series, **1**(1/2):3–34.
Papageorgiou, D., A. M. Choksi and M. Michaely (1990) *Liberalising Foreign Trade in Developing Countries: The Lessons of Experience* (Washington DC: World Bank).
Rodrik, D. (1990) 'Trade Policies and Development: Some New Issues', CEPR Discussion paper series no. 447 (London).
Romer, P. M. (1986) 'Increasing Returns and Long-Run Growth', *Journal of Political Economy*, **94**(Oct.):1102–1137.
Roubini, N. and X. Sala-i-Martin (1991) 'Financial Development, the Trade Regime and Economic Growth', NBER working paper no. 3876.
Stanchart Ghana Ltd (1995) *Clerk Recruitment* (Accra).
World Bank (1991) *Ghana: Progress on Adjustment* (Washington DC).

4 Trade Liberalization in Nigeria, 1970–93: Episodes, Credibility and Impact

Olu Ajakaiye and Adedoyin Soyibo

4.1 INTRODUCTION

At independence in 1960, the Nigerian economy was reasonably open, with a trade–GDP ratio of about 33 per cent. At that time, the import GDP ratio was 19 per cent, while the export–GDP ratio was 14 per cent. By 1965, the economy had become even more open, with a trade–GDP of 44 per cent, an import–GDP ratio of 30 per cent and an export–GDP of 13 per cent. Between 1960 and 1966, agriculture accounted for an average of 60 per cent of the GDP and 90 per cent of export earnings. During this period, Nigeria was essentially an exporter of crude materials made up of agricultural produce (cocoa, palm produce, groundnuts, cotton and rubber) and a few mineral products (mainly coal, tin and columbite).

Nigeria's imports as at 1966 were dominated by consumer goods, which accounted for about 50 per cent of total imports. Imports of capital goods and raw material accounted for about 25 per cent each. This composition of imports is a reflection of the incipient import-substitution industrialization strategy embarked on towards the end of the 1950s, when the various regions started attaining self government.

The emergence of crude petroleum as a major export during the 1970s immediately reduced the importance of agriculture as a contributor to GDP and foreign exchange earnings. The subsequent oil boom of the early to late 1970s altered the resource profile of the public sector very significantly. Specifically, since the mining sector is on the exclusion legislative list, crude oil taxes (corporate profit tax, royalties, and so on) as well as foreign exchange earnings accrued directly to the federal government. The immediate consequence of this situation was a change in the revenue allocation formula that de-emphasized the derivation principle – without much resistance, at least until recently – and emphasized issues such as need, even development and so on. Moreover, unlike agriculture, crude oil exports did not have direct implications for monetary policy. In particular, in order to finance the purchase of agricultural produce from the farmers through existing commodity marketing boards, the Central Bank of Nigeria (CBN) regularly advanced the market boards the necessary funds. As a result, the operations of the marketing boards had direct implications for money supply. On the other hand, crude oil mining did not require such financial support. The joint venture cash (JVC) calls denominated in $US represent government's share of the cost of crude oil extraction and as such, they do not have direct implications for the money supplied. Meanwhile, the fact that oil export earnings accrued to the federal government had implications for the conduct of trade policy. The associated relaxation of government budget constraints also influenced the conduct of fiscal, monetary and income policies, all which had implications for domestic absorption and imports.

Nevertheless, the emergence of crude petroleum in Nigeria did not alter the initial condition in terms of composition of exports as Nigeria remained an exporter of crude materials. All that happened was that crude petroleum replaced crude agricultural produce. It is significant to note, however, that whereas agricultural exports could have been reasonably responsive to trade policy, crude oil exports could not, because of the role of OPEC as well as the fact that government owns a substantial equity (60 per cent) of the major oil producing companies through the Nigerian National Petroleum Corporation (NNPC). The dominance of crude oil in total exports, clearly shown in Figure 4.1, implied that the bulk of Nigeria's exports became insulated from the influence of trade policy as far as response to export incentives were concerned. Thus, only imports could be influenced significantly by trade policy during the period between 1970 and 1993.

It follows that analysis of trade liberalization episodes, credibility and impact in Nigeria during most of this period relates more to import liberalization, and this has been the main focus of this study. The rest of the chapter is organized as follows: in Section 4.2, trade liberalization episodes are identified and their credibility analysed; Section 4.3 focuses on the regional integration aspects of the trade liberalization episodes, especially the ECOWAS trade liberalization scheme; the impact assessment of the episodes is contained in section 4.4; and Section 4.5 contains the summary and conclusion.

This study is based essentially on secondary data on relevant macroeconomic aggregates with supplementary data obtained from a survey of manufacturing firms that we conducted.

The basic features of the survey are as follows. Foremost, the sampling frame used for the survey of manufacturing firms was generated from three main sources: *Mini-Frame, 1988* of the Federal Office of Statistics (FOS); *Industrial Directory, 1994* of the Manufacturers Association of Nigeria (MAN); *Nigeria Exporters Directory, 1992* of the Nigerian Export

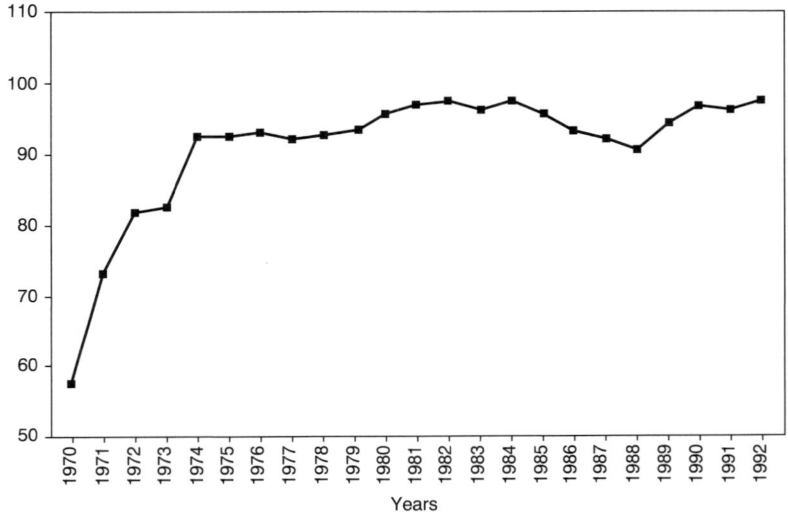

Figure 4.1 Contributions of oil to total exports, 1970–92

Promotion Council (NEPC). The *List of Quoted Companies, 1994* of the Nigerian Stock Exchange (NSE) and the *Listing of Industries* of the Central Bank of Nigeria (CBN) were also consulted. A total of 200 manufacturing firms were extracted from the first two sources and 80 from the NEPC directory. On reconciling the lists, it was found that very few exporting firms were outside the Lagos industrial zone. Indeed, only 46 exporting manufacturing firms could even be identified in the Lagos industrial zone. Accordingly, it was decided that a total of 40 exporting firms and 60 import-competing firms would be covered. In addition to classifying the firms as export manufacturing and import competing, we also grouped them into large, medium and small enterprises, using employments as a proxy for size.

The questionnaire was administered mainly by face-to-face interview, but in many cases the management of the firms insisted that questionnaires be lodged and an appointment fixed to meet the chief executive or the accredited representative for going through the questions. In a number of cases, appointments were declined because of the bulky nature of the questionnaire. There were also problems associated with change of ownership of sampled firms, especially after mergers or outright sale of firms, and similar problems.

Whenever such problems warranted a replacement of firms, the replacement was selected taking due cognizance of the characteristics of the firms to be replaced. In spite of these efforts, only 48 questionnaires were satisfactorily completed and suitable for analysis. Given the relatively small sample of responding firms, our inferences from these data are necessarily cautious. Indeed, for the present purposes, we rely more on analysis based on secondary data, with findings from primary sources introduced essentially to throw more light on the relevant issue under consideration.

4.2 TRADE LIBERALIZATION EPISODES AND CREDIBILITY ANALYSIS EPISODES

For the present purposes, trade liberalization will refer to import liberalization that may manifest itself in the substitution of less-distorting for more-distorting intervention, with the least-distorting intervention being a movement toward neutrality in the structure of relative prices. Collier *et al.* (1994) have classified three groups of approaches to measuring and identifying trade liberalization episodes. The first group has been called policy changes that may be measured through policy account and/or incidence measures. The former refer to an account of policy changes while the latter involves computing the non-tariff barriers as a proportion of SITC lines items. The second group is changes in relative prices that may involve the calculation of the following indicators: implicit, ratio of domestic to world terms of trade, and parallel market exchange rate premium. Indicators of changes in quantity, the third group of approaches, include trade intensity measures, changes in factor use and import counter-factuals.

It has been said that none of these indicators of trade liberalization is perfect. At the same time, the option of calculating all of the indicators may not be way out because there is no guarantee that the results will be mutually reinforcing. In any case, the data required to calculate all the indicators are unlikely to be available in most developing countries. There is, therefore, wisdom in selecting those indicators that are both feasible and relevant in the context of a specific economy. For our present purpose the method of policy account will be supplemented with the quantitative measures of implicit tariff index, trade intensity measures and import counter-factuals in identifying trade liberalization episodes in Nigeria during the 1970–93 period.

Policy Account

After the 1967–9 civil war, Nigeria resumed the active pursuit of the import-substitution industrialization strategy that had been adopted by the regional governments even before independence in 1960. The basic goal of trade policy remained essentially to offer effective protection to local industries by relying more on quantity restriction and less on tariffs.

Nevertheless, there were occasions when circumstances were such as to warrant abatement of the generally restrictive trade policy. Given the broad definition of liberalization to include import liberalization, a move toward neutrality in the structure of relative prices and/or the substitution of less for more distorting forms of intervention, the periods of abatement of restrictive trade policy represent trade liberalization episodes.

By the end of the civil war, there was considerable pent-up demand for goods and services that had been curtailed by the restrictive monetary, fiscal and trade policies necessary to free resources for prosecuting the war. The returning secessionists, who had suffered great deprivations, only added greater impetus to the demand. In such a situation, it was impossible to maintain the restrictive policies of the war era. Consequently, money supply grew at an average annual rate of 27.4 per cent between 1970 and 1976. Similarly, federal government expenditure grew at an average annual rate of 42.3 per cent over the same period.

In order to satisfy part of the pent-up demand, there was a generalized downward review of tariffs rates and removal of some quantitative restrictions in 1970. The restrictions on importations of machinery, agricultural equipment and spare parts were removed. There was a reduction in surcharge on imports from 7.5 per cent to 5 per cent as a part of the import liberalization policy. Tax exemptions were granted to exporters of manufactured goods. Foreign exchange controls in respect of repatriation of dividends and profits were relaxed.

This liberal trade policy posture was largely maintained in 1971, except that imports of goods, the local supply of which was considered adequate in terms of price and quantity, was subject to quantitative restrictions. Prominent among these were bicycle tyres and tubes, duplicating paper and maize. To complement this policy, duties on raw materials were reduced by between 10 per cent and 50 per cent. In furtherance of the anti-inflationary policy, the federal government established the National Supply Company, whose responsibility was to import large quantities of scarce consumer goods (the so-called essential commodities). The benefit of bulk purchase was expected to be passed on to prices, thereby helping to reduce the inflationary pressure of the post-civil war era.

In 1972 and 1973 there were relatively minor tariff changes, most of which were aimed at providing additional protection to local industries.

However, in 1974 there were substantial reductions in import duties on a wide range of commodities, especially industrial raw materials, vehicles and building materials, as well as several consumers goods.

In 1975 and 1976 licensing requirements for a wide range of goods were liberalized and the ban imposed on importation of several consumers goods was lifted. However, in order to offer protection to the two vehicle assembly plants, a quota was placed on the importation of cars under 2000cc. The quota was to represent the differences between the demand and the local production of such cars. Moreover, importation of agricultural machinery for land preparation and industrial machinery was duty-free. Import duties on other transport equipment, especially trucks, lorries, vans and their spare parts, were reduced from 33.3 per cent to 10 per cent.

Beginning in 1977, the liberal imports policy of the 1970–6 era started giving way to a more restrictive policy. For example, in 1977, not only were duties on a wide variety of imported finished goods raised, but import-licensing requirements were re-introduced for a number of consumer goods. Also, importation of several goods was prohibited. Prominent among such banned goods were cars above 2500cc, textile fabrics of all types, galvanized buckets, carbon paper and beer bottles. Meanwhile, duties on a wide range of imported raw materials were reduced and those on several others were abolished.

The aim at this initial stage was to re-orientate consumption patterns towards locally produced, import-competing goods as a way of reducing pressure on foreign exchange reserves, avoiding dumping, consolidating import-substitution industrialization and freeing foreign exchange for development purposes, especially in the social and infrastructural sectors.

Between 1978 and 1980, there emerged a severe balance of payments problem. As a result, the incipient restrictive imports policy was strengthened by raising import duties on many more commodities, placing several more under import licensing and banning many others. In 1979, for example, 25 items were placed under import licensing and 82 others were banned. This time, even imported inputs were not completely insulated from the import-restriction policy as duties on sheets and plates of iron and steel and completely knocked down refrigerators were raised considerably.

The more restrictive imports policy seems to have worked, as the balance of payments position showed signs of improvement between 1981 and 1983. However, only imports of raw materials were slightly liberalized during this period, while several competing imports were banned. For example, in 1981 government stopped issuing import licences for rice.

Meanwhile, between 1981 and 1982, there was a serious drain on foreign reserves, prompting the Economic Stabilization (Emergency Provision) Act, which was passed in April 1982. Under this Act there were tariff increases on 49 items, with imports of frozen chicken and gaming machines added to the list of banned imports. As well, 29 commodities that had been under open general import licence were placed under specific import licence.

By 1983, the restrictive trade policy posture was significantly reinforced as virtually all remaining imported finished goods (152) were placed under specific import licence. There was a general increase in import duties. In 1984, the open general import licence was abolished and more Draconian laws were promulgated against foreign exchange traffickers. Also, exporters who failed to repatriate export proceeds could be prosecuted. These measures were maintained in 1985.

The dramatic shift in policy the next year was predicated on the belief that the prolonged stagnation of the previous years was engendered by high levels of protection that encouraged inefficient producers. Implementation of the structural adjustment programme (SAP) began in September 1986. A major plank of the SAP is the liberalization of trade as a part of the overall strategy of enhancing the role of market forces in the co-ordination of economic activities. The adoption of the SAP, based on the classical notion of relying on competitive markets and private enterprise (Haberler, 1988), also implied a change in industrialization strategy from import substitution toward export orientation. Accordingly, the trade liberalization policy of this era closely approximates the movement towards neutrality in the structure of relative prices.

The first steps taken in the implementation of these liberal policies centred around the removal of price distortions by abolishing the import-licensing system, eliminating price controls and scrapping the commodity boards. The list of banned imports was reduced from 74 to 16 and the 30 per cent levy on imports introduced in January 1986 was abolished. Export duties were also abolished. The high point of the SAP was the liberalization of the exchange rate with the introduction of a second-tier foreign exchange market in September 1986. The intention was to provide appropriate price-based incentives to exporters and reduce the protection of local producers implicit in the over-valuation of the exchange rate. These policies were maintained during 1987. In addition, the duty draw-back/suspension scheme was introduced and advance payment of import duty was reduced from 100 per cent to 25 per cent. By 1988, a comprehensive tariff schedule was enacted into law. The tariff schedule was designed to last for seven years. It is significant to note that the schedule was intended to offer protection to local industries, implying a return to the pre-SAP import-substitution industrialization strategy. For example, while the interim tariff schedule introduced in 1986 provided 23 per cent protection compared to the 33 per cent that prevailed before then, the 1988 tariff provided 28 per cent protection (Faruqee, 1994). Furthermore, average tariff rates on imports of capital goods and raw materials were consistently below the overall average, while those on competing (final consumer) goods were generally above the overall average (Table 4.1).

This policy posture was retained with some modifications between 1988 and 1993. Given the resumption of the import-substitution industrialization strategy, amendments to the tariff schedules were generally geared towards increasing protection for local industries. Among the major modification were the introduction in 1988 of anti-dumping tariffs on roofing sheets, tomato paste and purée, aluminum coils, and batteries. In 1989, import duties on a number of intermediate inputs were reduced, while duties on imports of some goods also produced locally were raised. In essence, by 1988 the modification to the tariff schedule prevalent in the pre-SAP era had been restored.

By 1990, bans had also returned to the scene. This time, bans were imposed on exports of primary produce such as hides and skin and palm kernels, and the plan to ban export of cocoa by the end of 1991 was announced, all in a bid to use non-tariff measures to secure the market for inputs for the local processors of these agricultural products. In 1991, the amount set aside for duty draw-back was increased from n10 million to n50 million, the Nigerian Export–Import (NEXIM) Bank was established to finance export and the manufacturers-in-bond scheme was established. These were in addition to the regular practice of reducing duties on imported raw materials while raising those on imported finished goods. It has been estimated that by 1991, protection offered to local industries had reached 45 per cent (Faruqee, 1994).

In 1992, additional measures included the removal of duties on completely knocked down (CKD) components and spare parts for commercial vehicles, cement and inputs used in cement manufacturing. Also, import duties on fully built-up units of commercial vehicles were reduced as a part of the incentives package for the transport sector.

The policy of liberalized foreign exchange and the exchange rate were reasonably maintained. The banks were responsible for allocation of the foreign exchange and the exchange rate was not directly fixed, as was the case before SAP. A major development, however, was the attempt to close the gap between the officials and the parallel exchange rates on 5 March 1992, when the market rate was moved from n10 to $1.00 to n18 to $1.00. The immediate reaction of producers and distributors was to raise prices, and the associated massive inflationary pressure was largely responsible for the tariff reductions mentioned above. These policies were maintained in 1993 without any major change.

From the foregoing, the following significant trade liberalization episodes can be identified, namely, 1970–6, 1986–7, 1989, and 1992. The first, third and fourth episodes were essentially import liberalization through reductions in quantitative restrictions and lowering of tariffs on imports,

Table 4.1 Average tariff by main SITC sections, 1988–94

	1988	*1989*	*1990*	*1991*	*1992*	*1993*	*1994*
Food, beverages and tobacco	44.31	44.31	44.31	44.31	44.26	41.45	40.71
Mineral products	14.28	14.28	14.28	14.28	14.28	17.72	17.72
Chemicals and Chemical products	24.04	24.04	24.04	24.04	25.88	26.69	28.35
Resins and plastics	24.41	24.41	24.41	24.41	25.64	26.49	28.25
Hides, skins, leather	27.56	27.56	27.56	27.56	27.56	30.57	30.57
Wood and wood products	21.90	21.90	21.90	21.90	21.95	25.77	25.82
Paper/paper products	21.68	21.68	21.68	21.68	21.31	22.94	22.65
Textile products	58.90	58.90	58.90	58.90	55.45	52.29	49.06
Footwear etc.	39.69	39.69	39.69	39.69	39.69	37.31	37.31
Stone, cement, asbestos products	35.47	35.47	35.47	35.47	35.06	33.90	33.49
Base metal products	24.49	24.49	24.49	24.49	24.39	26.57	26.57
Machinery	19.10	19.10	19.10	19.10	19.10	22.33	22.16
Vehicles	23.49	23.49	23.49	23.49	23.49	24.77	24.77
Optical, photographic materials	26.34	26.34	26.34	26.34	26.34	27.60	27.60
Misc. manufactured products	39.95	39.95	39.95	39.95	39.95	37.42	37.32
Unweighted average	34.54	34.54	34.52	34.52	34.45	34.41	33.59

Sources: Computed from data contained in the *Federal Government Gazette* (1988).

Table 4.2 Distribution of imports, 1970–90 (%)

Year	*Non-fuel*	*Fuel*	*Manufactures*	*Total*
1970	13.09	1.00	85.91	100.00
1971	13.86	1.13	85.02	100.00
1972	14.10	3.20	82.70	100.00
1973	12.42	2.70	84.89	100.00
1974	12.51	3.40	84.09	100.00
1975	14.82	1.81	83.38	100.00
1976	16.45	1.93	81.63	100.00
1977	19.99	2.29	77.72	100.00
1978	16.99	2.00	81.01	100.00
1979	18.11	1.20	80.69	100.00
1980	18.06	1.67	80.27	100.00
1981	25.72	0.81	73.47	100.00
1982	26.38	1.16	72.46	100.00
1983	24.21	0.87	74.92	100.00
1984	19.74	0.55	79.72	100.00
1985	16.33	0.43	83.23	100.00
1986	23.89	0.89	75.22	100.00
1987	23.88	0.88	75.23	100.00
1988	23.88	0.89	75.23	100.00
1989	23.88	0.89	75.23	100.00
1990	22.45	0.74	76.81	100.00

Source: Underlying data obtained from *World Tables* (1994).

with emphasis on imports of raw materials and capital goods. The second episode, 1986–7, involved the drastic elimination of non-tariff barriers to trade and lowering of tariffs.

Quantitative Measures

Clearly, the policy account has been instrumental in dating the liberalization episodes as well as providing insights into the character of the episodes. However, since none of the methods so far proposed for identifying trade liberalization episodes is perfect, relying on the results from a single approach may create doubts. In order to reduce such doubts, it has been suggested that several methods should be applied (Collier *et al.*, 1994). For this reason, the method of policy account is supplemented with the quantitative measures mentioned earlier, beginning with the implicit tariff index.

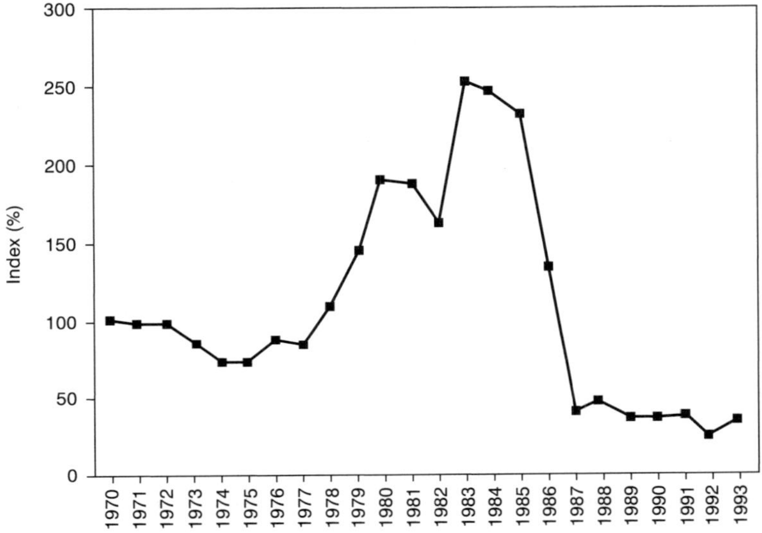

Figure 4.2 Implicit tariff index for manufacturing, 1970–93

Following Reinikka (1994), the implicit tariff index is derived by dividing the domestic (ex-factory) price index for a group of importables by their counterpart import price index. This index tends to fall when there is a trade liberalization episode. A common problem with this index is the difficulty in mapping from the SITC space into the ISIC space (Collier *et al.*, 1994). In the Nigerian context, however, an analysis of the composition of imports shows that during the period under consideration, imports or manufactures accounted for over 70 per cent of the total imports (see Table 4.2). Therefore, computing the implicit tariff index for manufactures should be a reasonable approximation of the reality. For this purpose, the index of GDP deflator for the manufacturing sector and import price deflators were derived from the national accounts statistics for the period between 1970 and 1973. A graph of the resulting implicit tariff index is shown in Figure 4.2. The indication is that the implicit tariff index confirms the major trade liberalization episodes identified by the policy account method. The implicit tariff index suggests, however, that there were mild trade liberalization episodes in 1977, 1982, 1984 and 1985. These episodes may reflect the influence of the dominance of imported raw materials and capital goods whose tariffs were generally lowered during the period under consideration.

Turning to the trade intensity measures, the ratios of import, export and total trade to GDP are supposed to rise if there is a trade liberalization episode. In the Nigerian context, however, we saw in Figure 4.1 that crude oil exports account for over 90 per cent of total exports during the period of interest. Since oil is insensitive to trade policy incentives, it seems reasonable to focus on import-GDP ratios for the present purpose. In this regard, it may be more illuminating to decompose imports according to the end-use because of the general tendency for discriminatory tariff policy in favour of capital goods and raw materials imports. Therefore, Figure 4.3(a)–(d) presents the import intensity ratios for the period between 1970 and 1993. Notice that the total raw material capital goods and consumer goods import intensity ratios increased in 1971. The ratios continued to increase after a dip in 1972 to peak in 1978. The ratios increased again in 1981, before embarking on a non-cyclical downward trend thereafter. The indication is that the import intensity ratios roughly confirm two of the liberalization episodes.

With respect to analysis of import counter-factuals, the import compression index, defined as the index of percentage difference between the actual and fitted values of a reasonable import demand function, is a useful measurement. A trade liberalization episode will be associated with a lower import compression index, as the difference between predicated and actual imports tends to narrow when imports is liberalized, *ceteris paribus*. For this purpose, an import demand function was estimated, and the results are as follows:

$$\underset{}{\text{LRIMP}} = \underset{(3.33)}{2.659} + \underset{(2.29)}{0.188\text{LRGDP}} + \underset{(2.95)}{0.490\text{LRIMP}\,(-1)}$$

$$\text{Adj. R-squared} = 0.87 \quad \text{D.W.} = 1.34$$

where:

LRIMP = natural log of real imports
LRGDP = natural log of real GDP.

Taking the antilog of the residuals between the actual and fitted values, and relating them to the actual, results in the import compression index shown in Figure 4.4. The indication is that the import compression index tends to confirm most of the liberalization episodes.

On the basis of these findings, there is considerable confidence in the trade liberalization episodes identified by the policy account method. It can therefore be concluded that a total of four trade (import) liberalization episodes occurred in Nigeria between 1970 and 1993. Out of these,

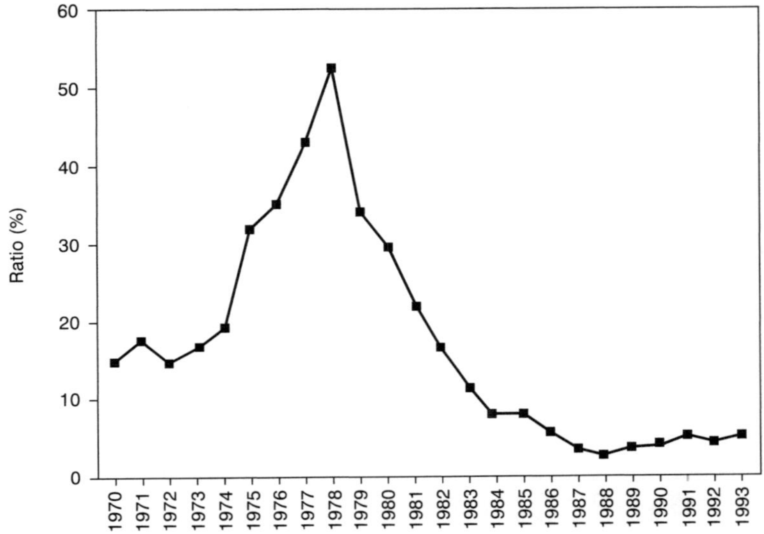

Figure 4.3 Import–GDP ratios, 1970–93 (a) All ratios

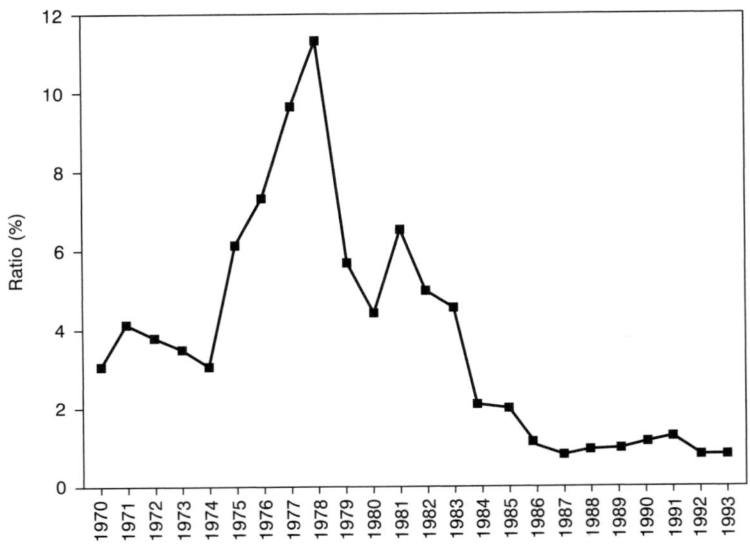

(b) Consumer goods

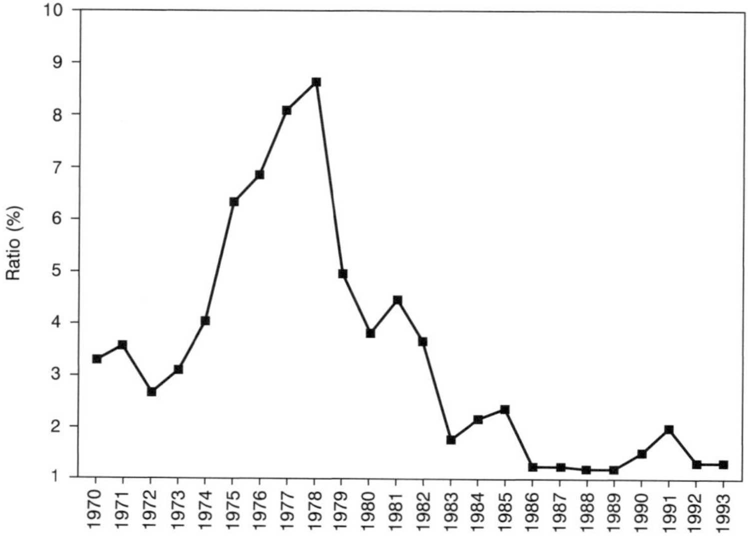

(c) Raw materials

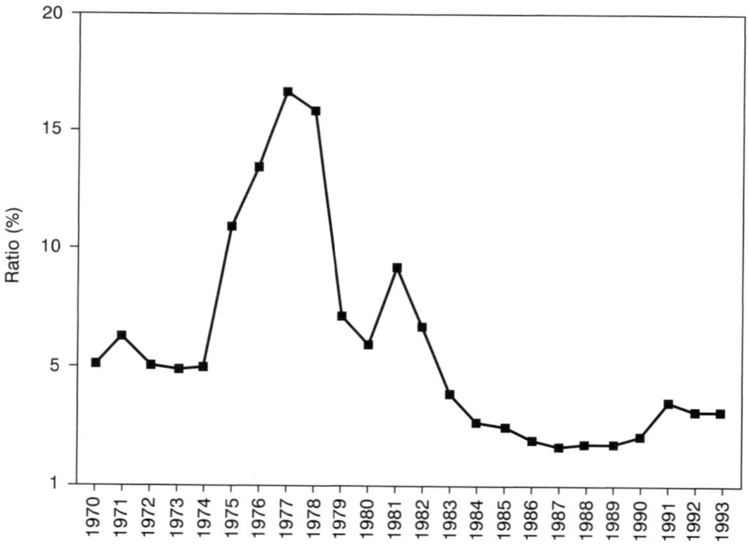

(d) Capital goods

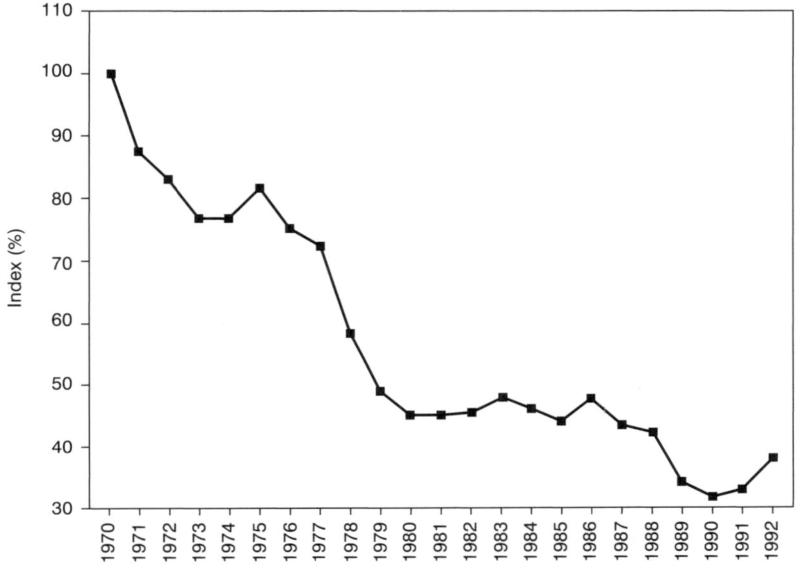

Figure 4.4 Import compression index, 1970–93

the 1986–7 episode was a result of the substitution of less for more distortionary intervention. In essence, the episode reflected the classical liberal policies of SAP. The other episodes were results of import liberalization involving a combination of tariff reductions and relaxation of non-tariff barriers to trade. It is significant to note that the last two trade liberalization episodes were conducted in an environment of a flexible (more market-determined) exchange rate regime. The trade liberalization episodes of the pre-SAP periods were carried out under a fixed exchange rate regime and an import-licensing system of foreign exchange allocation.

Credibility

From the foregoing, it is clear that it was difficult to sustain the various attempts to liberalize trade in Nigeria. It is therefore reasonable to expect that the response of the private agents to these policies might have been considerably influenced by their judgements regarding sustainability of a given trade liberalization episode. Accordingly, it is pertinent to examine the credibility of the trade liberalization episodes as well as indicators of

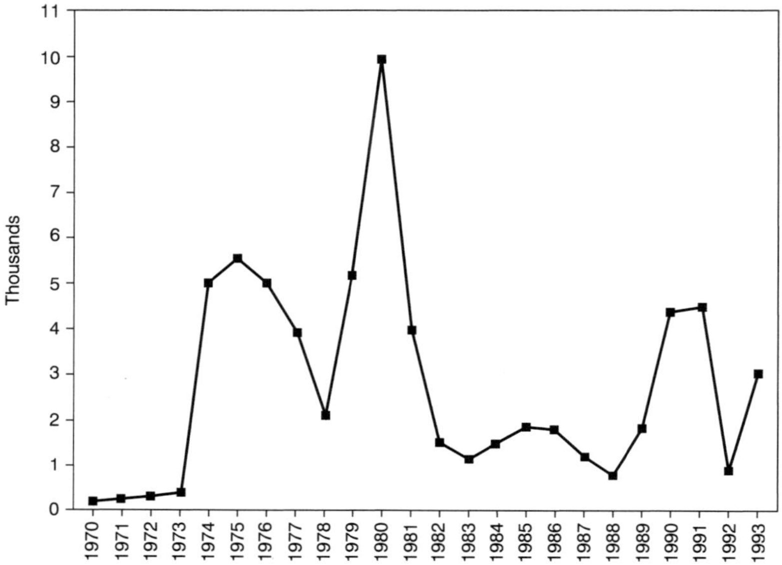

Figure 4.5 Nigeria's foreign reserves ($ million)

responses to them by private agents. For this purpose, indicators of credibility of trade liberalization episodes are measured and analysed.

According to Collier *et al.* (1994), a credible trade liberalization policy must satisfy three conditions: (1) macro-economic compatibility, (2) systematic forecastability and (3) time consistency. A credible trade liberalization episode satisfies macroeconomic compatibility conditions if it is payment and budget compatible. Payment compatibility requires that the policy be implemented along with complementary policies necessary to prevent deterioration of the balance of payments position, while budget compatibility requires that complementary policies be taken to prevent worsening of the fiscal balance.

A credible trade liberalization episode satisfies the systematic forecastability condition if the policies are such that economic agents cannot predict when policy reversal is imminent. The requirement here is that the trade policy is not conducted according to certain rules. Finally, a credible trade liberalization policy satisfies the time consistency condition if the authorities are able to resist pressures by interest groups to reverse a policy that redistributes the net benefits of the trade policy against them.

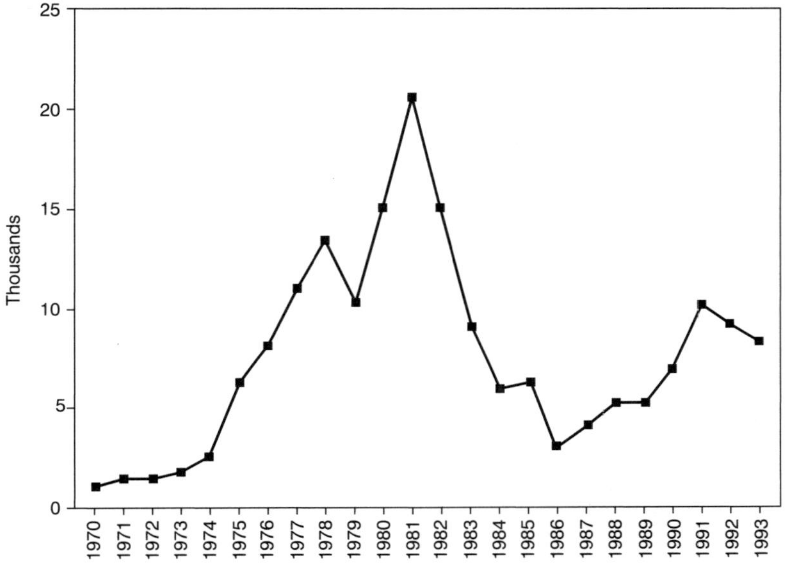

Figure 4.6 Real imports, 1970–93 ($ million)

Several indicators have been proposed for diagnosing the credibility of trade liberalization. In order to assess the credibility of the episodes already identified, many of these indicators are measured and analysed in the hope that they will also be mutually reinforcing, as was the case for the identification of the episodes.

Beginning with the payments compatibility aspects of the macroeconomic compatibility, if a trade liberalization episode is not accompanied by any appropriate monetary policy, then foreign reserves will fall, suggesting that the episode is not credible. A look at Figure 4.5 will suggest that the 1989 and 1992 trade liberalization episodes were credible. Yet they were reversed. Thus, a private agent that based its response to the 1989 and 1992 on the movement in foreign reserves would have been disappointed. However, the private agent would have correctly predicted the reversals that occurred in 1977 and 1988. The indication is that monitoring this outcome alone may not enable a discerning private agent to predict policy reversals correctly at all times in the Nigerian context.

Turning to the dollar values of real merchandise import, Figure 4.6 is illuminating. The expectation is that if a trade liberalization episode is accompanied by an increase in imports, then a necessary condition for

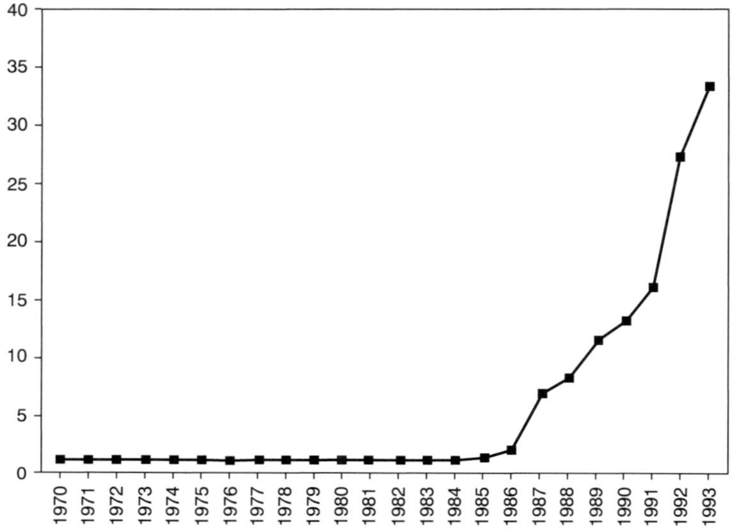

Figure 4.7 Nominal effective exchange rates, 1970–93

incredibility must have been established. From Figure 4.6, this hypothesis is not verified in the Nigerian case. For example, real imports increased systematically after 1972 but the policy was not reversed until 1977. Similarly, imports started falling in 1981, yet trade was liberalized in 1986–7, 1989 and 1992. The indication, again, is that a private agent monitoring the values of real imports for the purposes of ascertaining the credibility of trade liberalization episodes in Nigeria would have been misled.

With respect to the trend of the nominal (trade-weighted) effective exchange rate, the expectation is that a trade liberalization episode may be rendered payments compatible by exchange rate depreciation. Again, this does not seem to have been the case in Nigeria between 1970 and 1984, as can be seen from Figure 4.7. On the other hand, although the liberalization episodes of 1986–7, 1989 and 1992 were undertaken along with exchange rate depreciation, these episodes were reversed. Again, it follows that a private agent that monitors exchange rate policy for the purpose of deciding on the credibility of a trade liberalization episode in Nigeria could have been misled.

The budget deficit–GDP ratio has been proposed as another diagnostic indicator of payments and budget compatibility. If this indicator is falling during a trade liberalization episode, then the episode is cred-

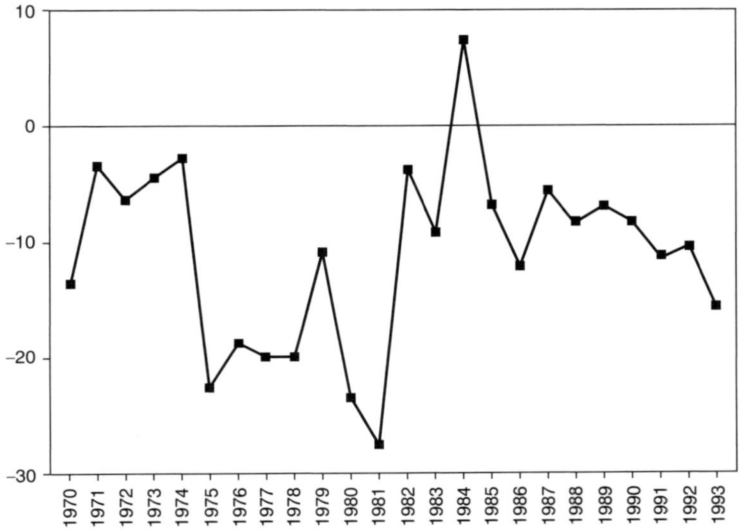

Figure 4.8 Deficit-GDP ratios, 1970–93

ible because it must have been accompanied by an expenditure-reducing policy or revenue-increasing policy or a combination of both. In the Nigerian case, this indicator seems reasonably able to predict imminent reversals of the liberalization. Specifically, the dramatic increase in deficit–GDP ratio between 1974 and 1975 shown in Figure 4.8 may suggest imminent policy reversal. Similarly, the deteriorating fiscal posture in 1988, 1990 and 1993 correctly predicts the policy reversals. Therefore, the budget deficit–GDP ratio seems to be a reasonable diagnostic of macroeconomic incompatibility of trade liberalization policy in the Nigerian context.

With regard to systematic forecastability, evidence suggests that the 1970–6 liberalization episode was initially a response to inflationary problem, and subsequently a response to the desire to protect local industries. Thus, even when the level of reserves was high between 1977 and 1980, there were not serious attempts to liberalize trade. Similarly, even though the level of reserves continued to decline after 1986, there were attempts to liberalize trade in 1989 and 1992 in response to the desire to protect local industries. The only liberalization episode that really resembles a change in policy rule is the 1986–7 episode. The new rule seemed to be liberalize trade in order to promote efficient resource allocation and

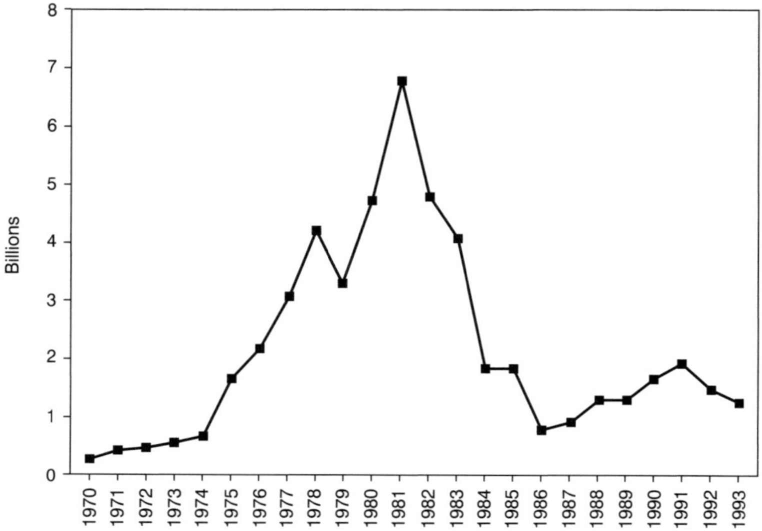

Figure 4.9 Dollar values, 1970–93 (a) Imported consumer goods

utilization. This episode was consistent with the underlying strategy of the SAP – namely, to enhance the role of market forces in resource allocation (FRN, 1986).

It is significant to note that the 1986–7 trade liberalization episode was not time consistent in the sense that it radically altered the distribution of benefits. Import-dependent producers were severely hurt by reduced effective protection through lower tariffs and a depreciated exchange rate. In response, they mounted pressure for policy reversal and a return to the earlier quo in trade policy formulation. (See Faruqee, 1994, for a concise discussion of this factor.) Consequently, the trade liberalization episodes of 1989 and 1992 clearly resemble that of 1970–6. The only difference is that quotas were effectively discontinued since the import-licensing system was resurrected. In its place, high tariffs on competitive imports (competing final durable and non-durable consumers goods) and relatively low tariffs on non-competitive imports (capital goods and raw materials) were occasionally supplemented with outright prohibitions as a strategy for protecting local industries.

The foregoing suggests that a private agent that monitored the deficit–GDP ratio might have been able to predict the reversal of the trade liberalization episodes identified in this study. It turns out that this ratio

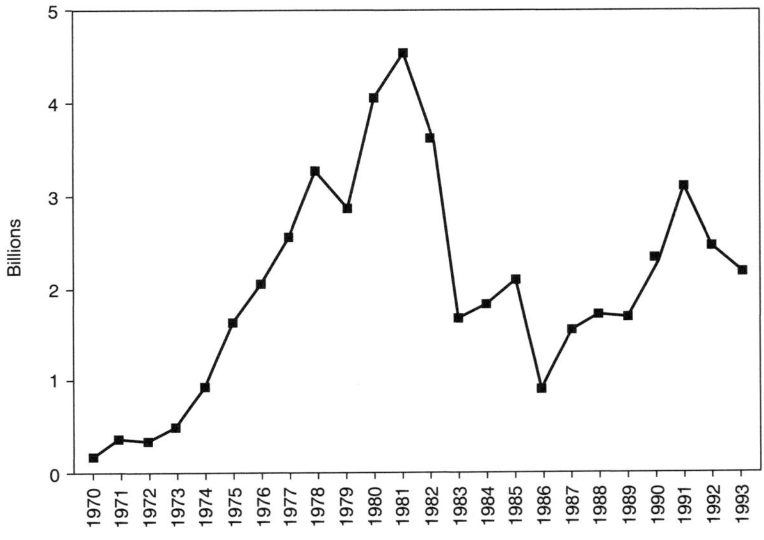

(b) Imported raw materials

has always been at the centre of the complaints by the organized private sector regarding macroeconomic policy, especially since the 1980s. It is therefore reasonable to expect that private agents might have responded to any of the incredible trade liberalization episodes. For this purpose, a number of the indicators proposed by Collier *et al.* (1994) for diagnosing consequences of incredibility have been measured. These indicators are imports of intermediate inputs, imports of consumer durable goods and commercial bank lending for imports. If a trade liberalization is incredible, then agents will tend to increase imports of intermediate and consumers durable goods during the liberalization period. In order to finance these imports, bank credit for imports should increase phenomenally during the liberalization episode.

From Figure 4.9(a) and (b), it can be seen that the pattern of inverted U-shaped curves of consumers goods and raw material imports between 1970 and 1993 are quite similar to those of export earning during the same period shown in Figure 4.10. This suggests that export earnings largely determined the level of imports of both consumer goods and raw material rather than speculative behaviour by the agents. Specifically, it should be observed that imports of both raw materials and consumer goods peaked in 1981 just as the export earnings did.

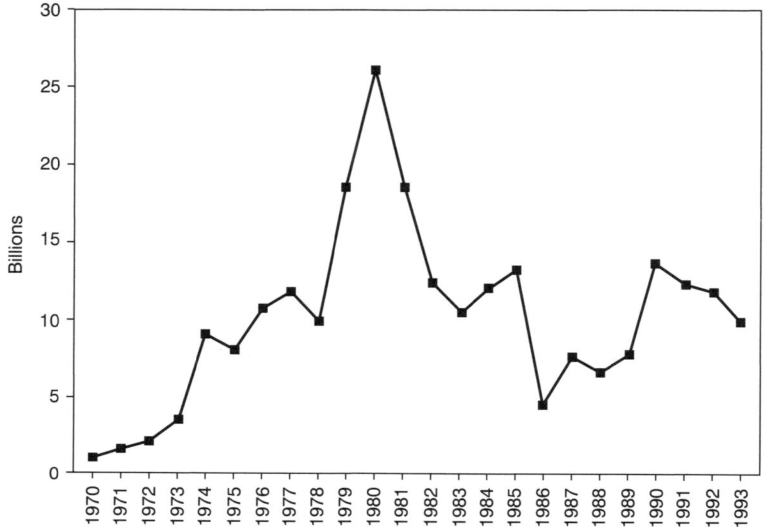

Figure 4.10 Dollar values of export earnings, 1970–93

The slight recovery of these imports since 1987 also reflects the slight recovery of export earnings during this period. In particular, the recovery of export earnings in 1991 as a result of the Gulf War is clearly reflected in the level of imports of raw materials. Correspondingly, the graph of commercial bank credit for imports has roughly the same shape as that for exports and the two categories of imports, as can be seen from Figure 4.11.

On the whole, the indication is that the trade liberalization episodes in Nigeria seem not to have encountered serious credibility problems to the extent that there was no conclusive evidence of significant speculation by the private agents. Nevertheless, the trade liberalization policies were reversed. The lack of credibility problem may have to do more with the strong influence of the organized private sector, which has been accustomed to operating in a protected environment. The Nigerian experience, especially in 1988, suggests that it will be difficult to alter unilaterally a policy rule designed to preserve a given level of protection, as already powerful producers are likely to secure quick reversal of the policy.

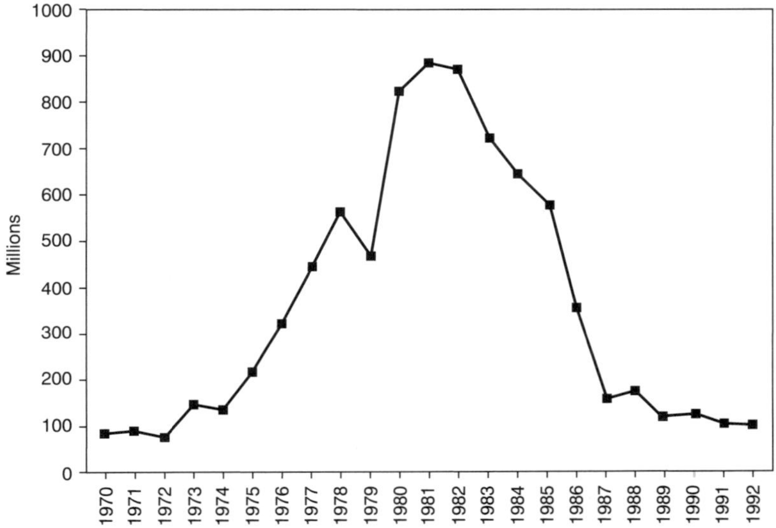

Figure 4.11 Commercial bank loans for imports, 1970–93

4.3 REGIONAL ASPECTS OF THE TRADE LIBERALIZATION EPISODES

Nigeria was one of the earliest countries to sign the ECOWAS treaty of 1975, but delays in ratifying the treaty by other member states made the treaty definitive two years later. The history of implementation of the ECOWAS trade liberalization scheme is well documented in Ogunkola (1995) and Obadan (1994a). The general indication is that the scheme was not implemented by many countries even after postponing the take-off date twice, from 1979 to 1989 and later to 1990. Obadan (1994a) has pointed out that one of the obstacles to the implementation of the ECOWAS trade liberalization scheme was the adoption of economic reform programmes by most member states during the 1980s and the associated jettisoning of long-term economic development planning and, hence, the regional integration programme.

Nigeria adopted a neo-liberal structural adjustment programme (SAP), which has universal trade liberalization as its core policy. Accordingly, there was a general tendency to eliminate non-tariff barriers to trade while tariff rates were supposed to be lowered universally. In this circumstance, preferential tariff schemes such as the one embedded in the

ECOWAS tariff reduction schedule of 1989 are inconsistent with the market forces doctrine of the SAP embarked on in 1986. Nevertheless, it should be expected that the unilateral trade liberalization policy of the SAP should affect Nigeria's trade with ECOWAS member countries, albeit fortuitously. Thus, the trade liberalization episode of 1986–7 should have positive effects on Nigeria's imports from ECOWAS countries.

The initial commitment to the SAP trade liberalization policies soon became unsustainable as manufacturers mounted pressure for the restoration of protective tariff policy. Thus, by 1988, the policies of the preceding couple of years were abandoned and protective tariffs were reintroduced. The maintenance of this policy stance probably made it sensible for the Nigerian government to embark on the implementation of the ECOWAS trade liberalization scheme in 1991, a year behind schedule.

Specifically, with effect from 1991, the government decided to remove duties and taxes from unprocessed products. In 1992 the government continued the ECOWAS scheme by approving the list of industrial products produced by specific companies in the relevant member country that would benefit from the 25 per cent annual tariff reduction. Thus, it should be expected that the implementation of the ECOWAS scheme with effect form 1991 will have a favourable impact on the share of ECOWAS countries in Nigeria's imports, exports and total trade.

4.4 IMPACT OF THE TRADE LIBERALIZATION EPISODES

The four trade liberalization episodes identified in Nigeria have been shown to be incredible, but they did not elicit significant speculative responses from the private agents. It has also been pointed out that three of the four episodes were implemented against the background of a fundamentally import-substituting industrialization strategy. Only the 1986–7 episode was implemented in connection with an attempted export-led growth strategy – which was abandoned soon afterward.

In this circumstance, the impact of the trade liberalization episodes has to be analysed in the context of the character of the policy. It should be noted that a trade liberalization episode under the import-substitution industrialization strategy may not be aimed at 'getting the prices right' in the tradeables sector. Rather, it may be aimed at increasing supplies, thereby reducing inflationary pressure, as was the case in Nigeria during the early 1970s. In that situation, imports of raw materials and capital goods need not decline and, hence, output of import-competing domestic producers need not fall and there might be no unemployment problems even in the short run. On the other hand, a trade liberalization policy designed to get the prices right can generate unemployment in the short run, as pointed out by Collier *et al.* (1994).

We assessed the impact of the trade liberalization episodes on growth of total imports and GDP against this background, using the technique of time series analysis. However, because of the nature of the episode, it is difficult to adopt the before and after approach of Papageorgiou *et al.* (1991). For instance, it is implausible to compare these performance indicators for three years before the 1970–5 episode with those of three years after it because of the civil war of 1967–9. Similarly, the years after the 1986–87 episode already include the 1989 episode, while the 1992 episode is clearly not amenable to such analysis. Therefore, the method of regression analysis is adopted. Specifically, the log of real imports and real GDP are regressed, respectively, on their lagged values and a dummy variable for each of the four trade liberalization episodes. The results are presented next.

The regression results in respect of real imports between 1970 and 1993 are as follows:

$$\begin{aligned} \text{LnRIMP} = \; & \underset{(0.19)}{0.079} + \underset{(20.49)}{0.988\text{LnRIMP}(-1)} + \underset{(1.57)}{0.254\text{D7076}} \\ & - \underset{(-4.94)}{1.148\text{D8687}} - \underset{(-0.54)}{0.183\text{D89}} - \underset{(2.16)}{0.728\text{D92}} \end{aligned}$$

R-squared = 0.97 D.W. = 0.76

Where:

LnRIMP = natural log of real imports
D7076 = dummy for the 1970–6 liberalization episode
D8687 = dummy for the 1986–7 liberalization episode
D89 = dummy for the 1989 liberalization episode
D92 = dummy for the 1992 liberalization episode.
All parenthesized figures are the t-statistics.

These results suggest that the 1970–6 trade liberalization episode had positive effects on real imports as expected while the other had negative effects. This should not be surprising, because the dummy variable may be capturing the influence of several other events that occurred during the period, especially the declining foreign exchange earnings and the massive depreciation of the exchange rate. The same explanation holds for the negative and significant coefficient of the dummy for the 1992 trade liberalization episode.

The regression results for the real GDP equation are as follows:

$$\underset{}{\text{LnGDP}} = \underset{(1.68)}{2.893} + \underset{(4.89)}{0.745}\text{LnGDP}\,(-1) + \underset{(0.46)}{0.026\text{D}7076}$$

$$+ \underset{(-0.43)}{0.033\text{D}8687} + \underset{(0.52)}{0.052\text{D}89} + \underset{(0.65)}{0.066\text{D}92}$$

R-squared = 0.68 D.W. = 1.87

where:

LnGDP = natural log of real GDP and
all other variables are as defined in the previous results.

These results suggest that none of the liberalization episodes had a significant effect on output. It is pertinent to mention that similar results were obtained in respect of the index of manufacturing output. The indication is that trade liberalization of the type witnessed in Nigeria between 1970 and 1993 did not exert significant influence on output or income generation. This should not be surprising, given the pivotal role of crude oil exports on the economic prospects of the country during this period. The insignificance of the effects of the trade liberalization episodes may also reflect the marginal effects of tariffs on the domestic cost of production such that even setting it to zero on imported intermediate inputs and capital goods imports did not amount to much in terms of incentives. This is especially so during the post-SAP era, where the exchange rate depreciation wiped out the cost advantages associated with lower tariffs.

A preliminary analysis of the survey data indicated that the cost of utilities (electricity, water, communications, fuel and so on) and transport accounted for over 86 per cent of the total indirect cost of production, which is rather high. Meanwhile, over 50 per cent of the responding firms indicated that they pursue cost-plus pricing. Since these indirect costs rose most drastically after the commencement of the liberalization policies in 1986, it is clear that they would have eroded the general competitiveness of the Nigerian manufacturing sector. Secondly, 25 per cent of the responding manufacturing firms indicated that they were exporting before but they were no longer doing so. Prominent among the impediments to export were foreign exchange difficulties, tariffs and licensing arrangements. Many of the responding manufacturing establishments were not even aware of the existences of the major export promotion incentives, as can be seen from Table 4.3. Column 2 of the table also shows

Table 4.3 Responding establishments that are aware of and benefiting from export promotion incentives (%)

Incentive	*Aware of incentive (%)*	*Enjoying incentive (%)*
Import duty drawback	37.5	3.5
Export tax rebate	39.6	33.0
Export retention	43.8	100.0
Export subsidies	56.3	6.7
Other tax privileges	52.1	38.3

Source: Survey data, 1994

that even fewer of them took advantage of the incentives as recently as 1994. These findings tend to corroborate the inferences from the regression analysis, as well as providing insight into some of the factors at work.

With respect to the impact of the trade liberalization episodes on the share of ECOWAS in Nigeria's trade, it seems reasonable to concentrate on the 1986–7, 1989 and 1992 trade liberalization episodes. Data on the direction of Nigeria's trade from which the share of ECOWAS can be computed are available only up to 1991, however, so the 1992 episode has to be excluded from the impact analysis. Accordingly, the shares of ECOWAS in Nigeria's imports and exports were each regressed on time and dummies for the 1986–7 and 1989 trade liberalization episodes.

Beginning with imports, the regression results are as follows:

$$\begin{array}{llll} \text{SHAREM} = 0.318 & + \ 0.012\text{TIME} & = 0.456\text{D8687} & - \ 0.330\text{D89} \\ \quad (2.76) & \quad (1.24) & \quad (2.26) & \quad (-1.19) \end{array}$$

$$\text{R-squared} = 0.37 \quad \text{D.W.} = 1.7$$

Where:

SHAREM = share of imports from ECOWAS countries in total imports
TIME = time trend and
all other variables are as defined earlier.

These results suggest that Nigeria's imports from ECOWAS countries benefited significantly from the SAP-induced trade liberalization episode. However, they do not seem to have benefited from the 1989 episode. A tentative implication is that import liberalization policy rooted in an import-substitution industrialization strategy may not be beneficial to the ECOWAS trade liberalization scheme. This is especially so since none of the ECOWAS member countries was in a position to supply the capital goods and raw materials imported by Nigeria during this period. Meanwhile, our survey results show that only 29 per cent of the imported raw materials used by the responding manufacturing firms in 1994 was sourced from the ECOWAS sub-region. The veracity of this deduction will remain preliminary until further testing becomes feasible, especially when data permit the inclusion of the 1992 episode in the analysis.

Turning to exports, the regression results are as follows:

$$\underset{}{\text{SHAREX}} = \underset{(1.06)}{0.338} + \underset{(8.67)}{0.229\text{TIME}} + \underset{(0.69)}{0.385\text{D8687}} + \underset{(1.50)}{1.157\text{D89}}$$

R-squared = 0.86 D.W. = 1.11

where:

SHAREX = share of ECOWAS in Nigeria's export and all other variables are as defined earlier.

These results suggest that the liberalization episodes had no significant effect on the share of ECOWAS in Nigeria's export. Our survey results tend to corroborate this indication. For instance, only 10 per cent of responding firms exported during 1994. Moreover, the firms indicated that foreign firms from outside the ECOWAS sub-region offer the greatest competition in the export market. This is not surprising, given the dominance of oil in Nigeria's exports and the relatively small contribution of the manufacturing sector to GDP, let alone exports. It is to be hoped that by the time the more elaborate ECOWAS trade liberalization scheme is fully implemented and the share of manufactures in total exports increases from its minuscule level of only 1 per cent as at 1992, this situation may be altered. This is especially so since many of the responding firms believe that there are barriers to regional imports. They indicated, however, that reduction in regional tariffs and changes in investment rules and licensing arrangements are among the major incentives that, if provided, could encourage them to expand trade in the ECOWAS sub-region.

4.5 SUMMARY AND CONCLUSION

In this study, an attempt has been made to identify significant trade liberalization episodes in Nigeria using the method of policy account and quantitative indicators. On the basis of policy account, four episodes were identified, namely, 1970–5, 1986–7, 1989 and 1992. It is important to mention that only the 1986–7 episode involved drastic elimination of non-tariff barriers to trade as well as generalized lowering of tariffs. All other episodes were characterized by reduction in quantitative restrictions and lowering of tariffs on imports, with the emphasis on raw materials. Upon analysis of the quantitative index of trade liberalization, particularly the implicit tariff index, the major trade liberalization episodes identified on the basis of policy were confirmed. In addition, the implicit tariff index suggest the existence of mild trade liberalization episodes in 1977, 1982 and 1985. These episodes may be reflections of the dominance of imported raw materials and capital goods in total imports, whose tariffs were considerably lowered during these periods.

In spite of the fact that there were reversals of trade liberalization policies in Nigeria during the period of analysis, the data suggest that, in general, there is no evidence of significant speculation by private agents. This lack of a credibility problem may have to do with the strong influence of the organized private sector, which has been accustomed to operating in a protected environment. Nevertheless, our survey of manufacturing establishments indicates that general policy reversals pose serious problems for effective corporate planning.

With respect to the impact of the trade episodes, evidence suggests that trade liberalization had limited impact on output, employment and income generation. Our survey data also show that only about 10 per cent of the total output of the responding firms is exported. Similarly, the impact of trade liberalization on regional integration was rather limited. These findings are not surprising in view of the pivotal role of crude oil exports in the economic prospects of the country. Since Nigeria's trade liberalization policies have been deeply rooted in the import-substitution industrialization strategy, the limited impact of the liberalization episodes on regional integration is also understandable. This is especially so because of the clear preference for imports of more sophisticated industrial raw materials and capital goods, none of which any of the ECOWAS member countries can produce, let alone export to Nigeria.

Analysis of the survey data suggests that the major impediments to trade promotion include shortages of foreign exchange and raw materials as well as tariff protection by the trading partners. Moreover, evidence suggests that only a limited number of the responding firms took advantage of the existing trade promotion incentives and many of them seem not to be aware these incentives exist. Therefore, there is a need to mount enlightenment campaigns to educate corporate bodies about the existence of the incentives. It is quite likely that the incentives are not significant enough, hence the apathy towards them, especially given the relatively low percentage of tariffs in the total production cost in an environment of high import dependence, shortage of foreign exchange, and high costs of funds, utilities and transportation. Presumably, if the ECOWAS member countries show more commitment to the implementation of the ECOWAS protocols, the inconsistencies between the ongoing adjustment policies and regional integration will gain more attention, and vigorous effort may be directed at resolving the inherent conflicts to the advantage of regional integration.

References

Bevan, D., P. Collier and J. Gunning (1992) *Nigeria, 1970–1990* (San Francisco, Calif.: International Centre for Economic Growth).

Brown, M. B. and P. Tiffen (1992) *Short Changed: Africa and World Trade* (London: Pluto Press).

Central Bank of Nigeria (CBN) (various issues) *Statistical Bulletin* (Lagos: CBN).

Central Bank of Nigeria (CBN) (1994a) 'Listing of Industries', mimeo (Lagos: CBN).

Central Bank of Nigeria (CBN) (1994b) *Major Economic and Financial Indicators* (Lagos: CBN).

Central Bank of Nigeria (CBN) (various issues) *Annual Report and Statement of Accounts* (Lagos: CBN).

Collier, P., D. Greenaway and J. Gunning (1994) *Evaluating Liberalization: A Methodological Framework* (Nairobi: AERC).

Collier, P. and J. Gunning (1994) *Zimbabwe Trade Liberalization* (Oxford: CSAE).

Egwaikhide, F. O. (1995) 'Trade Policy Reforms in Nigeria: A Historical Outline', in Nigerian Economic Society (1995) *External Trade and Economic Development in Nigeria*, ch. 3.

Ezenwe, U. (1995) 'An assessment of ECOWAS Experience in Intra-Regional Trade', in Nigerian Economic Society (1995) *External Trade and Economic Development*, ch. 14.

Faruqee, R. (1994) 'Nigeria: Ownership Abandoned' in I. Husain and R. Faruqee (eds), *Adjustment in Africa: Lessons from Country Case Studies* (Washington DC: World Bank).

Favaro, E. and C. Sapelli (1989) *Export Promotion and Economic Growth* (San Francisco, Calif.: International Centre for Economic Growth).

Federal Republic of Nigeria (1970) *The Second National Development Plan of Nigeria, 1970–74* (Lagos: Government Printer).

Federal Republic of Nigeria (1986) *The Structural Adjustment Programme for Nigeria, 1986–88* (Lagos: Government Printer).

Federal Republic of Nigeria (1988) *Official Gazette* (Lagos: Government Printer).

Federal Republic of Nigeria (various years) *Economic and Statistical Review* (Lagos: National Planning Commission, The Presidency).

Federal Republic of Nigeria (various issues) *Federal Budget* (Lagos: Government Printer).

Federal Office of Statistics (1988) 'Mini-Frame on Industries', mimeo (Lagos).
Federal Office of Statistics (1993) *Annual Abstract of Statistics* (Lagos).
Federal Office of Statistics (1995) *National Accounts of Nigreia, 1981–93* (Lagos).
Federal Office of Statistics (various issues) *Nigerian Trade Summary* (Lagos).
Federal Office of Statistics (various issues) *Review of External Trade* (Lagos).
Fields, G. (1988) 'Trade Strategies for the Poor: Adjusting to New Realities', in E. Berg (ed.), *Policy Reform and Equity* (San Francisco, Calif.: International Centre for Economic Growth).
Gavin, M. (1993) 'Adjusting to a Terms of Trade Shock: Nigeria, 1972–88', in R. Dornbusch (ed.), *Policy Making in the Open Economy* (EDI Seminar Series, Oxford University Press).
Haberler, G. (1988) *International Trade and Economic Development* (San Francisco, Calif.: International Centre for Economic Growth).
Manufactures Association Nigeria (1994) *Industrial Directory* (Lagos).
Nigerian Export Promotion Council (1992) *Nigerian Exporters Directory* (Lagos).
Nigerian Stock Exchange (1994) 'Listing of Quoted Companies', mimeo (Lagos).
Obadan, M. I. (1994a) 'The ECOWAS Trade Liberalization Scheme and Intra-Community Trade Expansion: Impact and Challenges', *Journal of Economic Policy* **1**(1).
Obadan, M. I. (ed.) (1994b) *Policies for Export and Economic Development: African and Asian Perspectives* (Ibadan: NCEMA).
Ogunkola, E. O. (1995) 'The Revised Treaty of ECOWAS: A new Wine in an Old Skin?', *African Journal of Economic Policy*, **2**(1).
Oyejidie T. A. (1975) *Tariff Policy and Development in Nigeria* (Ibadan University Press).
Oyelabi J. A. (1975) 'Tariffs, Domestic Prices, Effective Protection and the Structure of Trade in Nigeria', in M. Berger (ed.), *Industrialization Policies in Nigeria* (Munich: Weltrorum Verlag).
Papageorgiou, D., M. Michaely and A. M. Choski (1991) *Liberalizing Foreign Trade, Lessons from Experience in the Developing World* (Oxford and Cambridge, Mass.: Blackwell).
Phillips, A. O. and E. C. Ndekwu (1987a) *Structural Adjustment in a Developing Economy: The case of Nigeria* (Ibadan: NISER).
Phillips, A. O. and E. C. Ndekwu (1987b) *Economic Policy and Development in Nigeria, 1987* (Ibadan: NISER).
Phillips, A. O. and D. O. Ajakaiye (1991) *Nigerian Economy and Society: Economic Policy and Development, 1988–89* (Ibadan: NISER).
Phillips, A. O. and D. O. Ajakaiye (1993) *Nigerian Economy and Society: Economic Policy and Development, 1990–91* (Ibadan: NISER).
Reinikka, R. (1994) *How to Identify Trade Liberalization Episodes: An Empirical Study on Kenya* (CSAE WPS/94.10).
Shepherd, G. and C. G. Langoni (1991) *Trade Reform Lessons From Eight Countries* (San Francisco, Calif.: International Centre for Economic Growth).
Thomas, V. and J. Nash (1991) 'Reform of Trade Policy, Recent Evidence from Theory and Practice', *The World Bank Observer*, **6**(2):219–40.
World Bank (1994) *World Tables, 1994* (Washington DC: World Bank).

5 Trade Liberalization, Credibility and Impacts: A Case-Study of Kenya, 1972–94

Francis Mwega

5.1 INTRODUCTION

Kenya has implemented structural adjustment programmes (SAPs) since the mid-1970s. Included in SAPs were trade liberalization policies. These mainly involved reducing average tariff rates; narrowing their variance and replacing import quotas with import duties. These policies are likely to worsen the balance of payments by lowering the domestic price level and hence the real demand for money. They therefore must be supplemented by direct export promotion policies, currency depreciation, and contractionary fiscal and monetary policies.

This chapter analyses four main issues, utilizing the methodology suggested by Collier, Greenaway and Gunning (1993) for studying trade liberalization. Section 5.2 discusses the timing, magnitude and duration of trade liberalization episodes in Kenya since the early 1970s, Section 5.3 evaluates the credibility of these trade liberalization episodes, and Section 5.4 examines their economic impacts. Section 5.5, briefly discusses the extent to which trade liberalization was unilateral or undertaken in the context of regional and multilateral trade arrangements. While much of the analysis utilizes secondary data, these are supplemented by the results of a survey of 46 firms undertaken for this study.[1] Section 5.6 concludes.

5.2 TIMING, MAGNITUDE AND DURATION OF TRADE LIBERALIZATION EPISODES IN KENYA

Collier, Greenaway and Gunning (1993) suggest several ways to identify trade liberalization episodes. These include (1) a narrative of changes in policies and (2) a comparison of quantitative changes in relative prices (including the implicit tariff index) and trade-related quantities. They point out, however, that each of these measures has theoretical and/or practical problems, hence several of them may need to be employed in the hope that they confirm one another. Indexes of trade liberalization, more-over, may be uncorrelated across rankings, making their interpretation difficult.

A Narrative of Policy Changes[2]

Kenya experienced its first major balance of payments (BOP) problem in 1971 when there was a drastic rundown of reserves following an experiment with expansionary fiscal policies (King, 1979). The government reacted to this crisis by adopting for the first time restrictive trade policies where some imports were banned, others were placed under quota, and import licensing started to be used extensively for BOP support and to protect industries. Exchange control and import-licensing regulations were introduced in early 1972 against luxury and 'semi-luxury' imports, while foreign exchange allocation was denied for a wide range of non-essential items, including those manufactured locally. Other measures included restrictions on physically taking the Kenyan currency out of the country, restrictions on certain types of imports, and the imposition of a 5 per cent cash ratio (rescinded later). Use of tariffs was, however, still constrained by membership in the East African Community.[3]

In 1973, the system of import controls was partially liberalized following an improvement in the BOP. The backlog of import licences was eliminated in early 1973, while some items subject to quota were transferred to specific licensing and more liberal procedures were introduced in allocation of foreign exchange. Commercial banks were also asked to adopt a liberal credit policy.

The early 1970s also coincided with calls for less protection of the industrial sector if it was to break from the confines of a small market and thereby make a contribution to employment, foreign exchange earnings and the overall growth of the economy. Several studies (for example: Reimer, 1970; Phelps and Wasow, 1972; Hopcraft, 1972; World Bank 1975) showed that some industries were highly protected and that the system of protection tended to favour finishing touch industries.[4]

The country reacted to the adverse impact on the BOP of the quadrupling of oil prices in the second half of 1973 by tightening the trade control regime in 1974.[5] In addition, the liquidity ratio was increased from 12.5 per cent to 15 per cent and extended to NBFIs, interest rates were raised, and restrictions were placed on domestic borrowing by foreign companies.

The country was afflicted by drought and experienced a growth rate of only 0.9 per cent in 1975. However, most of the year was characterized by an appreciation of the shilling following that of the dollar, making imports relatively cheap. To improve the external balance, the peg of the shilling was changed to SDR and the shilling was devalued in October by 10.8 per cent. A manufactured exports subsidy was also put into effect (at a rate of 10 per cent) to compensate exporters for the bias against them caused by import duties which make it easier for manufacturers who substitute for imports to attract labour and capital away from those that produce for export. The government also took recourse to international financial institutions, and received an IMF loan of SDR 67.2 m in July 1975 under its Extended Fund Facility. It was cancelled after three months, however, when the agreed ceilings on government borrowing and on total domestic credit were exceeded.

In 1976–7, the country experienced an improvement in the BOP resulting from a large increase (80 per cent–91 per cent) in the world prices of coffee and tea. The better BOP position induced the government to relax quantitative restrictions by increasing the rate of licence approvals and the volume of licensed imports. On the other hand, foreign exchange controls were imposed against Tanzania and Uganda in August 1977 following the break-up of the East African Community.

The proceeds of the beverage exports boom were not sterilized and were fully passed on to the farmers. The resulting expansion in aggregate demand (which was compounded by an expansion in government expenditure) produced a serious BOP crisis beginning in 1978. Import bans, quotas, quantitative restrictions and an advance import deposit scheme were used to try to contain the situation. In 1979, the economy was also hit by the second oil shock when the price of oil doubled, leading to a full-blown BOP crisis in 1980.

The BOP problems again forced the country to seek conditionality loans, with the authorities promising in the fourth development plan (1979–83) to adopt a more open development strategy through such policies as the gradual phasing out of protective concessions to firms more than five years old, the cessation of the 'no objection certificate' given by local manufacturers to importers of competing imports, the provision of more export incentives and so on.

The government first went to the IMF. Terms for a two-year programme were agreed in August 1979 for SDR122.5 m but disbursements were delayed for a year, requiring the drawing of a fresh agreement. The delay forced the government to seek funds from the World Bank's structural adjustment lending (SAL) programme in 1980. The Bank was already in the process of designing an industrial sector credit, which it converted to an SAL programme by adding conditionalities. Among the conditions was the replacement of quantitative restrictions by tariffs and their rationalization (by 1983). Another IMF stand-by of SDR151 m was received in early 1982 followed by another in March 1983 (the first to be fully disbursed) and an SAL in 1982. The latter's conditionalities touched on virtually every sector of the economy, including picking up on the unfinished trade policy initiatives of SAL 1.[6]

The government was unable to implement these programmes successfully. The IMF stand-by and World Bank SAL programmes negotiated in 1979–82 were abandoned or poorly implemented, leading to the cancellation of IMF stand-bys as credit ceilings were exceeded. There was also a delay in the release of the second tranche of SAL 2 from March to December 1983, and a decision was made in 1984 not to continue with a new BOP support programme due to the limited progress with SAL 1 and SAL 2, but instead to focus on sectoral programmes.

It was envisaged, for example, that 20 per cent of the items in the more-restrictive Schedules IIA and IIB were to be shifted to the less-restrictive Schedule I each year. Due to a serious BOP problem in 1982, the entire import-licensing programme was temporarily halted. When the new foreign exchange allocation schedules were published in 1983, the process had been reversed, with the less-restrictive Schedule I having 24 per cent fewer items than before (Ng'eno, 1991). This poor record in implementing reforms has been attributed to inappropriate timing and design of the programmes, large macroeconomic imbalances – including inadequate use of the exchange rate policy – and lack of adequate political commitment by the authorities (UNDP/World Bank 1993; Mosley, 1994; Swamy, 1994).

The country experienced a mini-boom in coffee in 1986, which was not sterilized, leading to a serious BOP problem by the end of 1987. This led to recourse to an 18-month IMF stand-by in the second half of 1987, which was supplemented in 1988 by another loan under the IMF's structural adjustment facility and another in 1989 under its enhanced structural adjustment facility. Trade liberalization policies were mainly implemented under the World Bank's industrial sector credit covering the period 1988–9, later extended to 1990–1 under its exports development project.

These efforts at trade liberalization were somewhat more successful, as they benefited from the earlier experience, availability of better information, and better focus under the sectoral programmes. They extended beyond one credit programme even though they were hampered by continuing large budget deficits (Swamy, 1994). After the false start in the early 1980s, some strides in trade liberalization and export promotion were made after 1987. But there was a reversal in mid-1991 in the run-up to the aid embargo of November 1991 to December 1993 when all programme (BOP) support was suspended by donors until various socio-political and economic reforms were implemented. While there was no formal reversal of import liberalization – the items on the restricted list remained unchanged – approval time lengthened substantially, and licences were often granted for small amounts so that tariffs were no longer the binding constraint on many imports (UNDP/World Bank, 1993). At the Paris Consultative Group (CG) meeting in December 1993, the donors pledged to disburse approximately $170 m in 1994 provided a number of conditions were met, including continued progress in implementing the economic reform agenda. At the CG meeting of December 1994, a further $220 m was pledged for balance of payments support.

Tariffs

In 1980, a 10 per cent tariff surcharge was imposed on all imports and there were tariff increases on over 200 items. These reforms were continued in 1981, with tariff increases ranging from 2 per cent–90 per cent imposed on about 1400 items. There were also tariff reductions on about 20 items used mainly by export-orientated industries.

The tariff reductions started in 1981 gradually extended in the 1980s and 1990s to more import items, particularly under SAL 2 in 1983–4 and since 1987 under the World Bank industrial sector adjustment credit. The number of tariff categories, for example, was reduced from 25 to 11, while the maximum tariff rate was reduced from 170 per cent to 70 per cent over 1987–92. In June 1994, the maximum rate was reduced to 45 per cent and the number of bands to seven. In June 1995, these were further reduced to 40 per cent and to six, respectively. The average unweighted tariff rate declined from 41.3 per cent in 1989/90 to 34 per cent in 1992/93 (UNDP/World Bank, 1993).

As can be seen in Figure 5.1, tariff reforms implemented in the 1980s and early 1990s had some impact in reducing the effective tariffs. The collected tariff rates increased to a peak in 1982 and then generally declined over the rest of the period.

Quantitative Restrictions

Since the BOP crisis of 1971, Kenya has extensively used administrative controls to manage the balance of payments and to provide protection to some industries. Until their abolition in 1993, import quantitative restrictions in Kenya were mainly administered through import licensing. This was pervasive: the number of import products under licence increased from 228 in 1972 to 2737 in 1985, and in the mid-1980s the Import Management Committee was processing an average of 2000 applications for foreign exchange per week (Dlamini, 1987). Essential products were put in the less-restrictive licence categories while the non-essential products were put in the more-restrictive imports categories or completely banned. Import liberalization essentially involved a shift of items from the more-restrictive

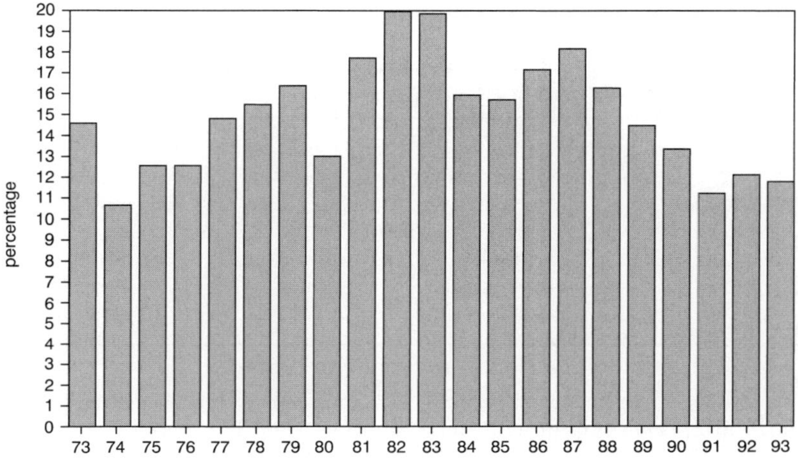

Figure 5.1 Collected tariff rates in Kenya, 1973–93

categories to the less-restrictive categories. Until the abolition of import controls in May 1993, the schedules were published annually.

Some progress was made towards relaxation of QRs, with an arbitrary mechanism such as the 'no objection' certificate eliminated in June 1980, while import items in the less-restrictive categories were increased. The share of quota-free imports increased from about a quarter in 1980 to a half in 1987 (Table 5.1).

The number of import items under quantitative restrictions further declined to 22.1 per cent in 1990/91, with the average lag between licence application and foreign exchange allocation reduced from six months to about three weeks (World Bank, 1990). The coverage of the restricted imports dropped from about 15 per cent in 1990/91 to 0.2 per cent in 1991/92 (UNDP/World Bank, 1993).

Reforms in the direct allocation of foreign exchange were continued in the 1990s. In August 1992, a 100 per cent retention scheme for exporters of non-traditional products was introduced; it was extended (at 50 per cent) to traditional exports (November 1992) and tourism (February 1993). The policy on retention accounts and the inter-bank foreign exchange market were reversed in March 1993, however, to contain the inflationary spiral following the floating of the shilling. The government accused the retention account holders of hoarding foreign exchange for speculative purposes when the country faced a serious balance of payments problem.

Table 5.1 Progress in relaxation of quantitative restrictions, 1980–7 (% of total imports)

	IA	*IB*	*IIA*	*IIB*
1980	24	19	43	14
1981	23	20	46	10
1982	25	19	46	10
1983	36	21	32	11
1984	30	17	45	6
1985	48	13	38	5
1986	48	10	35	7
1987	51	11	31	7

Notes:
IA: quota free; IB: licences issued by item, but usually readily available; IIA: bulk goods, permit require ministerial approval; and IIB: imports competing with domestic industry severely restricted

Source: Mosley (1994)

In May 1993, these reforms were re-introduced, with the retention accounts at a rate of 50 per cent (later increased to 100 per cent in February 1994) for exporters of both goods and services (so long as the proceeds were utilized or sold within three months, after which they would be sold to the central bank at the official rate before it was unified with the inter-bank rate), and import licences were abolished except for a short list of items that require prior approval for security, environmental and health considerations. Importers were, however, still required to provide documentary evidence of shipments or of actual importation and the sellers' final invoice before commercial banks could make the appropriate payments (CBK, 1993). In addition, all imports worth over Ksh 100 000 were still subject to pre-shipment inspection and a clean report of finding issued by a CBK-approved inspection agency.

Direct Export Promotion Policies

By the late 1970s it was generally agreed that the impact of the manufactured exports subsidy introduced in 1974 was quite limited because the rate was quite low (at 10 per cent of the fob value of goods manufactured in Kenya with a local value-added of at least 30 per cent) and payments were subjected to much delay. In the 1980s, one-third to two-thirds of the total subsidy payments accrued to four firms while the payments comprised only about 5 per cent of manufactured exports, hence the subsidy had minimal incentive value (World Bank, 1990). In effect, the subsidy was treated as a windfall by those few firms that received it rather than an incentive for increased exportation.[7]

There were numerous attempts to rectify this situation. For example the rate was increased to 20 per cent in 1980. Because of BOP problems, however, the scheme was suspended in June 1982. The subsidy was reintroduced in December 1982 at the rate of 10 per cent with a bonus (incremental) rate of 15 per cent to new exporters and those who increased their exports in the previous year. This bonus rate was abolished in 1985 and the basic rate raised to 20 per cent. In 1986 the items eligible for export compensation were reduced from 2000 to 700, but later increased to 1260. In 1990, exporters were permitted to process their claims through commercial banks to speed up payments while export firms were given the option to claim import duty/VAT exemptions on imported inputs rather than export compensation. The subsidy was eventually abolished in September 1993, to be replaced by the duty/VAT remission scheme for intermediate inputs.[8]

Other direct export promotion policies have included attempts to strengthen government export departments to expedite the handling and processing of the relevant export documents; support for regional trading arrangements; manufacturing-under-bond (since 1989) whereby production is done exclusively for the export market, simplifying the export documentation processing and facilitating the importation of inputs; and establishing export-processing zones (EPZs). EPZs were legislated in 1990 and two state-operated EPZs are being developed at Athi River and Mombasa. A private EPZ (Sameer Industrial Park) was commissioned in Nairobi in early 1991 and several others have been approved since then. A pre-shipment export financing facility was also introduced in 1992 but abolished thereafter following massive frauds through the so-called 'political banks' during the run up to national elections that year.

The Exchange Rate

The Kenya shilling was pegged to the British pound until December 1971 and to the $US until 1975. The official exchange rate remained fixed (at Ksh7.143) for much of this period (except for 1973, when it was slightly appreciated), with the other currencies reflecting cross rates against the dollar in the international currency market.

Between October 1975 and December 1982, the Kenya shilling was pegged to the SDR, which was considered to be relatively more stable than a single currency peg, especially following the floating of the US $ in 1973. During the SDR peg, the shilling was subjected to a number of discretionary devaluations. Following a combined devaluation of 31.3 per cent against the SDR in February and September 1981 and in December 1982 (from Ksh9.66 to 14.06 per SDR), the country adopted a crawling peg exchange rate regime in which the rate was adjusted on a daily basis against a composite basket of currencies of the country's main trading partners based on inflation differentials with these countries. The SDR peg was considered inadequate to maintain competitiveness of the Kenya shilling because the weights used did not reflect Kenya's non-diversified trade pattern. The currencies included in the SDR accounted for only 40 per cent of the country's combined exports and imports.

The efforts to liberalize the foreign exchange market were further continued in the 1990s. CBK introduced foreign exchange bearer certificates (forex-Cs) in October 1991 with a view to reduce capital flight and to tap the foreign exchange outside the domestic banking system. Forex-Cs were denominated and sold in convertible currency and entitled the bearer to future repurchase of the certificates at face value at the prevailing exchange rate without exchange control restrictions.

As they were negotiable and easily transferable from one holder to another, forex-Cs provided an alternative window to obtain foreign exchange, though at a premium over the official exchange rate. There was a severe shortage of foreign exchange in this period following the suspension of foreign aid to the country in November 1991 and the highly expansionary monetary stance in the run-up to the 1992 general elections. As a result a vibrant secondary market in forex certificates developed. The premiums on the certificates fluctuated between 20 per cent–40 per cent in the first half of 1992 (CBK, 1992), increased to 50 per cent in October 1992 and to a peak of about 75 per cent over the official exchange rate in December 1992 before declining as CBK placed impediments to their redemption.

The forex-C market collapsed and was phased out following devaluations of 25 per cent and 33 per cent of the official exchange rate in March and April 1993 and one of 6 per cent in May 1993. These substantially reduced the gap between the official rate and the market rate, and hence the premium on forex-Cs.

The foreign exchange market was further liberalized in August 1992 when an inter-bank market (operated by commercial banks) was introduced, with CBK pledging to finance only government imports and the servicing of the external debt at the official rate. The market exchange rate was to be determined by negotiation between banks and their clients and in transactions between banks. The two exchange rates were eventually unified in October 1993, thus ending the two-tier system.

By early 1995, the exchange rate was substantially determined by market forces, exchange controls on current account transactions were fully removed, and most exchange controls on capital account transactions were also abolished. The only remaining restrictions were on investment in shares and securities in the Nairobi Stock Exchange. Effective from January 1995, however, foreigners could purchase a maximum 20 per cent (raised to 40 per cent in June 1995) of the share capital of a locally-owned firm.

Quantitative Measures of Trade Liberalization

It is possible from the above policy account to identify various trade liberalization episodes in Kenya since the early 1970s. Inferences from actual changes in policies cannot be conclusive, however, as these policies move in opposite directions and interact with one another. This makes it difficult to identify the episodes with confidence, hence the need for quantitative measures of trade liberalization.

Our starting point is the study by Reinikka (1994a), whose objective is to develop an index that would identify trade liberalization episodes in Kenya in 1968 and over 1972–90. The study recommends the use of the implicit tariff index, derived by dividing the domestic producer (ex-factory) price index for a group of importable products with their counterpart import (world) price index. The implicit tariff index (1 + *ti*) reflects the difference between domestic and foreign prices for a given set of products (and hence the degree of protection) as derived from the expression

$$P_{di} = P_{mi} \cdot e\ (1 + t_i)$$

where P_m is import prices, *e* is exchange rate, and *ti* is the implicit tariff rate. In the base case, these were calculated for Kenya's manufactured goods excluding food, beverages and tobacco. Food-processing was omitted because it is more affected by price controls and includes maize, whose imports fluctuate much from year to year. Hence the estimated index is narrowly based, accounting for between a third and a half of manufacturing sector output in the study period.

Figure 5.2 shows the base case implicit tariff index calculated in this manner over 1972–93.[9] The index identifies seven trade liberalization episodes in 1973, 1975 (unlike Reinikka), 1977–81, 1983, 1985, 1988–90 and in 1993. The index hence shows that two distinct trade liberalization episodes occurred in the early to mid-1970s as well as one extended liberalization episode from 1977 to 1981 following the coffee boom. Thereafter there were three liberalizations episodes in the 1980s and one in 1993.

The base case implicit index seems to tie with the policy account above, even though it appears to exaggerate the degree of trade liberalization in 1977–81 following the coffee boom. Hence there is likely to be a bias in the computation of the index. The import price index (P_{mi}) is unlikely to have significant bias because of the mandatory pre-shipment inspection of Kenya's imports since 1972, which has prevented pervasive over-invoicing of imports. It is the Kenyan domestic price deflator (P_{di}) that is

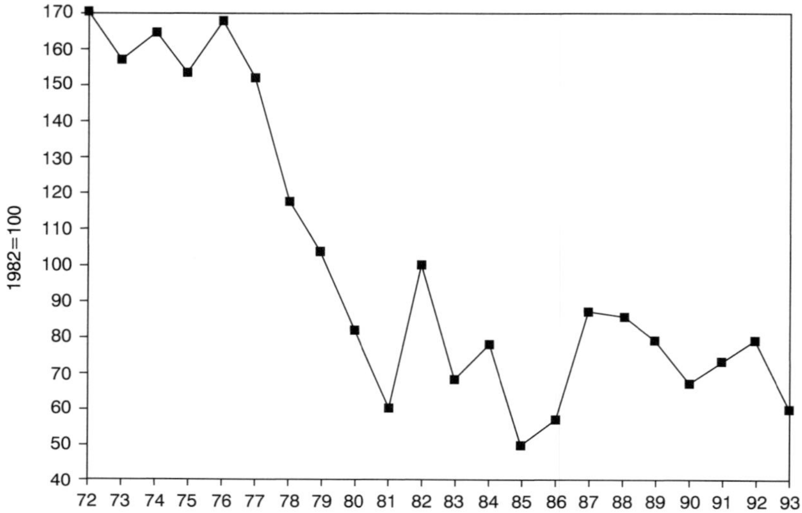

Figure 5.2 Implicit tariff index: total manufacturing *minus* food, beverages and tobacco, 1972–93

likely to be the main source of the bias. This may be attributed to increased supply of manufactured goods following the coffee boom that reduced their prices and hence the index, reflected in the rapid growth in the imports and manufacturing output during this period.

A criticism of the implicit tariff index is that: (1) it conceals information, especially of dispersion around the mean; and (2) empirical derivation is not easy, as it has to be obtained indirectly, while imports and domestic products in the index may not match, particularly for broad SITC and ISIC classifications. The composition of the products may also change over time and price deflators may contain biases that are difficult to detect or control. Hence, while the implicit tariff index has some promise, it needs to be evaluated in the context of other trade measures.

Though a number of the other indexes identity similar trade liberalization episodes as the base case implicit tariff index, they do not resolve the issue of whether protectionism increased or decreased during the 1970s, 1980s and early 1990s.

In contrast to the implicit tariff indexes, snapshots of effective rates of protection based on studies done in the 1960s, 1970s and 1980s suggest that the economy has become more protected over time. Sharpley and Lewis (1988), for example, standardized results from Reimer (1970) and

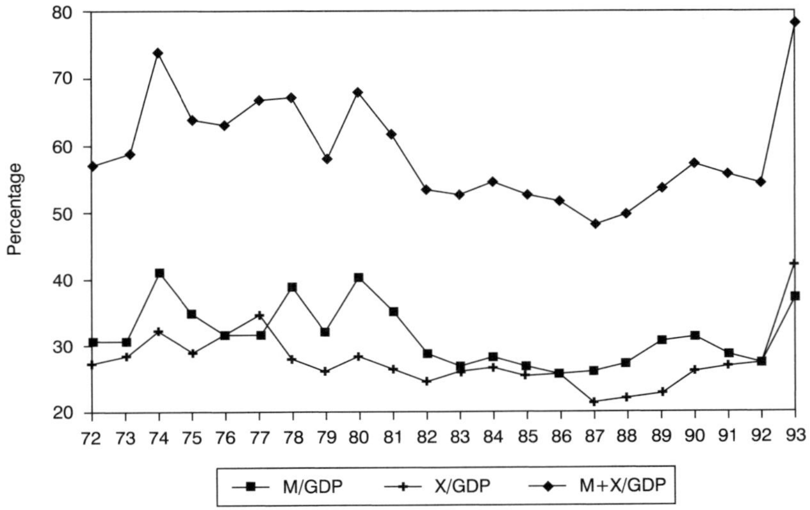

Figure 5.3 Evolution of Kenya's import, export and trade coefficients, 1972–93

the World Bank (1987) and concluded that the effective rate of protection increased from 31 per cent to 51 per cent of value-added between 1968 and 1985. Keyfitz and Wanjala (1991), on the other hand, traced the impact of tariffs through input–output tables and estimated the mean ERP of the manufacturing sector to have increased from 66.3 per cent in 1976 to 164.2 per cent in 1987. Reinikka (1994a) attributes much of the discrepancy between the base case implicit tariff index and snapshots of effective rates of protection to data problems arising from differential coverage of sectors and levels of their aggregation as well as the international prices that are utilized.

The evolution of Kenya's export (X/GDP), import (M/GDP) and trade ((X + M)/GDP) ratios also shows that the Kenyan economy became less open in the 1980s and early 1990s compared to the 1970s, although there was a substantial opening in 1993 (Figure 5.3). The reduction in openness reflects poor exports performance, particularly in the 1980s, leading to increased import compression. The import restriction index also suggests increased protectionism in the 1980s compared to the 1970s, but with substantial recovery in 1993. This index is given by the percentage difference between actual imports and predicted imports from an import demand function.

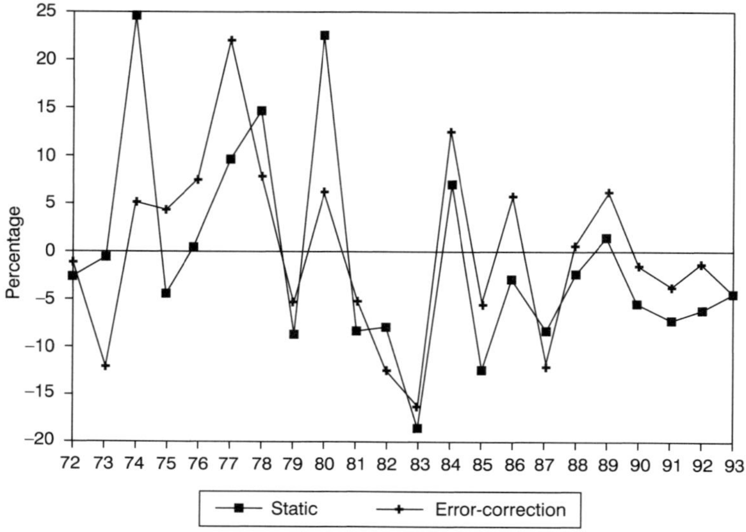

Figure 5.4 Import compression indices in Kenya, 1972–93

Kenya has until recently applied import restrictions widely to close the gap between the demand for imports and the supply of foreign exchange. During the periods of foreign exchange shortages, the volume of imports depended on the amount of foreign exchange importers could get. Estimation of an import demand function therefore has to incorporate explicitly forex reserves availability as a determinant of imports demand in order to derive the 'true' unconstrained elasticities. This combines the traditional imports demand model, which links real imports to domestic output and relative import prices, and the Hemphill (1974) imports supply model, which links real imports to lagged forex reserves and forex earnings.

Following Faini (1988), Moran (1989), Bruce and Ndii (1991) and Mwega (1993), static and error-correction models were estimated by two-stage least-squares with forex reserves and forex earnings used as instruments to replace relative import prices.

The following models were estimated over 1964–93:

$$\log RIM = \alpha_0 + \alpha_1 \log RGDP + \alpha_2 \log RPIM + u$$

$$\Delta \log RIM = \beta_0 + \beta_1 \Delta \log RGDP + \beta_2 \Delta \log RPIM + \beta_3 ECM_{-1} + v$$

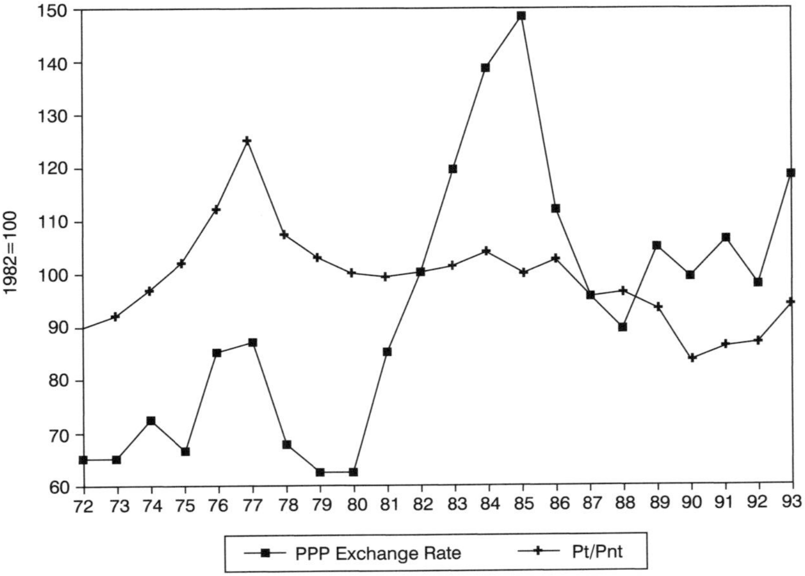

Figure 5.5 Evolution of real exchange rate indices in Kenya, 1972–93

where *RIM* is real imports, *RGDP* is real income, *RPIM* is relative import prices and *ECM* is an error-correction term from the residuals of the static co-integration equation.[10]

Figure 5.4 shows the import compression indexes calculated from the anti-logged residuals of the static and error-correction models.[11] Both indexes show increased import compression over time. The gap between actual and predicted imports in the static equation declined from 2.3 per cent in 1974–83 to −4.2 per cent in 1984–93. The error-correction equation shows less import compression between the two periods, with the gap declining from 1.2 per cent in 1974–83 to −0.3 per cent in 1984–93.

Another index to identify trade liberalization episodes is the real exchange rate, which may be a more reliable predictor of long-term economic performance than other measures of 'openness' (Helleiner, 1994). Figure 5.5 shows the evolution of two indexes of real exchange rate over 1972–93. The first is the purchasing power parity real effective exchange rate (REER) derived by deflating the domestic price level by the average for Kenya's main trading partners, both expressed in a common currency.[12] The second measure of real exchange rate was derived by dividing the price of tradeables

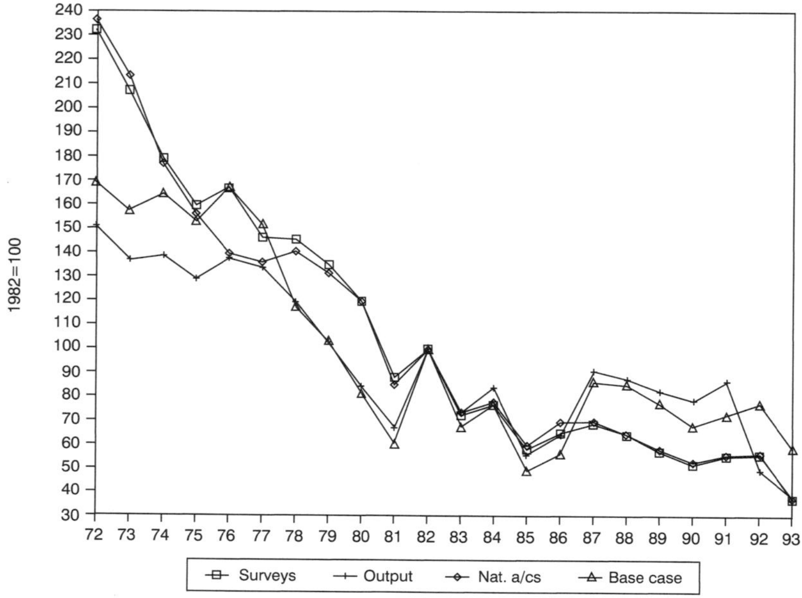

Figure 5.6 Implicit tariff index: total manufacturing output, 1972–93

(manufacturing, agriculture, forestry, mining and quarrying in the monetary sector) by the price of non-tradeables (services and the non-monetary sector) using data from the national accounts.

REER on average depreciated in this period. The second measure of the real exchange rate, on the other hand, shows general appreciation over time. These real exchange rate measures do not therefore resolve whether protectionism on average increased or decreased in Kenya between the 1970s and early 1990s.

One limitation of the base case implicit tariff index above is that changes in the index may result from variations in te prevailing economic conditions, or from changes in other policies rather than trade policy. This implies that the focus should be on the entire manufacturing sector, with changes in the implicit tariff index accepted as measures of incentives irrespective of their source (Collier, Greenaway and Gunning, 1993). Estimating the index for the total manufacturing sector also tests for biases in the domestic price deflator.

The implicit tariff index was therefore estimated with domestic price deflators from the total manufacturing output as well as from value added

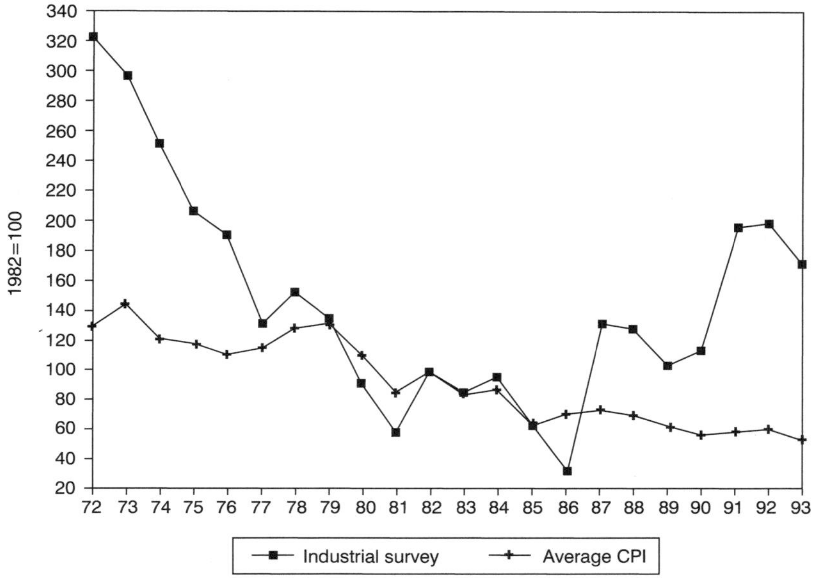

Figure 5.7 Implicit tariff index: clothes and footwear, 1972–93

as reported from industrial surveys and the national accounts. As shown in Figure 5.6, total manufacturing output shows relatively modest liberalization over time compared to both the base case index and the manufacturing value added and therefore seems to be more credible. The total manufacturing output index also identifies similar trade liberalization episodes as the base case index, except that the 1993 liberalization episode now commences in 1992.

In a further test of biases in the domestic price deflator, the implicit tariff indices were also calculated for clothing and footwear based on published data on the producer price index from the surveys of industrial production and the consumer price index (CPI). These two indexes, however, give conflicting results (Figure 5.7). The average Nairobi CPI data generally show sustained liberalization, especially after the coffee boom, while the industrial surveys data show liberalization until 1986 and increased protectionism thereafter.

Lastly, Reinikka (1994a) recommends estimation of an importables demand function and testing whether its elasticities are plausible or not. If they are not plausible, one can use plausible elasticities to derive the

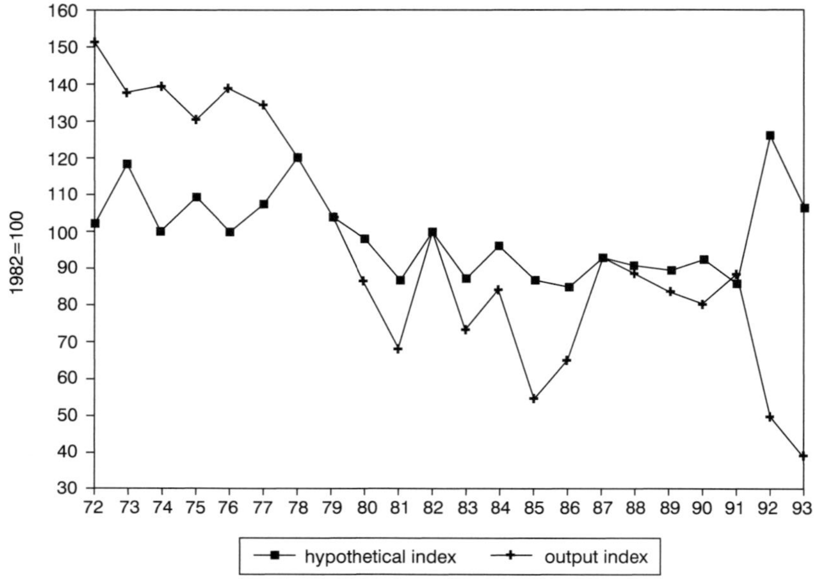

Figure 5.8 Hypothetical implicit tariff index, 1972–93

importables price series. The demand for importables (constant-price manufactured value added plus manufactured imports) was postulated to be a function of total expenditure (constant-price gross investment plus private consumption), the price of importables (the producer price calculated above for the manufacturing value added) and the price of non-tradeables (the non-tradeable components of CPI). Our estimated model gave implausible price elasticities. Except for the expenditure elasticity (1.231), own-price (−0.572) and cross-price (0.167) elasticities substantially deviated from the expected unit coefficients (Reinnika, 1994a). We therefore proceeded (following Reinnika) to derive a hypothetical domestic price series from the importables demand function on the basis of price elasticities of 1.231, −1 and +1, respectively, assuming a zero constant term (that is, subsistence consumption is zero). As seen in Figure 5.8, the hypothetical domestic price deflator yields less pronounced trade liberalization over time.[13]

To summarize the results, Figure 5.9 illustrates the percent proportion of indexes showing a trade liberalization episode out of the 14 indexes that were computed. A majority of the computed indices suggests that

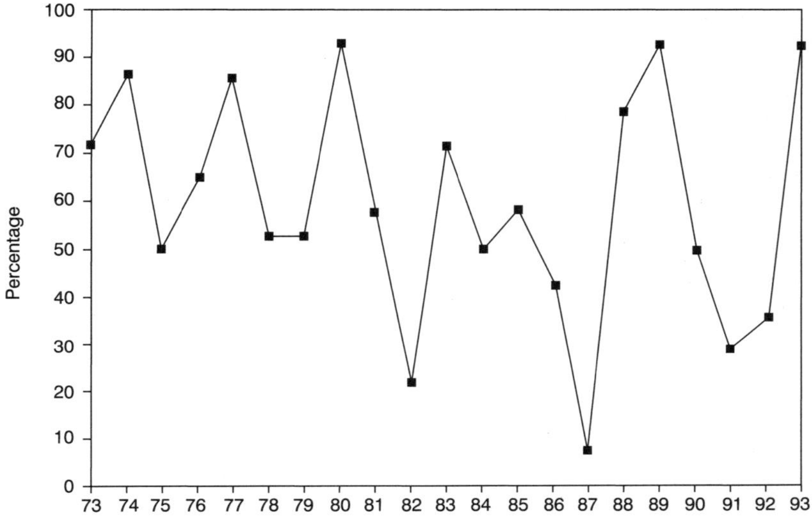

Figure 5.9 Proportion of the estimated indices indicating a trade liberalization episode in Kenya, 1973–93

there was trade liberalization in 1973 and 1974; during the coffee boom in 1976–7; and in 1980–1, 1983, 1985, 1988–9 and 1993 and undoubtedly extending to 1994.

5.3 CREDIBILITY OF LIBERALIZATION EPISODES IN KENYA

There are three necessary conditions for a trade liberalization to be considered credible:

(1) macroeconomic compatibility;
(2) absence of systematic forecastability; and
(3) time consistency (Collier, Gunning and Greenaway, 1993).

Trade liberalization is likely to affect the balance of payments adversely by reducing the demand for money. An exogenous trade liberalization is therefore likely to be macro-incompatible unless accompanied by policies to reduce money supply and/or to increase money demand. Macroeconomic incompatibility may also be due to misguided fiscal, monetary and exchange rate policies as well as expectations of an adverse external shock.

Systematic forecastability, on the other hand, occurs when the government is perceived to follow an endogenous trade policy rule (that is, QRs are utilized to manage the balance of payments). In this case, a trade liberalization induced by a positive TOT shock is considered temporary unless the shock is taken to be permanent.

Time inconsistency may occur when the government is judged to be of the redistributive type and cannot credibly commit itself to a free trade policy (Reinikka, 1994b). In this case, the public anticipates that the government will subsequently have an incentive to impose quantitative restrictions or increase tariffs and to distribute the benefits to its favoured group or groups. Time inconsistency may also occur when there is uncertainty about whether the government is a true liberalizer or a redistributive one and whether it favours lasting or merely temporary reform. The government might, for example, adopt liberalization policies in order to get programme aid, after which it will revert to trade restrictions.

Time inconsistency might also occur when there are conflicting goals between the public and private sectors regarding government spending. The private sector, for example, might anticipate that the government will finance its expenditure through an inflation tax (seigniorage) once people increase their real cash balances. Lastly, there might be time inconsistency if policies are determined by a political process through a majority rule and there is uncertainty about the winners and losers from trade liberalization.

Credibility has a large influence on the sustainability of trade liberalization efforts. When a trade liberalization episode is perceived to be incredible, private agents increase consumption or accumulate speculative inventories of temporary cheap imports in anticipation of higher prices in the future. Producers may also defer investment or reallocation of resources from non-tradeables and importables to exportables (given their irreversibility) until uncertainty about the future trade policy is resolved (Rodrik, 1992).

The Early Trade Liberalization Episodes

Substantive work has already been done on the credibility of the main liberalization episodes in Kenya in the 1970s and 1980s. Reinikka (1994b), in particular, has undertaken a detailed study of the credibility of (1) the endogenous import liberalization induced by the coffee boom of 1976–1977; (2) the exogenous import liberalization episodes of the early 1980s, focusing on the 1980 episode and the rationalization of import licensing in 1982, leading to the trade liberalization episode of 1983; and (3) the exogenous trade liberalization episode of 1988–9.

Reinikka's main conclusions (1994b) are that the 1970s and 1980s trade liberalization episodes were not credible, hence they ended with reversals. In general, reversals were preceded by a decline in foreign exchange reserves; stockpiling of foreign exchange and import licences; increased imports placed in bonded houses and declared through customs; higher exchange rate premiums as the parallel market was increasingly utilized to access foreign exchange; increased credit from the financial system to fund these activities; and a declining investment as decisions were deferred to the future. The exception was the 1976–7 episode, which witnessed considerable investment in the manufacturing sector, suggesting that investors expected a reversal and a tightening of QRs.

Even though the exogenous trade liberalization episodes in the early 1980s were mainly implemented as part of the policy conditionalities of the World Bank under SAL 1 and SAL 2, they faced problems of macroeconomic incompatibility and probably time consistency as a new government had just taken over (in 1978) when they were initiated in 1980. The 1988–9 episode was also perceived to be macro-incompatible as aid flows contracted and compensating devaluation was delayed. However, the reversal of this episode was implicit, as the items on the restricted list remained unchanged up to mid-1991. Approval time lengthened substantially, however, and licences were often granted for smaller amounts than requested (UNDP/World Bank 1993).

The 1993–4 Trade Liberalization Episode

The reversal of the 1988–9 liberalization episode culminated in the suspension of all programme (BOP) support in November 1991, and this was only restored at the Paris Consultative Group (CG) meeting of November 1993. At this, and the following meeting in December 1994, a combined balance of payments support of about $390 m was pledged, provided Kenya continued progress in the implementation of economic and political reforms.

The 1993–4 episode had both exogenous and endogenous elements. The policies that underpinned the trade reforms (and which are discussed in Section 5.2) were largely exogenous and were agreed to with donors before and during the programme aid suspension.

These trade policies were clearly macro-incompatible, as suggested by the increase in the forex-C premiums before they were phased out, and by the reversal of policies on the inter-bank foreign exchange market and export retention accounts in March 1993. The parallel exchange rate premium also increased from 109 per cent in 1991 to 138 per cent in 1992 (World Bank, 1995).

These trade reforms were made macro-compatible by the adoption of a very tight monetary policy and a substantial improvement in the balance

Table 5.2 Balance of payments performance in Kenya, 1990–3

BOP accounts as a % of GDP f.c.	*1990*	*1991*	*1992*	*1993*	*1994*
Current account	−6.3	−3.0	−1.4	2.1	1.8
Capital account:					
Private long-term	0.3	0.6	−0.2	−0.2	−0.7
Government long-term	1.2	1.2	−1.0	3.3	−2.0
Parastatal long-term	0.8	0.2	−1.2	−2.1	−1.8
Short-term	2.0	−0.2	−0.1	4.3	4.3
Total capital account	4.3	1.7	−2.4	7.3	−0.2
Overall balance	−2.0	−1.5	−3.9	9.4	1.6
Total monetary movements	2.0	1.5	0.0	−9.4	−1.6
Errors and omissions	−0.0	−0.2	−0.1	0.1	0.1

Source: Kenya, *Statistical Abstract and Economic Survey*, various issues.

of payments in 1993 and to a lesser extent in 1994. While the capital account in general worsened in 1991–2 following the aid embargo (Table 5.2), it improved dramatically in 1993. The current account also improved in 1993–4.

The improvement in the capital account arose from several sources.[14] First was reduced capital flight, as the incentive to over-invoice imports and under-invoice exports in order to retain foreign exchange abroad had diminished due to the introduction of the trade liberalization measures described above. There was also reduced demand for a parallel market channel as there were no longer binding restrictions on the flow of foreign exchange in the open market. Reduced capital flight, for example, was reflected in a decline in cross-border bank deposits by Kenyan residents, as the data in Table 5.3 show.

Second is increased private and official capital inflows (see Table 5.2). The largest increase was in short-term capital inflows repatriated to take advantage of the depreciation of the shilling and the subsequent relatively high returns on treasury bills and bank deposit rates that the country experienced in the second half of 1993. The high rates followed the application of a very tight monetary policy to mop up excess liquidity generated by the massive increase in money supply in the run-up to the December 1992 General Elections. The increase in short-term inflows continued to 1994, despite the appreciation of the Kenya shilling and the reduction in interest rates to more normal levels (see Figure 5.10). The introduction of the inter-bank market in August 1992 was accompanied by a large depreciation of the exchange rate, which reached a record low of Ksh81 to the US$ in July 1993 (compared to an official rate of Ksh36 at the

Table 5.3 Cross-border bank deposits by Kenyan residents, 1991–3

	Dec. 1991	*1992*				*1993*			
		Mar.	*Jun.*	*Sept.*	*Dec.*	*Mar.*	*Jun.*	*Sept.*	*Dec.*
$US bn	2.35	2.35	2.52	2.41	2.22	2.26	2.18	2.17	2.08

Source: IMF, *International Financial Statistics* (June 1994)

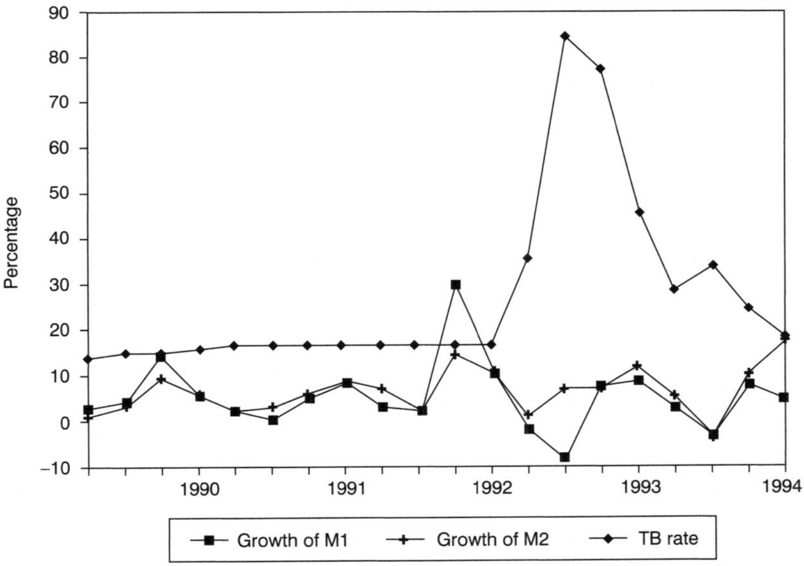

Figure 5.10 Treasury Bill rate and growth of money supply in Kenya, 1990:1–1994:4

end of the previous year). The Kenya shilling subsequently substantially appreciated, reaching a peak of Ksh35 to the US$ at the end of October 1994, about the exchange rate prevailing before the adoption of reforms two years earlier. By early 1995, the exchange rate had stabilized at about Ksh45 to the US$.

Third, the capital account was 'boosted' by the accumulation of external debt servicing arrears and by some unfreezing of programme loan disbursements in 1993.

The improvement of the current account balance was a result of increased foreign exchange earnings from exports of coffee, tea, horticultural produce and manufactured goods. The volume of all categories of exports substantially increased in 1993–4 (except crude materials in 1993 and mineral fuels in 1994), perhaps due to earlier depreciation of the Kenya shilling, and an increase in their international prices. The price of coffee in particular soared following a frost in Brazil that reduced its harvest. The price rose from an average of US$ 73 in 1992 to US$181 in 1994. Another important source of foreign exchange earnings was tourism and sale of goods and services due to the turmoil in neighbouring countries, particularly Somalia and Rwanda.

The substantial government and short-term capital inflows and the good performance in the export and tourism sectors led in 1993–4 to surpluses 'larger that ever previously recorded in both current and overall accounts' (*Kenya Economic Survey*, 1994). This was, however, accompanied by a low absorptive capacity for the BOP surpluses. There was a relatively low demand for imports, because of the earlier depreciation of the shilling and sluggish economic growth, which reduced per capita real incomes. Kenya's real economic growth plummeted in the 1990s to an average rate of only 1 per cent between 1991 and 1993 but recovered to a 3 per cent real growth rate in 1994. Reduced domestic consumption in turn caused a decline in the volume of intermediate and capital imports. High real interest rates also dampened demand and adversely affected the financing of imports.

Since these foreign exchange earnings are, to a large extent, temporary, the episode might *not* be credible and private agents would expect it to be reversed eventually. This is likely to be aggravated by the real appreciation of the shilling in late 1993 and 1994 with its adverse impact on exports.[15]

However, the episode may be sustained in the next few years before there is substantial pressure on foreign exchange reserves and before private agents pervasively adopt the speculative activities described above for the earlier episodes:

(1) coffee prices may remain buoyant for some time;
(2) recovery of import demand may be slow, as a result of slow economic growth; and
(3) resumption of programme aid after the 1993 and 1994 CG meetings has resulted in increased official capital inflows from bilateral donors and multinational institutions.

The government has also tried to improve its credibility by eliminating QRs and by making the Kenya shilling to a large extent convertible.[16]

Table 5.4 Indicators of performance in Kenya's external sector

Indices	*1990*	*1991*	*1992*	*1993*	*1994*
Export quantum:					
Total exports	122	126	126	148	167
Non-oil exports	143	135	141	164	196
Export price:					
Total exports	169	216	244	438	450
Non-oil exports	178	227	254	483	486
Import quantum:					
Total imports	119	111	107	116	144
Non-oil imports	126	119	114	113	159
Import price:					
All imports	238	265	307	496	445
Non-oil imports	287	318	359	611	536
Average coffee:					
KSh per 50kg bag	1932	2598	2641	6247	8201
Exchange rate per $	24	28	36	68	45
$US per 50kg bag	81	93	73	93	182

Note: 1982=100 for all the indices.

Source: Kenya, *Economic Survey*, various sources.

This implies that fiscal and monetary policies have to be compatible not only with trade policy but also with the exchange rate, hence requiring better fiscal discipline. An increase in macroeconomic imbalances will be reflected not just in a reduction in foreign exchange reserves, but in depreciation of the nominal exchange rate and inflation also. A convertible currency helps lessen the foreign reserves loss during a trade liberalization and hence strengthens credibility.

Among the published diagnostics utilized by Reinikka (1994b) to indicate non-credibility of trade liberalization episodes are: stockpiling of foreign exchange and import licences; an increase in the exchange rate premium as the parallel market is increasingly utilized to access foreign exchange (these two are no longer applicable because of the almost complete liberalization of the forex regime); a decline in foreign exchange reserves; increased credit from the financial system to fund these activities; an increase in imports of durable goods; and a decline in investment especially in the manufacturing sector as decisions are deferred to the future.

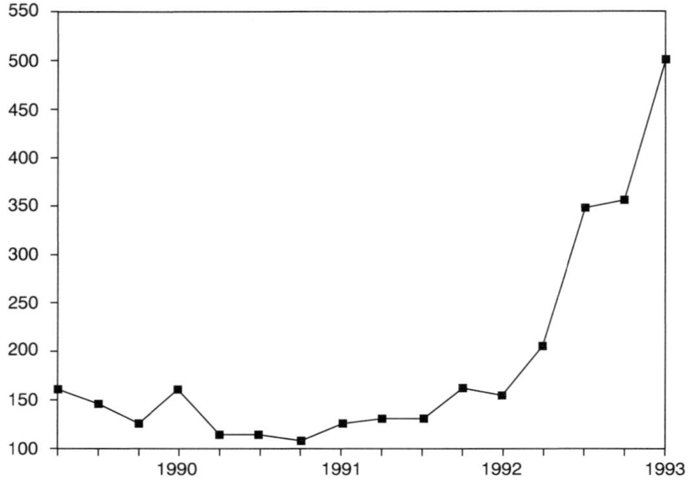

Figure 5.11 Foreign exchange reserves at 1982 import prices, 1990:1–1993:4

Table 5.5 Commercial bank credit to private sector (in KShs m. at 1986 prices)

	1991	*1992*	*1993*	*1994*
	24 164	23 902	17 282	17 974

Source: Kenya, *Economic Survey*, various years.

Foreign exchange reserves increased in real terms in 1993 as seen in Figure 5.11. Gross foreign exchange reserves remained above the four-month legally mandated import cover, although they declined from 6.5 in 1993 to 5.3 months' worth of import cover in 1994 (CBK, February 1995).[17] Similarly, real commercial bank credit to the private sector declined in 1993, with some recovery in 1994, reflecting the tight policies pursued in this period Table 5.5.

Second, non-fuel imports remained fairly constant in 1993 but increased substantially in 1994, although growth varied from one category of imports to another, with only miscellaneous manufactured articles increasing in both years (Tables 5.4 and 5.6). In 1993, the other increases were in imports of beverages and tobacco, chemicals, and manufactured goods.

Table 5.6 Imports quantum indices, 1990–3

	1990	*1991*	*1992*	*1993*	*1994*
Food and live animals	217	148	211	135	560
Beverages and tobacco	62	85	85	121	118
Crude materials, inedible	158	176	194	179	177
Mineral fuels	104	94	91	123	110
Animal and vegetable oils	150	154	176	138	176
Chemicals	97	113	115	131	124
Manufactured goods	108	112	99	114	114
Machinery and transport equipment	135	95	92	84	111
Miscellaneous manufactured articles	98	114	112	118	153

Note: 1982=100

Source: Kenya, *Economic Survey*, various years.

Table 5.7 Real GFCF in Kenya's private sector (K£ m.)

	1990	*1991*	*1992*	*1993*	*1994*
Total	398.77	398.49	383.36	391.29	434.41
Manufacturing	130.90	111.47	96.36	103.61	116.04

Source: Kenya, *Economic Survey*, various years.

In 1994 the other increases were in the imports of food and live animals, animal and vegetable oils and machinery and transport equipment. These imports could have been utilized to build inventories. In the field survey, finished goods and raw materials inventories of reporting firms increased by 15.8 per cent and 14.4 per cent, respectively, in 1994. The observed changes in the importation pattern in 1993 and 1994, however, suggest they were in response to fundamental factors rather than due to speculation.

Third, the real gross fixed capital formation (GFCF) by Kenya's private sector increased by 1.5 per cent in 1993 and by 11.0 per cent in 1994. GFCF by the manufacturing sector also increased in 1993 and 1994 after a decline in 1990–2 as the data in Table 5.7 show.[18]

From these diagnostics, it does not seem that there were significant speculative activities by private economic agents in 1993 and 1994. In the field survey, three-quarters of the respondents expected the number of their full-time employees to increase within one year and about a half

Table 5.8 Business expectations: anticipated change in key variables (%)

	One Year from now				*Three years from now*			
	Same	*Lower*	*Higher*	*Don't know*	*Same*	*Lower*	*Higher*	*Don't know*
Full-time employees	43.5	5.2	32.6	18.7	17.4	13.0	37.0	32.6
Local lending rates	15.2	21.7	28.3	34.8	8.7	19.6	19.3	52.4
The inter-bank exchange rate	13.0	28.3	21.7	37.0	6.5	19.7	10.9	62.9
The parallel exchange rate	6.5	8.7	10.9	73.9	4.3	2.2	2.2	91.3
Business tax rates	30.4	28.3	6.5	34.8	19.6	23.9	17.4	39.1
Personal tax rates	39.1	41.3	4.3	15.3	15.2	26.1	17.4	41.3
Inflation	15.2	28.3	32.6	23.9	10.9	15.2	26.1	47.8
Import duties on inputs	39.1	19.4	8.7	32.8	17.4	13.0	10.9	58.7
Import duties on consumer goods	39.1	15.2	8.7	37.0	13.0	15.2	13.0	58.8
Export duties	43.5	4.3	0.0	52.2	43.5	4.3	0.0	52.2

Source: Author's survey.

expected this to occur in three years' time. As shown in Table 5.8, the majority either had no clear expectations or did not expect adverse developments in the main policy variables. According to the field survey, of those who expected changes in the labour code, investment code, exchange rate policy, bank lending policy, the import tariff schedule and the business tariff schedule, the personal income schedule, and reductions in regional trade barriers, only in the last case did more than 10 per cent of the respondents expect the change to affect adversely their output or the number of full-time employees within to three years. However, as suggested by the decline in foreign exchange reserves in 1994, this situation may change in the near future.

5.4 IMPACTS OF TRADE LIBERALIZATION EPISODES IN KENYA

Trade liberalizations are undertaken on the assumption that they will ultimately improve exports and economic growth. This section therefore investigates whether there were discernible causal links between trade liberalization and economic performance, focusing on exports, output and total factor productivity growth. We also briefly assess the likely impact on the government budget.

Table 5.9 The trend growth in the volume of the various export components, 1964–93

	(%)
Food and live animals	4.5
Beverages and tobacco	7.6
Crude materials, inedible	1.1
Mineral fuels	−2.8
Animal and vegetable oils	−2.5
Chemicals	−0.7
Manufactured goods	1.3
Machinery and transport equipment	−6.6
Miscellaneous manufactured goods	0.6

Source: *Kenya, Economic Survey*, various years.

Trade Policy and Export Performance

The performance of Kenya's export sector has been poor in the last three decades. Exports grew much more slowly than the economy. While the real GDP grew at an average rate of 4.7 per cent over 1964–93, the trend growth in the volume of total and non-oil exports (estimated by regressing the log of exports quantity index on the time trend) was only 1.6 per cent and 2.9 per cent, respectively. Table 5.9 shows the trend growth in the volume of the various export components.

Faster economic growth requires substantial restructuring by increasing exports, savings and investment. This was not the case in Kenya. The structure of Kenya's final demand has changed little. As the data in Table 5.10 show, there were no marked shifts in the shares of exports (except 1993), savings or investment. Aggregate demand is still characterized by a large share of consumption and a low share of savings.

Trade liberalization is also usually expected to lead to a diversification of exports as new markets are discovered and new products become exportable. Dynamic effects during the liberalization process caused by resource flows into these new exporting firms can increase creativity and innovation, which in turn results in further diversification.

Coffee, tea and other agricultural products are still the dominant commodity exports, and primary products account for more than half of Kenya's total merchandise exports (see Tables 5.11 and 5.12). Petroleum exports are also important, although their importance has decreased over time. Their net contribution to forex earnings is also small, with the country mainly re-exporting petroleum products after processing. Tourism is an

Table 5.10 Structure of Kenya's final demand, 1970–93

% share in GDP	*1970*	*1992*	*1993*
Private consumption	60	68	66
Gross investment	24	17	16
General government consumption	16	16	13
Gross domestic savings	24	15	21
Exports of goods and services	30	27	42

Source: World Bank, *World Development Report* (1994/95).

important invisible export and since 1987 has overtaken coffee as the main foreign exchange earner in the country.

Exports of manufactures are relatively unimportant. The import-substitution industrialization strategy pursued earlier was not successful in increasing them. The share of manufactured exports declined drastically from 40 per cent in 1964 to 7.5 per cent in the mid-1980s; in the mid-1990s it comprised about 15 per cent of total exports. The decline in share of manufactured exports has been attributed to several causes. Exports to neighbouring countries declined, especially to Tanzania, where the volume of imports from Kenya has not yet reached the levels attained before the break-up of the East African Community in 1977. Other reasons are the growth in domestic demand for such products as paper; the anti-export bias of the trade policies; and supply constraints, especially the intermittent shortage of foreign exchange to purchase intermediate inputs (Lewis and Sharpley, 1988; Siggel, 1990).

Horticultural exports are an exception in Kenya's export performance. They rose from 4 per cent of total exports in 1970–4 to 11 per cent in 1985–9, with virtually all the increase going to industrial country markets (UNDP/World Bank, 1993). This is a sub-sector that could benefit from more directly targeted policies. Dealing with a perishable product, the industry faced many problems in the 1980s such as the high cost (and low quality) of packaging material because of import controls, and inadequate handling, cooling, storage and freight facilities.

This left Kenya's exports vulnerable to changes in terms of trade. The TOT index declined from 114 in the mid-1970s to 71 in 1990, though it did not increase to 86 in 1993. While the exports of coffee and tea have increased in volume, their prices either generally declined or remained stagnant. Both the volume and the price of petroleum exports declined in this period. Manufactures, which tend to have more robust prices, comprised only a small share of total exports, and therefore could not counteract the stagnation in the prices of the other products.

Table 5.11 Share in total exports by broad economic categories (%)

	1974–78	*1979–83*	*1984–88*	*1989–93*
Food and beverages	48.8	50.3	62.3	56.5
Industrial supplies	23.2	18.4	17.5	21.7
Fuels and lubricants	20.5	26.8	14.5	13.0
Machinery and capital equipment	1.5	0.4	0.4	0.7
Transport equipment	1.1	0.3	0.4	0.5
Consumer goods (nes)	4.9	3.8	4.9	7.5
Other goods (nes)	0.1	0.0	0.0	0.0
Total exports	*100.0*	*100.0*	*100.0*	*100.0*

Source: Kenya, *Economic Survey* (various issues).

Table 5.12 Quantities and prices of selected exports

Quantities	*1974–78*	*1979–83*	*1984–88*	*1989–93*
Coffee (tonnes)	79 340	86 994	103 780	92 624
Tea (tonnes)	63 304	84 905	121 357	172 039
Petroleum (million l.)	1 477	1 235	774	709
Canned pineapples (tonnes)	29 276	41 574	–	–
Beans and peas (tonnes)	15 541	31 261	n.a.	n.a.
Horticulture (tonnes)	–	–	154 178*	182 342
Export prices ($US/unit)				
Coffee (unroasted) (kg)	3.03	2.95	2.94	1.86
Tea (kg)	1.61	1.81	1.87	1.75
Petroleum (1000 l.)	92.73	226.20	175.03	177.55
Canned pineapples (kg)	0.53	0.63	0.67	–
Beans and peas (kg)	0.35	0.36	0.36	–
Horticulture (kg)	–	–	0.79†	0.87

Notes: * Average for 1987–93
† The data are for 1988.
n.a. = not available

Source: Kenya, *Economic Survey* (various issues).

Table 5.13 Destination of Kenya's exports

	1974–78	*1979–83*	*1984–88*	*1989–93*
Western Europe	43.2	40.7	48.9	43.1
Africa	29.3	28.0	25.1	28.4
Far East and Australia	7.1	10.8	9.7	12.3
USA	4.7	4.7	6.2	3.8
Middle East	2.3	4.0	3.4	3.0
Eastern Europe	1.8	1.1	1.1	0.5
Canada	1.6	0.8	0.8	0.8
Others	10.0	9.7	4.7	8.0
Total exports	*100.0*	*100.0*	*100.0*	*100.0*

Source: Kenya, *Economic Survey* (various issues).

There has also been little market diversification of Kenya's exports. Western Europe is still the largest single market, and has accounted for 40–50 per cent of Kenya's exports, followed by Africa (particularly Uganda and Tanzania), the Far East and Australia, the United States, and the Middle East (Table 5.13). More than 90 per cent of manufactures exports are still sold in developing country markets, most of them in Africa and the Middle East. (In the field survey, all exporting firms sold in the PTA/COMESA area, 19 per cent in the rest of Africa, 7 per cent in the Middle East, 15 per cent in Europe, 7 per cent in Asia and only 4 per cent in the United States.)

UNDP/World Bank (1993) and other studies attribute the overall poor performance of the export sector to domestic rather than external constraints, with incentives biased against exports, especially manufactured exports. The protective trade policies pursued in Kenya, by hindering the development of a more competitive environment, have produced a predominantly monopolistic/oligopolistic industrial market structure where firms earn large profits selling in the domestic markets and hence have little incentive to seek external markets. Our field survey found the main source of competition in the domestic market was domestic firms (67.4 per cent), with imports (23.9 per cent) far behind. Few firms adjusted their prices to the price of imports (8.7 per cent) or those of other domestic competitors (6.5 per cent). Many adjusted them as mark-up over cost (71.7 per cent), perhaps an indication of lack of competition. These firms to a large extent sold their products to end-users (76.1 per cent) relative to wholesalers (65.2 per cent) and retailers (43.5 per cent).

Kenya's industrial sector in the past relied heavily on domestic demand and import substitution, which clearly limited the scope of the industrial strategy. The World Bank (1990), for example, estimates the bias against non-traditional, non-oil exports and finds that it was 13 per cent more profitable in shilling terms (ignoring the impact of QRs) in 1980 and 10 per cent in 1989 to produce one dollar's worth of an import substitute than one dollar's worth of non-traditional exportable. Attempts at trade liberalization have not been credible and have been characterized by reversals. Trade liberalization policies have not been sequenced well or implemented adequately. Tariffication of QRs and reduction of tariffs were also undermined by loopholes in the tariff law, import duty avoidance, and illegal importation, and trade liberalization has been undermined by large budget deficits, which have averaged more than 5 per cent for most of the last two decades.

The impact of trade liberalization on exports is likely to depend on the nature of the accompanying policies, particularly a high and stable real exchange rate, compatible fiscal and monetary policies, and low distortions in factor markets (Nogues and Gulati, 1994). It is therefore difficult to verify empirically the causal linkages between trade liberalization and export performance *per se* – not least because, with an endogenous trade policy rule, causality may go both ways, with an export boom facilitating trade liberalization. To the extent that the economy became more liberalized from the early 1970s as suggested by the various indexes computed in Section 5.2, however, a worse export performance might have been prevented.

Using recursive least-squares (Hendry, 1989), we investigated for structural breaks in the volume of manufactured exports (SITC 5–8) from their trend in 1972–93 using the one-step Chow Test.[19] As seen in Figure 5.12, exports of chemicals (paints, enamels, soap and soap preparations, insecticides, and so on) increased significantly (at the 5 per cent level) from the trend during 1975–7. Exports of manufactured goods significantly deviated from the trend in 1974 (positively), in 1977–8 (negatively) and in 1993 (positively). Exports of machinery and transport equipment significantly increased in 1973, decreased in 1977–8 and 1983–4, and increased in 1993. Lastly, exports of miscellaneous manufactured goods decreased in 1975–7 and 1992 and increased in 1993. These results suggest that manufactured exports in general declined during the trade liberalization induced by the coffee boom of 1976–7 following the break-up of EAC and the temporary closure of the border with Tanzania, whereas they increased during the 1973–4 and 1993 trade liberalizations. The 1993–4 trade liberalization episode was particularly good for manufactured exports, although other extraneous factors were important.[20]

There were *no* significant structural breaks from the trend in the exports of food and live animals nor with crude materials (inedible) using the one-step Chow Test in the period 1973–93. There was however increased exports of beverages and tobacco from the trend in 1980, 1983,

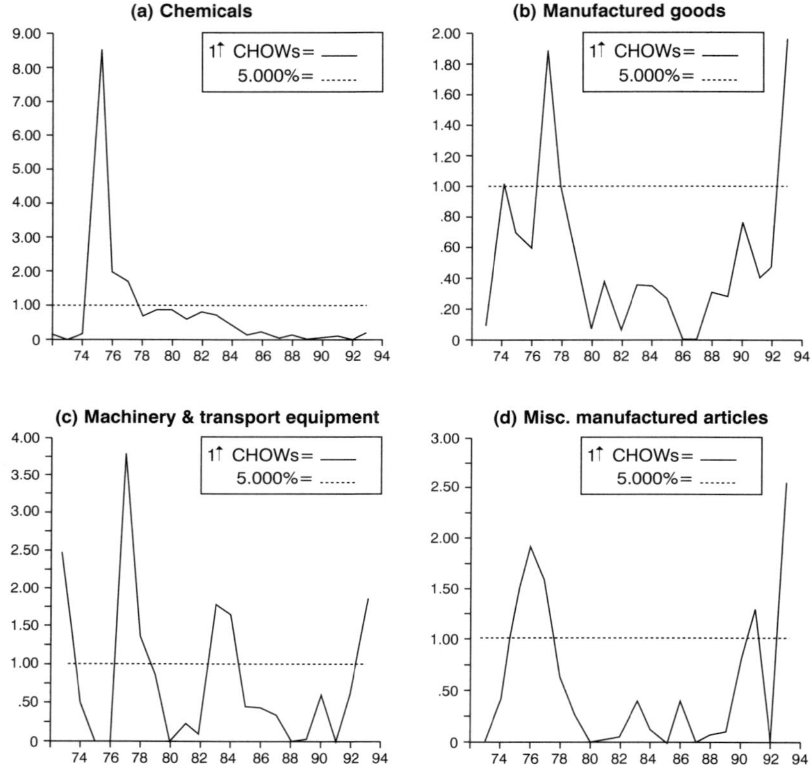

Figure 5.12 One-step Chow tests of structural breaks from trend in volume of Kenya's manufactured exports, 1974–94

1985–6 and 1993; mineral fuel exports in 1974 and 1976; and animal and vegetables oils in 1993. These are periods that nearly all the diagnostics in Section 5.1 identify as trade liberalization episodes.

Trade Liberalization, Output, Productivity and Employment

We investigate here whether the various episodes of trade liberalization had a discernible positive impact on economic performance in Kenya's manufacturing sector. This sector is likely to have a faster response as labour and capital are reallocated from non-tradeables and importables to exportables.

The positive impact of trade liberalization on total factor productivity and economic growth is attributed to a number of factors (Khan and Villanueva, 1990). First, trade liberalization permits a country to specialize more in those products in which it has a comparative advantage. The potential gains in this case are realizable when previous policies have discouraged export production (in support of import substitution) through taxation and other disincentives to generate a domestic price structure that is less favourable to exports than the international price structure (Helleiner, 1992). Second, trade liberalization enables a country to escape from the confines of a small domestic market. The larger market creates new investment opportunities and enables the exploitation of scale economies, learning-by-doing effects and increased capacity utilization, hence raising productivity and growth. Third, trade liberalization enhances economic growth by reducing X-inefficiency as domestic producers face more foreign competition, which induces them to adopt more efficient techniques of production and technological catch-up. This factor is postulated to be particularly important in developing countries, which have small domestic markets in terms of the purchasing power of their citizens, hence limiting investment opportunities and the exploitation of the various 'externalities'.

Many of these arguments cut both ways, however, with the net impact of trade liberalization on productivity depending on the specifics of demand shifts, ease of entry and exit, and the nature of foreign markets (Tybout, 1991). Uncertainty generated by more openness may also adversely affect productivity, particularly when liberalization policies are perceived not to be stable or credible.

Kenya has a small manufacturing sector that employed only about 14 per cent of the wage labour force in the early 1990s. It expanded faster than the rest of the economy, however, increasing the quantity index of manufacturing production by about threefold and the share of manufacturing in GDP from 10 per cent in the early 1960s to 13 per cent of GDP in the early 1990s.

The growth of the sector drastically slowed down in the 1980s and early 1990s (to 4–5 per cent per annum) after a rapid growth in the 1960s and 1970s. One cause of the decline in economic growth was a reduction of investment and its productivity. Until the reforms of 1992–3, this was attributed to increased political instability, cumbersome bureaucracy, price controls, constraints on repatriation of dividends, and shortages of foreign exchange that made acquisition of imported inputs uncertain or irregular (Friedrich-Naumann-Stiftung, 1992). Another factor includes reduced opportunities for easy consumer-goods-orientated import substitution.

This chapter has investigated whether total factor productivity growth (tfpg) was correlated with changes in trade liberalization indexes, where

Table 5.14 Factor productivity growth in Kenya's manufacturing sector (%)

	Labour	*Capital*	*tfpg*	*Total*
1965–73	3.8	5.1	2.7	11.6
	(32.8)	(44.0)	(23.3)	(100.0)
1974–83	3.3	3.2	0.7	7.2
	(45.8)	(44.4)	(9.7)	(100.0)
1984–93	1.9	1.0	1.5	4.4
	(43.2)	(22.8)	(34.1)	(100.0)

tfpg was measured by the difference between total growth and the combined contributions of the factor inputs. Manufacturing industries are postulated to have a well-behaved neoclassical production function of the form $y = y(A, L, K)$ where y = value-added; A = state of technology; L = labour; and K = physical capital. The growth equation can therefore be derived as:

$$\Delta \log y = A_0 + A_1 \, \Delta \log L + A_2 \, \Delta \log K + u$$

where A_1 and A_2 are the elasticities of output with respect to labour and capital, respectively, and u is a stochastic error term. This equation was estimated over 1965–93 and gave only one structural break in 1974 (at 5 per cent, based on Chow's one-step test using Hendry's recursive least-squares), when there was a drastic decline in growth following the first oil shock.[21]

Table 5.14 shows that productivity growth in the sector was dominated by labour and capital in the first two decades of independence (1965–83) and by labour and tfpg in the third.[22] Total factor productivity growth declined substantially in the second decade from about 2.7 per cent in 1965–73 to 0.7 per cent in 1974–83 but recovered to 1.5 per cent in 1984–93. The results also show that while the contribution of labour was relatively stable, that of capital declined substantially in the last three decades; this accounted for the non-significant capital coefficient in the growth equation.

Many variables have been investigated in the literature as potential correlates to tfpg. These have included growth of the economy, degree of exports orientation, import intensity, industrial concentration and level of protection (Tybout, 1991). There are several reasons why total factor productivity growth is likely to be positively correlated with growth in value added (the so-called Verdoorn's law). Faster growth permits the exploitation of scale economies, better use of factor inputs and absorption of new technologies through investment acceleration.

Apart from economic growth, many of the other variables are trade policy correlates. We therefore investigated whether changes in the various measures of the implicit tariff index were correlated with tfpg, given the sector's economic growth. None of the estimated equations showed any significant correlation between tfpg and the implicit tariff index over the period 1973–93.[23]

It is not surprising that changes in the indexes of trade liberalization did not have a significant impact on the tfpg of Kenya's manufacturing sector, given the poor performance of the sector in the last two decades. Trade liberalization did not induce a substantial change in the orientation of the manufacturing sector towards production for external markets to create a more balanced and diversified industrial structure.

These results, however, do not imply that trade liberalization had an adverse impact on the manufacturing sector. One of the reasons for resistance to trade liberalization is the concern that price changes brought about by trade reform would have negative effects on output in the industries facing stiff competition in the external market. Hence if real output grew more slowly in sectors where the quantity of imports rose more, it could be concluded that opening the economy would have negative (though temporary) effects on growth, depending on the flexibility and mobility factors of production (Coes, 1991).

We therefore tested whether more rapid growth in the quantity of imports (m) was associated with a smaller increase in real output (q) in the counterpart domestic industries. Of the four industries considered, the correlation between changes in real manufacturing output (nominal industrial output deflated by the domestic price index computed in Section 5.2 above) and the counterpart changes in the imports quantity index was positive in three industries and negative in one.[24] In machinery and transport equipment, the coefficient was also significant at the 10 per cent level, suggesting that this industry particularly benefited from increased access to imports through trade liberalization. Only in the case of miscellaneous manufactured goods is there some evidence that increased importation adversely affected real manufacturing output in the study period.

There was a drastic decline in wage employment growth in Kenya's manufacturing sector in the 1980s. We therefore analysed the correlation between employment in Kenya's large firms and the volume of counterpart imports over the period 1973–90. In chemicals and manufactured goods, the correlation is positive and significant at least at the 10 per cent level, suggesting that employment in these industries benefited from increased imports growth following trade liberalization.[25] This is consistent with the views that trade may open growth opportunities that, when used, increase labour demand. On the other hand, machinery and transport equipment and miscellaneous manufactured goods have negative coefficients that are significant at 5 per cent and 20 per cent respectively, indicating that they were adversely affected by import growth.

However, with chemicals and manufactured goods accounting for an average 83 per cent of total employment in the study period, these results suggest that trade liberalization may increase employment. This is consistent with the results of the field survey. Employment of full-time workers increased during the trade liberalization of 1992–4, although there was a large differential between exporting and non-exporting firms. Exporting firms increased employment by 20.7 per cent and non-exporting firms by only 2.1 per cent.

Trade Liberalization and the Government Budget

Trade liberalization involving tariffication of QRs can be expected to enhance tariff collections. Typically, however, a reduction of high protective tariffs can be expected to reduce import tax receipts. With many tariff reforms undertaken during periods of stabilization and fiscal austerity, the potential loss of tax revenues from lowering tariff rates is commonly perceived to be an important constraint on tariff reform.

There are three reasons why tariff revenues will not decrease one-for-one with decreases in nominal tariff rates (Pritchett and Sethi, 1994):

(1) to the extent that an import has some positive elasticity with respect to the tariff rate, the base of the tax will increase with a reduction in the tariff rate;
(2) the value of imports reported for the collection of import duties will increase with a decline in the tariff rate due to the reduced incentives for misdeclaration and smuggling; and
(3) the value of duty-exempted imports is likely to reduce with lower nominal tariff rates as the latter increase the share of non-exempt imports and reduce the incentives to lobby for exemptions. There is also less incentive to abuse the system by diverting imports to the exempt channel.

Using 1987 data for Kenya, Pritchett and Sethi (1994) show that there is only a weak relationship between the collected and official tariff rates. The collected rate increases much less than one-for-one with increases in the official rate. The maximum coefficient of the linear equation was only 0.49 with an R-squared of 0.25. The impact coefficient also declined as the official rate increased, with the coefficient estimated at 0.58 for a tariff below 60 per cent but a coefficient of 0.25 for a tariff above.

This suggests that reduction of nominal tariffs, especially from high levels, may have only a minimal impact on import tax revenues, especially

Table 5.15 Summary statistics of collected tariff rates by level of official rates in Kenya

(1) Official rate	*(2) No. of items*	*(3) Collected rate*	*(4) Coefficient of variation of (3)*
20	331	5	194
30	950	9	156
40	435	20	101
50	429	26	106
60	206	43	92
80	306	31	95
100	108	36	102

Source: Pritchett and Sethi (1994).

if this is accompanied by tighter procedures in assessing import values, granting exemptions and collecting revenue.

As can be seen in Table 5.15, collected rates are lower for items with higher tariff than for those with moderate tariffs. Moving high-tariff items to lower rates may actually increase import duty revenues if the collection performance at the lower rates is attained.

5.5 TRADE LIBERALIZATION IN KENYA: UNILATERAL, REGIONAL OR MULTILATERAL?

This section examines regional and multilateral trade arrangements and the extent to which Kenya's trade liberalization efforts were undertaken unilaterally. This is done briefly because some of these issues are discussed in detail in the regional case-studies elsewhere in this volume.

Kenya has been active in regional trade arrangements in conjunction with bodies such as the OAU and ECA (Ikiara, 1988). From 1964 until its collapse in 1977, Kenya, Uganda and Tanzania made up what was the East African Community. Among other achievements, members shared common services such as posts, telecommunications, railways, harbours and customs, and administered a common external tariff by which members enjoyed lower tariffs except for a few products to protect domestic industries. Until 1966, the members also shared a common currency and harmonized their monetary policies.

Kenya later participated in the formation of and joined the Preferential Trade Area for Eastern and Southern Africa (PTA), which was launched in July 1984. The objective of PTA was to encourage the growth of regional

Table 5.16 Share of Kenya's external trade (%)

	Exports				*Imports*			
	1985	*1990*	*1992*	*1994*	*1985*	*1990*	*1992*	*1994*
PTA/COMESA	22.0	16.0	20.1	37.1	1.5	2.8	2.8	2.4
Rest of Africa	7.3	5.7	6.8	7.5	0.5	0.2	0.4	11.3
Total	*100.0*	*100.0*	*100.0*	*100.0*	*100.0*	*100.0*	*100.0*	*100.0*

Source: Kenya, *Economic Survey* (various issues).

trade through reduction in tariff and non-tariff barriers as well as harmonization of fiscal and monetary policies. This initiative was extended to the Common Market for Eastern and Southern Africa (COMESA) in November 1993, with the objective of transforming PTA into a common market. There has also been some recent effort by Kenya, Uganda and Tanzania to revive the East African Community.

The operation of PTA/COMESA has not significantly improved Kenya's trade within the region except for (as discussed earlier) exports in 1993–4 as Table 5.16 shows. In the field survey, all exporting firms sold in the region but few imported from the region. Only about a third of the reporting respondents said there were barriers to exporting and a quarter said there were barriers to importing within the region, and that there were would be more intra-regional trade if these barriers were removed. Another 60.9 per cent said that it was easy to establish links within the region and that they were competitive with other firms with respect to labour costs (93.5 per cent), availability of capital (78.3 per cent) and production costs (86.2 per cent). The main barriers to exports were high tariffs (53.3 per cent), export-licensing arrangements (50 per cent), and others (72.7 per cent) such as damage of exports *en route*, pre-shipment inspection, restrictions on re-exports, and so on. The main constraints to importing from within the region were tariffs (50 per cent) and others (72.7 per cent) such as importation logistics, poor product quality and reliability, restrictions on certain types of imports such as scrap metal, and poor infrastructure. One major reason for the little intra-PTA/COMESA trade is to the limited diversity of the products that members produce.

Kenya is also a member of the various multilateral organizations that promote trade, such as GATT/WTO, the Lomé Convention and the United Nations Conference on Trade and Development (UNCTAD). Unlike the Lomé Convention and commodity agreements, Kenya has not actively participated in GATT either in terms of negotiators or in taking advantage of some of the preferences given to developing countries (Ikiara, 1988). No efforts, for example, have been made to inform or to encourage Kenyan producers about the GATT preferential trade arrangements or to encourage them to take advantage of the arrangements.

Since 1977, following the break-up of the East African Community, trade liberalization in Kenya has to a large extent been done unilaterally, although taking into account regional and multilateral trade arrangements. Tariff 'concessions' (of about 30 per cent), for example, are provided to imports from the PTA/COMESA area and regional considerations were cited for the abolition of the manufactures export subsidy in 1993. Unilateral trade liberalizations may facilitate regional integration and participation in multilateral trade arrangements in the future as trade barriers are gradually reduced (Collier and Gunning, 1994).

5.6 CONCLUSIONS

This chapter has analysed four issues. The first is the timing, magnitude and duration of trade liberalization episodes in Kenya. This is based on an account of policy changes and from various quantitative measures. The majority of the quantitative measures computed in the chapter suggests that Kenya experienced trade liberalization episodes in 1973 and 1974, during the coffee boom in 1976–7 and in 1980–1, 1983, 1985, 1988–9 and 1993, closely tying with the policy account.

The second is an analysis of the credibility of liberalization episodes. Since Reinikka (1994b) and others have done substantial work in this area, our analysis focuses on the 1993–4 liberalization episode. Given the government's poor past record with trade liberalization, this episode may *not* be credible, as it is based on temporary positive shocks on the balance of payments. For the reasons discussed in this chapter, however, the episode could be sustained for a time.

Third, the study investigates the economic impacts of these liberalization episodes on export performance, output, productivity, employment and the government budget. It is found that some trade liberalization episodes coincide with better export performance, although unidirectional causality cannot be inferred with better export performance perhaps facilitating trade liberalization under an endogenous trade policy rule. Trade liberalization does *not* seem to be positively correlated with productivity growth but is positively correlated with output and employment growth in the manufacturing sector.

Lastly, the chapter concludes that trade liberalization was largely unilaterally driven, although taking on board regional and multilateral trade arrangements.

Notes

1. The survey covered only Nairobi, but in all sub-sectors. The sampling frame was provided by the Kenya Industrial Research and Development Institute (KIRDI) *Directory of Kenya's Manufacturing Industries* (1993) and the Ministry of Commerce and Industry *Kenya Export Directory* (1993). Exporting and non-exporting firms were selected in proportion to the overall firm size distribution in the KIRDI directory.

   Among the characteristics of the sample firms, 73.9 per cent were unlisted companied, 8.7 per cent were listed companies 8.7 per cent were partnerships, and sole proprietorship and public and private joint companies each amounted to 4.3 per cent. Overall, 17.4 per cent were foreign-owned. Ethnically, 17.4 per cent were owned by Africans, 63 per cent by Asians, 17.4 per cent by Europeans and 2.2 per cent by Middle Easterners. About two-thirds of the firm owners were the founders of the business, the rest bought (4.3 per cent) or inherited it (30.4 per cent). About half of the owners had at least one other existing business of which 34.8 per cent were in manufacturing and 21.7 per cent were exporting. Exporting firms were deliberately over-sampled and constituted 65.2 per cent of the sample.
2. Parts of this narrative are based on Mwega (1994).
3. Kenya until 1977 participated in a customs union with Tanzania and Uganda, first under the East Africa, Common Services Organization and then under the East African Community (EAC). Under the latter import duties were assessed at about 30 per cent, with higher rates on luxury goods and lower (or zero) rates on intermediate and capital goods, though with specific and mixed duties to protect local industries such as footwear, textiles and cement (Barve, 1984).
4. The study by Phelps and Wasow, for example, showed that 43 per cent of their sample of consumer goods industries, 36 per cent of intermediate goods industries, and 18 per cent of capital goods industries had negative value-added at world prices.
5. Symbolically, for example, all persons leaving the country were required to declare and those returning to surrender foreign exchange to the monetary authorities effective from February 1974.
6. This paragraph is based on Mosley (1994).
7. In the industrial survey, 15.2 per cent of the firms said they had received export subsidies in the past; this is fewer than half the exporting firms.
8. In the industrial survey, 19.6 per cent of the firms said they received import duty drawbacks then and 17.4 per cent said they had received them in the past.
9. Three sets of published time series data are therefore required to calculate the base case implicit tariff index: (a) the value of manufacturing output; (b) the quantity index of industrial production; and (c) the import price index for manufactures weighted by their domestic shares.

   The manufacturing output data came from the Kenya *Statistical Abstract*. The latest data for this series were available for 1991, hence data for 1992 and 1993 were calculated by interpolation. It was also assumed that the share of food, beverages and tobacco in total manufacturing output in these two years is equal to that for 1991.

10. The justification for the error-correction model and the stability of the model are discussed in Mwega (1993).

    Real imports were measured by nominal imports deflated by the import price index; real income by nominal GDP deflated by the GDP deflator; and the relative import prices by the shilling import index deflated by the GDP deflator. The over-parameterized imports demand model was set at two lags for each of the explanatory variables including the lagged dependent variable.

11. The following are the results, with relative import prices treated as endogenous in both models.

Static model

Variable	*Coefficient*	*Std error*	*HCSE*	*T-value*	*Partial* r^2
Log RGDP	0.9048495	0.16276	0.24705	5.55951	0.5528
Log RPIM	–0.9570294	0.15021	0.18781	–6.37149	0.6189
Constant	4.1707704	1.21751	1.95059	3.42566	0.3195

$R^2 = 0.6237090$ $\sigma = 0.1272577$ $F(2, 25) = 20.72$ [0.0000] DW = 1.574

Error-correction model

Variable	*Coefficient*	*Std error*	*HCSE*	*T-value*	*Partial* r^2
ΔLog RIM 1	–0.5103762	0.18733	0.21446	–2.72450	0.2809
ΔLog RGDP	1.4785214	0.20691	2.33804	7.14580	0.7288
ΔLog RGDP 1	2.5586215	1.15885	1.58369	2.20790	0.2042
ΔLog RPIM	–0.6923938	0.16434	0.27328	–4.21310	0.4830
ECM 1	–0.5528559	0.18733	0.21619	–2.95123	0.3143
Constant T	4.1707704	1.21751	1.95059	3.42566	0.3195

$R^2 = 0.7824241$ $\sigma = 0.0984783$ $F(5, 19) = 13.67$ [0.0000] DW = 1.833

12. REER was derived from quarterly data averages. It was estimated as:

$$REERt = NEERt \, / \, (\sum Wjt^{*}CPIt/WPIjt)$$

where NEER was measured by:

$$NEERt = \sum Wjt^{*}Rt^{*}Ejt$$

where *Wjt* is current weights or trade shares of Kenya's 10 major partner countries at time *t*; *WPIjt* is the wholesale (producer) price index; *Rt* is the value of the one $US in terms of Kenya shillings; and *Ejt* is the value of one unit of currency of trading partner *j* in terms of the $US.

The sources of data were CBK publications (for *Wjt* and *CPIt*) and the IMF, *International Financial Statistics* (for *Rt*, *WPIjt* and *Ejt*).

13. We were unable to replicate Reinikka's results, with the hypothetical index highly sensitive to the data used.
14. See for example an article by Robert Shaw and David Ndii in the *Sunday Nation* of 9 October, 1994, titled: 'The Rising Shilling: What Causes, What Effects?'.
15. UNDP/World Bank (1993) find the real exchange rate the most important determinant of these exports. Other variables included were the relative price of exports; capacity utilization index measured by the ratio of actual to trend index of industrial production; and a dummy for 1986.
16. In June 1994, Kenya officially agreed to abide by the obligations of Article III of the IMF's Articles of Agreement to promote full convertibility of the shilling at least for current account transactions.
17. CBK and commercial bank foreign reserves (assets) were added and deflated by the import price index. The latter was linearly interpolated.

    Of the gross reserves, 3 and 2.1 months' worth of import cover were kept by CBK and commercial banks in 1994, from 2.8 and 3.5 months' worth of import cover, respectively, in 1993, to reflect the increased role of commercial banks in forex allocation.
18. The field survey suggested even faster investment growth. For the reporting firms, real GFCF (nominal GFCF deflated by CPI) increased by 3.5 per cent in 1991, 37.1 per cent in 1992, 96.8 per cent in 1993 and 22 per cent in 1994, perhaps reflecting the over-sampling of exporting firms.
19. This is calculated as:

    $$(t - T_1 - k)\ (RSS_t - RSS_{t-1})/RSS_{t-1}$$

    where T_1 is the size of the initialization sample and k is the number of explanatory variables. The test statistic is $F\ (1, t - T_1 - k)$ under the null of constant parameters, for $t = T_1 + M, \ldots, T_2$.

    Greenaway *et al.* (1994) criticize this approach on the grounds that any changes in economic performance following a trade liberalization are more likely to be modelled as a steady rather than a discrete transition. This is true for systematic and sustained trade liberalization where the impacts accumulate gradually over time. On the other hand, when trade liberalization is limited and is characterized by frequent reversals, as in the Kenyan case, it may be valid to assess the impact of a liberalization episode by looking for a structural break in the performance indicators.
20. In the field survey, the increase was dramatic. Of the 19 firms that reported dollar exports over the period 1992–4, exports increased by 59.2 per cent in 1993 and 152 per cent in 1994, increasing the share of their exported produce to 17 per cent. Ten of these firms were producing for the first time in this period.

    This was made possible by substituting domestic sales and utilizing the firms excess capacity. Of the reporting firms, exporting firms had less excess capacity (44.8 per cent) on a one-shift basis than non-exporting firms (61.1 per cent). Overall, 85 per cent of the firms were operating below capacity, and cited lack of demand (71.7 per cent) as the main reason for this, followed by high cost of credit (34.2 per cent), age of the machinery (18.4 per cent) and lack of credit facilities (18.4 per cent).

Exporting firms were also larger in size (average 173 workers and sales of Ksh265m.) than non-exporting firms (average 70 workers and sales of Ksh47m.).

21. Estimates of real capital stock data were derived from J. Vandemoortele, 'Kenya Data Compendium 1964–82', Institute for Development, Studies, University of Nairobi, occasional paper no. 44 (1984); and Long-range Planning Division, Ministry of Planning and National Development, 'Capital Stock Estimates for Kenya by Industry and Asset, 1972–1992', Technical Paper 92-02 (1992). The data for 1993 were estimated by the inventory method assuming a depreciation rate of 5.3 per cent for the manufacturing sector used in the latter publication.
22. Tfpq was estimated from the steady-state equation below. ΔLog y, ΔLog L and ΔLog K were lagged once and twice in the basic equation to even out business cycles and other shocks. The two lags were arbitrarily selected to conserve degrees of freedom.

$$\Delta \text{Log } y = \underset{(3.80)}{0.017} + \underset{(6.349)}{0.726} \, \Delta \text{Log } L + \underset{(8.680)}{0.539} \, \Delta \text{Log } K$$

$R^2 = 0.88 \quad DW = 1.68$

23. The results for the hypothetical implicit tariff index for example were:

Variable	*Coefficient*	*Std error*	*HCSE*	*T-value*	*Partial*	r^2
tfpg 1	–0.1656662	0.20095	0.43119	–0.82443	0.0384	
ΔLog y	0.2848091	0.20626	0.23368	1.38085	0.1009	
ΔLog *ITI*	0.0254475	0.04922	0.04586	0.51704	0.0155	
Constant	–0.0057967	0.01237	0.01089	–0.46875	0.0128	

$R^2 = 0.1045732 \quad \sigma = 0.0274332 \quad F(3, 17) = 0.66 \quad [.5868] \quad DW = 0.991$

Variable	*Coefficient*	*Std error*	*HCSE*	*T-value*	*Partial*	r^2
ΔLog y	0.1762446	0.15733	0.22591	1.12023	0.0652	
ΔLog *ITI*	0.0093003	0.04475	0.04921	0.20783	0.0024	
Constant	–0.0018540	0.01130	0.01154	–0.16404	0.0015	

$R^2 = 0.0687728 \quad \sigma = 0.0271880 \quad F(2, 18) = 0.66 \quad [0.5266] \quad DW = 0.959$

These results were somewhat supported by the field survey. There was no significant correlation between total factor productivity (with the production function estimated from gross output, market value of plant and equipment, and employment) and the share of exports in the 26 firms that gave data on the three variables.

Using Δ Log tfpg did not substantially change the results.

24. These results were:

Chemicals

$$\Delta \text{ Log } q = 11.690 + \underset{(0.802)}{0.162} \, \Delta \text{ Log } m \quad R^2 = 0.03$$

Manufactured goods nes

$$\Delta \text{ Log } q = 6.541 + \underset{(0.689)}{0.104} \, \Delta \text{ Log } m \quad R^2 = 0.03$$

Machinery and transport equipment

$$\Delta \text{ Log } q = 8.658 + \underset{(1.641)}{0.309} \, \Delta \text{ Log } m \quad R^2 = 0.14$$

Miscellaneous manufactured goods

$$\Delta \text{ Log } q = 31.833 - \underset{(1.225)}{0.358} \, \Delta \text{ Log } m \quad R^2 = 0.08$$

25. These are the results:

Chemicals

$$\Delta \text{ Log } L = 0.055 + \underset{(1.889)}{0.002} \, \Delta \text{ Log } m \quad R^2 = 0.19$$

Manufactured goods

$$\Delta \text{ Log } L = 0.047 + \underset{(1.714)}{0.001} \, \Delta \text{ Log } m \quad R^2 = 0.13$$

Machinery and transport equipment

$$\Delta \text{ Log } L = 0.004 - \underset{(1.857)}{0.003} \, \Delta \text{ Log } m \quad R^2 = 0.18$$

Miscellaneous manufactured goods

$$\Delta \text{ Log } L = 0.067 - \underset{(1.261)}{0.003} \, \Delta \text{ Log } m \quad R^2 = 0.09$$

References

Barve A. G. *The Foreign Trade of Kenya: A Perspective*. Transafrica Press, Nairobi, 1984.

Bruce C. A. and Ndii D. Framework for Macroeconomic Analysis (Applied to Kenya). Eastern Africa Department, Africa Regional Office, The World Bank, Working Paper Series 767, September 1991.

Central Bank of Kenya (CBK), Annual Report, various issues.

Central Bank of Kenya (CBK), Economic Survey, various issues.

Central Bank of Kenya (CBK), Monthly Report, various issues.

Coes, Donald, 1991, Brazil: Precedents and Prospects in Foreign Trade. In G. Shepherd and C. G. Langoni, *Trade Reform: Lessons from Eight Countries*, ICEG, 1991.

Collier, P., D. Greenaway and J. W. Gunning, A Methodology for the Study of Trade Liberalization. Paper Presented at the African Economic Research Consortium Launch Workshop on 'Regional Integration and Trade Liberalization', Nairobi, December 1–2, 1993.

Collier, P. and J. W. Gunning, Trade Policy and Regional Integration: Implications for the Relations between Europe and Africa. CEPR Discussion Paper No. 1012, 1994.

Dlamini A. T., Management of Foreign Exchange Reserves through Quantitative Controls: the Kenyan Experience. University of Nairobi M.B.A. research paper, 1987.

Faini R. *et al.*, Import Demand in Developing Countries. World Bank PPR Working papers, November 1988.

Friedrich-Naumann-Stiftung, *Blueprint for a New Kenya: Post Election Programme*. Nairobi, 1992.

Greenaway D. et al., Modelling Growth (and Liberalization) Using Smooth Transitions Analysis. CREDIT Research Paper No. 94/15, 1994.

Helleiner G. K., Trade, Trade Policy and Economic Development in very Low Income Countries. *Bangladesh Development Studies*, Vol. 20, No. 2 & 3, 1992.

Helleiner G. K. (ed.), *Trade Policy and Industrialization in Turbulent Times*. Routledge, London, 1994.

Humphill W., The Effect of Foreign Exchange Receipts on Imports of Less developed Countries. *IMF Staff papers*, Vol. 21, 1974, pp. 637–77.

Hendry D. F. *PC – GIVE: An Interactive Econometric Modelling System*. Institute of Economics and Statistics and Nuffield College, University of Oxford, 1989.

Hopcraft P., Outward-looking Industrialization: the Promotion of Manufactured Exports from Kenya. Institute for Development Studies (IDS), Discussion Paper No. 141, University of Nairobi, 1972.

Ikiara G. K., Kenya's Participation in Regional and Global Trade Arrangements. In J. Whalley (Ed.), The Small Among the Big, Vol. II, Centre for the Study of International Economic Relations (CSIER) Monograph, 1988.

Keyfitz R. and J. Wanjala, Optimal Tariff Reform for Kenya. Technical Paper 91–05, Ministry of Planning and National Development, 1991.

Khan M. S. and D. Villanueva, Macroeconomic Policies and Long-term Growth. AERC Special Paper No. 13, 1990.

King J. R., *Stabilization Policy in an African Setting: Kenya 1963–73*, HEB, London, 1979.

Moran, C., Imports Under a Foreign Exchange Constraint. *World Bank Economic Review*, Vol. 3, No. 2, 1989.

Mosley, P., How to Confront the World Bank and Get Away With It: A Case Study of Kenya, 1980–87. In C. Milner and A. J. Rayner, *Policy Adjustment in Africa*. MacMillan, 1994.

Mwega F. M., Import Demand Elasticities and Stability during Trade Liberalization: A Case Study of Kenya. *Journal of African Economies*, Vol. 2, No. 3, 1993.

Mwega F. M., Trade and Macroeconomic Policies and the Industrialization Experience in Kenya in the 1970s and 1980s, in G. K. Helleiner (ed.), 1994.
Ng'eno N. K., Kenya's Export Performance. In J. H. Frimpong-Ansah, S. M. R. Kanbur and P. Svenberg (eds), *Trade and Development in Sub-Sahara Africa*. Manchester University Press, 1991.
Nogues J. and Sunil Gulati, Economic Policies and Performance Under Alternative Trade Regimes: Latin America During the 1980s. . . .
Phelps M. G. and B. Wasow, Measuring Protection and its Effects in Kenya. IDS Working Paper, University of Nairobi, 1972.
Pritchett, Lant and Geeta Sethi, Tariff rates, Tariff Revenue, and Tariff Reform: Some New Facts. *The World Bank Economic Review*, Vol. 8, No. 1, 1994.
Reimer R., Effective Rates of Protection in East Africa. IDS Staff Paper No. 78, University of Nairobi, 1970.
Reinikka R., How to Identify Trade Liberalization Episodes: an Empirical Study on Kenya. Centre for the Study of African Economies, Working Paper Series/ 94.10, 1994a.
Reinikka R., The Welfare Cost of Speculation During Kenyan Trade Reform. Centre for the Study of African Economies, Working Paper Series/94.11, 1994b.
Rodrik, D., Conceptual Issues in the Design of Trade Policy for Industrialization. *World Development*, Vol. 20, No. 3, 1992.
Sharpley J. and S. R. Lewis, Kenya's Industrialization, 1964–84. IDS (Sussex) Discussion Paper No. 242, 1988.
Siggel E., Recent Industrial Growth and Development in Kenya: Constraints and Prospects for the Future. Paper presented to the 9th World Congress of the International Economic Association, n.d. but likely 1990.
Swamy, G., Kenya: Patchy, Intermittent Commitment. In World Bank, *Adjustment in Africa: Lessons from Country Case Studies*. Washington D.C. 1994.
Tybout J., Researching the Trade Productivity Link: New Directions. World Bank PRE Working Paper No. 638, March 1991.
UNDP/World Bank, Kenya: The Challenge of Promoting Exports, Washington D.C., 1993.
World Bank, *Kenya into the Second Decade*. Johns Hopkins University Press. Baltimore, 1975.
World Bank, Kenya: Industrial Sector Policies for Investment and Export Growth. Washington D.C., 1987.
World Bank, Kenya: Stabilization and Adjustment: Toward Accelerated Growth. Washington D.C., 1990.
World Bank, African Development Indicators, 1994–95.
World Bank, *World Development Report*, 1994/95.

6 Evaluating Trade Liberalization in Mauritius*

Beealasingh Dabee and Chris Milner

6.1 INTRODUCTION

In many ways Mauritius sits somewhat uneasily in a study of trade liberalization experiences in Africa. Indeed, it was not included in the recent World Bank study on adjustment in Africa (World Bank, 1994). It is not part of the continental land mass of Africa and the majority of the population of Mauritius are of Indian origin. But this could similarly be said of Madagascar, which was included in the above study. Mauritius is in fact included in the Africa region for many purposes, and is a member of the Preferential Trade Area for Eastern and Southern Africa/Common Market for Eastern and Southern Africa (PTA/COMESA) and of the Southern Africa Development Community (SADC). Probably the most persuasive argument for including Mauritius in the present comparative study is the fact that the country has expanded its non-traditional exports very significantly in the last decade (with exports accounting for 48 per cent of GDP and non-traditional exports accounting for 73 per cent of exports in 1993) and as a result is perceived as a successful liberalizer. An interesting issue to be investigated in this chapter is whether or to what extent this 'success story' is due to structural adjustment policies themselves or to Mauritius' ability to adjust over a longer period of time. The lessons to be learned by other African economies from the Mauritian experience depend critically on this.

The distinction between adjustment and the structural adjustment programme is drawn because the two may not be synonymous in the case of Mauritius; not because the programme of the 1980s was not associated with adjustment, but because the process of adjustment may have

* A research grant was made available by the African Economic Research Consortium (AERC) to the authors for this study. The authors gratefully acknowledge AERC's support.

Table 6.1 Policy account: Mauritius, 1970–95

1995	Mauritius joins the Southern African Development Community (SADC)
1994	Significant changes in tariff structure, large reductions in average rates and variability of tariffs
1993	Removal of all restrictions on transfers and payments for current transactions in the balance of payments
1992	Export permits abolished (except for prohibited goods) Approval of central bank no longer required for advance payment of imports Capital transfer tax of 15 per cent abolished for foreign investors. For nationals, tax reduced from 15 per cent to 5 per cent, transfers still subject to central bank approval PTA rules of origin amended so as to extend preferential tariffs to goods from member states, irrespective of whether manufacturing company controlled by nationals or not
1991	Import permits abolished (except for prohibited goods). Customs duty remissions on raw materials extended to non-EPZ manufacturing exporters
1985	Stamp duty increased from 12 per cent to 17 per cent
1983–5	Phasing out of quantitative restrictions on imports
1984	Mauritius becomes founder member of Indian Ocean Commission
1983	Import duties restored on non-basic food items and on consumer durables, affecting 4 per cent of total imports. Surcharge of 10 per cent on customs dues to keep imports down. Rupee delinked from SDR and linked to a trade-weighted basket
1982	Stamp duty on imports increased from 5 per cent to 12 per cent
1981	Second devaluation of rupee, by 17 per cent
1980	Stamp duty on imports increased from 2 per cent to 5 per cent
1979	Beginning of stabilization/structural adjustment programmes (to last till 1986) 23 per cent devaluation of rupee (part of IMF stabilization package) Introduction of stamp duty of 2 per cent on imports (EPZ, import-substitution industries, basic necessities exempted) Duty to be paid at time of order
1978	Abolition of import deposit scheme
1977	Import deposit scheme introduced, with 35 per cent of import value to be deposited; essential goods exempted
1976	Rupee delinked from £UK; new SDR link
1970	Export-processing zone (EPZ) established

Source: Data compiled by authors.

begun earlier. As the policy account chart (Table 6.1) shows, Mauritius did undergo a period of sustained stabilization and exchange rate adjustment starting in 1979, which was followed by a period of substantial import liberalization between 1983 and 1985.

This corresponds with the stand-by agreements, which extended over the period 1979–85, and with the structural adjustment loans (SALs) of 1981 and 1983. But attempts to reduce the trade regime bias against exports pre-date this episode of policy reform. Mauritius had operated an export-processing zone (EPZ) scheme since 1970. The presence of approximate free trade status and favourable fiscal incentives for export firms meant that Mauritius had acquired some (non-negligible) non-traditional export capacity by the beginning of the SAL programmes. (EPZ exports – mainly knitted textiles – already accounted for 24 per cent of total exports by 1979.) Thus one might date structural adjustment in a narrow sense to cover the period 1979–85. However, one should be aware, when assessing this relatively intense episode of liberalization, of the longer-term dimension of adjustment within the Mauritian economy from 1970 onwards. Indeed, one might view 1985 as a premature fixing of the end of the adjustment period, for the year 1991 ushered in a new wave of liberalization with the abolition of import permits, which freed virtually all categories of imports from a very pervasive import-licensing scheme. This was followed by the complete liberalization of foreign exchange (1993) and a major revision of the tariff structure (1994) that brought about significant reductions in the average level and variability of tariffs. Gradualism has in fact been a distinctive feature of the Mauritian liberalization episode.

In light of the above arguments, our study focuses on two distinct episodes – the 1979–85 liberalization/structural adjustment episode and the more recent 1991–4 liberalization episode. The pre-structural adjustment situation is conveniently represented, in Table 6.2, by some estimates of average rates of effective protection in the Mauritian manufacturing sector in 1980. In 11 out of 19 industries the rate of protection is in excess of 100 per cent, often well in excess. As we shall show more clearly in Section 6.2, although there was an apparent mixed strategy of import substitution and export promotion, there was a high degree of *de facto* anti-export and pro-import substitution bias within the trade policy regime at the start of the SAL period. From a discussion of the pre-structural adjustment trade policy regime we turn in Section 6.3 to a detailed analysis of the nature and extent of trade liberalization during the two episodes, using a number of incidence, price and quantity indicators of liberalization. In Section 6.4 we investigate the reasons for the sustainability of the reforms. This is followed in Section 6.5 by an assessment of the consequences of the liberalization episodes, and the regional dimension of

Table 6.2 Average rates of effective protection in Mauritian manufacturing sector, 1980

Sector	*ERP (%)*
Beverages and tobacco	123
Textile yarn/fabrics	77
Wearing apparel	99
Leather products	269
Footwear	158
Wood products	191
Furniture	130
Paper products	131
Printing/publishing	75
Chemical products	38
Rubber products	125
Plastic products	89
Non-metallic products	77
Iron/steel	154
Fabricated metal products	156
Machinery (excluding electrical)	62
Electrical machinery, and so on	179
Transport equipment	23
Optical goods, watches, and so on	266

Note: Average rates weighted by value added.

Source: Greenaway and Milner (1989).

trade reform is considered in Section 6.6. As official statistics currently available go up to 1994, or in some cases only to 1993, our assessment of the 1991–4 liberalization episode is relatively inadequate. However, this is complemented, in Section 6.7, by an analysis of a survey of Mauritian manufacturing enterprises that was carried out over the period July–September 1995. Finally, Section 6.8 provides an overall assessment of the Mauritian liberalization experience and the summary conclusions of the case-study.

6.2 PRE-STRUCTURAL ADJUSTMENT TRADE POLICY REGIME

The pre-structural adjustment trade policy regime is summarized in Table 6.3. It was typified by mixed and variable measures of import substitution,

Table 6.3 Pre-trade liberalization pattern of assistance to Mauritian industries

Sector	*Main form of assistance*	*Subjective ranking of protection levels*
Manufacturing – import substitution		
Large new activities (for example, foodstuffs, assembly of colour television)	Development certificate scheme, tariff and import quota protection	Assisted at a very high rate
Other	Import licensing and tariff protection	Assisted at high but variable rates
Manufacturing – export-orientated		
Wholly (for example, knitwear)	Export enterprise certificate scheme	Assisted, but at low rate
Partially (for example, furniture)	Tax rebate based on export growth	Disadvantaged at low rates
Agriculture		
Sugar		
large growers	Tax of 23.625 per cent on gross export receipts	Severely disadvantaged
small growers		Approximately zero rates
Rice	Subsidized exchange rate and subsidy payments on rice	Severely disadvantaged
Other agriculture		Approximately zero

Source: Compiled by the authors.

export promotion assistance for manufactured goods and non-traditional agriculture, and export taxation of the traditional export (sugar).

Import-substitution Measures

The development certificate scheme was initiated in 1963 – the pre-SAL legislation was set out in the Development Incentives Act of 1974 – and was designed to encourage the establishment of import-substitute industries in Mauritius. Its primary objective was to create employment in the manufacturing sector. Incentives to companies with development certificates (DC) included a tax holiday on corporate profits, exemption for a period from income tax on dividends, investment finance at preferential rates, investment allowances, and import duty relief (or exemption) on machinery, raw materials and semi-finished products. Protection from foreign competition was given through tariff and quota restrictions on imports.

Table 6.4 Pre-reform tariff system* in Mauritius

Fiscal duty	Varied by BTN classification (0–450 per cent)
Customs duty	Applied on some BTN classifications to countries that do not enjoy preferential treatment (5–50 per cent)
Stamp duty	Set at 12 per cent, payable on most goods at the time of import permit approval
Surcharge	A surcharge of 33.1 per cent on the sum of fiscal and customs duties and 10 per cent on the stamp duty
Duty exemptions	Might be granted to designated categories of importers

Note: * Specific ranges to 1984 values.

Source: Compiled by the authors.

At the start of the 1980s about 150 companies with development certificates (DCs) were in operation, employing a total of about 8000 people. The main concentrations of the manufacturing companies were in food and beverages and engineering. Both DC and non-DC firms received additional assistance/protection through tariff and non-tariff restrictions on imports.

The Mauritian tariff schedule, summarized in Table 6.4, was composed of five elements. These included general customs duty, preferential customs duty and fiscal duty. Imported commodities were subject to fiscal duty and general or preferential customs duty. All the major trading partners of Mauritius received the preferential rate. The (unweighted) average nominal rates shown in column 2 of Table 6.5 therefore record the visible (fiscal and customs) duties. Progressively, since the mid-1970s, a number of supplementary duties were also applied to all imports, including an import surcharge (10 per cent), a special levy (10 per cent) and stamp duty (12 per cent). The average nominal tariffs, inclusive of all supplementary duties, against competing manufacturing imports at the start of the reform period are listed in column 3 of Table 6.5.

In addition to import duties levied for general protective and revenue purposes, specific quota protection of up to 80 per cent of the domestic market was offered on a discretionary basis to companies with DC status. Import licensing was also used in a less-specific manner to provide protection for all local production in the manufacturing sector and non-traditional agricultural activity. Table 6.6 sets out some information on the coverage of the import-licensing policies in Mauritius in 1980. Note that coverage was at least 80 per cent of the value of imports in sections

Table 6.5 Average nominal tariffs in Mauritius, 1980

Activity	*Nominal tariff*	
	Fiscal and customs duties only	*All import-specific taxes*
Beverages	188	220
Tobacco	300	332
Textiles	13	45
Wearing apparel	4	80
Leather products	75	107
Footwear	50	82
Wood products	25	57
Furniture	88	120
Paper products	40	72
Printing	16	48
Basic chemicals	5	37
Other chemicals	29	62
Rubber	53	85
Plastic	20	52
Glass	40	72
Base metals	2	34
Fabricated metals	32	64
Lime etc.	51	53
Non-electrical machinery	19	51
Electrical machinery	41	53
Transport equipment	70	102
Watches and lenses	37	69
Arithmetic mean	*55.1*	*86.2*

Source: Compiled by the authors.

6–8 of the SITC (manufactured goods and machinery). It was also fairly high in the case of food and live animals, beverages and tobacco and oils and fats, all activities significantly covered by the DC scheme.

It should be noted also that there was significant escalation in scheduled tariffs, which was exaggerated further by the presence of quantitative restrictions generally on imports of final goods and the pervasive use of import duty exemptions on intermediate goods and raw materials for DC firms, and for other firms on a discretionary basis. This all contributed to the production of very high and variable (within and across industries) effective rates of protection for import-substitute activities (see Table 6.2).

Table 6.6 Coverage of import-licensing scheme in Mauritius, 1980

Category of imports (SITC)	*Estimated value of imports under licences (Rs m.)*	*Total value of imports (Rs m.)*
(0) Food and live animals	534 (49)*	1084
(1) Beverages and tobacco	26 (100)	26
(2) Crude materials (except fuels)	6 (3)	211
(3) Mineral fuels, lubricants and related materials	27 (4)	667
(4) Animal and vegetable oils and fats	92 (71)	130
(5) Chemicals	92 (29)	317
(6) Manufactured goods classified chiefly by material	1013 (82)	1228
(7) Machinery and transport equipment	649 (88)	736
(8) Miscellaneous manufactured articles	235 (80)	295
(9) Other commodities and transactions	4 (17)	24
Total	*2678 (57)*	*4721*

Note:
* Figures in brackets indicate percentages, in value terms, of goods under licences in each category of imports.

Source: Compiled by the authors.

Export Promotion Measures

The Export Processing Zone Act (1970) was intended to encourage the development of export-based manufacturing and processing industries in Mauritius through local and overseas investment. The incentives offered to companies under the Act included a tax holiday on corporate profits (longer than that available for DC firms), exemption from income tax for distributed dividends (again for a longer period than for DC firms), investment and export finance at preferential rates, investment allowances, and import duty exemption on machinery, components, raw materials and semi-finished products.

At the start of the reform period some 130 firms, employing about 24 000 people, were operating with EPZ status, with the vast bulk of the production being in spinning, knitting and made-up garments. Thus, although there was a strong bias in the policy regime in favour of import-substitution activities, and presumably also a bias induced by the natural protection that remoteness imposed upon the economy, the EPZ sector was significantly larger than the DC sector in employment terms. In production terms the picture is less clear, since manufacturing as a whole accounted for 14.9 per cent of GDP (at current factor cost) in 1979, but the EPZ sector accounted for only 3.4 per cent of GDP (with sugar-processing accounting for 3.9 per cent). But it should be recalled that the non-EPZ manufacturing contribution to GDP is measured here at policy-distorted (inflated) prices, whereas the EPZ contribution is measured at approximately world prices. The critical point to emphasize is that the export-orientated manufacturing sector had a presence in Mauritius prior to the import liberalization episode of the 1980s.

6.3 TRADE LIBERALIZATION IN MAURITIUS

Timing and Sequencing of Reforms

For reasons to be discussed in Section 6.4, trade liberalization in Mauritius has been a gradual process, with obvious implications for the sequencing of the reforms. During the first liberalization/structural adjustment episode (1979–85), the emphasis was on removal of quantitative restrictions and their conversion into tariff equivalents, whereas the more recent 1991–4 liberalization has seen the removal of all restrictions on current account transactions and the initial phase of tariff harmonization and reduction. Details of the reforms undertaken during these two liberalization episodes are indicated below, followed by a discussion of price and quantity indexes for the first episode and for the second episode wherever data are available.

The different policy instruments of the first liberalization are summarized in Table 6.7. A number of stages or sub-episodes can be identified from this table. During the period 1979–83 the emphasis was on macroeconomic stabilization and exchange rate adjustment. Indeed, during this period trade policies (in particular import duties) were used in a more restrictive manner; stamp duty on imports was progressively increased

Table 6.7 Summary of reforms in Mauritius, 1979–85

Policy instruments	*Initial reform*	*Subsequent reforms*
Import duties	Consolidation of some duties Lowering of average protection levels Reduced exemptions to duty Import surcharges in 1984–5	Intention to reduce spread of tariffs Intention to consolidate fiscal, customs and stamp duty into one tax (not fulfilled until 1994)
Quantitative import restrictions	QR removal from 1983 to 1985	Intention to introduce tariff equivalents (ultimately not fulfilled)
Export taxes/subsidies	Increased exemptions to sugar export tax Tax rebates for Manufactured exports by non-EPZ firms	
Exchange rate policy	23 per cent devaluation in 1979 followed by 17 per cent devaluation in 1981 Further depreciation of 45 per cent against $ between 1981 and 1985	
Institutional and other reforms	DC status phased out after 1984 Creation of investment and export promotion agency (MEDIA) Introduction of export credit guarantee (1981) scheme Negotiation of double taxation agreements	

Source: Compiled by the authors.

and an imports surcharge was applied in 1983. Trade liberalization did not start, therefore, until after 1983. The initial period of trade liberalization was concerned mainly with some liberalization of foreign exchange and import-licensing restrictions, and with the reform of the border taxation of imports. This latter element focused more on simplification of the duty structure rather than on reduction of average rates of duty. Indeed, import surcharges were increased further in 1984 and 1985 for fiscal reasons. A planned consolidation of some duties, the reduction of the spread of rates and reduced exemptions (for example, on intermediate imports) were aimed at reducing the spread and level of effective protection in import substitute sectors (though little progress was made on this). The main phase of import liberalization and reduction of protection for local firms came in the period 1983–5 with the progressive dismantling of quantitative import restrictions. The intention at the outset was to substitute tariffs for this non-tariff protection, but this did not subsequently materialize. The substitution appears to have been achieved in part by the managed revisions of import duties (in particular import surcharges) since the mid-1980s. In any case, it should be emphasized that DC firms have retained duty exemptions on raw material and intermediate imports, and still benefit from considerable tariff escalation.

The second episode of trade liberalization started in 1991 with the abolition of the import-licensing scheme, which had been maintained in spite of the import-liberalization measures adopted during the first liberalization episode. Since 1991, all commodities, with a few exceptions, have been imported freely. Furthermore, since 1993, all restrictions on foreign exchange transactions for the payment of imports have been removed and commercial banks no longer require the approval of the central bank for these transactions. Finally, changes in tariffs, planned during the first liberalization episode, were put into effect in 1994. The three taxes on imports (customs duty, fiscal duty and stamp levy) have been merged into a single customs duty. Tariffs have been harmonized; there are now 10 basic rates instead of 60. And the tariff rates have been significantly reduced, with the maximum rate being 100 per cent compared to (an overall combined rate of) 250 per cent.

Quantifying Changes in the Relative Incentives

It is possible to provide some information on the overall extent of trade liberalization on both a discrete and continuous basis. For the first liberalization episode, estimates of effective protection in 1990 are available that can be compared with the pre-reform estimates reported in Table 6.2. The post-reform estimates are reported in Table 6.8. Average rates of effective protection are in some non-export industries absolutely high,

Table 6.8 Rates of effective protection* in Mauritius (%)

Sector (with manufacturing breakdown)	*Total sales*	*Domestic sales*	*Export sales*	*Change in effective protection (relative to 1980)*
Food crops/fruit	21.7	23.5	–1.0	
Livestock/fish	12.2	13.7	–8.3	
Other agriculture	24.1	31.0	–2.6	
Mining/quarrying	19.9	21.6	–5.1	
Food	69.0	89.4	–	n.a.
Beverages and tobacco	182.2	184.4	–	+59
Textile yarn/fabrics	11.0	1.2	11.7	–66
Wearing apparel	4.4	52.7	3.5	–100
Leather products	8.2	27.2	7.1	–261
Footwear	88.2	96.0	–	–70
Wood products	37.6	77.8	4.0	–153
Furniture	241.2	259.2	–	+111
Paper products	57.3	76.7	5.6	–74
Printing/publishing	6.8	13.1	–	–68
Chemical products	20.5	25.7	–	–18
Rubber products	144.3	152.7	–	+19
Plastic products	59.3	73.0	–	–30
Non-metallic products	48.3	54.1	–	–29
Iron/steel	72.6	72.8	–	–81
Fabricated metal products	48.3	51.8	–	–108
Machinery (excluding eletrical)	3.2	9.1	–	–59
Electrical machinery and so on	180.5	218.2	–	–2
Transport equipment	3.7	4.4	–	–19
Optical goods, watches, and so on	11.9	14.0	12.1	–254
Jewellery and so on	9.0	13.8	9.5	n.a.
Other manufactures	6.1	17.4	5.3	n.a.

Notes:
* Averages weighted by value-added for 1989
† For sales by EPZ firms only in the case of manufacturers, and reported only where EPZ exports account for more that 25 per cent of net production; a nominal rate of 3.3 per cent is assumed for EPZ sales, which approximates the implicit subsidization associated with reduced taxation of profits.
n.a. not available

Source: Maxwell Stamp (1992) for 1990 estimates.

with rates in excess of 100 per cent in the case of beverages and tobacco, furniture, rubber products and electrical machinery. But in general, significant declines in rates of effective protection relative to 1980 levels are identified. In five industries the fall is at least 100 percentage points (wearing apparel, leather products, wood products, fabricated metal products and optical goods/watches) and there are six further industries where the fall is in excess of 50 percentage points. Indeed, the rate of protection is estimated to be higher in 1990 than 1980 in only three cases. It should be noted, however, that the average figures capture not only the effects of reduced protection but also the changes in the distribution of sales between the protected home market and export markets. The values for *effective* protection in domestic sales are rather higher than those in total sales, though even here it is clear that relatively low rates of effective protection prevail in the post-reform period. All (non-sugar) primary sectors and 14 out of 22 manufacturing industries have a rate of effective protection in domestic sales of less than 75 per cent.

The discrete measurement of liberalization based on pre-reform and post-reform levels of protection is a useful means of commenting on the extent of liberalization. It is less useful when wishing to comment on the precise dating of when the reforms affected relative prices.

In Table 6.9 we report some estimates from Milner and McKay (1996) of the movement of the real exchange rates for importables (RER_m) and exportables (RER_x) for the period 1978–89, where $RER_i = P_i/P_N$ and P_N is the price of non-tradeables. In the case of exportables, the real exchange rate fell steadily until 1982. This is consistent with the earlier discussion of policy events and with the first stage of stabilization in the policy episode. Indeed, the sharp increase in RER_x comes during the period 1983–6, which coincides quite closely with trade-liberalizing measures discussed above. In the case of importables, there is a rather more continuous pattern of appreciation over the whole reform period, with the real exchange in 1987 being about 20 per cent below its 1979 level. In fact, this evidence provides fairly good support for our initial dating of this liberalization episode. After 1987 (when QR liberalization was completed) the real exchange rates for each tradeable tend to reverse the experience up to 1987, with RER_x falling and RER_m rising between 1987 and 1989.

Changes in Trade Quantities

The stabilization episode of the early 1980s is captured by the import to GDP ratio recorded in Table 6.10; the ratio fell from 0.57 in 1980 to 0.42 in 1983. The ratio increased between 1983 and 1990, rising particularly quickly during the post-QR liberalization period from 1986 to 1988.

Table 6.9 Estimated real exchange rate for exportables and importables for Mauritius, 1976–89

Year	*Real exchange rates**	
	(Non-traditional) exportables† *(RER_X)*	*Importables*† *(RER_M)*
1978	0.947	1.094
1979	0.827	1.057
1980	0.763	1.031
1981	0.737	0.999
1982	0.782	0.902
1983	0.773	0.931
1984	0.904	0.902
1985	0.986	0.897
1986	1.065	0.926
1987	0.977	0.842
1988	0.929	0.859
1989	0.939	0.890

Notes:
* Annual averages are reported with Jan.–Jun. 1976 = 100. Values in excess of (below) unity imply a real depreciation (appreciation) relative to the 1976 level of the real exchange rate.
† Alternative estimates are reported by Milner and McKay (1996). Here we report the index that records a real appreciation during the liberalization episode.

Source: Milner and McKay (1996).

However, it would be difficult to ascribe all the increase in the import–GDP ratio to the 1979–85 liberalization measures. As Table 6.10 shows, there was a rapid growth of imports of intermediate and capital goods between 1984 and 1988. This was mostly due to the recovery of the EPZ in the early 1980s, as shown by the increasing ratio of EPZ exports to GDP over the period 1984–9. In fact, 50 per cent of the increase in the import–GDP ratio came from increased EPZ imports over that period. The increase in the import–GDP ratio from 1988 can also be partly explained by the increased imports resulting from the 30 per cent increase in salaries granted to the public sector. In addition, the introduction of fringe benefits in the form of duty-free cars and motorcycles for the public sector directly increased imports of these items.

Table 6.10 Volume and composition of Mauritian trade, 1979–94

Year	*Import–GDP ratio*	*EPZ imports GDP (%)*	*Share of imports (%)*		
			Intermediates	*Capital formation*	*Final consumption*
1979	0.52	7.6	57.7	12.1	30.3
1980	0.57	6.9	60.7	10.8	28.5
1981	0.49	6.6	62.0	9.5	28.4
1982	0.43	6.9	63.2	6.5	30.3
1983	0.42	12.0	64.3	8.7	27.0
1984	0.47	16.0	68.9	8.3	22.8
1985	0.52	30.3	69.2	9.2	21.7
1986	0.55	20.8	72.4	11.5	16.1
1987	0.60	21.7	67.6	14.5	17.9
1988	0.72	23.8	62.9	21.6	15.5
1989	0.70	23.6	66.2	16.1	17.6
1990	0.70	19.0	64.9	17.3	17.8

Year	*Export–GDP ratio*	*Share of exports (%)*	
		Sugar	*EPZ*
1979	0.39	61.8	24.1
1980	0.49	60.6	24.8
1981	0.37	49.6	33.2
1982	0.44	56.5	28.3
1983	0.44	57.8	28.2
1984	0.46	46.0	39.2
1985	0.51	41.0	46.6
1986	0.57	38.0	53.0
1987	0.61	36.3	55.0
1988	0.60	32.2	59.0
1989	0.58	31.8	58.4
1990	0.57	28.2	63.5
1991	0.54	27.5	62.9
1992	0.51	28.2	62.0
1993	0.55	22.6	62.0
1994	0.48	23.3	67.0

Sources: CSO, *Annual Digest of Statistics* (various issues) CSO, *Quarterly External Trade Statistics* (various issues).

The rapid increase in imports and exports that began toward the end of the first liberalization episode clearly corresponds to changes in the trade pattern expected from a successful liberalization episode. However, as argued above, more than 50 per cent of the increase in the import–GDP ratio between 1979 and 1985 was not the direct result of liberalization. Yet the liberalization measures of the 1979–85 episode clearly altered relative incentives. This must have given an impetus to the growth of the export sector. Unfortunately, we do not have a very satisfactory means of identifying the relevant counter-factual – that is, the trade volumes that would have existed with the same external and other environments, but without the trade liberalization measures.

The incidence of the 1991–4 liberalization episode cannot yet be assessed fully, as available data do not extend beyond 1994, or even beyond 1993 in some cases. However, it seems that the abolition of the import-licensing scheme in 1991 has had no significant effect on imports. The ratio of non-EPZ imports to total imports in fact declined slightly, from 72 per cent in 1992 to 71 per cent in 1994. It would be useful later to evaluate the impact of the 1994 tariff reductions, which significantly affected the prices of about 4400 products, mostly consumer goods.

Some of the effects of the 1991–4 liberalization episode may be picked up by the data generated by the survey of manufacturing enterprises carried out in Mauritius over the July–September 1995 period. An analysis of the survey data is included in Section 6.7.

6.4 THE SUSTAINABILITY AND CREDIBILITY OF LIBERALIZATION

The question of sustainability and credibility of trade liberalization arises because trade liberalization attempts are often aborted in developing countries. One explanation for their transitory nature is the temporary nature of the support granted by donor agencies to countries embarking on adjustment programmes (Collier and Gunning, 1994). The question of the pace of the reforms also arises. Again, in the case of donor-supported programmes, import liberalization is expected to move at a relatively quick pace, since the aid provided is temporary.

While it is true that trade liberalization was initiated in Mauritius as part of the SAL programme in the early 1980s, the government emphasized the sustainability of the trade reforms and was able to play down the question of pacing. This is why trade liberalization in Mauritius has been a gradual rather than an abrupt process.

Sustainability was accorded the highest priority by the government, even if it meant adopting apparently inconsistent policies. Thus, as quantitative restrictions were removed and imports liberalized in the early 1980s, various measures were adopted to keep down the level and value of imports. First, an import levy of 2 per cent was introduced immediately after the first devaluation of 1979. The levy was payable at the time of issue of import permits required for virtually all imports, excepting EPZ imports. As restrictions on imports were progressively removed, the import levy was progressively increased until it reached a figure of 17 per cent in 1985. On top of the import levy, a surcharge of 10 per cent on imports was introduced in 1983, and even though imports were liberalized in 1985, a very comprehensive scheme of import licensing was maintained until 1991. Finally, import permits were granted depending on foreign exchange availability. All these measures led to a decline in the dollar value of non-EPZ imports. These imports declined gradually from US$ 529 m in 1980 to US$ 390 m in 1986. Thus, every effort was made to restrain the import bill so as to maintain the sustainability of trade liberalization.

However, with the rapid expansion of the EPZ and tourist sectors, and with the inflow of substantial direct foreign investment from 1984, the level of foreign exchange reserves began to rise comfortably. From a low of US$41 m in 1984, there was a rapid and sustained increase to US$744 m in 1990. It became easier to obtain foreign exchange for imports, but the other restrictions described above remained. It was only in 1991 that the import-licensing scheme was abolished. The 17 per cent import levy was maintained till 1994 although, as from 1988, payment was required only when the imported goods arrived.

The sustainability of trade liberalization also made it credible. Furthermore, credibility was enhanced by the government through signalling: the rising level of foreign exchange reserves was constantly publicized as a reminder of sound economic management, especially with regard to the balance of payments. On one occasion, the government refunded an IMF credit tranche much before it was due. This was used as an additional signal to economic agents that there would be no policy reversals. Liberalization was credible, as indicated by the absence of any speculative accumulation of imports. When import permits were abolished in 1991, there was no marked change in the volume of imports.

According a high priority to sustainability allowed the government to play down the question of the pace of the reforms. For example, after the phasing-out of quantitative restrictions over the 1983–5 period, the World Bank was expecting a reform of the tariff structure to follow. However, the government argued that any further liberalization would be unsustainable, as the balance of payments and budget deficits would worsen. Since the end of the structural adjustment programme in 1986, government has had more leeway in negotiating with the World Bank and the IMF, with the result that reform of the tariff structure was postponed for a few years. It was only in July 1994 that a major revision of the tariff structure was introduced. The 1994 reduction in average tariffs was announced as the first phase of tariff reform. This gradual approach to reform helps to ensure that the reform is sustainable and to maintain the credibility of the reform.

6.5 CONSEQUENCES OF LIBERALIZATION FOR MAURITIUS

It was argued above that the rapid increase in exports, in particular manufactured exports from the EPZ sector, towards the end of the first liberalization episode may be partly attributed to the change in relative incentives brought about by the trade liberalization measures. These incentives no doubt led to changes in factor utilization, allocation and accumulation. Some of these changes are indicated below.

It must be stressed that the trade liberalization measures of the 1980s coincided with various favourable exogenous as well as policy-induced developments – which also had comparable effects on factor utilization, allocation and accumulation. The exogenous developments included economic recovery in the EC and the USA, resulting in the revival of EPZ exports and the rapid expansion of the tourist sector; favourable climatic conditions over the period 1985–90 leading to above-average sugar production; and significant inflows of direct investment into the EPZ from Hong Kong. Policy-induced developments included successful investment promotion; liberalization of the financial sector with the introduction of market-determined interest rates; the establishment of an offshore centre; the setting-up of a stock market; and upgrading of incentive schemes for exporters of manufactured goods and services. It is not easy to disentangle the effects of these developments from those of the liberalization measures of the 1980s.

Output Growth and Composition

The stabilization period of the reforms was identified earlier to be 1979–85. This was preceded by a period of deteriorating macroeconomic conditions in Mauritius. As Table 6.11 shows, the growth rate fell steadily from 1977 until 1980 (when large negative growth was experienced). With some success with stabilization and also a recovery of sugar prices, there was a return to positive growth in 1981 and 1982. But it was not until after 1983 that there was sustained accelerating growth. It is also after 1983 that we can identify a significant increase in the share of manufacturing and EPZ activity in GDP; the share of both increased each year until

Table 6.11 Growth and composition of output of Mauritius, 1977–94

		Shares in GDP of:*		
	Annual rate of growth of real GDP (%)	*Agriculture*	*Manufacturing*[†] *(EPZ) (%)*	*Construction*
1977	7.0	19.7	14.6 (2.7)	8.5
1978	4.0	17.8	14.6 (2.8)	9.2
1979	3.6	18.7	14.9 (3.4)	8.4
1980	–10.1	12.4	15.2 (4.3)	7.6
1981	6.4	14.3	15.7 (4.8)	6.7
1982	5.8	15.3	15.6 (4.5)	6.2
1983	0.4	13.8	15.8 (5.2)	6.2
1984	4.7	14.4	18.1 (7.2)	5.7
1985	6.8	15.3	20.6 (9.6)	5.6
1986	8.9	15.3	23.3 (11.6)	5.3
1987	8.4	14.6	24.6 (13.1)	5.3
1988	6.1	13.2	24.3 (13.5)	5.9
1989	4.5	12.5	23.6 (12.8)	6.4
1990	7.1	12.3	23.4 (12.7)	7.0
1991	4.3	11.4	22.9 (12.2)	7.3
1992	6.7	11.0	23.0 (12.3)	7.4
1993	5.0	9.7	22.9 (12.3)	7.5
1994	5.1	9.3	23.0 (12.4)	7.6

Notes:
* At current factor cost
[†] Includes sugar factories production

Source: CSO, National Accounts of Mauritius (various issues).

1987. The declining share of construction in GDP up to 1987 suggests that increasing factor utilization was the major source of growth up to this point. This is supported also by the evidence of unemployment (Table 6.12) and investment (Table 6.13).

Structure and Level of Employment

The rate of unemployment rose sharply during the stabilization period up to 1982 and 1983. Thereafter employment grew every year until 1991; the particularly sharp decline in the unemployment rate ($U/(E + U)$ in Table 6.12) came in the period 1985–9. Again this coincides quite closely

Table 6.12 Unemployment, employment,* and the structure of employment in Mauritius, 1977–91

	No. of people (000s)		*Share of employed labour force in:*	
Year	*Unemployed (u)*	*Employed (E)* *[u/(E + u)]*	*Agriculture*	*Manufacturing*
1977	14.6	194.8 (0.07)	33.5	17.1
1978	16.4	198.7 (0.07)	30.6	16.6
1979	22.8	199.4 (0.10)	29.8	17.8
1980	37.6	197.6 (0.16)	29.4	18.4
1981	60.1	196.0 (0.23)	29.0	18.9
1982	75.1	195.0 (0.28)	29.2	19.0
1983	70.7	194.0 (0.27)	28.8	19.8
1984	65.9	201.0 (0.25)	26.6	24.2
1985	58.4	215.0 (0.21)	24.4	29.2
1986	49.5	238.0 (0.17)	21.8	35.2
1987	39.0	259.7 (0.13)	19.3	38.5
1988	22.0	271.2 (0.08)	18.3	39.2
1989	15.4	273.2 (0.05)	17.5	39.4
1990	11.3	279.4 (0.04)	16.8	38.6
1991	11.0	280.3 (0.04)	16.2	38.6

Note:
* Employment in large establishments employing at least 10 workers.

Source: Data supplied by Ministry of Economic Planning and Development.

with the period of most intense trade liberalization. The composition of employment information, however, shows a rather earlier structural effect. Agriculture's share of employment remained fairly constant during the stabilization period 1979–83, and fell steadily thereafter. Similarly, manufacturing employment's share remained relatively stable up to 1983, but rose sharply after this point.

The growth in manufacturing employment, therefore, more closely coincides with the start of the trade liberalization period in 1983, with total manufacturing employment growing by over 25 per cent between 1983 and 1984.

Savings and Investment

Relative stagnation of (real) per capita incomes and high inflation at the start of the stabilization period (the annual inflation rate in 1980 being 42 per cent) forced down the savings rate in the stabilization period (see

Table 6.13 Savings and investment ratios in Mauritius, 1977–94

	*Savings Ratio** (%)	*Investment ratio*†
1977	19.3	27.7
1978	18.4	28.3
1979	19.5	25.7
1980	10.5	23.3
1981	14.8	21.9
1982	15.4	17.9
1983	17.1	18.0
1984	18.7	18.1
1985	21.6	18.6
1986	28.5	19.8
1987	27.4	21.6
1988	25.5	28.7
1989	23.1	26.6
1990	22.2	31.5
1991	24.1	28.9
1992	25.2	28.4
1993‡	24.2	28.8
1994§	23.3	30.9

Notes:
* Gross domestic savings as a percentage of GDP at current factor cost
† Gross domestic fixed capital formation as a percentage of GDP at current factor cost
‡ Provisional
§ Forecast

Source: Data supplied by Ministry of Economic Planning and Development.

Table 6.13). But this rose again steadily after 1982 to a peak in 1986 (when the savings ratio reached 28.5 per cent), and remained over 22 per cent for the whole of the period up to 1994. The investment ratio followed a similar pattern during the stabilization period up to 1983, but the recovery after that was much slower. Indeed, Table 6.13 shows that the sharp increase in the investment ratio did not come until after 1986. This is consistent with a view that the early post-reform period was marked by increases in utilization of existing capital (and some resource reallocation), rather than capital accumulation. Sustained policy reform and growth brought about new capital requirements and investment confidence in general after the completion of the first liberalization episode.

Table 6.14 Government revenue and expenditure in Mauritius, 1977–91

Year	*Total revenue (Rs m.)*	*Total expenditure (Rs m.)*	*Budget deficit (Rs m.)*
1977–8	1 718.8	2 087.2	–368.4
1978–9	2 205.3	2 439.9	–234.0
1979–80	2 594.3	2 902.1	–307.8
1980–1	3 445.0	3 805.2	–360.2
1981–2	2 220.9	3 336.2	–1 115.3
1982–3	2 802.6	3 973.0	–750.0
1983–4	3 060.8	3 743.2	–673.4
1984–5	3 396.2	4 276.5	–907.5
1985–6	4 128.3	4 444.9	–316.6
1986–7	5 202.6	5 125.0	77.6
1987–8	6 466.8	6 376.7	82.9
1988–9	7 630.5	7 482.8	147.7
1989–90	8 884.8	6 879.9	4.9
1990–1	10 150.9	9 979.5	171.4

Source: Taken from Greenaway and Lamusse (1994).

Fiscal Profile

Finally, we provide (Table 6.14) some information on the evolution of government finances over the reform period. The stabilization period saw a deterioration in the fiscal position, as revenues stagnated prior 1983. Again it is not until 1984/85 that the revenue-enhancement effects of growth of incomes and imports are evident. It should be recalled that the major liberalization of tariffs planned for the second half of the 1980s was not in fact implemented until 1994. This no doubt reflected in part the government's concerns about possible revenue-depletion from tariff reduction. But this caution may have helped to sustain the reform programme.

6.6. REGIONAL ASPECTS OF TRADE REFORM IN MAURITIUS

Trade liberalization in Mauritius has not influenced attempts at regional integration, although some recent moves towards regional integration have led to a degree of import liberalization.

Over recent years, Mauritius has been an active member of two regional groupings – the Indian Ocean Commission (IOC) and the Preferential

Table 6.15 Exports and imports of Mauritius within PTA/COMESA, 1982–93

Year	*Imports ($US m.)*	*Percentage of total Mauritian imports*	*Exports ($US m.)*	*Percentage of total Mauritian exports*
1982	9.35	2.0	1.80	0.5
1983	6.08	1.4	1.53	0.4
1984	7.75	1.6	3.33	0.9
1985	7.33	1.4	2.18	0.5
1986	7.92	1.2	2.21	0.3
1987	9.08	0.9	2.68	0.3
1988	8.85	0.7	3.47	0.3
1989	7.32	0.6	4.36	0.4
1990	19.54	1.2	6.84	0.6
1991	19.62	1.3	7.54	0.6
1992	31.95	2.0	10.40	0.8
1993	28.85	1.8	19.50	1.6

Source: Data obtained from Mauritius Export Development Investment Authority (MEDIA).

Trade Area for Eastern and Southern Africa/Common Market for Eastern and Southern Africa (PTA/COMESA) – and it has just joined the Southern African Development Community. The IOC, which was established in 1984, has five members – Malagasy Republic, Comoros, Seychelles and Réunion (a French overseas territory), and Mauritius. The IOC has so far concentrated on many areas of co-operation, and economic integration has not been given much importance. Hence there has been no attempt at trade liberalization within the IOC. However, some measures have been taken to increase the volume of trade among the members. These include, *inter alia*, the dissemination of information among traders and the increased availability of shipping facilities, lack of which seems to be the major obstacle to enhanced trade. As far as Mauritius is concerned, the IOC is not very important for its trade, as only 2 per cent of its trade is carried out within the IOC.

It must be noted that trade liberalization has taken place within PTA/COMESA. Mauritius has gradually reduced its tariffs on imports from other PTA countries. At present the imports benefit from a reduction of 70 per cent on import duties applied to other countries. It is expected that by the year 2000 all imports from other PTA countries will be allowed duty-free access.

The volume of trade Mauritius has within the PTA region remains fairly low. As Table 6.15 indicates, although imports have been increasing in more recent years, they still account for less than 2 per cent of Mauritius's total imports. Exports are much lower, but they have also been increasing in recent years.

Mauritius carries out only 5 per cent of its trade within the PTA/COMESA and the IOC. For historical reasons, most of the country's trade is with Europe, although some diversification into new markets in the region is actively pursued by government. Trade fairs and investment promotion campaigns have been intensified recently and double taxation agreements have been signed with a few countries.

6.7 ANALYSIS OF SURVEY DATA

As we have argued above, our assessment of the 1991–4 liberalization episode has been hampered by the lack of published data. An analysis of the survey data should therefore be quite useful. We first provide some background information on the survey.

Our proposed random sample of 100 firms included 35 EPZ and 65 non-EPZ firms, which included 15 small firms. EPZ firms usually produce exclusively for the export market, whereas non-EPZ firms produce mostly for the domestic market, with some firms exporting a small percentage of their output. Firms that refused to participate in the survey were repeatedly replaced until the field work had to be rounded up by mid-September 1995, when 81 firms had been interviewed – 24 from the EPZ and 57 from the non-EPZ sector. The various sectors covered by the 81 firms surveyed are indicated in Table 6.16. The EPZ is dominated by the textile and garments sector, whereas the non-EPZ sector is more diversified, producing import substitutes and non-tradeables.

It must be noted that it was decided to include relatively more non-EPZ firms in the sample because the direct impact of trade liberalization is felt by these firms. EPZ firms operate under a very liberal trade regime, completely exempted from the payment of import duties. Trade liberalization influences these firms through its effects on the non-EPZ sector. For example, a reduction in tariffs is expected to lead to a decline in employment in the non-EPZ sector, releasing labour and other resources for the EPZ sector.

Before presenting some of the important findings of the survey, we should point out that it was not possible to obtain all the data requested for reasons that may be specific to Mauritius. Given the small size of the domestic market, it is common to find that only a couple of firms produce a particular commodity for that market. For each of these firms,

Table 6.16 Sectoral distribution of manufacturing firms surveyed

Sector	*No. of firms*	*Total employment*
(a) EPZ		
Textile and ready-made garments	16	8909
Other	8	869
Total EPZ	*24*	*9778*
(b) Non-EPZ		
Textile and ready-made garments	11	1163
Food and beverages	11	1943
Metal products	10	972
Wood and furniture	6	419
Paper products	5	541
Footwear	4	92
Plastic products	3	32
Chemical products	3	341
Other	4	475
Total non-EPZ	*57*	*5978*

Source: Survey data.

information on sales, profits, inputs, investment, and so on, becomes quite strategic and is difficult to obtain. Even EPZ firms sometimes have a very small number of competitors based in Mauritius and it is understandable that some information cannot be released. Even when firms were willing to provide most of the information requested, they very often realized that searching for some of the require data put too much pressure on their time. Consequently, some of the results presented below may be affected by gaps in the data collected.

Employment and Employment Growth

Firms in the EPZ are much larger than non-EPZ firms. As shown in Table 6.16, EPZ firms on average employ almost four times as many workers as non-EPZ firms (407 compared to 105). The majority of non-EPZ firms are in fact relatively small, employing only up to 50 workers, whereas the vast majority of EPZ firms employ more than 100 workers, as shown in Table 6.17.

Table 6.17 Size distribution of manufacturing firms surveyed

Employment	*No. of firms*
(a) EPZ	
0–100	8
101–250	5
251–500	6
Above 500	5
Total EPZ	*24*
(b) Non-EPZ	
0–50	32
51–100	8
101–250	10
251–500	5
Above 500	2
Total non-EPZ	*57*

Source: Survey data.

A regression of the level of employment (EMP) of 63 firms shows that the level of sales (SALES) is an important determinant; whether the firm is an exporting firm – that is, whether it is an EPZ firm – is also important. The status of the firm is shown by a dummy variable (*DEPZ*). The results, based on OLS estimation, are shown below.

$$EMP = 45.5183 + 0.1122\,[\mathrm{E}{-5}]\,SALES + 141.1117\,DEPZ \qquad (6.1)$$

$$\begin{array}{llll} t & (1.9752) & (6.0146) & (3.4221) \\ P & (0.053) & (0.000) & (0.001) \end{array}$$

$R^2 = 0.41$ D.W. $= 2.1147$ $F(2,60) = 22.4147$

Mean of dependent variable = 146.8.

The results show that EPZ firms employ 141 more persons than non-EPZ firms. In fact, as EPZ firms have larger sales, they employ still many more workers. The coefficient on sales indicates that an increase in sales of Rs1 m increases employment by 1.12 per cent. These absolute figures may be difficult to interpret. It is more meaningful to consider the coefficient on sales in a regression using the double log form of Equation (6.1). The estimated equation gives:

Table 6.18 Changes in manufacturing employment, 1993–5

Sector	*No. of additional jobs*	*No. of jobs lost*	*Net change*
(a) EPZ			
Textiles and ready-made garments	788	950	–162
Other	186	2	+184
Total EPZ	*974*	*952*	*22*
(b) Non-EPZ			
Textile and ready-made garments	61	19	+42
Food and beverages	222	5	+217
Metal products	80	7	+73
Wood and furniture	100	0	+100
Paper products	85	90	–5
Footwear	1	15	–14
Plastic products	0	0	0
Chemical products	30	0	+30
Other	15	0	+15
Total non-EPZ	*594*	*136*	*458*

$$\text{LN}EMP = 5.6559 + 0.58808\ \text{LN}SALES + 0.55269\ DEPZ \qquad (6.2)$$

$$t \qquad (-7.1017)\ (12.0087) \qquad (2.4085)$$

$$P \qquad (0.000)\ (0.000) \qquad (0.019)$$

$$R^2 = 0.72 \quad \text{D.W.} = 2.0208 \quad F(2,60) = 80.4736$$

Mean of dependent variable = 4.0533.

An increase in sales of 1 per cent leads to an increase in employment of 0.6 per cent, suggesting that the manufacturing sector is still labour-intensive.

We can also examine the growth of employment, from figures for 1993, 1994 and 1995 collected during the survey. Table 6.18 confirms an important change in employment that seems to have set in at the national level. The EPZ, which was set up in 1970, has expanded fairly rapidly over the years to become a major employer. In 1990, 30.6 per cent of the total employment in large establishments (employing 10 or more workers) came from the EPZ. There was a decline in the number of jobs in 1993 (84 930 compared to 86 797 in 1990), the latest year for which statistics are available.

Table 6.18 shows that the employment creation in the EPZ considerably slackened over the period 1993–5. There has also been a decline in total employment in textiles and garments, the backbone of the EPZ since its establishment. This decline is not the result of national policies of trade liberalization, but is due to the increasing competition Mauritian EPZ firms have to face when exporting to the EU and to the USA, where EPZ exports have duty-free access. Table 6.18 also reveals that there is some diversification taking place in the EPZ.

From the survey data we can point out an interesting change in the trend of non-EPZ manufacturing employment. Over the period 1990–3, total employment in large establishments declined slightly, from 23 639 to 22 076 (an 8.3 per cent to 7.7 per cent drop). The survey shows, however, that during the same time, the non-EPZ sector contributed most of the increase in manufacturing employment. As shown in Table 6.18, employment increased in all non-EPZ industries except paper products and footwear. Import permits for the final goods produced by these industries were abolished in 1991 and tariffs have also been significantly reduced. An important question that arises is whether the increase in non-EPZ employment is related to the liberalization of imports over that period. This question is taken up below.

Regression analysis confirms the changes in employment growth summarized in Table 6.18. For 75 out of 81 firms surveyed, the change in employment over the period 1993–5 (*CHEMP*) is significantly related to the size of the firm and to whether the firm is an EPZ firm. The size of the firm is proxied by its total employment in 1993 (EMP93) and a dummy variable is used for EPZ firms (*DEPZ*). The results of OLS estimation give:

$$
\begin{array}{llll}
CHEMP = & 21.7125 & - \; 0.13285 \text{ EMP93} & + \; 33.2063 \; DEPZ \qquad (6.3) \\
t & (2.6716) & (-10.4007) & (2.2458) \\
P & (0.009) & (0.000) & (0.028)
\end{array}
$$

$$R^2 = 0.59 \quad \text{D.W.} = 1.9162 \quad F(2,73) = 54.2103$$

$$\text{Mean of dependent variable} = 5.75$$

According to the above results, employment creation is negatively related to the size of the firm.

Investment

The level of investment undertaken by EPZ and non-EPZ firms in 1994 is shown in Table 6.19. It is interesting to note that although employment has been declining in the textile and ready-made garments industries,

Table 6.19 Investment in manufacturing firms, 1994

	No. of firms Investing	*Investment (Rs m.)*
(a) EPZ		
Textiles and ready-made garments	12	46.8
Other	3	0.7
Total	*15*	*47.5*
(b) Non-EPZ		
Textiles and ready-made garments	8	53.0
Food and beverages	8	424.6
Metal products	5	11.3
Wood and furniture	5	8.3
Paper products	4	95.5
Footwear	2	0.2
Plastic products	3	0.9
Chemical products	2	23.0
Other	3	14.0
Total	*40*	*630.8*

Source: Survey data.

12 out of the 16 firms surveyed indicated that they undertook new investments in 1994, totalling Rs46.8 m. Although this represents a very small amount of investment, Rs5253 per worker, it is an indication that EPZ firms are increasing their capital intensity to face increasing worldwide competition.

A significantly greater proportion of non-EPZ firms invested in 1994. In fact, investment took place in all the non-EPZ industries listed in Table 6.19. However, more than two-thirds of the total investment in Rs 630.8 m was made in food and beverages alone. The average investment per worker for the whole non-EPZ sector was Rs105 520. This confirms that non-EPZ firms remain relatively more capital-intensive.

What is the likely impact of the investment on employment? Firms were asked whether they expected their employment levels to be higher in 1996 and in 1998. Surprisingly enough, EPZ firms in textiles and ready-made garments expect that employment would be at least 10 per cent higher in 1996. This seems to be at variance with the decline in employment noted in these industries over the period 1993–5. However, with the investment undertaken in 1994, it might be reasonable to expect employment to increase, since textile and garment industries are fairly labour-intensive.

Similarly, it is surprising to note that non-EPZ firms expect their employment levels to remain the same, given the high level of investment in 1994. However, non-EPZ firms are highly capital-intensive and the additional investments is likely to increase their capital-intensiveness.

Regression analysis confirms that non-EPZ firms invest significantly more than EPZ firms. The determining factors are the profit ratio (*PROFR*), defined here as the ratio of profits to the book value of plant and equipment, and the level of employment (*EMP*). The status of the firm is also important, as shown by the coefficient of the dummy variable (*NEPZ*), set to 1 for non-EPZ firms. The results of OLS estimation give:

$$\begin{array}{llllll} \text{LN}INV = & 12.0070 & -\ 0.55193\ PROFR & +\ 0.0065206\ EMP & +\ 1.4883\ NEPZ \\ t & (18.7514) & (-2.5081) & (4.2206) & (2.3529) \\ P & (0.000) & (0.057) & (0.000) & (0.024) \end{array}$$

$$R^2 = 0.37 \quad \text{D.W.} = 2.3820 \quad F(3,38) = 8.92 \tag{6.4}$$

Mean of dependent variable = 13.9401.

The negative coefficient on the profit ratio requires some comment. Usually, we expect a positive relationship between the profit ratio and investment. Assuming that the data collected are fairly reliable for profits and book value of plant and equipment, we know that non-EPZ firms are relatively more capital-intensive. As the book value of plant and equipment rises, the profit ratio declines. But the non-EPZ firms with declining profit ratios invest more on average, as they are relatively capital-intensive.

Trade Liberalization and Resource Allocation

As trade liberalization progresses, domestic firms usually encounter increased competition. The vast majority of non-EPZ firms (87 per cent) in our sample said they had faced greater competition from imports in 1994, a direct consequence of the import liberalization measures adopted since 1991. Higher competition from imports is likely to lead to a decline in the utilization of resources, which can be offset later if the firms become more efficient and more competitive.

Although EPZ firms are not directly affected by national trade liberalization policies, they have to face increased competition as world trade is gradually liberalized. About 80 per cent of EPZ firms noted increased competition in export markets. Again, more competition is likely to lead to a reduction in the utilization of resources in the first instance.

Regression results for 53 firms show that employment declines when firms (both EPZ and non-EPZ) face higher competition. Employment is determined by the stock of capital and equipment (*CAP*). Two dummy variables are included – one for the status of the firm (*DNEPZ* defined as before) and one for higher competition (*DCOMP*). The results of the OLS estimation are reported below.

$$EMP = 47.0140 + 0.2310\,[E-5]\,CAP - 130.4687\,DNEPZ - 170.5769\,DCOMP$$

t	(6.8133)	(3.6377)	(−2.9365)	(−3.4143)
P	(0.000)	(0.001)	(0.005)	(0.001)

$R^2 = 0.37$ D.W. = 2.3715 $F(3,49) = 11.2656$ (6.5)

Mean of dependent variable = 127.3774.

According to the above results, employment is expected to decline with higher competition. However, when Equation (6.5) is estimated for non-EPZ firms only, the coefficient of the *DCOMP* variable is not significant. This means that higher competition leads to some decline in employment, but this is not important. It must be remembered that employment is difficult to reduce for non-EPZ firms. On the other hand, they can easily reduce their investment levels if they face higher competition.

Equation (6.4) is therefore estimated again for 30 non-EPZ firms only. A dummy variable representing lower expected tariffs on imports of consumer goods is included. Again, however, it is seen that increased liberalization leads to a small decline in investment, but this decline is not significant.

Trade liberalization has not significantly brought down the utilization of resources in non-EPZ firms. In fact, these firms have considerably increased their investment and employment levels, as shown in Tables 6.18 and 6.19. The expansion of these firms may be partly explained by the fact that some of the goods produced are non-tradeables (for exam-ple, metal products for the increasing construction activity). Moreover, it must be noted that the bulk of additional employment and investment has taken place in the food and beverages industries, which traditionally have been highly protected (Tables 6.5 and 6.8), although recent liberalization measures might have slightly reduced their effective protection rates.

Credibility of Import Liberalization

Given the various import liberalization measures adopted since 1991, it might be feared that these measures are not sustainable and that import duties might be revised upwards – and that additional taxes might be raised through increases in income and corporate tax rates. However, as we argued in Section 6.4 above, trade liberalization has been credible right from the 1980s. The survey confirms this, as only 4 per cent of all firms in the sample expect increases in import duties and income and corporate taxes. The corporate tax was, in fact, reduced from 35 per cent to 15 per cent for all firms in June 1995, just before the survey was undertaken, yet there was no fear that this reduced rate would not be sustained. One reason for this is that important changes in taxes are announced some years ahead and there have been no reversals, except for import duties on furniture.

Regional Trade

The limited extent of regional trade is clearly indicated by the survey results. Only 12 of 57 non-EPZ firms export up to 10 per cent of their output to the region. EPZ firms do not export at all to the region. A significant proportion of non-EPZ firms (44 per cent) would like to export to the region but find various obstacles, mainly tariffs. Although Mauritius grants 70 per cent reduction in tariffs on regional imports, it seems that other countries in the region do not apply similar reductions in their tariffs.

6.8 CONCLUSIONS AND OVERALL ASSESSMENT

Output growth and trade performance in the post-structural adjustment and trade liberalization episode has been impressive. Relating this success to trade liberalization is of course convenient, but such an interpretation of events is not without its critics. Mauritius is often labelled as a special case because of its particular endowments and favourable external conditions.

In recent years external conditions have been conducive to growth in three regards.

(1) Under the Lomé Agreement guaranteed prices have been fixed for sugar. The EU is the principal consumer of Mauritian sugar, and provides a price that has been some three to five times the world price. (See Blake, Milner, Reed and Westaway [1994] for an assessment of the structural effects of a sustained increased in the price of sugar in the case of Mauritius.)
(2) Income growth in industrial countries in the 1980s has sustained a rapid expansion of the tourist sector. Between 1982 and 1988, tourist arrivals doubled to almost 240 000 per annum.

(3) The economy has benefited from footloose foreign direct investment (FDI). Though this is partly due to domestic policies, it has also been helped by external factors, in particular uncertainty regarding Hong Kong's and South Africa's political future, and the absence of tight MFN quotas applicable to Mauritius.

Both favourable external conditions and a more stable posture of macroeconomic policy during the 1980s were arguably necessary but not sufficient conditions for the growth and trade effects recorded in recent years. The principal stimulus came from growth-enhancing supply-side policies (including trade liberalization) that were directed at exploiting the economy's natural resources – relatively costly but well-educated labour and a stable political environment. An important element here was the existence of the EPZ. This was set up in 1970, but for some years its growth was disappointing. The analysis above would suggest that this was in part because up to the early 1980s the incentives to invest in the import-substitute sector reduced the incentive to invest in the EPZ. In the 1980s, further inducements to EPZ investment were offered, and the incentives to invest in the import-substitute sector have been reduced through trade liberalization. Protection of the import sector has as a result been reduced. At the same time barriers to FDI have been reduced. For example, double taxation agreements have been negotiated with a number of large industrialized countries, required documentation has been reduced and information services have improved. In addition, the infrastructure has improved significantly, not only for basic transportation, but also in terms of communication facilities and information technology.

The gradual transformation in Mauritius from an inward-orientated to an outward-orientated trade regime has been intervention-led rather than market-led (Greenaway and Milner, 1991). In the 1960s and 1970s relative incentives favoured the import-substitute sector. With the creation of the EPZ in 1970 the intervention-led export promotion phase began. Since that time, and in the 1980s in particular, the range of incentives available to exporters has increased. Moreover, protection of the import-substitute sector has fallen. It is important to note, however, that much of this intervention has been directed at freeing markets – and then allowing them to work. A key sector in this regard is the foreign exchange market. The willingness to allow real exchange rate depreciation to occur in the 1980s, and to allow the exchange rate to become market-determined, was crucial. In stimulating export growth this has probably been as important as trade liberalization. Thus, although the export orientation has been intervention-led, its success has rested, at least in part, on the loosening up of markets.

Finally, it should be emphasized that the shift over time to a more market-led development strategy has been facilitated in the Mauritian case by the efforts to maintain a political consensus for the reform agenda. The maintenance of this consensus was no doubt conducive to sustaining the reform programme. This may be another aspect of Mauritius's special case status, but it is nonetheless an aspect from which lessons can be learned.

References

Blake, A., C. R. Milner, G. Reed and A. J. Westaway (1994) 'Trade Shocks and Model Dimensionality: A CGE Analysis for Mauritius', paper presented to a workshop on *CGE modelling* at the Centre for African Economies, Oxford.

Collier, P., D. Greenaway and J. W. Gunning (1993) 'A Methodology for the Study of Trade Liberalization', paper presented at the workshop on *Regional Integration and Trade Liberalization*, Nairobi.

Collier, P. and J. W. Gunning (1994) 'Trade and Development: Protection, Shocks and Liberalization', in D. Greenaway and L. A. Winters (eds), *Surveys in International Trade* (Oxford: Blackwell).

Greenaway, D. and R. Lamusse (1994) 'Private and public sector responses to the 1972–75 sugar boom in Mauritius', mimeo.

Greenaway, D. and C. R. Milner (1986) 'Estimating the shifting of protection across sectors: an application to Mauritius', *Industry and Development*, **16**:1–22.

Greenaway, D. and C. R. Milner (1989) 'Nominal and effective tariffs in a small industrialising economy: the case of Mauritius', *Applied Economics*, **21**:995–1010.

Greenaway, D. and C. R. Milner (1991) 'Did Mauritius really provide a case study in Malthusian Economics?', *Journal of International Development*, **3**:325–38.

Maxwell Stamp (1992) 'Social, Economic and Environmental Impact of Industrialisation and Strategy Formulation, Report to the Government of Mauritius'.

Milner, C. R. and A. McKay (1996) 'Real exchange rate concepts and the measurement of liberalisation: some evidence for Mauritius', *Journal of African Economies*.

World Bank (1994) *Adjustment in Africa: Reform, Results and the Road Ahead* (New York: Oxford University Press).

7 Trade Liberalization in Tanzania: Episodes and Impacts

Benno Ndulu, Joseph Semboja and A. V. Y. Mbelle

7.1 INTRODUCTION: TRADE AND DEVELOPMENT – A REVIEW OF ISSUES

The relationship between trade and development has occupied a central place in the development debate over a long period. Indeed the vigour and interest characterizing it reflects both its perceived importance and continuing elusiveness in settling the main contentious issues on the theoretical and empirical fronts. Helleiner (1992) and Edwards (1993) undertake an admirable and comprehensive review of the key issues and empirical studies which preoccupy this debate affecting developing countries. What is particularly notable from this review is the continuing difficulties in obtaining reliable measures of trade policy and identifying more precisely the channels through which outward orientation affects growth. This is without prejudice to an apparent convergence of views (not consensus) that a reduction of barriers to international exchange promotes the growth of world trade and income more generally. This is evidenced at least by the strong association observed between reduction of such barriers and growth in trade since the last world war (Tanzi, 1995).

Although the gains from this growth are not equitably shared, they do provide opportunities to all to partake in them. South East Asian countries and a few others in Latin America have succeeded in exploiting these opportunities significantly and achieved spectacular growth rates in exports and income.

During the 1960s and 1970s the most influential thoughts affecting a dominant stance on trade policy in developing countries were those of Prebisch and Singer. Their thesis was essentially that secular decline of international prices for primary commodities, on which developing countries were most dependent for exports and income, led to a growing gap of incomes between the developing and the developed world. Diversification through industrialization was considered to be the key for closing this gap. Such industrialization, given the competitive disadvantage of late starters, could only be successfully achieved through protection based on the infant industry argument. The plethora of import-substitution industrialization experiments pursued in earnest across most developing countries well through the 1970s had their grounds on this thesis.

Other writers have noted, however, that excessive protection of industry in developing countries stifled productivity growth, encouraged industrialization at the expense of agriculture and exports, reduced savings, increased unemployment and led to very low rates of capacity utilization. They empirically supported these assertions through effective protection measures, anti-export bias measures and estimates of negative effects on income, exports and employment growth. Naturally these critics strongly advocated openness to international trade and complementary macroeconomic policies as essential to successful export-led industrialization and rapid growth. The key argument is that policies which do not discriminate against exports allow exploitation of comparative advantage; permit greater capacity utilization, exploitation of scale economies and employment generation as a result of expanded market opportunities. They also induce technological improvements and productivity growth in response to competition from abroad and through access to a larger menu of innovation taking place in developed countries. The public nature of such innovation makes it possible to access it without typically incurring costs of developing it (Baldwin, 1993). It is also argued that barriers to imports for protection of local industries are effectively a tax on exports because they raise the domestic resource costs for exports and lead to the appreciation of the real exchange rate thereby reducing international competitiveness and incentive to export.

The effectiveness of a liberalized trade policy stance or the lack of it has been empirically shown by these studies mainly by estimating its impact on export growth, particularly non-traditional exports in developing countries. The studies have largely related trade regimes to export growth, and in turn export growth to income growth, and claim an indirect causation in that direction. Some also added the impacts of the higher productivity export sector growth on overall growth. In addition to the productivity differential effect export externalities were shown to have a relatively stronger explanatory power for overall growth performance.

A lack of strong empirical evidence to support the link between export performance and growth has been a major weakness and a source of continuing controversies (Helleiner 1986 and 1995). Furthermore, the problem of simultaneity in the relationship has further undermined the strength of the conclusions reached with respect to direction of causation.

The simplicity of the regressions used in the relationships omitted other factors such as the role of world market conditions and trade strategy.

Esfahami (1991) and Helleiner (1990) instead emphasize the link between export growth and economy-wide growth through the alleviation of the foreign exchange constraint to imports, while others emphasize the problem of lumping together the effects of trade and macroeconomic policies. In this respect there are the difficulties of the identification of when quantitative restrictions are predominantly for macroeconomic purposes (protection of reserves) and when they are employed for protective purposes.

Overall, however, there is a strong trend towards trade liberalization in the world. Industrial countries have experienced a strong downward trend in tariffs, falling from about 40 per cent on average in 1950 to less than 5 per cent by the late 1980s, with continuance thereafter (Tanzi, 1995). The 1970s and 1980s, saw similar trends in developing countries, partly as a result of a 'light bulb' effect and partly on account of compliance to conditionality for external support. These trends are reflected in the rapid growth of world trade share in output due to a higher trade growth, at about 5.1 per cent per year compared to output growth of 3.0 per cent (Tanzi, 1995).

Drawing from the above review and the framework paper by Collier, Greenaway and Gunning (1995), our study will pay particular attention to the following issues. First is the distinction between what we consider to be pure trade policy (for example, external trade taxes) and other trade-related policies (for example, quantitative restrictions and exchange rate policy). In the case of the latter, we note that they could also be employed purely for the purpose of macroeconomic stabilization. In assessing the impacts of these instruments on economic performance and arriving at attribution to trade or macroeconomic measures, their main purpose for a given period of application will be taken into account. What perhaps reduces the significance of the distinction is the complementary nature of trade liberalization and macroeconomic stabilization policies in ensuring sustainable trade liberalization.

Second is the issue of methodological difficulties in identifying trade liberalization episodes. Those episodes prompted by policy initiatives in Tanzania have persisted over a long period but with a changing character. Reversals have tended to be partial rather than for the whole trade regime. For example, some upward revisions were made in tariff rates for revenue purposes in 1993, while the exchange regime became more liberalized and other quantitative restrictions further dismantled. A broad characterization of the episodes would thus have to employ some weights to the various instruments used. In particular there is a need to consider the relative weights attached to import liberalization, export promotion and exchange regime liberalization in the episodes as well as the timing and intensity of these features in trade liberalization, which vary over time. The effects of liberalization on various macro-aggregates also differ depending on the relative significance of these features. In the case of liberalization episodes which respond to temporary positive reversible shocks, the identification is more straightforward. Episodes based on policy initiatives, on the other hand, display much more variation in character over time.

Third is the assessment of the impacts of trade liberalization. The main methodological problems here relate to the issues of attribution and the key channels of transmission of effects. Whereas, as pointed out earlier, previous studies have focused largely on transmission to growth via exports, in a foreign exchange-constrained economy reduction in import compression and enhanced availability of basic goods might have a stronger effect on production and investment. Thus, for example, in response to the partial import liberalization under the Own-Funded Imports scheme introduced in 1984, agricultural and industrial production growth rose significantly in 1985 and 1986 prior to the intensive liberalization measures aimed at improved export performance implemented later. In fact, agricultural growth in Tanzania peaked during this period.

Export response, particularly of the manufacturing sector, followed the massive exchange rate depreciation after 1986, which significantly enhanced the profitability of export activities relative to those aimed at the domestic market (Ndulu and Semboja, 1995). This response was, however, again helped along by resumption of external resource inflows linked to compliance to the conditions for reforms. Import decompression effects made possible by sources other than the growth of the official export earnings have been an important part of the observed revival of real growth during the liberalization period.

In this regard we intend to distinguish, to the extent it is possible, the separate effects of import liberalization, export promotion and the liberalization of exchange regimes on the various macro-aggregates. We note here the significance of positive external shocks in prompting import liberalization compared to the large weight of deliberate policy initiatives in the other two features of trade liberalization. We will also distinguish the different channels through which these features affect exports, imports, incomes, productivity growth, employment and macroeconomic stability.

The fourth issue concerns the sustainability of trade liberalization. This crucially depends on the credibility of reforms being undertaken. Reforms may be perceived to be incredible in the absence of compatible macroeconomic policy measures, lack of capacity for policy surprise and time inconsistency of policy measures adopted (Collier, Greenaway and

Gunning, 1995). The key diagnostics and measures suggested focus on maintaining external balance through money supply restrictions to counteract reduction in the demand for money due to the expansion of demand for imports as domestic prices for imports decline with trade liberalization. The measures so adopted may be incompatible with each other, as the recent experience suggests. Massive sales of treasury bills at very high rates of return accompanied by speculative capital inflows to cash in on high differential domestic real interest rates with world capital market returns, have tended to create appreciation pressure on the local currency. This in turn has tended to put pressure on external competitiveness and profitability of exports. In the long run, as the speculative bubble bursts and reserves disappear, the current account balance may deteriorate, threatening the sustainability of the liberalization. There may thus be real trade-offs in the intensity of application of liquidity squeeze measures and exchange rate policy which introduce inconsistency in compatibility measures.

Section 7.2 describes the evolution of trade regimes in Tanzania since independence, highlighting the changes from closed to more open liberal regimes and the rationale for them. Section 7.3 characterizes trade liberalization episodes, highlighting their dominant features and motivation. Section 7.4 assesses the impacts of trade liberalization on exports, imports, productivity growth and fiscal balance. Furthermore, the section also assesses the impacts of and responses to liberalization and through regional trading arrangements. Section 7.5 concludes the study with an assessment of the sustainability of trade liberalization initiatives in the context of other policy and exogeneous pressures.

7.2 EVOLUTION OF THE TRADE REGIME IN TANZANIA: 1961–94

Tanzania has experienced significant changes in its external regime in the past three and a half decades. These changes mainly reflected stances in broader economic policy and strategies for development adopted by the country. Although there are numerous changes in the trade regime over the period, one can characterize them broadly into three periodic thrusts. These entailed a move from an open liberal trade regime during the first half of the 1960s, to a protected and closed regime during the late 1960s–early 1980s, and back towards a more open and liberal regime thereafter. Up to 1965, while the East African Currency Board was operational, the trade regime was relatively open, free of exchange controls, and with tariffs on imports mainly for protective purposes. The currency of the three East African countries was convertible under the Currency Board arrangement.

Following the dissolution of the Currency Board in 1965, the three countries introduced own currencies. Tanzania immediately introduced exchange controls to stem capital flight arising from the uncertainty originating from the break-up of the Board and soon thereafter from the adoption of socialist policy and its related nationalization campaigns. A series of restrictive measures governing trade and exchange were instituted during the late 1960s and 1970s in response to the emerging pressures from foreign exchange scarcity, tightening of a protective stance to assist import-substitution industrialization and a predisposition to controls under the tenets of a socialist economy. These measures included introduction of foreign exchange budgeting in 1971, and import licensing and external trade confinement to public agencies in 1972. This character of the regime persisted through to the mid-1980s, albeit with some variation in the tightness of restrictions, depending mainly on the availability of foreign exchange.

The move towards reinstituting a more open and liberal trade regime began in July 1984, with the Own Funds Import Scheme. Under this scheme, import licences were issued automatically, provided the importer used own funds, with no questions asked as to their source. Starting with a limited list, this was expanded to encompass a broad range of goods. Subsequent introduction of the Open General Licence System (OGL) and its expansion thereafter significantly added to the proportion of imports not subject to restrictions (Mbelle, 1993). Tariff reduction, dismantling of exchange controls and a steep depreciation of the local currency after 1986 combined to make the regime more open and liberal. The measures instituted after 1986 were to a significant extent prompted by compliance to conditionality related to the implementation of donor-supported economic reform programmes.

In order to have a more in depth characterization of the evolution of the trade regime in Tanzania, we group the trade policy measures into those which affect import liberalization, the liberal nature of exchange regime and export promotion. The mapping of specific policy accounts to these features is the main instrument adopted in this chapter to describe the evolution of the trade regime. Tables 7.1–7.3 present this evolutionary mapping of policy measures to the three regime features.

Flexibility to import is measured by two indicators, average effective tariff rate (revenue from import duty/value of imports) and the proportion of import licences issued on demand. In this regard higher tariff rates and tight import controls through licensing act as restraints to timely and flexible importation of goods. As Table 7.1 shows, average effective tariff rates (the ratio of import duty revenue to the value of imports) reached an early peak at the onset of the protective regime during 1966–9. The peak was reached in 1969 at nearly 18 per cent (Table 7.4). In

Table 7.1 Import flexibility

Period	*Average effective tariff rate (%)*	*Policy changes*	*Proportion of licences on demand (%)*	*Policy changes*
1966–70	15.1	–	0	Break up of East African Currency Board Tanzania shilling created 1966 Introduction of Exchange Control
1971–6	9.9	–	0	Introduction to foreign exchange budgeting Introduction of trade confinement and import licensing
1977–9	10.2	Break-up of East African Community common tariff arrangements	0	Relaxation of controls following 1977/78 coffee boom; however, no official change in policy
1980–3	7.8	–	–	Tightening of exchange controls and import licensing
1984–6	8.4	–	36.5	Adoption of Economic Recovery Programme 1986 (market forces emphasis) and introduction and expansion of own funds window
1987–92	5.8	Compression of rates and categories 'tariff liberalization'	45.2	Introduction of 'true' OGL in 1988 Introduction of forex bureaux in 1992
1993–4	4.1	Tariff rates raised but exemption increases in relation to investment promotion	100	Unification of exchange rates 1/8/93 and *de facto* abolition of licensing

Source: Compiled by the authors.

fact the scheduled tariff rates for competing imports were much higher, ranging up to 200 per cent (Ndulu *et al.*, 1987). The fact that average effective tariff rates were much lower partly reflected a composition of imports dominated by intermediate and capital goods which were charged significantly lower rates, exemption of duties offered to the public sector and foreign-funded projects as well as tax evasion on account of prohibitive rates. The subsequent decline in average effective tariff rates during the 1970s and early 1980s was a result of the growth of imports subject to exemption as the number of public enterprises and donor-funded projects increased. Deliberate policy efforts to reduce scheduled tariff rates began in 1987 after the adoption of economic reform measures in 1986. The aim was to rationalize the protective structure by reducing the rate categories and to induce compliance through lower rates. Although a temporary reversal occurred in 1993 when tariff rates were raised for revenue purposes, the effective tariff rates during 1987–94 were less than a third of those at the peak in 1969.

The second measure of import liberalization is the proportion of import licences issued on demand. In Table 7.1, this measure broadly reflects the official stance, although within it the ease with which licences were issued depended on the availability of foreign exchange. Thus during 1978–9 in contrast to the rest of the period 1970–83, almost all requests for foreign exchange were granted expeditiously. This was due to a positive external shock in the form of a commodity price boom which significantly relaxed foreign exchange scarcity. This period of relaxation was followed immediately by immense tightening of restrictions as a foreign exchange crunch bit during 1980–3. Not only were the import licences more difficult to obtain, but even when they were obtained, externalization of funds was not assured. In fact, during this period a large overhang of letters of credit built up with commercial banks. Policy changes in this sphere begun only in 1984 with the introduction of Own Funds Imports scheme. This resulted in the proportion of licences issued on demand reaching an average of 37 per cent during 1984–6. The introduction of the OGL in 1988 and later on the Foreign Exchange Bureaux in 1992 raised this average further to 45 per cent during 1987–92. A *de facto* abolition of controls in import licensing was implemented during 1993/94. Only a few items remain under the control list, mainly for health and security reasons.

The restrictiveness of the exchange regime is characterized by the premium on the official exchange rate. It measures the extent to which access to foreign exchange is restricted by exchange controls and is at variance with the public unrestricted demand for foreign exchange. As Table 7.2 shows, the first large increase in the exchange rate premium occurred during 1972–6. The official exchange rate remained more or less fixed during this period but restrictions in access to foreign exchange were introduced through the enactment of the Licensing Act in 1972. Private importers faced more stringent access and most often had to gain such

Table 7.2 Exchange regime

Period	*Premium (%)*	*Policy changes*
1966–71	31.1	First devaluation in 1971
1972–6	129.9	Devaluations in 1973 and 1975
		First OGL introduced 1972 for sourcing foreign exchange through normal export proceeds
		Private importers restricted
1977–9	91.8	Partial liberalization of imports following 1977/78 coffee boom
1980–4	232.3	OGL suspended 1982
		Introduction of own funds window 1984, private importers allowed
1985–6	440.8	Devaluation 1986
1987–92	85.9	Introduction of 'true' OGL in 1988
		Foreign Exchange Regulation Act of 1992 allowing bureaux to operate
1993–4	6.4	Forex auctions introduced July 1993
		Unification of exchange rates in August 1993

Source: Compiled by the authors.

access via official confinees. The foreign exchange crunch of 1973/74 occasioned by the first oil crisis led to further tightening of access.

The decline in the exchange rate premium during 1977–9 was a result of a partial relaxation of restrictions as foreign exchange availability improved with the coffee boom. The subsequent collapse of commodity prices, the second oil crisis, world recession and the post-effects of large import demand to service a war with Idi Amin's Uganda ushered in a severe tightening of controls leading to a steep rise on the premium during 1980–4. A further rise during 1985–6 resulted from the expansion of demand for foreign exchange as private importers were allowed to operate again under the Own Funds Imports scheme. Since then, a combination of a steep official devaluation of the local currency; relaxation of licensing controls under the OGL; introduction of the foreign exchange bureaux; foreign exchange auctions and ultimately adoption of interbank trade of foreign exchange; resulted in a virtual disappearence of the exchange rate premium by 1994. The remaining small margin probably reflects the differences in transactions costs between the parallel market and the other official sources as well as catering for capital account transactions currently not allowed.

Table 7.3 Export promotion

Period	*Export tax (%)*	*Policy changes*	*Promotional measures*
1966–72	2.1	—	—
1973–80	8.1	Export taxes, particularly on agricultural exports, raised	—
1981–5	0.3	Abolition of export taxes on most agricultural crops in a bid to raise producer prices with exchange rates still fixed	Presidential export award introduced 1981 Export rebate introduced in 1981 Export retention scheme introduced in 1983 Seed capital revolving scheme introduced in January 1985 Preferential interest rates to exporters introduced in 1985 Trade facilitation scheme introduced in 1981
1986–94	0	Export taxes abolished for all items	Duty drawback scheme introduced 1/7/88 Foreign exchange entitlement certificate introduced in 1990 Gold premium pricing introduced 1991 Export credit guarantee scheme introduced 1990

Source: Compiled by the authors.

Export facilitation, as shown in Table 7.3, is characterized by a combination of the level of explicit taxes levied on exports and the intensity of other promotional measures pursued to encourage export activities. As the table shows, the period 1966–72 was characterized by relatively low taxes on exports. This situation significantly changed during 1973–80, when effective export tax rates shot up to an average of 8.1 per cent. This shift accompanied the change in policy which heavily taxed agriculture to build industries. The negative impact this rise had on export volumes and the growth of parallel markets to evade heavy taxation, prompted a reversal of the stance in the early 1980s. Since the exchange rate remained more or less fixed and the local currency overvalued, the only recourse available then for raising official producer prices was to increase the share of world prices passed on to producers by virtually abolishing all export taxes on agricultural products.

Export promotional measures were, on the other hand, mainly targeted at non-traditional exports, predominantly manufactures. These were aimed at compensating for the negative effects of controls in the import and exchange regimes. They particularly included efforts to ameliorate the effects of the implicit taxation via overvaluation of local currency through preferential access to foreign exchange and tax rebates to improve the profitability of exports. Table 7.3 lists the complete set of measures instituted in this regard. As restrictions of the import and exchange regimes were subsequently relaxed, compensatory measures have become increasingly superfluous. The surge in non-traditional exports during 1986–90 was largely driven by real depreciation of the exchange rate, which significantly raised the relative profitability of exports.

Two other measures are used to confirm the above characterization of the trade regime. The first is a summary measure which can be used to characterize the evolution of the trade policy regime described above. This characterizes the regime's trade policy based on the ratio of domestic to world terms of trade (Collier, Greenaway and Gunning, 1995) or as in a similar measure of anti-export bias, which is the ratio of the effective exchange rate (EER) applied to the importers that applied to exporters (Edwards, 1993). The earlier approach, under conditions of no implicit tariffs, reduces to the ratio $(1 + t_m)/(1 + t_e)$ for a given ratio of foreign prices for exports and imports, where t_e and t_m are net export subsidies and import duties respectively. The latter approach, which takes into account import surcharges (n), other incentives to exporters (r) and import premium (PR) reduces to $(1 + t_m + n + PR)/(1 + t_e + r)$. For a given exchange rate, this ratio boils down to the ratio of domestic prices of imports to the domestic prices of exports. Tanzania has hardly used import surcharges as a policy instrument and other export incentives have been insignificant, having been mainly confined to exports of manufacturers which constitute less than a quarter of total exports. The measure we have adopted therefore is the ratio $(1 + t_m + PR)/(1 + t_e)$, where PR is the exchange rate premium. Table 7.4 presents the evolution of this measure and its components.

The evolution of the summary measure of anti-export bias confirms the above description of the evolution of the trade regime. It is clear from Table 7.4 that the effect of quantitative restrictions, here measured by the exchange rate premium, is the most dominant in the characterization of the evolution. Anti-export bias quickly builds up in the early 1970s with the onset of quantitative restrictions in 1972. It rises significantly above 1 (1 represents neutrality) in the next four years as these restrictions are tightened in response to the first oil crisis and increased exports taxes. The temporary sharp decline in the bias during 1978/79 matches the short-lived relaxation of import restrictions occassioned by the coffee boom, before a sharp tightening during the first half of the 1980s for

Table 7.4 Characterization of the evolution of the trade regime using the measure of anti-export bias

Year	t_m (%)	t_e (%)	*PR* (%)	$(1 + t_m + PR)(1 + t_e)$
1966	14.6	1.2	20.4	1.37
1967	16.8	1.9	21.8	1.41
1968	17.3	2.3	19.0	1.40
1969	17.9	2.4	21.8	1.43
1970	13.3	2.2	41.5	1.58
1971	10.6	2.1	62.5	1.77
1972	11.0	2.4	112.9	2.29
1973	12.2	5.2	106.6	2.30
1974	9.6	6.5	89.1	2.12
1975	8.3	5.5	183.6	3.09
1976	8.4	9.4	196.7	3.37
1977	10.8	12.3	171.4	3.22
1978	9.3	10.6	69.9	2.00
1979	10.5	8.9	46.0	1.72
1980	7.1	6.1	156.1	2.80
1981	6.6	2.1	233.3	3.47
1982	6.7	0.5	251.3	3.60
1983	9.4	0.3	255.5	3.66
1984	9.3	0.2	265.6	3.76
1985	8.6	0	477.0	5.86
1986	8.1	0	404.6	5.14
1987	6.5	0	180.1	2.87
1988	5.9	0	111.5	2.17
1989	6.0	0	78.4	1.84
1990	5.5	0	66.7	1.72
1991	5.7	0	43.8	1.50
1992	5.2	0	36.0	1.41
1993	4.1	0	5.3	1.09

Notes:
t_m = effective import duty rates
t_e = effective export tax rate
PR = exchange rate premium
The last column represents the anti-export bias measure, where 1 signifies neutrality

Source: Compiled by the authors.

reasons given earlier. A drastic reduction in export taxes did not offset the effects of the tightening of controls during this period as the index shot up to unprecedented levels. The liberalization of the import and exchange regimes subsequently resulted in achievement of a virtual neutrality of the trade regime by 1993.

The second measure is the effective rate of protection (ERP). Although this measure has been widely used to analyse the relationship between trade policy and the structure of the economy, it can also be used as a measure of incidence of trade liberalization. In the latter case it can be employed to trace changes in the trade regimes. High effective rates of protection have typically favoured import-substitution industries at the expense of agriculture and exports. Thus liberalization will be construed to have taken place when ERP has fallen.

Although a continuous measurement of ERP is not available for Tanzania, we present in Table 7.5 a few snapshots of effective rates of protection. These cover the periods 1966, 1984, 1986, 1989/90 and 1993. This range is adequate to highlight the main evolutionary features of the trade regimes. The main weakness of this trace is that the set of industries and their grouping is not consistent across the period. We are, however, able to discern the broad trends in the protective structure. From the table, the overall protection offered to the various activities increased between 1966 and 1984. Out of the 15 categories of activities, 8 showed large increases in ERPs. The period after 1986, in contrast, was characterized by a general declining trend of ERPs for almost all categories. By 1993 the effective rates of protection had declined by more than half for 8 out of 10 categories since 1986. The ERPs in this year were less than 25 per cent of the levels recorded at the peak of protection in 1984. This trend is consistent with the large tariff reduction pursued during the period of economic reforms.

7.3 TRADE LIBERALIZATION EPISODES IN TANZANIA: AN OVERVIEW OF EXPERIENCE AND POLICY INCIDENCE

Trade policy in Tanzania can be grouped into pure and trade-related policies. Taxes on external trade (imports and exports) constitute the main instruments of pure trade policies. Implicit tariff equivalents of quantitative restrictions and exchange controls make up endogenous trade policies. Whether such import restraints are targeted at sustaining external balance in place of exchange rate policy, as it happened in the first half of the 1980s, or used for protective purposes, for example during the 1960s and 1970s, the end result is that of implicitly taxing exporters. Tightening of controls raises the excess demand for foreign exchange in the marginal

Table 7.5 Effective protection rates for various activities

Activity	*1966*	*1984*	*Activity*	*1986*	*1989/90*	*1993*
1. Tobacco	528	316	1. Beverages and tobacco	83.8	63.7	35.00
2. Beer	187	1399	2. Food products	65.1	38.1	39.19
3. Canned fruits and vegetables	184	335	3. Textiles and apparel	55.4	36.1	24.67
4. Soft drinks	–23	5	4. Tanneries and leather	41.3	40.1	2.48
5. Textiles	269	240	5. Plastics and rubber (pharmaceuticals)	45.4	22.7*	2.64*
6. Tyres and tubes	270	59	6. Iron, steel and metal products	28.1	19.2	14.47
7. Soap	151	5258	7. Agriculture	24.0	31.7	35.00
8. Tanning and leather	130		8. Machines and transport equipment	25.0	17.6	8.00
9. Footwear	123		9. Rubber, glass, wood, paper, printing and cement	27.9	9.42†	2.85†
10. Metal products	93		10. Chemicals and fertilizers (pharmaceuticals – 1989/90)	1.6	–2.03‡	27.38‡
11. Glass products	31	424				
12. Paper products	26	6682				
13. Cement	12	101				
14. Sisal and jute bags	1					
15. Pharmaceutical products	0	2952				

Notes:
* Includes plastics and rubber only
† Excludes rubber
‡ Includes pharmaceuticals

Sources: Rweyemamu (1973), World Bank (1987), Ndulu *et al.* (1987).

segment of the market for foreign exchange, raising its premium. As long as exporters are required to surrender their earnings at the overvalued official exchange rate, and buy imports at domestic prices that fully adjust to the parallel rates, the premium is an implicit tax on exporters and a transfer to the holders of official import licences (Pinto, 1989). In the post-1986 liberalization the typical pattern has been to replace restrictive non-tariff barriers with real depreciating exchange rates and confine trade policy to its pure forms, mainly tariffs. This then prompts us to include the exchange rate policy as part and parcel of the trade liberalization process.

Pure trade taxes have not been a dominant instrument of trade policy in Tanzania. Indeed, effective tariffs on imports as opposed to those on schedules have been relatively low. At their peak, aggregate effective import duty rates (t_m) measured as the ratio of revenue from import duties to the value of imports, reached 18 per cent in 1969 and have declined steadily since then to reach 8 per cent prior to adopting tariff liberalization measures in 1988 pushing them even lower to an average of 4 per cent by 1993 (Ndulu and Semboja, 1994 and Table 7.4). Duty exemptions, particularly for capital goods, and tax evasion in the case of categories with prohibitive rates, were the main reasons (Ndulu *et al.*, 1987). Export taxes (t_x) likewise have shown a sharp decline after late 1970s and were virtually scrapped after 1980. The deviation of the trade regime from neutrality or the anti-export bias in terms of pure trade taxes, measured as $[(1 + t_m)/(1 - t_x) - 1]$, reached a peak of 26.3 per cent in 1977 before declining to 4 per cent by 1993. On the other hand, implicit taxation of imports measured by the exchange rate premium reached a peak in 1985 when the premium reached 477 exchange (Table 7.4). This phenomenal increase is associated with the tightening of import restrictions and exchange controls as the availability of foreign exchange drastically fell, combined with a passive exchange rate policy. It is not therefore surprising that liberalization measures have focused essentially on non-tariff barriers.

We can distinguish four main liberalization episodes in Tanzania's post-independence history. The distinction is in terms of the motivation for the liberalization, its longevity and intensity, the policy mix adopted in liberalization process, and its sustainability. The first episode was in 1978–9 prompted by the commodity prices boom of 1977–8 which substantially increased export earnings. It is important to underscore that this positive shock followed the negative one (the first oil crisis of 1973/74) combined with severe drought, in response to which import restrictions were tightened to an unprecedented intensity during 1975/76. Liberalization was mainly in the forms of relaxing import restrictions by offering import licences and foreign exchange virtually on demand. Policy fundamentals were left untouched, restrictions and exchange controls were still on the books. It was a temporary windfall-based episode which was quickly reversed with the commodity price collapse of 1979–80, the second oil price shock and diversion of the available foreign exchange to service the import requirements of the war with Idi Amin's Uganda. The parallel market premium during the episode declined sharply consistent with the reduced pressure on the parallel market demand (see Table 7.4). However, the anti-export bias of the regime remained high.

The second episode took place during 1981–5, and was aimed at mainly compensating for the penalties on exporters arising from the tightening of import controls and the pursuit of expansionary macroeconomic policy in response to widening resource gaps. The measures adopted were aimed at raising the profitability of export activities and facilitate exportation. Key among the measures were the introduction of the export retention scheme, which was introduced in 1983 to enhance access to foreign exchange by exporters, with retention rates ranging from 10–100 per cent. Export rebates were first introduced in 1981, ranging between 5 per cent and 25 per cent of the fcb value of exports. Other measures included selective subsidies to exporters, including preferential interest rates, and, most importantly, the scrapping of taxes on virtually all exports. Most of these measures were carried forward to later episodes but some of them became virtually superfluous as the exchange regime was liberalized, major import restrictions removed and exchange rate unification pursued (Ndulu and Semboja, 1995).

Partly overlapping with the second episode was the third episode, 1984–6, which was mainly in the form of partial import liberalization accompanied by internal trade liberalization measures. In July 1984 the government allowed the importation of selected consumer, intermediate and capital goods with own foreign exchange, no questions asked as to the source of financing. The disposal of such imports was to take place at market clearing prices. As a complement to this measure, confinement of trade to statal and parastatal bodies was relaxed to allow direct trade by private importers, and controls – particularly for imports – were dismantled. Own-finance import licences were provided automatically and the list of eligible items expanded rapidly thereafter.

By 1986 the value of own-finance imports exceeded total official export earnings and accounted for 64.7 per cent, 17 per cent and 40.5 per cent of total consumer, intermediate and capital good imports, respectively. This scheme has continued its operation to date and still accounts for about 20 per cent of a much expanded import volume. The significance of this episode lies centrally in paving the way for the later, more-intensive liberalization process. Sales of these imports at market clearing prices amounted *de facto* to an official acknowledgement of a much more depreciated exchange rate for imports. The subsequent depreciation of the official exchange rate reduced continued taxation of exporters without inflationary consequences, since prices had already adjusted. Participants had a sufficient range of exit options not to fear the consequences of reversals. To the extent that the increased supply of goods depressed domestic prices of imports and reduced the real demand for money, it created pressures for monetary contraction mainly via the official devaluation of the shilling for compatibility.

Although finance for these imports was not subject to the effects of the official exchange rate, subsequent official devaluation did raise domestic prices of imports as duty was assessed on a higher shilling value of imports. The burden of the increased shilling-per-unit tax of foreign currency used to finance imports must have been shared between the importers, in the form of reduced profit margins, and their customers, in the form of higher prices, depending on the price demand elasticities of the various commodities. It appears also that the scheme induced increased compliance to import duty collection as previously smuggled goods came into the open. Effective import duty rates rose by almost 33 per cent from an average of 6.7 per cent during 1980–3 to 9.1 during 1983/84–1986/87, without a corresponding increase in scheduled rates (Table 7.4). This might also have been a result of an increase in the proportion of private imports not subject to tax exemption. As a proportion of GDP, revenues from import duty also rose significantly during this period.

The fourth liberalization episode covers the period 1987 to date. As indicated above, the 1984–6 import liberalization measures had paved the way for an intensification of the process and the adoption of measures complementary to trade liberalization. The Economic Recovery Programme (ERP 1986/87–1989/90) adopted in 1986 with a resumption of donor support, had in it several measures aimed at the liberalization of external trade, together with macroeconomic policy measures. The process itself was characterized by an intensification of various measures over time.

Import liberalization was pursued on two main fronts, tariff liberalization and dismantling import restrictions. Until mid-1988, Tanzania's tariff structure was relatively complex, with 18 different main categories and wide rate dispersions ranging from 0 per cent to 200 per cent (Ndulu and Semboja, 1994). In mid-1988 the number of rate categories was reduced to rationalize the protective structure and their levels were reduced to mostly range between 0 per cent and 60 per cent, with higher rates for luxuries. In June 1990 further reforms in the tariff structure and levels were made. Five categories were retained, with rates ranging mainly between 0 per cent and 40 per cent, with a few at 60 per cent. In mid-1991 the tariff rates for intermediate and capital goods were set to zero, but were reinstituted in late 1993 due to obvious very adverse revenue effects.

The introduction of the Open General Licence system (OGL) in early 1988, for selective imports financed through the official window, considerably expanded the proportion of imports subject to automatic licensing. Over time the OGL was expanded from a positive list eligible for financing under the facility to the current small negative list. As a result, the proportion of imports subject to automatic licensing (including imports under own-funds, retention, and OGL schemes) increased from 19.4 per cent of the total in 1984 to 55.3 per cent in 1991. Virtually all foreign exchange from local and external sources is now channelled through a non-restricted import-licensing system. Import licensing has also virtually been scrapped and the import-licensing department at the Central Bank abolished. Licenses are now issued mainly for purposes of disclosure and gathering information.

The exchange regime has at the same time also been liberalized continuously since 1986, starting with the adoption of the General Retention Scheme, which allowed exporters to retain a specified percentage of their export earnings for importation of essential inputs and incentive goods as well as to service their foreign debt. In early 1992 the Exchange Control Act was amended to enable residents to hold foreign currency legally and open foreign currency-denominated accounts locally. This was accompanied by the introduction of *bureaux de change* which sold and bought foreign exchange at market-determined rates. At first, proceeds from export retention and privately earned/repatriated foreign exchange were the main sources of supply to the bureaux. Subsequently, with the unification of the official and bureaux rates beginning in 1993, the Central Bank auctioned its own foreign exchange and that provided for balance of payments support, adding significantly to the sources available to the bureaux. The bureaux and commercial banks have also increasingly become a major window for financing current account transactions, reducing the role of the administrative allocation of foreign exchange to an insignificance. The introduction of the interbank market for foreign exchange in 1994 has resulted in considerably deepening the market for foreign exchange. It is currently the main instrument for determining market-based exchange rate.

This impressive liberalization process suffered a setback in 1993, when the government raised tariff rates to plug revenue shortfalls. These shortfalls were themselves partly a result of an overshooting in the tariff liberalization. With the exception of consumer goods, the rates for all other goods were set to zero, significantly reducing the import duty revenue base. This occurred simultaneously with a granting of wide-ranging exemptions to private investors under the Investment Promotion Scheme. With relative stability of the exchange rate, the previous windfall compensation from rapid depreciation of exchange rate, which raised the local currency tax base, had disappeared. This revenue crunch remains a serious threat to the process of liberalization. The success of current measures to reduce exemptions and stem evasion will be crucial for sustaining the liberalization process.

7.4 IMPACT OF TRADE LIBERALIZATION ON ECONOMIC PERFORMANCE

Our assessment of the impacts of trade liberalization in Tanzania focuses on the post-1986 period. The short-lived liberalization episode of 1978/79, as pointed out earlier, was not accompanied by any fundamental policy changes and was quickly reversed with the disappearance of the windfall of foreign exchange receipts from the coffee boom. Again, although several export promotion measures were adopted during the first half of the 1980s, they were very limited in coverage and did not address the more serious issues related to the implicit taxation of exporters.

In this chapter we highlight the impacts of trade liberalization on export and import performance, and on macroeconomic stability. A preliminary assessment of industrial enterprise response to various liberalization measures will be made, based on the results from the industrial survey carried out in 1994. A brief assessment of the impacts on productivity growth is made, drawing from previous studies. We wish to underscore the fact that the period since liberalization measures were instituted is brief and therefore the assessment of the impacts might not fully reflect its range of potential effects, including in employment, which is a sore gap in this study.

Impact on Imports

Imports in current prices rapidly expanded during 1986–92. Although the revival in the growth of imports began in 1984 with the introduction of the Own Funds Imports scheme, this rate accelerated considerably after 1986 as external support resumed with the adoption of the Economic Recovery Programme. The import – GDP ratio rapidly climbed from 15.2 per cent prior to liberalization to 58.1 per cent by 1992 (Table 7.6). Measured in 1987 constant prices a rise in the import volume was also recorded, albeit at a less steep rate. Relative to the trough of 1983, on average real imports in the subsequent period were 42 per cent higher. The ratio of imports – GDP in constant 1987 dollars experienced a much less significant rise compared to the nominal ratio. This increased from a trough of 29 per cent in 1983 to an annual average of 33 per cent subsequently. This significantly lower ratio compared to the nominal average of nearly 42 per cent is explained by the differential valuation changes between imports and GDP at current prices on account of a steep depreciation of the exchange rate.

Broadly speaking, we can thus conclude, based on the 'before and after' evidence, that the relaxation of both import restrictions and the exchange regime restrictions, coupled with a significant rise in import capacity, led to increased imports. In order to provide a more accurate attribution to trade policy, however, we would need to disentangle the relative contributions of trade policy and autonomous increases of import capacity to the rise in imports. One difficulty in doing so stems from the fact that the rise in import capacity is partly policy-induced, through either

Table 7.6 Trade liberalization and imports in Tanzania

Year	*Imports current prices ($ m.)*	*Imports – GDP (current prices) (%)*	*Imports* (constant 1987 prices) ($ m.)*	*Imports – GDP*† *(constant prices) (%)*
1980	1353	26.3	1339.6	43.8
1984	886	15.2	942	29.9
1985	1021	14.8	1109.8	34.8
1986	1132	23.2	1217.2	36.2
1987	1078	30.6	1078.0	30.6
1988	1641	49.2	1562.9	41.3
1989	1442	50.8	1322.9	32.3
1990	1440	55.6	1200.0	27.4
1991	1599	50.2	1390.4	31.2
1992	1596	58.1	1352.5	29.3

Notes:
* Current prices imports deflated by import unit value index, 1987 = 100
† GDP at 1987 prices

Sources: Computations based on World Bank. *Development Indicators, 1994–95*, tables.

compliance to policy conditionality (including trade policy measures) or improved incentives to export and induced reverse capital flight.

For simplicity, we shall make a broad distinction of factors influencing real demand for imports between those that are directly trade policy-related and those that are not. Following Moran (1990) we specify an import demand function that incorporates the traditional determinants, income and relative prices, as well as import capacity constraints. The motivation of the relationship is the desire to minimize the costs of shortage of imports, given available foreign exchange and the demand generated by income and affected by changes in relative prices. We assume here that relative prices are exogeneous. In log linear form, the partial adjustment equation (Moran, 1990, pp. 283 and 284) is specified as:

$$\ln m_t = a_0 + a_1 \ln PDM_t + a_2 \ln y_t + a_3 \ln ft + a_4 \ln R + a_5 \ln m_{t-1} \qquad (7.1)$$

and

$$\ln PDM_t = \ln (PM_t^* + Z_t)/P \qquad (7.2)$$

Where m_t = real imports; PDM = domestic relative price of imports; y_t = real income; f_t = foreign exchange receipts; R = real reserves; Z_t = ln $(1 + t_m + PR)$; t_m = average effective import tariff; PR = exchange rate premium representing in this case non-tariff barriers; and P is the GDP deflator.

PDM, which is assumed to be exogeneous here, includes the effects of trade barriers, both explicit (t_m) and implicit (PR). It is the channel through which trade policy directly influences the real demand for imports. This influence can be directly estimated via the coefficient of PDM and the actual changes in t_m and PR.

From equations (7.1) and (7.2) the separate impacts of tariffs and non-tariff barriers can be obtained as follows:

$$d \ln PDM^* = d \ln PM + d \ln (1 + t_m + PR) - d \ln P \tag{7.3}$$

This simplifies to:

$$d \ln PDM = d \ln PM^* + \frac{t_m}{(1 + t_m + PR)} d \ln t_m + \frac{PR}{(1 + t_m + PR)} d \ln PR - d \ln P \tag{7.4}$$

This allows us to assess the separate impacts of tariff liberalization and reduction in non-tariff barriers on real demand for imports *ceteris paribus*. Given an estimated coefficient for PDM, a_1, from the import demand function and the average rates of changes for t_m and PR we can obtain these separate impacts.

Equation (7.2) was estimated by OLS to yield the following import demand function for Tanzania (1966–92).

$$\begin{aligned} \ln m_t = {} & \underset{(-2.7)}{6.1} - \underset{(-2.25)}{0.29} \ln PDM_t + \underset{(3.1)}{0.98} \ln y_t + \underset{(3.5)}{0.57} \ln f_t \\ & - \underset{(-1.4)}{0.04} \ln R + \underset{(0.7)}{0.12} \ln m_{t-1} \end{aligned} \tag{7.5}$$

$R^2 = 0.73$; Adj. $R^2 = 0.66$; F = 10.6;
SE of regression = 0.13

Domestic relative price of imports, real income and foreign exchange receipts (exports, net transfers and net capital inflows) have the correct signs and are statistically significant at 5 per cent or less. Income elasticity of demand for imports is unitary while the elasticities for foreign exchange receipts and import price are approximately 60 per cent and 30

Table 7.7 The estimated impacts of changes in tariff and non-tariff barriers

Period	*Import tariffs* (t_m)	*Non-tariff barriers (RP)*
(a) Changes in trade policy stance (Period averages of growth rates)		
1970–9	–0.037	0.21
1980–5	–0.010	0.64
1986–93	–0.0849	–0.36
(b) Impacts of changes on real imports		
1970–9	0.0009	–0.054
1980–5	0.00008	–0.178
1986–93	0.00231	0.095

per cent respectively. The results confirm the importance of import capacity constraints in determining the level of desired imports. They also confirm the significance of trade policy measures in influencing real import demand. The long-run import price supply response is 33 per cent obtained as $a_1(1 - a_5)$ where as $a_1 = 0.29$ is the short-run *price elasticity and $(1 - a_5) = 1.4$ with a_5 being the coefficient on the lagged dependent variable, m_{t-1}.

The above results can be used to assess the short-run impact of trade policy measures on real imports using the methodology outlined earlier. First we obtain the impact coefficients for each period as a product of the coefficient of PDM and the weighted growth rates of t_m and PR for each period. When this is multiplied by the actual rate of change of each policy measure, we obtain the impact of these changes on real imports – that is, holding all other determinants constant:

$$d \ln m = 0.29 \frac{t_m}{(1 + t_n + PR)} d \ln t_n, \text{ for tariff changes} \tag{7.6}$$

and

$$d \ln m = 0.29 \frac{PR}{(1 + t_n + PR)} d \ln PR; \text{ for changes in non-tariff barriers.} \tag{7.7}$$

The estimated impacts of changes in tariff and non-tariff barriers are presented in Table 7.7 for the various periods.

The estimated impacts in Table 7.7 point to two important conclusions. First is that the impact of tariff liberalization on real imports demand has been negligible in Tanzania. Even during the period when tariff rates were being reduced at an average rate of 8.4 per cent annually (1986–93), the impact on real import demand was hardly 0.2 per cent annually. Second, among the trade policy instruments, liberalization of import and exchange controls is most significant in influencing real imports. The estimates above show that the tightening of controls and the resultant phenomenal increase in the premium during 1980–5 led to a contraction of real imports at an average annual rate of 17.8 per cent. The relaxation of these controls during the liberalization period resulted in a sharp decline in the premium at an annual rate of 36.4 per cent, which in turn led to real imports rising at an average rate of 9.5 per cent.

Trade Liberalization and Export Performance

Three main effects of trade liberalization are highlighted here. They are all based on the contention that a fall in explicit taxation and particularly a reduction in non-tariff barriers reduce anti-export bias and raises the relative profitability of export activities. The Marshall–Lerner condition also stipulates that barriers to import are effectively a tax on exports, since they raise domestic resource cost of exports.

First, we proceed to assess the impact of liberalization on export orientation, which is measured as the ratio of exports to total production. The hypothesis is that as anti-export bias declines through reduction of both explicit and implicit taxation of exports, the proportion of output exported would rise.

Second, we assess the impact of liberalization on the diversification of the export basket. The hypothesis is that non-traditional exports are more responsive to a reduction in the taxation of exports, leading to expected rise in their share of total merchandise exports.

Third, as export supply would respond positively to a reduction in anti-export bias, we shall attempt to pinpoint the effects of trade policy measures relative to other policy reforms pursued during the liberalization period, so as to obtain a more precise attribution to the consequences of trade liberalization on exports. The increased supply is partly a result of actual increase in the volume of exports or bringing into the open of previously underground exports prompted by avoidance of excessive taxation on exports. In both cases the response is welfare-improving, since the latter case of bringing exports into the open would lead to a reduction in transactions costs associated with avoidance of taxation.

Table 7.8 shows a rapid rise in export orientation in the liberalization period, after a steep decline during 1980–5. The ratio of exports to DGP

Table 7.8 Trade liberalization exports of goods and non-factor services, 1980–93

	Exports to GDP (current prices)	*Exports to GDP (1987 constant prices)*	*Exports (current prices) ($ m.)*	*Non-traditional exports share in Total**	*Anti-export bias (1 = neutral)*	*Real exports (1987 constant prices)*
1980	13.2	19.5	676	29.6†	2.8	598.2
1984	7.1	13.0	413	22.2	3.8	408.9
1985	6.2	14.3	427	24.0	5.9	454.3
1986	9.1	12.3	446	21.0	5.1	413.0
1987	11.7	11.7	412	35.7	2.9	412.0
1988	13.8	11.9	459	35.5	2.2	450.0
1989	18.8	13.4	542	40.8	1.8	547.5
1990	20.5	12.9		33.1	1.7	563.8
1991	16.1	12.8	530	28.0	1.5	570.0
1992	20.8	14.7	513	30.6	1.4	681.0
1993	25.3		572	33.6	1.1	

Notes:
* Includes exports of manufacturers and non-traditional agricultural products
† 1981

Source: World Bank, *African Development Indicators 1994–95*; Bank of Tanzania, *Economic and Operations Reports*.

measured in current prices more than triples, from 6.2 per cent in 1985 to 21 per cent in 1992. A simple correlation between the anti-export bias index and export orientation for the whole 1966–92 period yields a statistically significant coefficient of 70 per cent. However, when this ratio is measured in constant prices, the recovery of export orientation is much more modest and takes place in earnest during the later part of the liberalization period. A ratio of real exports to GDP of 15 per cent is reached by 1992, but it is still significantly lower than the nearly 20 per cent achieved in 1980 (Table 7.8). The wedge between the current price and constant price ratios is mostly explained by the rapid depreciation of the local currency which affects the numerator and the denominator with a substantial difference. Nevertheless the rise in export orientation after a significant decline is notable even when measured in real terms.

More striking, however, is the very rapid response achieved in terms of the diversification of the export basket. The share of non-traditional exports (excluding minerals) rose sharply by almost twofold during 1986–90 (Table 7.8). This rise was essentially spear-headed by a rapid rise in the exports of manufactures and non-traditional agricultural export products. The response was occasioned by the rise in the profitability of exports due mainly to a steep exchange rate depreciation. In the case of manufacturers, this response was dominated by existing exporters who sold their products earlier, mainly in the domestic market. This market switching effect was in response to increased profitability of exporting. However, part of this response was by new entrants – both new and old producers into the export market (Ndulu and Semboja, 1995). A subsequent slow down of this diversification trend was a result mainly of a decline in the export of manufactures. Power shortages caused by a sharp fall in the water level in reservoirs for hydro-electric generation led to steep drops in capacity utilization and output. Further evidence of this response is reviewed later, based on the analysis of the survey of industrial enterprises' response to trade liberalization.

The export *supply response* to liberalization measures operate through three main channels.

(1) Since exports are presumed to be largely supply-constrained and in turn supply is assumed to be import-constrained, import liberalization will enhance capacity to export (export capacity effect).
(2) As internal terms of trade for exportables improve with reduction in both explicit and implicit taxation of exports, production for export will increase (resource-transfer effect).
(3) Devaluation of the shilling and reduction in export taxation raises the profitability of selling in the export market compared to the

domestic market, raising the proportion of output exported (export orientation or market-switching effect). This is in addition to the more general effects of enhanced competitiveness of Tanzania's exports in the world market, which would boost its share worldwide, particularly for non-traditional exports.

Real exports, measured in 1987 constant prices, rose at an average annual rate of 9.1 per cent during 1987–92 after registering a negative growth during 1980–6 (Table 7.8). Given the decline in export unit values averaging −2.3 per cent annually over the same period, current price exports registered a slow growth over the same period. The bulk of the revival in this growth was sourced from a rise in merchandise exports.

A good summary measure for the effects of a combination of the various liberalization policy stances, including compatible macroeconomic policies, is their impact on the real effective exchange rate. In turn, various studies, including those by Ndulu and Semboja (1995) and Badhuri *et al.* (1993), show that the single most important factor influencing Tanzania's export supply is the real exchange rate. Therefore, in order to assess the impact of trade liberalization on export supply response, we can combine these two relationships to obtain an indirect relationship between liberalization measures and export supply response. We do so in three stages.

The first stage is to determine the impact of the liberalization measures on the real exchange rate. Here, like Edwards (1993), we particularly emphasize the effects of explicit and implicit taxation on exports as well as contractionary macroeconomic policies required to sustain trade liberalization, and more specifically the effect of relaxing import restrictions as proxied by the fall in the parallel market premium which leads to a depreciation of the real exchange rate. Tariff liberalization will lead to a real depreciation assuming that the substitution effect between tradables and non-tradables will exceed the real income effect from tax cuts. Contractionary macroeconomic policy measured in terms of the decline in the excess of domestic credit growth over the depreciation rate of the nominal exchange rate, the growth of real GDP, and foreign inflation lead to the depreciation of the real exchange rate.

The second step is to estimate export supply responsiveness to the real exchange rate in a fully specified equation. Here we will invoke the small country assumption that Tanzania can export all its supplies to the world market. In addition, a separate effect of the capacity to export as measured by real output growth will be estimated.

The third step is then to assess the impact of the individual trade liberalization measures on export response through simulation. The indirect route of assessment is from the individual impact of import liberalization on the real exchange rate and in turn its effect on exports. This allows us to undertake a separate attribution to each policy instrument included. Furthermore, it also allows us to assess separately the relative importance of the impacts of pure trade policy instruments, endogenous trade policy instruments and complimentary macroeconomic policy measures.

In summary, the exercise entails:

(1) estimating the equation of the determinants of the real exchange rate. From this we obtain the impact coefficients of the various policy instruments on the real exchange rate;
(2) estimating the export supply function – from this we obtain the coefficient of the response of exports to real exchange rate changes;
(3) deriving the impacts coefficients for the individual policy instruments on export response as a product of the relevant coefficients from (1) and (2);
(4) assessing the actual change in the policy instruments over the liberalization period and estimating their impacts on exports.

This method was used by Ndulu and Semboja (1995) to assess the impacts of trade policy changes on the performance of manufactured exports in Tanzania as well as by Bhadhuri *et al.* (1993) to assess the impacts on total as well as various categories of exports.

We report in Tables 7.9 and 7.10 the estimated impact coefficients from both studies.

While significant differences in the magnitudes of impacts from the two studies exist, the main conclusion to be drawn from them are similar. The differences arise from choice of specification for both RER determinants and export supply equations.

The two sets of results point to the relatively larger impact of macroeconomic policy changes compared to either the pure trade policies or the so-called mixed policies. This is the case irrespective of the category of exports considered by Bhadhuri et al. It is also clear from the above results that the responsiveness of non-traditional exports to changes in each category of policy is higher than that of the traditional agricultural exports. Both sets of results show the insignificant impact of explicit taxes on export supply.

During 1980–5 a expansionary macroeconomic policy stance appears to have dominated the contraction of export supply via the influence of the overvaluation of the shilling. Explicit trade taxes, both the effective import tariff rates and export taxes as seen in Table 7.4, on average registered declines during this period. Quantitative restrictions were tightened

Table 7.9 Liberalization policy impacts on exports of Tanzanian manufacturers

Policy measure	*Impact coefficient**
Pure macroeconomic policy effects†	–0.132
Pure trade policy effects‡	–0.09
Mixed trade and macroeconomic§ policy effects	–0.102

Notes:

* The impact coefficient is the product of the separate effects of policy measures on RER (below) and the responsiveness of export supply to RER, estimated in a separate supply equation to be 0.68.

† Pure macroeconomic policy is defined as the excess of domestic credit growth over real output growth, rate of nominal exchange rate depreciation and inflation rate of trading partners. We assume here that the excess of domestic credit growth over real output growth drives inflation. Expansionary macroeconomic policy thus leads to real appreciation and in turn to a fall in exports. The estimated elasticity coefficient for macro-policy on RER is –0.193.

‡ Pure trade policy effects here represent import duty effects. Tariff liberalization leads to a real depreciation and induces exports. The estimated elasticity for import tax effect on RER is –0.132.

§ Mixed trade and macroeconomic policy is represented by the exchange rate premium. Depreciation of the nominal official rate – *ceteris paribus* – reduces the premium, while import restrictions raise it. The estimated elasticity coefficient for premium's effect on RER is –0.149.

Source: Ndulu and Semboja (1995)

to protect reserves and prevent deterioration in the external balance. In this sense they could be construed as being applied for macroeconomic stability rather than for trade policy purposes.

In the later period, however, the dismantling of quantitative restrictions and a rapid reduction in import duties were clearly applied for trade liberalization purposes. Nevertheless a contractionary macroeconomic policy stance was pursued vigorously at the same time, mainly through a steep exchange rate depreciation. On balance, even during this period the macroeconomic influence on the real exchange rate, and hence on the competitiveness and incentive to export, remained most dominant – at least until 1990.

One could initiate the analysis by taking it back further to include the determinants of the parallel market exchange rate premium to separate the current account and capital account effects and their attribution to the specific policy fundamentals.

Table 7.10 Liberalization policy impacts on Tanzanian export performance

Policy measure	*Impact coefficients**		
	Total exports	*Agricultural exports*	*Manufactured exports*
Macroeconomic policy†	–0.365	–0.365	–0.616
Import restrictions‡	–0.186	0.16	0.324
Export taxes§	–0.300	–0.300	–0.515
Parallel market rate**	–0.175	–0.175	–0.305

Notes:
* To obtain the impact coefficients, the coefficients below are multiplied with the respective export supply elasticities with respect to RER. These are 0.447 for total exports, 0.448 for agricultural exports and 0.78 for manufactured exports.
† Macroeconomic policy is measured as in Ndulu and Semboja (1995). The elasticity coefficient on RER is –0.791.
‡ Import restrictions are measured as the ratio of real imports to total supply. A rise in the ratio reflects tightness of import regime and leads to the appreciation of RER. Note that part of the effects measured through the exchange rate premium in Ndulu and Semboja (1995) are captured here. The elasticity coefficient on RER is 0.415.
§ Export taxes have a statistically insignificant coefficient of –0.66.
** Parallel market rate is the exchange rate premium here included as a marginal tax rate on exports. The estimated elasticity coefficient on RER is –0.391.

The above coefficients have been computed using the supply elasticities obtained from the multiple regression rather than the simple regression also presented by the author.

Source: Bhadhuri *et al.* (1993)

Trade Liberalization and Productivity Growth

There are three main arguments for productivity enhancement deriving from trade liberalization.

(1) Exposure to external competition reduces monopoly behaviour at firm level and is conducive to illiciting measures for cost effectiveness.
(2) On a more aggregate level, restructuring of production takes place as external competition and realignment of factor prices forces inefficient firms out and leaves more productive enterprises in existence. Technical efficiency is achieved from avoiding crowding in too many

firms producing at too low output, typically induced by protective measures (Mbelle, 1993; Ndulu and Semboja, 1994).

(3) Competitive pressure coupled with enhanced flexibility to import is conducive to innovation, and facilitates the development of product quality and core capabilities for the more efficiency-demanding export sector.

The assessment of the impact of trade restraints and liberalization on productivity was carried out by Ndulu and Semboja (1995) for the manufacturing sector as a whole and for a sample of enterprises in the textile sector. This assessment is done using a before-and-after approach. Trends in output per worker, capacity utilization rates, and cost efficiency were used to assess responses to both trade restraints and liberalization.

Sector-wide assessment shows that cost efficiency (measured as unit cost divided by an aggregate index of input prices) declined during 1980–5 due to steep decline in capacity utilization, wasteful use of 'subsidized' inputs and excessive stocks of imported inputs to hedge against shortages. Subsequently, however, in response to the rapid depreciation of the exchange rate, firms appear to have saved on costs of both exportables and importables. Allocative efficiency appears to have been prompted in response to changes in the input prices (ibid., p. 186).

Using data for the textile industry the study (ibid.) concludes that 85 per cent of the firms surveyed registered rather strong productivity growth in the post-liberalization period. This was in contrast to the poorer achievement in increasing capacity utilization rates. Cost efficiency improvements were registered by all firms surveyed, including those with declining capacity utilization rates. As the study by de Valk and Mbelle (1990) suggests, this was most likely to be due to a reduction in the utilization of high-cost imports by shifting to less import-intensive inputs and exportables. Moreover, with improved supplied under the liberalized regime, wasteful stockpiling was not necessary. It is also instructive to note that exporting firms registered relatively high labour productivity growth and capacity utilization rates in the post-liberalization period (Ndulu and Semboja, 1995, p. 187).

Trade Liberalization, External and Fiscal Balance

Here we focus on the impacts of trade liberalization on the external current account balance, overall resource balance and the fiscal deficit, using before and after comparisons. Table 7.11 presents these indicators as proportions of GDP.

The current account balance initially deteriorated as imports expanded rapidly after 1986. Expansion in exports followed later, with a two-year lag. Both ratios for the current account deficit and domestic resource shortfall to GDP rose steeply, from –6.6 per cent and –14.1 per cent in

1986 to –16.4 per cent and –35.1 per cent in 1990, respectively. The current account deficit thereafter declined significantly, mainly due to a rise in exports, net private transfers and continued inflows of external grants.

One phenomenon needs to be highlighted in this regard. Net private transfers, which were negligible before 1984, turned out to be a very significant part of financing imports. With the introduction of Own Funds Imports and the lifting of restrictions on private importers, a significant jump in net private transfers was registered. During 1985–7 these inflows on average financed a quarter of imports, up from an insignificant 2 per cent in 1980. With the introduction of *bureaux de change* and permission to hold foreign currency-denominated assets locally, net private transfers soared. Since 1993 these have reached the same level as the official merchandise exports. It is widely believed that these inflows are largely from the repatriation of proceeds from continued unofficial exports. When the domestic resource balance ratio to GDP is adjusted for these proceeds it is significantly less alarming and in fact shows a declining trend in the 1990s (Table 7.11).

On the fiscal front, the negative effects of tariff liberalization on revenue from trade taxes were more than offset during 1986–92 by a rise in the tax base from increased volume in imports and the positive change in local currency valuation of these occasioned by the steep depreciation of the exchange rate. The share of trade taxes in total revenue actually rebounded strongly during this period, rising twofold from the very low level of 3 per cent in 1984.

The following decomposition of the sources of growth of the revenue from import duty is instructive.

$$RMD = M\$.OER.t_m \tag{7.8}$$

$$gRMD = gM\$ + gOER + gt_m \tag{7.9}$$

where *RMD* = revenue from import taxes; *OER* = official exchange rate used for valuation of c.i.f. imports for taxation purpose; t_m = effective tax rate, *M$* = dollar value of imports.

We assume that increased compliance induced by the lowering of tax rates is reflected by an increase in c.i.f. imports disclosed for taxation purposes.

This simple approximate decomposition yielded the results in Table 7.12 for the period immediately before liberalization (1980–5) and the period after (1986–92).

It is clear from Table 7.12 that during 1986–92 the import tax revenue registered a very high growth rate in spite of an annual rate of decline of the average effective tariff rate. Exchange rate depreciation at an average

Table 7.11 Trade liberalization effects on external and fiscal balance

Year	*Current account balances ($ m.)*	*C/A ratio to GDP (%)*	*Resource balance to GDP (%)*	*Overall fiscal deficit to GDP (%) (excluding grants)*	*Prime* fiscal deficit to GDP (%)*	*Resource balance to GDP, adjusted for net private transfers† (%)*	*Taxes on international trade (% of total revenue)*
1980	–521	–10.1	–13.2	–11.4	–10.4	–12.8	17.6
1984	–359	–6.2	–8.1	–6.2	–10.1	–7.0	7.1
1985	–375	–5.4	–8.6	–6.9	–6.5	–5.2	8.6
1986	–321	–6.6	–14.1	–7.1	–8.8	–9.0	9.5
1987	–446	–12.7	–18.9	–8.2	–4.9	–10.0	16.1
1988	–376	–11.3	–35.4	–5.4	–6.3	–28.4	15.2
1989	–359	–12.6	–31.7	–6.1	–3.9	–25.3	12.5
1990	–426	–16.4	–35.1	–2.7	–4.2	–28.8	13.7
1991	–269	–8.5	–34.1	–2.7	–2.3	–21.3	16.5
1992	–297	–10.8	–37.6	–2.6	–2.4	–21.0	

Notes:
* Fiscal deficit includes grants but excludes interest payments on both domestic and foreign debt.
† The adjustment reflects the fact that the surge in net private transfers is a *de facto* repatriation by nationals of proceeds from unofficial exports.

Table 7.12 Results, 1980–5 and 1986–92

	Average growth of import tax revenue	*Average growth of imports ($)*	*Average rate of exchange rate depreciation*	*Average rate of change of effective tax rates*
1980–5	9.6	–0.7	13.9	–1.1
1986–92	52.8	9.5	53.4	–7.0

Note: The growth rates of the component factor add up to slightly more than that of the import tax revenues due to rounding off and measurement errors.

annual rate of 53.4 per cent in shilling terms and an average annual growth of 9.5 per cent for imports (in $US) more than offset the reduction in the effective tax rate. Nearly 85 per cent of this was accounted for by exchange rate depreciation. It should be instructive to note that as the exchange rate stabilized within a narrow band during 1994, this source of compensation for loss in revenue from tariff liberalization has become insignificant. Any further liberalization will thus have to be compensated by sources related to a rise in overall growth.

Industrial Firms' Response to Trade Liberalization

We present here a very brief analysis of the responses by firms to a questionnaire administered to them in August–September 1994 for discerning the impact of trade liberalization on their performance and strategies. The objectives are to highlight the characteristics of the firms interviewed and their major perceptions with respect to trade liberalization, and to determine any significant changes in behaviour *vis-à-vis* the changes in the trading environment.

The Survey: Sampling and Sample Size

Initially a decision was made to interview 175 manufacturing firms, 109 from Dar es Salaam, 18 from Arusha, 13 from Moshi, 13 from Mwanza and 9 from Morogoro. The six towns are the major manufacturing centres in the country. The firms were selected randomly using the list of firms appearing in the *1989 Industrial Survey*. Later on, six firms were added on the advice of the official from the Bureau of Statistics, who felt that their exclusion would be too conspicuous. Thus a total of 181 firms were earmarked for interviewing.

In terms of coverage, the selected sample structure was sufficiently representative. Following the ISIC classification, the following activities were earmarked for the interview: food (22 firms), beverages (7), tobacco (2), textiles (17), wearing apparel (11), leather (2), footwear (5), wood and products (9), furniture (13), paper and paper products (6), printing and publishing (14), chemicals (19), petroleum and petroleum products (1), rubber (6), non-metals (8), basic metals (3), metal fabrications (17) and machinery (19).

Response to the Survey

Out of 181 firms, only 81 responded adequately to the questionnaire. The nearly 50 per cent response rate is satisfactory considering the bulkiness of the questionnaire, its complexity and (sometimes) lack of clarity, the limited time provided for the exercise and the apparent fatigue among the respondents resulting from an overflow of researchers with similar questionnaires recently.

Characteristics From the 81 respondents, the following observations can be made.

(1) *Ownership* Out of 81 firms, 51 (63 per cent) are private and 30 (37 per cent) are public. Out of the 43 respondents, 70 per cent are wholly locally owned; only 4.8 per cent have at least 50 per cent foreign ownership. This suggests limited foreign ownership in the Tanzanian manufacturing sector.
(2) *Size* According to the Bureau of Statistics (BOS), firms are classified as small when they engage 1–19 employees, medium when they engage 20–99 employees and large when they engage 100 + employees. We adopt this definition for convenience and comparability.
   Out of 79 respondents who indicated the size of their firms, 25.3 per cent of firms are small, 30.4 per cent are medium and 44.3 per cent are large. Small firms contributed 2.5 per cent of total sales, medium firms contributed 3.3 per cent and large firms contributed 94.2 per cent. Thus large firms contributed the bulk of sales made by the firms surveyed.
(3) *Import intensity* We define import intensity as the proportion of raw materials imported. 46 per cent of 78 respondents indicated that they do not use imported raw materials. The results also show that import intensity is correlated with size. Of those not using imported raw materials, 41 per cent are small firms and 35 per cent are medium firms. 40 per cent of the 78 respondents have at least 50 per cent import intensity.

A Summary of the Findings

Utilization of Tax/Subsidy and Export Retention Schemes Nine, or 12 per cent, of 71 respondents benefited from import duty drawback in 1993. The majority (78 per cent) of the beneficiaries were large firms. Furthermore, 13 per cent of 53 respondents have benefited from import duty drawback in the past; the majority being large firms. The number of firms benefiting from duty drawn back has thus slightly increased.

3 per cent of 64 respondents benefited from export tax rebate in 1993. And 4 per cent of 50 respondents have benefited from this facility in the past.

Two per cent of 62 respondents benefited from export subsidies in 1993, and out of 49 respondents there were no beneficiaries of this facility in the past.

Of 66 respondents, 17 per cent utilized the export retention facility; the majority of these (64 per cent) being large firms. Of 51 respondents, 18 per cent had benefited from this facility in the past. There thus appears to be a slight decline in the use of this facility.

In short, the majority of firms, especially small firms, have not benefited from tax/subsidy/retention benefits granted during the trade liberalization period. This partly reflects a lack of awareness of their existence; partly the cumbersome procedures for obtaining rebates; and partly the superfluity of retention schemes in view of the fact that exporters do not now have to surrender their foreign exchange earnings to the Central Bank.

Export Participation Out of the 72 firms which responded to the questions on export participation, 22 (or 30 per cent) indicated that they were exporting part of their output in 1993. Of these 16 (72 per cent) were large firms, three were small and three others were medium firms. Of the exporting firms 12 (54 per cent) were private and 46 per cent were public. Three levels of export orientation were identified. Out of the 22 exporting firms, 11 exported 9 per cent or less of their output, 6 or 27.3 per cent exported between 10 per cent and 50 per cent of their output, while five exported more than 50 per cent of output. Large firms dominated the categories exporting 10 per cent or more of the output.

In response to questions on the history of export participation, 62 firms provided responses. Out of these, 30 indicated that they were currently (in 1994) exporting part of their output. Of these 19 (or 63 per cent) were private and the rest were public. Only 20 out of the 30 provided a history of export participation; 10 of these were exporting prior to 1980. One public firm started exporting in 1980–5 and nine (or 45 per cent) began exporting after the onset of liberalization. These new exporters were more or less equally distributed between the private (five) and the public sector (four).

Domestic Sales and Pricing A total of 79 firms responded to the questions on sales in the domestic market. Of these 95 per cent sold 50 per cent or more of their output in the local market. The key trading channels for their output were wholesalers followed by 'retailers'. It is rather revealing that most firms (about 70 per cent) still fix their prices through mark up. This applies almost equally to private and public enterprises. Only 10 per cent of the respondents indicated that they adjust their prices to keep in line with the price of imports, and another 7.5 per cent take market prices as given.

Sources of Competition to Industrial Enterprises The majority of the firms, whether private or public (54 per cent of 78), identified domestic firms as the main source of competition. These were followed at some distance by those (36 per cent of the total) who identified imports as the main competitor. Only four firms indicated that they faced no competition at all. The high weight placed on domestic competition is rather surprising, given the outcries often heard against cheap imports. It is nevertheless consistent with the high survival rates in the post-liberalization period. Only four firms out of the 78 singled out foreign competitors in export markets as the main source of competition.

These observations were confirmed by another question which took a longer-term view of sources of competition: 74 firms responded that they faced severe competition over the past few years. This time domestic competitors and imports received equal weight in response to separate questions regarding sources of competition. It is instructive to note that it was large firms that most often indicated imports as a source of competition. These firms have of late stepped up promotional activities, accounting for 94.6 per cent of all expenditures on product promotion.

Destination of Exports Out of the 30 exporting firms that gave information in response to this question the distribution of destinations for exports were as follows: Africa, 14 (or 47 per cent); Middle East, two (or 6 per cent); Europe, nine (or 30 per cent); and Asia, five (or 17 per cent). The frequency of Africa as an export destination is rather amazing, given the overall share of exports to Africa in the official statistics for the direction of trade. It appears that manufacturers trade more frequently within the region than exporters of primary products, a fact we confirm in a later survey reported in the next section.

Broad Conclusions from the Survey

The foregoing suggests two broad conclusions with respect to manufacturing enterprises' perceptions of the recent trade liberalization. First, there is a broad perception that export opportunities have expanded – as indicated by the increase in export participation and plans to export more in the future. For most part they do not make use of special payments-related incentives offered to exporters, given that these are now superfluous in view of the liberalization of the exchange regime. Second, manufacturers largely consider domestic competition as being the biggest pressure they face. While this is partly linked to increasing liberalization of internal trade, it is rather surprising that imports are not the single most important threat to their survival. This may point to the possibility that most imports are not competitive – for example, raw materials or capital goods not produced at home – or simply that most of them were quick to adapt to these pressures. We wish to single out textiles, which have faced immense pressures from imports. Even in this case, the manufacturers point more to 'unfair' competition related to tax evasion by importers rather than to imports *per se*.

Perceptions of Regional Groupings by Tanzanian Industrial Firms

A second survey was conducted in August–September 1995 to obtain the perceptions of industrial enterprises on the role of regional groupings in facilitating intra-regional trade. To accommodate multiple membership of Tanzania in three overlapping groupings, the survey sought to obtain impressions of membership of the recently revived East African Community which groups Tanzania with Kenya and Uganda; the Southern Africa Development Community, grouping Tanzania with nine other countries in Southern Africa; and membership in PTA/COMESA, grouping Tanzania with 20 other countries of Eastern and Southern Africa.

The questionnaire administered to a total of 108 firms sought to investigate three aspects related to intra-regional trade in the three groupings:

(1) to establish the extent to which Tanzanian industrial firms traded within each of the groupings both in terms of sourcing imports and as destinations of their exports;
(2) to establish whether or not Tanzanian firms were aware of the existence of these groupings and the role they played in facilitating trade among member countries; and
(3) to identify the major constraints faced in trading within the region and ways to address them.

Table 7.13 Participation of Tanzanian industrial firms within regional groupings

Trading with:	*No. of firms*	*% of total respondents*	*% of trading firms**
(a) East African Community (EAC)			
Kenya	18	16.7	26.5
Uganda	4	3.7	5.9
Total EAU	*22*	*20.4*	*32.3*
(b) PTA/COMESA excluding EAC countries			
Burundi	4	3.7	5.9
Mozambique†	2	1.9	2.9
South Africa†	6	5.6	8.2
Sudan	1	0.9	1.5
Zambia†	3	2.8	4.4
Zimbabwe†	5	4.6	7.4
Total	*21*	*19.4*	*30.9*

Notes:
* Total number of trading firms is obtained by adding those importing (43) and those exporting (25). Some double counting may ensue, since some firms may be doing both.
† These countries also belong to SADC.
41 firms indicated that they traded with countries outside these groupings. These represent 38 per cent of all respondents and 60 per cent of all firms engaged in external trade.

The focus on these issues was adopted against the background that the concerned governments in principle chose to focus mostly on preferential tariff treatment as the main integrating factor. Obviously the worries of revenue loss normally associated with such treatment appear to be insignificant, partly because of the small proportion of trade taxes associated with intra-regional groupings. In the case of Tanzania, for example, import duties from trade within PTA/COMESA (the largest of the three groupings) is less than 10 per cent.

The Characteristics of the Firms Surveyed

Out of the 108 firms which responded to the questionnaire, 70.5 per cent were private. 72.7 per cent of the respondents were located in the main commercial centre, Dar es Salaam, which also hosted about 50 per cent of those currently engaged in export trade. Out of the 93 respondents, 46.2 per cent were engaged in import trade, while only 26.9 per cent were engaged in export trade. 49.2 per cent of the respondents indicated plans to export in future mainly in response to increased opportunities for trade under the more liberalized environment.

Trade Participation within Regional Groupings

A surprisingly high proportion of those firms engaged in export and import activities trade within the regional groupings. 43 firms out of 68 engaged in external trade do so within the region encompassing all member countries in EAC, PTA/COMESA and SADC (Table 7.13). This compares favourably with the number of firms trading outside the region, which total 41. The average value of trade by each firm reporting such information is slightly higher for those industrial firms trading within the region than those trading outside it. These findings accord to regional trade a much higher importance for firms engaged in manufacturing than was earlier assumed. It is consistent with the findings of our earlier survey (Ndulu and Semboja 1995) of this study, in which 47 per cent of exporting firms indicated Africa as the destination of their products. Only if exports of primary products (accounting for more than 70 per cent of total exports) are included does regional trade become relatively insignificant.

Within the regional groupings involved, trade with EAC countries is most dominant, with Kenya being a trading partner for 18 out of 43 firms trading within the PTA/COMESA/SADC region. Proximity and historical trading ties are the key factors behind this dominance. If one includes other neighbouring countries sharing borders with Tanzania – that is, Zambia, Burundi and Mozambique – the total number of firms trading with this contiguous sub-region is 31 (Table 7.13) or 72 per cent of all firms trading in the region. This is consistent with the proximity argument as gravity models would predict.

Constraints to Regional Trading

Although 78.5 per cent of the respondents showed awareness of the existence of the regional groupings to which Tanzania belonged and their declared roles, less than 18 per cent considered them as arrangements facilitating trade within the region (Table 7.14). This may be indicative of the stronger influence of proximity rather than institutional arrangements for facilitating trade. Among the reasons given for this non-facilitating role are inability by these institutions to alleviate constraints to trade among the member countries. Table 7.15 shows the measures that these firms indicated member states could take to facilitate expansion of trade within the region.

Table 7.14 Firms perceiving regional groupings as facilitating trade (%)

	Exports		*Imports*	
	Yes	*No*	*Yes*	*No*
EAC	17.7	82.3	24.2	75.8
PTA/COMESA	17.5	82.5	15.0	85.0
SADC	15.3	84.7	5.3	94.7

Source: Survey data.

Table 7.15 Measures firms indicated would promote regional trade expansion (ten highest ranked)

Measure	*(%)*
(1) Improve communication network	16
(2) Reduce tariffs	12.5
(3) Promote products	11.1
(4) Cheapen transport	9
(5) Allow use of local currency*	7.6
(6) Reduce bureaucracies	6.3
(7) Reduce sales tax	5.6
(8) Facilitate payments	4.9
(9) Eradicate corruption at border posts	4.2

Note:
* Recently the governors of the central banks of Kenya, Tanzania and Uganda agreed on complete currency convertibility by December 1995.

Source: Survey data.

Of the reasons cited as 'other', the most highly ranked reasons are: the firm being purely domestic-orientated (35 per cent) no 'appropriate' materials within member countries (22.5 per cent) and low production (10 per cent).

The perception of the role of South Africa is that it is mainly seen as a competitor in trade rather than in a collaborator or neutral role, as Table 9.16 shows.

Most of these measures relate to alleviating non-tariff barriers to trade largely relating to lack of information for trading opportunities, transport bottlenecks, payments difficulties and bureaucratic constraints to trade

Table 7.16 Perceived role of South Africa in regional groupings

	EAC		*PTA/COMESA*		*SADC*	
	Importers from	*Exporters to*	*Importers from*	*Exporters to*	*Importers from*	*Exporters to*
Competitor						
Yes	35.6	35.6	31	39.1	28.7	39.1
No	64.4	64.4	69	60.9	71.3	60.9
Collaborator						
Yes	16.1	12.6	18.4	12.6	19.5	13.8
No	83.9	87.4	81.6	87.4	80.5	86.2
Neutral						
Yes	9.2	11.5	11.5	6.9	9.2	6.9
No	90.8	88.5	88.5	93.1	90.8	93.1

Source: Survey data.

and cross-border movements. It confirms the relatively insignificant role accorded to preferential tariff treatment which the regional institutions have tended to emphasize in the past. This comes as no surprise in view of the recent intensification of unilateral trade liberalization pursued by the member countries.

The above analysis would seem to suggest a need to reorientate the strategic focus of institutions charged with the task of facilitating regional trade. First, they should play down the earlier focus on preferential tariff treatment, given the rapid movement towards lower rates made by members unilaterally. In order to bolster the existing trade among member countries, these institutions ought instead to focus on facilitating movement of goods and people; setting up mechanisms for easy clearance of payments; providing information on opportunities to trade and harmonizing trade-related policies across member countries. Furthermore, there is a need for a more flexible arrangement in moving towards deeper integration to exploit historical ties and proximity within the groupings. The evidence of the differential intensity of trading among sub-groups would tend to argue for variable geometry arrangements for promoting trade. What is perhaps the most important lesson from the survey is the fact that enterprises are interested parties in these arrangements with substantial knowledge of what it takes to promote trade among themselves. It is a resource that needs to be tapped in the process of designing successful regional arrangements for facilitating trade.

7.5 SUSTAINABILITY OF REFORMS: A CONCLUDING ASSESSMENT OF SUSTAINABILITY OF TRADE LIBERALIZATION IN TANZANIA

Sustainability of trade reforms depends critically on the credibility of reforms being undertaken. If trade liberalization is anticipated to be temporary it induces hedging reactions by private agents through capital flight, illegal trade and inefficient stockpiling of imports in anticipation of reversals. The diagnostics of such perceptions are reviewed extensively by Greenaway and Milner (1993). They include signals related to the lack of compatible macroeconomic policy measures, systematic forecastability and time inconsistency.

The key diagnostics we intend to focus on here are foreign reserves, the ratio of fiscal deficit to GDP monetary control measures adopted (see Table 7.11). However we shall add trends in private net foreign transfers and private capital inflows as indications of perceived confidence economic agents have in the measures taken. As shown in Tables 7.11 and 7.17, these have increased substantially in the post-liberalization period. The former have been particularly important in the private financing of imports and the latter may be important for recent speculative holding of domestic financial assets.

Compatible policy measures pursued on the macroeconomic front have been in three main areas. First, they were aimed at maintaining external balance, mainly through money supply restrictions to counteract reduction in the demand for money resulting from the expansion of demand for imports as domestic prices for imports fell with trade liberalization. The earliest measure adopted was a steep depreciation of the shilling, which was devalued in real terms by more than 85 per cent in the last eight years, based on the trend of real effective exchange rate measured as $ units per shilling. This prevented a run on reserves and was helped along by a significant increase in external resource inflows. The exchange rate depreciation also significantly cushioned the reduction in revenue collections from lower tariff rates as the import tax base increased in local currency terms due to valuation changes. The other side of the coin is the increase in shilling-public expenditures due to revaluation of external obligations. The debt overhang has become particularly burdensome, as it has to be serviced at steeply devalued domestic currency.

The second measure was the reduction in the fiscal deficit and more importantly a reduced recourse to the monetization of the fiscal deficit. This is evident from the significant decrease in the ratio of the overall fiscal deficit (excluding grants) to GDP. This ratio has fallen from an average of –10 per cent prior to liberalization (1980–5) to –5.6 per cent thereafter. The prime deficit shows a similar trend. The decline in the overall deficit has been a result of a combination of an increase in revenue collection, particularly import duties, and a reduction in the rate of expansion of government expenditures. The increase in revenue from trade taxes was largely a result of valuation changes occasioned by a steep depreciation of the exchange rate. Inflows of external aid have reduced the recourse to financing the deficit via monetary expansion. This has been complemented more recently by borrowing from the public through massive sales of treasury bills.

The third measure has been a reduction in the rate of expansion of domestic credit, particularly during 1989–92. The continued pressures on monetary expansion appear to stem largely from a build-up of reserves and increases in foreign currency deposits in local banks. This is evident from the large difference in the recent growth rate of M_3 as compared to M_2 (Table 7.17). In this sense an increasing proportion of money supply is becoming autonomous and hard to control, given a limited range of sterilization options available.

In 1993 the central bank auctioned to exporters through a local purchase scheme a significant proportion of the gold reserves it had accumulated since 1991 and also part of the reserve accumulation from external inflows. The main aim of this intervention was to reduce liquidity in public hands and achieve sterilization of reserves. Depletion of the reserves during October 1993–January 1994 significantly reduced the scope of this measure. However, the introduction of the auctions of treasury bills which quickly became very popular, albeit at very high interest rates, performed the same function. Monetary growth in the following eight months significantly declined and reserves built up again to a comfortable position. But monetary expansion, mainly driven by private resource inflows, continues to exert large pressures on interest rates as measures to restrain liquidity expansion remain the only option pursued for sterilization. Partial financial disintermediation also ensues, through restricting credit and raising the reserve requirement of the commercial banks.

There are three concerns with respect to the sustainability of the ongoing liberalization process that need to be highlighted. The first relates to the liquidity mopping-up exercise currently being pursued. The sale of treasury bills at high interest rates has crowded out private credit, threatening a recession. It has also seriously led to a rapid build-up of public internal debt with potential dire consequences on investors' confidence as they anticipate higher taxes to service the increased burden in the future. There are also perceptions that this 'new' source of financing for the public sector deficit may breed fiscal indiscipline on the expenditure side, as it presents a soft option for financing uncontrolled expansion of the fiscal deficit.

Secondly, pressures on the real exchange rate appreciation are also

Table 7.17 Diagnostics for sustainability of trade liberalization in Tanzania

Year	REER index (1987=100)	Domestic credit (growth) (%)	Money supply growth (%)			Government deficit to GDP (%)		Reserves to imports (%)	Net private transfers to imports (%)
			M_1	M_2	M_3*	Overall (excluding grants)	Primary† deficits		
1980	143.2	24				–11.4	–10.4	11.6	1.6
1984	252.9	33	0.0	3.7		–7.9	–10.1	-56.8	7.1
1985	293.6	10	23.0	29.0		–6.2	–6.5	–13.5	23.1
1986	203.2	54	41.7	29.2		–6.9	–8.8	5.3	22.2
1987	100.0	50	31.6	32.0		–7.1	–4.9	4.2	29.1
1988	78.3	38	38.8	35.1		–8.2	–6.3	4.6	14.1
1989	68.6	33.4	26.0	29.5		–5.4	–3.9	8.5	12.6
1990	52.7	19.7	34.7	43.6		–6.1	–4.2	19.8	11.4
1991	56.4	19.1	22.4	26.9		–2.7	–2.3	20.2	25.5
1992	48.0	10.2	36.7	34.7	42.7	–2.6	–1.6	29.3	28.9
1993	45.3	63.9	32.9	28.8	39.3			12.0	
Average 1973–9						–11.0	–10.0		
Average 1980–5	223.6					–10.0	–10.7		
Average 1986–93	81.6					–5.6	–4.6		

Notes:
* M_3 includes foreign currency deposit accounts in local banks, beginning 1992.
† Deficit includes grants but excludes interest payments on both foreign and domestic debt.

Sources: Computed based on data from The World Bank, *Development Indicators 1994–95* for REER and net private transfers; The Bank of Tanzania, *Economic and Operations Reports* for the rest.

mounting as the relative scarcity of domestic currency increases. Fears of an overkill are real and export competitiveness and profitability are threatened. Increased speculative private resource inflows/repatriation to take advantage of the growing real interest rate differential with global capital markets are worrisome if the bubble bursts. These inflows have largely been directed at holding speculative financial assets rather than investment in the real sector, and add to the appreciation pressures on the real exchange rate.

Finally, the liberalization measures such as the relaxation of exchange controls, creation of bureaux de change, introduction of foreign currency deposit accounts and the development of the domestic financial asset markets have lowered the seignorage capacity of the economy by increasing the elasticity of substitution between base money and other financial assets. The revenue-maximizing rate of inflation will decline for a given level of income. The problem may become particularly serious if the liberalization process is not accompanied by a significant growth in income partly to offset this effect. In addition unification of the exchange rate takes away an implicit tax instrument, which in the absence of accompanying deep fiscal reforms must be compensated for by the inflation tax (Pinto, 1989, p. 322). The fiscal costs of the exchange rate unification thus entail the current account costs of the removal of the implicit revenue from overvaluation and the seignorage loss from the transition to a lower and a more elastic tax base.

References

Baldwin, R. E. (1993) 'Review of Theoretical Developments in Regional Integration', paper presented at the AERC workshop on *Regional Integration and Trade Liberalization* (Nairobi, December 1994).

Bhadhuri, A., L. Rutayisire and R. Skarstein (1993) *Evaluation of Macroeconomic Impacts of Import Support to Tanzania*, report no. 4/93 (SMU-University of Trondheim).

Collier, P., D. Greenaway and J. Gunning (1995) 'A Methodology for the Study of Trade Liberalization', paper presented at the AERC workshop on *Regional Integration and Trade Liberalization* (Nairobi, 1–3 December 1993).

de Valk P. and A. V. Y. Mbelle (1990) 'Textile Industry Under Structural Adjustment in Tanzania', mimeo (The Hague and Department of Economics, University of Dar es Salaam).

Edwards, S. (1993) 'Openness, Trade Liberalization and Growth in Developing Countries', *Journal of Economic Literature*, **21**:1358–93.

Esfahami, H. S. (1991) 'Exports, Imports and Economic Growth in Semi-Industrialized, Countries', *Journal of Development Economics*, **35**(1): 93–116.

Greenaway, D. and C. Milner (1993) *The Fiscal Implications of Trade Policy Reform: Theory and Evidence* (UNDP/World Bank).

Helleiner, G. K. (1986) 'Outward Orientation, Import Instability and African Economic Growth: An Empirical Investigation', in S. Lall and F. Steward (eds) *Theory and Reality in Development: Essays in Honour of Paul Streeten* (St Martin's Press).

Helleiner, G. K. (1990) 'Trade Strategy in the Medium-Term Adjustment', *World Development*, **18**(6).

Helleiner, G. K. (ed.) (1992) 'Introduction', in *Trade Policy, Industrialization and Development* (Oxford: Clarendon).

Helleiner, G. K. (1994) 'Trade Policy and Industrialization in Turbulent Times', in G. K. Helleiner (ed.), *Trade Policy and Industrialization in Turbulent Times*, ch. 1 (London: Routledge).

Mbelle, A. V. Y. (1993) 'Foreign Exchange Management During Structural Adjustment Programmes in Developing Countries: The Case of Tanzania', AERC Report.

Moran, C. (1990) 'Imports under a Foreign Exchange Constraint', *World Bank Economic Review*, **3**(2):279–95.

Ndulu, B. J. and J. Semboja (1994) 'Trade and Industrialization in Tanzania: A Review of Experience and Issues', in G. K. Helleiner (ed.) *Trade Policy and Industrialization in Turbulent Times* (London: Routledge).

Ndulu, B. J. and J. Semboja (1995) 'The Development of Manufacturing Export in Tanzania: Experience, Policy and Prospects', in G. K. Helleiner (ed.), *Manufacturing for Export in the Developing World: Problems and Possibilities* (London: Routledge).

Ndulu, B. J., *et al.* (1987) 'Import Tariff Study', report submitted to the Ministry of Finance, Economic Affairs and Planning. March 1987, Dar es Salaam.

Pinto, B. (1989) 'Black Market Premia, Exchange Rate Unification, and Inflation in Sub-Saharan Africa', *World Bank Economic Review*, **3**(3):321–38.

Rweyemamu, J. (1973) *Underdevelopment and Industrialization in Tanzania: A Study of Perverse Capitalist Industrial Development* (Nairobi: Oxford University Press).

Tanzi, V. (1995) 'Taxation in an Integrating World', Integrating National Economies Series (Brookings Institution).

World Bank (1987) *Tanzania: An Agenda for Industrial Recovery* (Washington DC: World Bank).

8 Trade Liberalization Policies in Uganda, 1965–95: Episodes, Credibility and Impact on Economic Development, with a Sample Survey of Enterprises Manufacturing Tradeables

Germina Ssemogerere and David Fielding

8.1 INTRODUCTION

This chapter evaluates Uganda's trade policies over the period 1965–95, with five objectives:

(1) to give a policy account of *whether* and *how* trade liberalization occurred:
(2) to identify the specific episodes when such liberalization took place;
(3) to weigh the *credibility* of the liberalization policies;
(4) to trace *the effects of liberalization on economic development*; and
(5) to examine any *supply response* to these policies from a sample survey of manufacturing enterprises producing tradeables for import-substitution and export.

Roots of the Current Interest in Trade Liberalization

The interest in liberalization is rooted in traditional international trade theory, which states that to maximize real income, a country should allocate its resources according to comparative advantage, at world market prices, so that the opportunity cost of producing exports does not exceed the real income earned, and the opportunity cost of producing import substitutes does not exceed the cost of comparable imports.

The arguments for protection, to nurture infant industries or diversify the economy away from complete specialization in primary exports subject to a secular decline in the terms of trade, made in the 1950s and 1960s, are regarded as exceptions under the least developed countries' special circumstances. These arguments do not raise an accepted (as yet) theoretical challenge to replace the orthodoxy of comparative advantage.

The voluminous literature review by Nicholas Stern (1989) pointed out that South-East Asia industrialized under a combination of export-promotion, to ensure efficiency, and protected import-substitution, to learn-by-doing at home in the local market. Furthermore, in the MDC's product differentiation by multinationals does not depend on the free trade orthodoxy.

However, economic stagnation, blamed on the pervasive distortions from the pro-import-substitution policies followed by many developing countries during the 1960s and after and the collapse of the centrally planned economies in Eastern Europe, have led to donor conditionality that ties liberalization of the trade regime to receiving balance of payments support and structural adjustment loans. This evokes once again the orthodoxy of comparative advantage as the guide to trade policy. It is this conditionality-based interest that lies at the root of the trade liberalization policies Uganda has followed since 1981, which are the subject of this chapter.

Working Definitions of Trade Liberalization

In their framework paper, Collier, Greenaway and Gunning (1994) defined trade liberalization as consisting of two distinct policy packages: the first is 'pure trade liberalization' – that is, putting in place 'neutral incentives' that do not discriminate between tradeable and non-tradeable sectors or between exports and import substitutes. This policy package seeks to lower the overall level of trade taxes; to apply the trade taxes uniformly across the board so as to reduce variance within the tax structure that can also be distorting; to limit the tax bands to the absolute minimum for administrative convenience; and to replace quantitative restrictions and licensing procedures with *ad valorem* taxes that work through the more transparent price mechanism, rather than arbitrary allocations.

The second policy package is 'exchange rate reform' or '*endogenous* liberalization', which, although taken for macroeconomic stabilization objectives, also changes the structure of relative prices of imports and exports, within the tradeable goods sector and between tradeables and non-tradeables, by realigning the real exchange rate.

In the Ugandan context, the distorting effects of the over-valued nominal exchange rate were considered more important, and to have outweighed the pure trade distortions – that most of the policy reforms were focused on exchange rate management.

A policy account of the two types of reform packages is presented in Section 8.2, starting with exchange rate management, then liberalization of the export and import trade regimes.

Effects of Trade Liberalization on Economic Development

Trade liberalization enables a small open economy to specialize according to comparative advantage, and to increase exports volume at given world market prices. Export expansion raises domestic income and employment via the foreign trade multiplier.

Participation in a larger world market promotes competition, which spurs the home country to improve the quality of output, generate new products and adopt cost-reducing technologies that increase total factor productivity.

For a small economy, the foreign market is essential to realize economies of scale, and optimal use of capacity of plant and equipment. The saving in unit cost is regarded by Edward Danison (1967) as a separate 'source of growth'.

On the import side, trade liberalization is often accompanied by import support from donors, which eases the foreign exchange constraint, allowing the home country to import essential consumer goods, thus relieving shortages and dampening inflation. It also makes possible the importation of essential inputs to enable import-substitution producers to utilize their plant and equipment fully. The foreign exchange from import support can also be sold to the public to raise non-inflationary budgetary revenue.

Trade liberalization is further expected to improve income distribution, by raising the value of the marginal product of labour, due to higher prices of the outputs produced by this labour and sold in more competitive markets. Additionally, trade liberalization reduces the rents from quota and licence-holders. Liberalization further improves the share of the export producers in the world market price by removing the implicit tax on exports imposed by the fixed nominal exchange rate and by increasing competition in exports marketing.

Empirical Issues

Much as trade theory predicts highly favourable effects of liberalization on economic development, there are as yet no reliable and unambiguous measures of such effects in the empirical literature. The difficulty of tracing the linkage between liberalization policies and economic development indicators is due to the policies' multiple effects, some of which run in opposite directions. The *net* outcome depends not just on the policies themselves, but also the art of implementation regarding timing, intensity of application and compatibility of well-synchronized packages. There is also some luck involved – not being derailed by exogenous shocks outside the control of policy-makers. Furthermore, unless other things remain equal, the empirical evaluator must be particularly careful not to attribute all the outcomes to liberalization, and neglect the effects of other policy reforms taken concurrently. The major empirical problems which are relevant to the Ugandan case are examined in Section 8.5.

Export Expansion and the Current Account

In a country exporting primary commodities, especially from tree crops like coffee, trade liberalization has no immediate effect on the volume of exports, since the short-run supply response is practically zero, except that from improved husbandry.

Planting is a permanent decision for a tree crop that takes four years to begin yielding a stream of output that will then last another 30 years. This kind of decision needs a package of supporting measures such as improvements in exports infrastructure, export financing, and so on, to convince private sector agents that the overall export incentives and environment have sufficiently changed to warrant making the permanent long-term investment. Therefore, liberalization, while necessary, is not sufficient; complementary measures also count for export growth.

Meanwhile, one must guard against drawing optimistic conclusions from an immediate increase in exports volume which is deceptive: it comes from either previously smuggled outflows or from decumulation of stocks, and dries up very quickly.

The same reasoning of making permanent decisions applies to fresh investment in new plant and equipment to manufacture exports. A permanent improvement in the exports environment, including institutions and infrastructure to support exports, must be forthcoming to convince private sector agents to invest.

For the underdeveloped country, liberalization must lead to the creation of new exports to improve the current account. This is particularly important to Uganda, whose export base is very narrow, with coffee alone contributing over 60 per cent of foreign exchange earnings.

If the marginal propensity to import out of current income is high, the increased nominal income from the temporary upsurge in exports leads to an increased demand for imports, and a worsening of the current account deficit, well before the new incentives are able to enlist a *genuine* supply response of new output from the field, especially that from tree crops or new factories. The evolution of this phenomenon is examined in the Ugandan case, where the major export is coffee, and where exports in manufacturing have to come from new productive capacity, since the manufacturing sector practically broke down during the civil strifes of the 1970s and early 1980s.

Import Composition, Productive Capacity and Donor Dependence

Liberalization eases the balance of payments constraint by making previously rationed imports available at open market prices, supplemented by outright donor support. The increased supply of imports relieves critical shortages of essential consumer goods and contributes to price stability. The supply also enables producers of import substitutes to obtain inputs and expand capacity utilization, output and employment. However, the relative importance of consumption versus producer imports inflows has been a subject of heated debate in Uganda, since the days of foreign exchange Window II in 1982.

Those opposed to the import of consumer goods at a faster rate than inputs point to a number of dangers, including development of a taste for import-intensive consumption at levels not sustainable without donor dependency on import support. They also cite the appreciation of the nominal exchange rate due to the generous foreign exchange inflows for import support, above the country's capacity to earn foreign exchange, which acts as an implicit tax on exports. Moreover, the lack of protection inherent in indiscriminate imports liberalization may jeopardize infant industries.

Those in favour of liberalization contend that the country needs foreign resource inflows to stabilize price levels, directly by increasing the supply of goods, and indirectly by raising non-inflationary revenue (Collier and Henstridge, 1993). Cost-reducing measures such as improvements to infrastructure, and technological and managerial training, should be the policies to replace protection in promoting import-substitution industrialization (Agricultural Secretariat, 1991).

The crux of the matter is that for import liberalization to be sustainable in an underdeveloped country, it should be used to promote a change in the country's productive structure to expand the capacity in a direction that improves the current account by import-substitution for those items the country can produce efficiently. Export expansion is also needed to earn foreign exchange to finance the import bill required for economic development (Kasekende and Ssemogerere, 1994).

The empirical issue of the effects of import liberalization on Uganda's economic structure is examined in Section 8.5.

Compatibility of Fiscal, Monetary, Exchange Rate and Trade Liberalization Policies

Liberalization reduces import prices in local currency. Economic agents previously dealing in imports find themselves with excess money balances, at the lower prices. A policy must be put in place either to increase the demand for, or to reduce the supply of, money to net out this excess liquidity. Otherwise, it will spill back into imports and worsen the current account, creating pressures to reverse import liberalization.

Increasing Prices and the Demand for Money In Uganda, currency devaluation, which raised the price of imports in local currency, has been the main tool for increasing the demand for money as the import regime was being liberalized.

Indirect taxes, in the form of excise duties and sales taxes, are also prevalent. Given Uganda's narrow tax base, indirect taxes have been going up, partly to replace the coffee export tax. The coffee tax was eliminated as international coffee prices sagged in the late 1980s but was temporarily brought back to control the effects of the coffee boom in 1992/94; it was again removed under the 1996/97 budget.

Tightening Money Supply: the SIPs programmes and interest rate policy The special import programmes (SIP I, II and III) financed by donor support, were intended to lower money supply in the hands of the public, by selling foreign exchange. The SIPs served two purposes simultaneously: to mop-up excess liquidity and to raise non-inflationary revenue.

A tight monetary policy, by sustaining high interest rates, reduces money supply and concurrently attracts autonomous capital inflow, which improves the external account. But high interest rates have a deflationary effect on private investment. For the public sector, government borrowing at high interest rates rapidly raises the local debt burden, which then necessitates foreign borrowing, higher taxes or printing money to repay. None of these options is desirable.

In Uganda, the relationship between autonomous capital inflows and high interest rates is unclear. It appears that capital inflows are due to improved security in some parts of the country, and a liberalized exchange rate and insecurity in neighbouring countries independent of interest rates. The higher interest rates are attributed to inefficiency in the banking system, which has failed to lower the cost of financial intermediation, rather than discretionary monetary policy. The high public debt burden also appears to have arisen from inefficient borrowing (Nyamalele-Bagamukhunda, 1996) and low tax revenue, independent of interest rate policy.

Section 8.4 puts together the fragments of evidence to examine whether there is any deliberate policy stance to synchronize fiscal, monetary, trade and exchange rate policies in a manner consistent with economic growth. The three-gap model of E. L. Bacha (1990) advocates foreign borrowing to ease the fiscal burden during adjustment. But in Uganda's case, the question is whether the current external debt levels are sustainable and should be increased by further borrowing.

Credibility of Trade Liberalization Policies

The literature points to three indicators on which private sector agents focus their attention in passing judgement on whether trade liberalization policies are credible. The first is macro-economic compatibility, which can be monitored through the resource balance on both the fiscal and external accounts. The other two, systemic forecastability and time consistency, are qualitative.

Systemic forecastability occurs if a government is prone to react to a crisis by interference in the market mechanism. This behaviour becomes perfectly predictable. This motivates destabilizing speculation from private sector agents that neutralizes the effect of trade policies. An attempt is made in Section 8.4 to trace whether there were any crisis-management policies taken by government during liberalization that were systematically forecast and neutralized. The analysis of this indicator depends so much on qualitative judgement, however, that it is unlikely to yield conclusive and indisputable results.

The second indicator, time-consistency, refers to the likelihood that reforms are permanent, given the political considerations and interests of the regime in power (Metzel and Phillips, 1996). Trade liberalization, to be sustainable, must change the economic interests and political balance to accept the new order. In Uganda, tariff exemptions and investment incentives are administered on an *ad hoc* basis to such an extent that both fiscal revenue and investor confidence are eroded! Section 8.5 attempts to trace the many changes in this area from the budget speeches and other sources (National Forum, 1996).

The third indicator of credibility monitors macroeconomic consistency. A rapid fall in foreign reserves, or a persistent balance of payments deficit, is a signal to private sector agents that policy-makers are likely to reimpose trade restrictions to protect reserves. Fortunately, in Uganda's case, reserves are building up steadily despite a current account deficit, partly because of large private remittances from abroad, the recent foreign exchange inflows from the coffee boom (Kasekende, 1994), and donor assistance.

Accumulation of a large fiscal deficit indicates that policy-makers are likely to print money, destabilize the price level, appreciate the nominal exchange rate and worsen the external account. Uganda's fiscal deficit, on the capital budgets, is funded by donors; the deficit is regarded as unsustainable by practically all analysts. The frequent changes in indirect taxes, especially the taxes on petroleum, beer and cigarettes, and the deployment of the extremely unpopular Anti-Smuggling Squad, appear to be strenuous efforts to raise revenue to replace the coffee export tax that was eliminated with liberalization. The move to conduct the budget on a cash basis since 1992 also shows policy determination to contain inflation. However, the upsurge in military expenditure has again called into question the government's ability to control the budget. The issues of macroeconomic compatibility with trade liberalization are examined in Section 8.4.

Exogenous Shocks and Trade Liberalization

During trade liberalization Uganda was plagued by two external shocks. The fall in the international price of coffee in fact accelerated liberalization of the coffee sector; in response, both the explicit and implicit taxes were removed and the marketing system was made more efficient by the dismantling of the monopoly of the Coffee Marketing Board (CMB) and the state-regimental co-operative system. The gains from liberalization in terms of higher producer prices to the farmers, however, were smaller than would have been the case under higher world market prices, apart from the times of the transitory coffee boom. Liberalization just managed to make the coffee sector survive!

The second and *repeated* external shock is from periodic droughts that affect Uganda's rainfed agriculture. Repeated droughts make food supply and food prices highly variable. Since food is a wage good for unskilled labour, high food prices, by increasing the cost of labour, implicitly lead to an appreciation of the real exchange rate. The policy efforts to depreciate the nominal exchange rate cannot correct for the foods effect since most foods, particularly staples, are 'non-monetary' and 'non-tradeable'. The effect of the drought on the gains from trade liberalization is examined in Section 8.5.

Outline of the Chapter

This Chapter consists of eight sections. Section 8.1 has outlined the issues to be investigated, their theoretical underpinnings and their associated empirical controversies. Section 8.2 narrates the policy account of trade liberalization in three parts: exchange rate reform, exports liberalization and imports policies. Section 8.3 uses a variety of indicators to identify the specific episodes of trade liberalization, such as the implicit tariff rate, changes in quantities, and so on. Then Section 8.4 presents the more qualitative discussion of credibility of trade liberalization policies, including moniterable resource balance indicators, and Section 8.5 traces the effects of trade liberalization on economic development.

Section 8.6 presents the findings of the response to trade liberalization of the producers of tradeables, from a sample survey of both export and import-substitution manufacturing enterprises. Section 8.7 draws the conclusions and makes policy recommendations from Uganda's experience. Section 8.8 is a brief summary of the chapter.

8.2 EXCHANGE RATE REFORM, EXPORTS, AND IMPORTS LIBERALIZATION: A POLICY ACCOUNT OF MAJOR DEVELOPMENTS 1965–95

Introduction

This section presents a policy account of the major development in the exchange rate and trade regimes over the period 1965–95, with the purpose of providing a background to the identification of trade liberalization episodes in Section 8.3.

The historical narrative is divided into three policy areas: evolution of exchange reforms, exports liberalization and imports policies. The section concludes with an overall assessment of the historical roots of trade and payments restrictions and the impetus for reforms.

Exchange Rate Reform

Uganda's exchange rate regime can be divided into four periods with distinct policy approaches:

(1) a rigidly fixed exchange rate with an emerging parallel market (1966–80);
(2) a managed float with attempts at exchange rate unification (1981–4);
(3) the civil war years with policy reversal (1985–7); and
(4) the drive to exchange rate unification (1987–93).

The description of these four approaches draws heavily on the work by Kasekende and Ssemogerere (1994).

(1) The Rigidly Fixed Official Exchange Rate Regime and the Emergence of a Parallel Market (1966–80)

Uganda attained independence in 1962 in an international environment of fixed exchange rates under the Bretton Woods System. From 1962 to 1966, the pre-independence policy simply continued; the East African Currency Board fixed the exchange rate to the UK pound sterling for all three countries, Kenya, Uganda and Tanzania. In this system, Uganda had no separate exchange rate policy.

In 1966, however, each country set up its own central bank to manage its monetary policy independently. Uganda fixed its shilling to the gold standard at a value of 0.12441 grams of fine gold per Uganda shilling (Kasekende and Ssemogerere, 1994). This was for convenience; there is no evidence of a conscious adoption of a fixed exchange rate policy.

In 1971 when the gold standard was abandoned by the IMF, Uganda shifted and pegged its currency at Ush 7.141268 per US$ 1.0. This lasted from 1971 to 1975.

As the US $ became volatile in the early 1970s, Uganda shifted again and pegged her currency at Ush 9.66 per SDR. The Uganda shilling remained fixed at this rate until June 1981, when the first SAPS package was adopted.

In the early years (1966–71) the rate of inflation was relatively low, as shown in column 10 of Table 8.1, by the CPI for the low-income consumer group. Save for the massive capital flight in 1968/69 just before the Obote I regime declared the 'move to the left' policies, and the military overthrow of that government in 1971, the economy functioned relatively well under the small-holder private sector-led agricultural growth. Import-substitution was promoted by the Uganda Development Corporation (UDC), which functioned as an efficient parastatal, with a high degree of autonomy (Glentworth and Wozei, 1972).

From 1972 to 1977, however, a number of events resulted in the misalignment of the nominal exchange rate, under a military regime that was not watchful to make the necessary adjustments. First, the expulsion of the Asians in 1971, and political insecurity generally, led to a massive exodus of skilled personnel. The industrial sector began to crumble. The scarcity of essential consumer goods that emerged led to rising inflation that pushed up the CPI from 43 per cent to 355 per cent over only five years (1972–8), as shown in column 10 of Table 8.1.

Second, the volume index of exports fell from 185 per cent in 1971 to 90 per cent in 1978, as the fixed nominal exchange rate under high inflation became over-valued and imposed an implicit tax on exports (Table 8.1, column 3).

Third, the producers of traditional exports – cotton, coffee, tea and tobacco – were paid fixed producer prices that were adjusted infrequently. Payments by the state-controlled co-operatives collecting system and the state export monopolies were often late. (These entities included the Coffee Marketing Board (CMB) for coffee and the Lint Marketing Board (LMB) for cotton.) The marketing and payments system imposed an additional inflation tax on exports producers as nominal producer prices in local currency were eroded by inflation.

Fourth, to the implicit, explicit and inflation taxes were added the inefficiency costs of the monopolistic marketing channels. Despite the fact that the unit value index of exports more than tripled, from 90 per cent to 399 per cent, as a result of good international coffee prices – especially in 1977 when the index rose to a record high of 446 per cent – the total value index of exports only rose from 155 to 241. Columns 3, 4 and 5 of Table 8.1 give the data. The quantity of exports supplied was not responding adequately.

Import prices rose steadily due to the oil shocks and high interest rates of the 1970s that caused many SSA countries balance of payments problems. The import unit value index rose from 14 per cent to 55 per cent in 1966–80. This led to a deterioration in the terms of trade index from 564 per cent to 448 per cent, as exports purchasing power fell.

The import volume index, however, declined from 269 to 153; the import value index more than doubled from 41 to 110. The relevant figures are in Table 8.1, columns 6–9.

As the export volume and value indexes deteriorated, at a time when the imports unit value, and total value indexes were rising, the country's balance of payments deteriorated sharply, especially over the years 1978–80. The country lost reserves in 1979–80. The data are given in Table 8.1 columns 1 and 2.

From 1976 onwards, adjustment policies were required to deal with the growing external disequilibrium. But since the regime in power was concerned with a civil war, which accelerated in 1978–9 and overthrew it, no attention was paid to economic management.

As the civil war grew, government printed money to finance it; between 1977 and 1980, 75–96 per cent of the fiscal deficit was financed by the banking system. Inflation rose sharply from 355 per cent to 1186 per cent as measured by the CPI (column 10 of Table 8.1).

The combined internal and external disequilibrium, as evidenced by hyperinflation and the balance of payments deficit, gave birth to serious exchange rate misalignment. There are no reliable data to trace when the parallel market in foreign exchange emerged. But stories refer to massive smuggling of exports to avoid the implicit tax, and of imports to earn the implicit subsidy by selling imports at the parallel market exchange rate, in a domestic market riddled with shortages of essential commodities after the collapse of the industrial sector from 1972.

The estimates of the foreign exchange premium shown in Table 8.2 are from various sources that put the figures from 14 per cent in 1966 to

Table 8.1 Balance of payments position, trade and price indexes, 1966–95

Year	Overall balance ($US m.) (1)	Change in gross reserves (2)	*Export indexes 1991=100* Volume (3)	Unit price (4)	Total value (5)	*Import indexes 1991=100* Volume (6)	Unit price (7)	Total import value (8)	Terms of trade (9)	The CPI (1991=100) low income group (10)
1966	149	–149	193	90	155	269	14	41	564	0.0013
1967	109	–98	191	93	158	264	14	40	577	0.0014
1968	80	–76	181	97	167	279	14	41	636	0.0015
1969	75	–70	208	90	157	298	14	44	587	0.0016
1970	2	–2	211	105	197	288	15	45	642	0.0033
1971	–17	+17	185	113	184	353	17	62	600	0.0037
1972	–0	+0	210	106	199	228	18	43	532	0.0039
1973	–3	+3	191	122	207	185	22	44	486	0.0043
1974	–14	+5	165	151	222	183	30	59	442	0.0074
1975	1	–11	146	138	179	167	37	57	363	0.0089
1976	3	–8	125	219	244	130	38	52	512	0.0139
1977	20	–10	104	446	413	219	40	92	1007	0.0195
1978	–43	–18	90	305	243	169	43	77	636	0.0335
1979	–62	+56	103	327	299	121	55	70	534	0.1061
1980	–176	+41	80	399	241	153	68	110	448	0.1186
1981	–187	–31	90	215	271	119	74	87	262	0.2032
1982	–33	–34	124	225	251	113	78	89	258	0.2740
1983	–36	–28	110	268	264	107	84	90	286	0.3320
1984	–59	+56	103	304	281	79	91	72	298	0.6671

1985	–67	+30	116	257	266	64	93	60	245	1.2737
1986	127	+1	108	306	295	103	90	92	305	5.8388
1987	–9	–19	111	234	230	147	86	126	243	15.3580
1988	8	–2	107	201	199	154	90	139	200	33.6152
1989	–62	+26	130	168	200	163	96	156	157	60.8673
1990	–108	–15	108	117	113	134	97	130	101	95.9349
1991	–122	–24	100	100	100	100	100	100	100	100.000
1992	9	–39	96	95	81	107	101	108	84	145.5035
1993	–106	–107	93	108	90	126	105	131	92	151.0167
1994	142	–169	149	198	264	123	106	131	167	171.8428
1995	107	–113								185.6000

Sources: The export, import and terms of trade indexes are from the Bank of Uganda, Research Department (1996). The CPI is spliced by The Department of Economics, Makerere University MA Programme (1996). The balance of payments data are from The Background to the Budget (Annual).

Table 8.2 Policy account of the evolution of the exchange rate premium and annual rate of inflation, 1962–80 and 1981–94

Period *(1)*	*Exchange rate policies* *(2)*	*Parallel market exchange rate premium (%)* *(3)*	*Real effective exchange rate index (1987=100)* *(4)*
1962	Fixed exchange rate under East African Currency Board	–	
1963		–	
1964		–	
1965		–	
1966	Break up of the currency board	14	
1967	Fixed exchange rate under the Gold Exchange Standard	14	
1968		14	
1969		14	
1970		43	
1971	Break-up of the Gold Standard	57	
1972	Fixed exchange rate	86	
1973		200	
1974		286	
1975		657	
1976		812	
1977		688 *	
1978		888	
1979		750 **	
1980	End of fixed exchange rate	850	
1981	Discrete devaluations	918	
1982	Managed Dual W_1 and W_2 float exchange rate regime		
1983		183	
1984	Exchange rate unification and W_1 and W_2	55	
1985	Action under forex shortage and civil war	366	
1986	Reversal to fixed exchange rate: serious policy debate	306	
1987	Massive devaluation & currency reform	288	100
1988	Discrete devaluations; crawling peg	118	170
1989		67	128
1990	Legalizing the forex bureaux	27	127
1991		21	128
1992	Auction system	8	124
1993	Exchange rate unification inter-bank market	0.01	110

Notes:
* The decline in the premium in 1977 reflects a coffee boom rather than exchange rate reform.
** The 1979 decline in the premium is not explained.

Source: Republic of Uganda, *Background to the Budget* (annual) (Kampala: Ministry of Finance and Economic Planning).

Kasekende and Ssemogerere, G. (1994) 'Exchange Rate Unification and Economic Development: the Case of Uganda 1987–1992', *World Development* **22**(8); UNDP/World Bank (1990), *Uganda: Agenda for Trade Liberalization*.

850 per cent in 1980. Given a distortion of this magnitude, it is understandable that liberalization in Uganda concentrated on exchange rate management or 'endogenous liberalization' as the key, rather than 'pure' trade policies.

(2) The Managed Float Exchange Rate Regime with Attempted Exchange Rate Unification (July 1981–April 1984)

The impetus for the early 1980s exchange rate reforms clearly originated from the IMF, as a condition for balance of payments support. In May/June 1981, the Obote II government drew up a financial programme whose key features were the restoration of confidence in the local currency by adjusting the nominal exchange rate and the eradication of price distortions in order to shift resources from parallel markets and smuggling into productive activities.

In July 1981, the shilling was unpegged from the SDR and devalued. The official exchange rate dropped from Ush 8.5 to Ush 76.97 per US$1.0 in one month, while the parallel market premium went from 918 per cent to 35 per cent between July 1981 and August 1982.

Unfortunately, the money supply grew by 50 per cent per annum between 1981 and 1982. Furthermore, foreign exchange, both to service the official debt and for private sector import requirements, was under-estimated and proved inadequate, despite strict foreign exchange allocation by the Money Market Committee of officials from the Bank of Uganda, the Treasury and commercial banks. In fact, private demand was shifting from the parallel to the official market, as cheaper foreign exchange was becoming available. Given continued inflation and excess demand for foreign exchange, it was impossible to locate an equilibrium exchange rate by devaluation alone.

In August 1982 a dual exchange rate system was introduced at two windows: W1 and W2. The lower-priced foreign exchange at W1 was obtained from the sale of traditional exports and public-sector cash loans. The proceeds were used to finance the public debt, contributions to international organizations and procurement of essential imports.

The higher-priced W2 foreign exchange came from earnings of non-traditional exports (which were very small) and an IMF loan to government (which raised substantial controversy). The W2 exchange rate was determined at a weekly auction; this higher rate served two purposes: to encourage non-traditional exports whose earnings were cashed at W2, and thus gradually increase the supply of foreign exchange to the economy, and to allocate the available foreign exchange more efficiently at this higher price.

Import restrictions were eased to ensure that importers bought the foreign exchange at the auction. The proceeds from W2 were used to finance the budget. These measures ensured consistency of exchange rate, trade and macroeconomic policies.

Under the dual exchange rate system, the W1 rate depreciated from Ush 99.3 to Ush 290 per US$1.0, while the W2 rate moved between Ush 300 and Ush 302 per dollar, over the same period (August 1992 to May 1994). The shift in the rates partly reflected a gradual loading of transactions from W1 to W2 as an increasing volume of foreign exchange was auctioned.

The parallel market premium, although dropping from 180 per cent in 1982 to 55 per cent in 1994, remained substantial; the actual parallel market exchange rate stood at Ush 466 per US$1.0 in May 1984. The underlying problem was money supply growth, which was 100 per cent per annum over the same period. Consequently, inflation, as measured by the CPI, which stood at 35 per cent in 1982 and fell to 21 per cent in 1983 (a year of fiscal discipline), then soared to 101 per cent by 1984 when monetary expansion was resumed to finance the civil war.

The W1 and W2 exchange rates where unified in May 1984, but the underlying fundamentals were not consistent. High inflation pushed up the parallel market exchange rate and the supply of foreign exchange at W2, mostly from the IMF, far exceeded the country's capacity to earn foreign exchange (non-traditional exports were just emerging).

The combined effect of monetary expansion to finance the civil war (which started immediately after the rigged elections in 1981 and accelerated by 1984) and the failure by government to reach a fourth stand-by arrangement with the IMF in 1984, which dried up the W2 resources, led to very rapid depreciation of the newly unified exchange rate, and the parallel market exchange rate, as well.

(3) The Civil War Years, Policy Reversal and Exchange Rate Policy Debate, 1985–7

In 1985 monetary growth stood at 139 per cent per annum. The parallel market premium went from 55 per cent to 306 per cent, reflecting serious exchange rate disequilibrium. By the year of the military take-over (1986), inflation had risen dramatically, as measured by the CPI (Table 8.1, column 10).

The auctioning of foreign exchange continued until the Obote II regime was overthrown, but the auction rate depreciated from around Ush 300 at unification in 1984 to Ush 1400 per US $ in February 1986.

The NRM government did not pay sufficient attention to macroeconomic stability or exchange rate policy at the beginning (in February), but by May the growing shortage of foreign exchange forced it to re-introduce the dual exchange rate system.

Essential imports were secured at Ush 1400/US$1.0. The supply of foreign exchange came from project aid and traditional exports. The 1400 rate was similar to the W1 rate; the bulk of official transactions took place at this rate. Private transactors were availed foreign exchange at 5000, while the parallel market exchange rate stood at Ush 6000/US$1.0.

The dual official exchange rate system was abandoned in August 1986, partly because it was an impractical mechanism to ration the increasingly scarce foreign exchange, and partly because of a growing debate in some influential NRM circles that it resembled the W1 and W2 system instead of breaking with the past.

A sharp policy reversal from a managed float system was put in place when a fixed exchange rate was administered at Ush 1400/US$1.0 from August 1986 to May 1987. Concurrently, budgetary control was weak, and this aggravated inflation. Several attempts to convene a donors' conference, independently of the Bretton Woods institutions, failed to raise the required foreign exchange. As the disequilibrium worsened, the NRM government had to turn to the IMF as well.

(4) The Drive to Exchange Rate Unification, 1987–93

The first reforms (1987–9) were part of a medium-term economic recovery programme 1987/88–1990/91 whose objectives were to restore positive real GDP growth to 5 per cent per annum, reduce inflation to 10 per cent per annum and achieve a sustainable balance of payments position by 1990/91. It was necessary to rehabilitate the entire economy and lay the foundation for future growth – that is, to rehabilitate the economic and social infrastructure and restore productive capacity in key sectors.

Foreign exchange was needed to import agricultural machinery, other inputs and animal drugs; equipment to repair trunk and feeder roads and electricity and water installations; commercial vehicles, particularly trucks, and railway rolling stock; and inputs for industries producing essential consumer goods, which were being rationed through the Resistance Councils (RC) system of local government (salt, sugar, soap, kerosene and iron sheets for roofing, for example).

The first steps consisted of discrete devaluations May 1987–October 1989, intended to narrow the gap between the official and parallel market exchange rates. The parallel market premium dropped from 288 per cent in 1987 to 118 per cent in 1988, and to 67 per cent in 1989. Concurrently, a drastic currency reform struck two zeroes off the existing currency and imposed a highly regressive tax of 30 per cent payable on converting the old into the new currency. This brought inflation down, with a fall in the CPI from 163 per cent to 85 per cent between 1987 and 1989. However, fiscal discipline was still weak; between May and November 1987, for example, the money supply tripled! In 1989, a crawling peg was adopted in an attempt to locate the market-clearing exchange rate.

The period 1987–9 is best regarded as experimental in liberalizing the key macroeconomic aggregates – exchange rate, price levels and interest rates. The trials specifically referring to trade liberalization are documented by the World Bank and UNDP (1990), *Uganda: An Agenda for Trade Liberalization*, country report no. 6. The debate over economic policy was still ongoing within NRM, regarding its ideology of a controlled economy and the IMF conditionality to liberalize in order to get scarce foreign exchange.

In 1990, however, the government issued two key policy documents: *The Way Forward I: Macroeconomic Strategy 1990–1995* and *The Way Forward II: Medium-Term Sectoral Strategies 1990–1995* (Republic of Uganda 1992 b,c) These documents are unique in that they made macroeconomic stability, particularly the control of inflation and exchange rate liberalization, the cornerstone policies to mobilize resources – local private savings and foreign exchange from exports earnings and capital inflow. Exchange rate reforms, trade liberalization and macroeconomic stabilization measures were made more consistent.

As liberalization was pursued consistently, more foreign exchange became available from foreign loans and grants, and was sold openly under the three special import support programmes of 1988–91. Foreign exchange bureaux were established in 1990 to cater for small private sector customers. The legalization of the bureaux gradually replaced the parallel market, and the premium dropped from 67 per cent to 20 per cent between 1989 and 1991.

The last two steps in foreign exchange liberalization covered the period January 1992–November 1993. First, official foreign exchange was auctioned to determine a market-based exchange rate. The second step was to unify the market institutions. Before November 1993, the foreign exchange market was segmented; the official market was administratively separate in the central bank where official donor funds were auctioned; the foreign exchange bureaus handled the transactions of small private customers on the open market.

In November 1993, the inter-bank market was established to operate alongside the bureaux. All authorized dealers in foreign exchange, including the bureaux, were free to determine their exchange rates according to supply and demand. The central bank used the weighted average midrate between the bid and offer rates to intervene to even out wide fluctuations to stabilize the market, or to pursue specific policy objectives, such as neutralizing rapid appreciation, which taxes exports.

Overall Assessment of Exchange Rate Policies

Fixed exchange rates and the controls to ration foreign exchange in Uganda are not related to any systematic development objective, such as the promotion of import-substitution industrialization. Acute shortages of foreign exchange, in a mismanaged macroeconomic environment, appears to be the root cause of exchange rate restrictions. Such environments prevailed in the 1970s under Amin's rule; in the early 1980s under Obote II and the civil war, and in the mid-1980s under the NRM government.

Given scarcity as the impetus for reform, exchange rate liberalization follows the conditionalities of the IMF. However, the sustainability of liberalization requires pursuit of a coherent and consistent macroeconomic policy – particularly to control inflation – and policies to increase the supply of foreign exchange. Inflation and the exchange rate premium move together as the balance of payments worsens.

The need to control inflation became understood in Uganda only gradually. Excessive government spending was at the heart of the very high exchange rate premiums in 1972–80 and 1984–9. The real effective exchange rate time series in the last column of Table 8.2 provide additional information on the importance of controlling inflation.

The need to expand a country's productive capacity to earn and conserve foreign exchange does not yet appear to be understood in Uganda. Part of the problem is the lack of coherent sectoral development policies, of which increasing the availability of own foreign exchange earnings should be one aspect.

The second part of the problem is the fact that adherence to the IMF conditionalities is followed by import support, grants and loans, which enable policy-makers to shelve and forget the foreign exchange constraint. The policy accounts of these issues are given below under export and import liberalization.

Export Liberalization: A Policy Account

This policy account is divided into four parts.

(1) We describe the major features of the export sector inherited at independence and the policies pursued up to 1970.
(2) We outline the distortions that practically wiped out most exports and narrowed the export base to one tree crop – coffee – between 1971 and 1980.
(3) In part (3) we cover the early exports policy reforms, 1981–5.
(4) We cover the policies of the recent period, 1986–95.

Uganda, as a small country in the international market which cannot influence world prices of its exports, has to concentrate on increasing exports volume to raise exports receipts, and on diversifying the exports base to cushion the stream of foreign exchange earnings from exogenous shocks.

We examine here how the policies affected the volume, measured by the exports volume index in Table 8.1 (column 3), and the country's ability to cope with external shocks, as reflected in the composition of exports in Table 8.3, which is divided into blocks corresponding to different policy regimes.

(1) The Exports Structure and Underlying Policies (1962–70)

Uganda inherited a diversified export base built to cater for various colonial interests. The most important source of foreign exchange was agricultural raw materials from the 'traditional exports': coffee, cotton, tea and tobacco, in that order of relative importance, contributed around 60 per cent to foreign exchange receipts in the 1960s (Table 8.3, block 1). This group of exports was encouraged to make the colonies self-sufficient by raising tax revenue and to contribute to the Second World War effort by availing raw materials.

The bulk of 'traditional exports', except estate tea, was grown by smalholders, who were assisted to improve husbandry practices by local chiefs who mobilized extension services for the timely planting, soil conservation, distribution of high-quality seeds, and proper drying and harvesting.

An Asian population, whose coming was originally encouraged by the colonial administration to build the East African Railway, grew in size and had easy access to capital, provided crop finance to export the traditional crops, as well as subsequent investment in exports-processing activities.

An autonomous co-operative movement (until 1970) was organized to assist farmers to share the benefits from the collection and marketing system for cotton and coffee.

Copper was the second single source of exports revenue, contributing, on average, 10 per cent to exchange rate receipts in the 1960s (Table 8.3, block 1). The copper mines at Kilembe were built with capital inflow from Canada and semi-killed labour from the Asian population. Mining also benefited from the high prices of the Second World War, the Korean War and the post-war policies of some Western countries such as the USA, using the commodity corporation to stockpile raw materials.

The third source of foreign exchange earnings consisted of a large collection of processed agricultural goods, such as cottonseed cake, edible oil, cigarettes, made tea and cotton fabrics, and other manufactured goods, such as fertilizers, soap, bicycle tyres and tubes, enamelled hollow ware,

Table 8.3 The composition of exports per block by policy regime 1968–95 in US$ M and by % of total value of exports

Traditional exports	*Block I: Inherited exports structure*						*Block II: Early 1980 reforms*						*Block III: Mid-level reforms*					*Block IV: Ongoing reforms*				
	1968	*1969*	*1970*	*1971*	*1972*	*1973*	*1980*	*1981*	*1982*	*1983*	*1984*	*1985*	*1986*	*1987*	*1988*	*1989*	*1990*	*1991*	*1992*	*1993*	*1994*	*1995*
Coffee	102	111	145	140	161	215.6	339	242	340.0	340	359.0	355.0	397	311	260	158	142	111.7	98.1	107	343	384
Cotton	42.2	35.9	50.1	50.3	52.6	48.0	4.3	2.2	3.3	11.6	12.4	15.4	5.1	4.1	3.1	0.2	5.7	11.7	9.2	5.5	3.6	9.9
Tea	10.6	13.3	13.5	13.6	18.0	1.5	0.3	0.3	0.8	1.2	3.2	1.1	3.2	1.9	1.2	0.4	3.5	6.7	7.7	11.1	11.8	8.7
Tobacco	0.4	2.4	1.1	1.9		1.7	0.3			0.9	1.5	0.3			0.6		2.1	4.5	3.5	7.0	8.8	7.3
Copper	15.9	25.6	23.6	19.7	16.1	15.6																
Other exports	5.4	6.0	6.9	4.9	4.4	6.4																
Animal feeds	2.9	3.8	3.8	3.0	6.5	4.5				3.2	4.5							4.0	3.8	5.2	10.5	8.9
Sugar	0.3	2.5	2.5	0.6																		
Maize and beans									0.6	11.3	10.1	3.1	1.1		0.3			5.1	7.5	32.3	39.0	30.1
Other exports							2.2	2.5	0.7	2.1	6.6	4.3	4.7	3.1	2.9	4.9		1.8	13	4.7	11.5	22.7
Barter trade (70% is coffee)															49.3	94.4						
Total exports value in US $M	179	201	24.5	234	260	293.7	346	247	346	370.0	397	379	411	320	322	252	179	147.9	194	201	460	561
Coffee as % of total exports value	56.8	55.4	59.3	60.0	62.1	73.5	97.8	97.9	98.2	91.8	90.4	93.6	96.6	97.1	92.1	97.8	69.8	73.9	73.7	62.9	74.6	68.5
Non-traditional as % of total exports value	4.6	6.1	4.6	3.4	4.2	3.7	0.6	1.0	0.4	4.5	5.3	2.0	1.4	1.0	5.9	13.2	0.0	23.6	21.9	34.4	20.2	26.9

Source: *Background to the Budget*. Various issues.

etc. This exports category, destined for the East African Market, contributed around 20 per cent to foreign exchange receipts. The remaining 10 per cent of exports receipts came from a variety of miscellaneous exports.

The policies that led to manufactured exports have a longer history. First, a price assistance fund, originally intended to stabilize the producer prices of primary exports, turned out to fix these prices below what the farmers could receive at the prevailing exchange rate from the world market. The savings from the fund were invested in infrastructure, particularly the Owen Falls Dam at Jinja. The availability of electricity encouraged export-processing and import-substitution industries. The marketing boards, the CMB and the LMB, collected the savings and export taxes.

On the eve of Independence the British Labour Party administration established autonomous corporations for the development of the colonies. The Uganda Electricity Board (UEB) and the Uganda Development Corporation (UDC) were set up under this policy (Glentworth and Wozei, 1972). The UDC actively promoted joint ventures between the Uganda government and foreign capital for investment in industry.

Industrial licensing (1948) was the third colonial policy, whose objective was to encourage the orderly development of industry by restricting investment to curve out a market where only one plant was viable. Industries like Nytil at Jinja, set up by Calico Printers of Britain, Uganda Cement Industries (UCI), and Tororo Industrial Chemicals and Fertilizers (TICAF) benefited from industrial licensing.

The East African Common Market, with its common external tariff to raise revenue, and other common services set up for the convenience of administering the colonies, enhanced the industrial licensing policy and enabled Uganda to have access to the common market for her large-scale industries (Namatovu, 1980).

The combined effects of colonial policy, the price assistance fund, and the high prices of raw materials offered during the Second World War and the Korean War, all enabled Uganda to create a diversified export base (Table 8.3). Consequently, the volume of exports grew steadily, from 193 per cent in 1960 to 210 per cent in 1972.

The trade regime was not without restrictions, however. The export duty was the single most important source of recurrent revenue, which was conveniently collected by the export marketing parastatal monopolies of CMB and LMB. The monopolies also levied the price assistance fund, which further reduced the share of smallholders in the world market price. Industrial licensing, and the East African common external tariff, gave substantial protection to industry. The exchange rate was fixed, as noted earlier.

The fact that the exports sector flourished, despite the restrictions, must be noted as important enough to warrant a re-examination of what else prevailed to neutralize the restrictive effects of the policy regime on exports performance.

The low rate of inflation kept the parallel market premium to at most 14 per cent, which minimized the implicit tax on exports. The autonomous organized co-operatives spread the benefits of marketing to the farmers until 1970. Crop finance from the Asian intermediaries was readily available, giving cash to farmers on delivering the crop and loans in kind to purchase key items like bicycles, iron sheets, and so on. The East African Common Market broadened import-substitution opportunities, allowing domestic firms to experiment with manufactured exports. Extension services ensured a reasonable level of productivity in peasant agriculture.

One may conclude that despite the lack of a conscious export-promotion policy, and despite trade restrictions, Uganda was able to respond to opportunities as they presented themselves, to build a prosperous and diversified export base.

(2) The Decline of Exports Volume and Narrowing of the Exports Base (1971–80)

The 1970s witnessed a tightening of the restrictive policies of the 1960s and an erosion of the positive aspects.

The exchange rate remained fixed in the middle of an acute shortage of goods, following the disruption of the industrial base, and a growing fiscal deficit. This led to rapid over-valuation and a parallel market premium that rose from 14 per cent in 1970 to 850 per cent by 1980 (Table 8.2). This huge over-valuation imposed a heavy implicit tax on exports, an outcome that is unrelated to the pursuit of any explicit positive policy objective, such as import substitution.

In 1969, the 'Move To The Left' policy package was put in place, with the objective of increasing government's control of the economy. The parastatals CMB, LMB and the Produce Marketing Board (PMB), for the local marketing of key grains, maize and beans, were tightly tied to the co-operatives by the Co-operative Act of 1970, giving the minister strict control over the appointment of co-operative administrators. Dividends to the co-operators dried up; farmers were paid late, at a fixed producer price that was eroded by inflation. These developments imposed a heavy inflation tax on exports producers.

Tax revenue from the manufacturing sector dwindled when the management of enterprises was allocated arbitrarily, and frequently changed hands. Smuggling, to enjoy the implicit subsidy on imports from the overvalued exchange rate, also reduced customs revenue. The export duty became the most important source of reccurrent revenue; it was harder to evade, because of the regimented co-operatives and export monopoly parastatals. The explicit export tax on coffee rose steadily as a proportion of recurrent revenue to an all-time high of 67 per cent in the 1985/86 fiscal year (Ssemogerere, 1992).

The combined effects of an inflation tax, an explicit export tax, an implicit tax due to the exchange rate premium, and the marketing monopoly of the co-operatives and parastatals created some dramatic negative effects on exports.

The share of the smallholder in the world market price of coffee at the market exchange rate, for example, was as low as 11 per cent in 1987 (Ssemogerere, 1992). For tea, the share of the producer in the world market price was estimated at 4 per cent and 8 per cent in 1980 and 1981, and remained below 30 per cent up to 1991 (Kaweesi, 1997).

Despite the fact that both tea and coffee are tree crops, the area planted under tea remained at 20 000 hectares, but the average rate of utilization of tea estates, as a percentage of installed productive capacity, was only 19 per cent (Kaweesi, 1997). The area planted in coffee fell from 229 000 hectares in 1971 to 192 000 in 1987, a decline of 31 000 hectares, as angry farmers uprooted coffee trees and used them for cooking fuel – despite the fact that uprooting was illegal (Ssemogerere, 1990).

Table 8.3 shows that the composition of exports dramatically narrowed. Coffee alone contributed 98 per cent to exports receipts and all other exports brought only 2 per cent by 1980, 1981 and 1982. The copper mines were closed, manufactured exports to Kenya and Tanzania practically disappeared with the collapse of the East African Community in 1974 (Namatovu, 1980).

Table 8.1 shows that the 1970s were generally years of good world market prices for coffee. For example, the unit price index stood at an all-time high of 446 per cent in 1977, and above 200 per cent between 1976 and 1988. The terms-of-trade index registered the most favourable historical record of 1007 per cent in 1977. However, the coffee boom that led to these developments in 1977 does not appear to have led to a relaxation of controls and a sharing of the benefits with producers. Certainly, the volume index of exports fell from 125 per cent in 1976 to 90 per cent in 1978, just a year following the boom, and to a record low of 80 per cent at the close of the restrictive policy regime in 1980.

In conclusion, therefore, Uganda's control regime narrowed the export base, by over-taxed exports producers, without pursuit of any tangible development objectives. The control regime was a carryover of post-independence controls to the highly distorted macroeconomic environment of the 1970s, which worsened the negative effects of these controls.

Both key qualitative indicators of exports performance shown in Tables 8.1 and 8.3 deteriorated: the export base narrowed, with the contribution of coffee to exports receipts rising from an average of 60 per cent in 1966 to 98 per cent by 1980. And the exports volume index dropped from 193 per cent to a record low of 80 per cent.

(3) The Early Reforms (1981–5) and Their Effects on the Exports Sector

As noted earlier, the impetus for economic reform in Uganda came from the need to comply with the IMF conditionalities.

Exchange rate devaluation in 1981–5 had some desirable effects: first, it reduced the parallel market premium from 850 per cent to 55 per cent, which lowered the implicit tax on exports; and second, the sale of foreign exchange at the depreciated exchange rate enabled government to pay farmers cash on delivering the produce. This, together with the concurrent budgetary control, lowered the inflation tax, and foreign exchange profits as a single item contributed 22 per cent and 8.5 per cent to recurrent revenue in the 1982/83 and 1983/84 fiscal years.

The second reforms raised producer prices upwards more frequently, as documented in Table 8.4. However, the increases, in real terms, were wiped out by rapidly rising inflation by 1985. In any event, the AGSEC repeatedly pointed out to government that the producer price increases did not cover the cost of production for most crops; this remained the case for robusta coffee until 1990, for example. The marketing system remained monopolistic, however; this made it unclear whether the entire administered price increases were being passed on to the export producer.

The effects of the reforms can be observed in Tables 8.1 and 8.3. The exports volume index rose from 80 per cent in 1980 to 116 per cent in 1985 in Table 8.1; this reflects a positive development. In Table 8.3, the contribution of non-coffee exports to total exports receipts also rose from 2 per cent to 6 per cent over the same period, indicating a positive attempt to return to a diversified exports base, and the fact that non-traditional exports receipts were allowed to be cashed at W_2, as noted earlier.

The positive developments are very limited, however, and must be interpreted with great care. First, most of the response in the volume index came from coffee that farmers diverted from smuggling and/or sold from existing stocks, as they were paid cash on delivery. Moreover, the period was too short to register an increase in exports from new planting, as traditional robusta coffee takes four years to mature. The response from tea was minor; it too came from rehabilitating existing shambas, as there was no new tea planting (Kaweesi, 1997).

No new investments to expand the processing and manufacturing capacities for export, particularly to the neighbouring countries, were reported either. This accounts for why the diversification remained so limited (Table 8.3, block 2).

Table 8.4 Real producer prices (Old Ush/kg)

Effective date of price increase	*CPI (1981=100)*	*Robusta coffee*	*Arabica coffee-bugishu*	*Non-bugishu arabica*	*Seed cotton*
09.05.81	100	20	37	32	15
11.11.81	92	38	71	61	33
07.05.82	111	45	84	73	36
09.05.83	148	41	70	59	33
01.07.83	153	52	91	77	39
21.12.83	170	60	104	88	53
10.06.84	181	72	130	100	70
29.10.84	250	84	140	110	72
24.06.85	502	54	84	72	12

Source: Real Ush/kg were calculated by deflating the nominal producer prices announced by government, the Kampala Cost of Living Index, low-income group 1981=100, using the values that matched the corresponding dates, in column 1.

It is fair to conclude that the reforms of the early 1980s were so limited that they did not induce any appreciable positive response of new investments in the exports sector. In any case, the intensification of the civil war in 1984–6 brought economic activities practically to a standstill.

(4) The 1986–95 Reforms and Their Effects on the Exports Sector

The NRM regime in February 1986 found an extremely weak exports sector, which the reforms over the period 1987–90 – best regarded as experimental – did not improve much.

- Exchange rate depreciation narrowed the parallel market premium from 288 per cent in 1987 to 27 per cent in 1990. This substantially reduced the implicit tax on exports.
- Uganda suffered a serious external shock over the period 1987–92, when the world market price of her major export, robusta-clean coffee plummeted from US$2.2 to US$0.9 per kg – that is, by more than 60 per cent. The price of arabica-clean fell from US$3.4 to US$1.09 per kg – that is, by around 68 per cent. Under these circumstances, a lingering parallel market premium of 27 per cent was extremely undesirable.

Barter trade (1986–9) The cornerstone policy the NRM government argued for at length in 1986–8 was barter trade. The rationale was that barter trade would open up new markets for traditional exports: tea, tobacco, cotton and surplus coffee not sold on the quota markets. Moreover, new exports that were not entering traditional markets could also enter via barter. These were: maize, beans, groundnuts and simsim and so on, and came to be called 'barter commodities'. The list was later extended to cover timber, cotton yarn, and hides and skins.

The conduct of barter trade protocols between government-to-government, and government-to-private companies was undertaken by parastatals: CMB for coffee, LMB for cotton products, PMB for produce, Uganda Tea Authority (UTA) for tea, Uganda Leather and Tannery Industries (ULATI) for hides and skins, and Uganda Hardware for timber. The history of these parastatals, except CMB and LMB, dates back to the 'Move to the Left' in 1969. In fact, the Obote II regime had also tried to revive barter trade through these parastatals.

The barter trade policy package was extremely difficult to implement, however. The sheer inertia of parastatals left many barter protocols unfilled. Except for coffee, the commodities, particularly produce, had no marketing logistics; for example, to gather sufficient quantities from smallholders, sort the produce by quality and transport it without deterioration. This lack of logistics left 70 per cent of barter protocols to coffee, thus limiting the contribution of the policy to export diversification. The barter values are recorded in Table 8.3, block 3, 1988 and 1989. The policy became discredited for being cumbersome, while producing meagre results.

Dual Licensing (1988–90) A second policy was dual licensing, undertaken as part of a 1988 agricultural non-traditional exports promotion programme conducted by the GOU and USAID. The idea was to export agricultural products and return imports of equal-value from the foreign exchange receipts. The implicit exchange rate of Ush 1000–Ush 1500 compared most favourably with the official exchange rate of Ush360/US$1.0. This was the key incentive. Additional incentives included simplifying export–import procedures to divert trade away from smuggling and into official channels and use of a special credit line from the BOU at the official exchange rate if imports were required as inputs into exports.

Dual licensing did not produce impressive results either. There was no data base to ascertain that the imports brought were of equal value to the exports receipts; some informed observers argued that the policy was used for capital flight. Moreover, the import–export cycle of three months led to very low turnover and tied up working capital. In the final analysis, an efficient exporter is not necessarily an efficient importer; on this count, the policy was inherently inefficient.

The estimates by Kasekende and Ssemogerere (1994) put the contribution of dual licensing to export receipts at US$13 million, US$21 million and US$21 million during 1988, 1989 and 1990, respectively. The policy came to be regarded as covert action to delay exchange rate reform, and was discredited by the end of 1990.

Foreign Exchange Retention Scheme (1989–90) A third policy was the foreign exchange retention account scheme, put into place in 1989. An exporter was allowed to open an account in which to retain 100 per cent of foreign exchange receipts, to be used at a later date to import commodities on the BOU approved list, or other commodities used as inputs into exports. The response by exporters was lukewarm: by 1990, only 29 accounts had been opened. The exporters could not trust the BOU to allow them to use their foreign exchange when they needed it, if the bank had other pressing commitments to meet. In other words, the foreign exchange retention account policy, as judged by private sector exporters, was not credible. It was quickly abandoned when the bureaux were legalized.

There is a catalogue of other minor reforms whose results are difficult to estimate singly; they are listed in Kasekende and Ssemogerere (1994).

The overall results of the policies, barter trade, dual licensing and retention accounts, are shown in Tables 8.1 and 8.3. Table 8.1 shows that the export volume index remained at around 108 per cent between 1986 and 1990. Under falling international prices of the major export, coffee, the unit value index fell from 306 per cent to 117 per cent over this period. Uganda failed to put in place a policy package to boost exports volume to make up for the decline in prices, with the result that exports receipts sagged from $US411 million to $US179 million in 1987–90 and to $US148 million by 1991, as shown in Table 8.3.

Liberalization of Exports (1991–5)

In this last period, two factors are key to explain exports performance. The 'Way Forward I' and 'Way Forward II' documents convinced government that exchange rate reform and macroeconomic stability were essential. The second impetus came from the results of nine special task force studies carried out under AGSEC supervision and fed into the Agricultural Policy Committee (APC) between 1989 and 1991. These studies generated the data required to measure policy distortions, using the policy analysis matrix (PAM) and other methodologies that are simple to explain to policymakers.

Table 8.5, for example, illustrates the meagre share of the producer price in the world price due to the implicit tax, the export duty and the marketing monopolies prior to 1990. Table 8.6 shows the distortions to comparative advantage, as measured by the domestic resource cost rations, which remained above 1.0 for the period prior to 1990, except for arabica coffee.

Table 8.5 Share of the producer in the world price (%) at the market exchange rate

Year	*Robusta clean*	*Arabica clean*	*Cotton lint equivalent*	*Made tea estates*	*Made tea outgrowers*
1987	12	12	22	12	30
1988	18	16	47	18	23
1989	14	12	38	31	23
1990	18	22	56	18	19
1991	40	81	62	19	20
1992	38	39	43	20	27
1993	35	47	63	35	31
1994	46	49	51	41	36
1995	–	–	–	54	–

Sources: Bank of Uganda, Agricultural Secretariat (1993); and Kaweesi (1997). Arabica and Robusta 'clean' represent the coffee commodities after the parchment is taken off. The 'made' quoted for processed commodities.

Taken together, the two factors – exchange rate reform and macroeconomic stability – convinced government to liberalize exports. All three major parastatal monopolies (LMB, CMB and PMB) were dismantled. Producer prices were decontrolled; they now follow international market prices. The exchange rate was unified in 1993, eliminating the implicit tax. The exports sector no longer pays export duties, (save for the stabilization tax on coffee to regulate the inflationary effects of the coffee boom in 1993 and 1994).

The results of liberalization are illustrated in Tables 8.1, 8.3, 8.5 and 8.6. Table 8.1 shows that the exports volume index was just beginning to recover in 1994. In Table 8.3, block 4, the entries of traditional exports values are considerably larger than in block 3 and so are the non-traditional exports entries. The contribution of non-traditional exports is beginning to register above 20 per cent while the share of coffee in exports receipts is coming down. Table 8.5 indicates that the share of the producer price in the world price has risen since 1991, although not consistently because of other constraints such as poor feeder roads, limited and expensive export finance, and so on, which create private localized marketing monopolies. In Table 8.6, the DRC ratios are below unity in 1992, reflecting a restoration of comparative advantages. The exports sector is still weak, however. Processing and manufacturing for exports have not been restored, due to multiple constraints of irregular and expensive electricity, water and telecommunications; the high cost of finance, and so on. The East African market is not easy to re-enter.

Table 8.6 Comparison of domestic resource cost ratios during liberalization

Commodity	*1989*	*1990*	*1992*
Coffee (robusta)	1.29	0.76	0.62
Coffee (arabica)	0.91	0.44	0.60
Tea	1.19	0.52	0.54
Cotton	1.62	0.62	0.89
Simsim	1.10	0.42	0.35

Source: Balayo (1992).

An influential study by the Private Sector Foundation (1996) on *The East African Open Border Potential Impact and Uganda's Economy* has costed the effects of the post-liberalization constraints on the competitiveness of a variety of exports and import-substitutes. Some of these data are reviewed in the sample survey of enterprises manufacturing tradeables in Section 8.6.

Imports Liberalization: a Policy Account

In contradiction of the widely held view in the SAPs literature, the policies to control the volume and composition of imports in Uganda do not appear to have been systematically motivated by the development objective to promote import-substitution industrialization. The emerging picture is that of *ad hoc* reactions to crises of foreign exchange scarcity created by either adverse terms of trade or insecurity and economic mismanagement. The tariff regime appears to have been determined by *ad hoc* policies to raise budgetary revenue.

The policy account of these developments is divided into four sections:

(1) import controls, licensing and foreign exchange allocation procedures;
(2) the tariff regime and unilateral changes in tariff structure;
(3) any consistency or otherwise of unilateral liberalization and economic integration; and
(4) a qualitative evaluation of the contribution of import policies to Uganda's economic development, in terms of increasing its capacity to earn/conserve foreign exchange and keep import dependence to sustainable levels.

(1) Import Controls and Allocation Procedures

The imports volume index 1991 = 100 in Table 8.1 (column 6) shows that Uganda enjoyed a rising volume of imports between 1966 and 1971, when inflation was low and the exchange rate – though fixed – was not over-valued. *Work for Progress: Second Five-Year Development Plan 1966/71* lay the emphasis in encouraging import-substition on attracting capital investment into joint ventures between the private sector and the UDC parastatal.

The import controls and foreign exchange allocation procedures, therefore, have their roots in exchange rate over-valuation and macroeconomic mismanagement, rather than the promotion of import-substitution *per se*, and are documented starting with the Structural Adjustment Programme of 1981.

The Money Market Allocation Committees (1981) Along with the devaluation of the shilling in 1981, as noted earlier, a money market committee was appointed to allocate foreign exchange. The requirements to service external debt and pay for government imports took priority. The balance of foreign exchange then went to private imports. However, given the ongoing rate of inflation, the still over-valued exchange rate and the shift of private agents from the parallel to the official market as news of foreign exchange availability from the IMF stand-by arrangement spread, the Money Market Committee found it impossible to clear the excess demand for foreign exchange.

The Dual Exchange Rate System (1982–4) A second device was to allocate foreign exchange via the dual exchange rate system, W1 and W2, over the period August 1982 to April 1984. This allocation system used the price mechanism to clear the excess demand for foreign exchange.

The private sector bought their foreign exchange at the W2 auction rate, while government obtained its foreign exchange at the lower W1 exchange rate. The two rates gradually moved closer to reflect the economy-wide scarcity of foreign exchange; simultaneously, the proceeds from W2 were used to finance the budget – as a non – inflationary source of revenue.

While raising the price of foreign exchange was the correct decision, macroeconomic management to reduce inflation was not pursued because of financing the civil war. The excess demand for foreign exchange, therefore, was not cleared.

A standing complaint about the dual exchange rate system is that the auction was indiscriminate. All importers qualified to obtain foreign exchange from the auction, regardless of the end-use of this scarce resource.

The concerns for policy-makers were, first, to ensure that the foreign exchange provided by the IMF was actually sold and the proceeds used to finance the budget. To accomplish this, the following import liberalization measures were taken.

(1) The 1 per cent commission to the Uganda Advisory Board of Trade and the 5 per cent deposit bond by importers were abolished.
(2) The 'no foreign exchange required' import licences for importers who had their own foreign exchange from the parallel market were abolished.
(3) Import licences were to be processed within five days.
(4) Customs duties were reduced.
(5) The commercial banks floated interest rates to promote lending.

A second policy concern was that the increased availability of goods would also reduce inflation. Whereas in the immediate run both concerns were valid, it still remained the case that the W2 foreign exchange was in effect a loan, to be repaid at some future date. Measures (2) and (3), which liberalized administrative constraints, were welcome: they improved efficiency.

Measures (1) and (4), which made foreign exchange cheaper, could have been streamlined for importers in activities that conserve/earn foreign exchange; this was *not* done.

To increase foreign exchange earnings, policy-makers relied on setting higher producer prices, as illustrated in Table 8.4, and lowering the parallel market premium to reduce the implicit tax on exports. Inflation ate away the increase in producer price. The share of the producer price in the world price of coffee, the major export, for example, was estimated at 23 per cent in 1983 and 14 per cent in 1984 (Ssemogerere 1992). A combination of monopoly marketing inefficiencies, inflation, the explicit export tax and the remaining 55 per cent parallel market premium, all continued to eat into the producer's price incentive. Investments into infrastructure to reduce production cost were not part of the policy package, for example.

When W2 ended, the country's capacity to sustain this level of supply of foreign exchange had not increased; the parallel market premium resurfaced.

The Inter-war Years (1985–7) The Obote II government continued the foreign exchange auction system until the regime was overthrown. The parallel market premium rose from 55 per cent to 366 per cent, reflecting the ineffectiveness of attempting to reduce excess demand by auctioning a limited quantity of foreign exchange under inflation. The imports volume index fell to all-time low levels of 79 per cent in 1984, just at the drying up of W2 resources, and 64 per cent in 1985 (Table 8.1).

Although the NRM re-introduced the dual exchange rate system in

May 1986, the continued excess demand spilled on to the parallel market at Ush6000/US$1.0. Attempts to fix the exchange rate at Ush1400/US$1.0 proved unworkable. Borrowing foreign exchange from the IMF had to be resumed with the SAPs package in May 1987.

Barter Trade, Dual Licensing and Retention Accounts (1988–90) We saw earlier that each of these systems of foreign exchange allocation was unworkable. Dual licensing (1988–9) was taken to avoid devaluation by giving a higher implicit exchange rate on exports earnings, through permission to allocate the foreign exchange proceeds to imports of equal value. This tied up working capital, and forced exporters to be importers. Barter trade sought to economize foreign exchange by paying for imports in terms of exports shipments. The lack of logistics to match export–import consignments of equal value made this allocation system inefficient and unworkable as well. The retention accounts were not perceived by private sector exporters to be credible, in the face of continued foreign exchange shortage at the Bank of Uganda.

The Open General Licensing System (May 1987–January 1990) This is the policy measure that attempted to articulate development objectives. The OGL was to allocated foreign exchange to those productive enterprises that met the following criteria:

- enterprises producing inputs for other priority sectors or goods for mass consumption
- enterprises that could generate substantial *tax revenue* through the sale of their outputs (sales tax)
- enterprises whose production process required few imported inputs
- enterprises whose production would facilitate exports expansion.

Despite the articulated objectives, the choice of the first 24 licenses granted did not meet the stated criteria. Only three enterprises, two for cement and one for crown seals, produced inputs. The rest of the enterprises produced consumer goods: five soap, three soft drinks, two beer, one cigarettes, four mattresses and six textiles.

The OGL did not improve the country's capacity to earn foreign exchange; none of the licensees produced exports! The agricultural sector, which generates Uganda's exports, was conspicuously excluded from the OGL. Nor did the OGL assist the country to conserve foreign exchange. Careful observers contend that some enterprises imported more than the three-months stock of imports they needed to fully utilize their productive capacity; this encouraged import-intensive production processes instead (Greenaway and Milner, 1993), without incentives to produce previously imported inputs locally. Since OGL imports were priced at the official exchange rate, enterprises bribed ovicials to be put on the OGL list, which grew larger, from 25 to 63 enterprises.

In summary, the OGL was neither open, nor general. Firms had to be selected, but the selection criteria neither fulfilled the stated objectives nor met the requirements of comparative advantage. The OGL was abandoned in 1990 in favour of the foreign exchange bureaux.

The Special Import Programmes (SIPs I, II and III) SIP I arose to speed up the purchase of foreign exchange allocated to private importers by the Import-Licensing Committee during January to November 1988. The committee had allocated US$ 53.606 million, but only US$21.2 million had been purchased. The committee had not examined the capacity of the applicants to pick up the allocations. SIP I sold a pre-determined amount of foreign exchange weekly, which was earmarked to particular sectors on a 'first-come-first-served' basis, solely dependent on the ability to pay. The funds were quickly exhausted. The drive to sell foreign exchange speedily led to liberalization of the qualifications. All applicants were eligible: firms, traders, distributors, agriculturalists, and so on. The only constraint was that purchasers of foreign exchange were not allowed to use bank credit, as this would spark off inflation.

SIP II, launched in June 1989, was even more directed at inflation control. It quickly disbursed foreign exchange to importers who could raise local cash without borrowing from the banking system. The money supply, as measured by M_2, dropped from Ush 60.2 billion to Ush 59.2 billion in one month! SIP II ended in September 1989 when the funds were exhausted.

SIP III lasted 14 months (February 1990–March 1991), during which US$98.8 million were sold to control inflation, which fell from 50 per cent per annum in January, just before the beginning of the programme, to 23 per cent per annum by June of the same year.

Some common observations were made about the SIPs by Kasekende and Ssemogerere (1994) and the UNDP/World Bank (1990). First, the SIPs were very effective in controlling inflation: they immediately led to a withdrawal of purchasing power from the public; the excess liquidity was turned into imported commodities, and the government secured non-inflationary revenue! To ensure speedy adjustment, the sale of foreign exchange under the SIPS led to considerable liberalization of import-restrictions. In this regard, the SIPs increased the efficiency of imports allocation. However, the SIPs added to the multiplicity of prices for foreign exchange. There were three exchange rates: the official over-valued rate; the SIPs rate; and the 'no foreign exchange required' parallel market rate for private sector customers who were rationed out of the SIPS market.

On the surface, foreign exchange under the SIPs appeared cheaper than that at the parallel market. However, private sector agents had to meet certain requirements, such as opening letters of credit at a commission of 2–3 per cent charged by commercial banks. Parallel market private agents enjoyed 10–20 per cent discounts on large purchases; they could also borrow to purchase foreign exchange. Discounts were not available on SIPs purchases, and borrowing was not allowed on SIPs I and II. *The SIPs were intermittent interventions*: they were not seen as permanent sources of foreign exchange; this stop–go phase could not encourage an efficient allocation of resources for long-term development.

For the country as a whole, one questions the desirability of fighting inflation with a loan from the IMF that encourages unsustainable import-intensive production and consumption levels. The lesson learned, overall, was to unify the exchange rate and control inflation so that a market-based exchange rate could equalize the demand and supply of foreign exchange.

The data in Table 8.7 provide a good indication of the process of imports liberalization. The 'own-resources' and 'no foreign exchange required' in rows 4 and 5 constituted the most liberal import flows, using foreign exchange purchased from the parallel market or from remittances by Ugandas working abroad. Although importers could not claim tax deductions because the parallel market was 'illegal' until 1990, when the bureaux were licensed, policy-makers acknowledged the existing scarcity of goods and left the prices of imports to be determined by the parallel market. This was the most important source of private sector financing: it contributed 30 per cent of total imports in 1987/88. This gradually declined to 5 per cent by 1994/95, as other foreign exchange sources were liberalized and opened to private sector agents.

Project and programme aid financed government requirements, the OGL and the SIPs allocations. This source financed 61 per cent of all imports at the beginning of the recovery programme in 1987, and rose to around 70 per cent in 1988/89 and 1990/91; it tapered off to 21 per cent by 1994/95. Most donor-funded imports are controlled because of the need to comply with procurement procedures, including tendering for large consignments, availability of counterpart funds, disbursement schedules according to donor conditionalities and accountability of the funds before the next consignment. The BOU is pushing to have the donors place their foreign exchange resources on the bureaux and inter-bank markets.

The restrictive barter, dual licensing and retention account allocations have all been scrapped. The bureaux, for small purchases, and inter-bank market for large purchases, rose in relative importance with liberalization, from 2 per cent in 1990/91 to 73 per cent by 1994/95. As this source emerged, own-foreign exchange, no-forex-required and the parallel market

Table 8.7 Imports liberalization, classified by source of financing ($USm.)

	1987/88	*1988/89*	*1989/90*	*1990/91*	*1991/92*	*1992/93*	*1993/94*	*1994/95*
(1) Total	622	776	596	546	449	533	719	1.085
(2) Project aid	305	419	187	218	169	176	199	230
(3) Programme aid	73	129	196	175	128	164	49	–
(4) Own resources	83	68	61	50	27	16	17	16
(5) No-forex	107	90	77	71	41	4	17	16
(6) Inter bank/bureaux	–	–	–	11	83	168	426	792
(7) Barter	38	48	42	22	1	–	–	–
(8) Other	16	23	34	–	–	–	14	–
Percentage of total								
(1) Total	100.0	100.0	100.0	100.0	100.0	100.0	100.0	100.0
(2) Project aid	49.1	54.0	31.4	39.9	37.7	33.3	27.7	21.2
(3) Programme aid	11.7	16.6	32.8	32.1	28.5	30.8	6.4	0.0
(4) Own resources	13.4	8.8	10.3	9.1	6.0	3.0	2.4	1.5
(5) No-forex	17.2	11.6	12.9	13.0	9.1	0.8	2.4	3.7
(6) Inter-bank/bureaux	–	–	–	2.0	18.6	31.6	59.2	73.0
(7) Barter	6.1	6.2	7.1	4.0	0.2	–	–	–
(8) Other	2.5	3.0	5.6	–	–	0.9	1.9	–

Source: Bank of Uganda, Research Department (1996).

shrank. The unified market-based exchange rate has become the most important mechanism for allocating foreign exchange since November 1993.

(2) The Tariff Structure: a Policy Account

Liberalization of imports, as a move towards free trade, pursues two objectives. The first is to move from quantitative restrictions and licensing to *ad valorem* tariffs that work through the price mechanism. This allows the most efficient importer to deliver the goods, instead of the monopolist quota holder; it also redistributes income from private quota-holders to government, which can now collect tariff revenue. The second objective is to minimize tariff bands, in order to reduce variance within the tariff structure and move towards uniform tariff rates that do not discriminate against economic activities. This improves both resource allocation and administrative efficiency.

Underdeveloped countries, including Uganda, add a third objective: to protect infant industries. Richard E. Baldwin (1969) insists that this is a non-economic objective. Baldwin's case against infant-industry protection by tariffs rests on the grounds that a subsidy should be used through which the country only incurs excess production cost over the period when the infant industry learns by doing, while avoiding excess consumption costs under tariff protection. However, the budgetary difficulties underdeveloped countries face make Baldwin's subsidy alternative impractical.

Uganda's fourth objective is to prohibit imports that violate some national criteria and international conventions the country is signatory to, by placing these imports on a negative list. For example, Uganda honours, but does not control, the donors' negative list; since this is a given, it is excluded from the policy account. Nevertheless, Uganda freely determines the government's component of the negative list, which in 1993 contained the items shown in Table 8.8. The negative list is inconsistent with the objectives of trade liberalization and is a source of repeated controversies. Items (1) and (3) consolidate the statutory monopoly of the two parastatals (UEB and UP&TC) by allowing them to be the sole importers of their inputs; this contradicts the efficiency objective of imports liberalization. With the exception of items (2) and (9), which can be argued for on non-economic grounds, the bans on the rest of the items would have protected the infant industries manufacturing these items locally. However, a ban creates extreme scarcity, which makes smuggling very lucrative; the manufacturers of the substitutes constantly complain about unfair competition, despite the bans. It would have been more efficient to set a uniform tariff to protect these industries: this would allow some competition by those importers who could pay the tariff, while at the same time providing government with tariff revenue.

Table 8.8 Uganda's negative import list

(1)	Uganda Posts and Telecommunications Corporation equipment
(2)	Firearms
(3)	Uganda Electricity Board specialized equipments
(4)	Beer, made with malt, with an alcoholic strength by volume of 80 per cent or higher
(5)	Soda, gaseous or carbonated drinks
(6)	Cigarettes
(7)	Motor vehicle batteries
(8)	Used motor vehicle tyres
(9)	Pornographic materials

Note: The above goods may not be imported unless prior authorization by the Minister of Commerce, Co-operatives and Marketing (now Minister of Trade and Industry) is given, as provided in the External Trade Act of 30 July 1953.

The Dramatic Change in Tax Structure during Liberalization Historically, Uganda's export tax rates, particularly on coffee, were much higher than the tariffs on imports. For example, the first three entries of row 11 in Table 8.9 show that in 1981/82, 1983/84 and 1986/87 the effective import tariff rates were only 1 per cent, 9 per cent and 3 per cent, while the effective export duty rates were 14 per cent, 71 per cent and 34 per cent, respectively. It was easier to collect export taxes, which consisted of the residual income earned by the export marketing parastatals, CMB and LMB, after compensating fixed margins to the participants in the commodity chain: marketing, processing, collection and the farmer (whose share was often below production cost).

Liberalization, which scrapped the monopoly of the marketing parastatals, plus the collapse of the international price of coffee in 1989–92, required a complete overhaul of tariff/tax rates. The Uganda Revenue Authority (URA), a quasi-independent body, was put in place in 1991 to streamline revenue collection and tax administration.

Export taxes were abolished, including the tax on coffee – this was necessary for the coffee sector to survive. Import duties and excise and sales taxes were raised instead. Liberalization, by eliminating price controls – including the fixed exchange rate – also formalized economic activities (from parallel markets), enabling the government to collect more income tax, Table 8.9, rows 4–8, increases in relative contribution to recurrent revenue (for imports, rows 4 and 8a) collectively, made the effective tariff rate rise to 13 per cent and 25 per cent in 1990/91 and 1994/95, as the effective export tax rate fell to zero!

The dramatic change in tax structure is riddled with many problems, however, including misclassification of imports, indiscriminate exemptions and smuggling.

Misclassification of Imports Some items are over-taxed, on the assumption that the consumption of the respective commodities is price inelastic. In 1991/92, for example, petroleum alone contributed 29.8 per cent to total recurrent revenue; it still contributes over 20 per cent to-date.

Because tariff rates are not uniform, there is an in-built tendency for highly taxed importers to evade the tax by misclassifying goods into lower tariff brackets. According to the Uganda Investment Authority, study by Maxwell Stamp (1993): 'many imports are deliberately misclassified by importers to take advantage of lower tariff rates applying to different commodities' (p. 41).

Exemptions The temptation to evade taxes is aggravated by the many exemptions granted for different reasons:

- Imports by many NGOs were exempt because the NGOs provided relief and other social services government was unable to provide immediately when it took over power in 1986.
- Imports for plant, machinery and construction materials not available in Uganda are exempt from duty under the Investment Code 1991, provided they are not more than five years old and the importer holds a licence intending to invest in Uganda, issued by the Uganda Investment Authority. The investor and expatriate staff are in addition exempt from duty and sales tax on motor vehicles and household effects for personal use. A report by the URA listed 293 enterprises granted such exemptions (1996).
- Imports for government projects and other donor-funded imports for project and programme aid are exempt from duty.
- Perhaps the most contentious exemptions are those granted at the discretion of the minister of finance because they open room for rent-seekers to apply political pressure to get exemptions. A local newspaper reported that after the minister signs the exemption list he leaves a blank space at the bottom, in which other non-authorized persons can add more exempt enterprizes for kickbacks (*The Monitor*, February – March 1995 issues).
- Certain other items listed in the Customs and Excise Tariff Handbook's third Schedule, which includes industrial inputs, and the Finance Bill 1992, which covers agricultural raw materials, are exempt from duty.

The Budget Speech 1996/97 claims to have eliminated practically all *ad*

Table 8.9 Changes in Uganda's tax structure during trade liberalization (as % contributions to recurrent revenue)

Source of revenue	1980/81	1983/84	1986/87	1990/91	1994/95
(1) *Income tax*	*17.1*	*6.7*	*11.4*	*10.2*	*14.6*
(2) *Indirect tax* of which	*73.9*	*88.9*	*86.3*	*88.4*	*83.8*
(3) Export tax	4.1	44.4	39.9	9.4	2.7
(4) Customs duty	*20.8*	*10.0*	*11.9*	*36.5*	*35.9*
(5) Petroleum products				26.6	22.5
(6) Other				9.9	13.4
(7) Excise duty	3.7	3.7	6.8	9.1	9.8
(8) Sales tax	39.0	19.0	25.3	26.9	25.7
(a) Imported goods				12.1	14.1
(b) Locally manufactured goods				14.8	11.6
(9) Other tax revenue	4.5	5.0	2.4	6.5	9.7
(10) No tax revenue	–	–	–	1.4	1.7
(11) Effective rates					
(a) Export tax	14.0	71.0	34.0	13.0	20.0
(b) Tariff	1.0	9.0	3.0	13.0	25.0

Sources: *Background to the Budget* (various issues). Effective rates are authors' own calculations.

hoc exemptions by requiring each ministry to budget for payment of the exemptions it grants. Government itself is to retain exemptions only on bilateral, United Nations and Multilateral Financial Institutions Agreements. The Investment Code 1991 is due for review by Parliament in 1996/97.

The effect of exemptions is to reduce the marginal import tariff rates claimed to be paid by importers. A comparison of column 1 of the effective tariff rates *actually paid*, and the marginal tariff rates *claimed to be paid* in column 2 of Table 8.10 gives some illustrative data on this problem. National Forum (1996) reports that a large section of the private sector and some senior civil servants expressed dissatisfaction that the reforms to eliminate exemptions are not being implemented effectively.

Smuggling The URA put in place an Anti-Smuggling Squad in 1991, staffed with army personnel who meticulously arrest cross-border traders with small consignments of sugar, salt, paraffin, beer, and so on and auction the consignments to demonstrate the determination of the URA to eliminate smuggling. The business community believes that smuggling

Table 8.10 A comparison of *ex-post* effective tariff rates (reduced by exemptions) and marginal tariff rates (claimed to be paid by imports) (%)

CCCN code (2 digit)	*Description of imported commodities*	*Ex-post effective tariff rate paid (%)*	*Marginal import tariff rate (%)*
39	Plastic and plastic articles	1.5	24.7
40	Rubber and rubber articles	5.8	11.6
48	Paper and paper products	3.4	16.4
56	Man-made fabrics	15.2	22.2
73	Iron and steel	3.8	42.0
85	Electrical machinery	6.3	22.0
94	Furniture	3.0	32.0

Source: Compiled from *Uganda: Tariff and Tax Policy Administration*, UNDP/ World Bank Mission Report (1 February 1993).

continues and that the Anti-Smuggling Squad should not mete out excessive force on small cross-border traders (National Forum, 1996).

It is extremely difficult and dangerous to collect data on smuggling to sort out the contentions. The old Ugandan problem appears to have resurfaced – unchecked large-scale smuggling persists because it is 'approved' by the regime in power. In the case of the NRM government, *The Monitor* (7 February 1997, p. 9) notes:

> Smuggling allows people to cheat. Taxi talk has it that those who make laws also break them. . . .
>
> In 1986, The NRM set up *DANZE Enterprises*, as a private company committed to participating in the market so as to make profits which will in turn be used to advance the objectives of the Movement. Its directors (all appointed by *the President*) had smuggled into the country large volumes of sugar, cooking oil, shoes, jute bags, bed sheets, blankets, sweaters, hoes, axes and matches. The company's record became more controversial when *the President* signed the royalties from his fast selling book, *Sowing the Mustard Seed*, to it.

On 12 March 1997, *New Vision*, the official NRM Government Paper also reported widespread smuggling of petroleum that has left the Petrol Station in Busia, Tororo, all the way to Busoga, empty! (This is repeated in the National Forum, *Report of the Working Group on Tax Policy and Administration* [1996] p. 12.)

Table 8.11 Duty collected, by tariff band (%)

Tariff band	*Imports value (% of total)*	*Duty collected (% of total duty)*	*Cumulative tariff revenue collected*
0	48.5	0.0	0.0
5	10.4	8.6	
10	12.5	21.0	29.6
15	0.7	1.7	
20	13.8	37.9	69.2
25	0.2	0.3	
30	9.0	19.0	88.5
40	3.0	7.0	
50	0.5	1.8	
60	0.0	0.0	
70	0.2	1.0	
80	0.0	0.0	
100	0.02	0.3	
150	0.04	0.7	
200	0.02	0.5	
	100	100	100%

Source: World Bank/UNDP (1990) *Uganda: An Agenda for Trade liberalization* ch. 3, 1988/89.

The Tariff Structure and Government Revenue Because of exemptions and smuggling, effective tariff rates are very low or nil on many items. Table 8.11 gives an idea of the proportion of tariff revenue collected in each tariff band in 1989. Over 48 per cent of imports had a zero tariff rate and about 30 per cent of tariff revenue came from the 0–10 per cent tariff bands; 88.5 per cent of tariff revenue was already collected by the tariff band of 30 per cent.

Table 8.11 is outdated – but, unfortunately, the data on tariff bands consistent with the changes in Table 8.9 are not readily available. Section 8.3 identifies the changes in average effective tariff and tax rates over the different liberalization episodes.

Some recent evidence suggests that between 1991 and 1995, tax exemptions to attract direct foreign investment yielded 0.01–0.46 benefit–cost ratios. Since these ratios are less than unity, the exemptions are an inefficient method of attracting investment.

To improve tariff revenue, Uganda should have moved to lower and uniform tariff rates during liberalization to ensure compliance and non-discrimination in resource allocation. The UIA-sponsored Maxwell Stamp

Table 8.12 Nominal and effective tariff protection under trade liberalization, 1985–

	Nominal protection		*Effective protection*		*Capacity utilization*	
	1985	*1992*	*1985*	*1992*	*1987*	*1994*
Beer (brewing)	–48	52	–55 –74	125	34.3	62.7
Leather (shoes)	–32	32	–	36	13.0	13.0
Paints:		48	–	131	3.9	34.8
Gloss	–8	–	–	–	–	–
Emulsion	–45	–	–20	–	–	–
Soft drinks	48	52	10 –40	134	–	–
Steel products	–35	42	–	56	21.6	22.4
Sugar	85	41	–	81	4.3	37.0
Tyres:		12	–	15	–	–
Bicycle tyres	57	–	59	–	1.5	0.0
Bicycle tubes	103	–	–	–	–	–
Textiles	–	22	–	–40	17.9	7.5
Fabrics:						
dyed	–88	–	–95	–	–	–
Printed	–81	–	–99	–	–	–
Unbleached	–73	–	–	–	–	

Sources: UNDP/World Bank (1990), *Uganda: An Agenda for Trade Liberalization* ch. 5; Ministry of Finance and Economic Planning, *Background to the Budget 1995/96*.

study (1993) estimated that government lost about 62 per cent of potential revenue because of exemptions. The loss of revenue must be higher and continuing when smuggling is also taken into account.

The Tariff Structure and the Protection of Infant Industries A relatively low and uniform tariff structure gives the most efficient protection to import-substitution industries, while minimizing the adverse effects of protection on exports growth and loss of tax revenue.

In Table 8.12, an attempt was made to assemble data on levels of nominal and effective protection rates over part of the liberalization period 1985–92. Unfortunately, there are few comparable items from the 1985 and 1992 studies. The studies gave the general impression that nominal protection increased in the early 1990s, as the tariff revenue base changed. This appears to be the case for beer, soft drinks and steel products, Table 8.12, for example. Effective protection increased as well.

In terms of nurturing infant industry growth, however, protection does

Table 8.13 Changes in imports structure during liberalization (%)

Import group	*1980*	*1986*	*1987*	*1988*	*1989*	*1990*	*1991*	*1992*
Consumer goods	46	47	40	41	42	43	40	44
Capital goods	43	34	42	41	38	40	38	33
Raw materials	11	19	18	18	20	17	22	23
Total	*100*	*100*	*100*	*100*	*100*	*100*	*100*	*100*

Sources: Bank of Uganda, Research Department (1995); and UNDP/World Bank (1990), *An Agenda for Trade Liberalization* (1990) ch. 4.

not appear to have achieved much. Capacity utilization by 1994 was 13 per cent for leather, 34.8 per cent for paints, 22.4 per cent for steel products and 37 per cent for sugar, despite high effective rates of protection of 36 per cent, 131 per cent, 56 per cent and 81 per cent, respectively, for these same products in 1992.

Table 8.13 traces the changes in the composition of imports during liberalization. Consumer goods averaged around 42 per cent over the entire period. Capital goods imports fluctuated widely, but tended to decline after 1987. Raw materials rose in 1989 and 1992. From this table, one cannot conclude anything about the effectiveness of import policy in changing imports to a pattern more conducive to import substitution.

The prevailing opinion in Uganda is that the tariff structure discriminates against exports. The one-snap-shot results of the URA-sponsored Maxwell Stamp study (1993) showed negative effective protection for all exportables. Unfortunately, there were no other studies for comparison to show how changes in the tariff structure during liberalization affected exports.

(3) Trade Liberalization and Regional Integration

Uganda is a member of the Preferential Trade Area (PTA), which has been in existence since 1982. The country is participating in the activities to turn the PTA into the Common Market for Eastern and Southern Africa (COMESA) by the year 2000.

Uganda used to be a member of the East African Community, which grew out of closer co-operation between the colonial governors of Kenya, Tanganyika, Uganda and the British resident representative of Zambia between 1928 and 1948, and became the East African Common Services Organization at independence, 1961–5. It was formalized by the heads of state of Kenya, Tanzania and Uganda in 1967 into the East African Community, which was broken up in 1974.

Lately, the idea of closer co-operation between the neighbouring countries is being entertained, though on a limited scale, through the agreement to establish a Permanent Tripartite Commission for co-operation between the Republic of Uganda, the Republic of Kenya and the United Republic of Tanzania, signed in Arusha in November 1993. This agreement takes into account and is harmonized with the PTA arrangements and the forthcoming COMESA (Article 9).

For the implementation of the Tripartite Commission, Uganda has agreed to the common text on identified areas of co-operation covering political cooperation to harmonize regional and foreign policies; border security, cattle-rustling, poaching, banditry and smuggling; facilitation of the movement of people across the common borders; co-ordination of security training and operations like joint patrols; and co-operation on legal and judicial matters.

The economic areas identified for co-operation cover: road and rail transport and the related infrastructure, inland water transport, ports and shipping, civil aviation, posts and telecommunications, and meteorology. The other sectors for co-operation cover trade, industry, agriculture and animal husbandry, energy, environment and natural resources, tourism, and wildlife.

Uganda has been a member of the Cross-Border Initiative (CBI) since 1992. The CBI seeks to reduce obstacles to cross-border activities. Under her current CBI action plan, Uganda grants 30-day temporary permits for the border populations and does not require visas for PTA countries.

Overall, the current integration initiatives are complementary to each other. The COMESA upgrades the PTA; the Permanent Tripartite Commission brings the three countries together especially in the areas of infrastructure and border security; and the CBI facilitates cross-border movements.

Uganda has progressively lowered her tariff barriers *vis-à-vis* the PTA and the agreements forming COMESA, by 70 per cent as at September 1994. The Budget Speech 1996/97 specified that the 80 per cent tariff reductions schedule required by COMESA was to be effected, and the harmonized commodity code published as a schedule to the Finance Bill by October 1996. Table 8.14 shows the status of implementation of the removal of non-tariff barriers and obstacles to intra-PTA trade: there is no inconsistency with trade liberalization, since all tariffs are to be eliminated by the year 2000.

However, the convoy, which is the most stringent non-tariff barrier, is *not* mentioned in Table 8.14! Before the vehicles carrying imported goods can form a convoy, goods have to be *completely unloaded off each vehicle, and inspected* to ensure that there are no smuggled items!

Table 8.14 Status of implementation on removal of non-tariff barriers and obstacles to intra-PTA trade at September 1994

Member state	*Full liberalization of import licensing or OGL*	*Liberalized foreign exchange allocation for PTA goods*	*Tax on foreign exchange*	*Quotas*	*Advance import deposit*	*Prohibitions on PTA goods*	*Visas issued at entry*	*Operating of border posts as required*	*Provide business travel allowance*
Kenya	Yes	Yes	No	No	No	No	Yes	Yes	Yes
Rwanda	Yes	Yes	No	No	No	No	Selective	No	Yes
Sudan	Yes	Yes	No	No	No	No	Selective	Yes	Yes
Tanzania	Yes	Yes	No	No	No	No	Yes	Yes	Yes
Uganda	Yes	Yes	No	No	No	No	Yes	Yes	Yes

Member state	*Import licenses demanded by other countries*	*Foreign exchange granted for advertising in other member states*	*Lack of sufficient wagons*	*Escort of trucks*	*Additional documents required to RCTD*
Kenya	No	Yes	Yes	Yes	Vehicle manifest
Rwanda	No	Yes	n.a.	No	No
Sudan	No	Yes	Yes	Southern Sudan Only	n.a.
Tanzania	No	Yes	Yes	No	No
Uganda	No	Yes	Yes	No	No

Source: Preferential Trade Area (PTA) for Eastern and Southern African States (1994), *Report of the Sixteenth Meeting of the Customs and Trade Committee PTA/TC/CT/XVI/8,* pp. 12–13.

Trade development Uganda is a net importer, obtaining nearly half (49 per cent) of her imports from Kenya, the single most important source of imports. The elimination of tariff barriers will lead to substantial loss of tariff revenue. A surcharge on all imports from COMESA of 10 per cent was put in place on 1 July 1996 to protect local manufacturers and compensate for the loss of revenue.

On the export side, Uganda earns hardly 1 per cent of her export receipts from SSA. Uganda's exports are largely agricultural raw materials: coffee, cotton, tea, tobacco and a handful of non-traditional exports.

To benefit from regional integration, Uganda needs to develop her manufacturing sector. However, this requires substantial investment in new plant and equipment to replace existing worn-out and obsolete machinery, which faces frequent breakdowns and lacks spare parts. In addition, Uganda needs to put in place reliable infrastructure, such as electricity, to enable the enterprises to make continuous production runs and raise capacity utilization rates.

Uganda exports maize and beans to her less-fortunate neighbours – Rwanda, Burundi, Zaire, Sudan and sometimes Kenya. But this trade is largely contingent upon the bad fortunes from drought or civil war of these neighbours, and the cash dollar payments of the World Food Programme, rather than deliberate export development policy, according to comparative advantage. The trade flows are *erratic* (Gordon, 1996).

(4) Conclusions on the Policy Account of the Imports Regime and its Development Implications

Imports liberalization is *not* straightforward. The foreign exchange controls and allocation procedures were eliminated by 1993, and replaced by the market-based exchange rate. However, tariff policy is *opaque*; it is riddled with *ad hoc* exemptions and smuggling and these prevent the tariff structure from maximizing revenue and protecting infant industries. The negative list, and donor imports, are still subject to controls.

The development impact of pure trade liberalization and exchange rate reform is still to be demonstrated. The reforms as pursued have *not* yet enabled the country to increase its capacity to earn/conserve foreign exchange, because they are not co-ordinated into a coherent import-substitution policy. Export-promotion measures are also still limited.

Since the controls of the trade and exchange rate regimes arose to cope with foreign exchange scarcity, the limitations of the liberalization policies to increase the country's capacity to handle its foreign exchange crises raises questions regarding the sustainability of liberalization.

Regional integration by the year 2000 is going to find Uganda *without sufficient new investments to export manufactured goods*, and with an inefficient import-substitution regime. How Uganda will react to this environment, is yet to be seen.

8.3 IDENTIFICATION OF SPECIFIC TRADE LIBERALIZATION EPISODES

The identification of trade liberalization episodes should be done using three measures:

(1) changes in prices, as measured by the implicit tariff rate, the parallel market premium, and the anti-export bias;
(2) changes in quantities, as measured by trade openness, shifts in investment, employment, and resource allocation among sectors; and
(3) a comparison of observed imports volumes with the counterfactual of imports, that would have prevailed without policy changes.

A serious note of caution is in order regarding the quality of data. The aggregate real GDP in constant 1991 prices has been re-estimated upwards to account for previously omitted output from small-scale and household enterprises, private building and construction, and a higher percentage of marketed food. The need to re-estimate was identified in the *integrated household survey (IHS) of 1992/93*. The adjusted time series were projected back to increase real GDP growth by 0.64 per cent over the interval 1987–93, and subsequently. This makes the real GDP time series discontinuous from 1986 back (*Statistical Bulletin* no. GDP/5).

The exports and imports data series from 1981 to 1995 were also re-estimated. The objective was to move from relying on trade-partner country data, which were inaccurate since some countries did not report their imports from and exports to Uganda in the international statistics, or only reported after a lag. Conversions between f.o.b. and c.i.f. values were also inaccurate. Barter protocols were often omitted. The trading partner exports figures had excluded Uganda's re-exports, which are required for national accounts purposes.

The re-estimates make the time series of exports and imports for 1981–95 discontinuous from those of 1965–80. According to the Statistics Department, even after the adjustments the exports and imports figures should be treated as minimum estimates because they exclude smuggling and cross-border trade (*Statistical Bulletin* no. EXT/1, *Imports and Exports*, Uganda). Further analysis of the inaccuracy of imports data is given by Kasekende (1994).

The inaccuracies of the imports data were discussed at a seminar organized by the BOU, where it was stated that an import-demand model would not be able to predict the counterfactual imports that would have materialized without the policy changes due to trade liberalization. Therefore, this indicator is omitted from the study.

Calculating the rate of inflation is another very serious problem. The raw data for 1965–95 come in three sets of constant prices: 1966, 1987 and 1991. At each change of the base year, the basket of commodities is different. The Department of Economics of Makerere University has spliced the CPI for the Low Income Group 1965–95, with 1991 = 100 as the best indicator of inflation, for its own teaching purposes The GDP implicit deflator and the middle-income and higher income CPIs are inconsistent. This study has therefore used the CPI, low-income group, 1991 = 100.

Another challenge is currency conversion. In 1987, the local currency was converted from old to new Uganda shillings, by striking off two zeroes and imposing a 30 per cent conversion tax. All the time series used in calculating the trade liberalization indicators in Table 8.15 were converted into new Uganda shillings for 1965–95. The adjustment for the 30 per cent conversion tax was *omitted*; it was shrinking and distorting the older series unduly.

After making several runs, it was decided to put all data – GDP, exports, imports, export duties and import tariff revenue – in *new current Ugandan shillings*.

Additional information from studies on the coffee sector, (1990), exchange rate unification (1994), and AGSEC-supervised studies on policy distortions in the agricultural sector (1989–92) was used to check the accuracy of the ratios in Table 8.15.

Uganda does not publish data on employment and investment by sector. The numbers available on employment in time-series form only span the period 1991–5; the data cover employment and the wage bill for just a few selected manufacturing establishments. The change in sectoral resource allocation and investment, therefore, was not calculated. Instead, an overall qualitative evaluation of the change in the structure of the economy, during the second liberalization episode 1987–95, is presented in Section 8.5.

Identification of Trade Liberalization Episodes

The identification of the liberalization episode uses only two types of data: the first type consists of changes in prices, as represented by columns 1, 2, 3 and 4 of Table 8.15; the second consists of changes in quantities as shown in columns 5, 6 and 7. Supplementary figures illustrate the intensity of each episode.

The 30 years are divided into five policy blocks: 1965–9, when distortions

Table 8.15 Indicators of trade liberalization episodes

Policy block	*Year*	*Effective import tariff rate (%) (1)*	*Effective export tax rate (%) (2)*	*Parallel market premium (%) (3)*	*Anti-export bias (4)*	*Exports–GDP (%) (5)*	*Imports–GDP (%) (6)*	*Trade openness (7)*
I	1965	22	7	14	1.3	25	20	45
	1966	22	10	14	1.3	25	19	44
	1967	22	11	14	1.3	25	18	43
	1968	24	10	14	1.3	23	18	41
	1969	20	12	14	1.2	23	17	40
II	1970	17	13	14	1.2	22	17	39
	1971	14	15	42	1.4	18	21	39
	1972	11	20	86	1.6	19	14	33
	1973	16	17	200	1.8	17	12	29
	1974	12	32	206	1.8	15	14	29
	1975	16	42	657	6	9	9	18
	1976	11	54	612	5.1	11	8	19
	1977	12	76	688	5.3	7	7	14
	1978	9	34	889	5.6	5	5	10
	1979	16	42	888	7.8	4	3	7
	1980	8	21	852	6.9	2	3	5
III	1981	5	14	918	8.6	2	4	6
	1982	6	46	183	2.6	1	2	3
	1983	8	71	106	1.9	1	2	3
	1984	2	64	55	0.9	2	6	8
	1985	3	70	366	2.9	1	2	3
	1986	4	84	306	2.4	1	7	8
IV	1987	5	37	200	1.7	1	17	18
	1988	2	17	118	1.6	1	15	16
	1989	3	18	67	1.7	1	8	9
	1990	4	13	27	1.1	1	8	9
	1991	6	2	21	1.1	6	7	13
	1992	21	0	8	1.1	5	7	12
	1993	26	0	0	1.3	7	17	24
	1994	28	3	0	1.3	10	18	28
	1995	25	0	0	1.3	10	18	28

Source: Own computations (1997); the raw data is in current *new* Uganda shs.

were minor; 1970–80, the controls period; 1981–4, the first liberalization episode; 1985–6, the reversal of the first episode; and 1987–95, the second liberalization episode. These dates coincide quite well with the policy account of Section 8.2.

The First Liberalization Episode (1981–4)

Uganda started immediately after independence (in policy block I), with an open economy where trade was 40–45 per cent of GDP, the anti-export bias was only 1.2–1.3 and the exchange premium only 14 per cent. The 'Move To The Left' policies of 1969–70 started the control regime, by the military government that took over in 1971; the economy deteriorated until 1980.

The first liberalization episode is dated 1981–4. The effective tariff rate on imports dropped by 3 per cent – column (1) of Table 8.15. The most dramatic change was the parallel market premium, which dropped from 918 per cent to 55 per cent – a drop of 863 per cent in four years! Anti-export bias dropped to practically zero by 1984 because of the large drop in the parallel market premium.

The quantity indicators in columns (5), (6) and (7) of Table 8.15 did not improve much, however. Given a rising effective export tax rate of 14–64 per cent, the exports–GDP ratio remained practically constant. The imports–GDP ratio rose only minimally, from 4 per cent to 6 per cent. Trade openness remained the lowest since 1965, between 6 per cent and 8 per cent in policy block II compared to 40–45 per cent in policy block I.

The main cause of failure to sustain the first liberalization episode was monetary expansion to finance the civil war that overthrew the Obote II regime in 1985.

The Years of Policy Reversal 1985–6

The years 1985 and 1986 were extremely chaotic. The Obote II regime was overthrown in July 1995, and its successor, the Okello-Lutwa regime, was overthrown in February 1996, when the NRM government took over power: two military take-overs in one calendar year!

Under the political chaos, hyper-inflation prevailed, pushing up the parallel market premium from 55 per cent to over 300 per cent. The NRM government interpreted the rising inflation to be caused by devaluation.

In June 1986, the NRM government made a sharp reversal and fixed the official exchange rate at Ush 1400/$US 1.0 for public sector transactions. Private consumer imports were rationed at Ush 5000/$US1.0, while the parallel market exchange rate stood at 6000.

Maintaining a fixed exchange rate under hyper-inflation and foreign

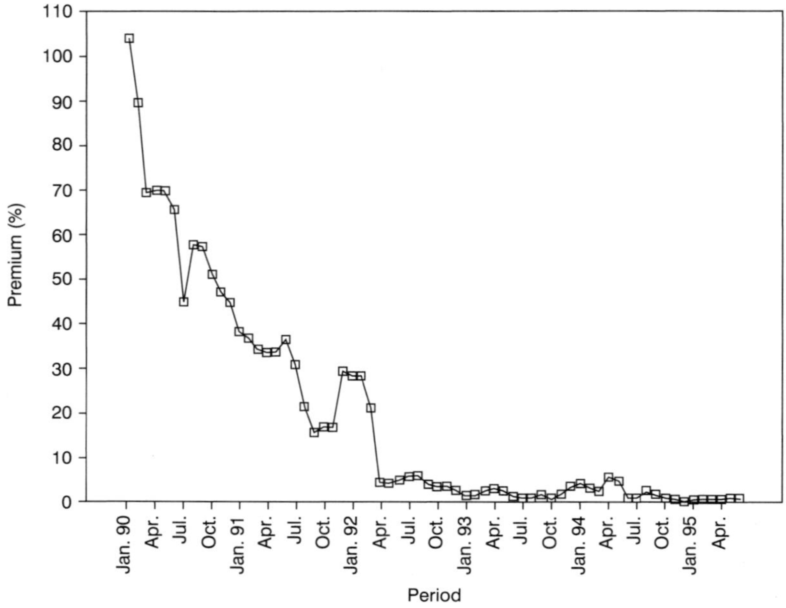

Figure 8.1 Exchange rate premium trend, January 1990–June 1995

exchange shortage proved impossible. The government had to scrap the policy reversal and turn to the IMF, under whose guidance it launched the *economic recovery programme 1987–91* for which foreign exchange was badly needed.

The Second Liberalization Episode (1987–95)

The second liberalization episode, while still ongoing, has made some dramatic accomplishments. The major dramatic evidence is exchange rate reform that removed the parallel market premium from 200 per cent in 1987 to zero in 1993.

Figure 8.1 shows a sharp fall in the premium for 1990–5 and Figure 8.2 shows the narrowing gap between the official and parallel market exchange rates over the same period.

The key to success was control of inflation, which fell from an average 108 per cent per annum over the period 1986/87–1991/92, to just 5.7 per

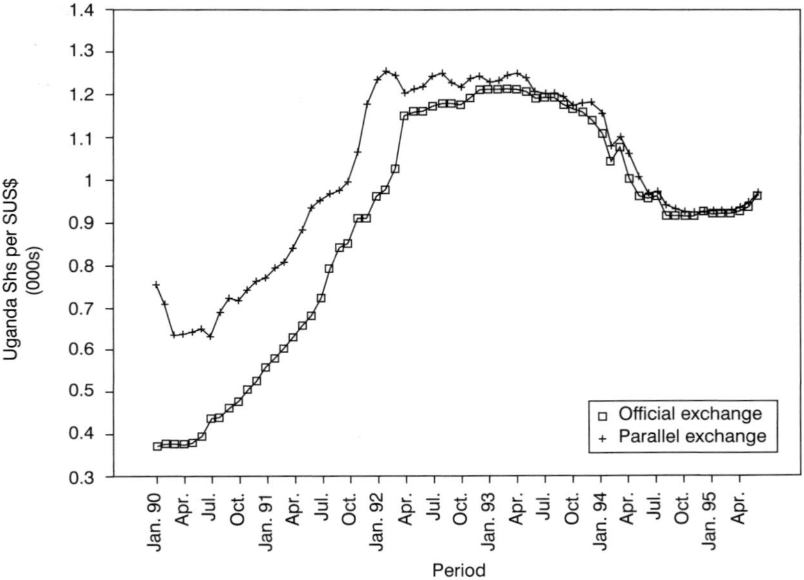

Figure 8.2 Exchange rate unification, January 1990–June 1995

cent per annum average over the period 1992/93–1994/95. Section 8.4 discusses how this macroeconomic consistency was achieved.

The reduction in anti-export bias was also remarkable. As shown in column (4) of Table 8.15, this fell from the record high of 8.6 in 1981 to 1.3, the level that prevailed in policy block I. This result maps perfectly into the policy account: the parastatal export-marketing monopolies, PMB, CMB and LMB, were dismantled; the export duty was reduced to zero; crop finance was turned over to commercial banks; the co-operative movement was given greater autonomy to compete by the 1992 Co-operative Act, which repealed the 1970 restrictive act; and producer prices were freed to vary with world market prices. However, the effect of the disappearance of the parallel market premium on reducing the anti-export bias is considered by most analyst to be the most important. The reduction of the effective export duty from 37 per cent in 1987 to zero by 1995 also helped to reduce the anti-export bias.

The picture on import liberalization is *opaque*. The effective import tariff rate rose from 5 per cent to 25 per cent (column (1) of Table

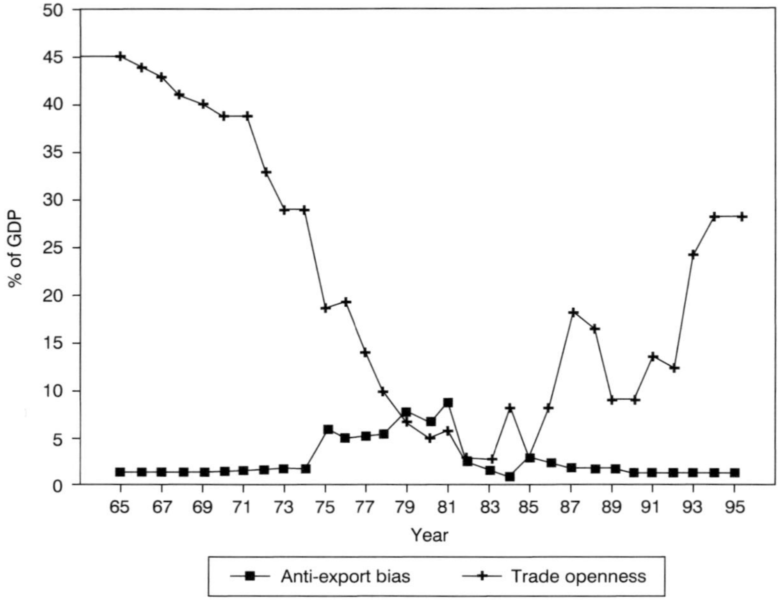

Figure 8.3 Indicators of trade liberalization (anti-export bias and trade openness)

8.15). This contributed negatively to the bias of the trade regime against exports. The granting of exemptions and the escalating smuggling, by reducing potential tariff revenue, are forcing the URA to levy steep tariffs on a few items: petroleum, beer and cigarettes (Table 8.1).

Whereas the imports–GDP ratio – Table 8.15, column (5) – has recovered to its height of 17–18 per cent in block I, the exports–GDP ratio – column (5) – is only registering 10 per cent, way below the 23–25 per cent average in block I when the regime was less controlled. Trade openness, though increasing, is therefore still limited; the increase is largely due to import intensity.

Figure 8.3 shows the relationship between the gradual fall in the anti-export bias and the rising, but still limited, increase in trade openness, relative to the very high level that prevailed in the 1960s but fell to practically zero by 1980.

Conclusions on Trade Liberalization Episodes

Did trade liberalization occur in Uganda? The answer is an unqualified yes: liberalization occurred in *two* episodes: 1981–4, and 1987 to the present.

The intensity of liberalization is most dramatic in the disappearance of the parallel market premium from 915 to 0. This is understandable; given the huge distortion in the price of foreign exchange, the policy effort was concentrated on exchange rate reform. The country gained indirectly as well: macroeconomic consistency reduced inflation, which was equally dramatic.

The reduction in anti-export bias from the 8.6, to 1.3, and the increase in trade openness from record low of 3 to 28, are both consistent with the trade liberalization episodes, but are less dramatic.

The relaxation of foreign exchange controls and allocation procedures was detailed: it scrapped the W2, OGL, SIPs, retention account, barter trade and dual-licensing schemes. Unfortunately, the country seems still to be unable to narrow the tariff bands, make the tariff rate uniform and reduce the tariff rates to levels that would remove the anti-export bias. Smuggling, tax exemptions and misclassification of imports all make the tariff regime *opaque*, and its purpose unclear.

8.4 THE CREDIBILITY OF TRADE LIBERALIZATION

The literature suggests three indicators on which private economic agents focus their attention in passing judgement about whether trade liberalization policies are credible: (1) macroeconomic compatibility; (2) systematic forecastability; and (3) time consistency.

The purpose of this section is to use the three indicators to weigh whether the liberalization episodes identified in Table 8.15 are credible. For the first episode, 1981–4, the discussion of credibility is brief, since we already know that it was reversed. The bulk of section 8.4, therefore, is focused on the second – and ongoing – episode, 1987–95.

Credibility of the First Liberalization Episode (1981–4)

The first episode was not credible, as diagnosed by the macroeconomic incompatibility indicators.

Table 8.16 gives the data on balance of payments incompatibility for 1981–5. The overall balance of payments deficit in 1981 was largely financed by the IMF to enable the authorities to build up reserves. As IMF financing fell, the country lost reserves in 1982, 1984 and 1985, a situation that could not be rectified because exports recovery was much slower, as the bulk of exports receipts still came from coffee, a tree crop (block II of Table 8.3).

Table 8.16 Balance of payments incompatibility indicators ($USm.)

	1981	*1982*	*1983*	*1984*	*1985*
Overall BOP	–187	–32	–36	–59	69
Financing:					
Change in gross reserves	–31	34	–28	56	29
IMF (Net)	125	82	85	–10	–90
Other (unspecified)	24	–15	–21	13	–7

Source: Republic of Uganda, *Background to the Budget* (1987/88).

Table 8.17 Fiscal incompatibility indicators (New USh.m.)

	1981/82	*1982/83*	*1983/84*	*1984/85*
Total fiscal deficit	(154)	(165)	(222)	(630)
Financing:				
External (net)	10	36	30	135
Domestic	144	130	191	496
Bank	133	114	(69)	539
Non-bank	11	15	261	(43)

Source: Republic of Uganda, *Background to the Budget* (1989/90).

The first episode was not fiscally compatible, either; Table 8.17 shows that throughout the episode, the fiscal deficit kept grew from Ush 154 m. to Ush 630 m. (new shillings). The bulk of financing the fiscal deficit, except for the 1983/84 fiscal year, came from the banking system – that is, printing money – which fuelled inflation. Taxes and the sale of foreign exchange at W2 did not raise sufficient revenue to finance the deficit, which ballooned because of the civil war.

The IMF withdrew the W2 resources in 1984, largely because government failed to achieve the fiscal and monetary reform targets.

There are no reliable data to indicate systematic forecastability. With regard to time inconsistency, perhaps one could simply remark that government's objective to survive the civil war was more important than its adherence to fiscal compatibility.

Credibility of the Second Liberalization Episode (1987–95)

The second episode, having lasted much longer, raises the question as to whether it is credible and likely to be sustained. This section presents

Table 8.18 Indicators of balance of payments compatibility, 1987/88–1995/96 (in $USm.)

	1987/88	*1993/94*	*1994/95*	*1995/96*
Total exports f.o.b	334	333	649	681
Total imports c.i.f.	–598	–841	–1367	–1541
Trade balance:	–265	–507	–717	–860
Factor income (net)	–18	–51	–63	–53
Current transfers:		492	107	799
Official		189	261	264
Private	266	303	355	535
Current account Balance:	–112		–164	–114
Medium and long-term loans (net)	189	182	286	229
Capital transfers		46	41	
Short-term borrowing (net)		–55	–22	75
				–83
Capital account balance:	121	173	305	220
Overall balance:	28	106	141	107
Financing:				
IMF credit (net)	–3	18	19	34
Change in gross reserves	–25	–107	–169	–112
Exceptional financing	–	–24	–22	–11
Residual financing	–	8	13	39

Source: Republic of Uganda *Background to the Budget* (1996/97) and (1992/93).

and analyses the data on macroeconomic compatibility and briefly presents the systematic forecastability and time consistency issues. These are brief because there are no reliable data to support an objective assessment.

Balance of Payments Compatibility

Table 8.18 contains the data on the balance of payments. Throughout the adjustment period, the trade balance has been negative. The adverse external shock reduced the price of coffee in 1984–91. The coffee boom reflected in the last two years has been short-lived. Export diversification away from coffee is still limited to just around 20 per cent of export receipts, (Table 8.3, block IV). Imports, however, have more than doubled since the beginning of the episode, from US$598 m. to US$1541 m.

The policies pursued have been consistent with liberalization – devaluation to a market-based exchange rate, raising of excise duties and sales taxes on imports; and high tariffs on excise commodities. These policies increased the demand for money, as did the three SIPs programmes.

The tariff regime, however, has not been systematically handled. Exemptions and smuggling are pushing imports to unsustainable levels, while not protecting import-substitution industries to economize on future imports. The policy-makers are not worried about import levels because current transfers, particularly the private component, have more than doubled over 1987/88–1995/96, from US$266 m. to US$535 m.

The country has also steadily accumulated gross reserves, from US$25m. to US$112 m.

However, careful observers still point to the persistent current account deficit, which cannot be eliminated unless the exports structure is changed to rely more on new non-traditional exports, relative to coffee. The IMF credit (net) has also increased from US$3m. to US$34 m. In a country sagged with an external debt of over US$3 bn this does not appear to be sustainable.

It is time to question how durable private current transfers are likely to be, particularly how sensitive they are to external shocks. The huge and growing magnitudes cannot all be coming from the earnings of Ugandan residents abroad, in a country rated to be under 'relative peace' to which these residents should be returning. It is more likely that Uganda is benefiting from *capital flight* from her unfortunate neighbours: Burundi, Rwanda, Sudan and Zaire. Whether this benefit is durable depends on the peace process in the troubled countries. There is further word that part of the private transfers reflect *unrecorded exports* receipts. There are no data, as yet, to analyse which of these arguments is more credible.

Meanwhile, however, exporters are complaining that the prevailing nominal exchange rate of around Ush 1000/US$1.00 is appreciated and taxing the development and diversification of non-traditional exports. In a land-locked country with poor infrastructure, a competitive exchange rate is badly needed.

On the imports side, the troubled neighbours may be using Uganda as an inlet for import requirements. The appreciated nominal exchange rate, exemptions and smuggling, all make the flow of imports much easier. Unfortunately, these forces make it extremely difficult to raise tariff revenue and to nurture an import-substitution regime that would enable the country to bring its use of imports to sustainable levels.

The underlying causes of the upsurge in private current transfers constitute a burning question for systematic enquiry along the lines of a possible 'Great Lakes' to generate answers that would enable Uganda to ensure balance of payments compatibility. A market-based exchange rate, sales and excise taxes on imports are necessary, but not sufficient to ensure balance of payments compatibility. The IMF import support simply masks the problem.

Table 8.19 Indicators of fiscal compatibility

	Average 1986/87–1991/92	*Average 1991/92–1994/95*
Recurrent revenue growth rates (% of GDP)	6.2	9.7
Total expenditure growth rates (% of GDP)	14.6	20.3
Domestic financing proportion (Bank)	1.2	–1.5
Growth in average level of M_2 (% p/a)	105.5	35.1
Average end-period inflation	107.6	5.7

Source: Republic of Uganda, *Background to the Budget* (1996/97), Table 6.1.

Fiscal Compatibility

Table 8.19 presents the data on fiscal compatibility from *Background to the Budget* (1996/97), on the occasion when the NRM government was reviewing its 'success' with macroeconomic stability over the past 10 years.

The government took the years 1986/87–1991/92 as times of failure to achieve macroeconomic stability because it was still financing the fiscal deficit from the banking system, which increased the money supply at an average rate of 105.5 per cent per annum and fuelled inflation at 107.5 per cent per annum.

In the 1992/93 fiscal year, the government decided to cut spending whenever recurrent revenue fell short of budgetary requirements. Concurrently, the Uganda Revenue Authority was created in 1991 to step up the revenue collection effort. Recurrent revenue rose from 6.2 per cent of GDP to 9.7 per cent. The increase in revenue and the strict control of expenditure dramatically changed the macroeconomic indicators. Money supply growth was brought down to 35.1 per cent per annum on the average while inflation fell to 5.7 per cent per annum. From government's point of view, this is spectacular success!

For fiscal compatibility, however, the following facts should be *highlighted*. Recurrent revenue still covers only recurrent expenditure plus another 14 per cent of revenue to allocate to development expenditure. This means that 86 per cent of development spending is donor-funded!

Second, the cuts raise many questions. Quite often they take the form of late payments to suppliers of government goods and services. This creates non-performing loans in the banking system! Other cuts involve paying salaries late – sometimes up to five months – particularly for the police and teaching services. This demotivates personnel. The non-payment of the Uganda Railways Corporation, for example, stands at Ush 24 billion.

Third, military expenditure is building up again. The government's unwillingness to settle civil war disputes by peaceful means is creating a budgetary crisis. Either the government will resort to printing money, and resurrect fiscal incompatibility as previous governments did to finance civil wars, or it will have to cut other budget lines substantially, bankrupting the financial sector, demotivating public sector employees and creating a recession.

The low rate of inflation should not be taken as an unambiguous indicator of macroeconomic management success, since a falling rate of inflation is also consistent with government non-payment of suppliers of goods and services.

With regard to revenue, tariff reform is overdue, to stop smuggling and minimize exemptions.

The value added tax (VAT) was instituted at 17 per cent in July 1996. The VAT has the desirable property of being uniform and non-discriminatory across economic activities. The VAT is gradually to replace the CTL and sales tax, which together contributed Ush 158 m. to recurrent revenue.

However, the VAT requires substantial investment in record-keeping; this eliminates most small-scale and semi-formal enterprises from the VAT (Sejjaaka, 1996). In addition, unfortunately, the introduction of the VAT was not properly administered, and the tax was collected at too many points. The refund system was longer than one month, tying up working capital. The commissioner of the VAT is not a member of the National Forum, a large informal pressure group whose meeting in 1995 he declined to attend! The end result was a two-week national strike, which had to be resolved by the president himself (Draft Report 1996, on Institutional Strategy for the National Forum).

Overall, therefore, while the government has taken serious steps since July 1992, with spectacular results, what is in place is not sufficient to ensure fiscal compatibility. It is essential, therefore, to improve the machinery for tax collection, including reform of the tariff regime, so that revenue can cover the development budget as well and the payment of the suppliers of public goods and services, to prevent a recession. The government must also reconsider its attitude towards the civil war to prevent this from blowing up the budget, as has happened in previous regimes.

Systematic Forecastability

This indicator is subjective. It involves imputing intent to the reaction of private sector agents, in situations where data are difficult to generate for ratification. It is therefore only discussed briefly.

Private sector exporters were not enthusiastic about opening foreign exchange retention accounts in the Bank of Uganda in 1988–90 because they perceived the policy as not credible. In the face of continuing foreign exchange shortages, the private sector exporters forecast that the Bank of Uganda would confiscate their foreign exchange. Over the two years, only 29 accounts were opened. The policy was scrapped in 1990 when the foreign exchange bureaux were open.

The special import programmes, (SIPs) over the period 1988–91 were also not regarded as credible sources of foreign exchange. Private sector agents regarded these as stop-gap measures to alleviate inflation. Concurrently, pressure was exerted on the open general licensing system (OGL), where applications went from 24 to 63, some using bribery, to import inputs volumes with more than three-months stock required for full-capacity utilization.

Other than the SIPs, and the retention accounts, the author was unable to identify other instances of systematic forecastability.

In its 1996 report, the National Forum alleges that frequent changes in tax structure create speculation (Issue 7, Recommended Action 7.5). This can be interpreted as the private sector systematically forecasting the direction of tax rate changes and stocking goods, or making arrangements to smuggle; this would imply that the existing tax structure is not credible. This is a researchable topic we are unable to cover, however. Only a few remarks about changes in taxes are documented in Table 8.20 under time inconsistency, to which we now turn.

Time Inconsistency

Time consistency tries to determine whether trade liberalization policies in place are likely to be upheld. This is a serious question, given that the impetus for Uganda's reform originated from the IMF conditionality. There is a possibility that the political interests of the regime may be changing from what they were in 1987.

In 1990, the IMF and the NRM government struck a common note in the documents, *The Way Forward I* and *The Way Forward II*. The government recognized that it could pursue its policy to build 'An Independent, Integrated, and Self-sustaining Economy' by mobilizing local resources (savings) and external resources (private capital inflow and exports earnings). The IMF's share in the kitty was to make the government agree that macroeconomic stability and a market-based exchange rate were the best means to mobilize savings, attract autonomous capital inflow and increase exports receipts. This common note was struck after hard bargaining from the economic recovery programme of 1987–91.

The government, after 10 years of 'successes', and having been 'elected', feels that it can go on its own. It appears more interested in shifting income distribution in favour of groups who, in its view, matter politically for its survival.

Table 8.20 Frequent changes in tax rates (by fiscal year)

	1987/88	*1988/89*	*1989/90*	*1990/91*	*1991/92*	*1992/93*	*1993/94*	*1994/95*
Income tax								
Threshold	50 000	50 000	240 000	480 000	480 000	600 000	840 000	1 200 000
Maximum rate on	60	60	55	50	50	40	30	30
Incomes equal or above per annum	1.2 m.	1.2 m.	1.2 m.	1.6 m.	2.6 m.	3.6 m.	4.2 m.	4.2 m.
Corporate tax rate	60	45	45	40	40	35	30	30
Sales tax rates								
1990/91	10		30		70		150	
1991/92	10	20	30	40	50	100		
1993/94	10	20	30					

Source: Republic of Uganda; Finance Bill 1994; and Ddumba and Hyuda (1994). Tax Performance, Reforms and Revenue in Uganda. Interim Research Report submitted to the AERC, June 1994.

The World Bank seems to have made the point clear that poverty reduction is politically important. Accordingly, as shown in Table 8.20, the income tax threshold has been raised from Ush 50 000 to Ush 1.2 m.

However, the frequent lowering of corporate tax from 60 per cent to 30 per cent amid exemptions, and the reduction in maximum income tax rate, 60 per cent to 30 per cent, show that government is squeezing the middle brackets in favour of the higher brackets.

The frequent sales tax changes can be interpreted as continuing efforts to raise revenue. If this is so, it does not tally with the rapid reduction in personal income and corporate tax rates, which are becoming regressive.

The privatization of parastatals is another area raising controversy. Since 1992, 25 parastatals have been privatized; by the end of 1996, however, only five were fully paid up (Kashugyera, 1997). This outcome is also inconsistent with the quest for budgetary revenue: it gives assets to preferred income groups at nominal prices. The extent of tolerated smuggling, for a government that cannot finance its development budget, is another example of inconsistent behaviour.

Whereas time inconsistency is a qualitative indicator on which it is difficult to pass conclusive judgement, students of the Ugandan economy are well advised to look carefully at the changing political interests of the NRM regime. On this issue one contributor to the Draft Report (1996) of the National Forum had this to say:

> Two years ago when the National Forum recommended the formation of a Ministry of Privatization and the President was there, it occurred within two weeks. Also when the National Forum recommended that the Ministry of Finance and Ministry of Economic Planning be merged, the merger was done immediately. Because the President was there. . . .
>
> In less developed countries, the *President* is everything. If you can link up to what the President wants, it goes through.
>
> The difficulty occurs, however, when the President does not attend, does not get involved, loses focus or does not follow up the policy recommendations.
>
> The President has been losing his focus on the economy and on policy matters. He is now looking more at foreign policy and other questions.
>
> The President has no interest in what the Forum is telling him. [The President refers to the incumbent President of Uganda.]

Overall Assessment of Credibility

Since 1987 when the current liberalization episode started, there has not been any reversal. Instances of systematic forecastability are few and their effects are negligible. One is therefore tempted to believe that the policy stance on trade liberalization is credible.

However, macroeconomic consistency indicators depict a tighter situation than the government's acclaimed success; exemptions, smuggling, the trend towards regressive income and corporate tax rates, privatized but not fully paid up parastatals, all point to *less determination to collect revenue to close the fiscal deficit*. Even more worrisome is the insistent refusal to settle the civil war peacefully, an orientation that has very grave budgetary implications.

Private current transfers, while allowing for a comfortable imports position, which is further eased by the IMF credits and accumulation of reserves, may well be appreciating the nominal exchange rate and stunting non-traditional exports growth. Furthermore, the liberal imports regime, under exemptions and smuggling, is making import substitution difficult.

8.5 THE IMPACT OF TRADE LIBERALIZATION ON ECONOMIC DEVELOPMENT

The discussion here is focused on overall GDP growth and change in the composition of output; trends in aggregate investment; changes in the manufacturing sector producing import substitutes; and changes in the volume and composition of exports.

The discussion is extremely limited and qualitative because of lack of long-term consistent data on the variables examined, as noted in Section 8.3. Moreover, not all observed changes can be attributed to trade liberalization. There was considerable peace, for example, particularly around 1990, when most of the economy was productive. Variations in weather are also important when 49 per cent of real output originates from rain-fed agriculture. The sharp changes in international coffee prices also affected growth. The data, unfortunately do not permit the netting out of the contribution of each factor to economic performance.

Changes in Aggregate Output and its Composition

In *The Background to the Budget* (1996/97) the government made its own assessment of the changes in real GDP, 1991 constant prices, and its composition, using the data in Table 8.21.

According to the government, macroeconomic stability has contributed positively to real GDP growth, from 5.2 per cent to 8.0 per cent per annum on the average. Most analysts put the average growth rate between 5 per cent and 6.2 per cent; the higher figure in the later years is partly due to the coffee boom, when the growth rate registered 10 per cent per annum.

Table 8.21 Changes in aggregate real output in 1991 constant prices during the second liberalization episode, 1986/87–1994/95

	Average 1986/87–1991/92	*Average 1992/93–1994/95*
(1) Growth in real GDP per annum (%)	5.2	8.0
(2) Growth in monetary GDP per annum (%)	6.7	9.5
(3) Share of total agriculture in real	53.0	49.0
(4) GDPShare of non-monetary agriculture (%)	29.0	25.0
(5) M2 as % of GDP	6.3	8.6

Source: Republic of Uganda, *Background to the Budget* (1996/97) Table 6.1.

The re-monetarization of the economy, which government attributes to price stability and the improved exchange rate, is indeed a gain from liberalization! The proportion of real monetary GDP grew faster than total GDP; the share of monetary agriculture remained constant at 24 per cent, while that of non-monetary agriculture shrank from 29 per cent to 25 per cent. This analysis is consistent with the data from the IHS, 1992/93, which pointed out that the marketed surplus of food has been rising: food is the largest component of agriculture.

The proportion of M_2 to total GDP rose from 6.3 per cent to 8.6 per cent per annum, on the average, showing greater willingness by the public to hold cash as inflation got under control. The shifts towards monetarization and exchange are all the more remarkable, given the limited investment in feeder roads and infrastructure noted in the Anti-Poverty Action Plan in the same issue of *The Background to the Budget* (ch. 7).

Changes in Investment and its Sectoral Allocation

While re-monetarization and the shrinkage of non-monetary agriculture are more clearly related to price stability and trade liberalization, the changes in investment are due to more factors: capital inflow, which may be due to peace at home; capital flight from the neighbours; and privatization and other policies. Unfortunately, the data on investment are limited, with reliable aggregate estimates starting only around 1991.

The proportion of investment to GDP is still low, below 20 per cent. The rising relative share of the private sector is due to privatization and the repossession of the custodian board properties by their former own-

Table 8.22 The composition of saving and investment

	1991/92	*1995/96*
Investment–GDP ratio	16.9	19.2
Public	7.9	6.9
Private	9.0	12.3
Domestic savings–GDP: excluding grants	2.3	16.1
Composition of investment:		
Structures–GDP	4.7	6.1
Equipment–GDP	1.9	3.0

Source: Republic of Uganda, *Background to the Budget 1996/97*. The figures on structures and equipment refer to the years in Table 6.1.

ers from whom they were confiscated in 1973 during Amin's economic war. The initial investment in structures is giving way to emphasis on equipment: this shift in the composition of investment is usually attributed to trade liberalization. Investment first went to structures (non-tradeables), and only picked up for the equipment (tradeables) after absorbing the shock of higher import prices when the subsidy from the over-valued exchange rate was removed (Table 8.22).

However, there is dispute within the business community that what is classified as 'equipment' contains imports of consumer goods, misclassified to avoid paying import duties. The dispute cannot be easily dismissed, given that the overall growth of the Index of Industrial Production is decelerating, as illustrated in Table 8.23, from 56 per cent in 1987/88 to 24 per cent in 1994/95. Most new investment goes to industry: apart from flower estates for export, investment in agriculture is minimal.

Capacity utilization is rated around 35 per cent on the average, despite the liberalized imports regime which should have facilitated the importation to acquire inputs. The private enterprise survey report (UMA/IBRD, 1995) notes the lack of working capital and the cost of inputs as leading obstacle to the procurement of imported inputs. Financial sector restructuring, which began in 1993, has raised collateral requirements, and slowed loans application procedures. This makes borrowing for development finance very costly. The tendency is to smuggle consumer imports for quick profits.

For the allocation of investment, the Maxwell Stamp report (1993) gives data on the number of projects approved by the Uganda Investment Authority. The allocation shows that 51 per cent of the new projects are orientated towards the domestic market (import substitution); 40 per cent are in non-tradeables and only 11 per cent are in exports. Given the

Table 8.23 The structure and growth of the manufacturing sector, 1987–95

Sub-group	*Weight in the Index of Industrial Production (1987 = 100)*	*1987/90 average growth rate per annum*	*1990/93 average growth rate per annum*	*1994/95 average growth rate per annum*
(1) Tobacco and beverages	26.10	55	10	36
(2) Food-processing	20.70	75	41	17
(3) Textiles and clothing	16.30	16	–20	–7
(4) Chemicals, paint and soap	12.30	84	85	34
(5) Timber, paper and printing	9.00	84	30	28
(6) Steel and steel products	5.30	8	140	25
(7) Bricks and cement	4.30	54	71	48
(8) Leather and footwear	2.30	–25	–9	69
(9) Miscellaneous	3.70	81	105	23
(10) All items	100	56	38	24

Source: Republic of Uganda, *Background to the Budget* (1996/97).

small size of the local market, it is understandable that industrial sector growth is decelerating.

Changes in Employment and its Sectoral Allocation During Liberalization

Existing employment data are virtually those of snapshots from the household surveys of 1989, and 1992/93, and the outdated human resources survey of 1989, when liberalization was just beginning. The limited figures show that between 1982 and 1992, agriculture's share in total employment fell from 83 per cent to 80 per cent; the share of industry also fell from 6 per cent to 3 per cent; while the share of services, particularly the informal sector, rose from 11 per cent to 17 per cent.

It is extremely difficult to attribute changes in employment to trade liberalization; retrenchment and privatization must also be examined. Real wages have risen in both rural and urban areas. But the information is extremely limited. For rural wages, data are given from the bi-annual sample surveys of the cost of production by the AGSEC. For urban areas, the data are from an annual survey of a few selected manufacturing establishments.

It is safer to conclude that the effect of trade liberalization on employment and its sectoral allocation is unknown. Van der Geest and Wignaraja (1996), who examined the effects of the SAPs on employment in SSA, came to similar conclusions.

Liberalization and Changes in Exports Structure

As noted earlier, trade liberalization in the exports sector was substantial! It consisted of removing the implicit, explicit and inflation taxes; dismantling the monopolies of exports marketing parastatals; and decontrolling producer prices of exports.

The change in exports volume is limited, however, as illustrated by the exports volume index in Table 8.2. Part of the problem is the adverse terms of trade that lowered coffee prices. A second problem is that newly-planted clonal coffee is just beginning to yield. In addition, there are constraints that were not touched by liberalization: lack of extension services and poor feeder roads in rural areas for agricultural exports; the high cost of development finance; and unreliable electricity, water and telecommunications for the manufacture of exports.

Trade liberalization, therefore, while necessary, is not sufficient to bring about a rapid increase in new investments to produce exports.

Overall Conclusion on the Effects of Liberalization on Economic Performance

The extremely limited time-series data only allow for tentative and speculative – remarks on how the economy may be responding to trade liberalization. This agrees with Sharer *et al.* (1995), who tried to model the response, and Loxley (1989), for an earlier attempt.

The effects of trade liberalization on investment are unclear. The bulk of new investment is going into import substitution for the local market (51 per cent). However, deceleration in the growth rate of the Index of Industrial Production (56–24 per cent overall), at the very time when investment in equipment is said to be increasing, and the liberalization of imports to improve capacity utilization, cast doubt on the accuracy of the data.

New investment in exports, practically all of which are agricultural, is very small (around 11 per cent); there appears to be hardly any *new* investment in manufactured exports, save for fish-processing, which is interrupted by environmental degradation of Lake Victoria, and the poor infrastructure for temperature control at Entebbe Airport.

The extremely limited data leave the effect of trade-liberalization on employment and productivity unknown.

8.6 A SAMPLE SURVEY OF RESPONSES OF MANUFACTURERS TO THE LIBERALIZED TRADE ENVIRONMENT

The objective of this survey was to document the response of 100 manufacturing enterprises producing exports and import substitutes to the liberalized trade environment. The survey took place in July–November 1995.

Since the common questionnaire for the study of the impact of regional integration and trade liberalization in SSA was long (23 pages) and complex, it was administered by skilled field workers from the Department of Statistics at Entebbe. The sample was restricted to large establishments that employed 20 or more persons, on the argument that these were more likely to keep records.

The survey settled for 84 establishment to begin with, rather than 100, because the costs due to *repeated visits* to complete the complex questionnaire rose very rapidly. Only 42 of the 84 establishments produced sufficient responses for data analysis, despite the repeated visits. Of the 42 enterprises, 15 exported while 27 produced import substitutes. Table 8.24 lists the enterprises by product category.

The proportion of the sample that failed to produce adequate responses (50 per cent) was so large that the reasons for failure had to be analysed. The remainder of this section is therefore divided into seven discussions:

(1) reasons for the inadequacy of 50 per cent of the sample;
(2) general information about the 42 enterprises that responded;
(3) response to the trade liberalization incentive structure;
(4) credibility, as assessed by the confidence of the enterprises in the liberalized policy regime;
(5) constraints of access to information and networking;
(6) labour market problems; and
(7) conclusions and policy recommendations.

Note that the labour market discussion compares some of the key problem identified in this survey with other surveys by UMA/IBRD (1995).

(1) Reasons for Lack of Adequate Response of 50 per cent of the Sample

Despite the fact that the questionnaire was delivered by the enumerators in person two weeks ahead, and followed with face-to-face interviews, 50 per cent of the establishments failed to provide adequate responses. Instead of just throwing away the 42 cases, it was decided to regard this as the first and most significant result (Table 8.25).

Table 8.24 No. of establishments in the sample by product classification (SITC)

Industry group	*No. of establishments*	*Product*
1520	1	Dairy products
1530	5	Coffee-processing*
1531	3	Grain-milling, maize
1534	1	Tea-processing*
1541	2	Bakery products
1549	1	Other food products*
1550	1	Manufacture of spirits*
1551	2	Manufacture of beverages, beer*
1554	2	Manufacture of beverages, soda*
1600	1	Cigarettes*
1721	1	Manufacture of textiles
1810	1	Wearing apparel
1920	2	Footwear
2109	1	Paper and paper products
2221	1	Printing and publishing
2411	1	Basic chemicals
2423	1	Pharmaceutical
2424	1	Soap*
2511	1	Rubber tyres
2693	1	Bricks
2710	1	Basic iron and steel
2811	1	Structural metal products
2899	1	Other fabricated metal products
2979	3	Other special purpose machinery
3230	1	Radios and TVs
3420	1	Motor vehicle bodies and trailers
3430	1	Parts and accessories of motor vehicles
3610	3	Furniture, foam products and mattresses
Total	*42*	

Note:
* Establishments that manufacture exports.

Source: Survey data.

Table 8.25 Manufacturing establishments classified by reasons for lack of adequate response to the survey questionnaire

Ownership of establishment	*Outright refusal*	*Firm shifted location*	*Management changed hands*	*Ownership disputes*	*No production due to lack of working capital*	*Closed due to operational problems, lack of demand, and so on*
Private and local	8	3	2	3	4	8 = 28
Private and Asian	6	0	2	0	1	0 = 9
Private and European	1	0	0	0	0	0 = 1
Government-owned	0		2			2 = 4
Total	*15*	*3*	*6*	*3*	*5*	10 = 42

Source: Survey data

We found three reasons for lack of adequate response – outright, refusal, operational problems and ownership disputes.

Outright Refusal

Outright refusal came from 15 of the 42 enterprises. It was expressed as lack of time to complete the questions, absence of the appropriate personnel to authorize release of the data, frequent rescheduling of appointments to frustrate the enumerator and outright closure of the factory or office gate. Although we shall never be sure about the causes of this hostile attitude, the enumerators advanced a number of plausible explanations.

First, 1995 was the year preceding the introduction of the VAT; this made the business community suspicious that the information requested might be used to assess the VAT. Second, 1996 was the year for presidential and parliamentary elections to which many businesses were pressured to contribute; the survey was regarded by some businesses as an assessment of their ability to contribute to the campaign. Third, a few businesses had non-transparent operations and did not entertain close observation. Fourth, locally-owned private sector enterprises complain that investment incentives are weighted in favour of new foreign investors despite the fact that the bulk of investment over the recent period was carried out by local private owners: this made many businesses hostile and led to distancing their operations from the government.

We could not rank these four plausible explanations in order of relative importance.

Operational Problems Leading to Closure

Operational problems leading to closure constituted the second most important reason for lack of adequate response, and affected 10 establishments, eight of which were private and locally owned. The operational problems most frequently quoted were: obsolete machinery subject to frequent breakdowns, lack of spare parts, and insufficient demand for the output due to inability to compete with imports after liberalization. Uganda's manufacturing sector needs to overhaul its plant and equipment in order to become competitive.

Related to operational problems is the *lack of working capital*, which affected five establishments. Exchange rate liberalization made imported inputs more expensive to establishments emerging from protection, with an import-intensive production structure. Financial sector restructuring that started in 1993 tightened loan application procedures, for example imposing higher collateral requirements, while the continuing inefficiencies of commercial banks kept lending interest rates high (19–28 per cent on average, compounded quarterly) despite falling inflation (around 5 per cent per annum). The combined effect of these changes was to make development finance scarce at the very time when manufacturing enterprises needed to restructure and modernize their operations.

Ownership Disputes

Ownership disputes and management changing hands are largely due to privatization; these factors may be more important now than in 1995, as privatization intensifies. Their effect was that access to records was impossible, or that records were destroyed altogether and non-existent. This affected six of the 42 enterprises in Table 8.25.

The shift of location was normal, and was the least important factor accounting for incomplete questionnaires. It affected only three enterprises.

In conclusion, the Ugandan environment in late 1995 did not provide an easy atmosphere in which to conduct a survey using a complex 23-page questionnaire. A National Census of Business Establishments planned for 1997/98 is advised to pay attention to some of the reasons listed in Table 8.25 if it wants to get a higher responses rate.

(2) General Background of the Enterprises Surveyed

The most recent census of manufacturing establishments is dated 1989. Since this is the only source from which to draw a sample frame, the survey had to cover establishments that were in existence prior to the second liberalization episode.

Of the 42 enterprises, 39 were in existence prior to 1989. Only three cases were established after 1991; these were added to increase the number of exporters.

The majority of ownership – 30 of the 42 enterprises is Ugandan. There is a case, therefore, for revising the Investment Code so that it can benefit foreign and local investors alike. A survey by the UIA (1994) also came to the conclusion that the majority of Uganda's investors are local.

Despite the care taken to pick large-scale enterprises with records, the majority of enterprises are small: 23 of the 42 enterprises started with less than USh 100 million worth of capital US$ (US$ 100 000). Of the 42 enterprises, 32 are still run by their founders, while two are inherited. Therefore, the size of enterprises has not grown much bigger since inception.

As regards legal status, 21 enterprises are owned by sole partners; nine are limited liability companies; and only three are joint ventures. Government is a shareholder in only three of the enterprises, a factor reflecting privatization. The rest of the enterprises are owned by co-operatives. A financial market is required to enable enterprises to access capital and expand in size, particularly into the joint-venture category where they can also benefit from foreign know-how and access to information on overseas markets.

On efficiency, 32 of the 42 enterprises operated below full capacity. Only five operated at full capacity; the rest did not state the capacity. Low capacity utilization is a chronic problem in Uganda's manufacturing sector, already noted in Table 8.12. The data giving the reasons for low capacity utilization in Table 8.26 should be brought to the attention of policy-makers – shortage of raw materials (19 responses) despite trade and exchange rate liberalization; lack of credit facilities (10 responses); and the high cost of credit (12 responses). These all suggest that the financial sector presents a serious constraint to manufacturing enterprises growth. Of the 42 responding enterprises, only 17 operate two shifts.

The pattern of investment in Table 8.27 follows that identified in Section 8.5. Buildings and structures came first, with 53 per cent of the total, compared with 32 per cent for plant and equipment in 1990. The proportions were reversed by 1994.

The analysis, of survey results, therefore, deals with small, relatively inefficient, old enterprises that find it difficult to secure finance. Investment to overhaul old plant and equipment is of recent origin.

Table 8.26 Reasons for low capacity utilization

	Lack of demand	*Machinery is too old*	*Labour is too expensive*	*Shortage of raw materials*	*Lack of credit facility*	*High cost of credit*	*Shortage of other foreign exchange*	*Other*
Yes	14	9	5	19	10	12	2	7
No	10	19	19	7	15	14	21	11
Not stated	8	8	8	6	7	8	9	14

Source: Survey data.

Table 8.27 Investment and finance of reporting firms (in new Ush.m.)

	1990	*1991*	*1992*	*1993*	*1994*
(1) Firm's Investment in fixed assets (total) for 42 enterprises	23 885 768	49 412 599	63 080 511	59 280 381	18 549 688
(2) Proportion of fixed investment in structure	12 786 939 (53.53%)	23 170 731 (46.89%)	32 104 743 (50.89%)	23 361 064 (39.41%)	5 278 178 (28.45%)
(3) Proportion of fixed investment in plant and equipment	8 135 324 (34.06%)	9 292 768 (18.85%)	11 892 330 (18.85%)	17 132 199 (28.90%)	10 396 407 (56.05%)

(3) The Response to the Trade Liberalization Incentive Structure

This is the most important section of the survey. The results should be interpreted with care, however, because only 15 of the 42 enterprises were specialized exporters. This is an extremely small sample.

Most firms (31 of 40) sold their output on the domestic market. The main competitors, therefore, were domestic firms (26 out of 42) in the local market. In the foreign market, 24 of 42 firms also cited domestic firms as the main source of competition.

The bulk of firms (29 of 42) determined their own prices plus a mark-up over costs in the domestic market. This is behaviour from monopolistic competition. Only three firms 'took prices as given', and only one 'adjusted prices in line with imports'.

Table 8.28 Value of exports by reporting firms ($US)

Value of exports in $US	*Previous year (1994)*	*Two years before (1993)*	*The year before trade liberalization (1989)*
0–999	33	10	13
1 000–4 999	1	1	1
5 000–9 999	1	1	0
10 000–19 000	1	0	0
20 000–49 000	1	1	1
100 000+	5	2	0
No. of firms responding	42	15	15

The increase in competition over the previous year (1993/94) also came from domestic producers, according to the 29 firms that responded. Another 16 cited imports from outside the region; and only five gave imports from within the region, as the source of increased competition.

On the exports side, only 15 firms responded. They had very little trade with the PTA. The increase in competition came from firms *outside the region*, as stated by five of the firms that responded. The destination of exports has not changed for 11 of the firms.

The value of exports is very small. However, the changes in position are of interest. In Table 8.28, for example, although 15 firms reported specializing in exports in 1989 and 1993, another 18 firms have since entered the export business, bringing the total to 33 in 1994. There are also more firms in the larger exports value categories: none in the category US$ 100 000+ in 1989, two for 1993 and five for 1994.

The response to the question of when the firm produced exports for the first time gives collaborating evidence. Of the 15 exporting firms, one exported in the 1960s; two in the 1970; three in the 1980s and nine between 1990 and 1995.

The response to the question whether the firms exporting now also did so in the past, indicates that 5 out of 42 exported only in the past.

Asked whether the currently non-exporting firms expected to export in the future, 25 (of 42) said yes.

Manufacturing firms, therefore, are increasingly interested in entering the exports business, and expanding the scale of operation. The interesting question for this study, therefore, is what is the root cause of this interest?

Table 8.29 Barriers to regional imports, as experienced by reporting firms

	Yes	*No*	*Not stated*
(1) Tariffs	10	7	25
(2) Licensing arrangements	7	10	25
(3) Quotas	1	16	25
(4) Foreign exchange difficulties	2	14	26
(5) Other	0	12	30
(6) Would you consider producing or trading in the region in the absence of these barriers?	13	3	26

Source: Survey data.

Table 8.30 Importance of policy changes

	Barriers to trade	*Barriers to investment*	*Access to foreign exchange*	*Trade regulations*
Very important	9	6	8	7
Important	5	2	3	7
Relatively important	9	13	9	6
Not stated	19	21	22	22

Source: Survey data.

With regard to barriers to trade, 7 (of 15) of the exporting firms indicated that barriers do exist; unfortunately, they did not categorize the barriers in the subsequent question. Only 1 firm mentioned *quotas*.

For barriers facing importing firms, the response was much better, as given in Table 8.29. The table indicates that 13 of 42 firms would enter production or trade within the region if the barriers were reduced. Tariffs are the biggest problem; as stated in Section 8.2, Uganda's tariff regime is opaque. The 'licensing problem' noted in the table refers to unnecessary run-around to get an operating licence, rather than to the authorities using the licence to restrict imports.

Table 8.30 suggests that the changes in barriers against regional trade are minor: few firms reported the changes as very important; most firms are in the non-responding category. Only 12 of 42 firms said 'yes' to the question 'Have you seen any policy changes, regarding the regional dimension to your trade in the last year?'.

Table 8.31 is very important for policy-makers. Most firms rate as 'very

Table 8.31 Incentives for expanding trade within the region

	Reduction in regional tariffs	*Reduction in general tariffs*	*Changes in investment rules*	*Changes in licensing rules*
Very important	18	11	11	9
Important	9	15	10	13
Unimportant	6	6	10	9
Not stated	9	10	11	11

Source: Survey data.

important' or 'important' the changes in incentives to encourage them to expand regional trade.

The overall conclusion regarding the changes in incentive structure is that improved policies are likely to encourage new firms to enter the exports business and existing firms to expand their operations. Within the region, policy changes, as perceived by the firms, have been minor. The tariff regime is singled out as an obvious barrier: policy-makers should clarify the objectives of the tariff regime, including how they want to use tariff changes to encourage regional trade.

Within the region, policy changes, as perceived by the firms, have been minor: but most firms suggest that improved policies are important, or very important, to encourage them to enter regional business.

(4) Business Confidence in the Liberalized Policy Regime

The response to this section of the questionnaire was not good: most firms are in the categories of 'had no idea' or 'no response'. (Table 8.32). This was the last section of a long questionnaire, and the responses might reflect fatigue.

An analysis of one question at a time indicates the following: 15 firms intended to keep the same level of employment a year from now, while five intended to have lower employment. None of the firms plans to expand employment.

For the *bank lending interest rates* question, 15 firms expected the rates to go down, six thought they would remain the same a year from now and only three expected them to go higher. Seven firms expected lower rates three years from now, while six expected higher rates, none expected the rated to remain the same. This response is realistic, in expecting lower rates in the future given the very high lending rates prevailing.

The response to the *exchange rate* questions (1.3 and 1.4) did not make

Table 8.32 Business confidence:
What is the most likely confidence level of the variable, compared with time of survey?

	Same	*Lower*	*Higher*	*No idea*	*No response*
(a) In one year's time					
(1) Number of full-time employees	15	7	0	5	15
(2) Local bank lending rates	6	15	3	9	9
(3) Official exchange rate	5	2	11	15*	9*
(4) Parallel market exchange rate	2	5	6	18*	11*
(5) Business tax rates	7	0	8	13	14
(6) Personal income tax rates	4	8	6	13	11
(7) The Rate of inflation	5	5	9	15	8
(8) Import duties on your inputs	0	3	5	15	19
(9) Import Duties on consumer goods	3	2	5	18	14
(10) Export duties	3	3	2	18*	16*
(11) Output of the firm	3	1	21	6	11
(b) In three years' time					
(1) Number of full-time employees	3	5	0	10	24
(2) Local bank lending rates	0	7	6	17	12
(3) Official exchange rate	2	4	4	20*	12*
(4) Parallel market exchange rate	3	2	0	24*	13*
(5) Business tax rates	3	0	6	18	15
(6) Personal income tax rates	1	5	5	18	13
(7) Rate of inflation	2	4	7	17	12
(8) Import duties on your inputs	0	2	3	20	17
(9) Import duties on consumer goods	0	1	5	21	14
(10) Export duties	1	3	1	22*	15*
(11) Output of the firm	0	0	17	11	14

Notes:
In the response to Section 6, p. 18 of questionnaire: same as now; lower or Higher, the (%) were not given. *The question did not make sense in the Ugandan context (there was only one market exchange rate; there are no export duties).

sense in the Ugandan context, with only one market-based exchange rate. That is why stars appear in the last two columns.

Eight firms expected *business tax rates* to be higher one year from now, and six firms three years from now. No firm expected the tax rates to go down. Seven firms expected the tax rates to remain the same a year from now, and three firms, three years from now. The expectation about tax rates, therefore, is pessimistic. Firms perceived the current falling corporate tax rates (Table 8.20) as *not credible*.

For *personal income tax rates* the picture is different. Four firms expected the tax rates would be the same a year from the survey date while one expected this three years on. For the optimists, eight firms expected lower personal income tax rates a year later, while five expected this three years on. The respondents expecting higher taxes were six for 'a year from now' and five for 'three years from now'. Given the trend shown in Table 8.20, optimism is reasonable.

On *inflation*, nine firms expected a higher rate of inflation in one year's time, while seven expected it in three years' time. This pessimistic view is surprising, given the very tight control of inflation since 1992, which the regime regarded as a great achievement. Fewer firms expected a lower rate of inflation – five expected it in one year's time and three expected it in three years' time. Only five firms expected the same rate of inflation to prevail a year later and two firms three years later. The persisting fiscal deficit and the attitude of government towards the civil war may well underlie private sector pessimism regarding inflation.

For import duties on inputs and consumers goods five firms in each case expected higher rates in one year's time, and three and five firms, in three years' time. No firm expected the same rates in three years' time; only two and three firms expected lower rates. For one year's time, three and two firms expected lower rates in each case, while none and three firms expected the same rates. The overall picture is pessimistic and consistent with the trend in effective tariff rates in Table 8.15, Section III, which are on the increase.

On *export duties*, the picture is different. Three firms expected the duties to remain the same in a year's time and three expected lower duties; only two firms expected higher rates. 'No-response' and 'no idea' were very high, however, suggesting that in the Ugandan environment of no export duties, the question did not make sense. The responses for three years' time are similar: one firm expected the same duties, three lower and one higher, with large numbers in the 'no idea' and 'no response' columns.

As to *whether output would expand*, most firms were optimistic: 21 expected higher output in a year's time, while 17 expected it in three years' time; none expected the same or lower output in three years' time. This optimism is probably excessive given the response of no increase in number of employees in a year's time and three years' time (question 1.1). The UMA/IBRD Survey (1995) also reported similar excessive optimism regarding how the firms saw their future growth.

Overall, the picture on employment, bank interest rates, inflation and import duties was pessimistic. The views on personal income tax, export duties and output growth were optimistic. The optimism, on balance, is therefore moderate.

(5) Information and Business Networks

This question is only treated briefly, with reference to Table 8.33, because most firms either did not state their views, or gave no response.

With regard to business location, availability of space (17), proximity to customers (15), access to new markets (12) and access to workers (11) were the leading responses, except for security (15). These responses are what one would expect even if networking was limited. For the location of the distribution centres, proximity to customers (13) and security of location (11) were the leading answers. The most surprising answer is (h) no response was recorded despite the fact that existing studies rate the infrastructure as one of the four most important constraints to growth, along with high taxes and high cost of finance (see Figure 8.4).

The results shown in Table 8.33 contain too few responses to allow a judgement about the importance of the effect information and networks to the enterprises' decisions.

(6) Labour and Other Cost Disadvantages of Ugandan Enterprises

Only two questions were selected from the labour market questionnaire: average level of education, and distribution of workers with more than secondary education. The data are presented in Table 8.34.

Uganda needs an educated labour force. The 'not-stated' responses in Table 8.34, last column, represents a shying away from stating their education because it was too low.

The second part of Table 8.34 is more telling. The columns thin out very rapidly, except for the management and administration categories. Hardly any technicians attend the university. Staff in the last four categories practically all stopped at vocational/technical levels, with the numbers of those who attended thinning out very rapidly. The largest column is that with 'no secondary education'.

The human stock itself, therefore, need to be upgraded if Uganda is to adjust to a competitive environment. The Capacity Building Working Group No. 4 of the National Forum is addressing the area of critical shortages in personnel.

Figure 8.4 ranks other constraints by order of relative importance from the UMA/IBRD Survey (1995). The shortest bars suggest that liberalization has made the exchange rate and trade regulations the least constraining. The longest are bars indicating that Uganda has a long agenda to assist the private sector to overcome these constraints.

Furthermore, Table 8.35 compares the cost of fuel in Uganda and Kenya: the dramatic change in tax structure in Table 8.9, plus the decontrol of

Table 8.33 Information and business networks of responding firms

	Primary	*Secondary*	*None*	*Not stated*
1. To what extent did the following considerations influence your decision about where to locate?				
(a) Government regulations	8	8	17	8
(b) Availability of space and cheap land	17	6	9	9
(c) Access to workers	11	14	7	9
(d) Access to new markets	12	9	10	10
(e) Proximity to customers	15	12	5	9
(f) Proximity to suppliers	8	14	10	9
(g) Proximity to competitors*	6	3	23	9
(h) Proximity to established infrastructure* (Water, electricity, etc.)	No	response	recorded	
(i) Relative security of the location	15	11	6	9
(j) Access to information about new markets, etc.	7	8	16	10
(k) Other (specify)	No	response	recorded	
2. Your offices and distribution centres (3.2)				
(a) Government regulations	1	6	20	14
(b) Availability of space and cheap land	8	8	10	15
(c) Access to workers	1	6	20	14
(d) Access to new markets	8	8	10	15
(e) Proximity to customers	13	10	3	15
(f) Proximity to suppliers	6	6	14	15
(g) Proximity to competitors	7	2	17	15
(h) Proximity to established infrastructure	No	response	recorded	
(i) Relative security of location	11	11	4	15
(j) Access to information	5	10	11	15
(k) Other	No	response	recorded	

Notes:
1. The responses came from 41 establishments (not 42).
2. Of the number of manufacturing plant locations 12 had one plant; 13 had 2 plants; 4 had 3 or more plants; 12 did not state the number of plants.
3. Of the establishments with separately located offices and plants: 16 had separately located offices from plants; 20 had offices and plants located together; 5 did not state separation of locations.

fuel prices since 1993, have led to very high fuel prices in Uganda. Uganda is best advised *not* to raise fuel taxes any further. The cost of fuel permeates the economy and adds to Uganda's already high cost disadvantage in the region.

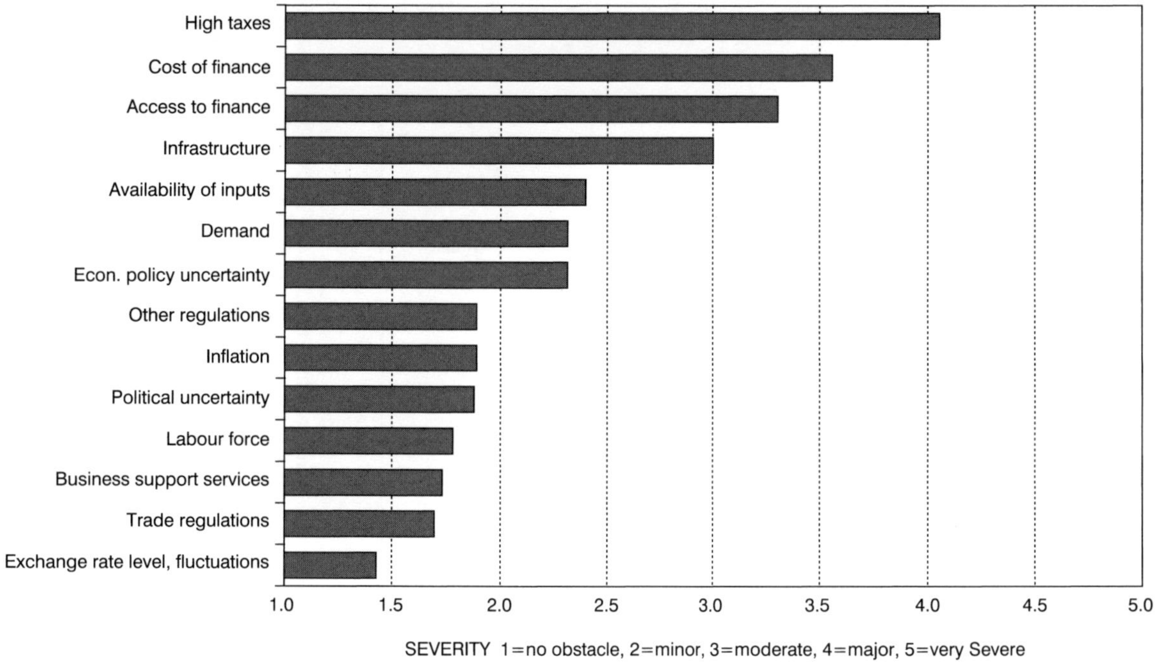

Source: UMA/IBRD (1995) *Survey of Manufacturing Enterprises*

Figure 8.4 Constraints to future operation and growth of Uganda enterprises

Table 8.34 Average level of education by employee category (per establishment)

Education levels	*None*	*Primary*	*Secondary*	*Above secondary*	*Not stated*
(a) Average level of education by employee category (per establishment)					
(1) Management	0	0	2	34	6
(2) Administrative/Clerical	0	0	9	27	6
(3) Commercial/Sales	0	1	11	22	8
(4) Supervisor/Foreman	0	1	15	19	7
(5) Technicians	0	1	11	23	7
(6) Maintenance	1	1	12	10	18
(7) Skilled Production Workers		3	13	14	12
(8) Other Production workers	3	11	12	4	12
(9) Apprentices/Trainees	1	7	3	6	14
(10) Support Staff	1	16	8	1	16
(b) Workers with more than secondary education by employee category (per establishment)					
(1) Management	7	2	6	27	
(2) Administrative/Clerical	11	10	10	11	
(3) Commercial/Sales	14	12	9	7	
(4) Supervisor/Foreman	12	11	16	3	
(5) Technicians	13	9	19	1	
(6) Maintenance	26	10	4	2	
(7) Skilled Production Workers	25	12	3	2	
(8) Other Production Workers	35	6	1	0	
(9) Apprentices/Trainees	37	4	1	0	
(10) Support Staff	39	3	0	0	

Source: Sample Survey of Manufacturing Enterprises (1995) Labour Market Questionnaire (p. 12) Question nos 15 and 16 were the only one to which meaningful responses were obtained.

8.7 CONCLUSIONS FROM THE SURVEY AND POLICY RECOMMENDATIONS

The emerging overall picture from the surveyed firms is as follows: most firms are small, old and inefficient, with low capacity utilization and difficulties in securing finance for inputs and for overhauling old plants and equipment.

Competition is with other domestic firms, where the bulk of output is sold. The firms set their prices with a mark-up over costs, reflecting the prevalence of monopolistic competition. However, the picture is likely to change with the improved policy environment. More firms are entering, or planning to enter, the export business. Those already exporting are

Table 8.35 The cost of fuels: Uganda and Kenya compared

Fuel (1 litre)	*Uganda (Ush)*	*Kenya (Ksh)*	*Ush equivalent of Kenyan cost*
Petrol	950	22.00	624.00
Diesel	850	24.15	470.00
Fuel oil	525	15.49	302.06
Kerosene	700	18.53	361.84

Source: Private Sector Development Programme: East African Open Borders Potential Trade Impact Study on Ugandan Economy (1996) Table 10.1: Comparative Factor Costs.

expanding business volume. Firms also expressed interest in entering the regional market, but many regarded the change in the policy environment as 'important', and 'very important' for them to follow up this interest.

For business confidence, the responses are inconsistent. The firms expect to increase output, but none expects to hire more labour, for example!

Continued improvement in the policy environment, therefore, is highly recommended, to consolidate the benefits from the second trade liberalization episode. The tariff regime in particular stands out as requiring immediate improvement. Furthermore, government should proceed to remove the other constraints not yet addressed by trade liberalization, such as improving the infrastructure, financial sector restructuring to make development finance available and affordable.

The conclusions and policy recommendations should be qualified in one major respect, however. They are based on a sample of enterprises that existed prior to 1989. This study highly recommends speeding up the planned census of business establishments 1997/98, which is required to provide a new post-liberalization sample frame from which samples can be drawn to study the effects of trade liberalization.

Table 8.35 specifically focused on the cost of fuels compared with Kenya: the dramatic change in tax structure (Table 8.9) plus decontrol of fuel prices since 1993 have led to very high fuel prices.

Figure 8.4 ranks other constraints by order of relative importance from the UMA/IBRD study. The shortest columns suggest that exchange rate and trade regulations are the least constraining. Despite trade liberalization, however, Uganda has a long agenda to assist the private sector.

Uganda is best advised not to raise fuel taxes much higher: the cost of fuel permeates throughout the economy and adds to her cost-disadvantage in the region.

Table 8.36 No. of people employed per class of business establishment

	No. of People Employed
0–9	1
10–19	2
20–49	3
50–99	4
100–199	5
200–499	6
500–999	7
1000+	8

Source: Republic of Uganda, Statistics Department (1989) *Census of Business Establishments*, and Uganda (1989) *Manufacturing Sector Report,* Table M13.

Factors Affecting Sample Selection

The latest Census of Business Establishments was taken in 1989. Therefore, only those establishments that existed prior to 1989 were considered, except the 10 cases that were chosen to substitute for the enterprises in the census that could not be located.

The survey questionnaire required a very wide range of data that could only be obtained from establishments that keep formal records. The sampling procedure assumed that the larger the establishment, the more likely it would be to have the capacity to keep formal records. On the basis of this assumption, the manufacturing establishments were classified by size, according to the number of employees, into eight classes, from 0–9 to 1,000+ employees per establishment. The establishments chosen for the survey were those falling within the size classes 3–8, with 20 or more employees, as indicated in Table 8.36.

Only manufacturing establishments were chosen: these fall within the ISIC (International Standard Industrial Classification) codes 1511–3699, inclusive. The establishment chosen are those manufacturing tradeables: import-substitution for the local market and manufactures for export.

The sample size was intended to be 100 establishments – 50 for import substitution and 50 for export. However, in Uganda there were very few export-manufacturers prior to 1989.

The factor responsible for the anti-export bias are documented in sections 2, 3 and 5 of the report. The intended sample, therefore, was adjusted to include 40 export and 60 import-substitution manufacturing enterprises.

The survey intended to cover four districts: Jinja, Kampala, Mpigi and Mukono, where 53.3 per cent of all manufacturing establishments in existence in 1989 were located. But because of the need to make repeated

Table 8.37 The size distribution of manufacturing establishments employing 20 and more persons in 1989

Size class by no. of employees	*No. of establishments by district* Jinja	Kampala	Mpigi	Mukono	*Total Number (6+3+4+5) in Sampling Frame*	*Total No. of Estab. in Uganda in Class Size*	*Sampling Frame as % of Total*	*Sampling Frame as % of Total Exch. Jinja*
(1)	(2)	(3)	(4)	(5)	(6)	(7)	(8)	(9)
1000+	0	1	1	2	4	5	80	not affected
500–999	2	3	0	1	6	7	86	57
200–999	2	8	3	3	16	21	76	67
100–199	10	10	1	1	22	33	67	36
50–99	10	25	5	14	54	103	53	43
20–49	18	102	33	31	184	343	54	51
Total	*42*	*144*	*43*	*52*	*286*	*512*	*56%*	*48%*

Source: Republic of Uganda, Ministry of Finance and Economic Planning, Statistics Department (1989), *Census of Business Establishments*; and *Uganda: 1989 Manufacturing Report*, Table M13.

visits to complete the lengthy questionnaire, the first budget disbursement was exhausted. It was decided to differ Jinja to the second budget disbursement (if this was still considered feasible by the AERC).

The sample frame as intended is shown in column (8) and the effect of excluding Jinja is shown in column (9) of Table 8.37. The distribution of establishments, by size category and by location, is laid out in columns (1)–(6) of the same table.

Supplementary Data Sources for the Sampling Frame

A Business Register, from the Statistics Department, compiled in 1990 and finalized in 1992, was used to identify exact street addresses, telephone numbers and so on. However, the Register does not distinguish between export and import-substitution manufacturing establishments.

A number of sources had to be consulted to identify exporters: the Exporters List from the Bank of Uganda; the Potential Exporters List from the Uganda Investment Authority; *Study of the Resources, Endowments and Comparative Advantage* (1993); the Export List for 1994; and the Monthly Survey of Industrial Establishment by the Statistics Department, Ministry of Finance and Economic Planning.

Sample Distribution by District

The data frame was stratified by economic activity and a sample for each stratum was selected using simple random sampling with random numbers.

Table 8.38 Sample size distribution by district: summary

District	*Exporters*	*Import-substitution*	*Total in the sample*
Kampala	20	36	56
Mukono and Mpigi	13	15	28
Percentage Distribution	33	51	84
Excluding Jinja	40	60	100

The sample size from each stratum was based on the weights of that stratum in the Index of Industrial Production, published annually by the Statistics Department. This information was supplemented by value-added percentages from the Census of Business Establishments.

For the size category 1000= employees, the sample enterprises were selected with certainty since there were very few establishments in the stratum.

The sample distribution by district is shown in Table 8.38.

References

Bacha, E. L. (1990) 'A Three-Gap Model of Foreign Transfers and the Growth Rate in Developing Countries', *Journal of Development* Economics, 32.

Balayo, A. J. (1992) 'An Assessment of the Impact of the Present Government's Trade Liberalization Policies on the Performance of Uganda Traditional Export Crops, Cereals and Grain Legume', case-study submitted to the FAO and the Bank of Uganda, Agricultural Secretariat.

Baldwin, R. E. (1969) 'The Case Against Infant Industry Tariff Protection', *Journal of Political Economy* **52**(3).

Bank of Uganda, Agricultural Secretariat (1991) *Competitiveness and Comparative Advantage of Uganda's Export Crops*.

Bank of Uganda, Agricultural Secretariat (1993) *Economics of Crop Production*, plus an addendum on 'Exchange Rate Appreciation and Exports Competitiveness'.

Bank of Uganda (1992) 'Export Credit Finance Scheme: Performance Survey Report' (December).

Collier, P. and M. Henstridge (1992/3) 'Uganda's Structural Adjustment Programmes' (Oxford University: Centre for the Study of African Economics, (unpublished).

Collier, P., D. Greenaway and J. Gunning (1994) 'A Methodology for the Study of Trade Liberalization', paper presented at the AERC Workshop on *Trade Liberalization and Regional Integration*, Nairobi, Kenya.

Danison, E. (1967) *Why Growth Rates Differ* (Washington, DC: The Brookings Institution).

Ddumba-Ssentamu, J. and M. Hyuha (1994) 'Tax performance Reforms and

Revenue in Uganda', a final research report presented to the AERC workshop, Nairobi.

Elbadawi, I. A. (1990) 'Inflationary Process, Stabilization and the Role of Public Expenditure in Uganda' (Washington, DC: The World Bank Macroeconomic Adjustment and Growth Division).

Glentworth, G. and M. Wozei (1972) 'The Role of Public Corporations in National Development: Case Study of Uganda Development Corporation and Uganda Electricity Board', *African Review*, **1**(3).

Gordon, H. (1996) 'Uganda Maize and Beans Marketing: Regional Exports and Policy Options Under Instability', Proceedings of A Workshop on *Equity and Growth Through Economic Research* (EAGER) organized by USAID (Kampala, Uganda).

Greenaway, D. and C. Milner (1993) *The Fiscal Implications of Trade Policy Reform: Theory and Evidence* (UNDP/World Bank).

Kasekende, L. etc. (1994) 'The Impact of Imports on Development in Low Income Africa, Uganda: Final Report' (Kampala: Bank of Uganda, Research Department).

Kasekende, L. and G. Ssemogerere (1994) 'Exchange Rate Unification and Economic Development: The Case of Uganda 1987–1992', *World Development*, **22**(8).

Kashugyera, L. (1997) 'Privatization in Uganda: A Case study of International Distilleries, Nile Breweries' Crown Bottlers 1992–1995', MA dissertation submitted to the Department of Economics, Makerere University.

Kaweesi, J. (1997) 'The Determinants of the Supply Response of Tea 1971–1995', MA Dissertation submitted to the Department of Economics, Makerere University.

Kiruki, S., H. G. Mahundi and J. C. Odomel (1994) 'The Resolutions of the Second East African Chiefs of Police Conference Held at Mombasa, Kenya 28–30 April 1994'.

Konrad Adenauer Foundation (1994) 'Revival of the East African Community', proceedings of a conference on *Ways and Instruments for Closer Cooperation Between Kenya, Tanzania and Uganda* (Kampala, Uganda).

Loxley, J. (1989) 'Uganda: Constraints on Economic Growth' (unpublished) University of Manitoba, Department of Economics.

Metzel, J. and L. C. Phillips (1996) 'Bringing Down Barriers to Trade: The Experience of Trade Policy Reforms', paper presented to the workshop on *Equity and Growth Through Economic Research* (EAGER), organized by USAID (Kampala, Uganda).

Monitor, The (Daily New Paper, English) Issues of February/March 1995; and 7 February 1997, p. 9.

Namatovu, G. (1980) 'Industrial Co-operation in the East African Common Market', PhD Dissertation submitted to Duke University, Department of Economics.

National Forum (1994a), Financial Sector Development', Progress Report (Working Group no. 3).

National Forum (1994b), 'Uganda's Investment climate and the Promotion of Investment: Progress Report and A Look Ahead', (Working Group no. 1).

National Forum on Strategic Management for Investment Promotion and Export Growth (1996) Reports of Working Groups 1 (Investment and Export Promotion) and 4 (Tax Policy and Administration).

Nyamalele-Bagamukhunda, C. (1997) 'The Relationship Between External Debt and Economic Growth in Uganda', MA Dissertation submitted to the Department of Economics, Makerere University.

Preferential Trade Area (PTA) for Eastern and Southern African States (1994) Report of the Sixteenth Meeting of the Customs and Trade Committee, Lusaka, Zambia 19–23 September 1994.

Private Sector Foundation (1996) *The East African Open Border Potential Impact and Uganda's Economy* (Government of Uganda and the UNDP, Private Sector Development Programme UGA/95/002).

Republic of Uganda (1987) *Rehabilitation and Development Plan 1987/88–1990/91* (Kampala: Ministry of Planning and Economic Development).

Republic of Uganda, Ministry of Commerce, Co-operatives and Marketing (1992a) Background Information Paper on Export Diversification Plan 1992/93–1996/97–2000.

Republic of Uganda (1992b) *The Way Forward I: Macroeconomic Strategy 1990–1995* (Ministry of Planning and Economic Development).

Republic of Uganda (1992c) *The Way Forward II: Medium-Term Sectoral Strategy 1991–1995* (Ministry of Planning and Economic Development).

Republic of Uganda (1993b) Agreement for the Establishment of a Permanent Tripartite Commission for Co-operation Between the Republic of Uganda, the United Republic of Tanzania and the Republic of Kenya (Arusha, Tanzania 30 November).

Republic of Uganda, Ministry of Finance and Economic Planning Statistics Department, '*Gross Domestic Product, Uganda 1984–1993/94*', Statistical Bulletin no. GDP/5.

Republic of Uganda (1993a): Statistical Bulletin EXT/1: 'Imports and Exports, Uganda 1981–1992' (Entebbe: Ministry of Finance and Economic Planning).

Republic of Uganda (1993c) Common text of Identified Areas of Co-operation Between the Republic of Uganda, the United Republic of Tanzania and the Republic of Kenya (Arusha, Tanzania, 30 November).

Republic of Uganda (1994a) 'Key Economic Indicators', 19th issue, November (Entebbe Statistics Department, Ministry of Finance and Economic Planning).

Republic of Uganda (1994b), 'Protocols on the Establishment of a Secretariat of the Permanent Tripartite Commission for Republic for Co-operation Between the United Republic of Tanzania. The Republic of Kenya and the Republic of Uganda' (Kampala: Ministry of Foreign Affairs).

Republic of Uganda (1994c) 'The Customs Tariff Import Duty Rates For Commodities Originating From Eastern and Southern African States (Amendment) order 1994' (Kampala: Ministry of Finance and Economic Planning).

Republic of Uganda (1994d), Statistical Bulletin no. IP/22 'Index of Industrial Production' (Entebbe: Ministry of Finance and Economic Planning).

Republic of Uganda (1994e). The Finance Statute, Supplement no. 6 (Entebbe: UPPC).

Republic of Uganda (1994f) 'Uganda's Proposal on East African Co-operation' (Kampala: Ministry of Foreign Affairs, 22 March).

Republic of Uganda (1990, 1991, 1992, 1993, 1994) The Finance Bill.

Sharer, R. L., H., DeZoysa and C. McDonald (1995) 'Uganda: Adjustment with

Growth, 1978–1995', *IMF Occasional Paper*, no. 121 (Washington, D.C.).
Ssemogerere, G. N. (1990) 'Structural Adjustment Programmes and the Coffee Sector in Uganda 1981–1987', research paper no. 1 (Nairobi, Kenya: Initiative Publishers for the AERC).
Ssemogerere G. N. (1992) 'The Effects of Uganda Government Pricing, Taxation, and Exchange Rate Policies on Coffee Production, Procurement and Export Performance', a case-study prepared for *Training Workshops on Agricultural Policy Analysis*, organized by FAO.
Ssemogerere, G. N. (1996) 'Employment and Labour Markets During Adjustment in Eastern and Southern Africa: The Cast of Uganda', proceedings of a workshop organized by the ILO (Kampala: Uganda).
Stern, N. (1989) 'The Economics of Development: A Survey', *Economic Journal* **99**:397.
Uganda: An Agenda for Trade Liberalization. UNDP–World Bank Trade Expansion Programme, Country Report No. 6.
Uganda Investment Authority (1993a) 'Study of Resource Endowments and Comparative Advantage: Uganda', by Maxwell Stamp PLC.
Uganda Investment Authority (1993b) 'Study of the Effectiveness of Policies, Facilities and Incentives for Investment Promotion', by Maxwell Stamp *et al.*
Uganda: Investment Authority (1994) 'Survey of Licenced Investors, Draft Report'.
Uganda Manufacturers' Association (1993) 'Income Tax Reforms, Trade Policy and Tax Administration Proposals'.
Van der Geest, W. and G. Wignaraja (1996), 'Structural Adjustment, Employment and Labour Market Institutions in Sub-Saharan Africa in the 1990s: A Review of the Literature' (Geneva: International Labour Organization).
World Bank/UNDP (1990) *Uganda: An Agenda for Change* (Washington, D.C.: The World Bank).

9 South Africa*

Michael Bleaney, Alan Hirsch, Merle Holden and Carolyn Jenkins

9.1 INTRODUCTION

By the standards of most of the rest of subSaharan Africa, South Africa is a large and developed country. Throughout the twentieth century gold has been the most important export commodity, and in the last two decades fluctuations in the gold price have been a significant influence on the whole macroeconomic environment. The international political isolation of the country in the apartheid era had wide-ranging effects, encouraging self-sufficiency as an aim of economic policy. It also fostered a protectionist trade regime designed to promote employment and high incomes among the relatively skilled and educated white minority. (South Africa's comparative advantage almost certainly lies in products that are intensive in less-skilled labour.)

A strategy of import-substituting industrialization has been in place since the first half of the twentieth century, but since 1970 the limitations of the policy have been increasingly recognized within South Africa. On the import side (as we show below), this has not been reflected in any significant reduction in the effective rate of protection, but protection has become more transparent, with a shift from import permits and quantitative restriction to tariff protection. On the export side, export subsidies were first introduced in the 1970s, and the system has been gradually refined and developed. These subsidies were a deliberate attempt to offset the anti-export bias of import protection. Nevertheless, the manufacturing sector remains very much orientated to the domestic market, and exports represent only a minor component of sales. Since the domestic market is relatively concentrated, South African manufacturing firms do not experience a very high degree of competitive pressure, and this is a handicap in an increasingly competitive world market.

* The authors would like to acknowledge the helpful comments of Jeff Fine and Charles Harvey on an earlier version of this paper. Any errors that remain are of course the authors' responsibility.

Since 1980 macroeconomic performance has been dismal. Growth, which had been rapid before 1970, decelerated to virtually nothing, and total factor productivity was declining in the last years of apartheid according to most estimates. Unemployment is very high, and inflation has been in the 10–20 per cent range since the early 1970s (although it did dip below 10 per cent temporarily in 1993/94). This weak economic performance parallels that of other middle-income countries (notably in Latin America) that have pursued an important-substitution strategy over a long period.

This chapter describes and assesses the process of trade liberalization in South Africa. It is divided into several sections. Section 9.2 provides an extended account of the development of South African trade policy, and Section 9.3 analyses the impact of trade liberalization on relative prices in the economy. In Section 9.4 we discuss the credibility of trade liberalization, both in the past and as announced by the new government. Section 9.5 considers the regional dimension.

9.2 HISTORICAL OVERVIEW OF TRADE POLICY

Introduction

A study by Bell (1992) identifies two trade liberalization episodes in South Africa. The first began in 1972 with the report of the Reynders Commission of Inquiry into South Africa's export trade, and the second in 1983 with the programme to replace quantitative restrictions with equivalent tariffs. During this second phase more vigorous export promotion policies were also implemented. It is possible that South Africa has now entered a third liberalization episode, with the lowering of tariffs under an agreement with the GATT. The process of trade liberalization has survived the change in government, which reduces the possibilities of a reversal of the process.

A striking feature of South Africa's trade liberalization is that , until 1995, it did not involve any import liberalization. The focus of earlier liberalization was the reduction of the anti-export bias, and, on the import side, the replacement of quantitative restrictions with equivalent tariffs and other duties. This distinguishes the process in South Africa from those in other African countries. A second distinction (and the two are in all likelihood connected) is that South Africa was not pressured into making changes as part of conditions attached to a loan. Trade policy has evolved in response to the perceived needs and problems of the economy, and has had the commitment of government and the support of the business community, virtually eliminating the credibility problem. A third noteworthy differences is that South Africa is to date the only

African country with a GATT offer. This signifies a new commitment to a more outward-orientated growth strategy.

What follows identifies three phases of active industrialization policy, beginning briefly with the adoption of a strategy of import replacement, and following with the shift in emphasis from expanding the manufacturing sector to generating a current account surplus. Because the succession of policy initiatives has been complex, a summary table in Appendix 9.A lists the developments chronologically. The account of policy changes is followed by a brief discussion of the nature of South Africa's liberalization experience.

Import-substituting Industrialization from 1925

Objectives

South Africa was one of the first world's current middle-income countries to explicitly adopt a policy of import-substituting industrialization (Levy, 1992). The 1925 Customs Tariff and Excise Duty Amendment Act initiated protectionist rather than revenue-orientated tariff policy; it extended protection considerably and affected a large number of industries that had previously not been affected (Kleu Report, 1983, p. 13).[1] The Act provided for 'moderate and selective' tariff protection, and empowered the Board of Trade and Industries (now the Board of Tariffs and Trade) to recommend tariffs for specific activities. Its recommendation were invariably accepted. With some exceptions, these powers continued into the 1990s.

ISI was expected to assist with developing greater economic independence from Britain and with creating employment for whites in manufacturing (Botha, 1973; Lumby, 1990). Further interventions followed, like the establishment of parastatal enterprises (for example, iron and steel in 1982) and development institutions (for example, the Industrial Development Corporation in 1940), and the introduction of quantitative restrictions (QRs) on imports in 1948. In fact, after 1948 import controls rather than tariffs were the main instrument of industrial protection (Lachman, 1974).[2]

Support for the new strategy was not undisputed. The Economic and Wage Commission appointed by the government within weeks of the passing of the 1925 Act (and which reported in January 1926) provided a jaundiced criticism of protection. The Customs Tariff Commission, appointed in 1934 to review the application and effects of the policy, argued that the strategy was not unequivocally beneficial; it found that there had been substantial gains in employment and industrial expansion, but that protection was having a weakening effect on initiative, risk-taking and competitiveness. (Wages, particularly of skilled workers, were higher than those for similar occupations in the UK, Australia, New Zealand and elsewhere, which raised domestic prices.) By that stage, however, many industries were reliant on protection for survival, and its maintenance had become a political issue. Justification for continuing was found in the increasing number of other countries pursuing similar policies.[3]

The 1958 Viljoen Commission (into the protection of industry) recommended that ISI be continued, but through the use of tariffs, rather than through QRs or subsidies. Nevertheless, QRs remained an increasingly important component of the protection programme (Hirsch, 1993). The threat of economic isolation from 1960 added to the strategic need for continuing ISI behind tariff and non-tariff barriers, especially for strategically important commodities.

Effects

Studies of the levels of protection provided by South Africa's tariffs structure prior to the 1970s conclude that tariff protection was indeed moderate (BTI, 1931; Holden and Holden, 1975; Lachman, 1974), although Holden and Holden found that effective tariff protection increased over the period 1956/57 to 1963/64.[4] What these studies do not consider, however, is the importance of import controls for the protection of domestic manufacturing. Estimates of the share of imports subject to import controls range from 50 per cent to 90 per cent (Levy, 1992). However, no study measuring the protective effects of import controls has been done for this period.

As a consequence of the protection of domestic industry, considerably diversification of the economy occurred, although the manufacturing sector that developed was highly concentrated (Meth, 1990). In a large measure the rules for protection encouraged this, usually being granted if a producer could supply at least 60 per cent of the domestic market (Holden, 1992b). A significant proportion of investment was the creation or expansion of parastatals, some of which were unprofitable but, like Mossgas and Sasol, were deemed necessary to maintain independence from the rest of the world. Private sector investment 'became too accustomed to being protected from price-cutting from abroad in times of international stingency' (AHI/SAFCI/SEIFSA, 1977, p. 24). Firms sustained high profit levels, even in periods of declining productivity, by rasing the prices of manufactures at a rate faster than that at which input prices were rising (Du Plooy, 1988), a practice that reduces competitiveness.

ISI also served to increase the country's dependence on foreign trade because of the need of the manufacturing sector to import capital and intermediate goods, necessitating greater export earnings to finance this. Between 1950 and 1970 the composition of imports changed, with capital goods as a proportion of imports rising from about 32 per cent to 41.5

per cent; a further 10 per cent of imports was made up of industrial raw material.[5] Controlled nominal interest rates and over-valued currency (which appreciated in the post-war boom) favoured imported capital and intermediate goods in production, while at the same time reducing the profitability of producing for export. The strength of primary exports, particularly gold, and ability of the country to attract foreign investment in the 1950s and 1960s made an inappropriate exchange rate policy appear sustainable. Manufacturing growth, however, began to slow at the end of the 1960s.

In summary, the effects of the ISI strategy from 1925 were:

(1) initially rapid industrial growth and diversification, which slowed at the end of the 1960s;
(2) industrial concentration;
(3) further industrial expansion increasingly dependent on the continuing ability to import capital; and
(4) a marked anti-export bias in manufacturing.

Initiatives to Reduce the Anti-export Bias from 1972

Objectives

The failure to expand exports, together with the recognition that ISI was no longer driving growth,[6] initiated a second major policy shift in the early 1970s with the appointment (1971) and reporting (1972) of the Reynders Commission of Inquiry into the country's export trade. The commission was required to make recommendations designed to improve the country's competitive export position and to identify for removal obstacles to export trade (Reynders, 1975). There was concern that South Africa was too dependent on a single commodity, gold (at that stage subject to a fixed price). In any event, imports were rising too rapidly for the trade deficit to be financed by gold exports and capital inflows. In addition, the export pessimism of the 1950s and 1960s had given way in the face of the achievements of the newly industrialized countries of South East Asia, which had achieved rapid economic growth through export promotion (or at least without biasing their economies towards import substitution).

The commission recommended the positive promotion of exports, especially of the manufacturing sector, as the long-term solution to future foreign exchange needs. It proposed that export incentives be offered to domestic producers to countervail the effects of distance from markets and the existence of subsidized exports from other countries (RSA, 1972).

Although the commission was criticized for ignoring what some saw as a contradiction of encouraging exports in the presence of a largely unchanged protective tariff and import-control structure (Ratcliffe, 1975), it initiated a more outward-looking trade strategy on the part of the government. A range of incentives to exporters was implemented by the government within a year of the publishing of the commissions's report. These included direct cash grants to exporters, tax concessions on export turnover and export profit, rail freight concessions, tax concessions on the disadvantage of using tariff-laden input, and rebates of import duties on imported inputs. In addition, direct controls on imports were partially relaxed from June 1972,[7] although this ceased in 1976 as manufacturers increased pressure for protection during the recession of the mid to late 1970s. Further assistance to exporters was given from 1978 in line with the Van Huyssteen Committee's proposals. The principal of uniformity of incentives to exporters was established at this time (Holden, 1990). The strategy was reinforced by the real devaluation of the rand in the mid-1970s, which went some way to correcting the over-valuation of the currency. This was not maintained when the gold price rose at the end of the decade, and the rand appreciated.

Effects

The Reynders Report initiated what has been called 'South Africa's first liberalization episode' (Bell, 1992, p. 6). Export incentives made the trade regime more neutral. The commencement of the dismantling of QRs and the devaluation of the rand in 1975 deepened the episode. Despite incentives to exporters, the policy pursued cannot be considered a full-blown strategy of export promotion. Protection of the domestic market continued, with import substitution proceeding in the production of intermediate goods (Holden, 1992a). The incentives were an attempt to redress some of the bias that existed against exports. Certainly in the years following the shift in policy, exporters grew in volume terms more rapidly than imports; from 1974 to 1984 the volume of merchandise exports, including gold, increased some 28 per cent. This does, however, reflect a period of rapid expansion in the late 1970s, with a fall in 1980–3, and recovery in 1984. The volume of merchandise imports fell by about 20 per cent.

However, these effects could be attributed to a real depreciation of the rand against the currencies of most of South Africa's major trading partners from 1974 to 1979 and a precipitous slide in 1984.[8] Furthermore, the growth in exports came mainly from an expansion in mining exports (from 57 per cent to 62 per cent of the value of total exports) and from beneficiated mining exports (in the category 'basic metals'). These recorded impressive growth, from around 5 per cent of total exports (15 per cent

Table 9.1 Exports as a % of total production

	1964	*1985*
Agriculture	24.0	23.7
Mining	87.0	66.0
Food, processed	17.4	10.3
Beverages and tobacco	6.0	1.1
Textiles	10.9	20.4
Clothing & footwear	4.8	4.3
Wood & wood products	2.7	7.4
Furniture	2.5	3.3
Paper and paper products	9.1	22.3
Printing and publishing	4.8	0.6
Leather and leather products	15.0	17.3
Rubber products	4.5	2.9
Basic chemicals and petrol	10.5	6.6
Non-metallic products	3.4	3.7
Basic metals	29.7	77.7
Metal products	3.8	2.7
Machinery, excluding electrical	9.1	11.6
Electrical machinery	3.4	3.4
Motor vehicles and transport	3.1	6.7
Miscellaneous (armaments)	22.4	63.2

Source: Central Statistical Services, *Quarterly Bulletin of Statistics* (various issues).

of manufactured exports) to 17.5 per cent of the total (52 per cent of manufactured exports) from 1974 to 1985. With few exceptions, production of most other categories of manufactures were sold mainly in the domestic market (see Table 9.1). There is no empirical evidence to suggest that basic metals received greater incentives to export than did other sectors, and yet the export performance of most other sectors in the economy failed to respond to the improved system of incentives (Holden, 1990).

In summary, the measures introduced during this period to reduce the anti-export bias were limited in scope, and less effective in promoting exports than a more appropriately valued exchanged rate. The import regime remained protectionist, not only during the 1970s, but through the 1980s as well. This is covered in more detail later. Between 1979 and 1983 there were, in fact, pressures for increased protection.

More Concerted Attempts at Liberalization from 1980

Objectives

In 1983 the move to liberalize trade by replacing QRs with import tariffs was resumed. The share of imports (by value) requiring import permits fell from 77 per cent in 1983 to 55 per cent in 1984 and to 23 per cent in 1985 (Levy, 1992). Also in 1985 the positive list of permitted imports was replaced with a negative list of imported items requiring approval, with unrestricted entry of all unlisted items (Holden, 1992a). Between 1985 and 1989 there was little decline in QRs, mainly because the protective effect of remaining controls was greatest for agriculture, historically the (previous) government's support base. In 1989 further reductions were implemented to bring down the proportion of imports covered by QRs to 15 per cent.

As in other countries, increases in tariffs were used to offset the effects of the removal of QRs on industry. These did not take the form of increases in *ad valorem* tariffs, but the creation of a non-transparent system of import reference prices (known in South Africa as 'formula duties'), the extent of protection increasing as the gap between an external reference price and the (lower) import price increases.[9]

During the 1980s, government commissions attempted to find a more effective system of export incentives to favour higher value-added manufactured exports. An important report was that of the Kleu Study Group, which was set up in 1977 to formulate a new industrial strategy. The Kleu Report (1983) recommended a move away from import replacement and criticized existing export incentives for neither favouring domestic intermediate inputs nor creating incentives for technological innovation. It also looked at the issue of uniform versus selective export assistance, pointing out that if the need of exporters for assistance were taken into account, selective assistance would be more appropriate, but that this might discriminate against more competitive exporters. If, on the other hand, uniform assistance were given, then some exporters would receive help when they did not need it, or when help would not lead to increased exports.

The government was not, however, in favour of completely free trade. A government White Paper issued in 1985 states:

> The government wishes to make it very clear that it has never espoused any so-called 'free-trade' policy. On the contrary, like all previous South African governments since 1924, and indeed earlier, it has decisively implemented a policy of protection for industry. Like previous governments, it has accorded protective customs duties, where justified, against competition from normally priced imports. This has continued to be done on a moderate and selective basis. (RSA, 1985, p. 14)

The White Paper recommended that protection be maintained, while simultaneously adopting policies to promote exports.

The debt crisis of 1985 necessitated a further shift in trade policy. Outflows of both long-term and short-term capital from 1985, together with the virtual cessation of inflows of both direct investment and loans, created a large and sustained deficit on the capital account of the balance of payments. This required action by the monetary authorities to turn the historical current-account deficit into a substantial surplus so as to enable the servicing of the foreign debt. The dual exchange rate system abolished in 1983 as part of the move towards more market-orientated policy by the South African Reserve Bank, was reintroduced; the value of the rand was permitted to fall against the currencies of all historically important trading partners; and deflationary policies to reduce domestic expenditure were implemented. The vigorous promotion of exports was also pursued, as is described below.

With the serious problems that emerged on the capital account of the balance of payments in 1985, a 10 per cent import surcharge was introduced, with the express intention of cutting imports drastically to generate current-account surpluses. In 1988 the surcharge was increased to rates of 60 per cent, 45 per cent and 15 per cent (depending on the type of commodity).[10] These rates were reduced by a third in March 1990 as the first step in phasing them out over three successive budgets. The promised reduction did proceed in the 1991/92 budget, but the final elimination did not materialize until 1995.

Towards the end of the 1980s the Board of Trade and Industry, which historically had responded sympathetically to private sector requests for tariff relief, began to move proactively towards reforming industrial policy. From 1987 the board responded less favourably to applications for tariff protection, supporting 65 per cent in 1987, 38 per cent in 1988 and 20 per cent in 1989. The board also began to devise a series of sectoral structural adjustment programmes with the aim of promoting exports. The first programmes, for motor vehicles and textiles and clothing, were introduced in 1989. Domestic producers in these industries were permitted to import duty-free inputs or finished goods if they exported a sufficient part of their output. This approach to redressing the anti-export bias has been controversial.

Officials within the Department of Trade and Industry (DTI) criticize it for creating increased administrative requirements (reported in Levy, 1992). Observers both within and outside the industries concerned claim it provides incentives for fraud in the form of fictitious exports (reported in Holden, 1992b). Shortly after the introduction of the first structural adjustment programme, the DTI indicated that they would be phased out over time, in favour of a uniform incentive programme.

In April 1990 the DTI introduced the general export incentive scheme (GEIS), replacing the export incentives of 1980. The GEIS provides economy-wide export incentives, related to value added and local content, as well as some protection against exchange rate fluctuations. Those industries with high value added and high local content have found that the GEIS provides considerable incentive to export.[11] The scheme is particularly designed to encourage the production and export of processed raw materials, but it excludes producers of indirect exports and appears to have overlooked the need to remove constraints on more labour-intensive exports. In 1993 South Africa successfully negotiated with the GATT both the maintenance of the GEIS and its extension to exporters of non-factor services for a period of five years, on the grounds that this would assist with post-apartheid reconstruction. This agreement was observed when South Africa signed an agreement with the GATT (see below) that included a commitment to a three-year phase-out beginning in April 1995. The GEIS is to be replaced by a newly-refined drawback scheme for exporters.[12]

Other developments in trade policy included the tax incentives under the so-called 37E programme introduced in 1991 to further encourage beneficiated exports,[13] and then removed in September 1993, as well as availability of 9 per cent loans from the IDC for exporters (the prime overdraft rate in 1991 was 20.25 per cent).

The import regime, however, remained protectionist throughout the 1980s. A government White Paper on industrial strategy issued in 1985 reported that although tariffs were flexible upwards, they had never been lowered. The coverage was extensive: *ad valorem* duties covered 83 per cent of the 11 544 tariff lines (Hirsch, 1993); formula duties applied to around one-sixth of all lines. Most rates were applied on an MFN basis, with very few goods entering at preferential rates. The result of selectivity in their imposition was a very large range of (nominal) tariffs, from zero (for some capital and primary goods) to over 600 per cent on certain plastic products to 1389 per cent for one particular fabric; of a representative sample of 32 developing countries, the coefficient of variation of South Africa's tariffs was the second-highest (Belli *et al.*, 1993).[14] The result of selectivity in their application was confusion among importers. Specific rebate programmes (and duty drawbacks in the 1980s) for exporters using imported inputs affected a large proportion of imports; the rules in some cases were so complex that they were not consistently applied, and duties were variable, changing from week to week.

The collected rates were, in fact, much lower on average than the statutory rates: only 9.2 per cent of the value of imports. The coefficient of variation was also lower, probably because there were no imports of goods attracting the highest tariffs – or of some zero-rated goods (Belli *et al.*, 1993). The incidence of protection was, however, roughly the same as in the statutory schedule, and typical of a strategy of ISI: manufacturing was the most protected sector, within which consumers goods were most protected.

Effect

It has been argued that the dismantling of QRs initiated South Africa's second liberalization episode (Bell, 1992). The process was continued with more effective incentives to exporters and supported by a more appropriate exchange rate policy. The liberalization was not unambiguous, however. The import surcharges introduced in 1985 had the effect of raising rates of effective protection substantially, and the compensating increase in tariffs to replace QRs placed an implicit tax on exports. These points are expanded immediately below.

In 1984 the average weighted rate of effective protection (including QRs) was estimated to be 30 per cent, with a high of 143.2 per cent for synthetic resins, plastics and synthetic fibres and a low of −1.0 per cent for (non-electrical) machinery (Holden, 1992b). The IDC estimates for 1988, which include estimates of the *ad valorem* equivalent of formula duties and the import surcharges, were an average effective rate of 70 per cent, with a high of 348 per cent for synthetic resins and a low of −1.0 per cent for (non-electrical) machinery. However, of the 71 subsectors, just over half, responsible for 54 per cent of value added in manufacturing, fell in the ERP range below 30 per cent (IDC, 1990, annex C, p. 58). Nominal rates of protection (including formula duties) remain moderate: at an average of 22 per cent for 12 000 tariff lines; 14 per cent if weighted by import value; and 20 per cent if weighted by value of production. There is, however, considerable variation across tariff lines (for a discussion of this, see Levy, 1992).

The degree of bias towards export promotion or import substitution was estimated for the period 1974 to 1987, the period over which QRs was replaced by equivalent tariffs (Holden, 1992c). The extent of the implicit tax on exportables as tariffs increased ranged from 34 per cent (if gold was excluded from the export price index) to 71 per cent (if gold was included). When the GEIS was introduced in 1990, it was estimated that the clothing industry, which received the most favourable treatment, would receive a maximum subsidy of 19 per cent of export turnover. The GEIS therefore only goes part of the way in offsetting the bias against exports.

Nevertheless, non-gold export volumes increased markedly after 1983, by an average of 7.7 per cent annually between 1984 and 1990, in spite of trade sanctions. Improved incentives alone were not responsible for the growth. The depreciation of the rand was important in stimulating exports;[15] movements in the real exchange rate appear to affect the supply response of exports, but not of import-competing sectors in South

Africa. At the same time, the recession in South Africa reduced domestic demand, making exports a viable option for manufacturers with excess capacity. It should be noted that although the growth in exports has been most rapid for industries characterized by large, capital-intensive firms, a World Bank study found that protection was higher in sectors with high employment levels than in sectors with high capital stock, and there is a statistically significant relationship between employment and protection levels (Belli *et al.*, 1993).

Current Trade Policy Reform

The report of the IDC (1990), a parastatal development bank, on tariff protection policy, recommended a broad-based, phased elimination of formula duties and their replacement with internationally accepted anti-dumping procedures and the lowering of *ad valorem* tariffs over five years to a maximum rate of 30 per cent (with the exception of small number of infant industries that could continue to need support). The recommendations were broadly welcomed, but were not adopted before the change in government. It is unclear as to how much real support they had in the National Party government (or the business sector). There were fears that the new government, which has close links with the trade unions, would be under pressure to reverse the reforms, opting for a more protectionist policy, particularly since protection actually favoured labour. However, both the Industrial Strategy Project, commissioned by the largest trade union body (ISP, 1993) and the framework for macroeconomic policy commissioned by the African National Congress (MERG, 1993) recognized the need for South Africa to become internationally more competitive. They recommended a more neutral trade regime: a simpler transparent tariff structure, with tariffs reduced in line with GATT requirements, and export incentives guaranteed for five years after the change of government. These recommendations have been implemented.

South Africa's offer in the Uruguay Round was the raising of the proportion of tariffs bound by the GATT from less than 20 per cent to just over 50 per cent and an increase in the percentage of duty-free lines to over one-quarter; the simple average tariff for industrial products would fall by one-third in a phased reduction programme (GATT, 1993). It was necessary for South Africa to revise its first GATT offer under pressure from the USA and Europe, which objected to the high protection wanted for the clothing, textiles and motor industries. A 45 per cent tariff on textiles was preserved, but the tariff on clothing was reduced to 45 per cent compared with the 60 per cent offered and the existing 100 per cent; the tariff on cars was reduced from 100 per cent to 50 per cent.

South Africa subsequently initiated a five-year tariff reduction and rationalization programme in 1995 (although clothing textiles and motor assembly were given eight years to adjust). The programme will decrease the government's tariff revenue by an estimated R600m. over five years, although there will be some savings as the GEIS is replaced with a new system of export incentives (the GEIS cost the government some R2bn annually). The number of tariff rates will be reduced from over a hunded to six, ranging from 0 per cent to 30 per cent, and discretionary changes in the system will no longer be possible.

Although the GATT offer is predicted to cause the greatest difficulties for the textile and motor industries, it did not prevent Ford US from purchasing a 45 per cent stake in South Africa's fourth-largest vehicle-maker in November 1994 (*Financial Times*, 29 November). Nor did it prevent the minister of trade and industry from announcing in September 1994 that these industries should expect tariff to be reduced to below those agreed with the GATT. In March 1995 the minister revoke an earlier commitment to provide R4.5bn in subsidies to textile producers,[16] and announced that tariff protection for the industry would be dismantled even faster than required (the eight-year target remains for many textiles, although some specific duties will go in four years).

Two further noteworthy developments occurred in 1995. In March the financial rand and capital controls on non-residents were abolished, without generating the anticipated outflows of capital (and consequent depreciation of the rand) that were anticipated. In June 1995 negotiations began between South Africa and the European Union over trade preferences. South Africa's request for Lomé status was turned down, but the country has been offered a free-trade agreement, with immediate access to Europe for most exports in return for phased exposure to European exporters. A free-trade agreement could lend credibility to and sustain the trade liberalization already underway, by locking in the trade policy even more effectively than is done by membership in the World Trade Organization (Jenkins and Naudé, 1995).

Comments on South Africa's Trade Liberalization

As has been shown above, South Africa's trade policy evolved from a serious commitment to industrial development behind protective barriers to an attempt to reduce the anti-export bias in the economy, without pursuing a full-blown policy of export promotion. More recently, the specific promotion of manufactures has begun to drive industrial policy. The piecemeal introduction of changes means that the trade regime has consisted of overlapping and sometimes contradictory policies.

Trade reform and liberalization refer to measures that move the economy closer to neutrality and greater liberality. If neutrality means that equal incentives are given to producers for the domestic and export markets, then South Africa made some moves in the direction of reducing the bias against exports in the 1970s, and more determined efforts in the latter half of the 1980s, although, even with the GEIS, this process is by no means complete.

Until the 1980s, QRs had been the most important instrument of protection. The replacement of government direct intervention in the form of QRs with tariff commenced in the 1980s and is all but complete (except for some agricultural products). However, they were replaced not with a transparent system of equivalent *ad valorem* tariffs, but with a complex array of formula duties. Effective rates of protection rose with the increased duties that replaced QRs and the import surcharges of 1985, and the devaluation of the rand raised the real effective protection level. Nevertheless, nominal rates of protection, even with formula duties, remained moderate.

Import liberalization began with the replacement of the positive list of permitted imports by a negative list of imports requiring approval in 1984. However, tariff reduction and the dismantling of the complex array of duties began only recently, as South Africa commenced its compliance with GATT requirements.

Any process of trade reform must be accompanied by appropriate exchange rate policy, since any over-valuation of the real exchange rate indirectly taxes tradeables, which receive little protection. South Africa adopted a more flexible and market-determined exchange rate regime in 1983. Within months the rand began its precipitous slide (in nominal terms, although it achieved a substantial real depreciation against most trading partners), an important contribution to the improvement in competitiveness of South African exports. The South African government did not, however, have a predominant objective for exchange rate policy, at least until 1988. It would be wrong, therefore, to suppose that the only goal was to manage the real exchange rate in such a way as to provide the right incentives to exporters and to those competing with imports. Objectives have included at various time the maintenance of a constant real gold price in rand, the control of inflation and the stifling of import demand. As a result, South African exporters and importers have had to cope not only with different movements of real exchange rates against different trading partners, but also with changes in the objectives of exchange-rate policy (Harvey and Jenkins, 1994). Since the end of the 1980s, exchange rate policy has been explicitly to maintain a favourable climate for exports.

The objectives of the industrial/trade strategy adopted have also shifted over time, from an imperative to reduce dependence on Britain and to create productive employment for whites, to the search for a stimulus to economic growth after the 'easy' stages of ISI were completed, and finally to the overriding necessity to ease pressures on the balance of payments. The sympathetic hearing from the Board of Trade and Industries received by individual companies' pleas for protection created a tariff structure that did not necessarily reflect any particular policy.

Finally, it should be noted that the reforms that have taken place in South Africa have not been part of a general and formal structural adjustment programme, and only very recently have the requirements of an external agency (the WTO) begun to drive trade reform. Changes have occurred in response to problems that have arisen in the economy. This has several implications.

First, the fact that the liberalization measures are designed domestically with the aim of addressing particular problems, means that the government is committed to each reform. Moreover, the government has generally achieved consensus through consultation with the business sector. Consequently there is domestically no significant credibility problem. Even with respect to a reduction in the overall level of protection, industrialists support the government's initiatives, although specific programmes have been vigorously criticized. The BTI has shown a willingness to resist lobbying pressures from the private sector over the last seven years.

Second, there is no ultimate free-trade goal towards which the government is moving. In fact, it has specifically distanced itself from such a position. Trade policy is evolving in response to the perceived needs of the economy and, in a limited measure, to pressure from the GATT. The South African government has usually moved at its own pace in implementing recommendations, even those of commissions appointed by the government. It appears to be continuing that tradition with respect to its implementation of the GATT agreement. The commitment to the GATT has the added advantage of reducing the possibility of a reversal of policy, therefore offering greater credibility to investors, both domestic and foreign.

9.3 THE IMPACT OF TRADE LIBERALIZATION

Protection against international trade changes the structure of relative prices in any economy, affecting the incentives to produce and consume individuals products. In Section 9.2 we described the evolution of trade policy in South Africa, and showed that there has been a sustained but gradual effort to reduce the anti-export bias of trade policy by subsidizing exports and making import protection more transparent (through without reducing the effective rate of import protection to any significant degree). In this section we investigate the impact of trade liberalization on relative prices by using three techniques:

(1) incidence analysis;
(2) regression analysis that attempts to correct for various possible influences other than trade policy on relative prices; and
(3) computable general equilibrium modelling, which we apply to the current programme of tariff reductions.

The results of all three analyses are consistent, in the sense that the impact of trade policy is rather small in every case.

(1) Incidence Analysis

Different trade policies may have differing effects on the incentives to produce importables and exportables in an economy. Incidence analysis is one method of estimating the overall effect on incentives of various trade policy measures.

The economy is assumed to consist of three sectors, importables, exportables and non-tradeables. The extent to which a tariff changes the relative prices of importables to exportables and non-tradeables is an indication of the real protection given to importables and a measure of the extent to which the tariff is shifted on to exportables and non-tradeables. Import protection has the effect of raising the price of importables relative to the price of exportables. The price of exportables is usually determined by world markets and tariff protection raises the price of importables. This increase in the relative price of importables is termed 'anti-export bias'.

In addition to increasing the relative price of importables, imports protection also increases the price of non-tradeables. When the price of importables increases, consumers switch expenditure towards non-tradeables, thereby increasing their prices. At the same time producers are encouraged to produce fewer non-tradeables when the price of importables increases. Both the demand and supply response in the market for non-tradeables to the increase in the price of importables creates an excess demand for non-tradeables and increases their prices.

The increase in the price of non-tradeables also reduces the relative price of exportables, making it relatively less attractive to produce exportables. Similarly, producers of importables find that their incentive to produce is reduced as the increase in the price of non-tradeables reduces the price of importables relative to non-tradeables. Therefore, the extent to which exportables bear the burden of protection is a function of the rise in the price of non-tradeables.

The impact of protection, or the incidence of protection, is measured in the following way:

$$p_n = -P_m + (1 - w)\, P_x \qquad (9.1)$$

$$p_n - p_x = w\,(P_m - P_x)$$

P_n is the proportionate change in the price of non-tradeables. P_m is the proportionate change in the price of exportables. The shift parameter (w) is a measure of the response in the price of non-tradeables relative to exportables to changes in the price of importables relative to exportables.

$$t^* = \Delta\,(P_m/P_n) \qquad (9.2)$$

and

$$S^* = \Delta\,(P_x/P_n) \qquad (9.3)$$

If we assume that free trade prices are normalized to unity, then *ad valorem* tariffs on imports and subsides to exporters raise the denominators in Equations (9.2) and (9.3). Whether the true protection and subsidy rates diverge from their nominal rates depend on how the price of non-tradeables changes. If d is the proportionate changes in the price of non-tradeables, then Equations (9.2) and (9.3) become:

$$t^* = (1 + t)/(1 + d) - 1 = (t - d)/(1 + d) \qquad (9.4)$$

and

$$s^* = (s - d)/(1 + d) \qquad (9.5)$$

The proportionate change in the price of non-tradeables is as follows:

$$\begin{aligned} P_n &= d = w\,P_m + (1 - w)\,P_x \qquad (9.6)\\ &= wt + (1 - w)s \end{aligned}$$

where w is the shift parameter, which is an index of the substitutability between non-tradeables and importables in production and demand (Greenaway and Milner, 1993). It can also be shown that w lies between one and zero.

Estimation

Equation (9.1) is estimated in double logarithmic form using price data so that:

Table 9.2 Estimation of the incidence parameter

Equation	*Independent variable*	*Coefficient period 1*	*Coefficient period 2*
Exports including gold	*lnPIMX*	0.707† (6.818)	0.801† (6.07)
Exports excluding gold	*lnPIMX*	0.341† (3.004)	0.756† (13.38)

Notes:
Cochrane Orcutt transformation used
† Significant at the 1 per cent level
t-statistics are in parentheses

$$ln(PNPX) = b_0 + b_1 ln(PIMX) + e \qquad (9.7)$$

PNPX is the price of non-tradeables relative to exportables and *PIMX* is the price of importables relative to exportables.

The price index for non-tradeables is computed through the use of quarterly sectoral GDP data, which is available in nominal and constant price terms (Holden, 1988). The prices of exportables and importables were taken from the export and import prices indexes published in the Reserve Bank, *Quarterly Bulletin of Statistics*.

The incidence parameter is calculated for two periods on quarterly data (Table 9.3). The first estimate was made by Holden in 1990 for data from 1974 to the first quarter of 1987. The second estimate uses the rebased national accounts data for the period 1985 to 1994. The incidence parameter is estimated for exports, which include and exclude gold exports.

In both periods incidence or shift parameter *w* is larger when the price of gold is included in the price index. During the earlier period when gold exports are excluded, the incidence parameter is estimated at 0.341. When gold exports are included, the parameter estimate rises to 0.707. In this period manufactured exportables did not benefit from the general export incentive scheme. Estimates of the incidence parameter for the later period are 0.757 and 0.801, excluding and including gold respectively.

These results indicate that when the price of gold is included in the price of exports, a substantial proportion of the protection given to importables is shifted in the form of an implicit export tax on to exportables. In this case exportables and non-tradeables are not close substitutes. On the other hand, when gold exports are excluded from the export price index in both periods, estimates of the incidence parameter are lower, demonstrating greater substitutability between manufactured exportables

Table 9.3 True rates of tariff protection and subsidy

Time period	*Incidence parameter*	*d*	*t*	*s*	*t**	*s**
1974–87	0.341	0.07	0.22	0.00	0.14	–0.06
1985–94	0.756	0.15	0.17	0.09	0.017	–0.05

and non-tradeables. The result is not surprising, as we would expect that the factors of production are less likely to be as sector-specific in the production of non-gold exports as they are in gold production.

For both non-gold exports and all exports the incidence parameter is higher during the later period. During this period the South African economy experienced an ongoing recession and limited the movement of the factors of production between the traded and non-traded sectors of the economy. This is then reflected in a rise in the estimate of the incidence parameter for non-gold exports and all exportables in the later period.

The true tariffs and true subsidy rates for non-gold estimates of the incidence parameter are calculated for both periods assuming average rates of nominal tariffs and exports subsidies (Table 9.3).

True protection in the period 1974 to 1987 is calculated at 14 per cent as compared with the average rate of nominal protection of 22 per cent in this period (GATT Trade Review, 1994). It is assumed that exports did not receive any meaningful subsidies in this period. The bias against exports is accordingly a high of -6 per cent. During the later period, despite the introduction of the general export incentive scheme and lower average tariff rates, the bias against exports is only marginally reduced, to -5 per cent. True protection is also low at 1.7 per cent.

(2) Regression Analysis

Trade liberalization is expected to influence the relative price of traded goods; if restriction on imports are reduced, they should be cheaper relative to domestic output. However, at an aggregate level, there may be additional influence on relative price because of the particular composition of imports. If, for example, imports are biased towards primary commodities, then commodity prices will influence the import price index relative to the consumer price index. As we show below, the movement in both import and non-gold export prices show some correlation with an index of primary commodity prices.

It is also possible that the effects of trade liberalization are seen in quantities as well as prices. One reason for this is that the change in policy causes new goods to be exported or imported. These goods will

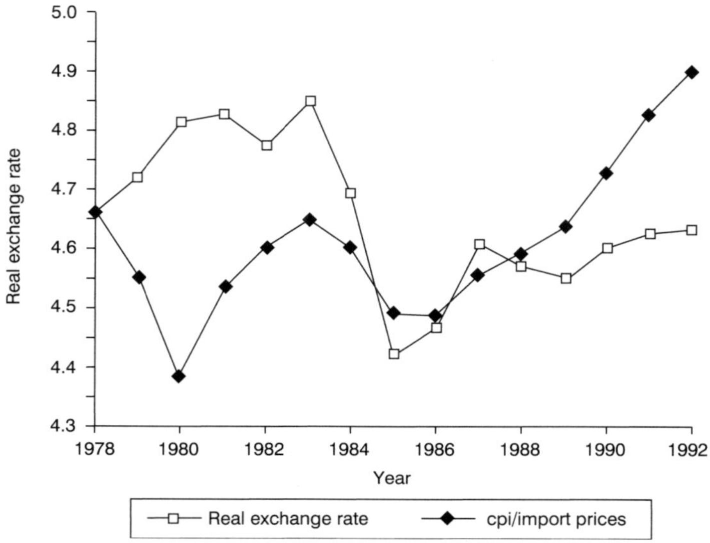

Figure 9.1 Relative import prices and real exchange rate, 1978–92

not appear in the pre-trade liberalization export and import price indexes, and consequently the shift in the incentive to trade is likely to be understated. Changes in quantities may, however, be an index of the lack of credibility of the liberalization, as importers seek to stock up before an anticipated policy reversal. However, we do not believe that credibility problems are significant in South Africa, since policy has shifted rather slowly and cautiously.

In the South African case, there is a major issue of the timing of trade liberalization. There has been a significant shift of policy over a long period of time, starting in the early 1970s, and with some retreats (for example, the imposition of imports surcharges in 1985). Over this period, there have been some sharp swings in the real exchange rate, whose impact can be seen in the trade figures. From an econometric point of view, this means that one cannot use a simple dummy variable to capture the change in policy, since the shift in stance was drawn out over such a long period. The approach adopted here is to try to model trade data using a variety of explanatory variables, and use a simple time trend as a possible proxy for policy shifts. This procedure has the disadvantage that a significant coefficient of the time trend is susceptible to a variety of other interpre-

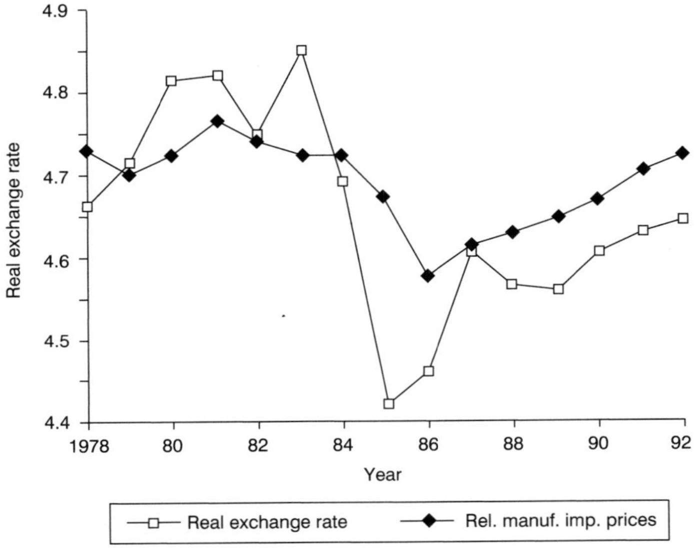

Figure 9.2 Relative price of manufactured imports, 1978–92

tations. In general, any omitted variable may be responsible for it. Consequently, any conclusions that are drawn depend heavily on the quality of the model used in the estimation. This having been said, however, the modelling process does yield some useful insights.

Relative Price Effects

Figures 9.1 to 9.3 present some data on relative prices and the real exchange rate from 1978 to 1992. The starting date is 1978 because the real effective exchange rate index was not calculated before that date. The graphs are constructed in such a way that there is expected to be a positive correlation between the variables. Thus the relative price of imports is expressed as the ratio of the consumer price index to the import price index (all variables are in logs).

Figure 9.1 looks at the relative price of total imports. This appears to be considerably lower (relative to the CPI) in 1992 (compared to 1978) than one would expect on the basis of the real exchange rate. In particular, relative import prices have fallen since 1987, while the real exchange rate has hardly changed. In the early part of the period, the most obvious

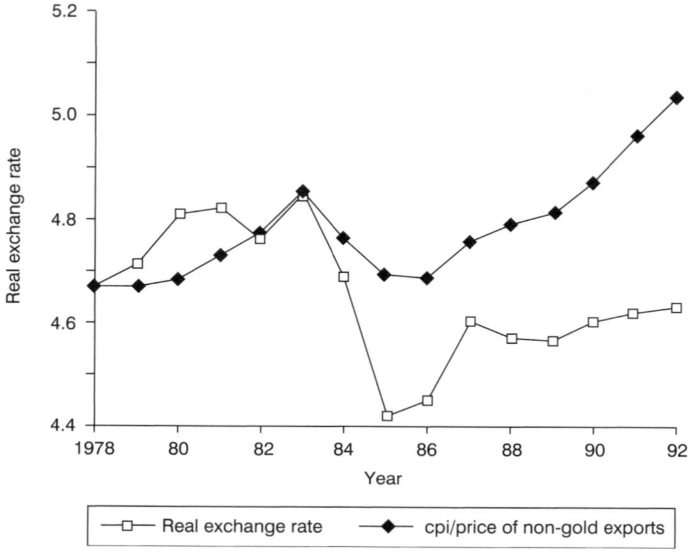

Figure 9.3 Relative price of non-gold exports, 1978–92

feature is the rise in import prices in 1979/80, which may reflect oil price effects (though in this case one would expect a sharp reversal in 1986, when oil prices collapsed).

Figure 9.2 examines the same issue but using data on manufacturing prices only. Relative to an index of the prices of manufactured goods produced and consumed in South Africa, the import price index of manufactures moves fairly closely with the real exchange rate, but is less volatile. Although there is a suggestion of a fall in relative import prices in recent years, this appears to be an accurate reflection of movements in the real exchange rate.

Figure 9.3 compares the relative price of non-gold exports with the real exchange rate. Non-gold export prices appear to have fallen quite considerably in relative terms since 1978 (this is also true if producer prices of manufactures are used as deflator instead of the CPI), and there is clearly some correlation with the real exchange rate.

If the relative price of aggregate imports (*RPM*) is regressed on the real exchange rate (*RER*) and the world price of non-fuel primary products relative to manufactures (*RPP*), then we get, for annual data 1978–92:

$$RPM = -0.966 + 0.00591t + 0.609RPM_{-1} + 0.549RER - 0.391RPP \quad (9.8)$$
$$\quad\;\; (-1.07) \quad (0.89) \quad (4.28) \quad (3.60) \quad (-2.47)$$

$n = 15$; R-squared $= 0.877$; $s = 0.055$ (t-statistics in parentheses)

All variables are in logarithms, t represents time and *RPM* is the consumer price index divided by the import price index, so that an increase in *RPM* represents a fall in the relative price of imports. It is clear that there are significant effects from the real exchange rate and the relative price of primary commodities; surprisingly, the real oil price is not significant in this equation, and is therefore not included. The time trend is insignificant.

A similar regression, using manufacturing prices only (and consequently omitting *RPP* as no longer relevant) produces the following results:

$$RPMMF = 0.604 + 0.00299t + 0.600\,RPMMF_{-1} + 0.257RER \quad (9.9)$$
$$\quad (0.74) \quad (1.40) \quad (3.54) \quad (3.74)$$

$n = 15$; R-squared $= 0.798$; $s = 0.027$ (t-statistics in parentheses)

Here *RPMMF* is the price of South African-produced manufactures for South African consumption divided by the price of manufactured imports. Once again the time trend is insignificant. Exchange rate effects are only about half as large as for the aggregate price index. This may reflect greater elasticity of import prices of primary products than of manufactures with respect to the real exchange rate, perhaps because of 'pricing to market' by importers of manufactures.

For the ratio of consumer prices to the price index of non-gold exports (in logs, *RPXNG*), the real exchange rate and the relative price of non-fuel primary products are also significant, but this time there is a significant time trend:

$$RPXNG = -0.523 + 0.000981t + 0.565RPXNG_{-1} + 0.500RER - 0.193RPP \quad (9.10)$$
$$\quad (-1.17) \quad (3.02) \quad (8.35) \quad (5.53) \quad (-3.27)$$

$n = 15$; R-squared $= 0.973$; $s = 0.021$ (t-statistics in parentheses)

Since the time-trend coefficient is positive, this indicates an unexplained downward trend in the relative price of non-gold exports that might possibly be attributed to increased export subsidies.

Volume Effects

We test for volume effects by investigating evidence of structural breaks in trade volume equations over the period 1960–92. For both imports and non-gold exports, we find that an equation estimated over the period 1960–78 forecasts remarkably well over the years 1979–92.

Import volumes 1960–92 The estimated equation is:

$$\underset{}{MVOL} = \underset{(-6.42)}{-3.58} = \underset{(5.86)}{0.242RPM} + \underset{(15.20)}{0.670Y} \qquad (9.11)$$

n = 33; R-squared = 0.927; Chow F(3,27) = 0.04; predictive failure F(14,15) = 2.80

Here *MVOL* represents the volume of imports and *Y* the gross domestic product (both in logs). As before, the relative price of imports (*RPM*) is defined as the consumer price index divided by the import price index (in logs), so the positive sign is as expected. The actual and forecast values when the equation is estimated up to 1978 only are shown in Figure 9.4. The Chow statistic is highly insignificant, but the predictive failure statistic is significant at the 5 per cent level (the value is 2.45). Since the forecast errors are not systematically of the same sign, this result is the effect of heteroscedasticity: the residuals are much larger in the later period. Since the predictive failure test is based on the squared forecasting errors, failure of this test can be triggered by heteroscedasticity rather than by structural change. This is clearly what is happening in this case.

Non-gold export volumes 1960–92 Here the equation is:

$$XNGVOL = \underset{(1.30)}{0.325} + \underset{(1.06)}{0.155XPR} - \underset{(-1.56)}{1.02YDEV} = \underset{(34.56)}{1.39YW} \qquad (9.12)$$

n = 33; R-squared = 0.976; Chow F(3,27) = 1.48; predictive failure F(14,15) = 1.20

Here *XNGOL* and *XPR* are, respectively, the volume and relative price of non-gold export (CPI divided by export price), *YDEV* is the deviation of South African GDP from a quadratic trend, and *YW* is OECD GNP (all in logs). Once again there is no evidence of structural instability at the end of 1978, with the Chow statistics and predictive failure statistics both insignificant. Actual and forecast values are shown in Figure 9.5.

The only result that might possibly be interpreted as evidence of trade liberalization effects is the trend fall in the relative price of non-gold

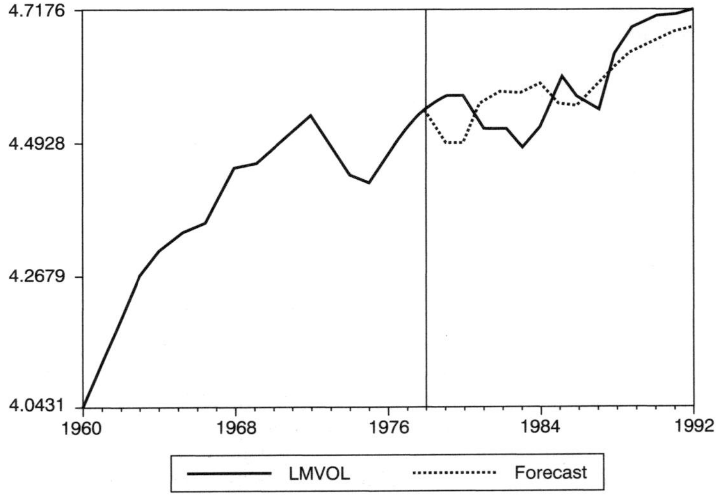

Figure 9.4 Plot of actual and static forecast(s)

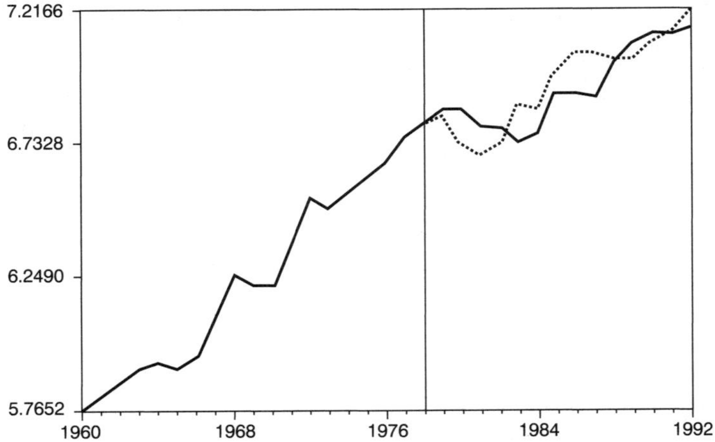

Figure 9.5 Plot of actual and static forecast(s)

exports over and above what is explained by real exchange rate depreciation and falls in world primary commodity prices. This may reflect export subsides; it may also however, be a consequence of price movements in the particular commodities South Africa exports, which may have fallen more than the price of a world basket of commodities.

(3) Computable General Equilibrium Estimates of the Liberalization

Nominal and Effective Rates of Protection in 1994 and Beyond

Table 9.4 shows the nominal and effective rates of tariff protection for 1994. These can be compared with those incorporating the tariff cuts and bound rates under the Uruguay Round. The manufacturing sector presently enjoys a weighted average rate of nominal tariff protection of 16.6 per cent. The rate is 6.4 per cent for the entire economy. Prior to the liberalization, nominal rates of protection ranged from a high of 84 per cent to a low of zero. Effective rates demonstrate a wider divergence ranging from a high of 892.6 per cent to a negative 6.9 per cent.

After the liberalization takes place it is anticipated and calculated by the Industrial Development Corporation that the rate of bound nominal tariff protection for manufacturing will fall to 10.8 per cent and that for the entire economy will decline to 4 per cent. The sectors experiencing the greatest changes in protection are tobacco (−64 per cent), clothing (−38 per cent), motor vehicles (−21 per cent), textiles (−18 per cent) and footwear (−14 per cent).

The IDC calculations of the effective rates of protection still show considerable variance despite the intended overall reduction in the level of protection (Table 9.4). Effective rates of tariff protection show dramatic changes in the competitive position of certain industries following the Uruguay Round. These changes arise, first, from the reduction of protection on inputs into certain industries that had previously been penalized, and second, from a reduced level of protection on their output. Overall levels of effective protection are reduced by the liberalization from 58.9 per cent to 34.7 per cent for the manufacturing sector, from 11.7 per cent to 7.2 per cent for the economy.

The IDCGEM Model

The IDCGEM model, a computable general equilibrium model developed at the Industrial Development Corporation, estimated the impact of the tariff proposals on the South African economy. This model makes the following assumptions:

Table 9.4 Nominal and effective rates of tariff protection (%)

	Nominal protection		*Effective protection*	
Sector	*1994*	*Uruguay*	*1994*	*Uruguay*
Agriculture	10.4	5.6	21.8	10.7
Gold	0	0	–0.2	–0.2
Other mining	4.4	2.5	7.0	3.7
Food	14.6	10.0	99.0	56.1
Beverages	23.0	10.2	43.1	19.0
Tobacco	84.2	19.4	257.1	129.2
Textiles	40.7	22.4	200.2	77.7
Clothing	75.6	37.2	847.5	131.8
Leather	15.5	10.9	106.5	61.9
Footwear	44.4	29.0	892.6	575.2
Wood	13.7	9.8	43.7	29.4
Furniture	24.3	19.9	129.0	96.1
Paper	11.4	6.8	40.5	21.7
Printing	9.8	6.3	23.6	14.7
Industrial chemicals	1.5	1.1	3.2	2.4
Other chemicals	14.1	8.2	110.2	48.7
Rubber	19.8	13.0	43.1	28.1
Plastic	20.6	15.9	55.7	44.8
Pottery	19.4	19.3	22.4	22.5
Glass	10.4	8.3	13.2	10.7
Other non-metals	9.6	7.3	16.8	12.9
Iron and steel	7.3	6.2	22.2	18.6
Non-ferrous	10.1	4.6	42.7	16.3
Metal products	12.9	11.2	32.1	28.2
Machinery	8.0	5.3	16.7	10.1
Electric mach	14.9	11.4	35.1	26.7
Motor vehicles	58.5	36.7	901.5	537.7
Transport equipment	6.1	4.0	10.2	6.5
Other manufacturing	13.5	10.3	52.1	37.4
Water and electricity	15.3	4.2	32.3	7.7
Construction	0	0	–6.9	–5.5
Trade	0	0	–1.1	–0.6
Financial	0	0	–0.3	–0.2
Other services	0	0	–0.6	–0.5
Servants	0	0	–3.1	–2.3
Government	0	0	–0.7	–0.4
Manufacturing	16.6	10.8	58.9	34.7
Total economy	*6.4*	*4.0*	*11.7*	*7.2*

Source: Industrial Development Corporation.

- fixed real government consumption
- constant post tax real wages
- fixed capital stocks in each industry
- less than full employment in labour markets
- endogenous balance of trade
- exogenous tax rates
- fixed exchange rates.

The model suggests that the consumer price index declines by 1.8 per cent as a result of the lower tariff levels. GDP increases by 0.4 per cent and employment by 0.5 per cent. The average nominal wage is predicted to fall by 1.81 per cent and the real average wage to rise by 0.004 per cent. The trade balance declines marginally while the government deficit increases by 3 per cent in real terms. This analysis assumes that there are no spread effects from the liberalization in other countries under the Round and that the static effects of the unilateral liberalization are relatively small. The sectoral results in percentage terms are shown in Table 9.5.

The manufacturing sectors that gain the most in volume of value added are basic metals, machinery, non-gold mining and other manufacturing. The sectors experiencing the greatest losses in value-added are transport equipment including motor vehicles and parts, followed by gold mining, footwear, rubber and textiles. The largest increases in imports occur in footwear (24.3 per cent), clothing (24.3 per cent), transport equipment (17.1 per cent), textiles (5.9 per cent), wood (4.3 per cent), beverages (3.1 per cent) and agriculture (2.3 per cent).

The sectors that experience above-average gains in employment are basic metals, agriculture, tobacco, non-gold mining and machinery. Employment is adversely affected in transport equipment, rubber, footwear and textiles. The motor vehicles and textile industries are significant employers of labour – the two industries together account for 10 per cent of the manufacturing employment. The predicted employment cuts arising from the trade liberalization in these two industries amount to 6256 workers.

Until the structure of the IDCGEM model is published and has been evaluated, it is difficult to be persuaded by the credibility of these results. Dramatic shifts are not predicted. However, it is important to bear in mind that the phasing out of the general export incentive scheme is not included in these simulations and therefore the predicted increases in exports may well be tempered by the reduction in present export incentives.

Table 9.5 Sectoral changes arising from the GATT offer (% changes)

Sector	Value added		Exports		Imports	Employment
	Volume	*Price*	*Volume*	*Price*	*Volume*	*Volume*
1 Agriculture	0.365	–0.593	3.141	–0.628	2.276	1.239
2 Gold	–1.731	0.019	–1.780	0.018	0.000	0.000
3 Other mining	0.722	–0.143	0.757	–0.202	0.912	1.147
4 Food	0.503	–0.916	2.812	–0.562	1.326	0.983
5 Beverages	0.221	–0.763	2.630	–0.526	3.076	0.893
6 Tobacco	0.649	–0.963	2.913	–0.583	1.393	1.166
7 Textiles	–1.158	–3.259	8.592	–1.718	5.952	–1.801
8 Clothing	0.460	–2.523	6.455	–1.291	24.289	0.570
9 Leather	0.432	–1.122	4.897	–0.979	1.646	0.784
10 Footwear	–1.430	–1.912	4.172	–8.034	33.161	–1.908
11 Wood	–0.126	–1.527	3.809	0.762	4.308	–0.221
12 Furniture	0.498	–1.571	4.201	–0.840	0.429	0.640
13 Paper	0.446	–0.560	1.886	–0.377	1.824	1.037
14 Printing	0.076	–1.250	3.225	–0.645	1.113	0.114
15 Chemicals	0.385	–1.241	4.355	–0.871	0.658	0.912
16 Rubber	–1.347	–2.995	7.167	–1.433	2.253	–2.537
17 Plastic	–0.144	–1.986	4.882	–0.976	–0.658	–0.285
18 Non-metal minerals	0.216	–1.272	3.523	–0.705	–0.098	0.485
19 Basic metals	1.264	–0.556	3.386	–0.677	0.046	2.012
20 Fab. metals	0.438	–1.050	2.986	–0.597	–2.070	0.622
21 Machinery	0.759	–0.995	3.087	–0.617	–0.296	1.046
22 Electrical machinery	0.115	–1.475	3.914	0.783	0.160	0.233
23 Transport equipment	–3.696	–5.652	21.013	–4.203	17.135	–6.407
24 Other manufactures	0.714	–0.676	2.228	–0.446	0.086	1.431

Source: Model results.

9.4 CREDIBILITY OF TRADE LIBERALIZATION

Many trade liberalizations lack credibility either because there is significant opposition to the policy or because the liberalization forms part of the conditions of a loan from the IMF or the World Bank, and the government's commitment to the policy is uncertain.

As we stressed above, in the South African case the approach to trade liberalization has been cautious and dictated entirely by domestic considerations, without any significant input from the IMF or the World Bank. The intellectual case for trade liberalization has been broadly accepted by the South African government, at least since the 1970s, when export subsidies were first introduced, and a significant shift took place in 1983 when the requirement to obtain import permits was replaced, for the majority of products, by a tariff system. The tariffs were designed to be equivalent to the quantitative restriction they replaced, and were supplemented by a system of formula duties that had the effect of setting a minimum import price. The formula element has, however, been allowed to atrophy, since the relevant prices have not been fully adjusted for inflation.

The use of export subsidies rather than tariff reduction and harmonization to achieve trade liberalization is unusual, and is probably related to the particular political circumstances of South Africa. Because of the international isolation of the apartheid regime, the government was concerned about dependence on imports, and one of the most appealing policy instruments available for influencing import dependence was the highly differentiated tariff regime. Because the government was unwilling to allow purely economic factors to influence the structure of imports, action on the export side was a more attractive option. Nevertheless, there has been significant shift to a more transparent import regime with considerably less reliance on imports permits.

These comments bring us to a more general point. In the apartheid era, South Africa was never in a normal peacetime situation, but existed in an atmosphere of semi-hostility or at least uneasy relations with many other countries, including many of its trading partners. The paramount policy objective was the survival of apartheid, to which all other aspects of policy were subordinate. Consequently it must have been well understood by business that trade policy could change swiftly and radically if threats to the regime appeared to make such changes necessary – as indeed occurred in the balance of payments crisis of 1985, when substantial import surcharges were introduced. One interpretation of this episode is that although there was also a substantial real devaluation at the time, trade policy was still being used as an instrument for addressing macroeconomic imbalances rather than to provide a stable, long-term framework for international trade. The use of trade policy for macroeconomic purpose is characteristic of restrictive trade regimes (Little *et al.*, 1993). Quantitative restrictions are particularly well adapted for this purpose, since they can be adjusted without any public announcement.

The problem of credibility of trade liberalization would seem to have three main aspects: (1) the greater transparency of import protection; (2) the subsidization of exports; and (3) prospects of significant further liberalization under the majority rule.

(1) Import Protection

Protection against imports was originally thought of in terms of effective protection analysis, with tariff equivalents being used to represent quantitative restriction. In the last two decades increasing emphasis has been placed on the 'new view' of protection, which recognizes the resources used in lobbying for increased protection. In this new view, the average rate of protection is less important than its dispersion and transparency. The less transparent a system of protection is, the harder it is to compare protection of different sectors, and the lower the political resistance to increasing protection for a given industry. With a highly differentiated tariff system, which implicity recognizes that not all industries have the same case for protection, it is likewise easier for a government to concede increased protection than under a uniform tariff regime. The thrust of this new view is that the return to investment in lobbying activities by firms may be greater than in cost-cutting or other efficiency-raising responses to import competition, with adverse effects on long-run productivity.

From the perspective of this new view of protection, South African trade policy has become more transparent with the transition from quantitative restrictions to tariffs. The system of QRs had been extremely non-transparent because of the necessity to obtain a permit for virtually any import delivery. If such imports consisted of products that were also produced by South African firms, there was always the possibility that these firms might lobby successfully for the permit to be refused. However, there was no effort, when the permit system was reformed and largely replaced by tariff protection, to reduce the dispersion of protection across industries. In fact, the opposite was the case: the introduction of formula duties with the transition to tariffs was intended precisely to ensure that particular industries did not suffer unduly – that is, that effective protection *at the sectoral level* remained substantially unchanged. Since the commitment to tariffication was widely discussed with industry before hand, and since a great deal of care was taken to ensure that sectoral interests did not suffer, there is little doubt that this move towards greater transparency of import protection was credible. This credibility was reinforced in the 1985 crisis, when the government chose to impose tariff surcharges rather than to extend quantitative restrictions.

(2) Export Subsidies

As explained in Section 9.2, export subsides were first introduced in the 1970s and have been maintained with several modification. With the introduction of the GEIS in 1990, the export subsidy scheme has become more general and less discriminatory between sectors. Since export subsidies are not permitted under GATT, the scheme is due to be phased out. Export subsidies represent an effort to render the trade regime more neutral, offsetting the impact of import protection by raising the price of exports not only relative to imports but also relative to non-tradeables. Although the scheme has existed long enough to be credible, the evidence suggests that the export market represents very much a sideline for most South African firms involved in it. The volume of non-gold export is negatively related to deviation of domestic output from trend (see Section 9.3), which implies that only when the domestic market is weak do firms in the manufacturing sector put efforts into exports.

In this context it is important to note some important structural changes that are taking place in South African exports. Traditionally, over 30 per cent of export receipts have come from export of gold (in 1980, the figure reached 45 per cent because of the high price of gold). However, since 1980, rapid expansion of production outside South Africa has held down the world price of gold, while for geological reasons South African production has remained static. The result has been a steady reduction in the real value of gold export earnings, to the point where in 1994 they only represented 21.6 per cent of the total. This has necessitated a reduction in the real exchange rate, most of which occurred in 1984/85. It is possible – indeed likely – that minerals and other primary products will remain a major component of South African exports (as is the case in Australia), and there was a rapid expansion of coal exports over the 1980s. Export earning from tourism are also increasing rapidly. However, the fastest-growing countries in the world have been able to expand their exports of manufactures at a rapid pace. The decline of gold earnings and the implied fall in the equilibrium real exchange rate mean that a wider range of South African non-gold production becomes potentially exportable if backed up by appropriate economic policies. Consequently, the issue of whether the manufacturing sector (or at least a significant section of it) can become export-orientated is a major question for the future. A radical reform of trade policy, including a commitment to a much more open regime, is probably necessary to achieve this. This raises the next question.

(3) Is the Commitment of the New Government to Further Trade Liberalization Credible?

In support of the argument that it *is* credible are the fact that a restrictive trade policy has been discredited by the poor macroeconomic performance of the 1980s and by the association of the policy with the apartheid regime, and that the government is concerned to expand employment of black labour. A more open trade policy would favour those factors in which South Africa is well endowed, which include relatively unskilled labour. However, the best organized labour interests are the trade unions, which tend to represent those already in employment; consequently they may lobby against too radical a trade reform because it threatens the interests of too many of their members.

Trade liberalization can be seen as part of a market-orientated strategy based on establishing attractive conditions for private investment, including monetary and fiscal restraint, a cautious approach to redressing the inequalities inherited from apartheid, and possibly privatization of state assets rather than the extensive nationalization the ANC advocated in opposition. The results of this programme will certainly fall short of the very high expectations of the ANC supporters at the time the new government was elected, and it is possible that opposition to a market-orientated strategy will increase with time. The government may gradually come under pressure to adopt more populist rhetoric and to make at least some gesture towards a more interventionist approach. Depending on the balance of political forces, this might initiate a slide towards a larger budget deficit (financed by money creation so that inflation increases), tighter exchange controls and the temptation to use trade policy to overcome short-term balance-of-payments problems.

To some extent, therefore, the credibility of trade liberalization is linked to that of the government's overall economic programme. In order to test whether there is a wider credibility problem, we compare long-term interest rates on government bonds with the rate of inflation over the period since 1989. Long-term interest rates should reflect inflationary expectations over the period to maturity of the bonds, so that if the markets view the probability of a future shift to a more inflationary policy as significantly greater than zero, interest should rise relative to the current rate of inflation. Table 9.6 shows long-term government bond yields, consumer price inflation and the implied real interest rate from 1989 until the first quarter of 1995.

From 1989 to 1992 bond yields and inflation were at levels typical of the 1980s, with an implicit real interest rate of under 2 per cent. However, from 1993 onwards, inflation fell to under 10 per cent per annum. (although it is now rising again, since the end of 1993). To some extent this may reflect a perception that the reduction in inflation is in part the result of temporary factors unrelated to long-term economic policy, such as the impact of recessions and the recovery of food output after the 1992 drought, but it is doubtful if this is the full explanation. There is also little evidence of a shift in the term structure of interest rates, so that the rise in long-term rates cannot simply be attributed to a tight monetary policy designed to facilitate the abolition of the financial rand. Accordingly, the increase in real interest rates suggests credibility problems for the new government.

Table 9.6 Long-term interest rates and inflation since 1989

Year	*Yield on long-term bond (%)*	*Consumer price inflation (%)*	*Implicit price interest rate (%)*
1989	16.90	14.68	1.94
1990	16.15	14.34	1.63
1991	16.34	15.26	0.90
1992	15.44	13.88	1.37
1993	13.94	9.75	3.82
1994	14.83	8.98	5.33
1995 (first quarter)	16.85	9.76*	6.46

Note:
* Inflation rate over previous four quarters.

However, it is not absolutely clear that slippage in monetary and fiscal policy would lead to a similar slippage in trade policy, even if, as is likely, it led to severe pressure on the exchange rate. For example, even if trade policy is tightened, this could be achieved by raising the lower tariff rates, not the higher ones, so that protection would become more uniform rather than less. In the South African context, the uniformity of protection is probably of greater significance than its level. The widespread recognition that South African industry was over-protected by the apartheid regime in pursuit of self-sufficiency, and the need for growth that is both faster and better adapted to the country's human resources, could be an important factor here. Indeed, the recent signals from the government suggests, if anything, an acceleration of the momentum towards trade liberalization, with ministers stating that tariffs may be reduced ahead of the programme agreed with GATT.

9.5 SOUTH AFRICA'S ROLE IN THE SOUTHERN AFRICAN REGION

Introduction

An implication of the political transition in South Africa is the new role seen for the country in the development of the Southern African subregion. In this area, as with domestic restructuring, expectations may be unrealistic. A senior official of a large bilateral aid agency said recently that with South Africa's joining of the Southern African Development Community (SADC), there are 'strong signals that the Southern Africa region is poised for tremendous economic growth and development'.[17] Even if this view is exaggeratedly optimistic, South Africa is clearly important in the sub-region. It dominates regional production, especially of manufactures, energy and financial services; it dominates regional trade; and it dominates regional transport. The country has been given the finance and investment portfolio within SADC, with responsibility for investigating the co-ordination of monetary fiscal and exchange rate policies within SADC countries. Because South Africa's domestic policies inevitably have consequences for the economies of the other SADC members, whose combined GDP is around one-fifth that of South Africa, a greater measure of policy co-ordination may reduce the impact of South African domestic policy on its neighbours.

The reintegration of South Africa into the region actually poses a dilemma. South African manufacturing firms are felt by other regional manufacturers to be a threat. All countries in the region are afraid of being swamped by South African trade and investment, or of losing foreign investment to South Africa. On the other hand, there is a possibility that South Africa could act as a catalyst for regional growth, being both a large market for regionally produced goods (including manufactures) and a reliable (though not necessarily cheaper) source of imports that is closer than Europe and North America. Access to the South African market should provide both competition (which should improve efficiency in production) and opportunities to gain from economies of scale. It is interesting to note that those countries in the region with the highest GNP per head (apart from South Africa itself) are the smaller neighbours that have a customs union agreement with South Africa, and therefore no protection from South African trade and investment.

South Africa's economic role in the region will make itself felt in the movement of commodities between countries (trade), in the flows of factors of production across country borders (investment and migration) and in changes in its real bilateral exchange rates with the currencies of neighbouring countries. There is not the space in this chapter to consider all of these issues. We shall therefore not examine labour flows, expect to say that South Africa is resistant to absorbing unskilled labour from its neighbours because of its own severe unemployment problems, and is likely to tighten procedures for closing its borders to illegal immigrants. At the same time, there is a brain-drain from the rest of Africa to South Africa, which is resented by both African governments and South African blacks, but not opposed by South African employers, who are anxious to raise the ratio of black to white employees and who need to ease the skilled labour shortage. This section focuses on trade and investment flows between South Africa and the rest of the region, and on the exchange rate, which not only influences these flows, but also transfers changes in South Africa's domestic economic policies to these countries indirectly.

Background: South Africa's Economic Size Relative to its Neighbours

South Africa is very large relative to its neighbours. Valued at 1995 exchange rates, its GDP is four times that of the other SADC countries combined, and almost half that of the whole of subSaharan African. It is responsible for almost two-thirds of the region's exports (and this excludes trade between members of the Southern African Customs Union (SACU,[18] which is also dominated by South Africa), and its purchases about half of the region's imports (again excluding intra-SACU trade). It generates and consumes more electricity than the rest of the sub-region combined, and in fact, has the capacity to generate electricity for the whole of Southern Africa. It supplies rolling stock to many of its neighbours (and has recently been invited to take over on a management basis the railways of Zaire, and possibly Mozambique and Zambia). Durban is reputed to be the largest port in the Southern hemisphere and Johannesburg is the continent's largest financial centre.

This is not to imply that South Africa does not have severe internal economic problems that need to be addressed: extreme inequality in the distribution of income and wealth; insufficient formal-sector job creation; inefficiency in (some) production; comparatively low productivity (high wages) skills shortages and poor basic education; weak income innovation; among others. The point is that South Africa's dominance in the region means that its influence is inevitably felt, and that South Africa's prosperity is important for regional welfare generally.

Regional Trade

South Africa's size relative to its neighbours has important implications for regional trade. First, the relationship is asymmetric in that South Africa is much more important to the region than the reverse. Secondly, South Africa runs, and will continue to run, a substantial trade surplus with each of its regional trading partners individually (as well as collectively). These points can be demonstrated by looking at exports and imports in terms of $US (see Tables 9.7 and 9.8). (Note that Mauritius, which joined SADC in 1995, is excluded from these tables.)

In Table 9.7, the trade flows recorded for South Africa are, in fact, SACU figures (including the exports and imports of the smaller SACU members to the rest of the world and excluding trade between South Africa and its SACU partners). This overstates South Africa's trade some-

Table 9.7 Exports and imports of goods and services of SADC countries (excl. Mauritius) ($USm.)

	1980	*1985*	*1990*	*1992*
(a) Exports				
Angola	n.a.	2 430	4 003	3 455
Botswana	748	889	2 251	3 090
Lesotho	364	283	555	614
Malawi	315	283	457	434
Mozambique	505	224	370	362
Namibia	1 753	965	1 431	1 264
South Africa	25 680	16 523	23 628	23 432
Swaziland	451	272	806	n.a.
Tanzania	770	437	548	555
Zambia	1 625	868	1 342	1 221
Zimbabwe	1 729	1 453	2 040	1 847
Total	*33 940*	*24 627*	*37 431*	*36 274*
(b) Imports				
Angola	n.a.	2 256	4 161	3 997
Botswana	954	847	2 388	1 507
Lesotho	482	369	776	954
Malawi	638	444	604	637
Mozambique	850	599	1 161	1 216
Namibia	1 887	1 094	1 676	1 178
South Africa	19 246	11 470	17 477	18 549
Swaziland	659	366	880	n.a.
Tanzania	1 421	1 178	1 667	1 510
Zambia	1 986	1 239	1 701	2 694
Zimbabwe	1 900	1 548	2 296	2 763
Total	*30 014*	*2 410*	*34 787*	*35 005*

what, but not significantly (by less than 5 per cent). Recently South Africa has started to record its own trade, treating the other SACU countries as foreign, but these data are not yet available. The South African figures are therefore included to demonstrate the order of magnitude of that country's trade flow relative to other countries in the region. In Table 9.8 the calculations excluding non-South African SACU trade and including intra-SACU trade have been made. Note that South Africa's exports to all other SADC countries are less than 15 per cent its total exports, despite South Africa's being a major exporter to the region.

Table 9.8 South Africa's trade with SADC countries in 1992 ($USm)

	Exports	*Imports*
Angola	121	n.a
Botswana	1112	56
Lesotho	260	15
Malawi	232	44
Mozambique	225	17
Namibia	365	133
Swaziland	200	78
Tanzania	9	3
Zambia	369	15
Zimbabwe	518	253
Total	*3409*	*615*

Sources: World Debt Tables 1994–94; national statistics; Imani Development (Harare) (1994).

Trade within the customs union is heavily orientated towards South Africa (although less so in the case of Botswana's exports). The smaller SACU members purchase about 10 per cent of South African's exports (by value); this is in the region of 75 per cent (in the case of Swaziland) to 95 per cent (in the case of Lesotho) of the total imports of these countries. With the exception of Botswana, the other members of SADC trade very little with the smaller SACU countries. In fact, this is more or less true for all SADC countries; they all trade comparatively very little with each other, but substantially with South Africa. Intra-SADC trade, excluding South Africa, is about 4 per cent of total SADC trade, while trade with South Africa is 25 per cent of total SADC trade. Even these proportions are understated, because they do not take into account informal trade: holiday-makers who return home with carfuls of goods purchased in South Africa and small traders who exchange handicrafts or labour for goods in South Africa were estimated to have been responsible for $US30m. of additional South African exports in 1990. Illegal trade is also not recorded. There are repeated report of trucks travelling north from South Africa, as far as Angola and Zaire, laden with goods to be exchanged for dollars, oil and other commodities.

South Africa's penetration of the Southern Africa region (officially) increased over 250 per cent in the period 1988–94, and its trade surplus with the region is growing. On its own this is not a problem, if the other countries of the region can finance this deficit by exporting elsewhere or with aid. Furthermore, since the value of the rand as fallen, the increased volume of exports from South Africa has occurred at lower $US values, providing a terms-of-trade gain for regional economies. Part of this considerable growth represents the recording of trade that was un(der)-reported during the sanctions period, when African countries did not want to be seen to be trading too freely with South Africa. Nevertheless, intra-regional trade is actually still understated, because it excludes trade within SACU (which is effectively treated by South Africa as domestic rather than foreign trade).

South Africa's trade regime has exacerbated the difficulties faced by its neighbours in gaining access to its significantly larger market. Although South African rates of effective protection are not particularly high for many goods,[19] is selectivity created a tariff structure characterized by large differences in tariff levels between and within sectors. Consequently, the moderate *average* level of protection in South Africa does not necessarily imply that the countries of the region have not faced a high tariff wall. In fact, the average nominal rate applying to consumer goods has been 32.1 per cent, which is ten percentage points higher than the average for all manufacturing (McCarthy, 1992). Table 9.9 shows nominal and effective rates of protection in 1990 for some products that are or could be produced in the region. In some of these industries, protection made penetration of the South African market without preferential access impossible. Moreover, South Africa has not hesitated to erect tariff barriers against neighbouring countries when their exports have been seen to threaten South Africa's interest, even against countries within SACU (car imports from Botswana in 1995) or in violation of a trade agreement (textile imports from Zimbabwe in 1992). South Africa's export regime has also been of concern to its neighbours, which were afraid that freer trade with South African would expose them to subsidized exports; incentives under the GEIS are payable on exports to all countries except the SACU partners.

These problems are now, in the main, temporary. South Africa has signed an agreement under the GATT that virtually eliminates QRs, reduces tariffs and phases out the GEIS. South Africa's offer in the Uruguay Round was the raising of the proportion of tariffs bound by the GATT from less than 20 per cent to just over 50 per cent and an increase in the percentage of duty-free lines to over one-quarter (GATT, 1993). The tariff reduction programme began in January 1995. Despite talk of accelerated and reciprocal tariff reduction within regional structures, preferential arrangements through SADC are very unlikely. In order to secure guaranteed access under predictable rules to the South African markets, neighbouring countries should look to securing comprehensive bilateral agreements with South Africa (Zimbabwe has already begun negotiation for the extension of the current outdated bilateral agreement with South Africa).

Table 9.9 Nominal and effective protection of selected South African industries, 1990

	Nominal protection	*Effective protection*
Pottery, china, earthenware	38	421
Clothing, excluding footwear	75	239
Knitwear: clothing	87	99
Textiles	40	94
Footwear	35	87
Knitwear: other	58	235
Carpets and rugs	30	161
Bakery products	25	139
Tobacco products	40	56
Non-alcoholic beverages	18	32
Furniture	25	44
Wood and wood products	20	37

Sources: IDC Annex C (1990); McCarthy (1992).

The trend of increasing South African penetration of the region does pose a threat to South Africa's competitors in Southern Africa, particularly Zimbabwe. Although Zimbabwe is a major supplier to the SADC countries, its trade with them did not grow much during the 1980s, while South Africa's trade in the region did. South Africa is now aggressively seeking markets in Africa, and is tapping into donor-funded projects, and region competitors will have to beat South African producers in terms of price, quality and reliability in order to win markets that may have been easier to gain during the 1980s. Zimbabwe firms say that it is difficult for them to compete in and with South Africa on quality. This is the result of a tightly closed economy for 30 years, which slowed technological advancement and capital replacement, and in many cases eliminated cheaper, better quality imports.[20]

It does not follow that South Africa will swamp regional markets. Regional competitors have some cost advantages over South Africa: cheaper labour; lower transport costs to countries to the north; and a better knowledge of local conditions, which reduces information costs. Obviously South African competition will most affect uncompetitive, inefficient or backward sectors, but some exporters in Botswana and Zimbabwe are already competing effectively in SACU countries, where South Africa holds the advantage of proximity and an integrated goods market. Moreover, strong post-sanctions demand for South African exports, together with increased domestic demand as the economy begins to show signs of growth, means that South Africa is hitting capacity constraints. There are therefore limits to the expansion of South African exporters in the short to medium term.

The asymmetry of the trade relationship between South Africa and its neighbours does not mean that the region is of no significance to South Africa. It is particularly important as a market for manufactured exports that may be less competitive in European, American or Asian markets, but which can compete in Africa because proximity reduces delivery times and affords better access to parts and servicing technicians. The range of South Africa's export to Africa is virtually as wide as the range of South African products, the most important being invisibles (services), food, steel, domestic appliances, building materials and paper products. In fact, almost two-thirds of South Africa's manufactured exports are sold to other African countries. For this reason, South Africa exporters are interest in the maintenance of trade links with the region, and South African policy-makers are anxious not to alienate neighbouring countries.

There is an additional reason why South Africa is treading cautiously and diplomatically within the region. There is a strong group in the government that is keen for South Africa to be seen as an African nation, rather than as an aspiring members of the so-called Western group of nations. This school of thought sees future relations with Africa as important and is willing, for example, to deal with Europe within African structures. This will be particularly important if Europe scraps Lomé and chooses to negotiate with regional structures.

Numerous factors will influence future trade between South Africa and the rest of Southern Africa. First, many of the regional countries are pursuing programmes of trade liberalization, usually with World Bank support. Although *not* under pressure from the World Bank, South Africa has eliminated the possibility of reversing its liberalization by signing an agreement under the GATT. The effects of unilateral liberalization taking place in several countries in the region will be to increase trade flows between them (as well as with the rest of the world).

Second, peace is now restored in Mozambique, which not only has implications for the region's transport routes,[21] but will also increase trade as Mozambique begins the process of reconstruction, funded by bilateral and multilateral aid donors. The restoration of peace in Angola, a potentially rich country, will also provide landlocked countries with closer access to a port and will increase the volume of intra-regional trade.

Third, South Africa's political transformation will improve that country's ability to receive trade delegations from and send them to the neighbouring countries and makes it possible for South Africa to tender for aid-financed projects in the region. This implies that South Africa's trade within Southern Africa may not yet have reached its potential, despite its being very large.

Fourth, once South Africa's relationship with the European Union is resolved, it may provide an opportunity for South Africa inputs to qualify for Lomé cumulation rules, even if South Africa is not granted full Lomé status. In other worlds, input of South African goods would count as 'local content' in the production of exports to Europe from neighbouring countries under the Lomé Convention.

The cumulative result of these factors means that South Africa's penetration of the region is likely to increase in the short to medium term. These factors are likely to be of far more importance than South Africa's joining SADC. Apart from SACU, African attempts at regional integration are notoriously unsuccessful at promoting regional trade. At any rate, the regional arrangements are a muddle (see Appendix 9.B). Their resolution is important as a tidying-up exercise, but will have little effect on promoting trade.

The factors that might offset the tendency to increased regional trade with South Africa are the lack of investment in South Africa, which means that South Africa is reaching capacity constraints, and the possibility of resentment at bilateral trade imbalances by the governments of smaller countries.

Regional Investment

South Africa's large trade surplus with the region will need to be offset by some flows in the opposite direction. In itself a continuing trade deficit with South Africa is not a problem if the smaller economies are running trade surpluses with other partners (or receiving aid that allows them to purchase from South Africa). However, the deficit with South Africa is growing and, for political reasons if not economic ones, there will need to be reverse flows. The freer movement of labour is one solution but, as stated above, this is not an option for the South African government. Alternatively, capital will need to flow from South Africa to its neighbours, either in the form of direct investment by South African firms (or multinational corporations based in South Africa), or in the form of finance. The latter will imply an extension of the South African financial system to its neighbours, developing *de facto* a monetary zone centring around the rand.

Currently, what little intra-regional investment there is occurs exclusively from South Africa outwards. Even during the period of tight capital controls, it was possible for South African investment to occur in the region. Historically, this was dominated by mining investment, although more recently it has occurred in other sectors, notably financial services, brewing and construction. Construction companies are particularly interested in positioning themselves to take advantage of their eligibility to tender for projects funded by multilateral donor organizations. In other sectors the primary objective of South African investment in Africa has been to obtain lucrative contracts, rather than to establish manufacturing concerns; South Africans are as nervous about investing in the rest of Africa as they are about domestic investment. An exception is Mozambique, where access to complementary agricultural raw materials has prompted large investments, usually in joint ventures with local entrepreneurs.

No exchange controls exist between SACU members, and members cooperate in exchange control procedures with outside parties. The rules for outward investments in Southern African countries tend to be more leniently applied than elsewhere, although any project that is demonstrated to contribute to SACU (South Africa) exports, or to substitute for strategic imports, has usually received approval. All profits generated offshore must be repatriated.

Flows of investment within the region are likely to be influenced by several factors.

(1) If South Africa signs an agreement with the European Union allowing its products to qualify as inputs to regional exports under the Lomé Convention, this will increase the incentive for South African firms to invest in other countries in the region in last-stage manufacturing, using South African inputs.
(2) South African firms wishing to produce in countries with which they currently trade may take the opportunity to purchase enterprises currently being sold off by the public sector under World Bank-supported privatization programmes. One of the attractions of this option lies in the fact that many public enterprises are currently monopolies.
(3) Direct investment from outside the region, to the extent that it is made in Southern Africa, is likely to be made in South Africa rather than the smaller countries.

The cumulative effect of these factors is that cross-border investment is more likely to be South African than to come from anywhere else. The flows are therefore unlikely to be significant in relation to the trade imbalances. Ironically, if these flows did become large, they would likely cause political resentment at the increased foreign ownership of domestic assets, a contributing factor to the nationalizations of the 1960s and 1970s.

Both trade and investment are hindered by exchange rate instability, and would therefore probably grow faster if more formal arrangements could be established to reduce the uncertainty associated with fluctuating exchange rates (Harvey and Hudson, 1993).

South Africa's Exchange Rate Policy and its Implication for Neighbouring Countries

South Africa adopted a more flexible and market-determined exchange rate regime in 1983. During the period 1981 to 1990, the value of the rand fell in real terms between 25 per cent and 45 per cent against the currencies of the major industrialized economies, and between 11 per cent and 35 per cent against the currencies of some East Asian countries. In sharp contrast to the real devaluations achieved against the industrialized countries, the rand was remarkably stable in real terms against the currencies of South Africa's main regional trading partners in the 1980s, generally appreciating modestly (9.1 per cent against the Botswana pula; 13.7 per cent against the Zimbabwe dollar over the period 1981 to 1990). The reason for this is that regional currencies track the rand because of the importance of South Africa for trade. However, the fluctuations of the rand have consequently carried costs for the neighbours by causing their currencies to fluctuate against those of other trading partners, especially in Europe and America *and Africa*, making other trade and investment more expensive.

Devaluations under structural adjustment programmes have exacerbated bilateral exchange rate instability between other regional trading partners. For example, when the Zimbabwe dollar was devalued in 1990/91, it virtually destroyed Botswana's textile sector (which has now recovered somewhat, but the costs were high).

In summary, then, the regional exchange rate arrangements are marked by long-term *real* stability of the rand against other currencies, with stable nominal rates with the Common Monetary Area and unstable nominal rates outside the CMA (except for Botswana).

Because of the asymmetry in their mutual relative importance as trading partners, it is unlikely that South Africa will ever achieve a competitive advantage in the region, other than very temporarily, through nominal devaluation (Harvey and Jenkins, 1994), while neighbouring countries may be able to devalue against the rand without fear of retaliation from South Africa.[22] For example, when Zimbabwe devalued in 1990 and again in 1991 as part of the structural adjustment programme, South Africa did not retaliate, because its exports to Zimbabwe were then less than 2.0 per cent of total exports. Increased competitiveness is at least partly responsible for the steady increase in Zimbabwe manufactured export to South Africa since 1991. Of course, as mentioned previously, no regional country trade exclusively with South Africa, and further falls in the value of the rand complicate the question of choosing the external value of regional currencies. Following a falling rand adds to inflationary pressures which, if not contained, erode any real exchange rate advantage achieved by devaluation.

There appears to be a compelling case for greater exchange rate co-operation in Southern Africa. The range of options extend from regular consolation (as at Basle for Western European countries) to full monetary integration. The best route would be to begin with regular consolation in order to increase mutual awareness of the effects of domestic policy on neighbouring economies. This would also defuse speculation about devaluations when central bank governors meet, if they do it regularly. Furthermore, there is greater role for the international financial institutions in taking account of the external effects of measures imposed as part of aid conditions.

9.6 CONCLUSIONS

South Africa has experienced not so much a trade liberalization episode as a gradual shift of trade policy in a more liberal direction, which may now accelerate with the advent of majority rule and the removal of international sanctions. Historically, South Africa has had a high level of import protection for many decades, and this remains the case. Import protection is highly differentiated and, under apartheid, was used as an instrument for controlling import dependence. The complex structure of import protection also means that the system is open to lobbying by sectional interests: an industry that feels itself to be under serious threat from import competition would expect a sympathetic hearing from the government. Export subsidies have been the principal instrument of trade liberalization in terms of reducing anti-export bias, and it is possible that they have contributed to the fall in the relative price of non-gold exports, which has been greater than can be attributed to other identifiable factors. Trade volumes, however, have remained remarkably close to what would have been predicted on past trends (after taking price and income effects into account).

The present situation could be summarized in the statement that, up until now, South Africa has taken no more than the preliminary steps towards a more fundamental trade liberalization. Announced future plans include a phased reduction of imports tariffs and the phased elimination of export subsidies, which will be replaced by a system of import duty drawbacks. All remaining quantitative restrictions on imports were abolished in December 1994. These measures still leave effective protection in the manufacturing sector at a level that is relatively high by OECD standards, although moderate compared to most developing countries. Rather more important is that dispersion of protection across sectors will not be greatly reduced, since six different tariff level are envisaged, and sensitive sectors are being allowed to phase in the new tariffs over longer than the standard five-year period.

This suggests that the South African government is hesitating to take the risk of a move to a much more uniform structure of import tariffs. Current plans effectively continue the cautious approach of the apartheid regime, and show signs of an acceleration of trade liberalization. There is not, however, a radical break with the past as has occurred in some other middle-income countries with a history of import-substituting strategy (for example, Mexico, Chile, Poland and the former Czechoslovakia) in opting for a much less discriminatory import regime and accepting the transitional costs in the expectation of making long-term efficiency gains. At present the government's energy is concentrated on overcoming the legacy of apartheid, and trade liberalization may become an increasingly attractive policy option because of its positive impact on the demand for unskilled labour and the anticipation that it will generate faster growth.

APPENDIX 9A

Table 9A.1 Evolution of trade policy in South Africa, 1925–95

Year(s)	**Policy change(s), important commissions, relevant event(s)**
1925–72	*The period of import-substitution industrialization (ISI)*
1925	Adoption of ISI with the Customs Tariff and Excise Duty Amendment Act
1948	Introduction of QRs
1958	Viljoen Commission recommends continued ISI, but using tariffs rather than QRs or subsidies
1969	SA government announces its intention to lift QRs under pressure from GATT and the IMF, but does nothing.
1972–83	*The first trade liberalization episode*
1972	Reynders Commission recommends export promotion.
	Export incentive measures are introduced.

1972–76	Some relaxations of QRs
1975–79	The rand is devalued
1978	Further assistance to exporters is introduced, in line with the Van Huyssteen Committee's proposals.
1979–80	Rand appreciates sharply
1983–91	*The second trade liberalization episode*
1983	The Kleu Study Group recommends a move away from ISI. The dual exchange rate system is abolished. The external value of the rand falls significantly.
1983–85	The reduction of QRs is resumed.
1985	Government White Paper recommends a dual approach to industrial policy: ISI and export promotion. Debit crisis; dual exchange rate system re-introduced. Substantial import surcharges introduced.
1987	BTI begins to move proactively towards trade policy reform.
1989	QR removal continues. Structural adjustment export incentives are introduced for clothing, textiles, automobiles and automobile components.
1990	General export incentives scheme (GEIS) is introduced. The phasing out of the import surcharges begins (not completed).
1991	An accelerated depreciation tax scheme is introduced.
Current	*The 'third' trade liberalization episode*
1994	The conversion of QRs to tariff is completed
1995	Import surcharges are eliminated. Tariff reduction in line with GATT requirements begins. The financial rand is abolished. Negotiations with the European Union over trade preferences commence.

APPENDIX 9B EXISTING REGIONAL TRADE ARRANGEMENTS

The Southern African Customs Union (SACU)

SACU was established in 1969 by Botswana, Lesotho, South Africa and Swaziland. Namibia become a member on achieving independence in 1990. Tariff revenues are pooled and shared according to a revenue formula, which has a considerable compensation element paid out by South Africa to the other, smaller members. All members except Botswana are also members of a common currency area. Although considered a success in terms of trade creation between the members, by the end of the 1970s it was apparent that all parties had reservation about various aspects of the agreement, and since 1982 the possible renegotiation of the agreement has been discussed (Mwase and Maasdorp, 1995).

The Preferential Trade Area for Eastern and Southern Africa States (PTA)

The PTA was established in 1983, and by 1993, 19 countries (see Table 9B.1) had joined the grouping. The original mandate of the PTA was quite large. Its objectives were to promote trade among member countries and to promote development in industry, agriculture, human resources and communications within and between members. Action has focused on trade promotion, the main instruments of which have been tariff preferences and the establishment of the PTA Clearing House. The achievements have been very limited.

COMESA

In 1993 a new treaty was drawn up by PTA members[23] establishing the Community of Eastern and Southern African States (COMESA). The intention is to create a free-trade area that will become a customs union with a common external tariff within 10 years and eventually evolve into a common market. Once the treaty has been ratified by 11 of its potential 22 members, the PTA will cease to exist. Member countries will follow the PTA programme of tariff reduction, although the COMESA treaty does contain a variety of new features, one of the most important being a provision for sanctions to be applied for non-compliance (including suspension or expulsion). There is nothing to suggest that the COMESA treaty will prove any more successful than the PTA arrangements, because trade potential between member countries is low and because member governments are no more willing to allow COMESA rules and promises to override their domestic interest than they were to submit to PTA requirements.

The Southern African Development Community (SADC)

SADC evolved out of the Southern African Development Coordination Conference (SADCC) established in 1980. The latter's objectives were to reduce the dependence of the region on the rest of the world (especially South Africa) and to promote regional co-operation in development projects. SADCC was never intended as a regional trade arrangement.

It worked rather well in bringing regional political leaders together and as a means for procuring foreign aid. The SADC Treaty (1992), however, is directly concerned with trade integration between its 10 members, reductions of tariff and non-tariff barriers to intra-SADC trade, greater co-ordination of external tariff, the creation of regional infrastructural authorities, and freer movement of capital and people. South Africa joined SADC in 1994.

The Cross-Border Initiative (CBI)

The CBI is not another independent attempt at regional harmonization. It is an attempt to address the regional dimension of trade liberalization and deregulation, which, it is argued, is missing from national structural adjustment programmes. The initiative was launched in July 1990 at the Maastricht Conference on Africa. Its objectives is to promote regional trade, factor mobility, and investment opportunities in the context of generally low trade barriers *vis-à-vis* the rest of the world. Several bilateral and multilateral donors (including the European Union, the IMF, the World Bank and the African Development Bank) have actively endorsed the initiative, as have 10 African countries. South Africa has participated in the discussions. Although there is a common plan of action, it is recognized that each participating country is at a different stage with respect to its trade liberalization and efforts at regional harmonization. The common plan of action recommends the elimination of all intra-regional trade barriers by the end of 1996 and the establishment of a common external tariff by the end of 1988. However, the initiative concentrates on regulatory impediments to regional trade and investment, recommending that needs to be done in order to increase cross-border trade and investments flows. Many of its recommendations are compatible with the aims of the PTA, SADC or national adjustment programmes, which it is not intending to replace (CBI, 1992).

Conclusion

The regional arrangements are a muddle. All members of the SADC, expect Botswana and South Africa also belong to the PTA. Eleven of these countries are also signatories of the CBI (which aims to promote trade and investment, but is not a formal grouping). South Africa is the dominant member of SACU, all the smaller members of which also belong to both the PTA and the SADC. Zimbabwe has bilateral trade agreements with three of the five SACU countries (South Africa, Botswana and Namibia) and the SACU countries have a free-trade agreement with Malawi. The overlapping memberships are recorded in Table B.1. The contradictions inherent in dual (or more) memberships have not yet been addressed.

Table 9B.1 Membership of regional trade groupings, 1995

Potential COMESA	*PTA*	*SADC*	*SACU*	*CBI*
Angola	X	X		
Botswana		X	X	
Burundi	X			
Comoros	X			X
Djibouti	X			
Eritrea				
Ethiopia	X			
Kenya	X			X
Lesotho	X	X	X	
Madagascar				
Malawi	X	X		X
Mauritius	X	X		X
Mozambique	X	X		
Namibia	X	X	X	X
Rwanda	X			X
Seychelles				
Somalia	X			
South Africa		X	X	obs
Sudan	X			
Swaziland	X	X	X	X
Tanzania	X	X		X
Uganda	X			X
Zambia	X	X		X
Zimbabwe	X	X		X

Note: obs = observer status.

Notes

1. Of course, revenue duties imposed previously must have had a protective effect, and some limited protective duties had existed in the former states prior to Union in 1910 (Botha, 1973).
2. The system of import control was initiated as a response to a serious balance-of-payments crisis in 1948, because of the restriction on tariff policy that had followed the entry of South Africa into the GATT negotiations in 1947. The system of import licensing was extended and formalized in 1949, and maintained until the early 1980s. In contrast to the active policy of import licensing, South Africa adopted a relatively passive policy with respect to exchange rate changes and tariff adjustments through the 1950s and 1960s (Lachman, 1974).

3. This was increasingly the case during the 1950s and 1960s as many developing countries adopted strategies of import substitution. The prevailing wisdom was based on post-war arguments supporting export pessimism, especially with respect to primary commodities (Prebisch, 1959; Nurske, 1959), and the expected future benefits of protecting infant industries.
4. A later (1978) study by Merle and Paul Holden estimated average rates of effective protection in 1964 as 15 per cent on consumer goods, 6 per cent on intermediate goods and 2 per cent on capital goods. This study, however, excluded the protective effect of QRs.
5. Although there has been a sectoral decline in overall import penetration, the level of import penetration in the crucial sectors of capital and transport equipment has remained extremely high, and has not declined over time, despite high levels of protection of these industrial sectors (see Kahn, 1987).
6. Empirical estimates of the contribution to growth show that import substitution was an important source of growth up to the mid-1950s during the 'easy' stages of ISI; thereafter, given the size of the domestic market, further import substitution in capital goods did not drive growth (Scheepers, 1969).
7. Under pressure from the GATT and the IMF, the government had announced its intention to lift QRs in 1969. When the GATT made provision for unbinding tariffs, QRs were gradually, although only partially, relaxed between 1972 and 1976 (Hirsch, 1993). This process was resumed in 1983.
8. The rand did rise sharply in value during the gold boom of 1979–80. This, and the combined effect of world recession in the early 1980 and the boom in South Africa in 1979–81, contrived to reduce exports, lending weight to the view that the exchange rate and the level of demand, were more important in determining the level of exports than the export incentives offered in the 1970s.
9. Applications for tariff relief are considered by the Board of Trade and Industry, which operates with substantial autonomy from the rest of the Department of Trade and Industry. Reference prices are often ruling Western European prices, implying that almost by definition countries exporting to South Africa at prices below those of firms in Western Europe or North America are treated as if they were dumping. The formula duties became less important over time, as the formulas were not adjusted for inflation.
10. According to a report on tariff protection policy published in 1990 by the Industrial Development Corporation the revenue from import surcharges in 1988 amounted to 7 per cent of the import bill; tariff revenue was 5 per cent of the value of imports (IDC, 1990).
11. Note that the GEIS payments were tax-free, at least until the 1994 budget.
12. It has been recognized that direct cash subsidies are unacceptable in terms of the GATT. There have been suggestions of additional benefits for small and medium exporters, like pre-shipment finance, research and development aid, and assistance with promotion and marketing.
13. Under Section 37E of the Income Tax Act, approved beneficiation projects that add value of at least 35 per cent to inputs may apply for advanced depreciation.
14. As Belli *et al.* (1993) point out, no statistic captures the variation in the

South African tariff schedule. All tariff rates above 400 per cent actually apply to only 26 tariff lines, and many of these products appear between products with significantly lower tariffs in the schedule. Sometimes one gram per square metre difference in the weight of a fabric can mean the difference between a tariff of 1389 per cent or 150 per cent.

15. During the period 1981 to 1990, the value of the rand fell in real terms between 25 per cent and 45 per cent against the currencies of the major industrial countries; and between 11 per cent and 35 per cent against the currencies of some East Asian countries. This contributed substantially to the improved competitiveness of South African exports. Note, however, that the rand did not depreciated at all against the currencies of its most important African trading partners (in fact, the rand generally appreciated against these currencies).
16. In 1994 the clothing and textiles industries, together with the South African Clothing and Textile Workers' Union agreed to accelerate the tariff reduction programme (from 12 years to 10) in exchange for R4.5bn in government aid to help with training and new investment. This agreement, known as the Swart plan, was jettisoned by the government when the Clothing Federation adopted a revised plan, proposing a two-year tariff elimination for textiles, claiming that it could then create another 65 000 jobs for very little capital expenditure.
17. For a summary of the membership of regional groupings, see Appendix B.
18. The South African Department of Customs and Excise records trade information for trade between the SACU (Botswana, Lesotho, Namibia, South Africa and Swaziland) and the rest of the world, without differentiating by member according to final destination or origin. It does not record trade between SACU members.
19. If 30 per cent is regarded as a moderate level of effective protection, over half of 71 subsectors, responsible for 54 per cent of value added in manufacturing, experience effective levels of protection of less than 30 per cent (IDC, annex C, 1990). Nominal rates of protection average 22 per cent.
20. Although there are considerable inefficiencies in South African manufacturing (and agriculture) after decades of protection, South African's response to the debt crisis in particular and trade sanctions more generally was to begin to reduce its anti-export bias and to attempt to become internationally more competitive.
21. South Africa is planning a large road corridor from Johannesburg to Maputo, and there is talk of eventually extending this to Gabon.
22. In Botswana, maintaining a stable real exchange rate against the rand has been a matter of deliberate policy. Despite having large budget and balance of payments surpluses at the time, Botswana has devalued on a number of occasions in order to prevent a worsening of its competitive position.
23. Additional signatories are Eritrea, Madagascar and Seychelles.

References

AHI/SAFCI/SEIFSA (Afrikaanse Handelsinstituut; SA Federated Chamber of Industries; Steel and Engineering Industries Federation of SA) (1977) *Survey of Gross Import Substitution Potential for South African Manufacturing Industry 1975–80* (Johannesburg).

Bell, T. (1992) 'Should South Africa further liberalize its foreign trade?', Economic Trends working paper no. 16.

Belli, P., M. Finger and A. Ballivan (1993) 'South Africa: a review of trade policies', World Bank Informal discussion papers on *Aspects of the South African Economy*, no. 4.

BTI (Board of Trade and Industries) (1931) 'The cost of living inquiry', report no. 125 (October).

Botha, D. J. J. (1973) 'On tariff policy: the formative years', *South African Journal of Economics*, **41**(4):321–35.

Central Statistical Services (CSS) (various issues) *Quarterly Bulletin of Statistics* (Pretoria).

Cross-Border Initiative, Eastern and Southern Africa and Indian Ocean (1992), Workshop to facilitate cross-border trade, investment and payments in Eastern and Southern Africa and the Indian Ocean. Report of the technical working groups published by the Commission of the European Communities.

Du Plooy, R. M. (1988) 'Productivity in South African industry', *South African Journal of Economics*, **56**(1):82–93.

Foroutan, F., C. Jenkins and C. Montenegro (1995) 'Regional trade preferences', in *Zimbabwe: consolidating the trade liberalization*, UNDP/World Bank Trade Expansion Program Country Report No.16 (Washington, DC: The World Bank).

GATT (General Agreement on Tariffs and Trade) (1993) *Trade Policy Review: South Africa*, vols 1 and 2. Geneva.

Greenaway, D., and C. Milner (1993) *The Fiscal Implications of Trade Policy Reform: Theory and Evidence*, UNDP/World Bank.

Harvey, C. and D. Hudson (1993), 'Post-apartheid regional financial and monetary cooperation', in B. Oden (ed.), *Southern Africa after Apartheid* (Uppsala: Scandinavian Institute of African Studies).

Harvey, C. and C. Jenkins (1994) 'The unorthodox response of the South African economy to changes in macroeconomic policy', in E. Bacha (ed.), *Economics in a Changing World*, vol. 4 (International Economic Association).

Hirsch, A. (1993) 'South African trade policy and its institutions', Industrial Strategy Project report, ch. 2.

Holden, M. G. (1988) 'The definition and calculations of real exchange rates: an application to South Africa', University of Natal Economic Research Unit, occasional paper no. 20.

Holden, M. G. (1990) 'The choice of trade strategy: past reflections and future prospects', in N. Nattrass and E. Ardington (eds), *The Political Economy of South Africa* (Cape Town: Oxford University Press).

Holden, M. G. (1992a) 'The high road to trade reform' *Indicator SA*, **10**(1):25–30.

Holden, M. G. (1992b) 'Trade reform: finding the right road', *South African Journal of Economics*, **60**(3):249–62.

Holden, M. G. (1992c) 'The structure and incidence of protection in South Africa', in P. Black and B. Dollery (eds), *Lending Issues in South African Microeconomics* (Southern Book Publishers).

Holden, M. G. and P. Holden (1975) 'An intertemporal calculation of effective rates of protection for South Africa', *South African Journal of Economics*, **43**(3):370–9.

Holden, M. G. and P. Holden (1978) 'Effective tariff protection and resource allocation: a non-parametric approach', *Review of Economics and Statistics*, **60**(2).

Holden, M. G. and S. B. Kahn (1990, unpublished) 'Foreign trade and balance of payments statistics in South Africa', paper presented to the Symposium on *Aspects of the Production and Use of Social-Economic Statistics* (Durban, May).

Imani Development (1994) 'Southern Africa: a region in transition. Presentation of trade and investments issues for Southern Africa', mimeo.

IDC (Industrial Development Corporation) (1990) *Ondersoek na die tarief beskermingsbeleid: ontleding van die tariefstuktur*, analytical document and five annexes (Sandton).

ISP (Industrial Strategy Project) (1993) 'A framework for industrial revival in South Africa', mimeo.

Jenkins, C. and W. Naudé (1995) 'The case for reciprocity in South African-European trade relations', *Development Southern Africa* 13(1), pp. 17–30.

Kahn, S. B. (1987) 'Import penetration and import demand in the South African economy', *South African Journal of Economics*, **55**(3):238–48.

Kleu Report (1983) *Report of the Study Group on Industrial Development Strategy* (Pretoria: Government Printer).

Lachman, D. (1974) 'Import restrictions and exchange rates', *South African Journal of Economics*, **42**(1):25–42.

Levy, B. (1992) 'How can South African manufacturing efficiently create employment? An analysis of the impact of trade and industrial policy', *Informal Discussion Papers on Aspects of the Economy of South Africa* (World Bank).

Lewis, S. (1987) 'Economic realities in Southern Africa (or, one hundred million futures)', IDS Discussion Paper no. 232, (Institute of Development Studies).

Little, I., R. N. Cooper, W. M. Corden and S. Rajapatirana (1993) *Boom, Crisis and Adjustment: the macroeconomic experience of developing countries* (Oxford University Press).

Lumby, A. B. (1990) 'Foreign trade and economic growth: during the inter-war years', *South African Journal of Economic History*, **5**(2):61–82.

McCarthy, C. (1992) 'South Africa as a co-operative partner in Southern African trade and investment', paper prepared for conference on regional economic integration organised by the Southern African Foundation for Economic Research (Harare).

MERG (Macroeconomic Research Group) (1993) *Making democracy work: a framework for macroeconomic policy in South Africa*, (Bellville: Centre for Development Studies).

Meth, C. E. (1990) 'Capital goods, "dependence" and appropriated technology', in N. Nattrass and E. Ardington (eds), *The Political Economy of South Africa* (Cape Town: Oxford University Press).

Mwase, N. and G. Maasdorp (1995) 'The Southern African Customs Union', paper prepared for the AERC conference on regional integration and trade liberalization in SubSaharan Africa, (Harare, March).
Nurske, R. (1959) *Patterns of Trade and Development*, Wicksell Lectures (Stockholm; Almguist & Wicksell).
Oden, B. (1993) *Southern Africa after Apartheid* (Uppsala: Scandinavian Institute of African Studies).
Prebisch, R. (1959) 'Commercial policy in the underdeveloped countries', *American Economic Review, Paper and Proceedings*, pp. 251–5.
Ratcliffe, A. E. (1975) 'Export policy in perspective', *South African Journal of Economics*, **43**(1):74–91.
Reynders, H. J. J. (1975) 'Export status and strategy', *South African Journal of Economics*, **43**(1):123–31.
RSA (Republic of South Africa) (1972) *Report of the Commission of Inquiry into the Export Trade of the Republic of South Africa*, Rp 69/72 (Pretoria: Government Printer).
RSA (Republic of South Africa) (1985) *White Paper on Industrial Development Strategy* (Pretoria: Government Printer).
Scheepers, C. (1969) 'The effect of import substitution on the volume and structure of South Africa's imports, 1926/27–1963/64', *Finance and Trade Review.*
World Bank (1993) *World Development Report* (Washington DC: World Bank).

10 Trade Liberalization in Zambia 1970–95*

Flora Musonda and Christopher Adam

10.1 INTRODUCTION

The 20 years following the onset of Zambia's economic crisis in 1974 witnessed two major trade liberalization episodes. The first lasted from 1983 to 1987 and was undertaken by the government of President Kaunda. As we shall discuss in this chapter, these reforms were not macro-compatible, principally because they were ultimately not credible. The second episode commenced with the re-opening of negotiations with the IMF in 1989 and the resurrection of earlier reforms. These were embraced in 1991 by the newly-elected MMD (Movement for Multi-Party Democracy) government of President Chiluba, and were strengthened by Zambia's ratification of the PTA/COMESA agreements on trade liberalization and regional integration. At the time of writing, the post-1989 reforms remain in place. While the reforms are compatible and credible, in the sense that there is no evidence of widespread hedging activity on the part of the private sector, weaknesses in the supply-side response to liberalization threaten to undermine the reforms.

The two liberalization episodes are separated by a sharp policy reversal that lasted from May 1987 until mid-1989 as Zambia attempted to pursue its own independent adjustment strategy outside the auspices of the IMF and World Bank. The policy reversal fully offset all the gains achieved in the 1983–7 period. It not only returned the economy to its pre-reform configuration, it also had quite profound effects on the structure of the second liberalization programme and on its credibility.

This case-study is based loosely on a four-phase partition:

* We acknowledge the support of Dr Mananga Ndulu in assisting in data collection in Zambia in 1995. We also acknowledge the co-operation of the Ministry of Finance and Economic Development, the European Union, and David Bevan for allowing the second author to draw on work done under the auspices of the CSAE/Government of Zambia project *Macroeconomic Modelling and Policy Analysis in Zambia*.

(1) the period up to 1985 and the emergence of a quota-ridden 'endogenous' trade policy characterized by a strong anti-trade bias;
(2) the implementation of trade and exchange rate liberalization during the period 1983–9;
(3) the reversal of the 1983–9 liberalization; and
(4) the current reform programme begun in 1989.

The process of liberalization can be characterized quite simply. The principal instrument of trade policy in Zambia and, throughout most of the period since Independence, the principal determinant of protection, has been the exchange rate regime. The tariff structure has remained relatively unchanged over the 30 years of Zambia's modern history, changing only twice during the entire period. The first change was the development of a relatively anti-trade tariff policy that evolved up to 1975, and the second was the process of liberalization started in 1984. This tariff reform was effectively suspended (but not reversed) during the 'growth from own resources' period of 1987–9 and then brought to a conclusion in 1992–4 with a rapid series of reforms.

The first part of this chapter consists of a detailed account of the evolution of trade and exchange rate policy (Sections 10.2 and 10.3), and an analysis of the movement in aggregate indicators of trade liberalization (Section 10.4) Section 10.5 reviews the Zambian trade liberalization in a regional context. The second part of the report consists of a more detailed analysis of the current liberalization programme. Section 10.6 reviews the evidence from the Trade Liberalization Survey implemented in August 1995. Sections 10.7 and 10.8 consider macro-compatibility and credibility of the current liberalization phase, and Section 10.9 concludes.

10.2 POLICY ACCOUNTS

Background

Zambia's transition from being one of the richest countries in Africa to one of the poorest took less than a generation.[1] On the eve of the multi-party elections in 1991, real per capita incomes had more than halved since 1970, gross national savings represented only 6 per cent of national income, as opposed to 18 per cent in 1970, while gross investment had fallen to less than 10 per cent of national income, down from almost 40 per cent two decades earlier. During the same period Zambia borrowed heavily, but with the downturn in commodity prices and growth its external indebtedness increased sharply. External debt peaked in 1993 at approximately $US7.3bn, about 230 per cent of GDP and just under $1000 per capita. Only Somalia, Mozambique and Tanzania had higher per capita debt burdens.

The causes of the decline in the country's fortunes are rooted in the combination of an economic inheritance that ensured dependence on the production and export of copper, and an inappropriate response to the macroeconomic shocks to world copper prices. At Independence in 1964 the United National Independent Party government of President Kaunda inherited a highly dualistic economy dominated by an enclave copper sector. The early years of the republic (1964–72) coincided with relatively high world copper prices and the government embarked on an extensive programme of capital formation, much of which was heavily import-intensive and capital-intensive, in the rest of the economy. The manufacturing and construction sectors grew at 10 per cent and 9 per cent per annum, respectively, over the decade from 1965 compared to the aggregate growth rate 2.4 per cent per annum (mining declined and agriculture exhibited only moderate growth of 2.5 per cent per annum).

From the perspective of the 1980s and 1990s, these growth rates are relatively high, but two additional factors need to be considered. First, the growth rates for manufacturing and construction were from a very low base; more importantly, the growth was achieved at low levels of efficiency. Gross domestic investment averaged 20 per cent of GDP from 1065–70 and approximately 35 per cent of GDP from 1970–4, but the non-copper investment boom did not translate into growth. The incremental capital–output ratio (ICOR), which is a measure of the efficiency of investment, was exceptionally low. The ICOR averaged approximately 60 (that is, a one-unit change in output requires 60 units of investment) indicating a chronic inefficiency on the part of the economy in transforming investment into growth. A comparable figure of approximately four for Indonesia for the period 1973–81 gives an indication of the scale of the inefficiency of investment in Zambia at this time.

The late 1960s, however, also saw a change in the political economy of Zambia and the emergence of an economic policy, based loosely on President Kaunda's conception of 'humanism', in which there was shift in emphasis towards concerns about the distribution of income and wealth rather growth. Thus, following the findings of the Brown Commission on wage levels in the mining sector, and the 1969 Mulungushi Declaration, which introduced widespread nationalization, economic performance began to stutter. State ownership became the dominant force in the Zambian economy, accounting for over 50 per cent of output in the manufacturing sector by 1975 and a similar share of formal sector employment. Around it emerged policies that limited competition in domestic markets, protected industry from external competition and saw an increasing proportion of output allocated by non-market mechanisms. Aggregate levels of investment began to decline and the public sector grew rapidly. Trade policy began to be increasingly inward-looking, creating barriers behind which state-owned enterprises rapidly expanded. These developments pre-dated the terms-of-trade shocks that hit the economy in 1974.

The crisis in Zambia was exacerbated by the government's policy response to the sequence of external shocks that hit the economy from the mid-1960s to the early 1980s. The temporary positive shocks to copper prices in the 1960s were incorrectly viewed as permanent, causing the government to revise its permanent income and thus increase consumption. Conversely, the permanent negative price and production shocks of the 1970s and the 1980s were treated as temporary and the government's response was to maintain consumption levels, draw down reserves and increase external borrowing. Even as the permanence of the negative shock was becoming apparent, deep-set reluctance to restore external balance placed the government on a course where trade policy and external borrowing were the principal instruments of macroeconomic adjustment. Thus at two crucial times the government incorrectly interpreted its external environment; as a consequence its policy choices were inappropriate and ultimately unsustainable.

Mineral Dependence

Copper mining has been the mainstay of the Zambian economy for the past 65 years. During the period before Independence in 1964 the economy developed primarily around a core of international mining companies,[2] who enjoyed a boom during the immediate post-Second World War period. Many of the structural problems facing the country now have their roots in the development strategies adopted at that time. The most significant was the creation of a highly dualistic agricultural sector, which emerged as a consequence of a policy that maintained the supply of low-wage labour to the mining sector. This was achieved through the combination of agricultural taxation that kept the price of the staple wage good low to consumers – achieved by strongly favouring the commercial 'line-of-rail' agricultural sector through high subsidies on fertilizer, for example – and by actively promoting labour migration from rural areas to the Copperbelt. Smallholder agriculture, and especially diversification within agriculture, were discouraged.

By Independence the copper sector had expanded dramatically. Production had reached approximately 675 000 tonnes per annum and accounted for 93 per cent of total exports, 71 per cent of government revenue and 40 per cent of GDP. Over the three decades since then, the copper sector has been in decline. Although not significantly diminishing its share of total exports since the collapse of copper prices in the mid-1970s, it has contributed significantly less to government revenue and GDP than

Table 10.1 The copper sector

Period	*CU**	*C/GDP*† (%)	*C/REV*‡ (%)	*C/X*§ (%)	*Price***
1965–69	653	42.3	60.8	93	194
1970–74	683	29.4	39.0	94	154
1975–79	651	14.2	3.2	91	83
1980–84	578	14.0	3.2	92	75
1985–89	459	14.0	8.2	85	73
1990–93	418	7.5	12.0	82	80

Notes: * Copper production in thousands of metric tonnes; † copper sector share of GDP; ‡ mineral taxes including corporate taxes as percentage of total revenue excluding grants; § share of copper in total exports; ** US cents per pound in constant 1982 prices.

Source: Government & the Republic of Zambia (GRZ).

before. Copper revenues' share of total revenue (excluding grants) fell from an average of 51 per cent in 1964–74 to less than 4 per cent in the following decade before recovering to around 10 per cent in the period since 1986 (Table 10.1).

Over the same time the share in GDP more than halved from around 36 per cent to just under 15 per cent. Aside from the obvious effects of the sharp fall in copper prices (see below), much of the decline in the sector reflects an erosion of Zambia's comparative advantage in copper. Production reached its historical peak in 1969 at 760 000 tonnes and has been declining ever since; by the early 1990s average production levels were around 400 000 tonnes per annum. Current reserves have declined in quality since the mid-1970s,[3] and have become increasingly expensive to mine as shafts have deepened and open pit reserves approach the end of their viable life. The lower than anticipated utilization of processing plant has increased operating costs. The declining comparative advantage of the sector has been exacerbated by a history of poor management of ZCCM, the parastatal copper mining company,[4] and a government policy towards ZCCM that has emphasized political and rent-seeking rather than commercial objectives. Copper production was (and is) at the centre of Zambia's political economy and as a consequence was the victim of frequent policy reversals (most notably in the area of taxation) and inconsistencies in the objectives of senior management, which were frequently at odds with the efficient operation of the sector.

Having said this, the outlook for the sector is not necessarily gloomy. Recent reassessments of the copper inventory[5] suggest that if sufficient investment is undertaken in the medium term then the economic life of the sector may be extended (at an annual production level of around 400 000 tonnes per annum) for a further 80 years. This is, however, dependent on the privatization of ZCCM,[6] since the government is unlikely to be able to raise the required investment capital without privatization.

The Origins of Trade Restrictions, 1974–85

Adverse External Shocks

The period from 1974 to 1980 was dominated by three adverse factors. The first was the consequences of the dramatic fall in Zambia's terms of trade, which was more severe than in any other sub-Saharan economy. Though it is common to think of the adverse terms-of-trade effect stemming solely from a fall in copper prices, the rise in import prices hurt the economy as much, not least because of the high capital-intensity of the production structure of the economy. Throughout the period from 1974 to 1980 the export price index was in fact higher than it had been in the period before 1974, and by 1980 export prices had regained their 1974 peak level. By contrast, import prices had doubled since 1974 and reduced the economy's capacity to import by almost 50 per cent. The 1974 capacity to import has not yet been regained (see Figure 10.1).

Second, the economy suffered as a result of military conflict in the region and the hardening of attitudes towards South Africa. In particular, the conflicts in Rhodesia, Angola and Mozambique sharply increased transport costs for Zambia's copper exports.

The third, and arguably most serious, problem facing Zambia at the time came from the policy response to the worsening terms of trade – the assumption that the terms-of-trade decline was due solely to a fall in export price and that it was temporary. As a consequence the government sought to maintain aggregate macroeconomic balance not by reducing the level or composition of consumption (either private or public) but instead through reductions in investment and recourse to external finance. Both were anticipated to be temporary measures. Thus consumption was broadly maintained at around 80 per cent of GDP from 1975 to 1980 while investment plummetted. This cut-back in absorption was still not sufficient to equate gross domestic expenditure (GDE) with gross domestic income (GDY) and the government was thus forced to increase its borrowing from overseas, particularly from commercial sources (Figure 10.2).

By 1980 the most acute phase of the terms of trade decline had passed. Having fallen by around 60 per cent in the five years to 1980, the terms of trade declined by only 15 per cent during the next five, primarily because

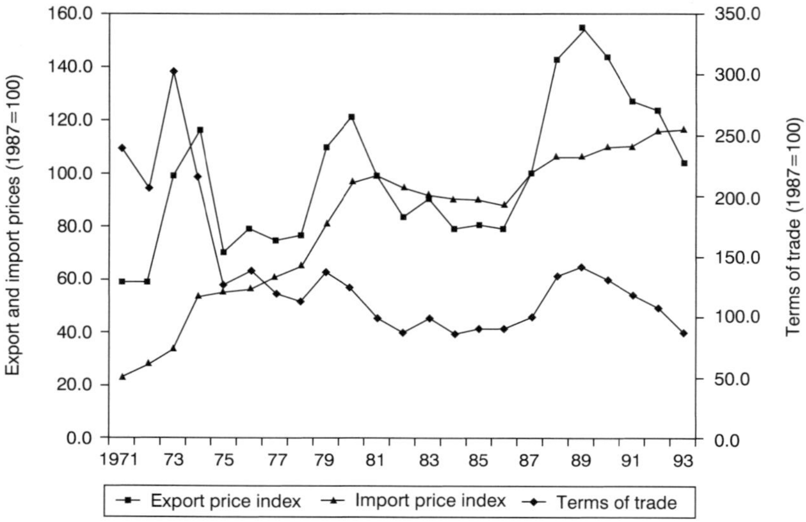

Source: World Bank World Tables (1995).

Figure 10.1 Export and import prices and terms of trade, 1971–93

of a steady decline in copper prices. However, it was at this stage that the consequences of the government's earlier strategy for the functioning of factor markets became marked. The exchange rate was fixed throughout most of the period (it was devalued in 1976 by 20 per cent and then in 1978 by 10 per cent). Interest rates were set administratively, and were negative in real terms, while public-sector real wages were raised by the presence of a large and highly-paid non-African labour force and through wage-leadership effects from the copper sector. As a consequence, capital and foreign exchange were relatively cheap at official prices and labour relatively expensive; given the endowments of the economy (capital-scarce and labour-abundant), factor prices were inappropriate and did not clear the factor markets. Macroeconomic compatibility was thus maintained through an endogenous trade and financial policy using quantitative controls to ration foreign exchange, imports and capital. Controlled markets such as these necessarily require mechanisms for allocating rationed supplies. In Zambia during the 1970s and 1980s the principal mechanism was through state ownership. Since capital and foreign exchange were effectively subsidized by the rationing mechanism, resource alloca-

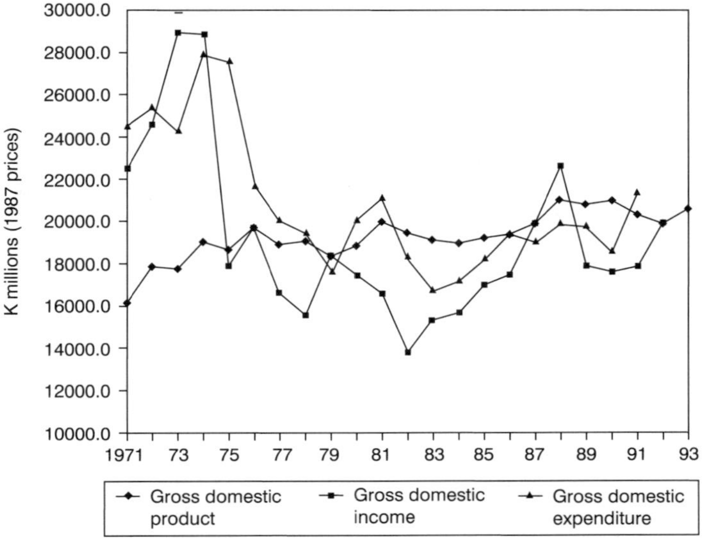

Source: World Bank World Tables (1995) and GRZ.

Figure 10.2 GDP, income and expenditure, 1971–93

tion in the state-owned enterprise sector became import and capital intensive.

The period up to the early 1980s witnessed occasional but unsuccessful adjustment efforts and the history of negotiation with the IMF and other agencies up to 1983 reveals a pattern of incomplete adjustment and only partial stabilization. The concentration on short-term stabilization rather than fundamental (and therefore less easily reversible) adjustment efforts meant that implementation was very closely related to the state of the current account; as economic circumstances improved following disbursement of aid facilities, adherence to their conditions weakened and in many cases policies were reversed. By 1983 there had been no significant alteration of the fundamental structure of the economy. In the face of an over-valued official exchange rate, external balance was maintained by administrative fiat and quantitative restrictions, while the domestic budget balance remained excessive, with expenditure swollen by high levels of consumer subsidy. By the early 1980s private creditors stopped lending to Zambia, short-term borrowing increased and debt service arrears began to emerge, precipitating a shift in bargaining power away from the government and towards the country's external creditors.

Trade Policy in Manufacturing

The politics and macroeconomics of economic policy in Zambia had a profound influence on the evolution of trade policy. In particular, the response to the external shocks that hit the country in the mid-1970s saw an increase in the reliance on direct controls on trade, used both to determine macroeconomic balances (that is, an endogenous trade policy response to incipient balance of payments deficits) and to influence the structure of protection afforded to industry. It is therefore fortunate that the production of an input–output table in 1975 allowed the computation of effective rates of protection for the year that turned out to be the last year in which the structure of domestic relative prices was largely determined by the explicit tariff structure. Thereafter, until the current reform period, the structure of relative prices increasingly reflected the consequences of quantitative rationing of foreign exchange and imports. The 1975 data therefore provide a convenient benchmark for trade policy.

The tariff policy developed in the period up to 1975 followed the model that was common elsewhere among developing countries. The range of nominal tariffs was high, ranging from 0 per cent to 150 per cent. A large proportion of goods were zero-rated (both for tariff duty and subsequently for import sales tax purposes), consisting of capital goods, heavy intermediate goods and 'essential' consumer goods. Intermediate inputs typically attracted duty of 10 per cent, while consumer durables attracted 50–100 per cent nominal duty (see Table 10.2) Motor vehicles, furniture and other luxury goods attracted the highest duty rates, 100–150 per cent.

The variable structure of the nominal tariff combined with the highly open nature of the economy meant that the level of effective protection differed sharply from the nominal protection, although there was a significant positive correlation between the two (Table 10.2). The World Bank produced estimates for 1975 showing average effective protection (weighted by value added) at approximately 160 per cent for the manufacturing sector. The range of subsectoral averages was from around 30 per cent for heavy intermediate goods and capital goods to 370 per cent for non-food consumption goods. This range, however, reflected a much higher firm-level variation in effective protection, which extended from –22 per cent to 1250 per cent.[7] The distribution of effective protection was similar to that of nominal protection in which consumer goods were afforded the highest level of protection, followed by light intermediates, capital goods and heavy intermediates.

Table 10.2 Unweighted mean tariff rates (%)

	1975		1981	1986	1992	1993	
	Nominal	Effective	Max.	Max.	Max.	Max.	Effective
Consumer goods							
Food products	40.1	2.9	41.5	48.9	42.6	36.1	24.0
Other non-food	37.6	17.5	44.5	48.7	47.1	39.5	46.1
durables	82.1	14.4	45.4	52.5	48.6	40.0	21.6
Intermediates		3.5					
Light	32.4		33.3	35.6	39.4	30.0	28.8
Heavy	16.5		33.1	36.9	42.5	34.4	22.5
Capital goods	7.9	5.7	58.3	67.2	38.3	33.3	21.3

Sources: World Bank (1984) and GRZ.

The Emergence of Quantitative Controls

Following the emergence of the macroeconomic crisis of the mid-1970s, the government turned increasingly to direct controls as a means of maintaining external balance. The primary instrument was the foreign exchange control regime, which sought to determine the aggregate level of foreign exchange availability as well as sectoral ceilings. The presence of such quantitative controls raised the market clearing price for traceable goods above the level implied by the tariff-augmented world price. As such the latter no longer indicated the extent of protection afforded to the tradeable manufacturing sector. The foreign exchange control regime that emerged during the 1970s and 1980s was both highly centralized and extremely inefficient. The Ministry of Commerce and Industry made allocations on a firm-by-firm and product-by-product basis. However, even when licences were granted by the Ministry of Commerce and Industry there was no guarantee that the potential imports would be realized, and indeed during 1983–5 import licences issued exceeded the foreign exchange actually available.

The binding constraint on foreign exchange allocation was the Bank of Zambia's release of funds. Given the overrun of import licences, the bank had to use its own criteria to chose among applicants for foreign exchange. This created a cumbersome and lengthy process that increased administrative costs and uncertainties in importing, but also reduced the speculative value of the import licence. This encouraged stockpiling and hoarding of goods rather than licences by importers. It also created a parallel market for foreign exchange at a higher exchange rate as the excess demand for foreign exchange could not be met by the official channel.

Importers were constrained by foreign exchange allocation and bans and tariffs were redundant.

The foreign exchange allocation system also produced important intra-firm effects. In particular, state-owned enterprises enjoyed preferential access to foreign exchange and therefore access to imports at increasingly over-valued exchange rates. This was to become a feature of the Zambian economy throughout the 1980s, but particularly in the period of the 'growth from own resources'. The legacy of this particular form of endogenous trade policy, which was so systematically biased in favour of the import-substituting SOEs, has profound implications for the evolution of the capital stock and the investment response to current reform programmes. It also provides an explanation for the difficulty experienced by the current government in implementing privatization.[8]

Aside from determining aggregate foreign exchange availability, the exchange control system, through the Import Licensing and Foreign Exchange Allocating Committees, determined the sectoral allocation of foreign exchange, thereby affecting the structure of protection afforded by the tariff schedule. The ranking of priorities for foreign exchange allocation – net of debt service in the early 1980s – was as follows:

(1) intermediate inputs for domestic production of 'essential' consumer goods (milled grain, edible oils, soaps, pharmaceuticals);
(2) final consumer products in the 'essential' items category;
(3) intermediate inputs for the copper sector, fertilizer production, public transport and coal mining;
(4) other intermediate inputs and capital goods;
(5) commodities that support development of the transport, communications and tourism sectors; and
(6) consumer goods.

The foreign exchange allocation system by and large mirrored and therefore reinforced the structure of protection afforded by the tariff structure, enhancing the protection to consumer goods and competing industrial intermediates (categories (4) to (6)), and thereby providing open-ended support to the domestic, import-substituting activities. The price-raising effects of the quantitative restrictions are difficult to measure, not least because the relevant price comparison is the market price of the actual or potential imports. However, estimates made in 1983 by the World Bank, based on a survey of market rather than declared prices, suggested that the actual protection afforded by the import controls was significantly higher than the notional protection afforded by the tariff structure. They estimated that the additional protection afforded to consumer goods (excluding essential foodstuffs) resulted in an approximate doubling of the notional rates of effective protection.

Price Controls[9]

Domestic price controls were steadily introduced in Zambia throughout the 1970s and 1980s, principally on agricultural 'essential goods' and the products of some parastatal companies. These were monitored by the Prices and Incomes Commission (PIC). Price controls were partially removed in 1982 on all non-agricultural products, leaving controls on maize meal, wheat flour and candles. The latter prices were set by the government, while all other prices were subject to *ex-post* review by the PIC. As is to be expected, the price controls on agricultural products represented a (distortionary) transfer from rural producers to urban consumers. Similarly the price controls on output of parastatal companies leveraged the effective protection afforded to those firms using the output of parastatals in their own production.

10.3 TRADE LIBERALIZATION

Episode I, 1983–7

Throughout the period from the late 1970s there had been attempts to put in place reform programmes – generally supported by IMF stand-by credits – but these generally met with failure.[10] Efforts at reform were consolidated following the (one-party) elections in 1983 and the government entered negotiations for what was to be the first full-blown economic adjustment programme. The programmes consisted of a series of IMF stand-by agreements, sectoral adjustment credits from the World Bank group, and Paris and London Club rescheduling arrangements. The reform programme consisted of an expenditure-reduction strategy concentrating on government expenditure, but the center-piece of the programme was trade liberalization based upon the introduction of a foreign exchange auction. Though uncoordinated and plagued by slippage and policy reversals, the reform programme came remarkably close to success.

Import Liberalization

The process of tariff adjustments during this period was based around a standard gradualist tariff 'concertina' programme. Reform was expected to consist of three components: (1) the reduction of tariff exemptions and raising of the minimum tariff for tariff-attracting imports; (2) the reduction of the maximum tariff; and (3) the contraction of the range of nominal tariffs. The 1984/85 tariff reform succeeded in implementing the first two of the components. The minimum tariff was increased to 10 per cent for all non-tariff-exempt goods and the maximum tariff was reduced from 150 per cent to 100 per cent for all goods (expect for tobacco, some vehicles, firearms and other miscellaneous luxury goods) in October 1984. The scope of exemptions was reduced at the same time.

The component that was not implemented was the unification of sales tax for domestic and imported goods. This was to be achieved by the introduction of an 'uplift factor' applied to the customs duty-inclusive landed price of imports, with sales tax levied on the enhanced price. The objective of the 'uplift factor' was to adjust import prices for the domestic wholesale margin borne by domestic producers. This element of the programme was not implemented until the resumed liberalization in 1992. Also not implemented at the time was the establishment of a tariff commission. This has not yet been done, although a number of later initiatives were implemented that assume the functions initially anticipated for the tariff commission.

The Foreign Exchange Auction

The centre-piece of the 1985 reform programme was the foreign exchange auction, which has been the subject of considerable examination.[11] During 1983 and 1984 a crawling peg devaluation strategy was pursued by the authorities. It involved step devaluations of 30 per cent in 1983 and 70 per cent in 1984, bringing about a real exchange rate depreciation of approximately 11 per cent in the two years before the implementation of the auction. Nonetheless, the parallel market premium continued to edge upwards towards 75 per cent. An export retention scheme was introduced in 1984, permitting non-traditional exporters to retain 50 per cent of their export proceeds for their own current account use.

In April 1985 a weekly foreign exchange auction system was introduced for all foreign exchange transactions (excluding government imports and debt service). The supply of foreign exchange was generated by ZCCM export earnings, export proceeds of the non-copper sector, aid inflows and other inflows. Just prior to the establishment of the auction in October 1985, the exchange rate was K2.2 per US$. In the first auction the rate depreciated by 55 per cent converging rapidly thereafter towards the rate established on the (illegal) parallel market.

While the auction was initially perceived to be a success – not least in removing the administrative burden on importers – the government's failure to establish a fiscal balance meant that the nominal exchange rate depreciated rapidly. By mid-1986 the rate had depreciated to K7.12 per US$, a nominal depreciation of 223 per cent. Over the same period the premium on the parallel market fell from 75 per cent to approximately 30 per cent, and the real exchange rate depreciated by close to 200 per cent. If we take the definition that exchange rate unification is a situation where the parallel market no longer plays a significant role in resource allocation decisions, the exchange rate in Zambia was approximately unified at a sustainable equilibrium real exchange rate by March 1986.[12]

Despite achieving an external balance – albeit precarious – the foreign exchange rate auction came under severe pressure. Concerned by the rate of depreciation on the market and the belief that the depreciation was fuelling cost-push inflation, the government began to express concerns about the functioning of the auction system. The auction was converted from a marginal to a Dutch basis (in an attempt to offset what was seen to be excessive bidding by the private sector)[13] but when this did not in itself reduce the rate of depreciation, direct intervention increased. Following a politically motivated reshuffle of senior officials at the Bank of Zambia in April 1986, the bank sought to stabilize the exchange rate by selling foreign exchange forward.[14] However, the private sector had already formed expectations that the forward selling by the bank was unsustainable and as a result the private sector demand for foreign exchange increased, rather than decreased. This drove the marginal price of the kwacha down, which increased the cost to the Bank of Zambia's forward foreign exchange purchase contracts. The losses incurred in this unsuccessful Ponzi-scheme intervention were monetized by the Bank of Zambia's increasing its claims on the government. It was this rapid expansion of base money rather than cost-push effects from higher imports costs that fuelled inflation,[15] which depreciated the nominal exchange rate further.

At the time it was also suggested the rapid depreciation of the auction rate was due to shortfalls in copper earnings and the failure on the part of external donors to maintain the supply of balance of payments support. It is true that during 1986 there were delays in disbursement by some of the donors. But copper earnings remained relatively stable, and if anything increased marginally during the latter part of the auction period. The lower than anticipated foreign exchange supply did not, therefore, render the reform macro-incompatible. Rather, it was the combined effect of the interventions by the newly appointed officials in charge of macroeconomic management and their consequences for fiscal balance and the growth in base money that led to self-fulfilling speculative behaviour on the part of the private (and public enterprise) sector and ultimately undermined the credibility of the market.

Reversal: the New Economic Reform Programme, 1987–9

With the functioning of the foreign exchange market undermined by a loss of credibility, the other early successes of the auction period were not sustained. In December 1986 riots broke out on the Copperbelt in response to proposals to remove consumer subsidies on maize as the government sought to address fiscal imbalances. The foreign exchange auction continued throughout the early part of 1987, being radically modified in January 1987 by the introduction of a second foreign exchange rate window.

The official rate, for government transactions and debt service, was fixed, while the second window remained auction determined. However, on 1 May 1987 President Kaunda announced that the externally driven programme was 'disintegrating the social fabric of the Zambia' and that a new programme, based solely on 'own resources' and to be known as the New Economic Recovery Programme, would be implemented. Zambia immediately suspended financial relations with the IMF and instituted a policy reversal. The principal features of the new programme were the abolition of the foreign exchange auction and the introduction of a fixed nominal exchange rate of K8 per US$ (the auction was suspended at a rate of K21 per US$); a moratorium on external debt service, limiting debt service to 10 per cent of exports net of allocations to government, ZCCM, ZIMOIL and IATA; and the re-introduction of import licences and other controls on goods and factor markets. While no explicit changes were made to the nominal tariff, the trade regime was once again distorted through the re-introduction of the fixed exchange rate and the reversion to quantitative foreign exchange allocations administered through the Foreign Exchange Management Committee (FEMAC). The export retention scheme was effectively eliminated. The ERS remained in name, but proceeds had to be surrendered to the Bank of Zambia and their subsequent use required FEMAC approval.

Restarting Liberalization: the Second Liberalization Episode, 1989–95

The New Economic Recovery Programme was not sustainable, both because it was incompatible and because it too was incredible. Ironically, however, the policy reversal occurred just as export prices rose for the first time since 1978/79 and the economy enjoyed a short terms-of-trade boom that improved by almost 25 per cent between 1987 and 1989. Had the boom occurred a few months earlier, or had the authorities maintained the auction, the unanticipated external income windfall would have boosted foreign exchange supply and might have been sufficient to restore the credibility of the auction system and hence re-establish the macro-compatibility of the liberalization programme. This was not to be, and the same external windfall (supported by the unilateral moratorium on external debt) generated a sustained improvement in the current account that rendered the policy reversal compatible in the short run and allowed the New Economic Recovery Programme (NERP) to last until the middle of 1989. However, by this time the domestic economic recovery programme was clearly failing. Factor and goods prices remained severely distorted, the parallel market premium soared to over 1000 per cent per annum in 1988, and total gross fixed investment fell below 10 per cent of GDP for the first time in the country's post-Independence history. President Kaunda was forced to re-open negotiations with the IMF and World Bank.

The 1989–95 Reform Programme

Following the resumption of relations between Zambia and the IMF, an orthodox stabilization programme was implemented. A maxi-devaluation of 63 per cent was instituted in 1989; a coupon system was introduced to reduce the budgetary cost of food subsidies; and most prices were decontrolled in June of that year. These actions paved the way for the economic reform programme in September 1989, which was converted into a full-blown adjustment programme in July 1990. In April 1991 the IMF introduced a debt forgiveness scheme known as the Rights Accumulation Programme (RAP).[16] Despite strong donor support, however, adjustment efforts were mixed during the most of the first two years of the programme, although some progress was registered in dismantling many of the domestic price controls and in re-establishing a liberalized foreign exchange and payments system (see below). The programme suffered a setback in the run-up to the first multi-party elections in 1991 when the UNIP government sought to engineer a pre-election boom, an event accompanied by a temporary cessation of aid flows by some donors in June 1991. The pre-election boom was unsuccessful and the government was defeated by the MMD in October 1991.

The victorious MMD government was quickly faced with two serious problems: (1) the consequences of the election boom; (2) the devastating effect of the drought that hit the region 1992. In retrospect the macroeconomic effects of the drought have been relatively transitory: the government managed to run a more or less fiscally neutral emergency drought budget, while emergency grain deliveries and other drought relief were very successful in alleviating famine. What proved more difficult was achieving fiscal stabilization. Despite the tight fiscal stance adopted following the 1991 elections, macroeconomic stability worsened rather than improved and the RAP targets were repeatedly missed.

From mid-1991 until mid-1993 the rate of domestic inflation increased markedly, reaching a maximum annualized rate of close to 400 per cent. Fiscal stability was eventually restored in late 1993 through the introduction of a cash budget proscribing the use of deficit financing from the central bank. The successful implementation of the cash budget halted inflation virtually in its tracks by mid-1993. Annualized inflation dropped from 385 per cent in July 1993 to 15 per cent in October and was briefly negative in November 1993 as a result of a reduction in reserve money growth due to complete sterilization of aid inflows, instituting controls over domestic credit to the public sector and, most dramatically of all, the achievement of a freeze on central bank credit to the central government. Despite a decline in domestic revenue from around 20 per cent of GDP to 13 per cent in 1993, the government engineered a deficit reduction of 8 per cent of GDP in two years. One consequence of the cash budget, however, was that with the decline in domestic revenue, there was a sharp increase in domestic debt financing, which, occurring concurrently with the liberalization of domestic interest rates and the *de facto* exchange rate unification, led to a sharp rise in nominal and real domestic interest rates. Real interest rates rose sharply during 1993 and were consistently in excess of 50 per cent per annum on short-dated treasury bills. Only by late 1994 had real rates declined to single-digit levels. These high interest rates contributed to a tight squeeze on domestic credit to the real economy, which has exacerbated the direct costs of adjustment faced by the industrial sector in response to new relative prices in both the goods and factor markets.

Trade Liberalization Measures

Broadly, the liberalization measures introduced under the economic reform programme in 1989, with the exception of the exchange rate regime, simply involved a restoration of the measures implemented five years earlier. Thus in the March 1991 budget the tariff reform process was re-started. The number of tariff rates was reduced to six and new minimum and maximum rates were set at 15 per cent and 50 per cent, respectively. A small number of tariff exemptions remained in place (especially fertilizer and essential foodstuffs), and the tariff rate on some luxury goods was kept at 100 per cent. In the 1992 budget the tariff concertina continued with the tariff schedule reduced to three rates (20 per cent, 30 per cent, and 40 per cent), the exemptions list further narrowed, and a 20 per cent 'uplift factor' applied to imports for computation of import sales tax.[17] This procedure was finally concluded in the 1995 budget with the reduction of the three tariff rates to 10 per cent, 15 per cent and 20 per cent, respectively, the abolition of the 20 per cent uplift factor on imports and its replacement with a unified sales tax rate of 23 per cent, in anticipation of the transition to a VAT in July 1995. Finally, in 1993 the government ratified the PTA/COMESA external tariff reduction agreement. This eliminated all non-tariff barriers for intra-PTA trade and committed the government to a schedule of tariff reductions on intra-regional trade. Starting from the tariff prevailing at the time of ratification, which in Zambia's case is the post-1982 level, individual external tariffs on goods originating within the PTA region[18] had to be reduced by 60 per cent in October 1993; by 70 per cent in October 1994; by 80 per cent in October 1996; and by 100 per cent in October 2000. Zambia has already implemented the 1993 and 1994 reductions.

The current reform programme focuses greater attention on liberalization measures aimed at stimulating the non-traditional export sector. As suggested earlier, the principal disincentive to the growth of this sector lay with the persistent real exchange rate over-valuation and the implicit tax this imposes on exporters. Increased attention is also directed towards administrative constraints to non-traditional exports. The most important of these, given the relatively high import dependence of the non-traditional export sector,[19] is the reform of the customs duty drawback scheme. Although in principle the scheme operated in accordance with international standards, in practice poor administration and budgetary restrictions have meant that duty rebates were rarely paid and in cases where they were, the delays involved reduced their real value substantially, eroding any incentive effects notionally afforded by the scheme. Modifications introduced in 1994 aimed to reduce the burden of proof for drawback, to permit drawback as credit against import tax liabilities and to include third-party exporters. Notwithstanding these reforms, there is still widespread discontent among exporters over the effectiveness of the duty drawback.

Of more profound consequence for the tradeables sector, and particularly the exports sector, was the introduction of VAT in July 1995. The VAT, which replaced the sales tax is levied at a rate of 20 per cent, represents a significant shift in incentive to the exportables sector. In addition to the removal of the cascade effect of the sales tax, exports are zero-rated, thereby providing relief on input taxes levied on intermediate inputs, which by Lerner symmetry is equivalent to the provision of a direct export subsidy.

Exchange Rate Liberalization Measures

The most important trade-liberalizing reform measures introduced in the current reform programme relate to the exchange rate regime. Following the experiences of 1987 the transition to full exchange rate unification was achieved without recourse to a foreign exchange auction. In February 1990, a dual window exchange rate was re-introduced. The official exchange rate for government imports, debt service and parastatal allocations was fixed at K28 per US$ and allocations were made FEMAC. The second window, which was also fixed, was initially priced at a rate of K40/US$, and was used for open general licence (OGL) imports. The OGL list, initially restricted to approximately 10 per cent of 1985 imports, was widened during 1990 and 1991 as the government gradually transferred a greater proportion of imports from the first to the second window. Concurrently, the two managed rates were progressively devalued and brought together. They were unified in April 1991 at a rate of K58/US$. Allocations of foreign exchange, however, were still made by the FEMAC.

The MMD government accelerated exchange rate reform. In its first budget in January 1992, it committed to a programme of weekly depreciations of the exchange rate; the rate converged rapidly towards the rate established on the export retention market, which, following the 1992 budget, had been further liberalized. The export retention allowance was increased to 100 per cent of gross earnings, although retentions had to be sold or used within 180 days. Subject to that restriction, the retention market was a price-clearing market for current account transactions. Less than six months later the OGL list switched from 'positive list' to 'negative list', and a *bureaux de change* market was introduced for current account transactions, thereby effectively removing the time limit restriction applying to the retention market. By December 1992 the OGL exchange rate was unified with bureau rates (although a transitional discount of 15 per cent applied to OGL purchases) resulting in a unified exchange rate by early 1993.[20] Finally, in January 1994 all capital account exchange controls were abolished. At this point the exchange rate was fully market-determined and the Bank of Zambia began to develop an inter-bank foreign exchange market.

The Level of Protection Following Liberalization

By the beginning of 1995 Zambia had completed the implementation of trade liberalization measures. In addition to the transition to a floating exchange rate and the removal of all quantitative controls and non-tariff barriers, the nominal tariff has been restructured, providing a significantly lower level of nominal protection across the bulk of trade, while the tariff relief afforded by the PTA/COMESA agreement has lowered intra-regional trade close to free-trade levels. The tariff reforms and removal of quantitative restrictions have led to a marked decline in effective protection. The final column of Table 10.3 reports estimates of effective protection

Table 10.3 Estimates of effective protection (%)

Category	*1975*	*1983*	*1993*
Consumer goods			
Food	127.5	165.9	165.2
Non-food	368.5	255.9	30.0
Durables	225.0	202.8	130.0
Intermediates			
Light	163.1	113.9	60.0
Heavy	22.0	44.3	50.0
Capital goods	35.2	62.5	54.0
All	161.9	140.0	57.0

Sources: For 1975 and 1983 World Bank (1984); for 1993 A. T. Kate, M. Thorne and C. Chileshe (1994).

computed by Kate *et al.* (1994) that suggest the weighted average effective protection afforded to manufacturing has fallen significantly since the pre-reform period.

With the exception of food, whose average rate of effective protection is inflated by an extremely high degree of protection for pasteurized milk and oil-seed, the structure of effective protection follows that for nominal protection, where the tariff increases with the degree of value added in the product. Thus, for example, in the textile sector the evidence suggests that grey cloth and cotton yarn receive low or negative protection, while finished fabrics enjoy effective protection of around 40 per cent and garments of around 50 per cent. Kate *et al.* (1994) further suggest that if it is assumed that there is significant leakage in the tariff, so that the effective nominal tariff is only 50 per cent of the notional tariff, the average level of effective protection falls to the relatively low level of 14 per cent.

The sharp temporary appreciation of the nominal exchange rate severely undermined the competitiveness of formerly protected firms and had serious, and possibly permanent, output effects. These results must be interpreted with caution for two main reasons. The first is that they have been drawn from a relatively small group of products (37), so that averages are based on a small and unrepresentative sample, and the second is that the estimates are single-point estimates taken from company records in 1993, a year during which macroeconomic relative prices were far from their equilibrium levels. A further extension of the analysis is required to map protection from commodities into the size and ownership characteristics of the manufacturing sector in Zambia. One far from surprising feature to emerge from the analysis by Kate *et al.* is that those products with the largest reduction in effective protection are typically produced in large-scale, state-owned sector, principally by companies falling under the ZIMCO group. Given the nature of the foreign exchange allocation system, which was biased in favour of allocating rationed foreign exchange to SOEs, it may also reasonably be expected that the change in *average* effective protection illustrated in Table 10.3 probably *understates* the loss of effective protection sustained by the state-owned manufacturing sector.

10.4 MEASURING TRADE LIBERALIZATION

In this section we present some of the aggregate evidence on trade liberalization. In the absence of detailed market prices for importables, and c.i.f. border prices for imports, which would be required to compute directly the actual wedge between domestic and world prices, we follow the methodology outlined by Collier, Greenaway and Gunning (1993) in developing proxy aggregate measures of trade liberalization by examining the wedge between domestic and world relative prices.

We start from the position that Zambia, being a small open economy, is a price-taker in the market of tradeable productions. Thus the domestic price earned for exportables is:

$$P_x = P_x^* e(1 - t_x) \tag{10.1}$$

where * denotes world prices, *e* is the nominal exchange rate and *tx* taxes on exports. For importables, the domestic price is given as:

$$P_m = P_m^* e(1 + \Theta) \tag{10.2}$$

where Θ is a measure of the protection afforded to domestic production of importables. This consists of the actual effective tariff on imports (t_m) and the price-raising effect of quantitative restrictions on foreign exchange. Re-arranging Equations (10.1) and (10.2) allows us to express the wedge between the world tradeable price ratio and the domestic price ratio as a measure of the degree of protection afforded to domestic producers by the stance of trade policy. We shall refer to this as the relative protection coefficient, which can be expressed as

$$q = (1 - t_x)/(1 + \Theta) \tag{10.3}$$

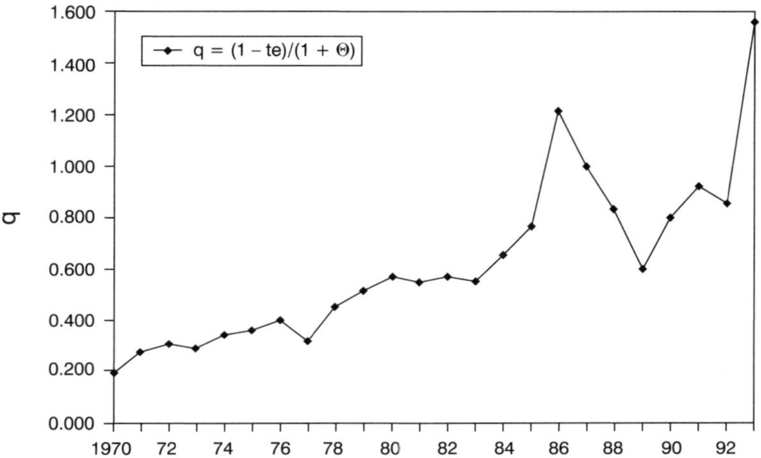

Note: A rise in q indicates a liberazation.

Figure 10.3 Coefficient of relative protection, 1970–92

From Equation (10.3) we note that a rise in q represents a decline in the coefficient of relative protection or a tendency towards a more liberal trade regime. We compute this coefficient for the period from 1970 to 1993, which spans the four main phases discussed above. Throughout most of the period under review, the only exportable good attracting price-distorting duty was copper. Even for this product, the export tax rate was non-zero only from 1969 to 1973, when copper was subject to a royalty, and from 1983 to 1988, when the mineral export tax was in effect. With the exception of 1970 and 1973, the effective tax rate on copper was, however, very low and stable. Movements in the relative protection coefficient are therefore predominantly determined by movements in the implicit protection afforded to importables. Figure 10.3 plots the evolution of the coefficient of relative protection.

The aggregate index clearly identifies the main liberalization episodes in Zambia. Thus, commencing in the late 1970s the index reflects the stagnant anti-trade environment. This persisted more or less unchanged during the phase of incomplete adjustment in the period from 1980 to 1984 and then the sharp and successful liberalization that occurred with the introduction of the foreign exchange auction in 1985. It is notable that the reversal following the introduction of the own funds programme

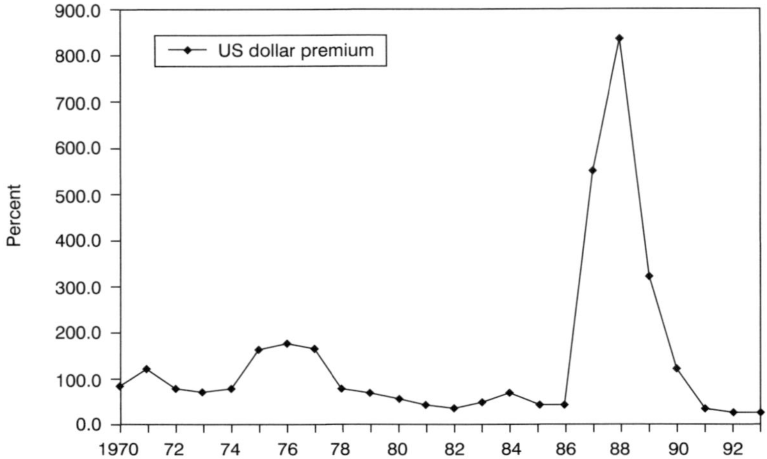

Source: Pick's Currency Yearbook.

Figure 10.4 Parallel market premium, 1970–92

in 1987 almost perfectly offset the liberalization gains obtained after 1983, and returned the economy to the status quo prevailing in 1980. Also clearly illustrated is the rapidity with which the liberalization has occurred in the current reform programme, particularly from 1992, when exchange rate unification was finally completed and the nominal tariff was further adjusted.

What is less appealing about the figure is the suggestion that the relative protection coefficient indicated a steady trade liberalizing movement throughout the period from 1970 to 1980, even though the policy accounts suggest that this period is associated with the emergence of an increasingly quota-ridden and restrictive trade structure. This is supported by the evidence from Table 10.3, which indicates that although effective protection on imports fell between 1975 and 1983, the fall was in the region of 12 per cent, significantly less than the amount suggested in Figure 10.3.

Two factors may possibly explain this counter-intuitive result. The first is that the parallel market premium was trending downwards from 1970 to 1980. As can be seen by comparison of Figures 10.3 and 10.4, there is a marked negative correlation between the premium and the measure of the relative protection. The reduction in the premium is not reflected in the policy accounts, but if the summary measure is correct, the reduction in the trade-retarding effects flowing from the foreign exchange regime moved the regime towards a more liberal stance. The second explanation is that the way in which the aggregate measure of relative protection is computed assumes that the composition of imports has not altered. For example, if the share of heavily protected importables declines in the domestic importable price index relative to its share in the world price index, this would (*ceteris paribus*) be reflected in a movement in the coefficient of relative protection towards liberalization. We do not have sufficiently disaggregated data on prices to isolate these composition effects.

10.5 THE REGIONAL DIMENSION OF TRADE LIBERALIZATION

Zambia is a member of all the major regional trade groupings, principally the Community of Eastern and Southern Africa (COMESA, formerly Preferential Trade Area [PTA]) formed in 1981 and the Southern African Development Community (SADC), formed in 1980. Zambia hosts the headquarters of COMESA.

Intra-regional Trade

In common with other African regional trade arrangements examined elsewhere in this project, the volume of Zambia's intra-regional trade has generally been low, with trade flows tending to reflect dependence on a small number of primary export commodities and a tendency for the metropolitan inheritance to dominate import supply. The exception to this is trade with South Africa and Zimbabwe (see Table 10.4).

The growing importance of sub-regional trade, especially with South Africa, is clearly seen. Preliminary estimates from SGS for 1994 indicate that this shift in trade patterns has been maintained and, if anything, increased.[21] Trade between Zambia and the PTA and SADC group (which excludes South Africa) is presented in Table 10.5.

With the exception of 1991, Zambia's trade with the PTA has consistently accounted for a relatively low share of total trade, averaging approximately 5 per cent of exports and 8.5 per cent of imports. However, there seems to have been a discernable increase in the share of the sub-region in total trade after 1991, when the trade liberalization measures re-introduced in 1989 were accelerated. The major trading partners within the grouping are Zimbabwe and Kenya. Exports to Zimbabwe and Kenya account for about two-thirds of total exports to PTA, while imports from Zimbabwe accounted for about 73 per cent of total PTA imports in 1988,

Table 10.4 Imports (%) by country of supply, 1992–3

Country	*1992*	*1993*
South Africa	26.8	41.6
Zimbabwe	6.5	6.5
Other African	2.8	2.1
UK	11.7	10.3
Germany	3.7	4.5
Other EU	8.5	6.8
Japan	4.5	4.1
Other Asia	4.8	2.9
USA	8.6	2.7
Other	22.1	18.5

Source: CSO, *External Trade Bulletin 1994.*

Table 10.5 Trade accounted for by PTA and SADC as share of total trade (%)

Year	*Exports*	*Imports*
1988	3.5	6.2
1989	3.2	11.9
1990	3.0	7.0
1991	10.8	7.8
1992	7.8	8.9
1993	4.3	8.5

Source: CSO *External Trade Bulletin 1994.*

increasing to over 75 per cent in 1993. Other countries that have become important regional trading partners of Zambia include Malawi, Botswana, Swaziland, Tanzania, Mozambique, Mauritius and Burundi. Much of this trade increased after trade liberalization measures were restored. As noted above, exports from Zambia to the PTA increased dramatically from 1990 to 1991.

The major development in regional trade, however, has been with South Africa, which is now Zambia's major import trade partner. This trade has increased since trade liberalization, with imports from South Africa accounting for 42 per cent of the total value of imports for 1993. While the trade with South Africa is biased towards imports, exports are also increasing, and given that South Africa has joined SADC this is quite an important potential market for Zambia.

Comparative Tariff Policy

As noted, Zambia is one of the countries that have ratified the PTA tariff reduction, with a 70 per cent relief on PTA-originating imports from October 1994, scheduled to increase to 100 per cent by 2000. Given that Zambia operates a relatively low average tariff, PTA relief brings the nominal tariff range down to a maximum of 12 per cent and a minimum of 6 per cent.

10.6 SURVEY EVIDENCE ON TRADE LIBERALIZATION

The Background to the Survey

The aggregate evidence presented so far suggests that current liberalization measures are relatively orthodox in their design and have been implemented comprehensively. An important question – in fact the fundamental question – is how the real economy has responded to the reform measures. Macroeconomic data on the structure and evolution of the real economy are extremely ill-suited to addressing this question. Not only are there considerable delays in the collection of aggregate sectoral data,[22] but increasingly macroeconomic data are likely to be plagued by severe measurement error (which is endogenous to the policy reforms being implemented).[23] These problems are already being seen in the divergence between different estimates of aggregate GDP.[24]

In order to examine the consequences of the current reforms on the manufacturing sector we turn in this section to the evidence from the 1995 Trade Liberalization Survey. Three sets of issues are important:

(1) the consequences of reforms for the structure, conduct and performance of firms;
(2) firms' perceptions about current and future reforms; and
(3) firms' planned behaviour and expectations.

With this focus we are able to secure some, albeit limited, dynamic perspective on the reform process in Zambia. However, it should be stressed that, by being a survey of the manufacturing sector only, it may also be prone to some of the biases inherent in using aggregate data.

The most obvious source of the bias comes from the conjecture that the two decades of import-substituting development strategy created an economy in which the manufacturing sector *in the aggregate* was too large relative to the agricultural sector. Under any conceivable adjustment strategy it might be expected that the manufacturing sector should decline relative to the agricultural sector and if growth were low, this would probably be accompanied by a decline in the absolute size of the manufacturing sector. Thus by concentrating only on the manufacturing sector, the survey will be biased toward activities that might reasonably be expected to be declining. This factor will need to be borne in mind in analysing the results of the survey.

The earlier sections of this paper discussed the policy accounts and the evolution of trade liberalization. However, it is worth recapping the principal components of the reform process in Zambia and the macroeconomic environment into which this survey fits. At the time of the survey, firms in Zambia were faced with full currency convertibility, on both current and capital accounts, low and broadly uniform tariffs on traded goods and virtually no (explicit) non-tariff barriers to trade. This had been the case for almost two years. At a regional level, Zambia had ratified the PTA/COMESA treaty and was committed to a reduction to zero of tariffs on intra-regional trade by 2000. The final component of the liberalization measures – the transition from a sales tax to a VAT – had just been implemented, albeit against a background of severe institutional problems within the Zambia Revenue Authority.

However, the macroeconomic environment was still far from stable. In early 1995 the tight fiscal stance that had been maintained since mid-1993 was lost and the much-anticipated graduation from the Rights Accumulation Programme was delayed. The country eventually graduated from the RAP to the enhanced structural adjustment facility (ESAF) in the final quarter of 1995, after having implemented additional revenue measures (that is, tax increases) and further tightened government expenditure in the second half of 1995. From a macroeconomic perspective, however, the stabilization looked difficult to sustain. Perhaps the most critical issue was the emergence of extremely high levels of tax evasion, not least of customs duties, which – aside from undermining effective revenue productivity – led to an increase in the volume of smuggled imports. Combined with the consequences of the stabilization efforts, namely high real interest rates and an over-valued real exchange rate, the manufacturing economy faced an extremely high level of competition. Moreover, a more problematic consequence of the delayed graduation was that there was extreme uncertainty over the future direction of domestic government policy, and the likely evolution of aid flows. Faced by such uncertainty, and the inherent irreversibility of investment activities, there was a high premium to waiting. As we shall argue below, the combination of these four factors seems to have severely compromised the real response to the liberalization measures.

Table 10.6 The structure of exports, 1989–94 (US$ million)

	1989	*1991*	*1994*
Traditional (metals)	1 279.5	1 041.2	965.2
(%)	(93.6)	(89.6)	(86.6)
Electricity	1.5	1.0	19.6
(%)	(0.2)	(0.1)	(1.7)
Agriculture	26.1	32.6	21.8
(%)	(1.9)	(2.8)	(2.0)
Manufacturing	59.1	87.7	107.5
(%)	(4.3)	(7.5)	(9.7)
Total	*1 366.2*	*1 162.5*	*1 114.1*

Source: Export Board of Zambia (1995).

The Sample Firms: Ownership, Structure and Performance

A sample of 100 firms was taken from the list of establishments provided by the Central Statistics Office (CSO) in Lusaka. The selection was not random, but was stratified with the objective of creating a sample that contained approximately 60 import-competing firms and 40 exporting firms in the manufacturing sector. The structure of production in Zambia, however, is such that it was difficult to identify 40 firms that export on a regular basis. Despite declining volumes, copper exports still account for over 85 per cent of total visible exports in 1994, while a large share of non-traditional exports is accounted for by electricity (13 per cent) and horticulture and floriculture (15 per cent). Manufacturing exports therefore constitute only 10 per cent of total Zambian exports (see Table 10.6).

Replacements to the sample were made in order to capture some exporting firms, but ultimately the sample contained only 16 firms that sold some proportion of their output on the export market. During the administration of the survey, further replacements were made when firms originally in the sample were found to be closed or were unwilling to participate.[25] The original sample had also included ZESCO, the Zambian Electricity Supply Company; due to its size, activity and statutory monopoly position this company was deleted from the sample. (ZESCO sold approximately $US20 m. of electricity to Zaire and Zimbabwe in 1994).[26]

The survey data were collected as a single cross-section of firms from the three line-of-rail industrial areas of the country: Lusaka and Kafue; the Copperbelt towns of Kitwe, Ndola and Luanshya; and the southern town of Livingstone, which is close to the border with Zimbabwe. In order to obtain a perspective on the dynamics of trade liberalization, firms were asked to report on a variety of indicators of their operation for the year prior to liberalization, which in the Zambian case was taken to be 1989,[27] the year the country re-activated its orthodox adjustment programme. Since that time the governments of President Kaunda (to 1991) and President Chiluba (1991–present) have pursued a programme of rapid liberalization.

As will become apparent, however, the relatively small size of the sample means that there are a number of limitations to the use of the data. In particular, the extremely high variances of many of the variables means that we are rarely able to establish results with a high degree of statistical accuracy. In general we must take the data as being at best supporting evidence rather than decisive evidence. Moreover, because of the heterogeneity of the sample we typically use the median as the measure of central tendency within the sample. Secondly, there are a number of aspects of the survey that rely on long-recall information and some that rely on long-distance expectations. We have no basis upon which to evaluate the accuracy of these data and therefore we do not rely on them excessively. Finally, we should be aware of the sample selectivity bias inherent in the survey. We are obviously sampling firms that are currently in existence and, moreover, were in existence when the CSO last updated its list of establishments. This therefore excludes firms that closed during the period and those that were established more recently. It is therefore a sample of 'established survivors'.

Location, Sectoral Distribution and Age of Firms

The 100 firms spanned eight manufacturing activities across four locations (see Table 10.7). Most firms were located in Lusaka and the Copperbelt (82 per cent), and the majority were concentrated in three sub-sectors, food, beverages and tobacco (27 firms), textiles and leather (28 firms), and chemicals (23 firms). Within each of the subsectors there is a considerable degree of heterogeneity. In some cases, particularly in the textile and leather sector, the sub-subsectoral differences in structure and performance are systematic. Thus, as shall be seen later, there are marked differences between the cotton yarn sub-subsector and the garments sub-subsector. In the case of the other subsectors (chemicals and metal manufactures, especially) there are no systematic differences and the sample size is just too small to justify disaggregation beyond the two-digit classification used in Table 10.7.

The sample firms are split more or less equally between Zambian and

Table 10.7 Sample firms

Two-digit sector code	*Location of enterprise*			*Total*
	Lusaka	*Copperbelt*	*Livingstone*	
Food/beverage/ tobacco	18	6	3	27
Textiles/leather	4	12	12	28
Wood/wood products	6		2	8
Paper/printing	3	1		4
Chemicals	11	12		23
Non-metallic minerals	1			1
Metal products/ Machinery	5	3	1	9
Total	*48*	*34*	*18*	*100*

Source: Survey data.

non-Zambian-owned firms. The African-owned firms (55 per cent of the total) are split more or less evenly between state-owned firms and private firms. Foreign firms are almost entirely wholly private, with only 5 per cent being joint ventures (with the Zambian government). Approximately 70 per cent of the private firms (both African and non-African- owned) are small, unlisted companies, partnerships or sole proprietorships. The remainder are listed companies, of which three-quarters are foreign-owned. To focus the analysis on a more meaningful set of distinctions, we simplify the firm classification, distinguishing only three types of firm: state-owned enterprises; domestic-owned private firms; and foreign-owned private firms. Foreign private firms are those whose owners are ethnically non-African, whether or not they are Zambian citizens. Foreign private firms therefore include both subsidiary operations of firms whose head- quarters (and decision-making) are located outside Zambia, and also those firms whose owners are non-African Zambians. As Table 10.8 suggests, there is no strong relationship between legal ownership status and the sector of operation of the firms, with the exception of SOE representation in the food, beverage and tobacco and the paper and printing sectors.

The average age of sample firms is 22 years, placing their median formation around 1973, just at the height of the copper boom (Table 10.9). A small number of firms in the sample – all of which are foreign-owned – were established prior to Independence in 1964, with the oldest three companies dating to 1929, 1935 and 1949, respectively; all of these are

Table 10.8 Firm ownership by sector

Two-digit sector code	*Location of enterprise*			
	State-owned firms	*Domestic-owned private firms*	*Foreign-owned private firms*	*Total*
Food/beverage/ tobacco	13	4	10	37
Textiles/leather	3	12	13	28
Wood/wood products	3		5	8
Paper/printing	1	1	2	4
Chemicals	6	7	10	23
Metal products/ Machinery	1	3	5	9
Total	*24*	*31*	*45*	*100*

Source: Survey data.

Table 10.9 Firm age by sector

Two-digit sector code	*Date of establishment*				
	1990–95	*1985–89*	*1974–84*	*1964–73*	*Pre-1964*
Food/beverage/ tobacco	2	2	6	17	
Textiles/leather	7		14	5	2
Wood/wood products		1	2	4	1
Paper/printing			2	2	
Chemicals	2	1	5	12	3
Non-metallic minerals					1
Metal products/ Machinery	1	2	1	4	1
Total	*12*	*6*	*30*	*44*	*8*

Source: Survey data (see also Appendix 10C, Table 10C.1).

still 100 per cent foreign-owned. Three-quarters of the sample firms were established between 1964 and 1984, and 12 per cent were established during the most recent phase of the economy's history. SOEs are somewhat older than domestic private firms on average (24 years as opposed to 16 years) reflecting both their rapid creation in the early post-Independence period, and the fact that virtually no state firms were created

Table 10.10 Sales by sector (K m.)

	Value of sales last period			
Two-digit sector code	*Mean*	*Median*	*Minimum*	*Maximum*
Food/beverage/ tobacco	352	202	1	1 517
Textiles/leather	1156	134	1	13 000
Wood/wood products	1040	94	0	7 475
Paper/printing	370	370	370	370
Chemicals	1588	880	9	10 668
Non-metallic minerals	125	125	125	125
Metal products/ Machinery	318	103	1	1 066
Total	*959*	*202*	*0*	*13 000*
Does the firm export at least some of its output?				
No	453	146	0	7 000
Yes	2663	456	1	13 000

Source: Survey data (see also Appendix 10C, Table 10C.2).

after the beginning of serious adjustment efforts began in the mid 1980s. Overall, however, the pattern of firm formation in the sample reflects what we know to be the case in the economy as a whole. Thus the period up to the Mulungushi Declaration was dominated by foreign firms and by the emergence of a rapidly growing SOE sector, while the decade following this was characterized by growth of private Zambian-owned firms, although the number of foreign-owned private firm continued to grow. No strong sectoral patterns emerge in terms of the time of firm foundation. Moreover, given the age of the firms, the vast majority of the non-government and non-listed companies are still owned and run by their founders – some 75 per cent of all companies.

Firm Size and the Structure of Production

The variance of firm size, either by sales or by employment, is extremely high (Table 10.10 and 10.11). Full-time employment ranged from 4 employees to 5000 while the value of sales[28] ranged from less than K1m. to K13 bn. in the previous year. The median firm, however, had sales in 1994 of approximately K200 m. (approximately $US300 000)[29] and total full-time employment of around 80 people. Due to the high variances

Table 10.11 Full-time employment by sector (no. of employees)

	Full-time employment			
Two-digit sector code	*Mean*	*Median*	*Minimum*	*Maximum*
Food/beverage/tobacco	257	50	10	1832
Textiles/leather	417	112	14	5000
Wood/wood products	191	80	12	763
Paper/printing	122	69	35	314
Chemicals	381	91	4	4875
Non-metallic minerals	52	52	52	52
Metal products/Machinery	59	43	16	115
Total	*304*	*80*	*4*	*5000*
Does the firm export at least some of its output?				
No	237	62	4	5000
Yes	578	147	15	4875

Source: Survey data (see also Appendix 10C, Table 10C.3).

within the sub-samples, it is not possible to reject statistically the hypothesis that firm size is constant across ownership status, but there is weak evidence that SOEs are substantially larger in terms of sales and employment than private sector firms, although, as we shall see below, their labour productivity is significantly lower. Within the private sectors, domestic firms are somewhat larger than foreign firms, but have a lower level of labour productivity. The sample is also relatively homogeneous across the manufacturing subsectors. Median sales values are slightly larger in the chemical subsector than elsewhere, while the textile sector seems to be the most labour intensive. Again, these results hold across all forms of ownership.

The sample data on the structure of production are relatively sketchy, with only just over two-thirds of the sample reporting data on their cost structure. From the data collected, however, intermediate inputs account for approximately 50 per cent of the total cost of production and value added for the remainder (Table 10.12). The aggregate input-output coefficients were relatively constant across the subsectors and across exporting and non-exporting firms. Roughly half of all inputs (one-quarter of the cost of production) are imported, with the import shares being highest in the textiles and chemicals sectors. Value added is more or less equally split between payments to labour (13 per cent) and gross profits (11 per

Table 10.12 Structure of production by sector

Two-digit sector code	*Input–output ratio (Median)*	*Imported raw material (Median)*	*Wages as share of sales (Median)*	*Gross profit margin (before depreciation and tax) (Median)*
Food/beverage/tobacco	0.79	0.14	0.08	0.13
Textiles/leather	0.78	0.30	0.16	0.10
Wood/wood products	0.82	0.20	0.26	0.07
Paper/printing	0.55	0.00	0.11	0.34
Chemicals	0.62	0.27	0.13	0.15
Non-metallic minerals	1.08	0.20	0.31	0.10
Metal products/Machinery	0.73	0.00	0.13	0.05
Total	*0.77*	*0.22*	*0.13*	*0.11*
Does the firm export at least some of its output?				
No	0.79	0.21	0.13	0.11
Yes	0.73	0.23	0.15	0.16

Source: Survey data (see also Appendix 10C, Table 10C.4.).

cent) with depreciation and taxation accounting for the balance of the cost of production. For the sample as a whole the mean net rate of profit on sales (that is, before depreciation and taxation) was 17 per cent, while the median rate was 11 per cent, with a range from a maximum profit rate of 90 per cent to a loss of 22 per cent.

There is no time series on firm profitability (either retrospective or prospective), but we can refer to the RPED survey results from von der Fehr *et al.* (1995), who find that the mean profit rate on sales across a similar sample of manufacturing firms (in food, textiles, wood and metal goods) was approximately 13 per cent. The printing and chemical sectors enjoyed a higher rate of profit (with a mean of 34 per cent) while the wood products and metal products and machinery recorded the lowest rates. An interesting feature of the data, possibly reflecting the small sample size, is that the profit rate in 1994 was highest for the SOE firms and lowest for the foreign private firms across all sectors. There was, however, a marked difference between exporting and non-exporting firms. The median all-firm profit rate for non-exporting companies was 11 per cent, while the median for the exporting firms was 16 per cent. Interestingly, however, the higher profitability of exporting firms is due not to higher profitability of the export-intensive sectors but rather the high profitability of exporting firms in sectors that have a low export exposure,

Table 10.13 Labour productivity by sector (K m.)

	Labour productivity (sales per full-time employee)			
Two-digit sector code	*Mean*	*Median*	*Minimum*	*Maximum*
Food/beverage/tobacco	5.24	.87	0.00	20.17
Textiles/leather	3.06	1.82	0.00	17.29
Wood/wood products	3.87	2.36	0.01	11.50
Paper/printing	1.18	1.18	1.18	1.18
Chemicals	10.13	7.27	0.02	31.43
Non-metallic minerals	2.40	2.40	2.40	2.40
Metal products/Machinery	4.09	3.55	0.01	9.27
Total	*5.38*	*2.50*	*0.00*	*31.43*
Does the firm export at least some of its output?				
No	5.41	1.91	0.00	31.43
Yes	5.29	4.69	0.08	17.29

Source: Survey data (see also Appendix 10C, Table 10C.5.).

particularly food, beverages and tobacco, and metal products, which combined account for only 14 per cent of the total number of exporting firms.

Factor Demands and Productivity

Unfortunately, data on firms' capital stock is very poor and it is not possible to compare capital–output or capital–labour ratios accurately across sectors and ownership. However, it is possible to derive some basic indications of comparative labour productivity across firms (Table 10.13), although even these indicators are seriously compromised by our inability to control for the capital intensity of the firms. Nonetheless, the all-firm mean level of sales is approximately K5.4 m. per full-time employee per annum (approximately $US8000), although the median is less than half this value at K2.5 m. There are very marked differences across sectors, ownership and markets. Foreign-owned firms are significantly more productive than either domestic private firms or SOEs, and this dominance covers all sectors of manufacturing. It is notable, however, that the domestic private sector firms are significantly less productive than their state-owned equivalents in all sectors except chemicals.

Exporting firms are also significantly more productive than those firms supplying the domestic market. Median productivity among exporting companies is K4.7 m. as opposed to K1.9 m. among the domestic-orientated firms. Part of the explanation for the large differences in labour productivity, particularly between domestic and foreign private firms and between import-substituters and exporters, may lie with the relative capital intensity of the firms. As we noted above, we do not have adequate survey data to draw reliable inferences on capital–labour ratios, but it is useful to note than when asked about the constraints to full capacity utilization, significantly more SOEs and domestic private firms than foreign firms felt that the age of their capital stock was an important constraint to their operations (Table 10.14). Similarly, all firms in the sample, regardless of ownership or of whether they were exporting or not, perceived broadly the same factors constraining their output. Overwhelmingly, firms reported a shortage of demand (at prevailing prices) for their products, most notably through competition from imports, and the extremely high cost of credit. Approximately 80 per cent of firms responding identified lack of demand as constraining their output, and 85 per cent also identified the cost of working capital. Less than half of firms identified *access* to credit as a constraint to full capacity utilization. Moreover, it is interesting to note that the majority of firms did not see high real wages or access to foreign exchange as major constraints to their operation, although domestic private firms perceived themselves to be constrained by somewhat higher real wages and less access to the domestic and foreign capital markets.

Liberalization and the Product Market

The textbook model of a compatible trade liberalization would take as its starting point an increase in the output of the exportable sector firms and a contraction in the output of import-substituting firms. Though the survey collected data on the level of output and firm-level expectations of the future growth of output, it did not collect information on the change in output over the period since the implementation of the adjustment programme. However, there is some partial information from the RPED report by von der Fehr *et al.* (1995), which suggests that approximately 60 per cent of firms experienced a decline in the real quantity of sales over the previous year (from 1993 to 1994) and that this decline was most marked among larger firms. The data do not, however, discriminate between exporting and non-exporting firms. We are therefore unable to infer with any degree of accuracy from the survey data (either the trade liberalization or the RPED survey) the output consequences of liberalization or how they differ between exportable and importable sectors. There is, however, some weak evidence from our survey on firms' expectations about the future direction of their output.

Table 10.14 Perceived constraints to full capacity operation

	Does the firm export at least some of its output?		Total*
	No*	Yes*	
Lack of demand			
Yes	53 (79.1)	12 (85.7)	65 (80.2)
No	14 (20.9)	2 (14.3)	16 (19.8)
Old capital stock			
Yes	32 (57.1)	8 (66.7)	40 (58.8)
No	24 (42.9)	4 (33.3)	28 (41.2)
Real wages too high			
Yes	11 (22.9)	4 (44.4)	15 (26.3)
No	37 (77.1)	5 (55.6)	42 (73.7)
Shortage of inputs			
Yes	20 (40.0)	6 (60.0)	26 (43.3)
No	30 (60.0)	4 (40.0)	34 (56.7)
No access to credit			
Yes	22 (44.9)	5 (55.6)	27 (46.6)
No	27 (55.1)	4 (44.4)	31 (53.4)
Cost of credit			
Yes	50 (84.7)	12 (85.7)	62 (84.9)
No	9 (15.3)	2 (14.3)	11 (15.1)
Shortage of foreign exchange			
Yes	11 (24.4)	3 (33.3)	14 (25.9)
No	34 (75.6)	6 (66.7)	40 (74.1)
Other			
Yes	14 (35.0)	4 (40.0)	18 (36.0)
No	26 (65.0)	6 (60.0)	32 (64.0)

Note: * Percentage in parentheses.

Source: Survey data.

The Export Market

Although all the firms in the sample produce tradeable goods, the majority sell their output only to the domestic market, with less than 8 per cent of the total output of the sample firms being exported. Moreover, the total exports of the sample firms are accounted for by only 15 firms, and only eight of the firms exported more than 50 per cent of their output. The export base of the sample is thus remarkably narrow.[30] This is not, however, a sample characteristic. The 1995 Audit of the Export Board notes that of the 84 significant exporters in the economy (excluding the mineral sector), over 70 per cent of the export value is accounted for by only nine companies.

Total 1994 exports by the sampled firms in US$ terms were approximately $26.9 m. or 18 per cent of total recorded 1994 non-traditional exports,[31] which were estimated by the Export Board to be approximately $148.5 m.[32] Within the sample, the textile and leather, and the wood products sectors accounted for the vast majority of total exports, the former at 86 per cent and the latter at 10 per cent. Total exports from the sample firms increased by $12.5 m. over the previous year (an increase of 87 per cent, but this total was still markedly lower than in the year prior to liberalization, when total exports from the sample were $90.5 m. The decline in recorded exports is due almost entirely to the collapse of a single former parastatal exporting firm, Kafue Textiles, which experienced a sharp decline in its total output during the period of liberalization. As we shall see, the collapse of Kafue Textiles' exports followed directly from the collapse of its share of the *domestic* textile market following import liberalization. Prior to liberalization, Kafue Textile's principal market was the (highly protected) domestic market, with the export share simply being determined by the excess of production over domestic demand. Trade and exchange liberalization lowered the domestic market price to a point where Kafue Textiles was unable to maintain its domestic market share. It subsequently reduced its production dramatically, which had a direct knock-on effect on the volume of production available for exporting (even though the share of its output that was exported had increased).

The experience of Kafue Textiles is repeated across the spectrum, particularly in the garment subsector of the textile industry, historically one of the most protected (and SOE-dominated) sectors of the economy, where output levels and therefore export volumes have contracted sharply. In contrast, the subsector that has shown the most dramatic export improvement is cotton yarn, where exports have risen dramatically since liberalization, albeit on the strength of one exceptionally productive and capital-intensive company in the sample. Even so, employment in the yarn subsector rose by 8 per cent from 1993 to 1994, while employment in the garment sector fell by a similar amount.

Excluding Kafue Textiles, however, the sample firms collectively enjoyed a sharp increase in their total export earnings after the beginning of the liberalization process, with total exports (at current $US) rising from approximately $2.4 m. on the eve of liberalization to approximately $8.7 m., an increase of about 260 per cent. Though this is an impressive turnaround, it should be noted that the total volume of non-traditional exports in Zambia remains remarkably low. Total non-traditional (visible) exports are approximately 13 per cent of total exports; the ratio has almost doubled since 1989, but this has been because of the fall in the value of traditional exports. Total visible exports fell by over 18 per cent from 1989 to 1995, principally as a result of the collapse in copper output. Thus while there has been a notable increase in the value of non-traditional exports from Zambia since the beginning of the current liberalization phase, this has been insufficient to offset the steady decline in traditional export supply. There is some evidence that a number of currently exporting firms began their life by supplying the domestic market and only switched into supplying the export market in the 1990s. Most exporting firms, however, have been established export market suppliers since their creation. Of the pre-Independence firms, approximately half sold their output to the export market, whereas of those firms established since Independence, less than one-fifth exported anything. Most interesting of all, not one of the firms established during the period from 1985 to 1989 has been involved in exporting (see Table 10.15).

Liberalization and the Consequences for Exporting

A key objective of the Zambian liberalization process, and established as an explicit goal in the government's sequence of policy framework papers, has been to stimulate the growth in the non-traditional export sector at the target rate of 15 per cent per annum in the constant dollar value. In reality, the growth has been somewhat lower than anticipated, averaging approximately 10 per cent per annum in *current* dollar prices. Export performance has, however, been stronger since mid-1993 than before, although still falling short of the PFP target growth rate.

It is appropriate, therefore, to consider whether this slower than anticipated non-traditional growth rate can be attributed to a policy failure, to weaker than anticipated effects of price reform or to other factors. Here the survey evidence takes us some way towards understanding the reasons for this outcome. One possible explanation is simply that the process of switching to the export market takes time and that as perceptions about the profitability of exporting develop, more firms see their best trading opportunities in external markets. Thus while 75 per cent of non-exporting firms have never exported any of their output in the past, a similar proportion of firms indicated that they expect to do so in the future. Unfortunately, the survey did not elicit the reasons why firms believed they would increasingly sell to export markets, so this claim is somewhat difficult to assess. However, it is interesting to note that, according to the survey evidence, even though there were trade-liberalizing reforms in the past, firms typically did not switch between domestic and

Table 10.15 Exports and export share by sector

Two-digit sector code	*Value of exports ($US) (Sum)*	*Value of exports pre-liberalization ($US) (Sum)*	*% Share of output exported (Mean)*
Food/beverage/tobacco	30 000	500 000	2.59
Textiles/leather	23 265 670	88 998 608	18.11
Wood/wood products	2 789 250	1 000 000	3.13
Paper/printing			
Chemicals	748 810	50 150	4.13
Non-metallic minerals			0.00
Metal products/machinery	56 000	4 000	7.78
Total	*26 889 730*	*90 552 758*	*7.67*

Source: Survey data

export markets. If firms were established with an eye to the export market, then they historically would supply that market regardless of changes in trade policy (and thus relative prices between domestic and export markets) and vice versa. In other words, the elasticity of substitution seems to have been low in the past, and we may therefore conclude that there is no strong reason to believe that this has changed. However, one possible ex post explanation comes from evidence presented above that previous trade reforms were not credible and hence we would not expect to have seen firms altering their behaviour. By this argument, then, the apparently high elasticity of substitution between supplying the domestic and export markets in response to the current reforms may reflect, in addition to possibly larger relative price effects, greater credibility of the reforms.

A second argument explaining sluggish reaction to reform is simply that the reforms have not proceeded 'far enough'. This claim may be supported by the evidence on the perceived constraints to exporting. Approximately 60 per cent of firms felt they faced constraints to exporting within the region, although the perception of being constrained in export markets was stronger among those firms that were actually exporting. As with the responses to the constraints on full capacity operation, the picture that emerges is one where quantitative constraints play little role in limiting export opportunities (for example, less than 10 per cent of firms felt that quantitative barriers played any role in limiting regional trade while less than a quarter of firms felt that access to foreign exchange still represented a constraint to their operations), but where price disincentives were important. Exporting firms still perceived that they faced high tariffs against their exports, with almost 90 per cent, indicating that it was the single most important constraint to their operations. All exporting firms identified the reduction of tariffs as important reforms, but over two-thirds felt that the reduction in regional tariffs, particularly by Zimbabwe and South Africa, was essential for their continued export activities (Appendix Table 10C.6).

A further constraint perceived by firms is the view that while they are competitive in terms of labour costs, exporting firms lose out in the face of high domestic (non-tradeable) production costs, particularly for transport and energy. These costs of production may not be expected to rise with liberalization (except as a result of second-order income effects), but historically they have been kept below their market clearing levels through explicit or implicit subsidies.[33] The reform measures implemented in the 1990s have included the adjustment of utility prices towards an average-cost pricing regime. In the case of energy and transport costs this has involved an explicit commitment to set prices at border prices. It should also be noted that the survey occurred at a time when the regional air transport system was in a state of flux following the closure of Zambia Airways. In all three cases, however, these (relative) price changes may be judged to be one-off adjustments.

The third possible explanation for the relatively modest response to trade reforms is the degree of uncertainty facing firms in the Zambian economy. As is borne out by the sample firms, there is a strikingly high degree of uncertainty as to the future direction of macroeconomic and trade policy. Firms were asked whether they expect policy reforms in the next 12 and 36 months in the areas of exchange rate policy, tariff structures and regional trade policy, as well as on the likely implications for their own firm operations. In not one case did the survey generate decisive responses. It is true that over a three-year period, the simple majority of firms expected some change (although a consistent 20 per cent of all firms claimed not to know about policy reforms), but in general the proportion of firms expecting policies to move in one direction was almost exactly balanced by firms thinking the opposite. Uncertainty was greater, however, in the area identified as having the greatest consequences for export performance, namely regional trade barriers. Although 85 per cent of firms believed that regional tariffs against their exports were too high (and too low against imports), only 47 per cent of all firms felt that rates would change, while 53 per cent either felt that there would be no change or were unsure as to what might happen (Appendix Tables 10C.7 and 8).

From a public policy perspective, these results are quite remarkable, not least in view of the fact that the current government has identified itself strongly with macroeconomic adjustment and liberalization. However, a moment's reflection would suggest that the results are consistent with the current state of policy-making in Zambia, where the direction of policy is intimately linked with conditional adjustment programmes developed by the donor community. As noted in the introduction to this section, the first five-year phase of the liberalization programme – which had been shaped by the RAP – was due to be completed in March 1995. Due to events at the beginning of 1995, the graduation from the RAP did not happen, and it was only late in the third quarter of 1995 that it seemed likely, even to senior officials, that a successful graduation to an IMF enhanced structural adjustment facility would occur. The step was finally taken in the last quarter of 1995 and the next five-year policy framework paper was presented only in early 1996. At the time of the survey, however, there was no clear articulation of the future direction of policy. Moreover, as the 1996 general election approached, there was growing uncertainty about the likely direction of policy either by the incumbent government during the run-up to the election, or beyond it.

Liberalization and Import-substituting Firms

Despite Zambia's earlier position as one of the most industrialized economies in Africa, its industrial sector, which was predominantly state-owned, was highly protected and heavily capital-intensive and import-intensive. Any trade liberalization programme, therefore, had to be accompanied by a significant contraction in the import-substituting manufacturing sector; this contraction, moreover, would occur rapidly as consumers switched demand in response to the removal of price and non-price barriers to imports. It is thus reasonable to assume that the most immediate effects of trade liberalization will be felt by import-substituting firms. This is particularly true in the case of Zambia, where import liberalization, while being offset to a significant degree by the initial real exchange rate depreciation, has been accelerated by two important factors:

(1) the appreciation of the real exchange rate that has occurred since mid-1993, has reduced the competitiveness of exports and the consumer price of imports; and
(2) the increase in trade and sales tax evasion. Imports that evade customs duties (which have been reduced as a result of explicit trade liberalization measures) also evade domestic taxes levied on the duty-inclusive c.i.f. price of the imports. As a consequence, the (weighted) average market price of imports is significantly lower than the tax inclusive price of import-substituting production.

These two factors have, as we shall argue below, led to an overshooting of the effective real exchange rate for import-substituting firms and a greater contraction in the import-substituting sector than would be warranted at an equilibrium effective real exchange rate.

This view is supported to some extent by the survey data, which suggest that non-exporting firms have borne the brunt of the costs of adjustment. Since the beginning of the liberalization process total full-time employment has declined by approximately 6 per cent overall. However, non-exporting firms have witnessed a 7 per cent decline in employment, with the exporting companies registering a small increase in aggregate employment. The principal contracting sectors are wood and wood products, chemicals, and metal products, none of which had any significant export market. These are the sectors, moreover, that have enjoyed the highest level of effective protection.

Firms' perceptions of domestic product market competition are dominated by notions of import penetration (Table 10.16, and also the following discussion on competition), with 60 per cent of firms seeing import competition as their main threat. Interestingly, however, of those firms identifying import competition as their principal source of competition, almost 70 per cent still indicate that they tend to employ a mark-up pricing rule rather than taking import prices as the reference for their output price, with only 30 per cent of firms identifying themselves as price-takers. Obviously there may be quality differences between products, but nonetheless this does indicate the extent to which profit margins are being squeezed as a result of the reduction of protection afforded by the trade regime. Firms seeking to price on a mark-up basis have significantly lower average profit margins.

Liberalization and Factor Markets

The previous section suggested that relative prices had moved substantially for the manufacturing sector and liberalization measures had induced marked changes in the degree of competition faced by these firms, particularly those operating in import-substituting sectors. We suggested that these changes reflected both the planned and anticipated effects of liberalization, but might also reflect the transitional effects of the adjustment process. Whether trade liberalization is welfare-improving (and ultimately sustainable) will depend to a large extent on the consequences of the liberalization measures for factor demands and growth. As we noted above, it is expected that the manufacturing sector would shrink in aggregate, although within the sector we expected a shift from the production of importables to exportables. The consequences for factor markets are threefold. Consider first the labour markets. Whether trade liberalization increases or decreases manufacturing employment will depend on the rela-

Table 10.16 Perceived sources of competition

	Does the firm export at least some of its output?		*Total**
	*No**	*Yes**	
Main source of competition in the domestic market			
None	1 (1.2)	4 (21.1)	5 (5.0)
Domestic firms	33 (40.7)	4 (21.1)	37 (37.0)
Importers	47 (58.0)	11 (57.9)	58 (58.0)
Increased competition from domestic producers			
Yes	62 (77.5)	10 (58.8)	72 (74.2)
No	18 (22.5)	7 (41.2)	25 (25.8)
Increased import competition from within region			
Yes	64 (81.0)	11 (64.7)	75 (78.1)
No	15 (19.0)	6 (35.3)	21 (21.9)
Increased import competition from outside region			
Yes	55 (72.4)	12 (70.6)	67 (72.0)
No	21 (27.6)	5 (29.4)	26 (28.0)

Note: * Percentage in parentheses.

Source: Survey data.

tive labour intensity of exportables to importables and the relative growth of these subsectors. The consequences for the average real wage in the sector follows directly from the factor demands, while the consequences for the skill distribution of manufacturing real wages depends more specifically on the relative skills composition of the exportable and importable sectors.

Similarly, expectations may be formed in respect of the capital market. Even in the short run when the sector is declining in aggregate, we may expect an increase in investment as the exportable firms expand their output, even though importable firms' output is contracting. Again, the consequences for the structure of the capital stock are ambiguous and will depend on the relative rates of growth and the capital intensity of production in the expanding and contracting sectors.

Labour Market

Since the commencement of liberalization measures in 1989, only 11 of the 100 firms have registered an increase in employment. Almost half of

Table 10.17 Change in employment

Two-digit sector code	*12-month growth in labour force* −10%–0%	0%–10%	10%–50%	Greater than 50%
Food/beverages/tobacco	17	1	2	
Textiles/leather	16	3	3	
Wood/wood products	5		1	
Paper/printing	2	1		1
Chemicals	14	1		
Non-metallic minerals				
Metal products/Machinery	2	2		
Does the firm export at least some of its output?				
No	45	4	5	1
Yes	11	4	1	
Total	*56*	*8*	*6*	*1*

Source: Survey data (see also Appendix 10C, Table 10C.9).

all firms have seen employment decline by more than 10 per cent from their pre-liberalization level, while 10 per cent of all firms (still in operation since the beginning of 1989) have seen their employment decline by over 50 per cent. It would seem that a large part of the decline in employment has occurred in the last 12 months before the survey (Tables 10.17). Given that there is a selection bias in the sample – we are only surveying firms that are currently in operation and therefore exclude firms that have closed down since the beginning of the liberalization period – this suggests a major contraction in (formal sector) manufacturing employment. It is true, however, that exporting firms have seen a significantly small decline in their employment over the period. While the median decline in full-time employment for the sample as a whole has been 6 per cent of the original work force, the median exporting firm has not changed employment at all.

For the data on business confidence, however, the vast majority of firms (79.7 per cent) did not expect employment to change any further over the next 12 months. Of those who did expect it to change at all, however, the majority expected further declines in employment. There was no distinctive pattern by the ownership status of the firms, but the sectoral spread of expected changes in employment again indicates that non-exporting firms were more pessimistic about their future employment levels.

Table 10.18 Real investment by sector (constant 1994 prices)

Two-digit sector code	*1994*	*1993*	*1992*	*1991*	*1990*
Food/beverage/tobacco	7052	1850	44 896	82 024	79 070
Textiles/leather	5511	18 602	11 613	5 346	3 540
Wood/wood products	4	25	35	27	15
Chemicals	829	625	3 214	2 732	1 202
Non-metallic minerals	2		26		75
Metal products/Machinery	30	82	126	71	60
Does the firm export at least some of its output?					
No	7 998	2 602	49 271	88 700	82 497
Yes	5 429	18 583	10 640	1 500	1 467
Total	*13 428*	*21 185*	*59 911*	*90 200*	*83 964*

Source: Survey data.

Evidence from a longer-term outlook is much less coherent, with no clear patterns emerging. To a considerable extent this reflects the difficulties associated with long-term forecasting, particularly in the presence of the considerable uncertainty over the future direction of trade and macro-economic policy.

The Capital Market

The data on investment is even more sobering than for employment. Although the sample size is small and therefore – given the lumpiness of investment activity – somewhat unreliable, the data suggest that investment levels rose quite sharply in the early stages of liberalization (1991/92), but fell off sharply thereafter. Overall, total real investment among the sample firms fell from almost K90 bn. in 1990/91 to less than K15 bn. in 1994, but in all sectors (with the exception of the food, beverage and tobacco sector) investment actually rose sharply from 1990 to 1992[34] (see Table 10.18). The subsequent decline has been most marked in chemicals and the food, beverage and tobacco sectors (which have the lowest export shares). In the textile sectors, 1992 and 1993 saw a sharp *increase* in the volume of investment, which has tailed off only in the most recent year. Examination of the data at the firm level suggests that this reflects the investment pattern anticipated by the trade liberation model in which the exporting firms in the yarn sector increased their investment quite rapidly while the textile and garments sector firms reduced their gross investment levels to zero.

We might expect liberalization to affect the cost of capital formation in a number of ways. The first is through the removal of the high levels

Table 10.19 Composition of real investment by sector

Two-digit sector code	*Mean ratio of tradeable to non-tradeable investment*				
	1994	*1993*	*1992*	*1991*	*1990*
Food/beverage/ tobacco	15.23	27.70	7.79	1.41	6.88
Textiles/leather	4.33	6.14	7.45	4.28	3.00
Wood/wood products	10.75	6.75	12.50	12.50	12.50
Chemicals	18.82	3.20	10.54	6.81	17.70
Non-metallic minerals			4.88		
Metal products/ Machinery	2.33	5.67			
Does the firm export at least some of its output?					
No	13.95	12.40	8.24	4.65	8.91
Yes	3.84	4.14	8.11	5.19	4.35
Total	*11.06*	*9.79*	*8.22*	*4.76*	*7.94*

Source: Survey data.

of protection afforded to imported goods. Thus we would expect the share of tradeable (imported) capital goods to decline in the total stock of investment. The second, is through the alteration of relative prices in the goods markets: we would expect the composition of capital formation to reflect the composition of capital in the growth sectors of the economy. The data on the composition of capital is, however, not sufficient to cast much light on the debate. The composition of investment seems to move in a broadly procyclical way for the textile sectors (that is, during the growth in investment, the share of tradeable capital increased) and in a counter cyclical fashion for other sectors (Table 10.19).

The collapse in investment among the firms seems to be closely related to the high real interest rates that emerged in 1993 following the stabilization measures enacted at that time. By 1994 the small volume of investment that did occur was predominantly financed from retained earnings (either personal savings in the case of sole traders or partnerships or corporate profits in the case of listed companies), which, as the previous sections have indicated, have been sharply squeezed over recent years. Only 18 per cent of firms used bank finance for capital formation. Of those that did, typically less than 30 per cent of the investment cost was financed from this source, with the vast majority of firms indicating that the cost of finance, rather than access to finance, has been the principal constraint to raising external finance for investment (Table 10.20).

Table 10.20 Reasons for not borrowing from banking system

	Does the firm export at least some of its output?					
	No	*%*	*Yes*	*%*	*Total*	*%*
Loan not required	6	(21.4)	1	(11.1)	6	(18.9)
Collateral too high	2	(7.1)			2	(5.4)
Interest rates too high	20	(71.4)	8	(88.9)	28	(75.7)
1993						
Loan not required	6	(20.0)	2	(18.2)	8	(19.5)
Collateral too high	1	(3.3)			1	(2.4)
Interest rates too high	23	(76.7)	9	(81.8)	32	(78.0)
1992						
Loan not required	9	(29.0)	2	(18.2)	11	(26.2)
Collateral too high	1	(3.2)			1	(2.4)
Interest rates too high	20	(64.5)	9	(81.8)	29	(69.0)
Fear of rejection	1	(3.2)			1	(2.4)
1991						
Loan not required	8	(33.3)	1	(11.1)	9	(27.3)
Collateral too high	2	(8.3)			2	(6.1)
Interest rates too high	14	(58.3)	8	(88.9)	22	(66.7)
1990						
Loan not required	8	(27.6)	1	(11.1)	9	(23.7)
Collateral too high	4	(13.8)	1	(11.1)	5	(13.2)
Interest rates too high	17	(58.6)	7	(77.8)	24	(63.2)

Source: Survey data.

Incentives, Regulation and Taxes: Some Microeconomic Evidence

By mid-1995 when this survey was conducted, Zambia had moved rapidly with the implementation of its trade, exchange rate and fiscal reforms. Trade licensing and export retention schemes were abolished early in the reform programme as were (explicit) non-tariff barriers. The only outstanding trade-related tax instruments, other than the tariff schedule itself, were the duty drawback system and the transition from a sales tax on imports to a value-added tax system.

The inefficient administration of the duty drawback scheme has frequently been cited as a serious deterrent to export development. The scheme is intended to provide drawbacks (that is, rebates) on duty paid on imported inputs consumed for export purposes. In practice, the administrative costs and delays, particularly during the period when domestic inflation was high, have been seen as a serious constraint to the successful operation of the scheme. The most common problems were verification[35] and the extent to which the real value of the drawback was eroded by inflation as a result of the delay by the government in rebating the duty paid. Unfortunately, the data from the survey do not cast light on the extent to which the effective duty drawback scheme deviated from the notional value of the scheme. The reported median relief is approximately 18 per cent, but it seems there may be some serious ambiguity in the question; it is not clear whether respondents were required to express the relief as a proportion of the export value or as a proportion of the total duties paid on inputs.[36] It is interesting to note that significantly more non-exporting firms than exporting firms claimed that they received duty drawback benefits. Given that the scheme is available to exporters only, this would suggest that the data are contaminated by firms' misinterpreting the duty drawback scheme as some other general form of incentives that provide for duty-free importation.

Although the VAT was not covered in the survey, we were in a position to follow up with a set of questions aimed at eliciting perceptions of the likely consequences of the VAT. The VAT was introduced on 1 July 1995, as a standard invoice-based tax levied on supplies of goods or services regardless of their country of origin. The VAT replaced a sales tax that covered only the manufacturing sector of the economy. The sales tax on imports was levied at 23 per cent on c.i.f. plus duty border price of imports closer to the prevailing domestic market price. Following the introduction of the VAT on imports, the uplift factor has been abolished, thereby removing a further element of protection afforded to domestic producers of importables. Taxable supplies, including imported goods, are subject to VAT at a standard rate of 20 per cent, whereas exports are zero-rated. A small number of goods (specifically maize and other essential commodities) are exempt from the tax. Businesses that are exporting are therefore entitled to recover the input tax on goods and services consumed in the production process.

At the time of the survey, the VAT was not fully implemented, particularly with respect to provisions for exporters. One area of concern focused on the implementation of the VAT refund schemes under the provisions of the budget. It was understood at the time of implementation that the gross receipts from VAT paid on inputs would be remitted to the Treasury as revenue, and that the Treasury would refund payments from the government's consolidated account to exporters. Refund payments would be made three months in arrears. The concern was that because of the requirement of the cash budget that expenditure could only be made if there was sufficient revenue to cover it, so the Treasury would delay in making VAT refunds.

We conducted structured interviews with 20 firms in Lusaka, chosen in respect of their earlier good response, proximity and consistency, which implied meeting the same person who responded at the earlier main interview. The interviews were conducted between 27 September and 2 October 1995. In many cases we managed to interview the same respondent as during the major interview. While it was too early to measure the functioning of the system directly as no refund had yet been made, we were able to assess firms' perceptions of the consequences of VAT. The main concerns were with the implementation of the tax and its administration. At this stage it appears that tax evasion by suppliers and competitors has limited the benefits of the tax. This is most marked in sectors where markets are being supplied by firms able to avoid taxes and duties; this is particularly the case in the garments sector. In these circumstances, the broadening of the tax base and the elimination of the uplift factor has squeezed the profits of tax-paying domestic producers.

At this stage few firms felt that the introduction of the VAT would have a major impact on export performance, not least because firms identified other factors as the binding constraint to their operations, and the fact that the VAT rebate for exporters was not due to commence until October 1995. More importantly, however, the experience of the VAT highlights the transitional costs borne by the formal manufacturing sector as a result of the collapse in the tax enforcement capacity of the government. In such circumstances, while the VAT may be expected to work well in principle, in practice it increases the implicit tax on informal production, thereby reducing the incentives to exporting and increasing the degree of effective protection faced by the importables sector.

Summary of Firm-Level Evidence

The evidence generated from the survey supports the evidence presented in the first part of this chapter that interprets the current trade liberalization programme as following a broadly standard trajectory. Domestic producers do not perceive themselves to be quantity-constrained in goods or factor markets, but they do perceive their operations to be constrained by stiff price competition as a result of trade liberalization and exchange rate over-valuation; high production costs, particularly working capital; and high transitional costs of adjustment. Their fears are exacerbated to a large degree by considerable uncertainty about the future direction of trade and macroeconomic policy in both domestic and regional markets. Although there is support for the view that the policy reform process is characterized by uncertainty, there is no evidence that the liberalization measures are perceived as incredible.

The consequence of these adverse factors is understated in the survey for the reason mentioned above, that the sample is biased towards successful – that is, surviving – companies and therefore understates the aggregate consequences for the manufacturing sector, although six of the original sample firms were on the verge of closure. Outside the sample, firm closures in the formal sector have been widespread. In Livingstone, 78 per cent of the garment firms in the town (14 out of a population of 18) closed between 1994 and 1995, while 20 per cent of the firms in the wood products sector and the sole firm in the fabricated metal products, machinery and equipment sector had closed. The same story emerges in other main manufacturing locations, with the garments sector suffering the highest proportion of closures. Overall it is estimated that some 25 per cent of formal sector manufacturing firms (by number of firms) have closed since the beginning of the current reform process. Running concurrently with this spate of closures is a rapid process of firm foundation, albeit on a significantly smaller scale. New firms are mainly concentrated in agricultural-related activities, services and trading, with very few in manufacturing. The number of entries was actually much higher than existing firms, but in different activities. One can therefore conclude that substitution of activities is taking place since trade liberalization, with people moving to areas they find more profitable. For example, there is an upsurge of agricultural-related activities, implying that more resources are directed to these activities and away from manufacturing.

10.7 MACRO-COMPATIBILITY AND TRADE LIBERALIZATION

Both trade liberalization episodes in Zambia were accompanied by a range of measures designed to ensure the compatibility of the reform. The interesting point of comparison between the two is that in the former case the reforms were ultimately unsuccessful because macroeconomic compatibility was undermined by a lack of credibility in the government's commitment to exchange rate reform. The reforms of 1989–95, on the other hand, seem to have been not only macro-compatible, but also credible, as the MMD government has been able successfully to establish its commitment to reforms. Contributing to this has been the high level of aid support. The government's commitment has also been buttressed by its ratification of the COMESA regional trade agreement, which binds Zambia to a pre-announced tariff reduction and commits it to avoiding non-tariff barriers.

Trade Liberalization and the Volume of Trade

Given the enclave nature of the exportable sector in Zambia, the impact of trade liberalization measures on the volume of traditional exports may be expected to be moderate. Copper does not lend itself to smuggling and thus changes in trade policy alter the profitability of the sector through their effect on the implicit taxation of net foreign exchange sales by ZCCM to the government. We may, on the other hand, expect the non-copper export sector to respond more sharply to trade-liberalizing measures. We shall discuss this below, but it should be noted that since non-copper exports account for such a large proportion of total exports (see Tables 10.1 and 10.6), liberalization-induced increases in non-traditional exports are likely to have only a marginal impact on the capacity to import. We would therefore expect the main impact of trade liberalization to be experienced through the import side.

The interesting feature, however, was that in both cases despite the liberalization measures – both the tariff reforms and the removal of foreign exchange rationing – the volume of imports did not increase. In fact, it continued to decline (Figure 10.5). This is even more surprising since both trade liberalization episodes in Zambia have been heavily aid-supported. Net aid flows to Zambia have been rising steadily since the mid 1970s (with the exception of the interregnum in 1987–9), but showed a marked upward movement during both reform episodes (Figure 10.6).

There are a number of possible reasons for the fact that even though both liberalization episodes were aid-supported, aggregate imports did not increase. First, the 1989–94 period was a time of declining terms of trade (which fell by almost 25 per cent from 1989 to 1993), so that while actual imports did not rise, measured relative to the counterfactual they were higher than they would otherwise have been. This accords with the textbook case of an aid-supported liberalization, although since the aid flow continues it is not yet possible to determine whether imports will fall to a sustainable no-aid level that would indicate compatibility.

This does not seem to hold in the case of the 1985–7 liberalization, where – even though there was also a significant aid inflow, and export volumes were increasing against relatively constant world terms of trade – import volumes remained more or less constant. Since the aid inflow clearly augmented the capacity to import and imports did not increase, the aid inflow must have been used to increase reserves or to finance debt service payments. To some extent both were the case in the earlier period, since the data on aid flows are computed as gross aid inflows net of amortization of capital only, and thus a component of the aid inflow was used to clear arrears on official debt and to service current debt.[37] As we shall also note below, there is evidence that this earlier period coincided with a sharp increase in domestic saving. Evidence from national accounts data indicates that private sector investment increased, but the foregoing suggests that the private sector was also accumulating (illegal) financial assets.

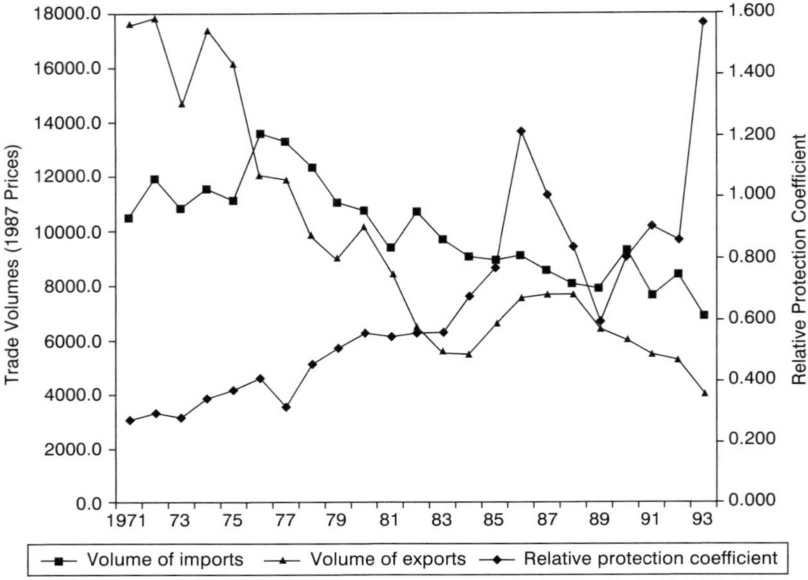

Source: World Tables (1995) and own calculations.

Figure 10.5 Trade liberalization and trade volumes, 1971–93

Setting aside the question of the aid inflow, other important characteristics of the liberalization episodes may be noted. First, although evidence on the composition of imports is available at present only for the first liberalization episode, we see a significant shift in import composition away from exempt and low tariff items (which received preferential access through the exchange rate allocation mechanism), such as food items, government imports and heavy capital goods, towards high tariff goods such as vehicles (Table 10.21). The second feature of the compositional shift at this time was the dramatic increase in the share of capital goods, especially vehicles, and construction materials. Combined with the sharp increase in private savings, which was dominated by inventory accumulation rather than fixed capital formation, this reinforces the view that speculative behaviour on the part of the private sector was widespread. A second feature of both liberalization episodes is that trade reform measures were budget improving, at least in terms of explicit revenue and expenditure items. The positive budgetary consequences of trade reform mean that ex post both trade liberalization episodes seem to have been payments neutral.

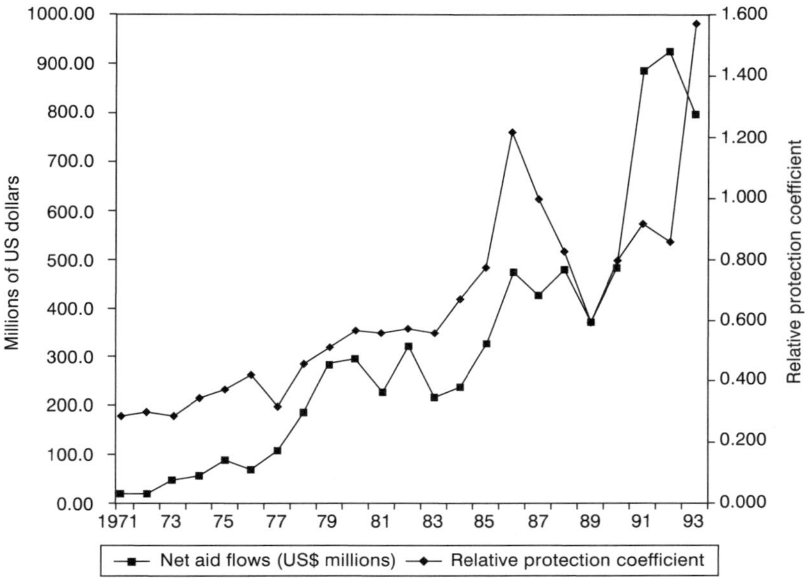

Source: World Tables (1993) and own calculations.

Figure 10.6 Trade liberalization and aid, 1971–93

Macro-compatibility was therefore achieved in part by increasing taxation (relative to the counterfactual). We now turn to the details of the fiscal effects.

The Fiscal Consequences of Trade Liberalization

In Zambia, the liberalization of trade has two main consequences. The first is the direct budget implications of the changes in the tariff. The second concerns the broader fiscal implications arising from exchange rate reform. We have not analysed the foreign exchange budget of the government during this period of the two liberalization episodes, which is required to assess the overall fiscal consequences of exchange rate unification.[38] In this section we shall therefore examine only the direct budget consequences of liberalization.

Figure 10.7, which plots the evolution of trade taxes against the coefficient of protection, indicates a strong positive relationship between liberalization and government revenue. A clearer picture, however, is observed in

Table 10.21 Imports classified by end use (FOB) (%)

	1980	*1981*	*1984*	*1985*	*1986*	*1987*	*1988*	*1989*	*1990*
Inputs in industries									
Agriculture, forestry & fishing	10.3	5.9	10.1	11.1	5.4	6.8	6.0	6.4	8.5
Mining & quarrying	6.5	7.9	6.2	7.5	11.9	11.0	10.2	9.8	8.9
Manufacturing	60.6	66.0	66.1	62.4	48.0	46.5	49.1	50.4	51.4
Construction	13.4	12.9	11.2	10.8	19.3	19.0	15.6	13.4	13.4
Electricity & water	3.0	2.5	1.1	2.4	3.1	2.5	1.8	2.3	2.3
Distribution	0.3	0.2	0.1	0.1	0.2	0.2	0.1	0.1	0.1
Transport & communications	5.4	4.7	4.4	5.1	10.6	10.2	12.8	6.6	9.0
Other services	0.5	0.3	0.7	0.7	1.6	3.8	4.3	11.0	6.3
Total intermediate goods	*100.0*	*100.0*	*100.0*	*100.0*	*100.0*	*100.0*	*100.0*	*100.0*	*100.0*
Fixed capital formation									
Agriculture, forestry & fishing	5.7	5.1	7.1	6.1	3.7	3.4	2.2	4.9	3.6
Mining & qarrying	28.3	26.5	27.0	31.9	25.2	21.8	14.6	11.8	7.9
Manufacturing	34.0	34.0	20.3	23.6	3.0	8.4	8.2	12.0	8.8
Construction	3.3	4.1	3.3	5.0	35.6	31.3	27.3	13.3	26.3
Electricity & water	5.2	4.6	6.7	6.1	3.9	4.5	8.4	4.4	2.1
Distribution	0.2	0.2	0.2	0.1	0.1	0.2	0.5	0.4	0.1
Transport & communications	17.1	18.4	21.1	12.1	20.1	20.1	25.1	35.1	37.8
Government administration	3.2	5.4	5.4	11.8	1.8	4.2	6.6	6.9	6.8
Other services	3.0	1.6	8.8	3.4	6.6	6.3	7.2	11.2	6.7
Total capital goods	*100.0*	*100.0*	*100.0*	*100.0*	*100.0*	*100.0*	*100.0*	*100.0*	*100.0*
Private & government consumption									
Food	24.9	17.1	20.4	19.0	11.4	8.1	7.9	9.1	3.9
Beverages & tobacco	0.6	0.4	0.8	1.4	0.7	0.7	0.7	1.2	0.9
Clothing & footwear	7.9	7.7	3.9	2.3	3.9	4.5	3.8	3.2	4.0
Fuel & light	5.0	2.5	6.4	3.7	4.0	2.6	1.7	6.7	25.3
Furniture & houehold equipment	17.8	19.3	27.5	32.3	16.1	23.3	32.8	27.7	23.0
Personal care & health	16.6	15.6	12.5	11.8	22.7	30.6	22.7	17.4	13.3
Transport & Communications	17.5	25.3	14.1	19.7	31.4	9.9	14.0	9.2	11.6
Education, recreation & entertainment	4.5	7.7	9.7	7.9	7.2	19.2	13.7	20.3	10.7
Other services	5.2	4.3	4.7	1.8	2.5	1.2	2.6	5.3	7.2
Total consumption goods	*100.0*	*100.0*	*100.0*	*100.0*	*100.0*	*100.0*	*100.0*	*100.0*	*100.0*
Sub-total shares									
Intermediate goods	54.7	57.1	60.6	58.4	39.6	44.3	44.6	40.4	35.2
Capital goods	25.3	22.9	19.7	24.0	42.9	42.9	35.9	36.8	43.7
Consumption goods	19.9	20.1	19.7	17.6	17.4	19.8	20.4	22.9	21.1

Source: Annual Statements of External Trade and CSO worksheets.

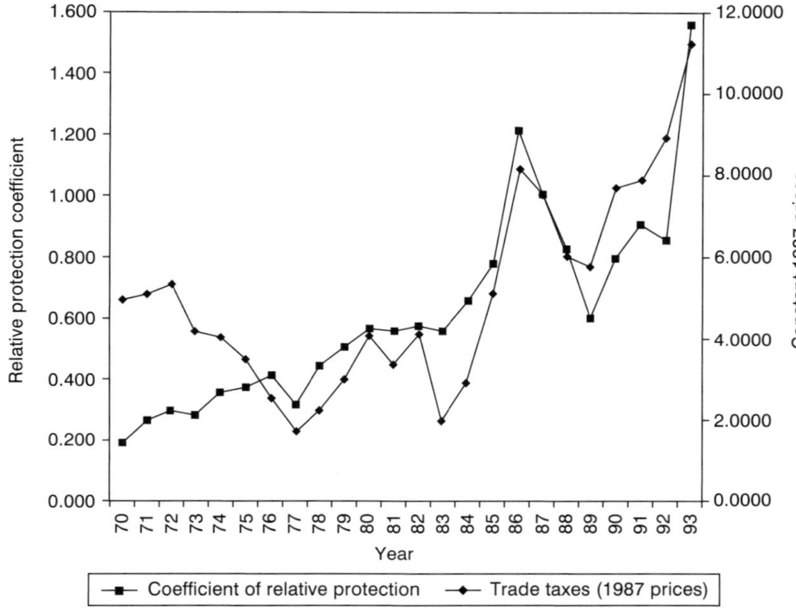

Source: World Tables (1995) and own calculations.

Figure 10.7 Trade taxes and coefficient of relative protection, 1970–93

Figure 10.8, where the components of revenue are expressed as a proportion of GDP. This illustrates three important features. First, by international and regional standards the average trade tax ratio over the period as a whole is relatively low.

Over the decade 1980–91, import taxes accounted for 2.5 per cent of GDP, less than 50 per cent of the sub-Saharan African average of 5.21 per cent over the same period.[39] Import sales taxes, which were introduced in 1977, have assumed an increasing role in raising the effective revenue yield on imports, so that by the end of the period the average revenue yield was just less than 5 per cent of GDP, bringing the total yield from taxes on international trade broadly in line with the rest of sub-Saharan Africa.

Given that the share of imports in GDP has fallen sharply since the mid-1980s, this rise in the trade tax yield reflects a sharp increase in the effective rate of tax on imports. The effective tax rate on imports (from

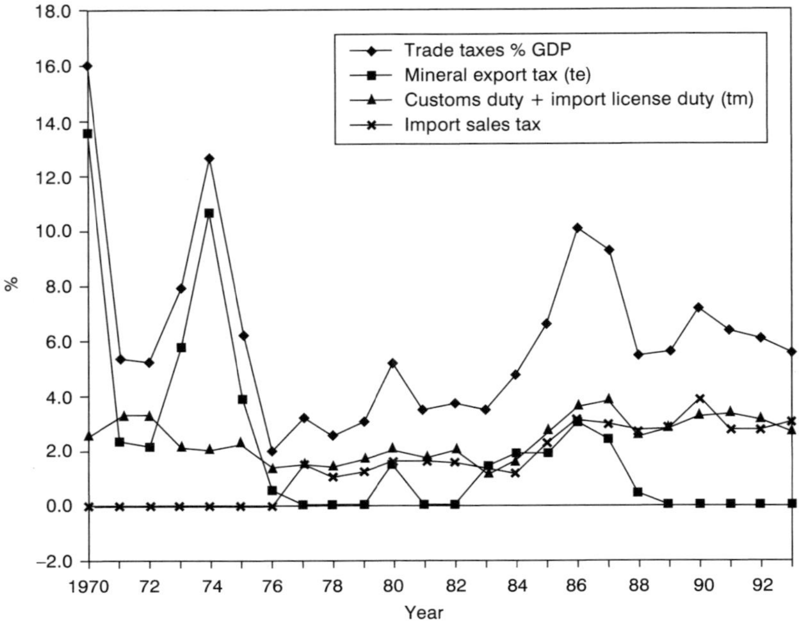

Source: CSO (various years).

Figure 10.8 Composition of taxes on trade, 1970–92

customs duties and import levy) increased from around 4 per cent during 1975–80 to 12 per cent by 1989–94. This is partly due to the change in import composition that has accompanied liberalization. During periods when quantitative controls were in effect, administrative allocations of foreign exchange were biased towards low-tariff essential goods and intermediate goods in favour of high-tariff consumer goods. The relaxation of quantitative controls led to an increase in the share of consumer goods in total imports, thereby increasing the average revenue yield on imports. However, the second factor leading to the increased effective tax rate is a consequence of the 'concertina' tariff restructuring, which has involved a reduction in the dispersion of tariff rates both through a reduction in the maximum tariff and an increase in the minimum tariff (Figures 10.9 and 10.10), although it is not possible to identify separately the revenue effects of the two reform components.

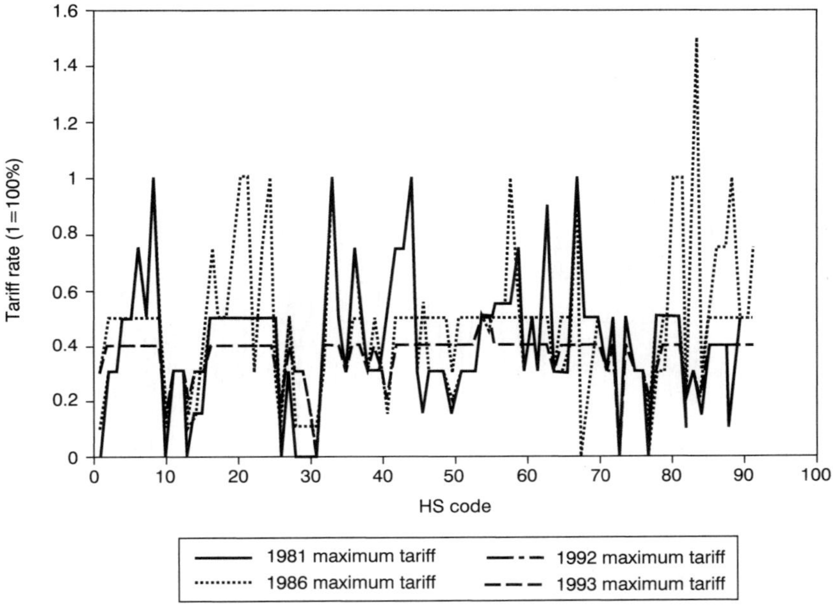

Source: SGS Database.

Figure 10.9 Dispersion of maximum tariff, 1981–93

The Fiscal Consequences of Exports Reform

Though trade liberalization appears to have been quite strongly budget-improving on the import side, the same cannot be said for export tax revenue. The importance of trade taxes on exports has declined markedly from the early 1970s, enjoying only a brief recovery in the mid-1980s. (Appendix 10B describes changes in the export tax regime in Zambia since 1964.) Given the nature of ownership in the copper sector, however, the incentive effects of changes in the tax regime are unlike those elsewhere in the economy. Output from the sector is wholly exported, the sector is a price-taking supplier, and since the sector has been wholly government-owned it has typically operated under soft budget constraints so that supply is determined principally by production and geological conditions. Moreover, taxation policy towards the sector has been determined in large part from the fiscal imperative of the government.

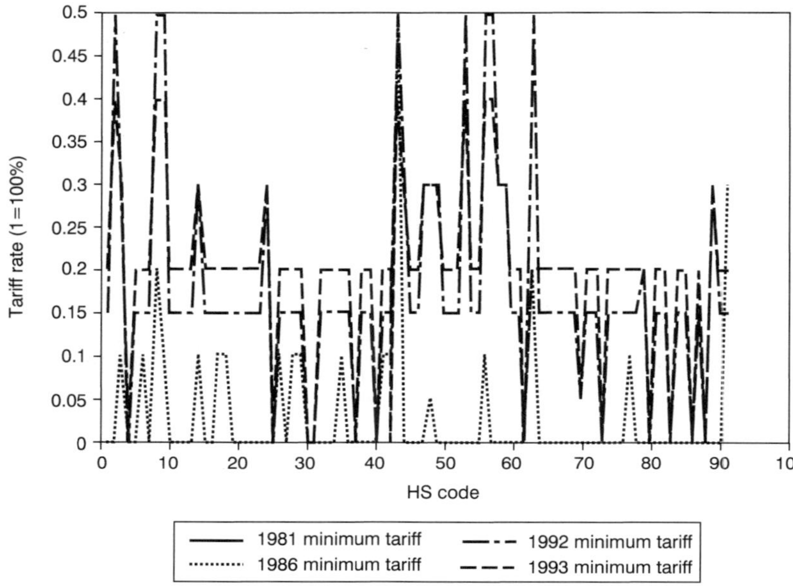

Source: SGS Database.

Figure 10.10 Dispersion of minimum tariff, 1981–93

Thus as the appendix indicates, taxation instruments have been changed frequently to maintain the flow of mineral sector revenue to the fiscus. However, the tax yield from the mineral sector has fallen dramatically since the early 1970s. During the high-price period of the late 1960s and early 1970s the mineral tax base was shifted away from a royalty basis towards a profit basis for taxation. As can be seen from Figure 10.8, the switch was of short-lived benefit as ZCCM's profits were eliminated in the 1970s and did not recover except for a short period during the temporary price boom enjoyed in 1988–90. The low profitability of the sector throughout the 1980s spurred the introduction of the Mineral Export Tax in 1983, which levied tax on the gross proceeds from mining. The Copper Revenue Tax, which functions as a super-tax based on the world copper price, was triggered in the early 1990s as world prices rose above $US1.00. As prices declined again in 1992 the tax yield from the sector returned towards zero.

10.8 THE CREDIBILITY OF LIBERALIZATION MEASURES

The credibility of trade liberalization episodes in Zambia is a story of sharp contrasts. As we noted, the liberalization of 1983 to 1985 serves as an example of a programme that seemed to be macro-compatible beforehand, but which was undermined by a lack of credibility that rendered the episodes incompatible. The current programme seems to be more credible in the short run, but faces the risk of reversal over the medium term. We shall discuss each in turn.

Episode I: Compatible but Incredible

There is only limited evidence with which to track the loss of credibility of the 1985–7 reforms, even though it obviously did decline. Time series data on the issue of import licences do not provide particularly valuable evidence on speculative activity. This is because throughout the period of controls, import licences issued by the Ministry of Commerce and Industry provided the holder with no option value. The Ministry of Commerce and Industry habitually over-issued licences relative to the number of licences honoured by the Bank of Zambia, which retained full control over quantitative foreign exchange allocation. Given the nature of the allocation system, therefore, import licences *per se* had limited perceived asset value.

We can draw on national accounts data showing that the period of the first reform programme coincided with a substantial increase in inventory accumulation (Figure 10.11). It is important, however, to view this evidence with some care. The national accounts definition of inventories represents a conflation of inventories of both inputs and final products, including copper awaiting export. As the just-published 1985 input–output table indicates, copper stocks held at the year-end were atypically high and therefore account for a large proportion of the high increase in inventory accumulation. Netting out finished copper stocks, however, it nonetheless remains that speculative acquisition of inventories does seem to have occurred prior to the collapse of the auction. This is further bolstered by the evidence from Table 10.19, showing the large increase in the share of transport and communication consumer imports (that is, vehicles) during 1986.

Episode II: Macro-compatibility and Hysteresis

The second liberalization episode presents us with a more complicated set of evidence. In one sense macro-compatibility has been achieved, but only after a protracted stabilization effort and with substantial balance of

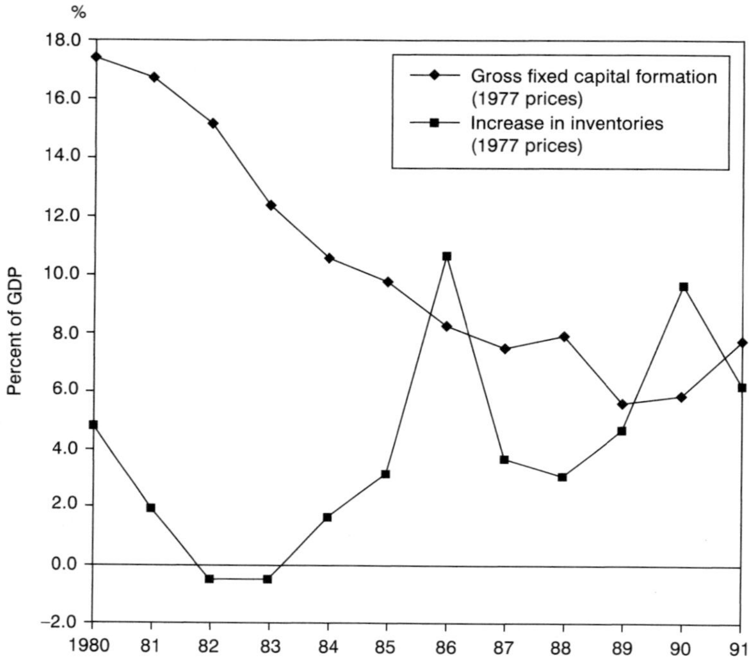

Source: World Tables (1995).

Figure 10.11 Fixed capital formation and inventories, 1980–91

payments support from the donor community. Although inventory accumulation seemed to surge in 1989, this apparently did not persist. A bigger problem for the success of the episode is that the liberalization of asset markets, combined with the temporarily high private and official capital inflows, resulted in a real exchange rate appreciation. This was particularly dramatic in the final quarter of 1993, when the nominal and real exchange rates appreciated by approximately 25 per cent (see Figure 10.12). Since then the real exchange rate has depreciated slightly, although persistent domestic inflation ensures that the real exchange rate still shows a tendency to be over-valued relative to its sustainable equilibrium. This raises a number of issues associated with the efficient adjustment in response to trade liberalization.

The sustainability of trade reform depends on the response of productive resources. Some sectors of the economy, such as the exportable sector,

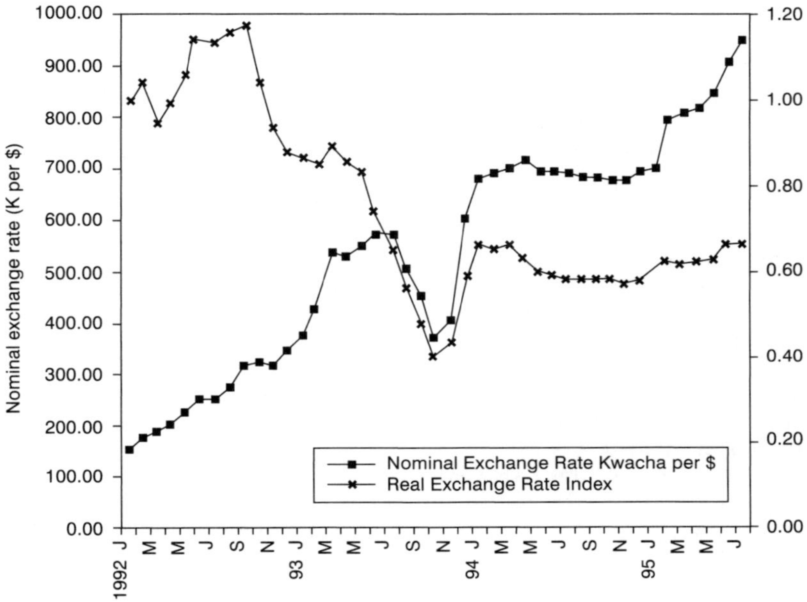

Note: A fall in the real exchange rate index represents a depreciation.

Figure 10.12 Nominal and real exchange rate indexes, 1992:1–1995:6

should be in a position to benefit from the liberalization, but (as has been noted) the anticipated supply-side recovery in Zambia's manufacturing and non-traditional export sectors has not emerged. In this final section we return to the four key components of the adjustment process in Zambia that bear most heavily on the sustainability, and thus credibility, of trade liberalization. The first two factors are the over-valuation of the real exchange rate and the high and variable real interests rates that prevailed from mid-1993 until 1995. Given the cost of working capital and the lower level of effective protection, importable sector firms have been unable (profitably) to match import prices, which, given the over-valued exchange rate, are low relative to their equilibrium level. The third issue relates to the consequences of endemic uncertainty over the stance of macroeconomic policy, while the final issue concerns the effects of the lack of synchronization in regional trade liberalization.

Temporary Real Exchange Rate Appreciation

It is clear that once trade liberalization policies have been implemented, formerly heavily-protected, import-substituting sectors become less viable at world prices and are therefore expected to shrink, with their resources reallocated to expanding sectors. This type of de-industrialization is an anticipated consequence of (and indeed an indicator of) successful liberalization. A temporarily over-valued real exchange rate, however, means that the deindustrialization may be significantly greater than required over the medium term, as viable but insolvent enterprises close down or switch from manufacturing to distribution. This is already quite common throughout the light to medium industrial sector, especially among the multinational firms whose former manufacturing has been substituted by distribution of imports from Zimbabwe-based manufacturing.

Is there evidence that the real exchange rate was *temporarily* over-valued in Zambia from 1993 to 1995? The combined effect of a number of factors indicate that it was.

First, the terms of trade showed a sharp improvement between October 1993 and mid-1995. Over this period, the world copper price rose by approximately 45 per cent from around $US0.80 to approximately $US1.15 per pound. The price increase reflects both demand factor – particularly from China – and the collapse of the Zaïrian supply. It was widely anticipated, however, that the price increase was temporary.

The second factor is aid inflows. Given the extremely large net aid flows to Zambia since 1989, the real exchange rate had obviously appreciated relative to its level in the absence of aid. This appreciation was not particularly relevant, since it is reasonable to assume that the country will remain aid-dependent over the foreseeable future. In this sense the aid-induced appreciation may be viewed as permanent. What was more relevant, however, was the short-run increase in aid flows that followed from the somewhat euphoric response of the donor community to political reforms at the end of 1993. Moreover, the volatility of the high gross aid inflows and disbursements that constitute the net aid flow to Zambia contributed to increased volatility of the nominal exchange rate.

Third, private capital inflows increased sharply following the reduction of inflation in 1993 and the abolition of exchange controls in January 1994. Private capital flows for 1994 were estimated to be approximately US$100, some 300 per cent higher than the mean private inflow since 1990. As we noted above, evidence suggests that this inflow was not being converted into fixed capital formation but rather was being held as claims against the government.

The increase in private capital flows reflected the regime shift in the conduct of fiscal and monetary policy since 1993. The consequence of this shift for the nominal and real exchange rate can be illustrated using a model first developed by Neary (1985). We take the case of two domestic assets, money and government bonds, where the latter are perfect substitutes with foreign financial assets. Domestic money, on the other hand, is not held by overseas residents and therefore can be thought of as a non-tradeable asset. Assume the demand for (broad) money is written as

$$m - p = \alpha y + \gamma i \tag{10.4}$$

where m, p, y and i are the (logarithm) of nominal money demand, the price level, real income and the interest rate on bonds. The link between the demand for money and the nominal exchange rate is first through the price level, which is defined as:

$$p = \beta p_{NT} + (1 - \beta)\, p_T \tag{10.5}$$

where $p_T = ep_T{}^*$ defines the domestic price of tradeable as determined by the price-taking assumption. For simplicity we can normalize the world price of tradeables to unity so that we can express Equation (10.5) as:

$$p = \beta p_{NT} + (1 - \beta)\, e \tag{10.6}$$

The second link between the exchange rate and money demand is through the interest rate. Increases in the domestic interest rate will have the effect of attracting foreign assets into the economy and lead to a substitution into domestic (non-tradeable) financial assets. In equilibrium the demand for money will equal money supply, denoted H, so that (with some substitution):

$$H = \beta p_{NT} + (1 - \beta)\, e + \alpha y + \gamma i \tag{10.7}$$

Since the exchange rate is flexible, then Equation (10.7) holds continuously. For equilibrium to hold, then any increase in the price of non-tradeables requires a decline (that is, an appreciation) of the nominal exchange rate for money market equilibrium to be maintained. The *MM* locus in Figure 10.13 plots money market equilibrium. Since the demand for money is the asset-market counterpart of the tradeable goods market it is not necessary to describe the tradeable goods market equilibrium. We do, however, need to describe the non-tradeable sector. This is illustrated by the *SS* locus, which plots combinations of p_{NT} and e that give equilibrium in the non-tradeable market. Points above the line correspond to excess supply.

Initial equilibrium is at *A*, where the real exchange rate is given by the

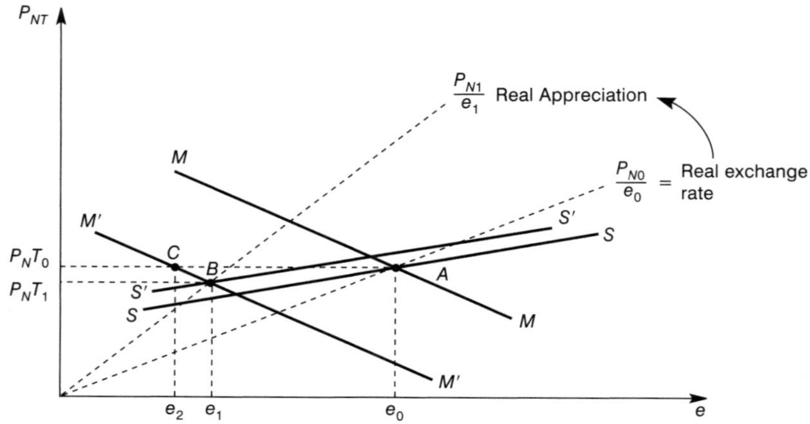

Note: Resource inflow shifts *SS* to *S′S′* and *MM M′M′* leading to real exchange rate appreciation $A \rightarrow B$. If non-tradeable prices are sticky, nominal exchange rate will overshoot its equilibrium ($e_0 \rightarrow e_2 \rightarrow e_1$).

Figure 10.13 Resource flows and real exchange rate depreciation

slope of the ray through *A*. Consider a positive shock. The resource inflow will increase the demand for non-tradeables and will shift the *SS* locus to *S′S′*. If the boom is temporary, the shift in the *SS* locus will be modest. However, the boom also increases *y* and thus increases the demand for money (Equation 10.4). Equilibrium requires that the price level falls. This involves an inward shift of the *MM* locus (by a larger amount than the movement in *SS*) and the economy will move to *B*, at which point the real exchange rate has appreciated.[40] The basic result therefore is that a recovery in the demand for money, *given a fixed nominal money supply*, will lead to an appreciation of the real exchange rate. The appreciation may or may not include a fall in non-tradeable prices. If there are rigidities in non-tradeable prices, then equilibrium in the money market will require that all the adjustment will fall on the nominal exchange rate and, as a consequence, nominal and real exchange rate overshooting (A → C → B).

The above results relate to the situation of a constant money supply (that is, where resource inflows are sterilized by the authorities) and a given demand for money function. It is possible to observe the same phenomenon without an explicit resource inflow, but rather as a result of an autonomous recovery in the demand for money. The argument carries over to a consideration of changes in the interest rate (or the interest elasticity of demand for money). Assuming that the demand for (broad) money is positively related to the interest rate, then rising interest rates will have the same consequences as a recovery in the autonomous demand for money, namely that the exchange rate must appreciate to ensure money market equilibrium.

There is strong evidence that from mid-1993 to early 1995 there was a sharp recovery in the demand for kwacha. For example, from September 1993 to July 1994 broad money rose by 60 per cent in nominal terms, while the price level rose by only 30 per cent. Even with quite large movements in the level of real income this still suggests a sharp increase in the willingness of Zambians to hold kwacha. Given this recovery in the demand for money, the right monetary policies adopted by the government had the consequence of generating a short-run exchange rate over-valuation.

Real Interest Rates and the Cost of Working Capital

As noted above, an important component of capital inflow is a surge in short-term private capital taking advantage of the high real interest rates in Zambia. While it should be clear that this will lead to a real exchange rate appreciation, it is probably worth revisiting the question of why real interest rates were so high over the period from 1993 to 1995 (Figure 10.14).

The *ex-post* real rate of interest is simply the nominal rate of interest less the rate of inflation,

$$r = i - \pi \qquad (10.8)$$

where r is the *ex-post* or realized real interest rate, i the nominal interest rate and π the relevant rate of inflation. If we denote the expectation of Equation (10.8) as the superscript e, and subtract it from the equation, we derive a relationship, Equation (10.9), that identifies three possible explanations for high *ex-post* real rates of interest,

$$r = r^e + (i - i^e) + (\pi^e - \pi). \qquad (10.9)$$

This shows that real interest rates may be high because of high anticipated (or 'required') real rates, higher than expected nominal interest rates, or lower than expected inflation. In the period from June 1993 to the end of 1993 the latter two terms may have explained the high interest rates as the market sought to come to grips with the dynamics of inflation and the operation of the treasury bill market. Over 1993 inflation and the nominal exchange rate would have been difficult for anyone to forecast; but as time proceeds, the argument that the market continued to make such large errors in its expectations is harder to sustain.

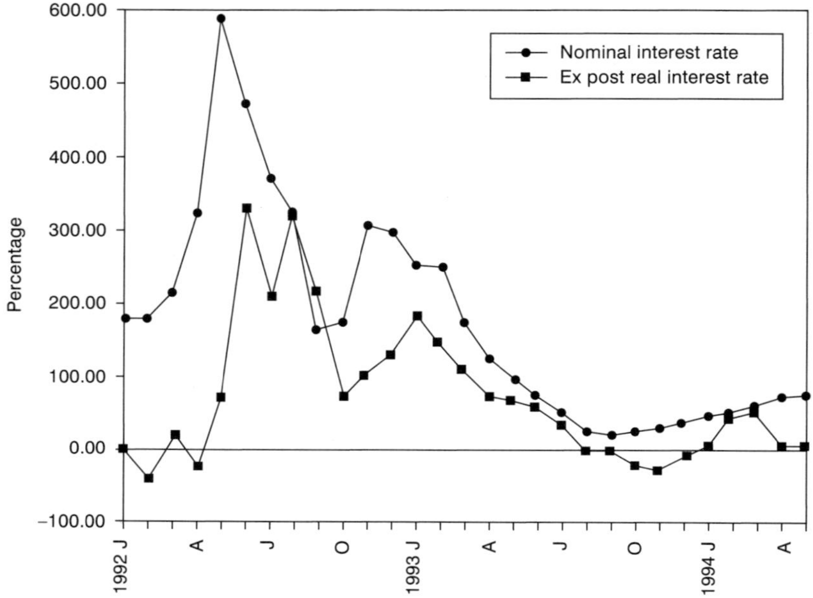

Figure 10.14 28-day treasury bill nominal and real interest rates, 1992:1–1994:6

The focus must therefore turn to the first term on the right hand side, the expected real interest rate. Why should it be high? To understand this we need to think about two cases, the first where there are capital controls and the second where capital controls have been removed. When there are capital controls, the high real interest rate may come about if there is a shortage of savings, an excess demand for those savings or a combination of the two. Thus with binding capital controls the loanable funds market is non-tradeable in the sense used above; the interest rate is simply that which equates domestic supply of funds (savings) with domestic demand (government borrowing through treasury bills). With high demand for funds emanating from the government's fiscal stance, and limited supply of savings (since the private sector has been dis-saving during the adjustment period), it seems entirely plausible that real rates are high for purely market reasons.

However, capital controls were removed in January 1994. What implications does this have for interest rates? The benchmark case here is the uncovered interest parity (UIP) condition, which simply says that funds will flow into and out of the country up to the point, where the expected, risk-adjusted return from investing in Zambia is equated to the return in the rest of the world. If the return in Zambia is higher than the rest of the world, funds will flow in and reduce the return. Thus, letting the asterisk denote the rest of the world, we have the UIP condition $i = i^* + \hat{E}^e$, where $\hat{E}^e$ is the expected depreciation of the domestic currency over the holding period. If the expected depreciation is positive, then domestic interest rates need to be higher than world rates to compensate the holder for the loss of value conditional on the depreciation. Notice that under the UIP condition, $i^e = i^{*e} + \hat{E}^e$ so that $(i - i^e) = (i^* - i^{*e})$. Noting also that the foreign analog of Equation (10.9) is $r^{*e} = i^{*e} - \pi^{*e}$, we can express the domestic anticipated real interest rate in terms of the real rather than the nominal exchange rate as

$$r^e = r^{*e} + (\hat{E}^e + \pi^{*e} - \pi^e) \tag{10.10}$$

The second term on the right-hand side is now an expression for the *expected* depreciation of the real exchange rate so that high *ex-ante* real domestic interest rates can be explained by high expected world interest rates, or because the real exchange rate is over-valued and investors expect a real devaluation over the holding period of the investment (that is, the treasury bill).

Consider the nominal UIP condition. If we use the US bond rate as a representative foreign interest rate, we find that there has been a relatively constant and large difference between the actual depreciation in the kwacha and that predicted by UIP. This difference could be explained by a number of factors: (1) it could be a risk premium on investing in Zambia; (2) it could occur because agents are consistently bad predictors; or (3) there could be other factors ensuring the UIP does not hold. These other factors principally include non-market determinants of interest rates. Since it is unlikely that the risk premium could be that high (it seems implausible given the very short maturity of the securities), this evidence still points to the presence of some non-market factors in the bill market, even though these factors seem to be diminishing rapidly.

Similarly, we could test Equation (10.10), which would compare the actual real depreciation with the expected. World interest rates at this time were probably higher than their historical trend due to the joint effects of the cost of German reunification and inflationary concerns in the US and other OECD economies, but this alone cannot explain the high rates in Zambia. On the other hands, the second factor, the expected depreciation of the real exchange rate, is interesting because it states that if the real exchange rate is perceived to be over-valued, then we would expect domestic real interest rates to be higher than world rates, even with capital mobility. Since we have indicated that the evidence leans towards assuming an exchange rate over-valuation, this result seems plausible.

To the extent that the real exchange rate appreciation is correctly perceived as temporary, this should not be cause for concern unless there are rigidities preventing an optimal response. There are a number of reasons why temporary appreciations may not induce appropriate responses, the most problematic for the productive sector being market imperfections that mean the productive sector cannot borrow to finance the loss of profits experienced during the temporary boom. For example, suppose there is a short-run inflow of foreign resources that appreciate the real exchange rate, but that firms in the tradeable sector, knowing the boom is temporary, choose not to alter their resource allocation. For the duration of the boom, these firms will face stiffer competition from imports and non-tradeable and will make losses relative to their pre-boom position. Conversely, importers and firms operating in the non-tradeable sector will enjoy super-normal profits. Ideally, the capital market would function in a way that temporarily transfers the savings from the sectors enjoying the temporary windfall to the sectors suffering its adverse consequences. If, however, the capital market is not prepared to lend to the (temporary) loss-making firms in this predicament – even though they are profitable in the long run – then these firms will close down. Thus, in these circumstances, even though the effect of the temporary boom on the real exchange rate is moderate, because everyone knows the boom is temporary and a high proportion of the resource flow is saved, the output cost may be large. This is clearly a case where the private sector may not be able to respond optimally to the shock, even though it knows how to do so. An important lesson is that just because the real exchange rate appreciation is moderate and the perceived misalignment is small, it does not mean that the costs of the misalignment are also small.

The output costs may actually be very dramatic if there are hysteresis effects associated with the closure of existing firms – when a factory is closed it is generally closed for good and will not re-open when better times arrive. In other words, temporary phenomena will have permanent effects as a result of their permanent impact on the capital stock. Similar effects may also be felt in the labour force, where it is well known that layoffs today generally reduce the probability of being re-hired tomorrow, not least because the value of the job-specific human capital declines and the worker or manager is therefore less employable at the previous wage. It is notable that in Zambia, it is the established tradeable goods firms – those represented in the main by ZACCI – that are most concerned by the adverse consequences of temporary real exchange rate movements. In part this may reflect effective lobbying by a powerful interest group. More probably it is because the membership of ZACCI is relatively more capital and skill intensive than the rest of the private sector, and is necessarily more vulnerable to costly hysteresis effects arising from temporary appreciations.

There is an increasing body of anecdotal evidence suggesting that in Zambia the transitional costs may be high. In 1994 sales in the large-scale sector contracted dramatically and capacity utilization continued to fall, while a number of companies stopped producing and turned to trading. However, the effect of trade liberalization has been different depending on whether the company is basically national or multinational or whether it produces mainly for the domestic or the export market. For multinationals, it has been easier to restructure their regional activities and turn to more trading than in the past. In the process of restructuring, certain production lines in Zambia have been given up. Local companies have scaled down production, or even closed down completely, and turned more to trading in order to sustain their existence. The export-orientated companies have indicated increased sales, especially those that were already established in the market before liberalization.

Uncertainty and the Option Value of Waiting

Trade liberalization measures, in particular those that lead to a change in inter-sectoral relative prices, may create incentives for investment in potentially expanding sectors (such as non-traditional exports and agriculture). They may also be expected to increase the incentive to invest in existing traditional sectors to the extent that reform leads to greater availability of intermediate inputs (including credit) and through higher levels of demand. The central concern in the Zambian liberalization programme is that despite the extensive adjustment to relative prices there has been a very limited investment response. If national accounts figures are to be believed, aggregate investment in 1993 was estimated to be approximately 8 per cent of GDP,[41] and though no official figures have yet been produced for 1994 there is little evidence that investment is picking up. Traditional indicators of increased activity, such as cement sales, electricity consumption and, of course, employment, all suggest that activity in 1994 remained at or slightly below the level recorded in 1993.[42] Even more worrying is the evidence that despite an improvement in the agriculture terms of trade over the period of the adjustment programme, crop acreage seems to have declined in 1994, with the principal cause being cited as 'uncertainty as farmers react to the privatization of input financing and crop marketing'.[43]

It is important to stress that this stagnant investment behaviour is not a temporary phenomenon, but rather the continuation of a relatively

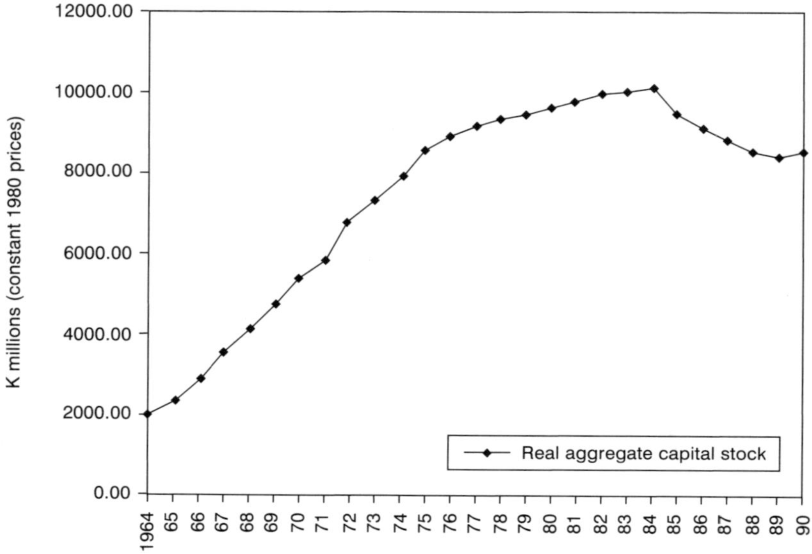

Source: Ministry of Finance and Economic Development CGE Modelling Project.

Figure 10.15 Real aggregate capital stock, 1964–90

long-term trend in the Zambian economy, the consequence of which is a gradual decline in the country's capital stock. Figure 10.15 illustrates the severe decapitalization of the economy. In the face of relatively constant real output prices, if the capital–labour ratio is falling, the only way for employment to be maintained, let alone increased, is for real wages to fall. Stimulating investment and improving its quality (so that a higher marginal product of labour and thus greater level of output is secured from a given unit of investment) are clearly central to reversing the output decline and halting the continued decline in average real wages. Indeed, unless this reversal is achieved relatively soon, the consequences for the political economy of Zambia may be severe as the austerity measures that have characterized the adjustment programme cannot be sustained for long in the face of worsening aggregate conditions and, possibly more seriously, in the face of widening perceived income and wealth inequality.

Investment is typically irreversible and sector-specific: once made, it is either difficult to reverse or can be reversed only with significant cost. Since the profitability of investment is determined by its expected net present value of future earnings, the irreversible investment decision is a function of uncertainty about the future evolution of prices, costs, taxation and even government policy. Often, however, investment can be delayed and there may be some benefit in doing so. The capacity to delay an investment decision makes it analogous to a *call option* in finance. The option costs the investor (in terms of the return forgone today and the possible loss of 'first-mover advantages') but it conveys benefits by offering the flexibility to choose a time to invest as uncertainty resolves itself. The net effect of this cost and benefit is referred to as the *option value*. This argument is symmetrical. In many cases disinvestment from a firm or a sector carries with it costs that cannot be avoided once the decision to dis-invest is undertaken. These may be thought of as exit costs (decommissioning, redundancy costs, and so on), and just as investors may exercise the option to wait rather than invest in a new project, so existing stakeholders may choose not to disinvest until uncertainty resolves itself.

In circumstances where private sector investment is characterized by irreversibility and high levels of uncertainty, arising from endemic uncertainty about prices as well as about the future direction of policy, relative prices and simply-calculated profits may be expected to move a long way without triggering an investment response as the value of the option to wait remains higher than its exercise price. There is an important rider to this result, referred to as the 'bad news principle', which suggests that 'good' and 'bad' news have different effects on the value of options. In particular, the adverse effect of bad news (that is, an increase in the probability of a disadvantageous outcome) has a greater impact on investment than the positive effects of 'good news'. In other words, reducing 'downside' risk and uncertainty may be expected to have a much greater impact on stimulating investment that would increase the 'upside'.

As a final comment it is important to note that this methodological approach carries over to considering resource reallocation in other factor markets. Most notably we may think of the labour market where similar considerations are at work; despite large changes in real wages between sectors, labour does not seem to have moved, reinforcing the view that the labour market in Zambia is prone to rigidities. However, if we acknowledge that both labour demand and labour supply decisions are characterized by irreversibility – because of the costly acquisition and maintenance of sector-specific skills – firms and individuals will exercise the option to maintain their current labour allocation rather than undertake costly reallocation that may turn out to be incorrect.

We distinguish between two broad classes of uncertainty. The first can be termed *stochastic uncertainty*, by which we mean the general uncertainty with movements in world prices and other factors that are essentially exogenous to Zambia. The second class of uncertainty we can refer to as *policy-related uncertainty*. This category can be sub-divided further into:

(1) uncertainty associated with the aid process and the future aid strategy of the donor community, particularly concerning the future of the external debt burden;
(2) uncertainty concerning the direction of domestic economic policy; and
(3) uncertainty over the managerial capacity of government in the new economic control regime. This third type is important in the present situation, where reforms have introduced new markets and new operating procedures and have confronted government with new regulatory challenges.

Running through all policy is an inherent time inconsistency. Unlike investment, policy is generally reversible and in many cases governments may have an incentive to change policy after the private sector has responded. However, knowing that the government has the capacity and often the incentive to change the policy stance in the future, the private sector will anticipate this change. As a consequence, the private sector reaction today may not be one that would be desired by the government. It may be unhelpful to concentrate only on this venal representation of the problem, as it is a problem that spans the entire domain of government action. By dint of its sovereignty, a government is empowered to respond to events and to shift its policy stance as new pressures arise. In many circumstances to fail to do so would be viewed as a derogation from duty. The consequence of this flexibility, however, is that the government cannot commit itself not to respond to changing events in the future. Even if the government would prefer the consequences of the no-response policy – in order to make binding commitments and thereby reduce the uncertainty faced by the private sector – it will be under great pressure to respond to immediate consequences. All governments are faced with this conflict between being able to commit themselves to future policy action (such as a policy of low taxation on profits) and retaining the flexibility of action required to respond effectively to unforeseen (and unforeseeable) events. The problem confronting policy-makers is that the difference between *ex-ante* and *ex-post* incentives is that it induces undesirable change in the behaviour of other actors.

All intertemporal decisions encounter time inconsistency problems. The areas of stimulating private sector investment and privatization are prime examples, since the private sector is aware that once the asset has been sold, the government has the incentive to 'change the rules of the game' in a manner that alters the return to the private investor. The changing of the rules could be malign, such as a renationalization, but could be indirect, operating through a change in the tax, tariff or exchange rate regime, or indeed through more benign routes. It is hard to judge the likelihood of wholesale renationalization, given the change in the worldwide economic consensus, but as evidence from other countries indicates, this uncertainty may not be trivial.[44] However, it is probably not worth concentrating on this aspect too much. Of greater consequence seems to be the 'benign' causes of time inconsistency in policy, which may lead to private investors adopting a 'wait and see' stance. These include the consequences of the government's response to external shocks and to other developments in the economy, and the consequences of error and uncertainty emerging from the process of learning new methods of conducting economic policy. We can consider each in turn.

Force Majeure The fast pace of policy reform in Zambia has meant that it has not always been possible for the government to adhere to policy commitments, not has it been possible to anticipate correctly the joint fiscal consequences of the myriad policy changes that are made. The most obvious example is the severe erosion of seigniorage revenue in 1991 to 1993 and the continued failure to increase the yield from the ZIMCO companies, which obliged government to increase the sales tax and excise duties on petroleum products above the levels of initially anticipated in the ERP documents. Similarly, the on–off process of liberalization of maize marketing and financing acts as a profound disincentive to private firms' participation in this sector. In such cases the need to fine-tune (or occasionally alter radically) policy as events unfold represents an obvious time inconsistency.

Learning by Doing The transition from a centrally controlled policy regime to a market-orientated system has placed the government process under considerable strain as the bureaucracy attempts to reorientate towards the implementations of new policy. It is inevitable that in the process errors will be made, adversely affecting prices and returns to private investment. For example, soon after its implementation it became clear that the Investment Promotion Act permitted excessive tax allowances and it had to be hurriedly repealed and reformed. It is to be anticipated that the introduction of VAT and the further development of arm's-length regulation and open-market operations in the money and foreign exchange markets will bring with them transitional difficulties and an increase in policy uncertainty.

It is important to note that the impact of such policy transition effects (policy incoherence) is asymmetric in terms of the uncertainty confronted by the private sector. This is an example of the so-called 'bad news principle' noted above, where increasing the probability of adverse outcomes increases the value of the option to wait while the consequence of increasing the probability of favourable outcomes does not alter the investment decision.

Aid and Uncertainty In aid-dependent economies such as Zambia, an important source of uncertainty comes from the impact that aid flows (or their absence) have on the economy's external balance and the trajectory for the real exchange rate. Over long periods in the past, real exchange rate volatility was avoided through the pursuit of unsustainable borrowing strategies and the use of tariffs and quotas to respond to external balance crises. Having implemented trade liberalization, the government has forgone the use of quotas, *ad hoc* tariffs and foreign exchange rationing as ways to achieve external balance. Since the economy remains rationed in commercial international capital markets and is thus unable to raise short-term commercial stabilization capital, real exchange rate adjustment (to restore external balance) will be effected solely through domestic price and nominal exchange rate adjustment.

The other principal determinant of the real exchange rate is the flow of official aid capital. Though in aggregate relatively small, the net aid flow has two damaging features. First, as is well known, the net flow in the past has often been very volatile, putting considerable stress on the macroeconomic management capacities of the authorities. Second, and more problematic, is the expected future of the aid relationship in Zambia. The country has come to the end of the current programme and is awaiting the final negotiation of the ESAF, while many bilateral agencies are beginning to exhibit severe aid fatigue and are expressing doubts about the effectiveness of their aid programme, both its level and composition.[45] Perhaps more than at any other time in recent years, the private sector is unclear as to the donor community's commitment to Zambia.[46]

Financial Liberalization Trade liberalization is occurring at a time of significant changes in domestic and foreign asset markets. This will have a number of implications for privatization. At a traditional level, asset market liberalization will alter comparative rates of return to different assets, which may be expected (at least in the short term) to reduce the relative attractiveness of loans to former SOEs. Although one of the initial components of financial liberalization is the removal of ceilings on permitted bank lending rates, it is often the case that the return to private sector lending actually falls following financial liberalization relative to other investment. Thus, post liberalization, banks are able to hold wealth in terms of interest-bearing foreign assets (at a time when world interest rates are comparatively high) as well as in government securities, which, until early 1995 at least, yielded comparatively high real returns and were relatively liquid.

Against this, a number of factors reduce the attractiveness of lending to the private sector, especially when viewed from an options perspective. Domestic credit to the private sector is relatively irreversible. Although there is some securitization of investment (through the Lusaka Stock Exchange), credit is typically based on a limited collateral basis and loan recovery may be costly if the return on the loan fails to materialize. Moreover, the variance of returns to lending to the private sector is high. One of the consequences of reform has been to alter the structure of markets and to remove the traditional signals of credit-worthiness of borrowers (such as access to foreign exchange, upon which banks have in the past been able to base their lending decisions); uncertainty as to the likely return to investment is therefore high. In this environment, all investors, including banks, will find that the value of their option to wait will be high. This uncertainty may be particularly large in respect of lending to former SOEs. As noted above, there is evidence that this waiting behaviour is widespread in the financial sector where, even though the return on government securities has fallen sharply, banks have remained extremely liquid.

10.9 CONCLUSION

A major challenge of trade liberalization is to assure a level of compatibility with trading partners. Zambian manufacturers, for example, experienced transitional problems associated with the lack of synchronization in trade liberalization between Zambia and its principal trade partners, Zimbabwe and South Africa. Exporters in those countries enjoy considerable trade policy advantages in their penetration of the Zambian market, often with the support of export incentives from their home country. The macroeconomic constraints to rapid adjustment exacerbate this problem.

Internally, the high-interest rate strategy adopted to maintain price stability and internal balance may not be macro-compatible over the medium term, since the continued pursuit of this strategy will undermine the current balance. By making the costs of transition prohibitive and forcing up working capital and investment costs, output, exports and tax revenue will continue to decline, putting further pressure on the fiscal balance, increasing the borrowing requirement and further increasing interest rates. A vicious circle will ensue. The private sector may come to view the policy as incredible and will as a consequence take hedging positions against the government. Such positions may prove to be self-fulfilling so that again compatibility and stabilization will be lost.

APPENDIX 10A: SUMMARY OF TRADE LIBERALIZATION AND RELATED MEASURES IN ZAMBIA, 1983–95

Table 10.A1 Summary of trade liberalization policies and their implementation

Programme	*Policy action and implementation*
Episode 1 1984–7	
Exchange rate	
1983–4	*Managed float with crawling peg devluations* Step devaluations implemented in 1983/84. Nominal devaluation of 30 per cent in 1983 and 70 per cent in 1984
	RER depreciation approximately 11 per cent, 1983–5
1985	*Foreign exchange auction* See text for details, pp. 462–3.
	Own-funds import scheme Introduced on schedule; parallel market premium reduced to 45 per cent
Import policy	
1984	*Minimum tariff increased to 10 per cent* Implemented in October 1984 for all goods except those covered by minimum tariff
1985	*Maximum tariff reduced from 150 per cent to 100 per cent* Implemented October 1984 for all goods except tobacco, some vehicles and miscellaneous luxury goods
	Scope of minimum tariff extended Implemented December 1984
	Exemptions from import duties reduced Implemented January 1985
	QRs on imports eliminated Implemented in conjunction with foreign exchange auction
	Sales tax for imports and domestic goods unified Proposal to introduce 'uplift factor' for imports not implemented
1986–7	*Tariff commission established* Not implemented

Export policy	
1985	*Export retention scheme introduced* Implemented, with exporters entitled to retain 50 per cent of gross export proceeds for use on own current account imports; restrictions still applied to capital account transaction; export retention could not be official traded.
1986	*Export Board created* Implemented in 1986, but board under-funded and not effective
Episode 2 1987–9	
Exchange rate	
1987 January	*Single window auction abandoned* Auction abandoned at 67th Auction; replaced by dual window (fixed official window and auction-determined second window)
May	*Auction abolished* Exchange rate fixed at K8.00 per dollar, following 160 per cent revaluation
	Establishment of Foreign Exchange Management Committee (FEMAC)
1988–June 1989	*Discrete devaluations* Official rate depreciated by 25 per cent in November 1988 to K10; and by 60 to K16 in 1989; RER appreciation of 100 per cent between 1988 and 1989
Import policy	
May 1987–89	*QRs re-introduced* No change to notional tariff; reintroduction of quantitative controls through FEMAC; bias in allocations towards SOEs
	Moratorium on official debt service Maximum of 10 per cent of foreign exchange allocated to non-IATA debt service; Zambia declared ineligible to use IMF resources in September 1987
Export policy	
	Export retention scheme modified Exporters required to surrender all export proceeds and seek FEMAC permission to acquire funds for inputs

(continued on page 528)

Table 10.A1 *continued*

Programme	*Policy action and implementation*
Episode 3 1989–94	
Exchange rate	
1990 February	Reintroduction of dual window exchange rate official window for government, parastatal allocations, allocations made by FEMAC at fixed rate of K28/$; second window, at managed but depreciated rate of K40/$, for open general licence (OGL) imports
1990/91	*Gradual transfer of OGL imports from first to second window*
1991 April	*Unification of dual windows at OGL rate of K58/ $* Direct allocation of government imports; unified OGL rate still managed
1992 April	*Export retention allowance increased at 100 per cent* Retentions can be sold, but must be sold or used within 180 days.
September	OGL list switched from 'positive list' to 'negative list'.
October	*Bureaux de change market legalized*, for current account transfers only
December	*OGL rate unified with bureau rate*, although transitional discount of 15 per cent applied to OGL purchases and relaxation of 100 per cent up-front kwacha cover for OGL sales
1993 October	OGL discount eliminated
1994 January	All capital account exchange controls abolished
Import policy	
1991 March	*Number of tariff rates reduced to six* New minimum and maximum rates set at 15 per cent and 50 per cent; a small number of exemptions granted (especially fertilizer and essential foodstuffs) and some luxuries kept at 100 per cent tariff
1992 March	*Tariff schedule reduced to three rates (20 per cent, 30 per cent and 40 per cent* Exemptions kept for

	crude oil, fertilizer, maize, newsprint, books, educational and medical,; exemption from tariffs implies exemption from sales tax
	20 per cent 'uplift factor' applied to imports for computation of sales tax Sales tax levied at 23 per cent; with imports subject to uplift, raises sales tax rate to 27.6 per cent; uplift designed to reflect the equivalent domestic costs of wholesaling.
1989–92	*QRs removed with liberalization of OGL* QRs remain on residual 'negative list' covering firearms, ivory, etc.
1994	*Ratification of PTA/COMESA external tariff reduction agreement* All NTBs have been removed and individual external tariffs have to be reduced by 60 per cent by October 1993; 70 per cent by October 1994 (both implemented by Zambia); 80 per cent by October 1996; 100 per cent by October 2000; reduction in tariff levels as at date of ratification
Export policy	
1989–93	*Export retention liberalized* See above
	Promotion of export board
1994 March	*Duty drawback scheme modified* – to reduce burden of proof for drawback; to permit drawback as credit against import tax liabilities; and to include third-party exporters, but still regarded as ineffective
1995 July	*Introduction of VAT* Planned introduction of VAT will classify exports as zero-rated for tax purposes, allowing exporters relief on input taxation

Source: World Bank (1993); Kate *et al.* (1994); Bank of Zambia (various issues).

Table 10.A2 Summary of price intervention in agriculture

1930s to 1989	Though government intervention in the agricultural sector long pre-dated Independence (see Davies, 1933), there was a distinct increase in intervention in the years from 1964 to 1982. In 1970, the government introduced district floor prices for producers of maize, groundnuts, sunflower, soya beans, cotton, wheat, rice and tobacco. During the 1970s the floor prices also served as the ceiling prices, but in 1982 farmers were allowed to seem prices above the floor. However, since the marketing boards were all parastatal monopolies, the floor prices continued to prevail, at least for small-holder farmers. Commercial farmers, through the Commercial Farmers Bureau, had some power to negotiate prices, although PIC approval was required to all price negotiations.
1989–1994	
1992	Removal of consumer subsidy on breakfast and roller meal; subsidies briefly reintroduced during the drought in 1992 and 1993
1992–5	Liberalization of other agricultural markets; fertilizer subsidies were ended in March 1992 and marketing and financing were moved gradually to market basis. Implementation has been slow as a result of the adverse effects of drought in 1992/93. Net subsidies to agricultural marketing and financing (non-collection of crop-financing loans) were approximately 2 per cent of GDP in 1993–4.

APPENDIX 10B: TAXATION OF THE COPPER SECTOR

Tax revenue from the principal export sector of the Zambian economy has been generated from a number of instruments, covering both royalty-based production taxes, traditional export taxes and a combination of turnover and profit taxes.[47] Table 10.B1 illustrates the tax instruments employed and the revenue collection over the 1980s.

Table 10B.1 Export taxation

Instrument	*Coverage*	*Rate and description*
Royalty tax	1964–9	13.5 per cent of London Metal Exchange Price (abolished 1969)
Mineral tax	1969–86	51 per cent of profits (abolished 1986)
Income tax	1964–9	Levied at different rates per mine
	1969–90	Levied at 45 per cent on profits after mineral tax and mineral export tax paid
	1990–	Computed at 45 per cent of actual copper price if price is less than $1/lb; and 45 per cent of notional profits at copper price $1/lb for prices in excess of $1/lb; excess profits taxed by *copper revenue tax*
Mineral export tax	1983–8	Levied on gross receipts of mineral export sales at 4 per cent (1983); 10 per cent (1985); 13 per cent (1986); 3 per cent (1987) (abolished 1988)
Copper revenue tax	1990–	Payable on gross receipts from sales in excess of $1/lb; later referred to as *excess copper earnings taxation*; tax rate set at 60 per cent on revenue to $1.05; 70 per cent to $1.10; 80 per cent to $1.15; 90 per cent to $1.20; 100 per cent on sales in excess of $1.20
Dividend tax	1973–	20 per cent withholding tax on dividends

Source: Aron (1992).

APPENDIX 10C: SUPPLEMENTARY TABLES

Table 10C.1 Firm age by sector and ownership status

	Date of establishment				
Two-digit sector code	*1990–95*	*1985–89*	*1974–84*	*1964–73*	*Pre-1964*
(a) State-owned enterprise					
Food/beverage/tobacco			5	8	
Textiles/leather			2	1	
Wood/wood products					
Paper/printing				1	
Chemicals			1	4	1
Non-metallic metals					
Metal products/machinery		1			
Total		*1*	*8*	*14*	*1*
(b) Private – domestic					
Food/beverage/tobacco	2			2	
Textiles/leather	4		7	1	
Woo/wood products		1	1	1	
Paper/printing			1		
Chemicals	2		3	2	
Non-metallic metals					1
Metal products/machinery			1	2	
Total	*8*	*1*	*13*	*8*	*1*
(c) Private – foreign					
Food/beverage/tobacco		2	1	7	
Textiles/leather	3		5	3	2
Wood/wood products			1	3	1
Paper/printing			1	1	
Chemicals			1	1	
Non-metallic metals					
Metal products/machinery	1	1		2	1
Total	*4*	*4*	*9*	*22*	*6*

Table 10C.2 Sales by sector and ownership status (K millions)

	Value of sales last period			
Two-digit sector code	*Mean*	*Median*	*Minimum*	*Maximum*
(a) State-owned enterprise				
Food/beverage/tobacco	449	264	1	1 517
Textiles/leather	2 733	453	142	7 604
Wood/wood products				
Paper/printing	370	370	370	370
Chemicals	3 342	965	53	10 668
Non-metallic minerals				
Metal products/machinery	126	126	126	126
Total	*1 484*	*383*	*1*	*10 668*
Does the firm export at least some of its output?				
No	762	343	1	7 000
Yes	4 914	4 267	453	10 668
(b) Private – domestic				
Food/beverage/tobacco	72	14	1	202
Textiles/leather	521	61	1	5 365
Wood/wood products	147	27	13	400
Paper/printing				
Chemicals	591	557	11	1 200
Non-metallic minerals	125	125	125	125
Metal products/machinery	1	1	1	1
Total	400	32	1	5 365
Does the firm export at least some of its output?				
No	210	28	1	1 200
Yes	1 157	134	1	5 365
(c) Private – foreign				
Food/beverage/tobacco	312	297	10	989
Textiles/leather	1 397	318	7	13 000
Wood/wood products	1 576	161	0	7 475
Paper/printing				
Chemicals	895	861	9	2 000
Non-metallic minerals				
Metal products/machinery	573	573	80	1 066
Total	*1 013*	*293*	*0*	*13 000*
Does the firm export at least some of its output?				
No	412	216	0	2 000
Yes	2 515	548	79	13 000

Table 10C.3 Full-time employment by sector and ownership status (no. of employees)

	Full-time employment			
Two-digit sector code	*Mean*	*Median*	*Minimum*	*Maximum*
(a) State-owned enterprise				
Food/beverage/tobacco	466	331	20	1 832
Textiles/leather	455	204	60	1 100
Wood/wood products				
Paper/printing	314	314	314	314
Chemicals	1 124	297	55	4 875
Non-metallic minerals				
Metal products/machinery	24	24	24	24
Total	*605*	*279*	*20*	*4 875*
Does the firm export at least some of its output?				
No	364	222	20	1 832
Yes	1 807	1 074	204	4 875
(b) Private – domestic				
Food/beverage/tobacco	19	20	10	27
Textiles/leather	716	268	14	5 000
Wood/wood products	133	110	12	278
Paper/printing	35	35	35	35
Chemicals	76	35	4	264
Non-metallic minerals	52	52	52	52
Metal products/machinery	89	89	78	100
Total	*329*	*65*	*4*	*5 000*
Does the firm export at least some of its output?				
No	339	78	4	5 000
Yes	278	42	15	890
(c) Private-foreign				
Food/beverage/tobacco	80	34	13	443
Textiles/leather	133	81	32	752
Wood/wood products	225	50	14	763
Paper/printing	69	69	48	90
Chemicals	122	70	25	540
Non-metallic minerals				
Metal products/machinery	53	40	16	115
Total	*119*	*50*	*13*	*763*
Does the firm export at least some of its outout?				
No	83	47	13	540
Yes	236	129	41	763

Table 10C.4 Structure of production by sector and ownership status (K millions)

Two-digit sector code	*Input-output ratio median*	*Imported raw material ratio median*	*Wages as share of sales median*	*Gross profit margin (before depreciation and tax median)*
(a) State-owned enterprise				
Food/beverage/tobacco	0.78	0.23	0.09	0.14
Textiles/leather	0.52	0.10	0.11	0.04
Wood/wood products				
Paper/printing	0.55	0.25	0.11	0.34
Chemicals	0.38	0.26	0.20	0.15
Non-metallic minerals				
Metal products/machinery		0.00	0.38	
Total	*0.70*	*0.24*	*0.12*	*0.15*
Does the firm export at least some of its output?				
No	0.73	0.24	0.10	0.15
Yes	0.52	0.22	0.21	0.09
(b) Private – domestic				
Food/beverage/tobacco	0.60	0.04	0.05	0.11
Textiles/leather	0.78	0.38	0.16	0.12
Wood/wood products	0.72	0.14	0.39	0.08
Paper/printing				
Chemicals	0.55	0.10	0.17	0.18
Non-metallic minerals	1.08	0.20	0.31	0.10
Metal products/machinery	0.57	0.50	0.16	0.05
Total	*0.76*	*0.18*	*0.15*	*0.11*
Does the firm export at least some of its output?				
No	0.78	0.20	0.16	0.11
Yes	0.74	0.12	0.08	0.27
(c) Private – foreign				
Food/beverage/tobacco	0.92	0.09	0.09	0.05
Textiles/leather	0.79	0.28	0.17	0.04
Wood/wood products	0.86	0.54	0.13	0.05
Paper/printing		0.00		
Chemicals	0.77	0.48	0.12	0.14
Non-metallic minerals				
Metal products/machinery	0.74	0.00	0.09	0.24
Total	*0.80*	*0.23*	*0.13*	*0.05*
Does the firm export at least some of its output?				
No	0.86	0.18	0.13	0.05
Yes	0.76	0.23	0.15	0.10

Source: Survey data.

Table 10C.5 Labour productivity by sector and ownership status (K m.)

	Labour productivity (sales per full time employee)			
Two-digit sector code	*Mean*	*Median*	*Minimum*	*Maximum*
(a) State-owned enterprise				
Food/beverage/tobacco	3.36	1.43	0.00	19.16
Textiles/leather	3.83	2.37	2.22	6.91
Wood/wood products				
Paper/printing	1.18	1.18	1.18	1.18
Chemicals	8.23	5.07	0.19	28.57
Non-metallic minerals				
Metal products/machinery	5.25	5.25	5.25	5.25
Total	*4.68*	*2.37*	*0.00*	*28.57*
Does the firm export at least some of its output?				
No	4.64	2.37	0.00	28.57
Yes	4.87	4.57	0.19	10.17
(b) Private – domestic				
Food/beverage/tobacco	6.93	0.54	0.08	20.17
Textiles/leather	1.26	0.23	0.00	6.03
Wood/wood products	1.61	1.09	0.10	3.64
Paper/printing				
Chemicals	8.87	7.14	1.10	17.40
Non-metallic minerals	2.40	2.40	2.40	2.40
Metal products/machinery	0.01	0.01	0.01	0.01
Total	*3.50*	*0.82*	*0.00*	*20.17*
Does the firm export at least some of its output?				
No	3.69	0.68	0.00	20.17
Yes	2.73	2.50	0.08	6.03
(c) Private – foreign				
Food/beverage/tobacco	7.42	5.14	0.37	19.77
Textiles/leather	4.67	3.41	0.18	17.29
Wood/wood products	5.22	4.80	0.01	11.50
Paper/printing				
Chemicals	12.34	10.34	0.02	31.43
Non-metallic minerals				
Metal products/machinery	5.56	5.56	1.85	9.27
Total	*7.18*	*5.39*	*0.01*	*31.43*
Does the firm export at least some of its output?				
No	7.36	4.80	0.01	31.43
Yes	6.73	5.83	0.81	17.29

Table 10C.6 Perceived constraints to export expansion

	Does the firm export at least some of its output?		
	*No**	*Yes**	*Total**
Are there barriers to exports			
Yes	36 (55.4)	13 (76.5)	49 (59.8)
No	29 (44.6)	4 (23.5)	33 (40.2)
Tariff barriers			
Yes	40 (85.1)	12 (85.7)	52 (85.2)
No	7 (14.9)	2 (14.3)	9 (14.8)
Licensing arrangements			
Yes	9 (23.7)	4 (40.0)	13 (27.1)
No	29 (76.3)	6 (60.0)	35 (72.9)
Forex restrictions			
Yes	7 (18.9)	4 (44.4)	11 (23.9)
No	30 (81.1)	5 (55.6)	35 (76.1)
Export quotas			
Yes	4 (10.8)	1 (11.1)	5 (10.9)
No	33 (89.2)	8 (88.9)	41 (89.1)
Most important constraint to exporting			
Tariffs	34 (89.5)	14 (87.5)	48 (88.9)
Licensing arrangements	2 (5.3)	2 (12.5)	4 (7.4)
Other	2 (5.3)		2 (3.7)

Note: * Percentages are in parentheses.

Source: Survey data.

Table 10C.7 Perceptions of policy change one year ahead (%)

	Does the firm export at least some of its output?		
	No	*Yes*	*Total*
Labour regulations			
Yes	36.7	31.3	35.5
No	58.3	62.5	59.2
Can't tell	5.0	6.3	5.3
Investment code			
Yes	41.7	52.9	44.2
No	50.0	41.2	48.1
Can't tell	8.3	5.9	7.8
Exchange rate policy			
Yes	30.5	47.1	34.2
No	59.3	52.9	57.9
Can't tell	10.2		7.9
Bank lending policy			
Yes	32.2	31.3	32.0
No	55.9	56.3	56.0
Can't tell	11.9	12.5	12.0
Tariff schedule			
Yes	37.9	50.0	40.5
No	51.7	43.8	50.0
Can't tell	10.3	6.3	9.5
Corporate tax schedule			
Yes	35.7	40.0	36.6
No	57.1	53.3	56.3
Can't tell	7.1	6.7	7.0
Personal tax schedule			
Yes	35.7	40.0	36.6
No	60.7	53.3	59.2
Can't tell	3.6	6.7	4.2
Reduced regional trade barriers			
Yes	47.3	50.0	47.9
No	43.6	43.8	43.7
Can't tell	9.1	6.3	8.5

Source: Survey data.

Table 10C.8 Perceptions of firm-level and macroeconomic changes

	Does the firm export at least some of its output?		
% change	*No*	*Yes*	*Total*
Output expected to decline by (%):			
No change	72	16	88
0–10	2		2
10–25	6	1	7
25–50	1	2	3
Output expected to rise by (%):			
No change	63	14	77
0–10	3	2	5
10–25	9	1	10
25–50	6	1	7
More than	50	1	1
Employment expected to decline by (%):			
No change	61	15	76
0–10	10	1	11
10–25	5	1	6
25–50	5	2	7
Employment expected to increase by (%):			
No change	74	17	91
0–10	2		2
10–25	3	2	5
25–50	1		1
More than 50	1		1
Inflation expected to fall by (%):			
No change	68	17	85
0–10	8		8
10–25	2	1	3
25–50	3		3
More than 50		1	1
Inflation expected to increase by (%):			
No change	62	17	79
0–10	7		7
10–25	7	2	9
25–50	4		4
More than 50		1	1
Import duties on inputs expected to fall by (%):			
No change	66	14	80
0–10	11	1	12

(continued on page 540)

Table 10C.8 *continued*

% change	*Does the firm export at least some of its output?* No	Yes	*Total*
10–25	2	4	6
25–50	2		2
Import duties on inputs expected to rise by (%):			
No change	73	19	92
0–10	4		4
10–25	1		1
25–50	3		3
Duties on consumer goods expected to fall by (%):			
No change	73	15	88
0–10	6	2	8
10–25	1	2	3
25–50	1		1
Duties on final consumption goods expected to rise by (%):			
No change	71	18	89
0–10	7		7
10–25	2		2
25–50	1	1	2

Source: Survey data.

Table 10C.9 Price-setting and profitability

Price-setting	*Profit as share of sales* *Mean*	*Median*
Domestic market		
Price-taker	0.21	0.10
Mark-up over costs	0.12	0.07
Price discriminate	0.03	0.07
High to signal quality	0.13	0.13
Export markets		
Price-taker	0.15	0.09
Mark-up pricing	0.01	0.02
Price discriminate	0.23	0.20
Negotiate with buyer	0.10	0.11

Source: Survey data.

Table 10C.10 Change in employment (%)

Two-digit sector code	*Mean*	*Median*	*Maximum*	*Minimum*
(a) Since liberalization				
Food/beverage/tobacco	–0.90	0.00	0.43	–0.67
Textiles/leather	0.18	0.00	5.00	–0.73
Wood/wood products	0.11	–0.07	1.20	–0.60
Paper/printing	0.15	–0.05	0.94	–0.24
Chemicals	–0.17	–0.16	0.14	–0.58
Non-metallic minerals	–0.26	–0.26	–0.26	–0.26
Metal products/machinery	–0.27	–0.33	0.00	–0.40
Does the firm export at least some of its output?				
No	–0.01	–0.07	5.00	–0.67
Yes	–0.13	0.00	0.14	–0.73
Total	*–0.03*	*–0.06*	*5.00*	*–0.73*
(b) Over last year				
Food/beverage/tobacco	–0.05	0.00	0.43	–0.74
Textiles/leather	–0.03	0.00	0.33	–0.47
Wood/wood products	–0.07	0.00	0.23	–0.60
Paper/printing	0.24	0.01	0.94	0.00
Chemicals	–0.09	–0.05	0.08	–0.34
Non-metallic minerals	–0.12	–0.12	–0.12	–0.12
Metal products/machinery	–0.13	0.00	0.08	–0.40
Does the firm export at least some of its output?				
No	–0.05	0.00	0.94	–0.74
Yes	–0.03	0.00	0.33	–0.47
Total	*–0.05*	*0.00*	*0.94*	*–0.74*

	Change in employment since liberalization			
	Less than –50 per cent	*–50 per cent to–10 per cent*	*–10 per cent to 0 per cent*	*0–10 per cent*
Food/beverage/ tobacco	1	5	10	1
Textiles/leather	3	2	10	1

(continued on page 542)

Table 10C.10 *continued*

	Change in employment since liberalization			
	Less than –50 per cent	*–50 per cent to–10 per cent*	*–10 per cent to 0 per cent*	*0–10 per cent*
Wood/wood products	1	1	1	1
Paper/printing		2	1	
Chemicals	2	10	5	1
Non-metallic minerals		1		
Metal products/ machinery		3	1	
Does the firm export at least some of its output?				
No	5	23	22	1
Yes	2	1	5	2
Total	*7*	*24*	*27*	*3*

	Change in employment since liberalization (%)		*12-month growth in labour force (%)*	
Two-digit sector code	*10–50*	*Greater than 50*	*Less than –50*	*–50–10*
Food/beverage/tobacco	1		1	6
Textiles/leather	2	1		6
Wood/wood products		1	1	1
Paper/printing		1		
Chemicals	2			7
Non-metallic minerals				1
Metal products/ machinery				3
Does the firm export at least some of its output?				
No	4	3	2	21
Yes	1			3
Total	*5*	*3*	*2*	*24*

Source: Survey data.

Notes

1. More comprehensive studies may be found in Davies (1993); Gulhati (1989); World Bank (1984); and Bates and Collier (1993).
2. Anglo-American Corporation of South Africa and Roan Selection Trust International, a subsidiary of AMAX Corp of the USA but incorporated in the UK.
3. Gulhati (1989) reports that it took 43 tonnes of ore to produce one tonne of finished copper in 1973 and 53 tonnes in 1983.
4. State acquisition in the mining sector began in 1969 with the presidential declaration that 51 per cent of equity in mining companies (existing and new) would transfer to the state but at a fair book value. From 1 Jan 1970 the foreign-owned companies were reorganized into Nchanga Consolidated Copper Mines (NCCM) and Roan Consolidated Mines. The government's own holding company, ZIMCO, held a 51 per cent controlling interest in the companies. From 1973 the government began to take a more active role in management of NCCM and RCM and in parallel created the Metal Marketing Company, MEMACO. MCCM and RCN merged as of 1 March 1981 as ZCCM, which was 60.3 per cent owned by ZIMCO with the minority shareholding spread between Anglo-American and the remainder being held by offshore investors.
5. See Keinbaum Development Services GmbH (1994).
6. See Adam and Bevan (1995).
7. It makes very little sense to put any weight in the extent of the range, as it tends to reflect in large measure the high level of instability in disaggregated input–output coefficients. See Adam (1994).
8. See Adam (1999).
9. This section is taken from World Bank (1984).
10. The main events of each of the episodes discussed here are summarized in Appendix 10A, Table 10A.1.
11. See Bates and Collier (1993).
12. See Aron and Elbadawi (1997).
13. The shift to a Dutch auction also improved the fiscal position of the government, which – as the seller of foreign exchange – was able to capture the consumer surplus from bids above the marginal price.
14. This involved the Bank of Zambia committing to supply a greater amount of foreign exchange than was available. This forced the marginal price down (that is, the kwacha was less depreciated) but led to the development of a foreign exchange pipeline with an uncertain delivery cost to the government. As the marginal rate continued to fall, the government had to purchase foreign exchange at a higher rate of exchange than it had already sold it for. This not only increased the losses incurred by the government, but the need to meet previous sales contracts led to a squeeze on the uncommitted foreign exchange, which could be sold on the market.
15. By 1985, it has been suggested, the official exchange rate was wholly inframarginal, so that a reduction in the premium as a result of exchange rate unification did not alter the marginal price of imports to the consumer, although it did have major redistributive effects, particularly on the SOE sector.
16. This programme-within-a-programme established quarterly short-term

macroeconomic targets for reserve money, the nominal exchange rate, domestic credit and international reserves, the fulfilment of which permitted the government to accumulate the right to extinguish outstanding arrears to the IMF. Only once these arrears were cleared could Zambia qualify for access to the IMF's enhanced structural adjustment facility (ESAF). It was anticipated that sufficient rights would be accumulated by the end of the five-year ERP to warrant clearance of all outstanding arrears to the IMF.

17. Sales tax was levied on taxable goods, both domestic and imported, at a rate of 23 per cent. The 20 per cent uplift resulted in the effective sales tax rate on the landed, duty inclusive price of imports rising to 27.6 per cent.
18. To qualify for COMESA tariff reductions goods must: (1) be wholly produced in a member state; or (2) be produced in the member states but where the c.i.f. value of any foreign (that is non-COMESA) materials used does not exceed 60 per cent of the total cost of all materials used in the production; or (3) be produced in member states from foreign materials but where the value of such inputs do not exceed 55 per cent of ex-factory cost of the goods; or (4) be of particular economic importance of the member states and containing not less than 25 per cent value added.
19. See Audit of the Export Board (1993).
20. There remained a small discount on the exchange rate at which OGL transactions were executed, reflecting the higher transactions costs associated with that model.
21. SGS data are based only on imports with a shipment value greater than $US5000 for which pre-shipment clearance is required from the country of supply.
22. The CSO in Lusaka only published the 1985 Input–Output Table in 1995. It is unlikely that a comprehensive IO table for the early 1990s will be produced before 1997.
23. This will be the case if the survey frames used by the CSO to collect data become increasingly less representative of the true structure of the economy. The regular CSO surveys (for example, for the construction of the Index of Industrial Production) are dominated by medium-sized to large firms in the traditional import-substituting manufacturing sector. For example, if liberalization leads to the shrinkage of the large-scale to medium-scale sector and an increase in the small-scale sector, CSO data will be biased towards indicating a greater contraction output than is actually occurring.
24. See World Bank (1994).
25. Given the small manufacturing firm population in Zambia, many firms in this sample had already been interviewed under the three waves of the RPED survey, as well as many other firm-level studies carried out by the World Bank, UNIDO and the PTA/COMESA secretariat in Lusaka.
26. Export Board of Zambia, *Exporter Audit Report 1995.*
27. As indicated earlier, it is difficult to exactly the commencement of liberalization measures.
28. Throughout we take sales as the best measure of the 'supply' of the firm. Firms were asked to report both sales and production and to provide information on the change in inventories. Responses were much more complete on sales levels than on production while revaluation problems meant that

their was little reconciliation between sales and production plus net reduction in inventories.

29. At an average exchange rate for August 1994–August 1995 of K/$ 673.
30. Almost 50 per cent of the exports from the sample firms is accounted for by a single firm.
31. Non-traditional in Zambia consists of all exports excluding metals (copper, cobalt, zinc and lead).
32. Export Board of Zambia, Exporter Audit, 1995 (May 1995).
33. For example, through subsidization of the state-owned utilities.
34. We have used the investment deflators computed by von der Fehr *et al.* (1995) in their study of the RPED data.
35. For example, firms supplying both domestic and export markets have found it difficult to claim for duty drawback on that proportion of inputs used for the export market if the original import consignment was undifferentiated.
36. For example, only eight companies replied to this question (even though 21 claimed to receive benefits from the scheme. Of these eight companies, three reported the relief as 23 per cent (the value of the nominal sales tax on imports avoided); two firms reported the relief as 5 per cent; and the remainder reported the relief as between 75 per cent and 100 per cent.
37. This was true also of the second liberalization although in this case the resource flow (that is, the resource transfer net of interest and arrears) was significantly higher.
38. See Kiguel and O'Connell, *World Bank Research Observer* (1995).
39. See Bevan, Adam and Chambas (1998).
40. As the figure is drawn, the fall in the aggregate price level reflects the combination of a small fall in the price of non-tradeables and a large fall in the price of tradeables as a result of the nominal exchange rate appreciation. This is what happened in the third quarter of 1993 in Zambia.
41. CSO Annual Report for 1993 (January 1994).
42. Local cement sales from Chilanga Cement fell by 10.4 per cent and electricity consumption, excluding ZCCM, rose by approximately 2 per cent in the year, while formal sector employment continued to gradually decline. (All figures from Bank of Zambia Monthly Real Economic Statistics, December 1994.)
43. Draft GRZ Letter of Intent to IMF (March 1995).
44. The two most commonly cited examples are the oft-repeated concern about the policy stance of a future Labour government in the United Kingdom and also the now-celebrated case of the telecommunications of Jamaica. In the case of the latter – which is fully documented in Adam *et al.* (1992) – the spectre of possible renationalization were Mr Michael Manley who had presided over the initial nationalization of the telecommunications industry in the early 1970s and the then Leader of the Opposition, to return to power allowed the buyer to demand an extremely favourable bargain. This included a 25-year monopoly with guaranteed rate of return and the requirement that the Government of Jamaica post US$-denominated bonds in an escrow account in Washington, DC, callable if the buyer's monopoly position was jeopardized.
45. See, for example, the extensive reviews of aid to Africa undertaken in the past year by Sweden, Canada and the United States.

46. Notice how the intrinsic time-inconsistency problem discussed above can contribute to the emergence of unfulfilled donor expectations and donor fatigue. Consider the case where *ex-ante* aid inflows are designed to improve infrastructure, thereby enhancing the return on private capital and stimulate private investment. Because of the presence of the capital taxation problem, the prospect of future taxation of profits will mean that the private sector investment that the aid is expected to stimulate will does not materialize and as a result the aid flow turns out, *ex post,* to be either perpetual consumption transfers which do not contribute to growth, or aid-financed white elephants.
47. This section draws heavily on J. Aron (1992).

References

Adam, C. S. (1994) *On the Stability of Input–Output Coefficients in Zambia 1964–1985*, mimeo, Centre for the Study of African Economies, University of Oxford.

Adam, C. S. (1999) *Privatization in Zambia: Issues in Regulation and the Macroeconomics of Transition* in J. A. Paulson (ed.), *The Role of the State in Key Markets* (London: Macmillan).

Adam, C. S. and D. L. Bevan (1994) *Investment, Uncertainty and the Option to Wait*, mimeo, Centre for the Study of African Economies, University of Oxford.

Adam, C. S., D. L. Bevan and G. Chambas (1993) *Revenue Productivity in Sub-Saharan Africa*, mimeo, Centre for the Study of African Economies, University of Oxford.

Adam, C. S., W. P. Cavendish and P. S Mistry (1992) *Adjusting Privatization: Case Studies from Developing Countries* (London: James Currey).

Aron, J. (1992) *Political Mismanagement of a Mining Parastatal: the Case of ZCCM*, mimeo, Centre for the Study of African Economies, University of Oxford.

Aron, J. and I. Elbadawi (1997) *The Parallel Market Premium and Exchange Rate Unification: A Macroeconomic Analysis of Zambia* in Kiguel, M., *et al.* (eds), *Parallel Exchange Rates in Developing Countries* (London: Macmillan).

Bank of Zambia, *Statistical Fortnightly*, Lusaka (various issues).

Bank of Zambia, *Monthly Real Economic Statistics*, Lusaka (various issues).

Bates, R. H. and P. Collier (1993) *The Politics and Economics of Policy Reform in Zambia* in R. H. Bates and A. O. Krueger (eds), *Political and Economic Interactions in Economic Policy Reform: Evidence from Eight Countries* (Oxford: Blackwell).

Central Statistical Office, Government of the Republic of Zambia, *External Trade Bulletin*, Lusaka (various years).

Central Statistical Office, Government of the Republic of Zambia, *Annual Report*, Lusaka (various years).

Collier, P., D. Greenaway and J. W. Gunning (1993) *A Methodology for the Study of Trade Liberalization*, mimeo, Centre for the Study of African Economies, University of Oxford.

Davies, J. M. (1993) *Modern Industry and the African* (London: Macmillan).

Export Board of Zambia, *Export Audit*, Lusaka (various years).

Government of the Republic of Zambia, *Letter of Intent to the IMF*, March 1995.
Gulhati, R. (1989) *Impasse in Zambia: the Economics and Politics of Reform*, EDI Case Study No. 2 (Washington, DC: World Bank).
Kate, A. T., M. Thorne and C. Chileshe (1994) *Effective Protection and Domestic Resource Costs in Zambia*, UNDP/UNIDO Report.
Keinbaum Development Services GmbH (1994) *Strategic Options for the Privatization of Zambia Consolidated Copper Mines* (Lusaka).
Kiguel, M. and S. A. O'Connell (1995) 'Parallel Exchange Rates in Developing Countries', *World Bank Research Observer*, vol. 10.
Neary, P. J. (1985) *Real and Monetary Aspects of the Dutch Disease* in A. Jugengenfelt and R. Hague (eds), *Structural Adjustment in Developed Open Economies* (London: Macmillan).
Picks Currency Yearbook (1993) (New York: International Currency Analysis Inc.)
von der Fehr, N-H. *et al.* (1994) *The Zambian RPED Enterprise Database*, mimeo, Department of Economics, University of Oslo, February.
World Bank (1984) *Zambia: Industrial Policy and Performance*, Report 4436-ZA (Washington, DC).
World Bank (1993) *Zambia: Prospects for Sustainable and Equitable Growth*, Report 11570-ZA (Washington, DC).
World Bank, *World Tables* Oxford University Press and World Bank, Washington, DC (various years).

11 Trade Liberalization and Regional Integration in Zimbabwe

Mthuli Ncube, Paul Collier,
Jan Willem Gunning and Kupukile Mlambo

11.1 INTRODUCTION

Both the overall level and the geographic composition of Zimbabwean trade has been subject to major policy changes. From 1965 until 1991 a combination of foreign exchange controls and trade restrictions created a large import-substituting manufacturing sector and implicitly taxed agricultural exports. Despite the growth of manufacturing, overall GDP per capita declined during the 1980s. Concerned by the lack of growth, in 1991 the government embarked upon trade and exchange rate liberalization as the core of a more wide-ranging economic liberalization programme. The geographic composition of trade was affected during 1965–80 by world sanctions against Rhodesia, which artificially increased the share of trade with South Africa, and during 1980–94 by SADC policy of reversing this dependence. Only since 1995 has policy towards the geographic pattern of trade ceased to be governed by these overriding political considerations. South Africa is now seen both as a major potential market if the high protection against Zimbabwean produce can be reduced, and as a major potential competitor in the SADC market as the restrictions against South Africa are removed.

This chapter focuses upon four aspects of trade policy. Section 11.2 considers the macroeconomic compatibility of the liberalization, and its underlying credibility. Trade liberalization will rebound on the balance of payments and on the budget and either of these might become unsustainable unless there are offsetting policy changes that restore payments and fiscal compatibility. The credibility of the change in trade policy can be called into question either by a failure to make these offsetting changes, or by a perception that the balance of political advantage lies in policy reversal. Section 11.3 sets the trade liberalization into the wider context of economic liberalization and focuses upon the interaction of the trade liberalization with the financial liberalization. Trade liberalization affects financial liberalization through a variety of mechanisms. For example, during foreign exchange rationing, the allocation of foreign exchange was the most reliable indicator of credit-worthiness, so that liberalization causes a loss of information for the banks. Financial liberalization also affects trade liberalization. The sharp increase in interest rates differentially disadvantages those firms with long lags between purchases of inputs and sales of output, characteristics associated with international trade.

Section 11.4 investigates the resource allocation consequences of the liberalization with particular focus upon the manufacturing sector. Whereas the original manufacturing sector was heavily import-substituting and so might be expected to contract as a result of trade liberalization, it is *a priori* an open question whether resources would shift out of the manufacturing sector in its entirety or whether an expansion in export-orientated manufacturing would enable the sector in aggregate to grow. The manufacturing sector might also become more labour intensive as a result of factor price changes arising from the liberalization, so that employment might increase relative to output. A feature of the analysis is its use of detailed survey data for the manufacturing sector, partly collected specifically for the study. The effect of liberalization on the Zimbabwean manufacturing sector is potentially of wider significance for African trade policy. If the sector is successful in reorientating to exports then there is some basis for the hope that other small, inward-orientated manufacturing sectors can transform themselves. If, however, it is unsuccessful, then since Zimbabwe has better infrastructure and a better-educated labour force than most other African countries, prospects elsewhere may be bleak.

Section 11.5 turns to the regional context of the trade liberalization, again keeping the focus primarily upon manufacturing. Zimbabwe is a net exporter of manufactures to the region and a net importer of manufactures from the rest of the world. The section considers how the new political landscape might affect trade in manufactures. This section summarizes and concludes the analysis.

11.2 THE MACROECONOMICS OF THE LIBERALIZATION

We begin with the macroeconomic aspects of the trade liberalization. About half of the liberalization attempts in Africa have been reversed. With such a high incidence of reversal, private agents do not automatically regard a liberalization as permanent; rather, they assess the credibility of policy maintenance. Concerns about the course of future policy introduce a second dimension to resource reallocation: in addition to the inter-sectoral reallocation which trade liberalization is intended to induce, agents engage in inter-temporal reallocation. We analyse the extent to which the Zimbabwean liberalization has been credible to well-informed private agents.

The consequences of limited credibility of a trade reform can be highly damaging, inducing socially inefficient inter-temporal reallocation through portfolio switches. Private agents are liable both to speculate, by hoarding imports, and to delay investment.

Speculative behaviour has been evident at various stages of the reform process. In the first half of 1991 there was massive speculation by traders. When items were first placed on OGIL some firms imported several years' worth of inputs, clearly fearing that the liberalization would only be temporary. There are two ways in which the hoarding of imports can be temporarily attractive: better availability and lower price. The hoarding of goods imported under OGIL was probably motivated by fears that the improved availability was only temporary. Alternatively, hoarding might be motivated by the expectation that a range of imports are currently unsustainably cheap. An example of such hoarding is the timing of imports of textiles and cars around the 1991 devaluation. As shown in Table 11.8 (p. 594) there was a substantial peak in imports of these durable goods in the third quarter of 1991, presumably just ahead of the devaluation. Similar behaviour was reported of the devaluation at the end of 1993. This devaluation was widely anticipated, and indeed was virtually pre-announced one month in advance. This induced deferral of exports and prepayment for imports. The counterpart to this was that subsequent to the devaluation import demand was weaker than expected and exports were stronger, permitting an appreciation in the Export Retention Scheme (ERS) rate from 8.5 to around 8.1 between January and April. A similar phenomenon occurred around the 1991 devaluation. Between the second and fourth quarters, the two quarters that straddle the devaluation, merchandise imports fell by 24 per cent, whereas merchandise exports increased by 18 per cent.

While there were evidently speculative purchases of imports, evidence on the deferral of investment due to policy uncertainty is more difficult to discern. We therefore consider the circumstances in which private agents will have doubts over the maintenance of trade liberalization policies. A trade liberalization can be less than fully credible if government behaviour is predictable in terms of some theory and the theory predicts that the liberalization will be reversed. Predictable reversal could occur in Zimbabwe due to three circumstances: (1) time inconsistency; (2) payments incompatibility; and (3) fiscal incompatibility. A further way in which liberalization might be less than fully credible is if government behaviour is seen as unpredictable but sufficiently volatile that there is a reasonable expectation that no policy change will persist for long. Volatile behavior is usually based on either political factionalism, giving rise to the shifting of power between opposing viewpoints, or sheer muddle. We consider these in turn.

Is the Zimbabwean Liberalization 'Time Inconsistent'?

Time inconsistency is a potential political trap. If the trap exists, then the very actions that would lead to the success of liberalization in economic terms, would lead to its being reversed politically. Essentially, in studying time inconsistency we must put ourselves in the shoes of a private business person and investigate how he or she regards the rational motivation behind government policy. The business person asks, 'does the government have a rationale for liberalizing now and subsequently reversing the liberalization?' For example, cocoa farmers in Ghana might well interpret trade liberalization as a trap to lure them into replanting cocoa. For many years cocoa had been very heavily taxed, farmers had not replanted, and so the yield from the tax gradually withered away. At this point the government had an incentive to remove the tax, because it lost little revenue, in the hope that farmers would replant. However, farmers might reasonably fear that were they to replant, the government would again have an interest in high cocoa taxation. Note that farmers do not need to regard the government's tax cut as a deliberate ruse. The current government might genuinely promise continuing low taxation. However, were farmers to replant, some future government would have an interest in restoring the high tax regime for precisely the reason it was introduced in the first place. In this example, a Ghanaian trade liberalization would be 'time inconsistent': investment would not occur in the export sector despite the liberalization.

Zimbabwe is much less seriously affected by time inconsistency than Ghana. First, whereas in Ghana the high export taxation regime had a powerful political rationale, in Zimbabwe the control regime was to an extent accidental. The present government inherited the control regime from the UDI period and has, albeit belatedly, chosen to dismantle it. In other words, there would probably never have been a control regime but for the peculiar political circumstances of UDI. The control regime does not represent a natural political equilibrium.

Secondly, the politics of decontrol was predominantly internal rather than being imposed by donor conditionality. The driving force was the conversion of the Confederation of Zimbabwean Industries (CZI) during 1987 from being pro-control to being pro-liberalization. The manufacturing sector had lobbied for protection prior to UDI, since as the import-competing sector it was the natural beneficiary. However, during the mid

1980s it came to see the inward focus of the regime, and particularly the inability to gain access to foreign exchange, as the binding constraint upon growth. At its 1987 conference it backed liberalization. Skalnes argues that the *de facto* one-party rule in Zimbabwe increases the influence of well-organized and articulate pressure groups relative to numerically large but unorganized social groups. The conversion of CZI helped the minister of finance, at the time virtually the only important figure to support liberalization, to persuade other ministers to adopt liberalization. The other powerful lobby, the Commercial Farmers Union, had an obvious interest in liberalization. Hence, the two best-organized lobbies in the country were pro-liberalization, not just as a short-term strategy, but for the long term. As shown above, the manufacturing sector benefited from liberalization in its first phase of input liberalization. Hence, its support in that early phase is not hard to explain. However, the CZI has maintained its support, lobbying only for changes around the edges of the policy, as liberalization has moved through the second phase during which the sector suffered considerably.

The only element of time inconsistency comes from the foreign aid linked to the liberalization programme. This has the potential to appear as a deal in which reform is the price the government pays in return for the aid. Since Zimbabwean per capita income is too high for the country to be a long-term substantial recipient of aid, the aid can be recognized as temporary, and if the government's motivation for reform were simply to receive the aid, then the policy would be predicted to be reversed once the aid inflow ceased. Again, this does not appear to be a serious consideration given the circumstances in which the Zimbabwean liberalization was conceived. The government did not start the liberalization from a position of economic crisis, and so was not desperate for aid. Further, to some extent the aid inflow has made subsequent policy reversal more difficult, because simply to roll the debt over will require adherence to conditionality, so that reversal would now carry some penalty in the form of accelerated debt repayment.

To conclude, the Zimbabwean liberalization cannot reasonably be seen as time inconsistent by well-informed private agents. This is not to say that there is no probability of policy reversal, but that there is no political trap whereby economic success would lead to political failure.

Is the Zimbabwean Liberalization Payments-incompatible?

A trade liberalization will tend to worsen the current account of the balance of payments unless offset by other policies. The most pertinent offsetting policy is the exchange rate, and this has been the main strategy of the Zimbabwean government. Reform has been achieved through a series of trade-liberalizing devaluations. Payments incompatibility arises if the exchange rate and trade policy changes become misaligned. Quite a common policy error in African trade liberalizations has been for trade restrictions to be liberalized too generously relative to the depreciation of the exchange rate, giving rise to an unsustainable balance of payments deficit.

The first phase of the liberalization, October 1990–August 1991, showed some symptoms of being payments-incompatible. During this period there was virtually no depreciation of the real exchange rate and exports were also virtually constant (in US$ terms). Yet merchandise imports were substantially liberalized, increasing in dollar terms by 24 per cent relative to their level during the two years prior to liberalization. As a result, the current account deteriorated from balance in 1989 to a deficit of around US$500 m by 1991. During this phase imports were therefore unsustainably cheap and smart agents speculated by purchasing them. The manufacturing sector was the major beneficiary of this cheap inputs phase, which is consistent with the evidence on increased profitability discussed above.

The second phase of the liberalization began with a devaluation that was both necessary, given the need to restore compatibility, and in all probability sufficiently large to have achieved its purpose. However, the drought and the financial liberalization both had powerful effects that obscure the picture. The drought probably accounts for the severe drop in GDP of 7.7 per cent. Such a temporary fall in income is an appropriate circumstance in which to borrow, and the current account deficit in 1992 amounted to US$842 m. To express this as a percentage of GDP we need to use an exchange rate, and at the time the official rate was overvalued. An approximation to the equilibrium official rate is arrived at by assuming that the rate as of January 1994 of Z$8.5 to US$1.00 was market-clearing. Deflating back to 1992 by inflation, so as to keep the real exchange rate constant, this yields an average rate for 1992 of Z$6.14. Using this exchange rate, the 1992 payments deficit was 20.1 per cent of GDP. Not only was this an enormous amount, but the increase over the 1991 deficit was itself 8.4 per cent of GDP. Since the GDP drop during the drought was 7.7 per cent, whereas the long-term growth rate had been 3.4 per cent, the shortfall of actual income from expected was around 11.1 per cent. Hence, the increased deficit accommodated around three-quarters of the shortfall. While an appropriate response to the drought, this incremental deficit was on top of an already large underlying deficit at a level that was evidently unsustainable. The high level of external financing may account for the strong appreciation of both the official and the ERS real exchange rates between September 1991 and the end of 1992, by which time three-quarters of the real depreciation achieved by the 1991 devaluation had been eroded.

In the context of a payments deficit of 20 per cent, it is evident to intelligent private agents that there will subsequently be either a depreciation or a tightening of trade restrictions. Hence, there are powerful motives both for the speculative hoarding of imports and foreign financial assets, and for the deferral of investment due to uncertainty. However, the financial liberalization dramatically raised the cost of hoarding by increasing both nominal and real interest rates. Loan rates from banks approached 50 per cent. At such rates the only speculation that is viable is in response to rumours of imminent devaluation. The correct perception that the policy stance would necessarily be modified in order to restore compatibility did not provide a precise timetable for policy change because the government was able to maintain a high level of reserves through borrowing. Hence, the policy was sustainable in the short term, and the information that it was not sustainable in the longer term did not provide an opportunity for profitable speculation at such high interest rates.

By limiting speculative import hoarding and the acquisition of foreign financial assets, the high interest rate policy temporarily appreciated the equilibrium exchange rate. The current account deficit would have been ever larger without the high interest rate policy.

In the third phase (mid-1993 to mid-1994) output recovered and so foreign borrowing was reduced. The current account deficit for 1993 fell to US$282 m, so that not only had the 1992 increment been reversed, but around half of the underlying deficit had been corrected. The devaluation of end-1993 re-established the real exchange rate at close to its level immediately after the 1991 devaluation and at least in the short term probably achieved something close to current account balance. By April 1994 there was virtual convergence between the official and the market rates. Because the market rate reflected equilibrium only in the current flow of transactions, as opposed to any changes in asset positions, the rate of Z$8.1–8.2 was probably influenced by the same unwinding of speculative trading positions taken in the run-up to the devaluation as occurred during 1991. The underlying equilibrium rate was therefore probably a few per cent more depreciated. However, this was clearly not sufficient to induce speculative hoarding of imports and foreign assets.

Hence, by early 1994 the policy stance was approximately payments-compatible, and so in this respect not a source of incredibility. During 1994 there was a strong real appreciation in the exchange rate once it had become market-determined. However, this probably reflected a terms of trade improvement as Zimbabwe's principal exports all appreciated on world markets. This terms of trade appreciation, which is quite likely to be temporary, had Dutch disease effects equivalent to a temporary aid inflow. The import substitute sector was thus doubly affected by liberalization and this temporary export boom. Since compatibility was achieved through a coincidental and probably temporary improvement in the terms of trade, the sustainability of trade liberalization in terms of the balance of payments is yet to be tested in more normal conditions. Presumably the nominal exchange rate will depreciate quite substantially post-boom so as to restore the real exchange rate and it is during this depreciation that the commitment of the government to the liberalization will be put to the test. The compatibility of the liberalization during 1994 was in contrast to the second phase of liberalization, during which policy was sufficiently payments-incompatible to have induced speculative hoarding, had it not been for high interest rates, and may well have generated substantial policy uncertainty.

Is the Zimbabwean Liberalization Fiscally Incompatible?

A liberalization that causes substantial deterioration in the budget may give rise to expectations that it will prove unsustainable in an analogous way to a deterioration in the payments deficit. The trade and exchange rate liberalizations have long-term effects on revenue and expenditure and also have transitional effects.

The government has retained quite high taxation of imports through duties, taxes and surcharges and so to the extent that trade liberalization expands trade it will enhance revenue. While reductions in these tax rates would probably reduce revenue, the trade reforms to date have primarily removed quantitation restrictions. Estimates on the effects of the 1994 tariff reductions suggest that with an unchanged composition of trade, revenue would barely be altered. The effect of trade liberalization on the expenditure side of the budget will have been to increase it, since the government will normally be a net purchaser of foreign exchange. However, since the government is also a major employer, the fall in real wages discussed below will have substantially reduced its expenditure.

Turning to the transitional effects, the export retention scheme was a potential claim on the budget as long as exchange rates were not unified. This is because they represented the right to buy at the official exchange rate. To honour this right the government had to buy (or forgo selling) the foreign exchange at the market rate. Hence, the cost involved is the difference between the two exchange rates, which in January 1994 was about 5 per cent but by April had fallen to 1 per cent. As of January 1994 there were US$300 m of ERS outstanding, representing a potential maximum cost of Z$320 m. However, the actual cost was much lower because little ERS was cashed before unification.

A related liability consists of the outstanding import licences, including the PTA allocations. These entitle the holder to purchase foreign exchange at the official exchange rate and so, as with the ERS, involved as of January

1994 a 5 per cent subsidy on the face value of the licences. The extent of outstanding licences was not known because at the time of the devaluation there was no complete tracking system. Licences were valid until June 1994. As with ERS, the extent of the liability depended on how many were cashed prior to exchange rate unification.

The ERS system as of December 1993 amounted to an implicit export tax of 11 per cent offset by an explicit selective export subsidy of 9 per cent. The implicit tax worked through the 50 per cent of export earnings that the government retained and paid for at the official exchange rate, which was some 22 per cent below the market rate. Hence, an exporter lost 22 per cent on half of export earnings. This implicit tax of 11 per cent did not appear as tax revenue. Partly, it appeared as reduced government expenditure, since the government was able to purchase its own imports using this cheap foreign exchange. To the extent that the government did not use all this foreign exchange, the Reserve Bank could sell it. However, since it sold it at the official exchange rate, it was conferring an implicit subsidy on importers. The net benefit to the government was thus only on its own foreign exchange expenditures. This was probably substantially offset by the selective 9 per cent subsidy to exporters, which was a claim on expenditure. In January 1994 the implicit export tax rate fell to 2 per cent, since the premium was only 5 per cent and the government retained only 40 per cent of export earnings, while the export subsidy was removed. By April 1994 the implicit export tax rate was negligible. The net effect of these changes is difficult to predict, but appears to be small in the longer term. However, there is an adjustment cost, as the withdrawal of ERS entitlements was not syncronized with the benefit conferred by devaluation. Although both changes were made effective from 1 January 1994, ERS entitlements were based on the physical export of the good over the border, whereas the devaluation benefit accrued on payment. Since payment might typically be three months later than export, exports that crossed the border in the fourth quarter of 1993 benefited from ERS and also received the devaluation benefit. An approximate estimate of the maximum cost of this effect is 5 per cent (the maximum cost of ERS as discussed above) of US$500 m (export values per quarter), or Z$200 m.

A potentially serious liability consists of the forward exchange rate cover provided until recently by the Reserve Bank at highly subsidized rates. For example, forward cover for the US dollar over 12 months was provided at 11.2 per cent, whereas the rate charged by commercial banks was 28 per cent. The magnitude of this resulting liability is uncertain but may be on the order of Z$1 billion. The scale is contingent upon inflation and the resulting currency depreciation.

Though the above fiscal changes are not substantially adverse (with the exception of the forward cover) they occur in a context in which a large and inflationary fiscal deficit was already likely. By 1995 the deficit was around 10 per cent of GDP. While this size of deficit had been common during the 1980s, the financial liberalization has closed off most of the non-inflationary means of domestic financing. A large fiscal deficit is important in the context of trade liberalization because of its inflationary consequences. At the microeconomic level, the high interest rates it generates inflict cost shocks that may undermine the trade liberalization. At the macroeconomic level a deficit that is seen as unsustainable potentially threatens the credibility of the entire liberalization programme.

By 1995 the policy stance was therefore fiscally incompatible. However, there are two factors that make this less likely to induce serious doubts over the maintenance of the liberalization programme.

First, the government has already made significant efforts to reduce expenditure. For example, the national accounts show that at constant prices there was a 14 per cent reduction in public administration between 1991 and 1992. Allowing for relative price changes, there was a further 11 per cent fall in public administration in units in GDP, so that in a single year the cost of public administration fell by 24 per cent. Second, private agents know that governments will tend to defer expenditure reductions until after elections. In effect, they recognize the public expenditure levels as time inconsistent rather than doubting the maintenance of the liberalization policy. Taken together, these factors make the fiscal deficit less damaging for investment.

Is Zimbabwean Economic Policy Volatile?

So far we have suggested that the liberalization does not currently suffer limited credibility either from time inconsistency or payments incompatibility, and that the fiscal problem is somewhat less damaging than it looks at first sight. These eliminate the sources of predictable policy change. There remains, however, a different basis for investor uncertainty, namely policy volatility. In this respect there may be some cause for concern.

The incentive system has been subject to frequent change (which in part has been the price of gradualism), and its operation has been haphazard. This may give rise to a low degree of supply response. There is indeed some evidence that firms failed to see the many steps of the liberalization as constituting a logical sequence of 'gradualism' and instead read them as policy volatility. We summarize the main instances of policy reversal.

(1) Some of the items placed on OGIL were later removed (for example, cement) rewarding those firms that had hoarded.

(2) The January 1994 announcement of tariff changes (many to a level of 100 per cent) has been widely interpreted either as a tariff increase (which it was not), or as enabling the government to make such an increase in the future, and thereby indicating an intention to do so.
(3) The FCAs for individuals were initially tradeable but were then restricted. This was seen by some in the private sector as a step back.
(4) The government announced a 25 per cent limit on foreign ownership. This was first interpreted as applying to incremental acquisitions, then raised to 35 per cent but made inclusive of existing ownership, and then returned to the first interpretation, which, however, was then reviewed. Rule changes are inevitable in a reform process, and sometimes changes will be mistaken and so need to be reversed. However, the government was perhaps insufficiently mindful of the ambiguous signals reversals give to the private sector.

11.2 FINANCIAL SECTOR REFORM AND TRADE LIBERALIZATION IN ZIMBABWE

Institutional Reform and Agency Problems

In this section we discuss the effect of financial liberalization on trade activity in Zimbabwe. Using data from 80 countries, King and Levine (1992, 1993a, 1993b) found significant correlation between the degree of development of the financial sector and high rates of economic growth. It seems from their findings that financial sector development precedes economic growth, making it a prerequisite for growth. The role of the financial sector in economic growth takes various forms. Apart from pricing resources for investing in positive NPV projects, the financial sector gives investors the opportunity to diversify risks in uncertain investments. The sector also facilitates the allocation of resources towards more efficient investment activities and those that are more innovative. The rationing of credit towards efficient activities increases value-added in the economy, thus contributing to economic growth. From the study, the financial sector can only effectively play the above roles under financial liberalization.

The findings of the King and Levine study serve as a motivation for analysing financial liberalization in Zimbabwe, and its role in enhancing trade activity and growth in general. Our approach is both theoretical and empirical. We shall analyse the behaviour of financial institutions in relation to the parties in conflict (agency problems) and the rationing of credit. Then we shall discuss the development of financial markets in Zimbabwe in relation to the agency and credit rationing issues.

Trade liberalization and exchange rate devaluation are aimed at adjusting relative prices to induce resources to shift towards the export sector and away from low value-added (and often import-dependent) import-substitution sectors. An efficient financial sector is crucial in determining whether firms can take advantage of these relative price changes, both in the short run (via trade financing in the goods market) and the medium term (via investment financing). Thus the central research question in this chapter is whether the financial liberalization measures implemented in Zimbabwe since 1991 reinforce or impede the effects of the trade and exchange rate liberalization measures.

We begin with a theoretical discussion of agency problems and asymmetric information issues that we believe are important for understanding the depth of institutional reform in the financial sector. It is the case that financial sector reform that concentrates on getting relative prices right is incomplete without complementary institutional reforms. In this section we summarize the theoretical arguments.

The Fisher Separation Principle argues that under perfect capital markets there is separation of consumption and production decisions. Managers can make investment decisions that maximize wealth for the owners, and there is no conflict of interest or asymmetric information between parties. Capital market prices are a sufficient signal for production decisions, while consumption decisions are left to the owner, who uses the capital market to maximize utility. The real world, however, is different. There is no separation of consumption from investment. The parties involved are always in conflict, a phenomenon that may detract from optimal decision-making. The real world is also characterized by asymmetric information, and other market imperfections such as transaction costs.

The firm can be seen as a nexus of contracts among various parties, such as shareholders, bondholders, employees and general taxpayers. While most stakeholders have fixed claims from the firm, the equity holders (owners) have residual claims. This gives rise to potential conflicts among the parties, where each party seeks to maximize benefit at the expense of the other. The incentive conflicts are known as 'agency problems'. The agency approach to the firm's capital structure problem contradicts the Modigliani–Miller Theory, which argues that the capital structure of the firm is irrelevant. In reality, agency costs do have an impact, making optimal capital structure possible under certain conditions.

Agency problems detract from the efficient operation of an enterprise. Departures from efficient investment strategies are detrimental to economic growth and development. Thus, the economic and financial environment that fosters efficient contracting among parties with diverse interests also promotes efficient allocation of resources and economic development. It turns out that in the context of the subject matter of this chapter – African finance – the social agency conflicts become the most important considerations in financial reform and regulation. At the centre of agency problems is that private actions undertaken by inside decision-makers are not readily observable by outside parties. Let us consider each type of agency problem in turn.

Managerialism

Managerialism refers to self-serving behaviour by managers. But, under separation of ownership and control, the operations of the firm are conducted by managers who typically lack major stock-ownership positions. The potential conflict arising between managers and owners manifests itself in several dimensions. The management-stockholder conflict leads to managerial propensity for expanding a span of control in the form of 'empire-building' at the expense of the capital contributors or owners, for unduly conservative investments in the form of seeking safe (but inferior) projects to maintain the safety of wage compensation and their own survival. In the parlance of managerial agency, such opportunistic behaviour has come to be known as 'excessive perquisite consumption'. Since management has partial or no ownership in the firm, it may exert less effort (or shirk) and have incentives to acquire excessive perquisites, such as luxurious offices, furniture, company cars, than if it had to bear all of the costs.

Debt Agency

This implies that there is a potential conflict between the firm's owners and its creditors that distorts efficiency. The debt contract may induce managers, working on behalf of owners (equity-holders), to make investment and financing decisions sub-optimally by departing from the principle of value maximization. This happens when equity-holders and creditors are disjoint classes of investors so that the primary concern is to maximize equity value over the cash flows that arise in the non-bankrupt states of nature.

Suppose that the firm raises some of its funds from the owners (equity-holders) and the remaining from debt financing borrowed at a fixed obligation. In the good states of nature, no matter how high the firm cash flow earnings, the debt-holders still receive only their fixed pay-off. Owners capture all the gains above the debt obligation. Thus, equity can be thought of as a call option granting the holder the right to buy the assets of the firm at an exercise price equal the right to buy the assets of the firm at an exercise price equal to the debt obligation. Then the value of equity (E) is given by $\mathrm{E} = \max\{0, V - [D\}$ while that of debt (B) is $B = D - \max\{0, D - V\}$, where V is the value of the firm and D is the face value of debt. Notice that the value of debt is reduced by the imbedded put option whose value increases with the riskiness of investments. The value of the firm satisfies put-call parity.

In such a case management, working in the best interests of existing shareholders, has an incentive to alter the riskiness of the firm's investment activities. Riskier investments, if successful, will benefit shareholders. But risky investments that fail will reduce the value of collaterilization to debt-holders, with the resultant decline in the value of outstanding debt. Indeed, when the firm goes bankrupt, limited liability allows stockholders simply to walk away from it, shifting all the risk to creditors. The risk incentive debt agency has come to be known as 'risk-shifting'. This problem manifests itself in the form of what has come to be known as 'under-investment'.

As mentioned earlier, the consequences of agency problems are harmful to the owners of the firm, and lead to economic inefficiency and wealth destruction. It is in the best interests of owners to resort to control mechanisms that move the operation of the firm toward full efficiency of the Fisherian variety. The control mechanisms should be built into the corporate governance system, contractual mechanisms, and markets for corporate control and takeovers. The mechanisms are discussed in Haugen and Senbet (1988), and Senbet and Seward (1994). The mechanisms include effective use of boards of directors, efficient design of management compensation, market for corporate control (mergers and takeovers), use of short positions in warrants and convertibles (see Barnea, Haugen and Senbet [1985] and Green [1984] for details), and the design of corporation tax.

Social Agency

Social agency leads to over-investment and makes the case for an efficient design of deposit insurance schemes and capital regulation in the form of capital adequacy ratios. Formal models on the nature and impact of social agency are presented in John, John and Senbet (1991) and John, Senbet and Sundaram (1994). The point is that, even in the absence of debt in the firm's capital structure, limited liability provisions are enough to give equity-holders incentives to shift risk to society, since limited liability allows them to 'walk away' in the bad states. The equity-holders still possess a call option with zero strike price, since the share price is bounded below at zero. The firms over-invest in risky technologies relative to social welfare goals. Hence the rationale of protecting depositors via deposit insurance schemes and the need to curb their excessive choice of risky projects by setting capital adequacy rules. However, the danger of ill-designed deposit insurance schemes, in the form of intermediaries shifting risk to society by taking on even more risky projects that still leave depositors protected, is not to be ignored. The deposit insurance institution or government is left with the task of meeting depositors' claims.

Equally important, is the prohibitive nature of capital adequacy ratios that are set too high. These could stifle entry of new firms and indeed force the exit of smaller banks, the corollary being the growth of large and fewer banks that extract monopoly profit from the market.

The Zimbabwe Experience on Agency Issues

In this section we shall evaluate Zimbabwe's experience with the agency problems discussed above with a view of offering solutions. In this respect we shall focus on three issues: (1) capital adequacy requirements; (2) deposit insurance; and (3) competitive banking. Issues of deposit insurance and bank regulation are inextricably linked to bank capital adequacy requirements (see Santomero, 1990; Eisenbais, 1990; Berlin, Saunders and Udell, 1991; John *et al.*, 1991).

Capital Adequacy Requirements

With sufficiently high capital adequacy ratios, a banking institution is covered for any unexpected portfolio shocks so as not to call into question the structure and operation of the deposit insurance safety-net. However, that requires enforceable adequacy-disclosure rules, surveillance mechanisms to detect unwarranted risk, and transparent and efficient bank payment systems. The extent of banks' risk taking beyond the optimal level, as well as the value loss due to risk-shifting, are functions of bank equity capital. The higher the bank capital the lower the extra risk taken, and the higher the Pareto efficiency loss. Capital adequacy provisions allow the bank to pursue investment activities within its investment opportunity set. They allow the bank to take on extra risk with higher returns that is limited to some level by the bank's own incentive. The policy implication of this is the implementation and enforcement of capital adequacy requirements, as opposed to mandatory restrictions on risk levels, which may yield inefficient allocation of resources.

Let us evaluate the experience of Zimbabwe against the ideal situation. In Zimbabwe the bench-mark scenario hardly obtains. In 1992 Zimbabwe commercial banks had risk-weighted ratios between 5.3 per cent and 11.8 per cent, while the four merchant banks had ratios varying from 4.7 per cent to 12.1 per cent (see Adam and Ncube, 1994). It is clear that some banks have low capital adequacy ratios, far below the 12 per cent or so advocated by the Basle Accord Agreement. Some of the banks have ratios as low as 4 per cent, and the highest ratio is about 10 per cent. In Zimbabwe loan risks could be higher – so much so that the Basle Accord proposed ratios may indeed be too low. Of course, there is a danger in setting too high capital ratios that are prohibitive to entry into the market. The negative corollary is the shrinking of the banking sector, when the economy requires a larger and more competitive banking sector.

The Zimbabwe banking sector fails to meet the prescriptions of optimal capital regulation. Low ratios that prevail, as well as mandatory restrictions on asset risk choices, imply that banks are not afforded adequate opportunity to exploit activities within their investment set. The banks are able to take risks far beyond the optimal level. Therefore, Zimbabwe should consider adopting prudential regulation along the lines of the Basle Accord. Adequacy ratios of more than 12 per cent would be appropriate, since the risks inherent in the economy may be much higher than perceived. Higher capital adequacy ratios would also allow banks to require less collateral.

In Zimbabwe, the supervisory role is not centralized. Banks operate under the legal framework of the Banking Act (1948),[1] amended in 1976, under both the Reserve Bank, through the Inspector of Banks, and the Ministry of Finance through the Registrar of Banks and Financial Institutions. This lack of regulatory focus destracts from effective enforcement of regulatory requirements and results in overlap of jurisdiction. The Reserve Bank should be given more supervisory powers and resources. This would complement its central roles in implementing sound monetary policy and being the lender-of-last resort.

Implicit Deposit Insurance (Too-Big-To-Fail)

Implicit deposit insurance in Zimbabwe exists in the form of 'too-big-to-fail' (TBTF) guarantee. The TBTF nomenclature is attributed to the head of the Federal Deposit Insurance Corporation (FDIC) in the USA after the rescue of Continental Illinois in 1984. To save jobs and depositors' assets in the late 1980s, the Bank of Credit and Commerce International (BCCI) in Zimbabwe was taken over by the government after its collapse on an international scale.

There are some major weaknesses in the TBTF policy implemented in Zimbabwe. First, it encourages excessive risk-taking by banks, at no cost for the banks, thus exacerbating moral hazard problems and increasing systemic risk. The TBTF policy means the government charges the banks no insurance but has to pay depositors when it takes over the bank. The bank insiders receive a transfer of wealth from taxpayers. Given the already large budget deficits in Zimbabwe, such a cost can only exacerbate public sector debt.

Second, to the extent that the TBTF policy only targets larger banks, neglecting small ones, it encourages the growth of large monopolistic banks. The Zimbabwe financial markets need to have a more competitive banking sector, but the TBTF priciple undermines that. Given the inherent weaknesses of the TBTF policy, Zimbabwe should move away from the policy and introduce deposit insurance. At the same time, one should be wary of replacing TBTF with the ill-designed deposit insurance systems of the advanced economies whose deficiencies are well-decoumented. For instance, if Zimbabwe implements a flat-rate deposit insurance system, the financial system will be more unstable, as opposed to the ultimate goal of reducing systemic risk.

High Collateral Requirements

High collateral requirements, which are prevalent in Zimbabwe financial markets, have implications for both credit rationing and capital adequacy. The role of collateral is to sort the risky borrowers from the safe ones, thus achieving a separating equilibrium in the demand for credit. This issue has been analysed by Bester (1985) and Chan and Kanatas (1985). Once the risky borrower is able to meet the high collateral requirements, bank rationing is obviated. The arguments presented may not seem robust to a competitive banking environment. However, in Zimbabwe banks have a proclivity to collude rather than compete, which makes the notion of a representative bank, as the models of Bester, and Chan and Kanatas assume, all the more plausible. Therefore, a borrower rationed by one bank cannot obtain credit from another bank. Sequential credit applications to banks produce the same result.[2]

High collateral requirements could also be a product of the absence of capital adequacy requirements. High collateral can be regarded as a substitute for capital requirements in the sense that both insure against default by borrowers. Therefore, we can also analyse the collateral problem as a means of reducing the risk-shifting agency costs arising as a result of conflict between creditors and borrowers, by using the analytical frameworks in the previous sections. However, there is a deeper issue here in the sense that high collateral requirementes favour those borrowers with relatively high assets in place. Entrepreneurs with high growth opportunities and intangible assets are more likely to be rationed out of the credit market due to high collateral requirements. The corollary is underinvestment in the economy, with the resultant adverse consequences on economic growth, as small and new entrepreneurial investors get squeezed out. Indeed, unduly high collateral requirements are a reflection of a failed financial system that is devoid of efficient and credible contracting among businesses and capital contributors.

Credit Rationing

In this section, we use the Stiglitz and Weiss (1981, 1983) exposition, and an extension of it by Adam and Ncube (1994), to explain the nature and consequences of asymmetric information between banks and borrowers. In their analysis Adam and Ncube argue that, prior to liberalization, the heavy import dependence of the Zimbabwe economy made the availability of foreign currency a binding constraint on investment decisions, so that the demand for domestic credit became derived demand. This period experienced 'disintermediation' arising from the fixed interest rates, which did not facilitate savings or direct demand for credit. Hence, the foreign currency constraint became the arbiter for rationing credit.

The basic assumption is that domestic credit is used as working capital and, since interest rates were controlled prior to liberalization, this demand is inelastic to interest rates. During this period firms tended to invest using internal funds in the form of retained profits, and only working capital was borrowed. This behaviour seems consistent with the *Myers–Mailuf Pecking Order Theory*, which argues that external financing is least preferred by firms. Working capital was utilized for importing vital raw materials, which in turn required access to foreign currency. Thus, demand for domestic credit under the fixed interest rate regime is *derived* from the demand for foreign currency. Because financial institutions are not adequately informed about the quality of borrowers, they view access to foreign currency as a way of resolving the adverse selection problem on quality of borrowers. Borrowers with foreign currency, or indeed those with claims to it,[3] are classified as 'good risk', and those without are classified as 'bad risk'.

Prior to the liberalization programme, the constraint facing the economy was the availability of foreign exchange. At the same time the economy was so heavily import-dependent that this transmitted foreign exchange rationing across the economy as a whole. Furthermore, the domestic credit market operated under administrative allocation procedures at controlled interest rates, which combined with foreign exchange rationing and resulted in a moribund domestic financial sector. Thus, since access to foreign currency represented a credible signal in the economy that divided borrowers into good risk and bad risk categories, domestic complementary requirements (including working capital) were typically made available at the controlled interest rate to firms with access to foreign exchange. This established one of the key features of the financial repression regime, shifting the onus of decision-making on credit rationing form the market to the government and its delegated institutions.

During this period the banking sector was (and it still is) perceived to be conservative and too cautious in its lending policies. Although the sector consists of a large number of institutions, the dominant lenders were (and are) the British-model commercial banks. Credit allocations were predominantly to the larger established firms and traditional export sectors, such as minerals and tobacco, while the provision of venture capital, particularly to the smaller, indigenous sector, is virtually non-existent.

Despite the relative sophistication of the financial institutions, including the equity market, the corporate sector is very heavily leveraged (that is, high debt to equity) and the debt of the sector is predominantly in the form of overdraft rather than fixed interest and fixed term loans. This is a typical *Hicksian overdraft economy*, which is bank-dominated rather than market-dominated in its supply of capital. Liberalization occurred at a time of severe negative shocks in the real economy, which has been compounded by a very tight anti-inflationary monetary policy. The drought of 1992 reduced agricultural output by about 24 per cent, and due to the high linkages in the economy, the decline in agricultural production had repercussions on the manufacturing and transport sectors. In 1993, manufacturing output fell by 25 per cent in the first six months. Export volumes (measured in $US terms) fell by 4 per cent in 1992 but were expected to rise by 11 per cent in 1993, although in value terms the 15 per cent fall recorded in 1992 was unchanged in 1993. The fall in output in 1993 was partly due to depressed demand, but also the effects of the credit squeeze. Let us say more about the Adam and Ncube (1994) argument.

The basic assumption of the model is that the demand for domestic credit is solely a working capital demand and that it is relatively inelastic with respect to the domestic interest rate. Firms require financing to cover their production and trading over time. Then, the demand for working capital is a function of import requirements, value-added and also the market into which the firm sells. For convenience we can concentrate on the case where working capital is required to finance imported intermediates and to provide post-shipment financing for the export market. Then demand for domestic credit by the private sector is derived demand, being more a function of the demand for foreign currency (that is, demand for imports) and less a function of domestic interest rates. In Zimbabwe, prior to liberalization, the rationing system for foreign exchange placed the economy in a perpetual state of excess demand for foreign exchange, a phenomenon that was made worse by controlled interest rates set below the world level in real terms. One corollary of this was that, conditional on foreign exchange availability, there was no excess demand for working capital at the prevailing availability of foreign exchange. In this pre-liberalization period, access to foreign credit became a strong screening signal.

At the controlled interest rate level seniorage revenue from implicit financial repression accrue to government since it was paying below world market interest rates. Recent estimates of the value of this source of revenue by Giovannini and de Melo (1993) suggest that during the 1980s between 4 per cent and 7 per cent of GDP per annum accrued to government as a result of policies of financial repression.

Let us examine two issues of liberalization. The first is the liberalization of the current account, which simply affects the availability and price of foreign exchange. The second liberalization is full capital account liberalization, with a fully flexible exchange rate, so that for any given exchange rate, domestic nominal interest rates adjust to ensure that the (risk adjusted) domestic real interest rate is equal to the world interest rate (an interest-parity relationship). In addition, we consider the effect of domestic monetary policies.

The current account liberalization without any alteration to the domestic interest rate will have two effects. The first is to increase the local domestic credit requirements to finance the same dollar equivalent input requirements. The second effect is that firms respond to the devaluation by switching output from the domestic to the export market, resulting in higher demand for foreign currency. Increases in the domestic interest rate will reduce the quantity of working capital demanded, although empirical evidence would suggest that in aggregate the demand for working capital is interest inelastic. For individual firms the quantity of working capital required is determined by a Leontief production function. Firms will respond to an increase in the interest rate by increasing their credit (and reducing profit), while at the margin, the increase in interest rates will force some firms to exit the market altogether. Hence in aggregate the interest elasticity will be low.

Now let us consider the supply of credit from financial institutions. From the standard Stiglitz–Weiss argument, the domestic banking sector operates under imperfect information, so that its expected profits do not increase monotonically with the interest rate. Beyond a certain point, the return to the bank begins to fall. This is because at higher interest rates the probability that the borrower will default on the loan increases. Thus even if there was an excess demand for credit at a particular interest rate, the banks would not raise interest rates to satisfy this excess demand. There are two basic reasons why this relationship exists.

The first concerns adverse selection effects whereby the mix of applicants for loans alters as the interest rate increases. Initially, rising interest rates will increase the expected, return to the bank as all borrowers repay their loans. However, as interest rates continue to rise, they reduce the expected profits of all firms, starting with the 'safe' ones. These firms will, at the margin, drop out of the market because they cannot afford to borrow at the going rate. Risky borrowers are less sensitive to the interest rate, since if they are going to default, the interest rate plays no role in their expected return. Risky borrowers remain so that the composition of the banks' lending portfolio is skewed towards lending with a higher risk of default. The expected return to the lender thus falls.[4] The second cause for credit rationing is an extension of the former but describes the case where successful borrowers undertake riskier activities with the credit extended to them. Finally, it is important to note that when there are different groups with different (perceived) characteristics, the lending rate will be set so that the expected return is equal to the cost of funds of the bank, and rationing is applied differently across the groups. Thus credit rationing may be complete for one group, bind at the margin for another, and be ineffective for a third group. It is worth making the obvious point that increases in interest rates will not affect the 'redlined' group and will affect the other two groups only – with its major impact on the marginal group.

We have alluded to the fact that one of the features of the foreign exchange rationing of the pre-liberalization period is that it offered the banks a good mechanism for screening good borrowers from bad borrowers. Because foreign exchange licences were allocated on an activity basis, receipt of the licence revealed to the bank additional information about the activities to be financed. This offered partial protection against both the adverse selection and incentive effects. By being able to screen out the Akerlof 'lemons', banks could use the foreign exchange allocation signal to separate good borrowers from bad.

Now, consider what happens to the credit supply function of the banks following liberalization and the interest rate shock. First, we would expect the trade and exchange rate liberalization measures to increase the profitability of credit to the private sector, if the credit availability favours the expanding sectors. On this basis, the supply of credit may be expected to increase. However, the most fundamental change is that when foreign exchange is allocated on the inter-bank market, the primary constraint facing the economy disappears. From the perspective of the banks, however, the removal of the foreign exchange rationing mechanism deprives them of a signal as to the credit-worthiness of borrowers, and more importantly their projects – which will have changed following trade liberalization. The banks are therefore faced with an informational problem of separating good borrowers (and projects) from bad ones. Since in the past this problem did not confront the banks to the same degree, the capacity to screen is relatively low. This produces the classic Stiglitz–Weiss backward bend in the credit supply function.

Another issue to note is that the liberalization of the capital account, and particularly its impact on domestic asset markets, will lead to a portfolio reallocation on the part of the financial sector away from loans and advances (in aggregate) and towards other financial assets, including foreign assets. Prior to liberalization, domestic interest rates were fixed. Due to the existence of capital controls this rate could be maintained at below the world interest rate indefinitely and government would earn implicit revenue on the spread between the domestic interest rate and the world deposit rate (that is, the rate that current holders of government debt would have to earn if they were to continue to hold domestic debt rather than deposit their funds offshore). Capital account liberalization will, if accompanied with relaxations on asset holdings, shift domestic real interest rates towards world rates, and thus the credit supply curve of banks will shift inwards as a result of their portfolio reallocation.

Yet another issue is that, in the short term, the domestic interest rate shock reduces the loanable funds of the banking sector in two ways. The first is the direct effect of a credit squeeze in attracting loanable funds from the credit market to the money market. Banks therefore switch into government and reserve bank securities. The second impact is that the adverse effects of the high real interest rates on the profitability of firms will lead to a rise in bankruptcy and default problems. The banks therefore are required to divert a greater proportion of their loanable funds to the accumulation of reserves.

Credit Demand and Investment Pattern

Working Capital Requirements of Firms

Detailed information on the structure of capital requirements in the industrial sector is difficult to obtain, although data from RBZ and from the Regional Programme on Enterprise Development first-round survey provide a snapshot of the structure of capital allocations.

Table 11.1 illustrates the allocation of total domestic credit to the non-government sector on the basis of 1990 national accounts data. Most notable is the very close link between credit share and the share of total GDP, although agriculture receives more than its GDP share and manufacturing less. Although not reported in this table, the only other sector that receives significantly more than its GDP share is the distribution sector. However, both these sectors receive credit subsidies through the domestic credit allocation system. This aggregate does not, however, distinguish between sectors that are domestically-orientated and those that are orientated toward the export markets. The main export activities in Zimbabwe are tobacco, textiles, basic metal and exportable manufactures; for each of these sectors there is evidence that they have a higher import dependence and are generally more dependent on inputs (Table 11.2).

Based on these data it seems that export firms are significantly more dependent on inputs and imports than their sectoral averages (that is, agriculture and all manufacturing). Since the need for working capital arises from the existence of production lags and the requirement to pay

Table 11.1 Structure of production (%)

Sector	*Share of GDP*	*Share of credit*	*Intermediate inputs*	*Import component*	*Value-added*
Agriculture	16	22	44	10	56
Mining	5	6	26	10	74
Manufacturing	28	24	62	18	38
Construction	3	2	64	13	36
Services	22	25	28	14	72
Total	*100*	*100*			

Source: Adam and Ncube (1994) p. 14.

for inputs in advance of receipt of sales proceeds, it seems reasonable to infer that the export sectors being both more import dependent and also facing longer payment lags will be relatively more dependent on working capital than the rest of the economy. These requirements obviously differ dramatically across sectors and size of firms. For example, larger firms are often likely to be able to acquire longer terms on their input credit than they extend on their own sales. In this case the funds from sales arrive before the costs of sales are financed. On the other hand, if receipt of export proceeds is slower than the payment of input costs (both domestically sourced and imported) then working capital requirements increase. Since we do not have data detailed enough to examine these issues, we cannot accurately determine working capital requirements. For the tobacco sector, however, there are already well developed trade financing facilities available. It is thus the textile and manufactured export sectors that seem to be most vulnerable to the effects of a squeeze on working capital. Whether we can draw this inference depends to a large extent on the actual form of credit use. We have assumed that working capital is principally used to cover intermediate inputs, particularly imported inputs. Table 11.3 provides a breakdown of total credit by end use, which confirms the view that the bulk of credit to the industrial sector (with the exception of the mining sector) is allocated to working capital and trade financing activities.

To investigate the relationship between access to credit and firm size, we turn to the RPED report (Gunning, 1994b). Credit in Zimbabwe for both working capital purposes and capital investment is heavily skewed towards larger and older firms. For example, while over 90 per cent of firms with over 100 employees have secure overdraft facilities with the commercial banks, this falls to 60 per cent for firms with between 11 and 100 employees and to 22 per cent for small firms. Similarly, over 80 per

Table 11.2 Exported goods (%)

Sub-sector	*Share of exports*	*Intermediate inputs*	*Import component*	*Value-added*
Tobacco	20	44	10	56
Textiles	7	64	17	36
Manufacturing	31	51	23	49
Basic metals	16	52	21	48

Source: Adam and Ncube (1994) p. 15.

Table 11.3 Decomposition of lending by end use (%)

Sector	*Capital Investment*	*Raw materials*	*Trade and other finance*
Agriculture	43	43	14
Mining	79	20	1
Manufacturing	31	53	26
Distribution	31	49	20
Construction	43	46	11
Transport	43	29	28
Services	36	46	18
Private	63	6	31
Total shares	*40*	*45*	*15*

Source: Adam and Ncube (1994) p. 15.

cent of firms established before 1979 have overdraft access, yet fewer than 40 per cent of firms established since independence enjoy that facility.

Medium-term Credit

Access to the correct mix of medium-term capital is no less important than working capital to the viability of the export sector. Trade liberalization establishes new relative prices both in terms of sectors of the economy (for example, resources would be expected to follow the demand shift from the importable to the exportable sector) and also in terms of the composition of investment goods (that is, from reliance on tradeable to the non-tradeable capital goods). Thus liberalization will establish the conditions for an investment boom, which requires financing if the investment is to be implemented. Moreover, savings are also required to finance the recapitalization of the manufacturing sector following the severe recession and adverse interest rate shocks of 1992/93 that

Table 11.4 Sources and uses of investment finance (%)

Item	*Retained earnings*	*Loans*	*Overdraft supplier credit*	
Land	28	10	62	
Building	25	5	60	
Equipment	28	29	38	5

Source: Adam and Ncube (1994) p. 17.

undermined the profitability of much of the industrial sector in Zimbabwe.

Investment enjoyed a boom in the early part of the liberalization period and this continued throughout the period to 1993. Generally, however, based on the RPED, the investment boom was in the development of existing capacity and upgrading the same product. Only 16 per cent of total investment was allocated to new products. However, since some of the upgraded investment constitutes retooling existing processes for the export market, this is not problematic.

Investment is predominantly funded through three sources – retained earnings, loans and overdrafts, and parent company finances. The distribution is given in Table 11.4.

The size distribution is also important, with small and medium firms financing a disproportionate amount of investment from their retained earnings.

Other Capital Markets

The market of medium-term capital has been particularly unattractive over recent years. The equity market was used only infrequently for capital accumulation until 1991, and there is currently no market in corporate bonds. Crowding-out effects of the central government and parastatal deficits, and the continued high and variable nominal interest rates, have sharply depressed the demand for domestic debt both from the formal sector (where term-lending is relatively infrequent) and also on concessional lines of credit. For example, commitments and disbursements by the ZDB in 1993 were only 30 per cent of their level in 1992 and 50 per cent of the 1991 level. Moreover, a number of long-term foreign credit facilities aimed at investment have remained undrawn because of the costs of local counterpart funds (for example, the ADB Industrial Restructuring Credit). Allied to this, the high domestic interest costs and the removal of the RBZ forward cover makes foreign debt financing of investment prohibitive at present. On the supply side, the current high interest rates and their associated uncertainty have made the financial sector reluctant to take long positions, even in government debt. As well, the dramatic rise in corporate insolvencies and the consequent rise in bad debt provisions have further reduced investible funds from the banking system.

A frequently noted characteristic of the financial sector in Zimbabwe is that while financial institutions are relatively mature, the financial markets are relatively underdeveloped, particularly in the flow of information on borrowers and the capacity for the sector to manage credit risk. This is particularly true for lending activity to the small and medium-sized business sector, where there is only one institution, ZDB/ZDF, providing term capital (that is, of greater than three-year maturity). This is due in large measure to the inheritance of the sector and its evolution in the context of an economy where the principal constraint facing the industrial sector was availability of foreign exchange. Successful access to foreign currency entitlements provided the principal signal of creditworthiness. The financial sector then fulfilled a relatively passive role, providing credit to an established and often heavily protected import-dependent sector.

The financial sector has therefore been relatively inexperienced in screening, monitoring and risk management capacities, and as a result lending practices are likely to maintain their bias towards larger, established, capital intensive clients (who in the past were relatively low-risk borrowers due to their protected market position). To the extent that it is these firms that are restructuring their capital stock to supply the export market, this is not a problem. This situation is not unique to Zimbabwe; a recent study of financial liberalization in Ecuador suggests that, although financial liberalization was pursued, there was a shift in credit towards larger and older firms. Liberalization also reallocated credit towards more efficient firms. Preliminary evidence from the Zimbabwe Development Bank indicates that this process is also occurring in Zimbabwe. Prior to 1991, the bulk of ZDB term-lending was for expanding existing import substituting capacity. Since then, there has been a sharp switch towards new expansions and retooling for the export market.

For small and medium enterprises, the voluntary credit-rationing behaviour of the financial sector means that financial liberalization is unlikely to improve access to the capital market for these firms. It may indeed worsen the situation. The facilities established to ease this credit constraint, such as the ZCGC facility mentioned above and the Venture Capital Company of Zimbabwe, are thus of central importance to this sector, particularly if their collateral requirements are less severe than those of the rest of the financial sector. For the latter, the collateral requirements typically imposed on term-lending are prohibitively high for smaller firms. In the absence of a track record or a guarantee from another bank (which amounts to the same thing), banks seek 100 per cent collateral coverage, usually on immovable tangible assets.

Direct Equity from Merchant Banks

During the height of the interest rate squeeze in 1992/93, the merchant banking sector was forced to take up equity in a number of client firms facing financial distress. The equity injection by the merchant banks allowed trade credit to continue to flow (from the commercial as well as merchant banks) and reduced the leverage of these firms. Although this action was undertaken in crisis situations by the merchant banks, it does point the way for policy interventions by the government and reserve banks aimed at facilitating the eventual deepening of the equity market. Such interventions would also improve the ability of enterprises to access working capital from the commercial banks. One option open to the government would be to develop an investment rust, possibly by increasing its equity participation funds made available through ZDB and the Venture Capital Company, that would provide equity injections into the corporate sector. Given the likelihood that the economy remains vulnerable to high levels of interest rate volatility, improving the gearing of export-orientated firms seems to offer a high return to the government.

The Zimbabwe Stock Exchange

Like many stock exchanges in lower-income economies, the ZSE has existed for a considerable period of time but at a low level of trading activity. The exchange opened in 1896, but the current structure dates from 1946, and was formalized in 1974 when the Stock Exchange Act was passed. Equities are traded on a call-over system among about eight brokerage firms, and the exchange trades industrial and mining shares, as well as government, municipal and ZESA stocks. There are 66 listed firms with a market capitalization of Z$16 billion, which is about 40 per cent of GDP. Approximately 85 per cent of investment (by volume) is from institutional sources who buy-and-hold, thus accounting for low trading activity. At present there are eight registered brockage firms, the oldest ones being Edward's & Company Stock Brokers (Pvt) Ltd., and Sagit Stock Brokers (Pvt) Ltd.[5]

The market was relatively quiet throughout the 1980s (in terms of turnover, new issues and price volatility), but from the introduction of the ESAP, the market enjoyed a dramatic boom. The market also experienced a sharp increase in the value of new equity issues on the market in 1990 and 1991. The market reversed in 1992 as a result of high domestic interest rates, shifting demand away from equities to the money market; the severe drought-induced recession also put downward pressure on the market (see general macroeconomic discussion).

The most notable feature, though, is that despite the continued high interest rates, there has been a continued growth in the volume (in US$

terms) of new equity issues, and the outlook for 1994 suggests that new issues will exceed the level of 1993. During the first nine months of 1994, Z$1.1 billion worth of shares were traded. A major stimulus to this was the liberalization in January 1994 of foreign access to the equity market. Since Janaury 1994 foreign investors (and resident FCA holders) are permitted to invest in listed and unlisted companies in Zimbabwe up to a threshold of total foreign shareholdings that does not exceed 35 per cent of total equity. Dividend flows from the investment may be remitted at a rate of 100 per cent (after withholding taxation has been charged).

Although much of the growth in the ZSE may be ascribed to stock adjustments to the level of prices, the openness of the market provides new opportunities for capital to be raised by currently heavily levered firms.

Money and Foreign Exchange Markets

Central to transition to a market-based financial system is the relationship between the financial sector and the Reserve Bank. One of the most important components of the financial sector reform concerns the new operating procedures adopted by the Reserve Bank of Zimbabwe in its operations with respect to the money and foreign exchange markets. The institutional aspects of the operation of the RBZ in both markets is particularly important to the credibility and efficiency of the reform measures.

The Money Market

The money market in Zimbabwe consists of the RBZ, the four discount houses (a fifth will start trading soon) and the commercial banks. The latter are referred to collectively as the reserve institutions. The discount houses have historically been the primary market-makers in domestic money and paper, and are the only institutions with access to the RBZ rediscount window. They have broadly the same role and status as the London discount houses.

The treasury bill market is conducted weekly, with an average of Z$55 million sold by tender by the RBZ. The tender is on a *Dutch Auction* basis (top-to-bottom auction) with the Reserve Bank maintaining a reserve price. In contrast, government stocks (that is, long-term debt) are sold on an occasional basis.

Prior to 1991, domestic monetary policy operated within a tightly controlled regime in which the binding constraint in the economy was foreign exchange. Monetary policy was therefore relatively passive, particularly in the conduct of the Reserve Bank of Zimbabwe. Since 1991, the discount houses have not been required to underwrite the government's treasury bill issues. Moreover, following pressure from the commercial banks, the RBZ's overnight window was opened to the commercial bank sector, thereby eliminating the discount houses' monopoly access to the RBZ. The *quid pro quo* for access is that the reserve institutions are obliged to accept in full issues of the Reserve Bank special bills, RBZ's principal liquidity management instrument. Reserve Bank bills are tradeable seven-day liquid assets, but do not qualify as reserve assets. Banks may borrow directly from the RBZ to finance the reserve bill issue at a rate marginally above the overnight rate. Reserve bills have been used periodically to control liquidity; currently, the outstanding stock is about Z$300 million.

The Reserve Bank's trade in bills of exchange has undergone significant reforms, and the decline in bill rediscounting has been replaced by the overnight market. Prior to 1991, the RBZ operated a passive programme of bill discounting, accepting paper of varying quality and for a range of activities, many of which included personal imports and luxury consumer durables. It was felt that the bank was financing too many non-core activities, particularly since it is generally more common for central banks to discount paper on a liquidity rather than an activity basis. While the RBZ has moved toward a liquidity basis for rediscounting, it has as part of the pro-export policy maintained an open window for 'class A' paper, which consists exclusively of trade-financing paper (that is, post-shipment financing). The market in lower grade paper, to the extent that it exists, is made by the financial institutions without a rediscount facility.

An important feature of the treasury bill market is the absence of underwriting of issues. Unsold bills are not taken up by the RBZ. Government does, however, have access to an overdraft facility with RBZ, at a rediscount rate that has been higher than the T-bill rate over most of the period. Recently, however, the term structure has changed so that the rediscount rate has been lower than the T-bill rate. The general practice in the gilts market, prior to 1991 was that the RBZ would follow the government budget by advising the financial sector on the timing, value and maturity of its interventions in the gilt market. Since 1991, the increased uncertainty in public finances – and in particular in inflation – has led the RBZ to suspend this method and replace it with periodic 'canvassing' of the market for new issues to ascertain maturity requirements of the sector. Not surprisingly, maturities have shortened and demand from the traditional holders of gilts – the insurance and pension funds – has declined. This is due to the fall in the liabilities of these institutions arising from the combination of retrenchment and recession effects, rising AIDS-related deaths, and in the shorter term, switches into the money market. The secondary market in government gilts remains very small, particularly in longer-dated securities that carry significant lower coupon rates and which can only be sold at significant capital losses to the seller.

Since 1991, and particularly since 1993, the Reserve Bank has begun to adopt more aggressive operating procedures in all its markets. The most direct has been the switch from a lender-of-first-resort to a lender-of-last-resort stance. Under the former method the RBZ stood ready to discount any volume of paper at the rediscount rate. The measures adopted in May 1993 coincided with the introduction of the overnight rate to the commercial banks and a change in stance in rediscounting procedures. Overnight funds are available up to any limit desired, but are allocated on a price basis, so that the overnight rate represents the marginal cost of liquidity to the financial sector. In order to avoid excess demand for short-term liquidity, redeposits of short-term funds are permissible but at zero interest rate unless the entire sector is in surplus. If any institution is in deficit, the redeposit rate is zero. The overnight market is thin and thus potentially volatile. It is estimated that the volume of funds placed on the overnight market is $100 million, although this can vary from between Z$400 million to net credit balances of similar amounts. At the same time as the introduction of the overnight market, the RBZ stopped making markets in a number of instruments in the expectation that the financial sector itself would become the principal market-maker. The RBZ continues ready to discount treasury bills and 'Class A' bills of exchange. However, in a marked departure from earlier operations it has withdrawn from other bills of exchange, negotiable certificates of deposit, and significantly from government gilts and parastatal paper other than AMA bills.

The shift in the balance of power in the money market has been dramatic. Prior to reforms, the financial sector seems to have dominated the market. The RBZ passively accepted bills of exchange within a relatively fixed interest rate regime. Recently, however, the RBZ has become more proactive in the market, aggressively managing liquidity using the reserve bills, and declining lower-grade bills and other paper. The Reserve Bank has established itself as a dominant player, capable of taking a credible and independent stance in the money market at least in the short term. This was illustrated most clearly in the conduct of monetary policy in 1992 and 1993.

The Foreign Exchange Market

Prior to December 1993, each authorized bank in Zimbabwe had a foreign currency limit set on a daily basis. Surplus funds at the end-of-day trading were sold to the Reserve Bank at the official exchange rate. The announcements of 1 January 1994 radically transformed this arrangement for the period of January to the end of June 1994. Under the Corporate

FCA rules all export proceeds were split 40 per cent, which was sold to the RBZ at the official rate, and 60 per cent, which was sold in the inter-bank market (or held in the FCA account). Only central government imports and debt service, fuel imports, and ERS and import licence overhangs were sourced from the official rate. All other requirements, including those of the RBZ and parastatals, had to be sourced from the market. Under the new operating procedure the RBZ could intervene in the market on two criteria. First, as lender-of-last-resort, to ensure that authorized dealers do not face liquidity problems. More relevantly, the RBZ could intervene in the market to influence the rate through open market operations. This latter intervention, which is not unusual, has caused quite serious problems in the market as the authorized dealers (ADs) seek to unravel the RBZ policy objectives. The following is an explanation from the perspective of the RBZ.

The Reserve Bank's announcement of 1 January 1994 seemed to have exceeded the private sector's expectations as to the extent of the liberalization, and as a consequence engendered some scepticism as to whether the policy could be sustained. An additional consequence was that the authorized dealers were not yet prepared to deal with the market. In order to assure a smooth transition to a full-blown inter-bank market, the RBZ has maintained a relatively high profile in market management. During the period from 1 January to 7 February 1994, the authorized dealers and the RBZ met daily to set rates. The rate was set around the official rate, with the banks trading within a band around the RBZ rate. After 7 February, the RBZ withdrew from the daily meetings although it continued to advise the ADs of its official rate. Moreover, it advised the market on a confidential basis as to the status of the market – that is, whether it was long (excess supply of dollars) or short (excess demand). On the basis of this information the market set the daily rate.

During the first six months of 1994, the full working of the inter-bank market was constrained by a number of factors. First, there was the continued compulsory surrender of 40 per cent of export proceeds, which meant the inter-bank market remained influenced by the activities of the government. Second, although there was a commitment to unify the official with the market rate, the Reserve Bank remained a major player in the market, a status that was strengthened by the informational advantage it held. The ADs had only limited knowledge of the state of the market. In addition, they did know that the RBZ maintained a policy rule that involved market interventions. This meant that the rate stayed close to the RBZ 'indicative rate'. Finally, the ADs did not seem to have developed the informational framework required to determine independently the status of the market.

From 1 July 1994, the two-tier exchange rate system was abolished. In addition, exporters were allowed to retain 100 per cent of their export earnings. This resulted in the alleviation of the foreign exchange constraint. In the budget of July 1994, the government announced that these changes mean that:

> our current account transactions are fully liberalized and the Zimbabwe dollar is on the road to convertibility. Attention is now focussed on the capital account with a view to liberalizing this area as well. The shortage of foreign currency is now behind us.

Innovations in Trade Finance

The flagship of financial liberalization since 1991 has been the deregulation of interest rates, which has led to a sharp rise in both nominal and real rates. The important question is how far financial liberalization has enhanced firms' ability to take advantage of the relative price changes from non-tradeables to the tradeables sector afforded by trade liberalization. We can distinguish between the *flow effect* (trade financing) and the *stock effect* (investment) of financial liberalization. In market terms this boils down to *factor* and *goods* markets effects. This section considers the flow effects. Trade liberalization has shifted relative prices by making exports more competitive, and trade financing plays a complementary role in enabling firms to fully exploit that advantage.

How does trade financing link with the *credit rationing* arguments of Adam and Ncube (1994) above? The strategies reduce the domestic credit requirements and increase the demand for foreign currency at a given level of domestic credit from the level dictated by 'crowding-out'.

Next we discuss the mitigating trade financing strategies.

Offshore Financing

To avoid the effect of a hike in interest rates, merchant and commercial banks and other institutions involved in trade finance have resorted to cheap offshore financing facilities. Up to US$5 million can be borrowed offshore without clearance from the authorities. Because banks can share the risk with trade guarantee firms they are able (since 1990) to provide the finance to firms at 5–10 per cent interest rates as opposed to about 30 per cent in the domestic market. Even when we add transaction costs of 2–4 per cent, the difference is not trivial. One large merchant bank indicated that before 1990 risk-sharing reduced their exposure to as low as 15 per cent, and credit guarantee companies abroad took 50 per cent of the risk. That allowed them to put together a cheap loan package for their exporter clients. The sectors that have benefited from the facility are textiles and tobacco. During this period bureaucracy came in the way of providing broad and effective financing. The drought in 1992 affected the facility due to the high indebtedness of companies. Of late, the International Finance Corporation (IFC) has provided up to US$25 million for trade financing, which has been distributed to various banks. The African Development Bank has also provided additional resources via the Zimbabwe Investment Centre (ZIC).

Whereas one of liberalization's salient objectives is to encourage and nurture participation by new small firms in the tradeables sector, offshore financing seems to be biased towards the larger, established firms. The larger firms obviously appear to be 'good risks' to banks, which goes some way in reducing the *adverse selection* problem in the loan market. Hence small firms are left to source the domestic market, leaving them exposed to interest rate risk, a price rationing mechanism. Therefore, small firms face quantity rationing in the offshore loan market and price rationing in the domestic market.

Pre-shipment and Post-shipment Financing

Regarding pre-shipment and post-shipment financing by banks, the bias is towards post-shipment financing, which most small and medium-size firms can access once they produce letters of credit. Access to pre-shipment financing is restricted, and where available it is up to about 180 days. Through its export financing scheme, the Reserve Bank also provides pre-shipment and post-shipment cover against confirmed export orders. Typically this costs LIBOR + 2.5 per cent. Commercial banks are involved, being obliged to underwrite the exporters' liability to the Reserve Bank. The banks are rather severe in their choice of beneficiaries to the scheme, making it virtually inaccessible to small firms.

The logic of banks' bias to post-shipment cover can be explained by our credit-rationing argument. At the pre-shipment stage there is an adverse selection problem, since the banks cannot accurately assess whether the firm has a guaranteed external market or not. Thus they ration credit and turn away applicants. In the post-shipment stage, with confirmed letters of credit, firms will have demonstrated that they are 'good risks', and thus reduced the adverse selection problem. Hence post-shipment cover is preferred by banks.

Credit Guarantee Schemes

Some of the surplus funds in the banking system are being used by the Zimbabwe Credit Guarantee Corporation (CGC), under the aegis of the Reserve Bank, to support small, export-orientated firms. Currently CGC has up to Z$400 million available at a 5 per cent interest rate over the next two years. This represents an improvement from the Z$100 million available in 1993 at 15 per cent interest, most of which was used for low-cost refinancing of loans. The CGC facility requires complementary financing/collateral from the banking sector, and the Reserve Bank guarantees up to 75 per cent of it. The banks use their normal screening procedures, which has resulted in the failure to acquire complementary funding and subsequent under-utilization of the scheme. *Ab initio*, the scheme looks like a risk-sharing scheme between the banks and the Reserve Bank, but the binding constraint is still the stringent commercial bank screening that undermines the risk-sharing objective.

Credit for small exporting firms is also available from the Small Enterprise Development Corporation (SEDCO) and PTA Bank, which have US$70 million at their disposal. The Zimbabwe Development Bank's (ZDB) development fund via equity participation also provides a line of credit. However, at ZDB, for instance, the rejection rate for credit applications is still as high as 15 per cent at the processing stage, and 60 per cent at the earlier enquiry stage.

Financial Innovation

Prior to 1 January 1994 the Reserve Bank offered foreign exchange cover to exporters for up to eight years and to non-exporters for up to five years at a 75 per cent discount of the full cost of the implied contract. The forward contracts that were issued just before 1 January will have to be honoured up to the year 2001. Exporters benefited and still benefit from the fixed and over-valued exchange rate provided by the forward contracts. The forward cover is not consistent with interest-rate-parity and constitutes a subsidy for importers. The cover, which ignores the current decline in the exchange, means the RBZ has to absorb the losses from client's arbitrage activity, exacerbating government financial distress.

After 1 January 1994, banks began to provide foreign exchange forward contracts for the firms involved in the external sector. The cover is based on the spread between domestic and the LIBOR, and is anything from three to twelve months. If r_d is the domestic interest rate, r_f is the foreign interest rate, e_s is the spot exchange rate, and e_f is the forward exchange rate, then interest parity means that:

$$e_r = e_s + r_f - r_d. \tag{11.1}$$

Put simply, if parity holds, no one should make arbitrage gains by borrowing abroad at the foreign interest rate, converting that to domestic currency at the spot exchange, lending in the domestic market at the domestic interest rate, and then paying back the loan when it matures, at the forward rate. One expects the banks to charge importers at least the difference between the domestic and foreign interest rates. For instance, for a 12-month forward cover, the cost could be as high as 25–30 per cent. The Reserve Bank's scheme, which did not adhere to this rule, was cheaper, costing only about 8–12 per cent.

New investment in the gold mining sector has been discouraged by the high cost of borrowing under interest rate liberalization. Exporters will be able to access cheap offshore pre-export financing in the form of gold loans. The interest rate on these loans is as low as 1–2 per cent per annum. Commercial banks and other banks, as well as the IFC, are involved in providing these loans. To hedge the exposure in their positions firms will have available call and put options. In future one would expect this facility to replace the Gold Equilization Account completely. The scheme will be extended to other precious minerals such as platinum.

A gold loan is denominated in gold bullion, so that the borrower pays by delivering to the lender a specific amount of bullion, taking amortization into account. The lender could be the Reserve Bank itself, lending out its reserves. When the mining company receives the physical gold bullion from the lender, it sells it at the spot market. The cash made from the sale is then used for investment. Interest payments of the loan are done over a specified period, with the principal paid in bullion. Since interest payments depend on the price of gold, borrowers gain when the gold price falls. Borrowers face increased interest payments when the gold price rises. Credit risk is increased. However, this can be mitigated by the lender requiring a letter of credit from a major trading bank, which is secured by the borrower's assets. The borrower also pays a fee for the letter. The borrowers can hedge themselves against volatility in gold prices using options and forwards. A put option, for instance, insures the producer against a fall in the gold price. The Reserve Bank, being the sole buyer and seller of gold, would have to manage part of the market for options and forwards, with banks (local and international) managing part of the market.[6]

The surplus funds held by the financial sector increased from Z$467.2m in January 1993 to Z$610.0m in November 1993. In terms of percentages, commercial banks hold the bulk of the funds. The portion held by commercial banks changed from 84.7 per cent in January 1993 to 79.5 per cent in November Merchant bank holdings increased from 7.7 per cent to 10.6 per cent and those of building societies from 7.6 per cent to about 10 per cent during the same 11-month period.

It is the intention of government to channel surplus funds towards small and medium-size firms at favourable interest rates. However, banks discriminate against such firms. Banks divert the funds to their large traditional customers, refinancing their loans at lower interest rates. The benefit to the small investor has not materialized. It is not obvious either that the CGC will effectively channel funds to the small investor if commercial banks still reserve the right to screen investors in the scheme.

Financial support for small export-orientated businesses needs to widened. The Agricultural Finance Corporation (AFC), which is seeking independent bank status, supports small agricultural projects. There also exists the Collective Self Finance Scheme (CSFS) whose members are small farmers mortgaged to institutions such as the AFC. The CSFS provides loan guarantee schemes and its capital base originates from members' fees, shares and donors' contributions. The CSFS and AFC should consider taking equity in small enterprises, much smaller than those of the Venture Capital Company of Zimbabwe (VCCZ) and ZBD.

Government-owned institutions such as SEDCO are under-capitalized. One reason cited is the lack of greater autonomy from government, which seems to restrict direct lending to small enterprises. The way forward is to give SEDCO autonomy under its own act.

11.4 RESOURCE ALLOCATION AND MANUFACTURING

Aggregate Effects

The direct effect of a trade liberalization that reduces restrictions on imports is to lower the domestic price of imports. This in turn lowers the average price level. Faced with a lower price level, private agents need to hold less domestic money in order to finance their transactions. This fall in the demand for money creates an incipient excess supply: people in aggregate want to hold less money and more goods. Their attempt to buy more goods increases imports and thereby worsens the current account of the balance of payments.

If the government cannot finance such a deterioration in the balance of payments because of limited foreign exchange reserves, it must coordinate the trade liberalization with with other policy measures that offset the payments deterioration. The combination of trade liberalization with other policies that keep the balance of payments constant is termed a *payments-compatible* liberalization. Faced with an excess supply of money, the government can adopt policies that either raise money demand or reduce money supply. In Zimbabwe the main strategy has been to raise money demand through devaluation. Devaluation increases the price of imports, directly offsetting the effect of the liberalization. This combination of the exchange rate and trade policy is called a *trade-liberalizing devaluation*. A trade-liberalizing devaluation has inter-sectoral resource allocation effects that are distinct from either a trade liberalization with a fixed exchange rate or a pure devaluation. It is the policy package most pertinent to Zimbabwean experience.

A trade-liberalizing devaluation changes domestic relative prices. In particular, it immediately raises the domestic price of exports relative to other goods and services. This price change gradually induces resources to shift into the export sector from the rest of the economy. In response to this resource shift, there is a second and gradual relative price change within the rest of the economy. Domestic production of non-tradeables and importables gradually declines, but the expansion of the export sector only replenishes the supply of importables (through the greater supply of foreign exchange, which finances extra imports). Hence, non-tradeables rise in price relative to importables. This induces a secondary resource shift out of importables into non-tradeables. Once all these reallocations have been made, the export sector is unambiguously larger, and the import-substitute sector unambiguously smaller, whereas the change in the non-tradeable sector cannot be determined a priori.

Effect on Investment

Prior to liberalization, imported capital goods are artificially cheap for those able to obtain import licences, because trade restrictions on other goods appreciate the exchange rate. In Zimbabwe this was to an extent offset by high tariffs. However, a trade-liberalizing devaluation removes this implicit subsidy. This induces those previously receiving licences to substitute the purchase of non-tradeable capital goods such as buildings. Hence, whereas in consumption there is a shift from the purchase of non-tradeables to imports, in capital formation there is an opposite shift from imported capital goods to non-tradeables. This produces an expansion of the non-tradeable capital goods producing sector, namely the construction sector. While firms are adjusting to their newly-desired capital stocks this effect might be quite powerful. Although in simple analyses of adjustment the resource movement is sometimes described as being from the non-tradeable sector to the tradeable sector, the combination of effects might be better described as a shift within the tradeable sector from import-substitute production to exports and a shift within the non-tradeable sector from consumer non-tradeables to construction. The net movement between the tradeable and non-tradeable sectors, if any, is ambiguous.

Effect on Aggregate Output and Employment

A trade liberalizing devaluation should tend to raise output by improving the allocation of imported inputs. This is particularly important in Zimbabwe because almost all imports were intermediate goods and their allocation prior to liberalization was by an administrative system that could not possibly have sufficient information to avoid gross allocative inefficiency. Firms were constrained by lack of reliable access in a timely fashion to appropriate inputs. However, because the price of imported inputs rises, firms that had access to them lost the rents over-valuation conferred.

A second effect is on real wages of unskilled workers. In Zimbabwe real wages of the unskilled rose sharply in 1980–2 to unsustainable levels as a result of an administered wage policy, and have since been gradually falling in response to high unemployment. This erosion of real wages has been assisted by inflation. To the extent that the liberalization has been inflationary, it has therefore accelerated the fall in real wages. While the trade liberalization is not, of itself, inflationary, the financial liberalization that accompanied it has been so. Certainly, inflation has increased faster during the liberalization than prior to it, and so it is reasonable to conclude that the liberalization has contributed to the decline in real unskilled wages. Note that this is not a decline in the equilibrium real wage, but rather an acceleration in what was already a gradual adjustment to the equilibrium. Such an adjustment raises employment. The transfer from wages to profits may also raise savings.

Both of these effects happen to benefit the import-substitute sector (which is largely coincident with manufacturing) because it is more intensive than other sectors in imported inputs, and because it is more subject to disequilibrium wages for unskilled workers than other sectors. If the manufacturing sector has been really badly hamstrung by high wages and controls on inputs, then it is possible that this effect more than outweighs the relative price changes among importables, exportables and non-tradeables. Thus, the resource reallocation effects of a liberalization are not clear-cut. Although the manufacturing sector loses *vis-à-vis* the export sector in terms of relative prices, it will disproportionately benefit from other effects. What can be concluded, however, is that the manufactured export sector should be particularly favoured, since it benefits both from the relative price effect and from the decontrol and wage-reduction effects. Within manufacturing, there should therefore be a pronounces shift into exports. At the other end of the scale, those parts of the manufacturing sector that had the most privileged access to imported inputs at implicitly subsidized prices will suffer the most since they have least to gain from decontrol and much to lose from the removal of the subsidy.

This suggests that the most complex resource reallocation effects are likely to be within the manufacturing sector. We therefore make this the particular focus of our attention in analysing the resource allocation effects of the liberalization to date.

The Impact of Trade Liberalization on the Zimbabwean Manufacturing Sector

We analyze the impact of liberalization on the manufacturing sector first by attempting to measure the changes in relative product prices and factor prices. We then turn to the consequences for manufacturing investment, output and profitability, relying mainly on survey data.

Relative Product Prices

At least initially we would expect that a compatible trade liberalization would turn relative prices against manufacturing. The data with which to measure this are currently rather limited. The most direct measure of domestic relative prices of manufactures to non-tradeables comes from the consumer price index and its components. Table 11.5(a) shows the price index for the composite of the manufactured goods that are reported in the CPI, namely clothing, footwear, furniture and household goods. Between 1990 and 1991 there was virtually no change in the price of these manufactures relative to consumer goods as a whole, but by 1994 there had been a fall of nearly 20 per cent. This is consistent with the timing of the various liberalization measures: prior to September 1991, the liberalization did not provide a significant opportunity for additional manufactured imports, although it did begin to ease the importation of inputs for manufacturing. Further, during 1992 and the first half of 1993 the economy was severely affected by drought. The resulting drop in personal incomes must have reduced expenditure on durables, causing a demand collapse in much of the manufacturing sector. These two factors, demand collapse plus a relaxation of imports, may explain the sharp decline in the relative price of clothing, footwear, furniture and household items to the CPI.

The measurement of relative prices using CPI data has the advantage of permitting the analysis to be much more recent than for other measures. However, it covers only a limited range and is contaminated by changes in consumer taxes. The most pertinent measure of the incentive for domestic factors of production, if it is done accurately, is the deflator for value-added in manufacturing, relative to the deflator for GDP as a whole. This is shown in Table 11.5(b). While the data unfortunately only go up to 1992, this does includes a full calendar year subsequent to the first major devaluation. It appears to tell quite a different story: the price of a unit of value-added in manufacturing rises relative to that for GDP as a whole by around 12 per cent between 1990 and 1992. Hence, the value-added price rises at a time when the consumer price falls. This may simply reflect data inadequacies. However, it is consistent with the effect of deregulation discussed above, whereby the manufacturing sector

Table 11.5 Relative prices for manufactures

(a) Consumer prices

	all CPI		*Clothing & footwear and furniture & household goods/ CPI*
1990	100	100	100
1991	122.4	123.3	99.3
1992	162.1	175.2	92.5
1993	189.6	223.6	84.7
1994	218.9	273.4	80.1
1995 (Jun.)	62.6	327.1	80.3

(b) Manufacturing value-added

	GDP deflator manufacturing	*GDP deflator all sectors*	*Relative price manufacturing/all*
1980	27.1	30.1	90.0
1990	100	100	100
1991	131.6	127.1	103.5
1992	202.0	180.6	111.8

Sources: (a) derived from the consumer price index;
(b) derived from the national accounts.

uses its imported inputs more efficiently, thus permitting both a higher price to be paid to domestic factors of production per unit of output, and a lower price to consumers. There is therefore at least some tentative evidence that the manufacturing sector was making better use of imported inputs. This is supported by the profits data we consider later.

Hence, at least on average during 1992 the manufacturing sector appears to have been a net beneficiary of the liberalization as far as the value-added data are concerned. The greater freedom to break production bottlenecks by importing inputs more than compensated for reduced product prices. However, the consumer price data show that subsequent to the expiry of the value-added data, relative product prices continued to turn against manufacturing, and this may have squeezed value-added prices.

Table 11.6 extends the relative price analysis from manufacturing to the export sector. Table 11.6(a) shows the relative price of mining value-added. This suggests that between 1990 and 1992 (the most recent data) there was no change in this relative price and hence a fall relative to the manufacturing deflator. Not only is this implausible, it is contradicted by stock exchange data that give clear evidence that the devaluation benefited mining and hit manufacturing. Between August 1991 and January

Table 11.6 Relative prices for exports

(a) Mining value-added

	GDPdef, minerals	*GDPdef all sectors*	*rel price minerals/all*
1980	45.9	30.1	152.4
1990	100	100	100
1991	131.7	127.1	103.6
1992	181.9	180.6	100.7

(b) Exports value-added

	GDPdef, exports	*GDPdef all sectors*	*rel price exports/all*
1980	34.3	30.1	113.0
1990	100	100	100
1991	143.0	127.1	112.5
1992	224.1	180.6	124.1
1993	288.9	223.2	129.4

(c) Real exchange rate

	Exchange rate/CPI
1990(3)	100
1990(4)	100.7
1991(1)	99.7
1991(2)	96.4
1991(3)	83.5
1991(4)	65.9
1992(1)	71.4
1992(2)	82.5
1992(3)	90.4
1992(4)	90.5
1993(1)	82.1
1993(2)	82.8
1993(3)	84.6
1993(4)	86.6
1994(1)	72.6
1994(2)	81.3
1994(3)	83.6
1994(4)	84.3
1995(1)	88.8
1995(2)	91.8

Sources: (a) derived from national accounts; (b) derived from World Bank data; (c) derived from IFS.

1992, the mining index rose in nominal terms by 38 per cent whereas the industrial index fell by 36 per cent.

Table 11.6(b) shows the same measure for exports as a whole. This yields a substantial change in favour of exports of 25 per cent over the same period, which increased to nearly 30 per cent for 1993. However, these data are less solidly based than those for mining. Table 11.6(c) gives an approximate calculation of the real exchange rate. It shows the domestic price level facing a Zimbabwean recipient of US$1, quarter by quarter. The table is an indicator of the incentive for exporters and the costs for importers not allowing for *ad hoc* taxes, subsidies and special schemes. There is some reason for thinking that resources may be fairly insensitive to *ad hoc* measures, because firms doubt whether the schemes will be maintained long enough to warrant changing production plans. Hence, the incentive provided by the exchange rate may be particularly important. As can be seen, there was no significant change in the real exchange rate prior to the devaluation of 1991. For its first year, the liberalization was therefore simply a matter of a relaxation of quotas. Although at its peak the devaluation reduced the real exchange rate by a third, by 1992 (third quarter) this had largely been eroded by inflation. The devaluation of January 1994 did not fully restore the earlier devaluation and was itself fully eroded by September 1994. A comparison of the second quarter of 1995 with the third quarter of 1990 (the position just prior to the start of liberalization) indicates that exporters were receiving 11 per cent more in real terms for a dollar of exports, and conversely importers were paying 11 per cent more. The expectations reported in our survey of manufacturing, conducted in mid-1995, were that the real exchange rate would further appreciate over the coming year, fully eroding these modest changes in incentives.

From its commencement in October 1990 until the first major devaluation of September 1991, the trade liberalization unambiguously benefited the manufacturing sector. As shown in Table 11.6(c) the real cost to firms of imported inputs did not rise, but inputs became more easily available. An indication comes from the industrial share price index, which in real terms (deflated by the CPI) appreciated by 46 per cent between its 1990 average and its peak at the end of August 1991. Before considering its effects subsequent to the devaluation, we turn to factor prices.

Real Wages

An additional route by which liberalization would benefit manufacturing would be that to the extent that it generated inflation it would thereby lower the real wage. Although a trade-liberalizing devaluation need not lower the real wage, in the Zimbabwean context the entire liberalization package has probably had such an effect.

Real wages in manufacturing rose in the aftermath of independence, peaking in 1982. Over the next five years they declined at an annual average rate of 2.7 per cent.[7] This process of wage decline can be interpreted as an unwinding of the wage premium over the supply price granted by the government in the early 1980s. Unions were too weak to win this premium for themselves or even fully to defend it. However, they were able to prevent nominal wage cuts and to get partial compensation for inflation. Thus, the decline in real wages was broadly a function of inflation.

Prior to liberalization, inflation averaged 16 per cent per annum. Between September 1990 and September 1994 (the most recent data point for wages) inflation increased substantially, probably largely because of the financial liberalization, so we would expect real wages to decline more rapidly. As shown in Table 11.7, in the two years subsequent to the liberalization (October 1990) they declined by around one-third. If we treat as the counter-factual the situation of the 1980s – 2.7 per cent real wage declines per annum – the liberalization would be responsible for two-thirds of this decline and the remaining third would have happened anyway. To some extent this may over-attribute the decline to the liberalization since the drought was itself not only inflationary, but tended to reduce real wages by lowering the demand for labour. However, the fall in real wages preceded the drought and persisted after it.

Bringing together the price effects for manufacturing labour and manufacturing output between September 1990 and September 1994, both declined sharply relative to the CPI, but wages by more than output. Taking September 1990 as 100, output prices fell to 78, while wages fell to 67. We would expect this to induce increased employment relative to both capital and output and this has indeed been the case. As discussed below, the survey found evidence of a fall in manufacturing investment, whereas national data on manufacturing employment for August 1994 show that it had already surpassed its previous peak. Substitution of labour for capital is being induced by the reforms, not just by the cheapening of labour relative to output, but more dramatically by the increased cost of capital relative to output. Whereas the price of manufacturing output has fallen relative to the CPI, the cost of imported capital has risen relative to the CPI, as shown by the 12 per cent depreciation in the real exchange rate, and the cost of financing such a purchase from borrowing has risen much more substantially. The indicator of a substitution from capital to labour is that of falling labour productivity: the average worker has less equipment and so produces less. This fall in productivity has indeed occurred: employment has risen more rapidly than output, with labour productivity declining by around 7 per cent. Hence, whereas output prices have declined from 100 to 78 and wages from 100 to 67, unit labour costs have fallen by less than wages to 73.

Table 11.7 Mean earnings in manufacturing

	Real (index)
Jun. 1990	100
Sep. 1990	107.2
Dec. 1990	125.8
Mar. 1991	101.2
Jun. 1991	100.5
Sep. 1991	100.5
Dec. 1991	110.3
Mar. 1992	88.5
Jun. 1992	85.5
Sep. 1992	84.9
Dec. 1992	93.1
Jun. 1994	62.5

Source: *Quarterly Digest of Statistics*, various issues.

This conjunction of falling labour productivity and low investment in the manufacturing sector may superficially appear disturbing, but it is a sign of health as long as it is in the context of growing overall employment. The crucial failure of the manufacturing sector prior to liberalization was to provide satisfactory dynamism for employment opportunities. The former incentive regime diverted national resources into capital formation, which replaced jobs. Under the new incentive regime those resources are released and production is achieved by increased employment. The next stage, however, is to induce job-creating rather than job-replacing investment.

Output and Profitability

Manufacturing output, which had been growing at 4 per cent per annum for the preceding six years, started to decline very severely in the month following the 1991 devaluation. It reached a trough in April 1993 and by late 1994 had surpassed its previous peak. In the following six months it contracted again by 25 per cent. During the first contraction all sectors of manufacturing declined, so that although there were substantial differences in performance, there was not a reallocation between sectors within manufacturing until 1994.

The path of aggregate manufacturing output is mirrored by the stock exchange index for industrials, which, from its peak in real terms of 146 in August 1991 (1990 = 100), dropped continuously to a trough of only 29 in May 1993. The industrial share index and industrial output both began to recover at the same time: between May 1993 and November 1994 the industrials index fully recovered to be back to 100 (in real terms), only to decline again by 8 per cent in the next six months, reflecting the renewed decline in output. Some of the recovery in the stock market was due to the opening of the market to foreign investors in July 1993. However, between then and the end of 1993 the value of foreign acquisitions amounted to only 1 per cent of the capitalization of the equity market. Moreover, the bulk of the recovery had occurred by that stage so this effect may not have been dominant.

Bringing together the stock market, output and relative price data, there appear to have been four phases during the liberalization.

October 1990 to August 1991 In this phase the manufacturing sector benefited from liberalization of inputs without suffering either increased competition from imports of final goods or higher prices for imported inputs. The combination of exchange rate over-valuation sustained by import restrictions constituted an input subsidy to the sector. The continuation of the subsidy in the context of a more efficient allocation of inputs may account for the 46 per cent appreciation of the stock exchange industrials index over this period.

August 1991 to April 1993 In the second phase the manufacturing sector suffered a fourfold negative shock:

(1) devaluation reduced the inputs subsidy;
(2) the introduction of the effort retention scheme increased competition from imports;
(3) the drought caused a demand collapse; and
(4) the domestic financial liberalization caused interest rates to rise from around 10 per cent to over 30 per cent.

Offsetting these negative shocks was the gradual reduction in real wages.

The first of these shocks, the subsidy removal effect, which was directly related to the trade liberalization, was not particularly large. This is implied by the relative price data of Tables 11.5 and 11.6. For example, within a year of the 1991 devaluation the real exchange rate had reverted to within 10 per cent of its pre-devaluation level.

The second shock, the introduction of the effort retention scheme, provided a legal window for the purchase of unrestricted foreign exchange. As this window was expanded, the price of foreign exchange on the ERS market fell. The real exchange rate through the ERS doubled between the fourth quarter of 1991 and the first quarter of 1993. The net effect of the expansion and cheapening of the ERS market on the cost of imported inputs for manufacturing was probably negative. The expansion of ERS implied an offsetting contraction in the supply of subsidized foreign exchange, and so gradually at the margin more inputs had to be purchased on the ERS market, whereas initially they had all been subsidized. The devaluation shock reduced the value of the subsidy per unit of officially purchased foreign exchange, and the ERS shock reduced the subsidy by reducing the amount of foreign exchange could be officially purchased. In addition to its impact on input costs, the effort retention scheme enabled final manufactured goods to be imported. As ERS foreign exchange became progressively cheaper, imports became increasingly competitive, providing a further squeeze on domestic manufactures. However, as shown in Table 11.8, the relaxation of import restrictions did not give rise to an upsurge in consumer imports. On the contrary, up to mid-1992 (the latest data point) such imports fell after the introduction of the effort retention scheme.

There are three reasonable explanations for this fall in consumer imports. First, consumers might have anticipated the gradual further liberalization in the form of the expansion of the ERS, with its implication that the ERS real exchange rate would fall so that imports would become cheaper. This would certainly have been a rational expectation, as indicated by the halving of the ERS real exchange rate and by the fall in the domestic relative price of importables noted in Table 11.5(a). An anticipation of cheaper imports would induce a postponement of their purchase. The other explanations are in terms of the remaining shocks. The increase in interest rates associated with the financial liberalization encouraged household savings and constituted an incentive to switch portfolios from consumer durables to financial assets. Finally, the drought caused a temporary fall in household incomes and induced a reduction in assets, both financial assets and consumer durables.

It is not possible to disentangle the effects of the various shocks during this phase. However, their net effect for the manufacturing sector was evidently devastating, as indicated both by the fall in output and the collapse in equity prices.

May 1993 to November 1994 During this third phase of the liberalization, the drought ended and the Reserve Bank acted to reduce nominal interest rates. The devaluation at the start of January 1994 moderately increased the cost of imported inputs purchased with official foreign exchange, but this real depreciation of official foreign exchange was offset by continued real appreciation of ERS foreign exchange. By April 1994 the two rates had converged at around Z$8.1 per dollar, which was a real appreciation in the ERS rate since May 1993 of over 10 per cent. Hence, the subsidy of imported inputs had by April 1994 been completely

Table 11.8 Imports of selected manufactures (US$m)

	Textiles	*Cars*	*Other vehicles*
1991 (1)	15.0	9.1	26.3
1991 (2)	12.8	8.9	44.0
1991 (3)	16.3	18.8	38.7
1991 (4)	12.0	12.0	39.3
1992 (1)	5.1	12.4	25.6
1992 (2)	7.1	10.3	20.7

Source: Derived from *Quarterly Digest of Statistics*, Table 9.5 and IFS.

removed without a substantial further cost shock. Between April and November 1994 inflation appreciated the real exchange rate, restoring it to its pre-devaluation level. During this phase there was a strong recovery in employment, output and, on the basis of equity prices, in the prospects for profitability. Indeed, by November 1994 equity prices and output had fully recovered to their levels at the start of the liberalization. However, this recovery was far from uniform since substantial parts of the manufacturing sector were intrinsically uncompetitive.

Renewed Contraction of Output During 1995 This fourth phase was driven partly by the closure of firms that had reached the limits of their financing, and partly by the further reversal of the interest rate declines and real exchange rate depreciation of 1994.

The RPED and AERC Surveys

We now turn to survey evidence. Many of the data we will use are from the survey conducted under the aegis of the World Bank's Regional Programme on Enterprise Development (RPED). Three rounds of panel data are now available, collected in June–July 1993, June–July 1994 and June–July 1995. The first two rounds have been extensively analyzed (Gunning, 1994a; Gunning and Mumbengegwi, 1995) but analysis of the third round started only recently. The second source of data is the survey conducted as part of the AERC Regional Integration and Trade Liberalization study. In Zimbabwe this survey was conducted jointly with the third round of the RPED survey. While in this chapter we make little use of the 1995 RPED data, we do report on the results of the AERC survey. We will also make some use of a complementary survey: the second round of the GEMINI survey.[8]

We first briefly describe the RPED survey and then use it to analyze the economic performance of manufacturing firms in the period 1992–4, with special emphasis on investment and on changes in employment. We also quantify the extent to which firms are exposed to increasing competition. Finally, we focus on the export performance of firms, particularly the evidence from the AERC survey on regional trade.

The RPED survey is conducted in eight African countries. The Zimbabwe study is a joint effort of the Free University in Amsterdam and the University of Zimbabwe. The survey contains very detailed firm-level information on sales, employment, investment, wages and earnings. While most of the data refer to the current year, for many variables earlier data were collected as well. For example, employment data were collected for 1981, 1986, 1991, 1993, and 1994. The survey also has considerable detail on the constraints experienced by different types of enterprises, including the extent to which they are affected by government regulations. In many ways this is an ideal data source. It has been used extensively in the studies collected in Gunning (1994b) and Gunning and Mumbengegwi (1995). Here we focus on the survey evidence on economic change in response to trade liberalization.

The first round of the survey was held in June–July 1993 and covered 201 enterprises in four selected sub-sectors. Both informal and formal sector firms were included but a minimum size of five workers (including owners) was imposed. Not all manufacturing was covered. The survey was limited to four selected sub-sectors with the sample consisting of 49 firms in the food sector, 26 in woodworking, 88 in textiles and clothing, and 38 in metalworking (Table 11.9).

In the case of formal sector firms, the sample was drawn from the list of manufacturing enterprises maintained by the Central Statistical Office. This CSO list contains in principle all registered firms. Since the CSO's coverage for smaller firms is likely to be incomplete, the list was used as a sampling frame only for firms with at least 50 employees. For smaller firms we used the first round of the GEMINI survey, conducted in August 1991. This covered over 5000 firms throughout the country but only a small number (107) engaged in one of the four manufacturing sub-sectors and satisfied our minimum size criterion.

Two limitations should be noted. First, structural adjustment is likely to lead to the founding of new firms, but the survey cannot capture this aspect of firm dynamics, since smaller firms (up to 50 employees) can be included only if they were founded before August 1991. Hence only a small number of firms established since the beginning of ESAP are included.[9] Secondly, very small firms (those with fewer than five workers) were excluded from the survey.

The distribution of firms in the original sample over sectors and over the two size classes defined by the sampling method is shown in Table 11.9. For each firm the probability of being included in the sample was

Table 11.9 Manufacturing firms in the RPED survey, 1993, by size and sector

Employment	*Food*	*Wood*	*Clothing*	*Metal*	*Total*
More than 50	31	16	54	23	134
Up to 50	18	10	34	15	67
Total	*49*	*26*	*88*	*38*	*201*

proportional to its size (measured in terms of employment) so that the size distribution in the sample differs from that in the population, large firms being overrepresented. This resulted in the size distribution shown in Table 11.10. Note that the 134 firms with at least 50 employees are all formal in the sense of being registered. Over half of the surveyed firms (115) were located in Harare, 54 were in Bulawayo (in the south) and the remaining 32 were in smaller centres.

The sample for the 1995 AERC survey was the same as the sample in the third round of the RPED survey, the two questionnaires being administered in the same interview. The 1995 sample was slightly smaller than in 1993, some firms having gone out of business or refused to participate in the survey. The AERC sample consisted of 192 firms: 47 in food (compared to 49 in the original 1993 survey), 26 in wood (26), 85 in textiles and garments (88) and 34 in metal (38).

Economic Performance During Liberalization

An obvious question is whether the reforms have led to a change in resource allocation. We can investigate this using the survey data on changes in the allocation of capital and labour between sectors. One of the most interesting results of the survey is that most firms continued to invest during the period of adjustment. Indeed, for each year of the ESAP period 60 per cent or more of the firms in our sample reported positive investment. Since the literature suggests that structural adjustment may well have a negative effect on investment, particularly if reforms increase policy uncertainty,[10] this is remarkable. However, even if firms continue to invest, resource shifts can be minor. We therefore estimate the extent to which the capital stock changed over the period.

In spite of the fact that investment data were collected this is far from straightforward. The survey recorded data on both the replacement and the sales value of the capital stock, as estimated by the respondent, usually an owner, director or manager of the firm. Obviously, these are not hard data: there is only a very thin market in second-hand capital goods

Table 11.10 Size distribution of surveyed firms in 1993

Employment	*No. of firms*
up to 10	40
11–50	27
51–100	39
101–250	47
over 250	48
Total	*201*

and some respondents clearly found it difficult to give an estimate of the value of their capital stock. This was particularly the case for the value of land and buildings. We therefore restrict the analysis to the third component of the capital stock, equipment.

The replacement value does not take depreciation into account. Our starting point is therefore the sales value of equipment, as reported in the 1995 survey. The value of the capital stock in earlier years is calculated recursively from:

$$K_t = (1 - \delta)\, K_{t-1} + \mu\, I_{t-1} \qquad (11.2)$$

where I denotes equipment investment, δ the rate of depreciation and μ the ratio of the sales and the replacement value of new capital goods. In a perfect market for capital goods μ would, of course, be equal to 1: the sales price for new equipment would be equal to the purchase price; that is, to the replacement value. At the other extreme, if there is no market for used capital goods then μ would be equal to zero. The problem in applying the recursive relation is that we have observations on I but not on δ and μ. We have therefore experimented with a range of values for these parameters. Table 11.11 shows the results for a 10 per cent depreciation rate and values of μ ranging from 0.4 to 0.7. Using the capital stock estimate for 1995 and the investment data for the intervening years we estimate the 1990 capital stock. The table shows the (observed) 1995 capital stock as a percentage of the (estimated) 1990 value.

Clearly this index is very sensitive to the chosen value of μ. For μ = 0.4 the capital stock would have remained virtually constant over the five-year period, gross investment just offsetting depreciation, while for μ = 0.7 the capital stock would (implausibly) have more than doubled. However, the sectoral pattern is insensitive to changes in μ; in all cases the capital stock has grown most in textiles and garments and least in the metal sector.

Table 11.11 Sensitivity of capital stock growth estimates: capital stock in 1995

Sector	*μ = 0.4*	*μ = 0.5*	*μ = 0.6*	*μ = 0.7*
Food	103.8	128.0	167.1	240.3
Wood	108.3	136.8	185.7	288.9
Textiles/garments	117.6	156.4	233.3	459.3
Metal	76.5	82.6	89.8	98.3
Total	*102.3*	*125.3*	*161.5*	*227.1*

Note: Index 1990 = 100 for various values of μ (δ = 0.10).

Table 11.12 Capital stock 1990–5

Sector	*n*	*1990*	*1991*	*1992*	*1993*	*1994*	*1995*
Food	28	100	103.4	109.9	115.9	125.6	128.0
Wood	15	100	124.5	141.0	148.8	141.1	136.8
Textiles/garments	53	100	109.7	162.8	177.6	166.5	156.4
Metal	25	100	94.7	97.1	89.8	86.1	82.6
Total	*12*	*100*	*104.3*	*122.8*	*128.1*	*128.0*	*125.3*

Note: Index 1990 = 100
δ = 0.10, μ = 0.5.

Table 11.12 gives the year-to-year results for the case δ = 0.10, μ = 0.5.[11] These estimates suggest that there was a spurt of investment in textiles and garments in the early liberalization phase (1992 and 1993) and that, except in the food sector, the capital stock has been declined in the last two years.

The average gross investment rates implied by our estimates are: 15.1 per cent per annum for food, 16.5 per cent for wood, 25 per cent for textiles and garments, only 6.2 per cent (that is less than the assumed depreciation rate of 10 per cent) for wood, and 14.6 per cent for the entire sample. The sensitivity analysis of Table 11.11 shows that such estimates must be treated with great caution. However, what is clear is that: (1) investment has been concentrated in textiles and (2) investment rates have started to fall. This last result is plausible: interest rates have risen sharply and the credibility of the reform programme has suffered during the last two years as the budget spiralled out of control.

Changes in employment are shown in Table 11.13. The survey data indicate that for the firms in the sample employment grew substantially

Table 11.13 Employment 1991–5

Sector	*n*	*1991*	*1992*	*1993*	*1994*	*1995*
Food	37	100	114.7	107.9	116.7	118.2
Wood	22	100	132.4	121.5	136.5	128.2
Textiles/garments	74	100	122.2	121.3	121.9	122.9
Metal	32	100	106.6	100.2	95.6	92.3
Total	*165*	*100*	*119.5*	*115.7*	*118.6*	*118.4*

Note: Index 1991 = 100.

in the first year after the introduction of the reforms, contracted the following year and then recovered, stabilizing at a level some 18 per cent above the 1991 employment level. While this may appear encouraging, it should be kept in mind that there is a selection effect: the sample consists of firms already in existence in 1991 that managed to survive until 1995. For those firms employment grew. Obviously, employment contracted (to zero) for firms that did not manage to survive during this period and grew in start-up firms.

With this qualification, manufacturing appears to have become more labour-intensive. Employment rose during the liberalization phase by 12 per cent relative to the capital stock.

Even though employment has stagnated, firms expect a quick recovery. The survey included questions on expectations, for both a one-year and a three-year horizon. The mean expected change in the volume of sales in the year from July 1995 was 30 per cent. Employment was expected to increase by 15 per cent in this period. Respondents expected an exchange rate depreciation of only 12 per cent (at a time when inflation was running at over 20 per cent and it was clear that a fiscal crisis was imminent). It is not clear how this result should be interpreted. Either firms expected the fiscal problem to be resolved by a reversion of trade liberalization instead of further exchange rate adjustment, or their expectations must be considered irrational.

We now classify firms by the percentage of output exported (in the period 1991–5) rather than by sector. Table 11.14 reports our estimates of changes in the capital stock, based as before on the reported investment data and using the parameter values $\delta = 0.10$ and $\mu = 0.5$. The table shows that the capital stock has changed in a way largely unrelated to export orientation. The capital stock actually appears to have *fallen* in the (small) group of firms that exported in excess of 40 per cent of their output. Employment, like investment, does not show a clear relation with the extent to which a firm exports (Table 11.15). In the aggregate, em-

Table 11.14 Changes in capital stock, 1989–93, weighted means, by % of output exported

	0%	*Up to 20%*	*20–40%*	*Over 40%*	*Total*
1990	100	100	100	100	100
1991	97.6	103.4	99.1	110.3	102.1
1992	92.6	118.9	113.0	101.8	107.4
1993	87.4	123.8	126.4	95.6	108.5
1994	92.1	123.2	127.7	87.1	108.4
1995	89.7	122.1	124.9	80.0	106.1
n	23	51	11	13	121

Note: $\delta = 0.10$, $\mu = 0.5$.

Table 11.15 Changes in employment, 1991–5, weighted means, by % of output exported

	0%	*Up to 20%*	*20–40%*	*Over 40%*	*Total*
1992	111.9	114.0	107.9	121.1	119.5
1993	112.8	108.7	96.9	123.8	115.7
1994	134.2	115.9	99.4	128.6	118.6
1995	127.2	118.3	97.7	129.8	118.4
n	37	61	11	15	165

ployment grew in 1992, contracted sharply in 1993 (partly as a result of the drought) and recovered in 1994.

We may conclude that the survey evidence indicates that firms have become more labour-intensive, but have not reallocated resources towards exports. This is consistent with the relative price changes noted above: factor prices have altered considerably in favour of labour, but product prices have changed by only a few percent and even this is not expected by firms to persist.

How does this compare with the second round of the GEMINI survey? That survey covered micro and small-scale enterprises (MSEs), defined as activities with up to 100 workers and with a wider sectoral coverage than we have used; only agriculture, mining and forestry were excluded. The survey found an increase of employment in the MSE sector (14.4 per cent) over the 1991–3 period. However, this growth is largely a rural phenomenon and is concentrated in trade, transport and services. Employment in manufacturing MSEs grew very little (0.4 per cent per year in 1991–3). Trade liberalization had a positive impact on the sector: MSEs benefited from improved availability of imported inputs while apparently not being harmed by competition from imports.[12]

The GEMINI report does not present a breakdown of employment growth by sub-sector, but it does show annual growth rates for the number of enterprises. For food this growth rate is minus 14 per cent; hence in this sub-sector MSEs were much harder hit than the larger firms covered by the RPED survey. The number of woodworking firms declined by 1.6 per cent per annum, a result very similar to the RPED finding. For textiles and metal the GEMINI survey finds substantial growth in the number of firms: at rates of 4 per cent and 20 per cent; respectively. The GEMINI evidence indicates that this indeed occurs. But, remarkably, firm start-ups are not concentrated in the exportable sector (textiles and clothing) but in the importable sector (metal working). In that sense the GEMINI data serve as a warning: the RPED survey indicates growth of exporting firms but (by construction) excludes new firms. The GEMINI evidence suggests that new firms are not concentrated in the export sector.

Returning to the RPED data, we now consider whether exporting firms are growing faster. Risseeuw (1995) has analyzed firm growth (in terms of employment) for the period 1991–4. Of the traditional variables in the analysis of firm dynamics, size and age, he finds a significant effect for size, proxied by employment at the beginning of the period.[13] Risseeuw also finds a strong effect for the dummy variable 'exporting'. Firms engaged in exporting grew substantially faster and the effect is highly significant. Risseeuw's analysis implies that (at least after 1986) there are no sectoral effects. Growth rates differ between sectors but this simply reflects differences in variables such as size. Once we control for such variables sectoral dummies become insignificant in the growth rate regression, except for metal: growth in the metal sector is significantly lower.

Curiously, Risseeuw finds quite different effects for firms exporting only in 1992–3 (Table 11.16) and those exporting in both of the last two years. Leaving that aside we may note that the sum of the two coefficients is 0.035. This suggests that exporting firms grew at about 3.8 per cent per year versus 0.3 per cent for other firms. Hence, controlling for differences in size and sector, exporting firms have grown a little more rapidly than other firms, but this has not been a sustained development.

The surveys also provide direct evidence on the extent to which the liberalization has removed obstacles. We consider three pieces of evidence. First, the trade and exchange rate regime no longer seems to reduce capacity utilization. Mumvuma and Zhou (1995, Table 4.3) investigated the constraints on capacity utilization. They report that 'shortage of imported raw material and intermediate inputs' was considered unimportant by 88 per cent of firms; only a small number of firms listed it as a moderate (8 per cent) or severe (4 per cent) obstacle. Secondly, Bade (1995)

Table 11.16 Growth of firms, OLS results for 1991–4

	coeff.	*T*	*sig.*
constant	0.337	3.21	**
size	−0.112	−2.87	***
size^2	0.009	2.47	***
D black owners	−0.072	−1.51	*
D metal	−0.064	−3.03	***
D export 1992/93	0.074	2.73	***
D export 1992/93 and 1993/94	−0.039	−1.36	*
Mean of dependent variable	0.028		
Adjusted R^2			

Notes:
Dummies are denoted by D.
Significance levels: *** 99 per cent, ** 95 per cent, * 90 per cent

Source: Risseeuw (1995), Table 5.

shows that government regulations are becoming increasingly unimportant. Labour regulations were still reported by many firms as a constraint on temporary output adjustments but the number of firms that see this as a problem fell sharply between 1993 and 1994. Similarly, foreign exchange regulations, a major constraint in Zimbabwe prior to ESAP, were unimportant by 1994 (Table 11.17). Finally, financial liberalization has reduced the impact of credit rationing. The Round II data indicate that out of 202 firms, only 33 can be considered rationed in the sense that they report that they expect not to be able to get a formal sector loan while having used their overdraft facilities to their maximum. Of these 33 firms, five reported that they had no cash flow problems, another five that they did not need a loan. Only eight firms had been refused a loan (Bade, 1995, pp. 76–7). Credit rationing therefore seems to have lost its bite. Again, this change is recent: there was more evidence of the importance of credit rationing in the Round I data.

Indirect evidence is provided by the AERC survey. The questionnaire contained questions on the respondent's business contacts: people who are regularly met and considered useful in terms of information, advice and, possibly, help in case of a crisis. Table 11.18 shows, for different firm sizes, how many people were considered useful in this sense and how many of these belonged to groups such as bank officials, politicians, professionals or civil servants. Not surprisingly, 'bank officials' and 'other professionals' are the main sources of useful contacts for re-

Table 11.17 No. of firms reporting problems with regulations in 1993 or 1994 and reported changes

Restrictions with respect to:	*Improvement*	*No change*	*Deterioration*	*Problem 1993*	*Problem 1994*
Joint ventures	18	30	1	10	4
Profit repatriation	23	24	0	21	8
Forex for business travel	102	19	1	50	6
Foreign loans	38	16	0	15	6
Payment of fees to non-residents	23	18	0	12	7
Payment of technology licences and royalties	23	16	0	15	6

Source: Bade (1995).

spondents in large firms. What is striking, however, is the relative importance of 'civil servants'. For the smallest firms they even account for 20 per cent of the useful contacts. Contacts with civil servants appear to be particularly important for firms with between 100 and 250 employees. For this group of large firms, civil servants account for over 40 per cent of the useful contacts. Presumably, regulations and other government interventions are still so important that firms cultivate contacts with the ministries and obtain much of the information they consider useful from civil servants.

Competition

Firms were asked about the number and size of their competitors and the sources of the competition they faced. The 1994 results indicated significant market concentration. Notably only a third of the firms reported that they took market prices as given or adjusted their own prices in line with import prices.

Domestic competition was considered as 'not important' among the factors taken into account in the firm's price-setting decision by 30 per cent of the firms in the survey. Competition from imports was called 'unimportant' by 68 per cent of the firms. However, a substantial number of firms, about a quarter, listed imports as the main source of competition. This is a remarkable change; in the Round I data only 14 firms (15 per cent) reported imports as the main source of their competition: none in the food sector, only one in wood, six in textiles and seven in the metal sector.

The survey also collected information on entry and exit of competing firms. These data suggest an increase in domestic competition. Almost half of the firms reported new firms entering the market in the period June 1993–June 1994. Many firms reported a loss of market share as a

Table 11.18 Useful business contacts, 1995 (mean number considered useful)

Size of firm	*No. of firms*	*Useful contacts*	*Bank officials*	*Politicians*	*Civil servants*	*Employees of NGOs*	*Other professions*
Up to 5	35	8.8	0.7	0.7	1.7	0.5	4.0
5–10	23	14.0	0.6	0.7	1.6	0.4	7.3
10–100	25	27.4	2.5	0.6	2.0	0.7	7.0
100–250	30	49.7	5.7	2.1	21.6	1.5	16.4
Over 250	36	47.4	7.8	1.6	3.2	1.8	16.9
All firms	149	30.3	3.8	1.2	6.0	1.0	10.5

Table 11.19 Domestic competition as perceived by firms in the 1995 AERC survey (% of firms)

Sector	*Domestic competition considered a serious problem*	*Domestic competition intensified in last year*
Food	41	59
Wood	29	50
Textiles	21	33
Metal	25	53
Total	*28*	*45*

result of the entry of these new firms, particularly in the case of firms in the textile sector (where 60 per cent of firms reported a loss of market share) and garments (63 per cent). The data suggest that by 1994 there was considerable competition in the garment industry, where 24 out of 57 firms stated that an important competitor had exited from the market in the past year. Also, as noted in the previous section, exporting in all sectors increased, so that firms are not only exposed to more competition in domestic markets but also in export markets.

The AERC survey gives more recent evidence (Table 11.19). In 1995, 51 out of 183 firms reported that they saw competition from local firms as a serious (that is 'large' or 'severe') problem. Domestic competition is clearly increasing: almost half of the sample reported that competition intensified during the past year. Similarly, about of the firms reported that the competition they faced from imports intensified between July 1994 and July 1995 (Table 11.20).

Table 11.20 Import competition as perceived by firms in the 1995 AERC Survey (%)

Sector	*Import competition considered a serious problem*	*Import competition intensified in last year*
Food	15	52
Wood	0	10
Textiles	39	58
Metal	31	64
Total	*27*	*51*

Export Performance and Constraints

The AERC questionnaire contained a number of questions on regional trade, in particular trade with South Africa and with fellow PTA countries. The responses show that in recent years a large number of firms have started to export. For those firms for which we can date the start of their exports, there appear to be many recent starters: 37 per cent in 1991 or later. Also and possibly more important – of the firms not currently exporting, the majority (56 per cent) expect to become exporters. In many cases South Africa is seen as the most attractive export market, but many firms reported growth in other African markets as well. In the AERC survey many respondents stressed that exporting to neighbouring countries has become much easier with recent trade and exchange rate liberalizations in those countries. In particular, many stressed that the problem of getting paid by the customer as a result of foreign exchange restrictions is rapidly disappearing.

In order to measure growth in exports we confine the sample to those firms that have been exporting for at least five years (Table 11.21). This is still a large group: 100 firms, or half of our sample. For this group there has been export growth, with large intersectoral differences. The food and wood sectors have shown very rapid growth (from low starting levels), exports of the metal sector show no clear trend, and textiles and garments (the sector that dominates the total) has shown growth in the last two years with exports in 1994/95 about 16 per cent higher in real terms than in 1990/91. Taking the sample as a whole, growth in exports over this period is 19 per cent in real terms.[14] Hence some growth has occurred, but it appears to be quite modest. Also, quantities are quite modest, except for textiles. The mean value of exports in 1994/95 was Z$0.9m in the food sector, Z$2.8m in wood, Z$10.4m in textiles, Z$1.3m in metal. The mean export value for all exporting firms in the AERC survey was Z$5.6m.

Table 11.21 Value of exports, 1990/91–1994/95 (index of weighted mean real value of exports for firms exporting throughout the period, 1990/91 = 100)

Sector	*No. of firms*	*1990/91*	*1991/92*	*1992/93*	*1993/94*	*1994/95*
Food	24	100	157	221	294	227
Wood	12	100	111	228	547	569
Textiles	46	100	80	102	115	116
Metal	18	100	92	92	125	101
Total	*100*	*100*	*81*	*104*	*118*	*119*

Table 11.22 Exports 1990–5, share of selected markets (%)

Sector	*PTA*	*South Africa*	*Europe*	*USA*
Food	95	3	–	–
Wood	13	26	58	1
Textiles	15	24	39	19
Metal	58	37	–	4
Total	*60*	*14*	*17*	*8*

The destination of exports is shown in Table 11.22. Note that there are very large differences between sectors. South Africa is an important market for all sectors except for food exports, which go almost entirely to other African markets.[15] A substantial part of the exports of the textiles and garments sector goes to developed countries, with the American and European market accounting for almost 60 per cent of exports. The European market is also important for furniture and other wood exports. Note that in the aggregate African destinations dominate; they account for 74 per cent of Zimbabwean exports.

The responses reveal that in spite of the trade liberalizations of the last decade, regional tariffs are still perceived as a major obstacle to intra-regional trade. For example, 105 out of 144 firms reported that reductions in regional tariffs would be important (30) or very important (75) in terms of encouraging them to expand trade within the region. The importance of regional tariffs is stressed particularly in connection with the tariffs imposed by South Africa on textile exports by Zimbabwe. Many Zimbabwean firms see the possible removal of this tariff (which many of them consider likely) as a major opportunity for expanding exports. While tariffs are seen as important impediments, changes in investment or licensing rules are considered relatively unimportant – in either case only 17 per cent of firms reporting that such a change would be very important for them. Other potential obstacles to regional exports (licensing arrangements, quotas, foreign exchange difficulties) are listed as barriers by only a small number of firms. Similarly, when firms report barriers to regional imports, tariffs are considered by far the most important barrier.

The importance of regional trade barriers is confirmed by econometric analysis of the survey data reported by Gunning and Oostendorp (1996). They estimated a fixed effects regression to explain investment behaviour. Explaining the estimated fixed effects in terms of expectational variables they found two highly significant variables. One of these measures reductions in regional trade barriers. Firms which expected such reductions were found to be more likely to invest (and to invest more) than other firms. In other words, perceived regional trade barriers are one of the reasons for low investment rates. The other expectational variable which turned out to be important measured the expected change in the exchange rate (Z$ per US$). Gunning and Oostendorp found that firms expecting a depreciation were more likely to invest. This may reflect the effect of depreciation on the profitability of the production of tradeables or alternatively the expectation that the government will restore compatibility through exchange rate adjustment rather than by introducing trade restrictions. Whatever the reason, the survey data provide the first strong evidence of expected exchange rate adjustment favourably affecting investment rates.

We have already noted that firms report that import competition has increased. This also applies to imports from within the region – one-third of the firms reported that import competition from PTA or SADC countries had increased in the past year – and to exporters – within export markets, one-third of the firms state that their main competitors are firms from within the region. Again, competition in these regional markets appears to have increased during the past year.

11.5 TRADE LIBERALIZATION WITHIN A REGIONAL CONTEXT

Introduction

In this section we shall analyse the performance of Zimbabwe's exports and imports in the Eastern and Southern African Region (ESAR), namely the Southern African Development Community (SADC), the Community of Eastern and Southern Africa (COMESA, formerly PTA), and South Africa.

Within the southern Africa region, Zimbabwe has one of the relatively more developed and sophisticated industrial, agricultural and financial structures – probably second only to South Africa. The economy and exports are also well diversified. For example, Ncube (1994) has shown that within SADC, Zimbabwe has the lowest Gini–Hirschman concentration index for exports, 0.3626, while that of South Africa including Namibia is 0.8931. This supports the view that Zimbabwe's export sector and indeed the economy at large is well-diversified.[16] In 1992, the manufacturing sector accounted for 24.3 per cent of GDP, followed by agriculture, which accounted for 10 per cent. The size of Zimbabwe's GDP is very small, however, compared to that of South Africa, which produces almost 82 per cent of the weighted regional GDP. Zimbabwe's contribution to the weighted regional GDP is 5 per cent. Nevertheless, relative to other countries in the region, the economy of Zimbabwe, especially its manufacturing sector, is quite large. According to Ndlela (1994), Zimbabwe's manufacturing sector is 50 per cent larger than those of Kenya and Zaire, three times larger than that of Swaziland, and ten times larger than those of Botswana, Malawi, Mozambique and Tanzania. However, the structure of manufacturing production is inward-looking, with most firms producing for the domestic economy. At the beginning of the economic reform programme in 1990, Zimbabwe exported only 11 per cent of manufacturing output. Second, Zimbabwe's exports have always been dominated by the European Union (EU) and other countries outside SAR. In 1992, the EU plus the rest of the world (ROW) accounted for 68 per cent of Zimbabwe's exports, with 33.75 per cent going to the EU. Exports to ESAR constituted 32.49 per cent of the total exports in value terms.

The size and relative development of the industry and physical infrastructure in Zimbabwe within the region, and the domination of its trade by countries outside the southern African region, suggest the following conclusion, which will be the main focus of analysis in this section: that Zimbabwe is a net exporter of manufactured goods within the region, and a net importer of manufactured goods with the ROW. The analysis will proceed as follows. First, we analyse the orientation of Zimbabwe's trade with the countries in the region, and explain these trends by examining the role of trade policy and institutional arrangements in promoting regional trade (that is, multilateral and bilateral trade agreements). Second, we examine the industrial mix of Zimbabwe's exports and imports within ESAR. Finally, we discuss the implications of an independent South Africa for Zimbabwe in terms of competition in regional markets.

Orientation of Trade

Recorded trade between Zimbabwe and the ESAR in 1992 totalled Z$2081 m in exports and Z$3178 m in imports. Of these totals, South Africa accounted for 42.3 per cent of Zimbabwe's exports to the region, while SADC and COMESA accounted for 51.1 per cent and 41.2 per cent, respectively. In the case of imports, South Africa accounted for as much as 86.1 per cent of Zimbabwe's imports from the region, while the shares from SADC and COMESA were only 12.3 per cent and 8.9 per cent, respectively.

Table 11.23 shows the trends in Zimbabwe's trade with the region between 1986 and 1992. What is interesting from the table is the growing importance of SADC and COMESA markets to Zimbabwean producers, especially as a destination for exports. In 1986, Zimbabwe's trade with SADC and COMESA stood at Z$335 m and Z$214 m, respectively. By 1992, the value of trade generated between Zimbabwe and SADC had increased fourfold, to Z$1453 m, while its trade with COMESA had increased sixfold to Z$1458 m. South Africa has nevertheless remained Zimbabwe's main trading partner, despite efforts within SADC and COMESA in the 1980s to reverse this phenomenon. Zimbabwe's trade with South Africa was worth Z$3617 m in 1992.

If we combine Zimbabwe's exports to South Africa and SADC, and to South Africa and COMESA, we find that in 1986 South Africa accounted for 51 per cent of Zimbabwe's exports to the former, and 57 per cent of exports to the latter. By 1992 these ratios stood at 45.3 per cent and 50.4 per cent, respectively, indicating the growing importance of these markets to Zimbabwe. In the case of imports, the domination of South Africa in the Zimbabwean market is obvious. In 1986, South Africa accounted for 73 per cent of Zimbabwe's imports from SADC and South Africa, and by 1992, this ratio had increased to 87.5 per cent. For COMESA, South Africa accounts for over 82 per cent of Zimbabwe's imports from these two areas. Thus, while Zimbabwe has over time managed to diversify its exports away from South Africa, it has not been able to reduce its reliance on imports from South Africa. As a result, Zimbabwe has always maintained a trade deficit with South Africa, and a trade surplus with SADC and COMESA.

The orientation of trade between Zimbabwe and the region is governed by a number of factors, which include national tariffs and the trade regime, and multilateral (COMESA and SADC) and bilateral (South Africa, Botswana, and Malawi[17]) trade arrangements. We shall discuss these two factors in turn.

The Evolution of Zimbabwe's Tariff Policy

For many years, trade policy in Zimbabwe was dominated by the foreign exchange allocation system instituted to prop up the import-substitution industrialization strategy. Tariff and other trade taxes played an insignificant role in resource allocation. Tariffs operated more as a way of raising

Table 11.23 Zimbabwe: regional trade (Z$000)

	Exports			*Imports*		
Year	*SADC**	*PTA*	*RSA*	*SADC**	*PTA*	*RSA*
1986	205 458	157 246	211 091	129 955	56 771	351 159
1987	280 317	209 667	185 427	141 185	53 372	361 457
1988	411 585	330 053	248 110	227 780	79 084	425 948
1989	512 005	349 595	289 781	293 074	96 081	691 410
1990	715 146	577 208	321 667	232 914	114 491	902 074
1991	805 217	579 340	479 921	341 176	165 032	187 197
1992	106 264	867 972	880 567	390 853	590 146	273 696

Note: * SADC excludes data for South Africa.

Source: *Digest of Statistics* (Harare: CSO various issues).

government revenue, accounting for over 14 per cent of total government revenue, than as a form of protection. However, with the introduction of the economic reform programme, and the subsequent abolition of the system of discretionary allocation of foreign currency in December 1993, the tariff has emerged as the primary determinant of the structure of protection in Zimbabwe. Its evolution has, however, been within the context of the economic reform programme and trade liberalization in general, rather than as a way of promoting regional integration and trade.

Two important duties operational in Zimbabwe are the customs duty, imposed on a selected number of goods, and a surtax, introduced for the first time in 1982, that covers all goods imported into the country. Zimbabwe operates a very complex tariff schedule, with suspension of duties and exemptions applied to a variety of products and imports from different countries. Suspension of duty is governed by a number of regulations enacted over time, including Customs and Excise (suspensions) Regulations 1993; Customs and Excise (PTA) (suspension) Regulations, 1993; Republic of South Africa Trade Agreement Regulations 1993; and Customs and Excise (suspensions) (Amendment) Regulations, 1994.

In addition, the excise and tariff handbook lists more than 45 customs procedure codes dealing with a variety of exemptions from import duties and surtax. These range from duties and surtax on imported goods for construction of approved projects, to surtax on goods imported by statutory bodies. In the 1994/95 budget, government also removed customs duties on all goods of a capital nature, except motor vehicles.

For those duties that are operational or effective, the policy of government is to reduce them within the context of the economic reform programme, and to a limited extent within the context of regional integration. The country currently operates the following tariff levels, ranging between 5 per cent and 30 per cent: consumer goods, 30 per cent; raw materials and intermediate goods, 10 per cent; and capital goods, 5 per cent. In the 1994/95 budget, government also reduced customs duties for textiles from 10 per cent to 5 per cent, while duties on clothing, which ranged from 20 per cent to 35 per cent, were reduced across the board to 15 per cent.

In Zimbabwe, trade policy has evolved within the context of a general trade liberalization programme. It is therefore difficult to answer the question of how trade policy changes have affected regional trade. Existing studies on the incidence of trade policy in Zimbabwe therefore tend to consider Zimbabwe's trade in general. That notwithstanding, the results of these studies have some important implications for regional trade. We shall review some of these studies, and compare the results with those found by researchers in other countries within the region.

The earliest information on the policy content of Zimbabwe's trade regime came out of a study by Jansen (1982), who used firm-level manufacturing sector data to calculate domestic resource cost and effective protection coefficients for Zimbabwe's manufacturing. The relevant results of this study, which use effective protection coefficients (EPC), are summarized in Table 11.24. We have ranked the manufacturing sub-sectors, from those receiving low or negative protection, to those receiving high effective protection. The table shows that, in general, tariff levels were rather low, suggesting that tariffs were not used as the main instrument to restrict imports. Protection was provided through the controls on foreign exchange and investment, and quantitative import restrictions. Jansen's results show that only three sub-sectors could be classified as enjoying excessive protection – namely, paper, printing and publishing (EPC = 1.87); metals and metal products (EPC = 1.77); and textiles (EPC = 1.74). With the exception of textiles, Zimbabwe imports very few of these products from the region. On the other end of the scale, foodstuffs, a sector likely to face regional competition, received the lowest effective protection (EPC = 0.86), followed by beverages and tobacco, which enjoyed marginal effective protection rates of 1.04.

Another study on the incidence of trade and industrial policy in Zimbabwe was done by Ratnayake (1994) for the government of Zimbabwe. The study, carried out after the introduction of the reform programme, offers useful insights into the changes that may have taken place since the 1982 Jansen study. The results of this study are summarized in Tables 11.25 and 11.26, where the former gives the sample statistics of protection in Zimbabwe, and the latter shows the uneven sectoral incidence of nominal and effective protection. The standard deviation of effective protection is

Table 11.24 Distribution of industries according to EPC, 1982

EPC ranking	*Classification*	*Industry*	*EPC*
Below 1.00	Negative protection	Foodstuffs	0.86
1.00–1.25	Marginal protection	Drinks/tobacco	1.04
		Non-metallic	1.25
1.26–1.50	Moderate protection	Clothing/footwear	1.28
		Chemicals	1.29
		Wood/furniture	1.38
		Transport	1.49
Above 1.50	High protection	Textiles	1.74
		Metals	1.77
		Paper, printing	1.87

Source: Compiled from Jansen (1982).

four times as high as the standard deviation of nominal protection on output, and eight times as high as the standard deviation of nominal protection on inputs. Table 11.26 shows that five of the nine sub-sectors listed received nominal protection rates above 30 per cent, while only one (non-metallic minerals) received a nominal protection rate below 20 per cent. The average protection rate for the whole manufacturing sector was found to be a modest 24.97 per cent.

In Zimbabwe, tariff rates imposed on imports of manufactured goods are higher than the tariff rates on intermediate goods and raw materials. In basic metal industries, the study reported a nominal protection rate on outputs that was more than double that on inputs. In general, the protection on intermediate inputs is low, ranging between 10 per cent and 22 per cent. The average nominal protection rate on the manufacturing sector was 13 per cent.

Ratnayake also reported effective protection rates for Zimbabwe's manufacturing sector, at both the 2-digit and 4-digit classification levels. The effective protection rate (ERP) measures the net impact of trade policies by comparing value-added in domestic prices to value-added measured at border prices. It is therefore a useful measure for assessing the impact of trade policy on domestic producers, since resources will tend to flow towards industries with relatively higher effective rates of protection. According to the study by Ratnayake, the sub-sector receiving the highest rate of effective protection is the basic metal industries (ERP = 157.1 per cent), with a rate that is twice as high as that of the manufacturing sector as a whole. The high ERP for basic metals mostly

Table 11.25 Sample statistics of protection in Zimbabwe, 1994

	Effective rate of protection	*Nominal protection rate on:*	
		Output	*Inputs*
Simple mean	64.45	29.29	16.33
Weighted mean	69.91	24.97	13.66
Median	53.65	32.00	17.94
Standard deviation	67.57	15.72	8.09
Coefficient of variation	104.85	53.69	49.56

Source: Compiled from Ratnayake (1994).

Table 11.26 Sectoral incidence of protection in Zimbabwe, 1994

Industry	*Nominal protection rates (%)*		
	Inputs	*Outputs*	*ERP (%)*
Food, drinks and tobacco	12.71	24.01	105.51
Textiles, clothing, footwear	13.32	23.90	39.77
Wood and wood products	17.99	33.76	62.32
Paper, printing, publishing	21.72	35.04	47.88
Chemicals, petroleum products	16.77	32.72	50.33
Non-metallic minerals	12.64	18.84	32.85
Basic metal industries	10.59	27.87	157.07
Fabricated metal products	21.12	30.36	52.33
Other manufacturing	20.38	40.75	61.47
Total manufacturing	13.65	24.97	69.91

Source: Summarized from Ratnayake (1994).

reflects the low protection on intermediate inputs and raw materials, rather than that the sector receives high protection. For example, the nominal protection accorded the output from this sub-sector is the fourth lowest. The only country within the region likely to suffer from this high level of effective protection is South Africa, which accounts for over 16 per cent of Zimbabwe's capital goods imports. SADC (excluding South Africa) and COMESA each account for about 0.4 per cent of Zimbabwe's capital goods imports.

The next sub-sector enjoying high protection is food, drinks and tobacco, which received an ERP of 105.5 per cent, suggesting that in this sub-sector, the value-added is over four times what it would be under free trade. There is therefore a deliberate attempt by policy-makers to increase local value-added in food, drinks and tobacco. The high ERP results may appear puzzling at first, especially given Jansen's 1982 study that found negative effective protection. The high figure reflects the wide intra-sectoral variations of protection. Effective protection on tobacco, which accounts for a large share of Zimbabwe's exports to the region, received an effective protection rate of 32 per cent, while packed and graded tobacco received an effective protection rate of −3.98 per cent. Within the food industry, canned, frozen and dried foods received a negative effective protection rate (−58.3 per cent), suggesting that the value-added in this and similar industries is lower than it would have been under free trade. The food, drinks and tobacco sub-sector is important in regional trade. Zimbabwe imports over 47 per cent of its food, beverages and tobacco from the eastern and southern African region, for example dried (or *kapenta*) fish from Malawi. It also sells 38 per cent of its food, drinks and tobacco exports to the region.

Textiles, clothing and footwear, which is an important sector for Zimbabwe in regional trade, and is probably the most efficient in the region (see Ndlela, 1994), received the second-lowest effective protection rate (ERP = 39.77 per cent), after non-metals, whose effective protection rate is 18.8 per cent. Within the sub-sector textiles have the lowest effective protection rate of 30 per cent, while clothing, whose imports are banned, enjoys an ERP of 85 per cent.

Within the region, the Zimbabwean economy is not as heavily protected as the study by Ratnayake suggests. In Table 11.27, we report on the comparable measures for four countries within ESAR. Average nominal tariff rates in Zimbabwe are comparable to those of South Africa and Tanzania, higher than those in Uganda, and lower than those in Kenya. Zimbabwe's average nominal tariff rate is lower that of sub-Saharan Africa in general: unweighted average tariff rate of 32 per cent, and an import-weighted tariff rate of 35 per cent (World Bank, 1993, Table 6.13).

In summary, we can say first that Zimbabwe, as indeed is the case with other ESAR countries, does not appear to have a specific policy to promote regional trade. The growth of Zimbabwe's trade in the region indicates the country's proximity to these countries, and its relative level of development. And the growth of imports, especially from SADC, reflects the improvement in information flows within the region; in Zimbabwe, this is the work of ZIMTRADE.

Second, Zimbabwe operates a very complex tariff schedule with a wide dispersion of effective protection rates within manufacturing. The wide

Table 11.27 Comparative measures of nominal protection (%)

Country	*Mean*	*Median*	*Maximum*	*Standard deviation*	*Coefficient of variation*
Uganda	20.0	20.0	200	0.0	0.0
Kenya	20.0	35.0	170	21.25	53.8
Tanzania	29.8	29.0	25	16.6	55.7
South Africa	29.0	–	1389	43.0	153.4

Source: Belli, Finger and Ballivan (1993).

range of rates suggests the possibility of resource misallocation, as heavily protected industries divert resources from efficient ones. The high protection rate afforded basic metals also suggests that the tariff regime remains biased in favour of import substitutes. Finally, there is no evidence that the tariff is designed to provide protection to any sector or particular input. This is puzzling, given that countries like South Korea used tariff and non-tariff barriers to protect selectively particular sectors, while at the same time making use of a variety of instruments to ensure that exporting firms face international prices on tradeable inputs (see World Bank, 1993).

Zimbabwe's Regional Trade Agreements

Zimbabwe has participated in preferential trade agreements in the region since the days of the Federation of Rhodesia and Nyasaland, established in 1953. Currently, Zimbabwe is a member of SADC and COMESA. However, bilateral trade agreements have been more important to Zimbabwe than multilateral arrangements. Table 11.28 shows that much of Zimbabwe's trade in the region is with South Africa and Botswana. In 1992 Zimbabwe imported goods worth Z$2737 m from South Africa, which was seven times and four times more than its total imports from SADC and COMESA, respectively. From Botswana, Zimbabwe imported goods worth about Z$154 m, or 39.4 per cent of its imports from SADC.

It is not surprising that South Africa and Botswana dominate Zimbabwe's trade in the region. For many years trade relations between Zimbabwe and these two countries were governed by bilateral trade agreements that gave the partners in the agreements preferential access to each other's markets. In the case of the trade agreement with South Africa established in 1964, the levels of preference available to Zimbabwe varied between 25 per cent and 30 per cent, while the level of preference given to South African firms over those from other countries was between 2.5 per cent and 20 per cent. These agreements constituted significant levels

Table 11.28 Zimbabwe: trade with SADC and South Africa (Z$000)

	Exports			*Imports*		
Country	*1986*	*1989*	*1992*	*1986*	*1989*	*1992*
Angola	3 164	5 793	22 832	31	1 516	38
Botswana	73 319	185 745	332 598	77 868	232 827	154 225
Lesotho	447	3 542	2 725	137	198	1 023
Malawi	20 875	80 086	206 624	6 697	8 347	13 695
Mozambique	54 424	90 278	216 591	647	2 368	25 780
Namibia	0	0	10 718	0	0	4 222
Swaziland	446	1 541	6 245	2 206	18 142	88 809
Tanzania	4 269	18 086	15 477	431	4 437	30 961
Zambia	48 514	126 934	248 837	41 938	25 239	72 100
Total SADC	205 458	512 005	106 264 7	129 955	293 074	390 853
South Africa	211 091	289 781	880 587	351 159	961 410	273 696 6
Total RSA+SADC	416 549	801 786	194 323 4	481 114	125 448 4	312 781 9
RSA % of total	50.676	36.142	45.316	72.989	76.638	87.504

Source: *Digest of Statistics* (Harare: CSO) various issues.

of preference, given that COMESA is still talking of achieving a 50 per cent cut in tariffs among member states by 1996.

The lapse of these agreements in 1992 was a major blow to Zimbabwean industry, and has been cited as a major handicap to growth in domestic output and exports by most Zimbabwean industrialists (see Gustafsson *et al.*, 1994). The hardest-hit sector was textiles and clothing, which suffered an imposition of duties soon after the lapse of the Zimbabwe–South Africa preferential trade agreement. Before 1992 Zimbabwean cotton textile exports carried a tariff of 10 per cent, now the general tariff level is 45 per cent. For clothing, the tariff before 1992 was 5 per cent, now it is 90 per cent. Since 1992, the textile sector has retrenched over 8000 workers, while several companies have been forced to close or go into liquidation. The biggest blow came in 1994 when Cone Textiles, the biggest textile firm in Zimbabwe, and employing 4500 workers, was forced into liquidation.[18] The bilateral trade agreement with South Africa is currently under negotiation, but it faces strong opposition from the textile and clothing industry in South Africa, who see it as an export of South African jobs to neighbouring countries.[19]

Zimbabwe's regional trade is also likely to suffer as a result of the polarization of relations between Zimbabwe and some of her COMESA partners, especially Zambia. Trade relations between Zimbabwe and Zambia reached a very low point in 1993 when Zambia banned a number of imports from Zimbabwe. In 1993, Zambia imposed a ban on pork products from Zimbabwe on the grounds that the southern parts of Zambia were infected with swine fever. This ban, however, applied to exports brought in over land, and not those entering Zambia from the airport, which was an expensive option for Zimbabwean producers. The estimated cost of this action was a loss of export revenues worth Z$3 m for Zimbabwe between January 1993 and August 1994 (ZIMTRADE Newsletter, 1994). In 1994 Zambia also banned dairy products and other related products from Zimbabwe, citing too much fat in Zimbabwean milk as the reason. In July 1994, the ban was changed to a 16 per cent duty on milk and related products.

The trade rift with Zambia is a culmination of a long-standing resentment against Zimbabwe within COMESA. Zimbabwe has been accused of being more interested in exporting to, than importing from, the region, hence it has a growing trade surplus with the region, which has irked its partners. In addition, countries in COMESA resent the fact that Zimbabwe is falling behind other countries in abiding by the annual targets of reducing duty on each other's goods. In reality, however, the preferential effect for a COMESA member country of a 50 per cent reduction in tariffs by 1996 is of limited significance. As discussed above, Zimbabwe's average tariff levels range between 5 per cent and 30 per cent, which in itself is not an indication of Zimbabwe's commitment to COMESA or SADC. It should be viewed within the context of the structural adjustment and trade liberalization programme, which commits Zimbabwe to reduce its external tariff to 30 per cent on average by 1995.

The unsettled state of Zimbabwe's bilateral and multilateral trade[20] arrangements, and the effect this is having on domestic production – especially in textiles – suggests that while overall trade liberalization is important, institutional factors are important as well.

The Industrial Mix of Regional Trade

Data in Tables 11.29 and 11.30 illustrate how the sectoral make-up of exports and imports differs across various areas. Table 11.29 shows that for the EU and other countries outside the SAR, drinks and tobacco constitute Zimbabwe's largest exports in value terms. Drinks and tobacco accounted for 40 per cent of Zimbabwe's exports to the EU, 46 per cent of exports to other countries, and 35.3 per cent of the country's total exports. The next largest export to EU and other countries comes from manufactured goods classified by materials. Table 11.29 also shows that

Table 11.29 Zimbabwe: industry shares of regional exports, 1992 (% of group total)

Sectors	*SADC*	*PTA*	*RSA*	*Region total*	*EU*	*ROW*	*Grand total*
Food & live animals	17.36	14.43	6.27	12.36	6.98	1.65	6.93
Drinks & tobacco	8.05	10.56	34.07	18.9	40.04	46.4	35.32
Crude materials excluding fuels	5.13	2.94	14.4	8.76	11.45	16.77	12.37
Mineral fuels/ lubricants	1.51	1.48	0.16	0.85	0	0.31	0.38
Animal, vegetable oils & fats	1.47	1.8	0.03	0.76	0.03	0	0.26
Chemical & related products	12.1	14.76	2.92	7.73	0.29	1.07	2.97
Manufactured goods classed by material	33.95	34.67	23.5	31.33	31.71	27.38	30.13
Machinery & transport equipment	11.54	14.03	4.68	8.77	0.27	0.3	3.04
Misc. manufactured articles	8.3	4.69	12.68	9.64	7.97	2.95	6.82
Communications transact, NES	0.59	0.64	1.29	0.9	1.26	3.17	1.79
Total exports	*100*	*100*	*100*	*100*	*100*	*100*	*100*

Source: CSO, *Quarterly Digest of Statistics* (Harare, 1994).

drinks and tobacco, followed by manufacture goods and crude materials (excluding fuels), dominate Zimbabwe's exports to South Africa. This information is useful in that it shows that although Zimbabwe is a net exporter of primary goods to South Africa and the developed world, its manufactured exports are also significant.

However, coming to the SADC and COMESA, the picture changes. Manufactured goods clearly dominate Zimbabwe's exports to these two markets. In 1992, manufactured goods accounted for 34 per cent of Zimbabwe's exports to the SADC, and 35 per cent exports to COMESA. Food exports constitute the next biggest export item, accounting for 17.4 per cent of Zimbabwe's exports to SADC. This was in line with Zimbabwe's portfolio as regional food security co-ordinator in the former SADCC.

Table 11.30, which presents the structure of imports, shows a reverse picture. Manufactured goods, machinery and transport equipment dominate Zimbabwe's imports from the EU (79.6 per cent of total EU imports), the rest of the world (38.8 per cent) and total imports (53.3 per cent). Imports from SADC and COMESA are dominated by food and live animals. In 1992, food imports accounted for 32 per cent of Zimbabwe's

Table 11.30 Zimbabwe: Industry shares of imports, 1992 (% of group total)

Sectors	*SADC*	*PTA*	*RSA*	*Region total*	*EU*	*ROW*	*Grand total*
Food & live animals	31.66	41.76	6.34	9.42	0.75	25.08	14.33
Drinks & tobacco	0.14	0.1	0.94	0.82	0.26	0.02	0.31
Crude materials excluding fuels	17.94	16.83	3.55	5.5	2.13	5.94	4.82
Mineral fuels/ lubricants	3.13	4.38	6.25	5.78	0.71	21.73	11.76
Animal, vegetable oils & fats	0.89	0.07	0.87	0.86	0.33	1.84	1.17
Chemical & related products	6.28	4.43	22.11	19.97	13.44	5.59	11.68
Manufactured goods class by material	26.85	18.08	28.23	28.4	11.13	7.33	14.24
Machinery & transport equipment	4.78	5.72	25.39	22.67	64.33	28.96	36.43
Misc. manufactured articles	2.04	1.71	2.37	2.39	3.95	2.01	2.62
Communications transact, NES	6.29	6.92	3.95	3.19	2.97	1.5	2.64
Total imports	*100*	*100*	*100*	*100*	*100*	*100*	*100*

Source: CSO, *Quarterly Digest of Statistics* (Harare, 1994).

imports from SADC and 42 per cent of imports from COMESA. However, in 1992, Zimbabwe also imported a significant amount of manufactured goods from SADC (27 per cent of total imports from SADC) and COMESA (18 per cent). Manufactured goods account for as much as 56 per cent of Zimbabwe's imports from South Africa, followed by chemicals and associated products (22 per cent). Food and live animals account for only 6.3 per cent of imports from South Africa.

We can then conclude that Zimbabwe exports mostly manufactured goods to SADC and COMESA, and mainly primary products to South Africa and the developed countries. On the other hand, manufactured goods account for a larger share of Zimbabwe's imports from South Africa, EU and other countries, while primary goods account for a larger share of imports from SADC and COMESA.

Similar information can be obtained from Tables 11.31 and 11.32, which show the proportion of each category of exports and imports to and from different external trade markets. From Table 11.31, we can note that SADC accounts for most of Zimbabwe's food exports (42 per cent, followed by

Table 11.31 Zimbabwe: structure of export shares by sector, 1992 (% of total exports in each industry)

Sectors	*SADC*	*PTA*	*RSA*	*Regional total*	*EU*	*ROW*	*Grand total*
Food & live animals	41.582	27.879	12.437	57.968	34.004	8.028	100
Drinks & tobacco	3.781	4	13.263	17.386	38.26	44.354	100
Crude materials excluding fuels	6.877	3.184	16.002	23.008	31.241	45.751	100
Mineral fuels/ lubricants	65.763	51.907	5.833	72.606	0	27.394	100
Animal, vegetable oils & fats	95.544	94.829	0.917	96.461	3.38	0.159	100
Chemical & related products	67.608	66.525	13.529	84.561	3.279	12.16	100
Manufactured goods classed by material	18.694	15.401	10.723	33.794	35.526	30.68	100
Machinery & transport equipment	62.927	61.74	21.172	93.657	3.028	3.315	100
Misc. manufactured articles	20.213	9.196	25.57	45.933	39.451	14.616	100
Communications transact, NES	5.476	4.805	9.936	16.406	23.79	59.804	100
Total exports	16.59	13.384	13.748	32.492	33.75	33.759	100

Source: CSO, *Quarterly Digest of Statistics* (Harare, 1994).

the EU (34 per cent) and COMESA (28 per cent). The ESAR accounts for almost 58 per cent of Zimbabwe's food exports. A larger share of Zimbabwe's chemicals, manufactured goods, machinery and transport equipment goes to SADC and COMESA. In 1992, the SAR accounted for 94 per cent of Zimbabwe's exports of machinery and transport equipment, while the EU took only 3 per cent, and the remaining other countries accounted for 3.3 per cent.

Table 11.32, on the other hand, shows that Zimbabwe's imports from SADC and COMESA as a share of total imports by industry are dominated all-round. These two markets account for a small amount of Zimbabwe's total imports, and in all categories as well. South Africa is an important source of imports for Zimbabwe in a number of product groups, but especially in drinks and tobacco (75 per cent of total imports), manufactured goods (48 per cent), and miscellaneous manufactured articles (25 per cent).

Table 11.32 Zimbabwe: Structure of import shares by sector, 1992 (% of total of total imports in each industry)

Sectors	*SADC*	*PTA*	*RSA*	*Regional total*	*EU*	*ROW*	*Grand total*
Food & live animals	7.629	7.278	10.704	18.455	1.363	80.181	100
Drinks & tobacco	1.549	0.835	73.929	75.484	21.863	2.653	100
Crude materials excluding fuels	12.849	8.715	17.797	32.017	11.524	56.458	100
Mineral fuels/ lubricants	0.918	0.93	12.854	13.791	1.563	84.646	100
Animal, vegetable oils & fats	2.629	0.159	18.08	20.709	7.306	71.986	100
Chemical & related products	1.857	0.948	45.765	48.021	30.057	21.923	100
Manufactured goods classed by material	6.511	3.17	47.942	56.004	20.402	23.594	100
Machinery & transport equipment	0.453	0.392	16.854	17.474	46.099	36.427	100
Misc. manufactured articles	2.692	1.625	21.895	25.603	39.349	35.048	100
Communications transact, NES	8.229	6.542	36.184	44.531	29.361	26.109	100
Total imports	3.454	2.498	24.183	28.081	26.103	45.816	100

Source: CSO, *Quarterly Digest of Statistics* (Harare, 1994).

Competition with South Africa

At the beginning of this section we noted some of the disparities between Zimbabwe and South Africa in terms of GDP levels and size of the manufacturing sector. When trade issues are also considered, the disparities are even more glaring. South Africa currently exports to at least 48 countries in Africa, 41 of which are in sub-Saharan Africa (SSA). Almost 75 per cent of South Africa's exports to SSA go to SADC and COMESA. In 1990 South Africa's exports to COMESA totalled US$1.2 bn, compared to Zimbabwe's exports to COMESA the same year which totalled US$38 m.

These disparities have led to the widespread belief that South Africa's entry into SADC and possibly into COMESA will displace the exports of countries such as Kenya and Zimbabwe, which account for most of the intra-COMESA trade. However, whether or not such a displacement takes place, it is important to note that Zimbabwe has competed against South

Africa in regional markets for some time now. Within SAR, Zimbabwe's largest export market includes Botswana, Mozambique, Malawi, Namibia and Swaziland. In these markets, Zimbabwean firms have always faced competition from South African products. Even more importantly, in Botswana, Swaziland and Namibia, Zimbabwean firms have exported at a disadvantage *viz-à-vis* South African firms, which enjoyed a zero tariff rate under the Southern African Customs Union (SACU). Zimbabwean firms are particularly competitive in textiles, leather and footwear, and foodstuffs. South Africa, on the other hand, is strong in less labour-intensive industries like machinery, iron and steel, and transport equipment.

To be able to make stronger conclusions about that relative competitiveness of Zimbabwean and South African firms in the regional markets, we need information on the relative efficiency of different industries at the firm level in both countries. Unfortunately, we have no such information regarding South Africa.[21] However, a review of efficiency studies in Zimbabwe will give us an indication of the relative competitiveness of the Zimbabwean manufacturing industry. Debates on the relationship between trade policy and efficiency have been around for some time now. The idea was first introduced by Adam Smith, who argued that one of the gains from trade was increased labour productivity due to scale economies. This idea has been revived by the 'new trade theorists' such as Helpman and Krugman (1985) who have incorporated ideas of increasing returns to scale and market structure into the analysis.

A number of studies on the efficiency of the manufacturing sector have been carried out in Zimbabwe. The first was by Jansen (1982), who applied the domestic resource cost (DRC) methodology to show that a high proportion of Zimbabwean industry, especially the capital goods sector, was largely inefficient. The DRC score for metals and metal products was 2.41, and for the whole manufacturing sector it was 1.27. While the study itself was controversial, especially in its recommendation that the inefficient industries should be closed down, it also provided interesting results. One important finding was that there was a wide dispersion of DRC efficiency scores within the sub-sectors and the manufacturing sector as a whole. For example, although the metal industry was generally inefficient, within the sub-sector such industries as agricultural implements were found to have DRC values below unity. In foodstuffs, the overall most efficient sector, according to jansen within DRC = 0.88, two of the six industries had DRC scores above unity.

The next studies to use the DRC methodology were by the World Bank (1989), and applied to capital goods and fertilizer firms. These studies found a high level of efficiency in Zimbabwean manufacturing. In the fertilizer industry, the DRC scores for the three firms were 0.72, 0.91, and 0.28. In capital goods, the Bank divided the sector into import sub-

Table 11.33 Zimbabwe: DRC for selected capital goods

Product	*Import substitution*		*Exports*	
	Net of capital costs	*Including capital costs*	*Net of capital costs*	*Including capital costs*
Rolling stock	0.27	0.44	0.35	0.57
Steel casting	0.52	0.71	0.60	0.81
Steam roller	0.74	0.97	0.96	1.23
Electric motor 75kW	1.32	1.52	1.63	1.86
Fasteners	0.41	0.70	0.48	0.80
Transformer 100KVA	0.55	0.58	0.65	0.80
Urban bus	0.06	1.06	1.21	1.85
Agric implements	0.49	0.65	0.60	0.77
Trailers	0.42	0.58	0.45	0.62
Weighted average	0.54	0.79	0.57	0.77

Source: World Bank (1989).

stitutes and exports; the results are contained in Table 11.33. The study found that only urban bus assembly and electric motor had scores above unity. Second, a rather surprising result was that the DRC values for import substitutes and exports were not significantly different, leading the Bank to comment that: 'The conclusion that the capital goods industry in Zimbabwe is largely efficient is puzzling, since the same pervasive policy interventions in other African countries have led to disastrous result'.

The World Bank went on to suggest that with such high levels of efficiency there was really no need to continue the protectionist policies of the past. The sector was already so efficient that trade liberalization would make the sector even more efficient. However, the salient point is equally important, that the protectionist policies established to prop up the import-substitution regime did not lead to the evolution of a highly uncompetitive manufacturing sector. Zimbabwe is therefore ready in certain industries to compete against South Africa.

The studies using DRC methodology were largely concerned with allocative efficiency. However, Adam Smith's original case for gains from trade relied on technical efficiency arising from increased division of labour (Rodrik, 1992). As part of the Regional Programme for Enterprise Development, which collected firm-level data for 202 Zimbabwean manufacturing firms, Mlambo (1995) calculated technical efficiency indexes for the sector using a stochastic frontier production approach. The study showed that the firms in the sample operated below the boundary of their production possibility sets. It found mean efficiency to range between 60 per cent and 63 per cent. While these figures may appear low relative to those in developed countries, they are comparable to those in other developing countries. For example, for Brazilian industry, Lee and Tyler (1978) found the technical efficiency score to be 62.5 per cent, while Meeusen and van den Broeck (1977) found the mean efficiency in the French textile industry to be 90.9 per cent. This suggests that although Zimbabwean firms may be inefficient relative to those in developed countries, by developing countries standards, they are relatively efficient. Thus the trade liberalization programme on which Zimbabwe has embarked should be conducive to improvements in productivity growth and technical efficiency.

11.6 CONCLUSION

Prior to the trade liberalization, the structure of Zimbabwe's economy was unusual, with an efficient export enclave of commercial agriculture and mining alongside a protected economy including a large and diverse manufacturing sector. The central changes in trade policy were the shifts from rationed access to foreign exchange and extensive bans on imports, to market-based allocation of foreign exchange and rights to import subject only to tariffs, which were themselves reduced.

We first focused on the macroeconomic compatibility of the liberalization and whether it was credible. The economic roots of a credibility problem lie in balance of payments or fiscal deterioration. The Zimbabwean liberalization was for a while undoubtedly payments incompatible. The balance of payments deficit, exacerbated by the drought, was some 20 per cent of GDP during 1992 when properly measured, implying a manifestly unsustainable rate of debt accumulation. However, by unifying the exchange rate and establishing an inter-bank market, the government created an institutional mechanism that would automatically, unless prevented by government intervention, correct payments deficits.

While the payments incompatibility was resolved, the liberalization became increasingly fiscally incompatible. By 1996 the fiscal deficit was running in excess of 10 per cent of GDP. The deficit had not been caused directly by the trade liberalization. The financial liberalization had enormously increased domestic debt service, and the phase of payments incompatibility had increased foreign debt service. There were some indications that this was starting to undermine the credibility of the liberalization. Real interest rates on government debt increased substantially, possibly suggesting some fear of default. Our survey found that firms were anticipating a substantial appreciation of the real exchange rate, so that part of the relative price effects of the trade liberalization would be undone. This might reflect a belief that the deficit would be financed by continually rising interest rates inducing a capital inflow.

The remaining roots of a credibility problem are political. In particular, a liberalization supported by a temporary influx of aid, as happened in Zimbabwe, might be induced by the desire to get the aid rather than to liberalize trade. With such a motivation, the liberalization might be reversed once the aid is exhausted. In a large and complex organization like a government it is possible to find instances of most shades of opinion, and undoubtedly in Zimbabwe the government included some reluctant liberalizers. However, the primary motivation appears to have been a perception both within government and the manufacturing sector that policies needed to change radically in order to escape from stagnation.

From credibility we turned to the interaction with financial liberalization. The ending of rationed foreign exchange allocation removed the indicator banks had relied on to estimate credit-worthiness. Faced with the increased riskiness of lending, rational banks would shift their portfolios into liquidity. Credit available for firms would thus contract. Yet the exchange rate depreciation increased the local currency cost of imported inventories, so that the demand for credit rose as the supply fell. Firms were thus faced not only with more expensive credit but with more severe shortages of credit. The firms most adversely affected by this were exporters since they had received priority in the rationed foreign exchange regime and tended to have the longest lags between payment for inputs and receipt of sales.

The resource allocation effects of the liberalization work partly through the relative price changes brought about by the changes in trade policy and the exchange rate, and partly by the changes in interest rates and creditworthiness. We identified four phases of liberalization. In the first, from October 1990 until the devaluation of August 1991, the liberalization of imported inputs increased the profitability of import-using manufacturing, but worsened the balance of payments and was unsustainable. During the second phase, from the devaluation until mid-1993, a conjunction of events devastated the industrial sector. A severe drought cut demand, while the exchange rate and financial liberalizations administered a cost shock. During this phase there was an 80 per cent fall in the stock market index for the industrial sector. In the third phase, from mid 1993 to late 1994, the ending of the drought, a reduction in interest rates, and the attainment of a liberalized trade and exchange rate regime enabled a rapid recovery. In the fourth phase, during 1995, interest rates rose and the real exchange rate appreciated, causing renewed contraction in output.

The aggregate data for the manufacturing sector reveal large changes in relative factor prices but small changes in relative product prices. Real wages in manufacturing fell by more than a third, whereas the cost of capital rose due to higher interest rates. By contrast, the real exchange rate was, by late 1995, almost back to its level of 1990, and the expectations revealed in the mid-1995 survey were for substantial appreciation. At the aggregate level there are some indications that this change in factor prices increased the labour intensity of production, as might be expected, with employment rising relative to output.

The survey data for manufacturing bear this out. Although it is difficult to estimate changes in the capital stock, the central estimate is that employment increased by 12 per cent relative to the capital stock between 1990 and 1995. While there were changes in factor utilization, there was little indication of a resource shift to exports within manufacturing. The survey found no clear relationship between changes in investment and employment and the export performance. However, deregulation has had an effect. Regulations are no longer seen as important constraints on firms' operations. Competition, particularly from imports, is rapidly becoming important. Firms report increased competition in export markets and also in the domestic market, both from imports and from other Zimbabwean firms. Yet in spite of the extent of deregulation, firms rely heavily on contacts with civil servants.

The data in the AERC survey on regional trade show that the South African market is important for all sectors other than wood. With the exception of South Africa, intra-African trade is not very substantial. First, where it appears to be important, in the food sector, exports are determined by special circumstances (deliveries to donor agencies for distribution in refugee camps) that are unlikely to be permanent. In the metal sector PTA markets are important, accounting for close to 60 per cent of exports, but exports of this sector are fairly small. An interesting finding is that tariffs are the sole remaining substantial barrier to regional trade but this barrier is seen as very important. The removal of South African tariffs on Zimbabwean exports (particularly of textiles but also of furniture) is now probably the key to inter-regional export growth.

The sectors that export most are wood and textile. For these sectors exports to developed countries are much more important than intra-African exports. The US and European markets account in each case for close to 60 per cent of exports. In this sense the perception that the Zimbabwean manufacturing sector exports primarily to South Africa and other neighbouring countries is simply mistaken.

The survey provides the only evidence on investment rates. Our estimates suggest that investment was substantial in the early years of the reform programme but fell in 1994 and 1995. We have suggested that this may be due either to high interest rates or to the risk of policy reversal. In either case, this reflects of the fiscal crisis that built up during the liberalization.

APPENDIX

Table 11A.1 Zimbabwe: structure of exports, 1992 (Z$000)

Sectors	*SADC*	*PTA*	*RSA*	*Region total*	*EU*	*ROW*	*Grand total*
Food & live animals	184 457	123 670	55 172	257 145	150 840	35 613	443 598
Drinks &	85 524	90 491	300 037	393 308	865 516	100 338	226 221
tobacco						6	0
Crude materials excluding fuels	54 500	25 236	126 821	182 347	247 593	362 587	792 527
Mineral fuels/ lubricants	16 089	12 699	1 427	17 763		6 702	24 465
Animal, vegetable oils & fats	15 630	15 513	150	15 780	553	26	16 359
Chemical & related products	128 571	126 511	25 728	160 811	6 236	23 125	190 172
Manufactured goods	360 723	297 186	206 904	652 089	685 503	592 012	192 960
class by material							4
Machinery & transport equipment	122 579	120 268	41 243	182 440	5 899	6 457	194 796
Misc. manufactured articles	88 298	40 174	111 699	200 653	172 340	63 848	436 841
Communication transact, NES	6 276	5 506	11 386	18 801	27 263	68 535	114 599
Total	106 264	857 254	880 567	208 113	216 174	216 229	640 517
exports	7			7	3	1	1

Table 11A.2 Zimbabwe: structure of imports, 1992 (Z$000)

Sectors	*SADC*	*PTA*	*RSA*	*Region total*	*EU*	*ROW*	*Grand total*
Food & live	12 372	11 803	17 358	29 929	22 105	13 002	16 216
animals	6	0	3	0		96	91
Drinks &	540	291	25 774	26 316	7 622	925	34 863
tobacco							
Crude materials	70 131	47 571	97 140	17 476	62 904	30 816	54 583
excluding fuels				1		5	0
Mineral fuels/	12 225	12 374	17 109	18 357	20 801	11 267	13 311
lubricants			4	7		27	05
Animal, vegetable	3 477	210	23 913	27 390	9 663	95 211	13 226
oils & fats							4
Chemical &	24 537	12 526	60 476	63 456	39 718	28 969	13 214
related products			1	4	0	5	39
Manufactured goods	10 494	51 094	77 265	90 259	32 880	38 024	16 116
class by material	0		8	1	4	9	44

(*continued on page 628*)

Table 11A.2 *continued*

Sectors	*SADC*	*PTA*	*RSA*	*Region total*	*EU*	*ROW*	*Grand total*
Machinery &	18 678	16 176	69 484	72 041	19 005	15 018	41 228
transport equipment			1	8	91	07	16
Misc. manufactured	7 989	4 823	64 988	75 992	11 679	10 402	29 681
articles					1	7	0
Communication	24 610	19 566	10 821	13 317	87 807	78 082	29 906
transact, NES			4	5			4
Total	39 085	28 266	27 369	31 780	29 542	51 851	11 317
imports	3	1	66	74	68	84	526

Notes

1. Other financial sector legal acts are Reserve Bank (1965), Building Societies Act (1965), Pension Funds and Provident Societies Act (1976), Stock Exchange Act (1974) (amended in 1989), Companies Act (1976), Insurance Act (1987), and Post Office Savings Bank Act (1965).
2. Choudry (1991) develops a model where rationed borrowers can apply to several banks, sequentially.
3. Claims to foreign currency in Zimbabwe, called Export Retention Schemes (ERS), could be traded; after the unification of the exchange rates (official and inter-bank) in July 1994, their purpose ceased.
4. Adverse selection problems may be more severe in competitive banking systems where applicants apply to more than one bank. Here, if one bank raises its loan rate it knows that only those firms denied credit at other banks will apply.
5. The current chair of the stock exchange is from Edward's & Company.
6. Cluff Resources (Zimbabwe) was granted the first gold loan on 26 November 1993, and the loan was advanced by the PTA Bank. The loan was worth 52 000 onces and raised nearly $20 m when the gold was sold on the cash market. Part of the loan will be used to develop underground activity at the Freda Rebecca mine in Bindura at a cost of $14 million, and the remainder will be used to pay off the high-interest debt owed to local banks. The interest payment on the gold loan is expected to be nearly $3.7 m in total (5.6 per cent). The payments will be in gold over four years (up to 1 January 1998), in eight equal instalments, starting in January 1995, after a one-year grace period.
7. Statistical Yearbook 1989, Table 4.9 for average earnings, deflated by the lower-income consumer price index.
8. We are very grateful to Lisa Daniels for making the report on this second GEMINI round (Daniels, 1994) available to us.
9. This is not quite true for the final sample, since in some cases firms selected for replacement turned out to have started recently.

10. See, for example, Collier and Gunning (1992).
11. Gunning and Pomp (1995) use the data for new firms to derive an estimate of as the ratio of the sales value of equipment and the value of start-up investment. They arrive at a median value of 0.4.
12. Daniels (1994), pp. xi, 47. More than half the firms reported that it had become easier to obtain inputs since 1991; only about 10 per cent increased competition from imports.
13. Of the explanatory variables size stands for employment at the beginning of the period, and the other variables are dummies, indicating whether the firm's owner is black and whether the firm is engaged in exporting. Note that only a single sectoral dummy 'metal' is included; once we control for the other variables all other sectoral differences become insignificant.
14. In the absence of the export price index, nominal export values have been deflated by the CPI. Clearly, this is not satisfactory.
15. Food exports include substantial sales to donor organizations for relief operations. Recently Zimbabwe has supplied much of the food distributed in Rwanda and the refugee camps in neighbouring countries.
16. From Ncube (1994), Table 14.3, p. 271, the Gini-Hirschman indexes for other SADC countries are: Botswana (0.8497), Malawi (0.6441), Mozambique (0.5225), Tanzania (0.4292), Zambia (0.9325).
17. The preferential trade agreement between Zimbabwe and Malawi lapsed after the two countries acceded to the PTA treaty in 1982.
18. Part of the problems facing the textile sector also emanated from the removal of export incentives by government, and the high interest rates.
19. See the F & T Weekly (1 September 1995), which argues that 'The lowering of tariff will further increase administrative problems with Asian countries which use Zimbabwe as a conduit to dump cheap goods in South Africa. There is also some concern that SA's textile and clothing companies will be tempted to move their factories to Zimbabwe where labour costs are a mere 20% of those in South Africa. Labour unions to the north are more accommodating' (p. 34).
20. There are rumours within policy circles in Zimbabwe that the country plans to rescind its ratification of the COMESA agreement as proposed by the 1994 SADC summit in Botswana, which recommended that member states of SADC terminate dual membership of the two markets. These rumours have been met with disappointment, as Zimbabwe contributes over 11 per cent of PTA's budget. Although the rumours may eventually prove incorrect, they are nevertheless important in that they indicate the general uncertainty with which Zimbabwe has approached the whole issue of regional integration, preferring in general to put more effort into bilateral trade arrangements.
21. For South Africa, we only have total factor productivity (TFP) indexes calculated for different manufacturing subsectors. Between 1972 and 1990, TFP for overall manufacturing was 0.55. At the subsectoral level, the leading industries were jewellery (4.12), paper (3.17), other manufacturing (2.48), basic non-ferrous (2.16), tobacco (1.39), and industrial chemicals (1.32). TFP indexes in textiles and clothing were 0.35 and 0.47, respectively, while wood and wood products, and furniture had negative indexes of −0.25 and −0.51, respectively. (See Belli *et al.* 1993.)

References

Adam, C. S. and M. Ncube (1994) 'Financial Liberalization and Trade expansion in Zimbabwe', June, unpublished paper, The World Bank, Washington, DC and CSAE, University of Oxford

Akerlof, G. A. and P. M. Romer (1993) 'Looting: The Economic Underworld of Bankruptcy', *Brookings Papers on Economic Activity* (2):1–73

Bade, J. (1995a) 'Infrastructure and Regulations', ch. 5 in J. W. Gunning and C. Mumbengegwi (eds) (1995)

Bade, J. (1995b) 'Finance: Credit and Indebtedness', ch. 8 in J. W. Gunning and C. Mumbengegwi (eds) (1995)

Barnea, A., R. Haugen, and L. Senbet (1985) *Agency Problems and Financial Contracting* (Prentice-Hall, Inc.)

Belli, P., M. Finger and A. Ballivan (1993) 'South Africa: A Review of Trade Policies', *World Bank Discussion Paper* no. 4 (Aug.)

Berlin, M., A. Saunders, and G. F. Udell (1991) 'Deposit Insurance Reform: What are the Issues and What Needs to be Fixed', *Journal of Banking and Finance*, **15**:735–52

Bester, H. (1985) 'Screening vs. Rationing in Credit Markets with Imperfect Information', *American Economic Review*, **75**:850–5

Bhattacharya, S. and A. V. Thakor (1993) 'Contemporary Banking Theory', *Journal of Financial Intermediation* 3:2–50.

Brown, R. H. and S. M. Schaefer (1994) 'The Term Structure of Real Interest Rates and the Cox, Ingersoll, and Ross Model', *Journal of Financial Economics*, **35**:3–42

Buser, S. A., A. H. Chen, and E. J. Kane (1981) 'Federal Deposit Insurance, Regulatory Policy and Optimal Capital Structure', *Journal of Finance* (Sep.): 51–60

Chan, Y. and G. Kanatas (1985) 'Asymmetric Valuations and the Role of Collateral in Loan Agreements', *Journal of Money, Credit and Banking*, **17**:84–95

Chigumira, G. and N. Maphosa (1995) 'Competition and Market Structure', ch. 6 in J. W. Gunning and C. Mumbengegwi (eds) (1995)

Choudry, B. (1991) 'What is Different About International Lending?', *Review of Financial Studies*, **4**:121–48

Collier, P. and J. W. Gunning (1992) 'Aid and Exchange Rate Adjustment in African Trade Liberalisations', *Economic Journal*, **102**:925–39

Daniels, L. (1994) 'Changes in the Small-Scale Enterprise Sector from 1991 to 1993: Results of a Second Nationwide Survey in Zimbabwe', GEMINI Technical report no. 71, (Mar.)

Diamond, D. W. (1984) 'Financial Intermediation and Delegated Monitoring', *Review of Economic Studies*, **51**:393–414

Diamond, D. W. (1991) 'Monitoring and Reputation: The Choice Between Bank Loans and Directly Placed Debt', *Journal of Political Economy*, **99**:688–721

Eisenbais, R. A. (1990) 'Restructuring Federal Deposit Insurance and the Federal Safety Net', paper prepared for the Academic Consultant's Seminar, Board of Governors, Federal Reserve (Mar.)

Giovannini, A. and M. de Melo 'Fiscal Revenue from Inflation Tax' American Economic Review (1993)

Green, R. C. (1984) 'Investment Incentives, Debt, and Warrants', *Journal of Financial Economics*, **13**:115–36

Grossman, S. and O. Hart (1986) 'The Costs and Benefits of Ownership: A Theory of Vertical and Lateral Integration', *Journal of Political Economy*, **94**:691–719

Gunning, J. (1994a), 'The Manufacturing Sector in Zimbabwe: Survey Evidence on Growth, Adjustment, and Vulnerability', unpublished paper (Department of Economics, Free University, Amsterdam)

Gunning, J. W. (ed.) (1994b) 'The Manufacturing Sector in Zimbabwe: Dynamics and Constraints', final report on the Round I RPED Survey data, Apr. (Free University, Amsterdam)

Gunning, J. W. and C. Mumbengegwi (eds) (1995) 'The Manufacturing Sector in Zimbabwe: Industrial Change under Structural Adjustment', final report on the Round II RPED Survey Data, Jan. (Free University, Amsterdam and University of Zimbabwe, Harare)

Gunning, J. W. and R. Oostendorp (1996) 'What Drives Investment? Panel Data Evidence from Industrual Firms in Zimbabwe', paper presented at the Workshop on *Investment in Africa* Oxford (Apr.)

Gunning, J. W. and M. Pomp (1995) 'Growth, Adjustment and Resource Allocation', ch. 2 in J. W. Gunning and C. Mumbengegwi (eds) (1995)

Gustafsson, A., D. Durevall and K. Mlambo (1994) *Evaluation of the Swedish Balance of Payments Support to Zimbabwe* (Stockholm: SIDA)

Haugen, R. and L. Senbet (1978) 'The Insignificance of Bankruptcy Costs to the Theory of Optimal Capital Structure', *Journal of Finance*, **33**:383–93

Haugen, R. and L. Senbet (1988) 'Bankruptcy and Agency Costs: Their Significance to the Theory of Optimal Capital Structure', *Journal of Financial and Quantitative Analysis*, **23**:27–38

Helpman, E. and P. Krugman (1985) *Market Structure and Foreign Trade: Increasing Returns, Imperfect Competition, and the International Economy* (Cambridge, Mass.: MIT Press)

Jansen, D. (1982) *Zimbabwe: Government Policy and the Manufacturing Sector* (California: Larkspur)

John, K., T. John, and L. Senbet (1991) 'Risk-Shifting Incentives of Depository Institutions: A New Perspective on Federal Deposit Insurance Reform', *Journal of Banking and Finance*, **15**:895–915

John, K., A. Saunders and L. W. Senbet (1994) 'A Theory of Capital Regulation and Bank management Compensation', unpublished paper, College of Business, University of Maryland, College Park

John, K., L. W. Senbet and A. K. Sundaram (1994) 'Corporate Limited Liability and the Design of Corporate Taxation', unpublished paper, College of Business, University of Maryland, College Park

King, J. R. and R. Levine (1992), 'Financial Intermediation and Economic Development', in C. Mayer and X. Vives, *Financial Intermediation in the Construction of Europe* (London: CEPR)

King, J. R. and R. Levine (1993a) 'Finance and Development: Schumpeter Might be Right', *Quarterly Journal of Economics*, **108**:717–38

King, J. R. and R. Levine (1993b) 'Finance, Entrepreneurship and Growth: Theory and Evidence', *Journal of Monetary Economics*, **32**:513–42

Lee, L. F. and W. G. Tyler (1978) 'The Measurement and Sources of Technical

Inefficiency in the Indonesian Weaving Industry', *Journal of Development Economics*, **9**:43–64
Meeusen, W. and J. van den Broeck (1977) 'Efficiency Estimation from Cobb-Douglas Production Functions with Composed Error', *International Economic Review*, **18**:435–44
Mlambo, K (1995) 'Measurement of Technical Efficiency in Zimbabwean Manufacturing Firms: An Application of the Stochastic Frontier Model', in J. W. Gunning and C. Mumbengegwi (eds) (1995)
Mumvuma, T. and H. Zhou (1995) 'Constraints to Capacity Utilisation', ch. 4 in J. W. Gunning and C. Mumbengegwi (eds) (1995)
Ncube, M. (1991) *Development Dynamics: Theories and Lessons from Zimbabwe* (London: Avebury)
Ncube, M. (1994) 'The Dynamics of Trade and Economic Relations in Southern Africa', in A. Atsain, S. Wangwe and A. G. Drabek (eds) *Economic Policy Experience in Africa: What Have we Learned*? (Nairobi: AERC)
Ndlela, D. B. (1994) *Economic Integration in Southern Africa: Challenges and Opportunities for Zimbabwe*, Zimconsult report prepared for the Africa Development Bank, Harare.
Rajan, R. G. (1992) 'Insiders and Outsiders: The Choice Between Informed and Arm's-Length Debt', *Journal of Finance*, **47**:1367–1400
Ratnayake, R. (1994) *Effective Protection of Manufacturing in Zimbabwe* (Centre for International Economics)
Risseeuw, P. (1994) 'Firm Growth in Zimbabwe 1981–1993', ch. 4 in J. W. Gunning (ed.) (1994b)
Risseeuw, P. (1995) 'Firm Dynamics 1991–1994: a Closer Look', ch. 12 in J. W. Gunning and C. Mumbengegwi (eds) (1995)
Rodrik, D. (1992) 'Does Trade Liberalization Really Help?', in G. K. Helleiner (ed.), *Trade Policy, Industrialization and Development: New Perspectives* (Oxford: Clarendon Press)
Santomero, A. (1990) 'The Capital Issue in Perspective', paper presented at the Board of Governors, Federal Reserve (Mar.)
Senbet, L. and J. Seward (1994) 'Financial Distress, Bankruptcy and Reorganisation', in R. Jarrow, V. Maksimovic, and W. Ziemba, *Finance* (North-Holland Research Volume)
Sharpe, S. (1990) 'Asymmetric Information, Bank Lending and Implicit Contracts: A Stylized Model of Customer Relationships', *Journal of Finance*, **45**:1069–87
Stiglitz, J. and A. Weiss (1981) 'Credit Rationing in Markets with Incomplete Information', *American Economic Review* **71**:393–410
Stiglitz, J. and A. Weiss (1983) 'Incentive Effects of Terminations: Applications to the Credit and Labour Markets', *American Economic Review*, **73**:912–27
World Bank (1989) *Zimbabwe, The Capital Goods Sector, Investment and Industrial Issues*. (Washington DC)
World Bank (1989) *Zimbabwe, An Industrial Sector Memorandum* (Washington DC, May)
World Bank (1993) *The East Asian Miracle: Economic Growth and Public Policy* Research Report (Oxford University Press)

Contents of Volumes 1, 3 and 4

Volume 3 Regional Case-Studies

Volume 4 Synthesis and Review

Index

Notes: 1 Entries in **bold** type refer to chapter subjects which are by country. Sub-entries under chapter headings are in text order rather than alphabetical.
2 Page numbers in **bold** type refer to illustrative figures or tables.
3 The term 'country studies' refers to studies on which individual chapters of the book are based.